CROSSCURRENTS

CONTEMPORARY POLITICAL ISSUES

THIRD EDITION

CROSSCURRENTS

CONTEMPORARY POLITICAL ISSUES

THIRD EDITION

EDITED BY

Mark Charlton
Trinity Western University

Paul Barker
Brescia College

Université d'Ottawa
BIBLIOTHÈQUES

LIBRARIES
University of Ottawa

I(T)P Nelson

I(T)P An International Thomson Publishing Company

Toronto • Albany • Bonn • Boston • Cincinnati • Detroit • London
Madrid • Melbourne • Mexico City • New York • Pacific Grove • Paris
San Francisco • Singapore • Tokyo • Washington

I(T)P® **International Thomson Publishing**
The ITP logo is a trademark under licence
www.thomson.com

DB#1514202

JA
88
.C2
C65
1998

Published in 1998 by

I(T)P® **Nelson**
A division of Thomson Canada Limited
1120 Birchmount Road
Scarborough, Ontario M1K 5G4
www.nelson.com

Canadian Cataloguing in Publication Data

Main entry under title:

Crosscurrents : contemporary political issues

3rd ed.
First ed. published under title: Crosscurrents 1.
ISBN 0-17-605614-9

1. Canada – Politics and government – 1993–   . 2. Canada – Social policy.
I. Charlton, Mark William, 1948–   . II. Barker, Paul, 1953–   .
III. Title: Contemporary political issues

FC630.C76 1998   971.064'8   C98-930130-3
F1034.2.C76 1998

Publisher and Team Leader	Michael Young
Aquisitions Editor	Nicole Gnutzman
Production Editors	Bob Kohlmeier and Jim Gifford
Project Editor	Jenny Anttila
Production Coordinator	Brad Horning
Interior Design	Marc Henderson
Cover Design	Rocket Design
Composition	W.G. Graphics and Alicja Jamorski
Cover Illustration	Joe Fleming

Printed and bound in Canada
1 2 3 4 (WC) 01 00 99 98

Contents

Contributors   ix

Introduction   xi

PART ONE: CANADIAN SOCIETY AND POLITICAL CULTURE

1. **Can native sovereignty coexist with Canadian sovereignty?**   2

   YES   JOHN A. OLTHUIS AND ROGER TOWNSHEND, The Case for Native Sovereignty   5

   NO   THOMAS FLANAGAN, Native Sovereignty: Does Anyone Really Want an Aboriginal Archipelago?   9

2. **Is the political culture of Canada becoming Americanized?**   19

   YES   PAUL NESBITT-LARKING, Canadian Political Culture: The Problem of Americanization   21

   NO   ANTHONY A. PEACOCK, Socialism as Nationalism: Why the Alleged Americanization of Canadian Political Culture Is a Fraud   39

3. **Should individual rights take precedence over collective rights?**   55

   YES   PIERRE TRUDEAU, Values in a Just Society   57

   NO   PAUL MARSHALL, The Importance of Group Rights   62

4. **Are Canadians tory-touched liberals?**   70

   YES   NELSON WISEMAN, Tory-Touched Liberalism: Political Culture in Canada   72

   NO   JANET AJZENSTAT AND PETER J. SMITH, The "Tory Touch" Thesis: Bad History, Poor Political Science   84

PART TWO: THE CONSTITUTION AND FEDERALISM

5. **Is the Canadian Charter of Rights and Freedoms antidemocratic?**   96

   YES   ROBERT MARTIN, The Canadian Charter of Rights and Freedoms Is Antidemocratic and Un-Canadian   98

Contents

NO PHILIP L. BRYDEN, The Canadian Charter of Rights and Freedoms Is Antidemocratic and Un-Canadian: An Opposing Point of View 103

6. **Is constitutional reform necessary? 109**

YES KATHY L. BROCK, The Need for Constitutional Reform 111

NO MICHAEL LUSZTIG, Megaconstitutional Reform Is Not Desirable 121

7. **Must national standards be *federal* standards? 134**

YES ROGER GIBBINS, Decentralization and the Dilemma of National Standards 136

NO RONALD MANZER, "And Dog Will Have His Day": National Standards in Canadian Social Policy 147

8. **Should Quebec be recognized as a *distinct society* in the constitution? 160**

YES PAUL DE VILLERS, Why We Must Entrench Quebec's Francophone Heritage 163

NO LINE MAHEUX, Why the Distinct Society Idea Is Tearing Canada Apart 167

9. **Do Canada's tax laws treat women fairly and equally? 174**

YES JUSTICE CHARLES GONTHIER, Opinion in *Thibaudeau v. Canada* 176

NO JUSTICE BEVERLY McLACHLIN, Opinion in *Thibaudeau v. Canada* 186

10. **Is it time for Canada and Quebec to part? 201**

YES DAVID J. BERCUSON, Why Quebec and Canada Must Part 203

NO DAVID T. KOYZIS, Why Political Divorce Must Be Averted 211

PART THREE: INSTITUTIONS

11. **Is the doctrine of individual ministerial responsibility workable? 220**

YES KENNETH KERNAGHAN, Is the Doctrine of Ministerial Responsibility Workable? 222

NO HUGH SEGAL, Ministerial Accountability: Confronting the Myth 232

12. **Does the institutionalized cabinet provide for good government? 242**

    YES CHRISTOPHER DUNN, The Utility of the Institutionalized Cabinet 244

    NO PAUL BARKER, Problems with the Institutionalized Cabinet 264

⧖13. **Should party discipline be relaxed? 278**

    YES DAVID KILGOUR, JOHN KIRSNER, AND KENNETH McCONNELL, Discipline versus Democracy: Party Discipline in Canadian Politics 280

    NO ROBERT J. JACKSON AND PAUL CONLIN, The Imperative of Party Discipline in the Canadian Political System 286

14. **Do the courts practise judicial self-restraint? 292**

    YES PETER H. RUSSELL, Canadian Constraints on Judicialization from Without 294

    NO F.L MORTON, Judicial Policymaking Under the Charter 306

15. **Should Parliament review Supreme Court nominees? 318**

    YES F.L. MORTON, Why the Judicial Appointment Process Must Be Reformed 320

    NO H. PATRICK GLENN, Parliamentary Hearings for Supreme Court of Canada Appointments? 327

PART FOUR: POLITICAL BEHAVIOUR

16. **Are political parties necessary? 338**

    YES G. GRANT AMYOT, Democracy Without Parties: A New Politics? 340

    NO VAUGHAN LYON, Parties and Democracy: A Critical View 355

17. **Should representation in Parliament mirror Canada's social diversity? 377**

    YES TIM SCHOULS, Why Group Representation in Parliament Is Important 379

    NO JOHN H. REDEKOP, Group Representation in Parliament Would Be Dysfunctional for Canada 392

18. Do referendums enrich democracy? 407

YES BRIAN NEEDHAM, A Better Way to Vote: Why Letting the People Themselves Take the Decisions Is the Logical Next Step for the West 409

NO MARK CHARLTON, The Limits of Direct Democracy 416

19. Should Canada adopt proportional representation? 428

YES JOHN L. HIEMSTRA AND HAROLD JANSEN, Getting What You Vote For 430

NO PAUL BARKER, Voting for Trouble 441

PART FIVE: PUBLIC POLICY

20. Does Canada need the CBC? 454

YES DAVID TARAS, We Need the CBC 456

NO BARRY COOPER, Rethink the CBC 459

21. Should Canada's universities be privatized?

YES DOUGLAS AULD, The Overregulation of Higher Education 466

NO WILLIAM BRUNEAU, Privatization in School and University: Renewal or Apostasy? 472

22. Is workfare sound public policy?

YES MICHAEL KRASHINSKY, The Role of Workfare in the Social Safety Net 488

NO ERNIE S. LIGHTMAN, Workfare: It's Jobs, Not Pathology 506

23. Is employment equity fair and necessary?

YES CAROL AGÓCS, Employment Equity: Is It Needed? Is It Fair? 520

NO JACK ROBERTS, Employment Equity—Unfair 532

Appendix: How to Write an Argumentative Essay, by Lucille Charlton 545

Contributors Acknowledgments 551

List of Contributors

Carol Agócs teaches in the political science department at The University Western Ontario.

Janet Ajzenstat is a professor of political science at McMaster University.

G. Grant Amyot is a professor of political science at Queen's University.

Douglas Auld is president of Loyalist College and Conjunct Professor at Trent University.

David J. Bercuson is a professor of history at The University of Calgary.

Kathy L. Brock is a professor of political science at Wilfrid Laurier University.

William Bruneau teaches in the Faculty of Education at the University of British Columbia. He is also president of the Canadian Association of University Teachers.

Philip L. Bryden is Associate Dean of the Faculty of Law at the University of British Columbia.

Barry Cooper is a professor of political science at The University of Calgary.

Paul De Villers is the Liberal Member of Parliament for Simcoe North and parliamentary secretary for intergovernmental affairs.

Christopher Dunn is a professor of political science at Memorial University.

Thomas Flanagan is a professor of political science at The University of Calgary.

Roger Gibbins is a professor of political science at The University of Calgary.

H. Patrick Glenn is a professor of law at McGill University.

Charles Gonthier is a justice of the Supreme Court of Canada.

John L. Hiemstra is a professor of political science at The King's College, Edmonton, Alberta.

Robert J. Jackson teaches politics at Carleton University.

Kenneth Kernaghan is a professor of political science at Brock University.

David Kilgour is a Member of Parliament for Edmonton-Strathcona and speaker of the House of Commons.

David T. Koyzis is a professor of political science at Redeemer College, Hamilton, Ontario.

Contributors

Michael Krashinsky teaches economics at Scarborough College, the University of Toronto.

Ernie S. Lightman is a professor of social work at the University of Toronto.

Michael Lusztig is a professor of political science at Southern Methodist University.

Vaughan Lyon teaches politics at Trent University.

Line Maheux is a senior policy advisor for the Reform Party of Canada.

Ronald Manzer is a professor of political science at the University of Toronto.

Paul Marshall is a professor of political theory at the Institute for Christian Studies, Toronto.

Robert Martin is a professor of law at The University of Western Ontario.

Beverly McLachlin is a justice of the Supreme Court of Canada.

F.L. Morton is a professor of political science at The University of Calgary.

Brian Needham is an editor with *The Economist* magazine.

Paul Nesbitt-Larking is a professor of political science at Huron College, The University of Western Ontario.

John A. Olthuis is a lawyer who has acted as legal counsel to various First Nations on land claims, aboriginal rights, and constitutional issues.

Anthony A. Peacock is a professor of political science at Utah State University.

John H. Redekop teaches political science at Trinity Western University.

Jack Roberts is professor emeritus of law at The University of Western Ontario and adjunct professor of law at Osgoode Hall Law School.

Peter H. Russell is a professor of political science at the University of Toronto.

Tim Schouls is a doctoral candidate in political science at the University of British Columbia.

Hugh Segal is Resident Fellow, School of Policy Studies, Queen's University and former advisor to the Conservative Party.

Peter J. Smith is a professor of political science at Athabasca University.

David Taras is director of the Canadian Studies Program at The University of Calgary.

Roger Townshend is a lawyer specializing in native issues.

Pierre Trudeau is a former prime minister of Canada.

Nelson Wiseman is a professor of political science at the University of Toronto.

Introduction

In the first edition of *Crosscurrents: Contemporary Political Issues,* we stated our desire to develop a collection of readings that would not only challenge students to think through a number of contemporary political issues but also foster in students an understanding of and tolerance for the views of others. To achieve this, we felt that a text structured in the form of a debate or dialogue on leading political issues provided an ideal format. We find it gratifying that a number of our colleagues have shared this goal and have used the first and second editions in their introductory political science or Canadian politics courses.

Changes to this edition. In preparing a new edition of *Crosscurrents,* we have maintained the basic structure and format of previous editions. The revised text addresses twenty-three issues. For each issue, an introduction provides the reader with the necessary background and places the subject in the context of more general principles of concern to the study of politics. Two essays then present conflicting viewpoints. Finally, a postscript offers a short commentary on the debate and suggests readings for students to explore the topic further.

To keep abreast of changing political issues and to respond to the many helpful comments from colleagues who have used the second edition, we have made significant changes to this volume. Fifteen of the twenty-three issues are new. The majority of the readings were written especially for the book, and thirty-one of them are new. Some of the authors from the second edition revised their articles, providing substantially updated material. We believe that readers will find the articles to be much more engaging because the authors enter more directly into debate with one another.

From the comments of the reviewers, it is clear that *Crosscurrents: Contemporary Political Issues* is used in general introductory courses and in Canadian politics courses to about the same degree. Therefore, we have tried to select topics appropriate to both and have retained the public policy section that covers a variety of issues. People that use the text in an introductory course may find the public policy section more helpful in the early part of such a course, which often deals with ideologies and concepts relating to rights and the role of the state in society.

A note for first-time users. In introducing the first edition of *Crosscurrents* we set out our rationale for developing a reader using the debate format. We still believe that the rationale for using this format for teaching introductory courses is as strong as ever and bears repeating for those who may be picking up this text for the first time.

There are three good reasons, we believe, for using the debate format. First, studies have shown that students learn and retain more information when they are engaged in an active learning process. Yet the reality in most Canadian universities is that students in introductory courses face ever larger class sizes, which militate against discussion and active student involvement. While students generally come to political science courses with a great deal of interest and enthusiasm, they frequently find themselves slipping into a pattern of simple note taking and passive learning.

Second, most introductory political science courses must of necessity address abstract principles and concepts and cover a great deal of descriptive material concerning processes and institutions. At the same time, students come to these courses expecting that they will discuss and debate what is going on in the chaotic world of politics. Unfortunately, it is often difficult for them to relate the debates of everyday political issues to the broader and more abstract principles encountered in their introductory courses. Without a reference point, discussions of contemporary issues may seem more like interesting "current events" digressions with little direct relationship to the overall propositions being dealt with in the lectures.

Third, students frequently bring to their readings an uncritical awe of the authority of the published word. When confronted with a series of readings by the leading authorities on each subject, there is a strong temptation for students to think that the text presents the "final" word on the subject. They assume that further discussion and debate can add little new to the issue.

With these thoughts in mind, we have endeavoured to develop a collection of readings that will serve as a resource for a more interactive style of teaching, whether it be in classroom or tutorial discussion situations or in a more formal debate setting. Because of the flexibility of the format, *Crosscurrents* can be employed in the classroom in several ways.

(i)   Some may wish to assign the chapters simply as supplementary readings reinforcing material covered in lectures, and to use them as points of illustration in classroom lectures or discussions.

(ii) The readings may be used as a departure point for essay assignments in the course. To encourage students to develop their critical skill, they could be asked to write an assessment of the arguments and evidence presented in one of the debates. Alternatively, students could select one side of the debate and write an essay developing their own arguments in favour of that view. We have included, as an appendix, instructions on writing an argumentative essay.

(iii) Others may wish to use the readings as a means of organizing weekly discussion sessions into a debate format. On each topic, two students may be asked to argue the case for opposing sides, and these arguments could be followed by group discussion. This format requires students to adopt a particular point of view and defend that position. Because the necessary background material is provided in the readings, this format is very easily adapted to large courses where teaching assistants are responsible for weekly tutorial sessions.

ACKNOWLEDGMENTS

We would like to express our appreciation to the many reviewers who offered very helpful comments and suggestions including the following: Chaldeans Mensah, Grant MacEwan Community College; William Matheson, Brock University; Martin Westmacott, University of Western Ontario; and Leonard Preyra, Saint Mary's University. We are particularly indebted to those authors who graciously agreed to write original essays or revise earlier ones specifically for this volume, as well as to the authors and publishers who have granted us permission to use their published work. In addition, we want to acknowledge the excellent support of Mike Thompson and Jenny Anttila of ITP Nelson in helping us to bring this project to completion. The careful and detailed work of Sarah Weber as copy editor was also much appreciated. Finally, we would be remiss not to mention the patient support of our families who, in their indirect way, have contributed to this volume.

Mark Charlton, Langley, B.C.
Paul Barker, London, Ontario

ABOUT THE EDITORS

Mark Charlton teaches political science at Trinity Western University, Langley, British Columbia. Professor Charlton received his Ph.D. in political science from Laval University, where he studied as an Ontario–Quebec Fellow. He is author of *The Making of Canadian Food Aid Policy* (1992) and co-editor of *Crosscurrents: International Relations in the Post–Cold War Era* (1993). He has also published a number of articles in *International Journal, Etudes Internationales, Journal of Conflict Studies,* and the *Canadian Journal of Development Studies.*

Paul Barker teaches political science at Brescia College, London, Ontario. Professor Barker received his Ph.D. from the University of Toronto. He has written articles on public policy that have appeared in *Canadian Public Administration, Canadian Public Policy,* and the *Canadian Journal of Law and Society.*

PART ONE

CANADIAN SOCIETY AND POLITICAL CULTURE

Can native sovereignty coexist with Canadian sovereignty?

Is the political culture of Canada becoming Americanized?

Should individual rights take precedence over collective rights?

Are Canadians tory-touched liberals?

Can Native Sovereignty Coexist with Canadian Sovereignty?

✔ **YES**
JOHN A. OLTHUIS AND ROGER TOWNSHEND, "The Case for Native Sovereignty"

✗ **NO**
THOMAS FLANAGAN, "Native Sovereignty: Does Anyone Really Want an Aboriginal Archipelago?"

In Canada, the subject of aboriginal rights has never been high on the political agenda. Most Canadians have a vague awareness of the deplorable living conditions on many Indian reserves, but that is about all. The demands of natives for land, greater autonomy, and even self-government have received little notice. More "immediate" issues such as constitutional reform, Quebec separatism, western alienation, or free trade with the United States have usually pushed Native issues off the list of urgent public issues.

However, the dramatic events surrounding the Oka crisis of 1990 did more to change public perceptions of native issues than any other single event. Reacting to municipal plans to expand a local golf course onto traditional native lands, armed Mohawk Warriors began erecting barricades in an effort to stop the work. The protest soon escalated into a full-scale confrontation between the Quebec provincial police and Mohawk Warriors, in which one police officer was killed. Soon a second set of barriers was erected on the Kahnawake reserve near Montreal as a demonstration of support. As the situation appeared to become more violent, Quebec Premier Robert Bourassa called in the Canadian armed forces to restore order to Oka. For the first time in twenty years, Canadian troops were deployed against fellow citizens.

For federal and Quebec officials, the issue was straightforward. The Mohawks, in using arms and barricades to press their case, had broken the law and needed to be brought to justice like any other citizens who had committed illegal acts. Land claims and other grievances would be settled only when arms were surrendered and the lawbreakers brought to justice. But the Mohawks rejected this view. It was not just a matter of land claims that was at stake. It was, the Warriors claimed, a question of sovereignty. The Mohawks occupied sovereign territory that had never been surrendered to any British or Canadian government. Thus the

Mohawks had every right, as any other sovereign nation, to take up arms to defend themselves. It was the police and army who were acting illegally.

At the heart of native grievances is the Indian Act, 1867, which set the tone for successive federal government dealings with natives. Under this act, elected Indian band councils, not traditional political institutions, deal with the Department of Indian Affairs and Northern Development. Band councils are granted limited powers, but all financial decisions are ultimately subject to the approval of the minister responsible for Indian Affairs. Thus sovereignty remains undivided and concentrated in the hands of Ottawa. Band councils are like fledgling municipal governments, able to exercise only those powers specifically delegated to them.

Native leaders have long argued that this relationship is humiliating and paternalistic. The real aim of the Indian Act, they argue, has been to use the band councils as an instrument for destroying traditional native institutions and for assimilating and integrating natives into the larger Canadian society. For moderate native leaders, the solution has been to negotiate some greater delegation of powers to the band councils. But for a growing number of native leaders this is not enough. Only when the full sovereignty of Indian nations is recognized will natives be able to overcome their degrading colonial status.

In the wake of the Oka crisis, native issues were suddenly given a more prominent place on the Canadian political agenda. The government of Brian Mulroney appointed a royal commission on aboriginal questions, and gave native leaders an increasingly prominent role in discussions leading up to the constitutional proposals of 1992. The Charlottetown Accord appeared to address many native concerns. The accord included a recognition of the inherent right of aboriginal people to self-government and the commitment to make these aboriginal governments one of three orders of government along with Ottawa and the provinces. Federal and provincial governments would have committed themselves to negotiating self-government agreements with those native bands that wished to do so, while a series of future First Ministers' Conferences were promised to give ongoing consideration to aboriginal constitutional issues.

However, many remained sceptical of the accord. Non-native critics wondered what a third order of government meant. What form would native self-government take? How would it mesh with the notion of a sovereign Canada? At the same time, many natives felt that the accord had not gone far enough. After all, the accord stated that aboriginal laws could not be inconsistent with those Canadian laws that are deemed essential to the preservation of peace, order, and good government. This was hardly a recognition of native sovereignty.

With the defeat of the referendum, many of the questions surrounding the issue of native sovereignty were left unresolved. In October 1996, the Royal Commission on Aboriginal Peoples published its five-volume report. Although the comission made over four hundred specific proposals, the report has quietly passed from public attention. This complacency was due in part to the lukewarm response of the Liberal government, which stated that the estimated $30-billion cost of implementing the report's recommendations was too great to accommodate in the present economic circumstances.

In the following essays three specialists in native issues debate the meaning of native sovereignty and its relationship to the concepts of a sovereign Canada. John Olthuis and Roger Townshend, lawyers who have done extensive work on native land claims and aboriginal constitutional issues, set out the case for native sovereignty. Thomas Flanagan of the University of Calgary argues that the demand for native sovereignty as it is posed by native leaders is incompatible with the continued existence of Canada.

✔ **YES**

The Case for Native Sovereignty
JOHN A. OLTHUIS AND ROGER TOWNSHEND

There is a great divide in perceptions between aboriginal people in Canada and non-aboriginal people. The non-aboriginal Canadian takes as self-evident the legitimacy of the Canadian state and its jurisdiction over Canadian territory. The average aboriginal person, on the other hand, views much of the power exercised by the Canadian state as illegitimate, oppressive, and as infringing on the powers of First Nations. To the extent that non-aboriginal Canadians are aware of this perception among aboriginal people, they are likely bewildered by it and have trouble seeing either a reasonable basis for it or any practical ways in which such a view could be acted on. Yet it is precisely this divergence of views that has caused and will continue to cause confrontations in the political area (such as regarding constitutional amendments) and confrontations on the ground such as at Kanesatake (Oka).

Although non-aboriginal Canadians rarely question the legitimacy of the Canadian state, most thoughtful people would likely be distressed at how flimsy the logical justification for Canadian sovereignty indeed is. There is no question that prior to European contact native nations in North America had stable cultures, economies, and political systems. They unmistakably exercised full sovereignty over their lands, although in somewhat different ways than did European nations. It would be arrogant and ethnocentric to recognize only a European model political organization as a sovereign state. The initial contact of Europeans with native nations generally treated them as allies or as enemies, but in any event, as nations to be treated as equals with European states. How then did this change? International law then and now recognized changes in sovereignty based on conquest, discovery and settlement, or treaty.

There is nothing in Canadian history that could qualify as a conquest in the international law sense. Treaties with First Nations fall into two rough categories. There are "peace and friendship" treaties, which, if anything, reinforce the concept of the equal nationhood of First Nations. There are also treaties that read as land transactions, which by their silence concerning matters of jurisdiction would seem to provide little help in rooting a claim that they are a source of Canadian sovereignty. Furthermore, there are vast areas of Canada where there are no treaties whatsoever. Thus the invocation of treaties is wholly unsatisfactory as a foundation of Canadian sovereignty. What is left is the doctrine of discovery and settlement. The difficulty with this is that it was intended to apply only to lands that were vacant. Its initial application to a claim of European jurisdiction required the step of considering the aboriginal people as legal nonpersons. In fact, the "discovery" of the Americas sparked lengthy theological and judicial debates in Europe about whether indigenous people indeed were or should be treated as humans. Thus the only justification for Canadian sovereignty (of course, inherited from British sovereignty) that has an air of reality to it requires, as a precondition, a judgment that aboriginal people are not human. This is surely repugnant to thinking Canadians.[1]

Despite the logical flimsiness of its assertion of sovereignty, the British (and later the Canadian state), after an initial period of nation-to-nation dealings, has treated aboriginal people as subjects and indeed as less than equal subjects. After the onset of European settlement, Canadian Indian policy has been aimed at assimilating aboriginal people into Canadian society. This integration was to be achieved on an individual level and preferably to be achieved by entry into the working-class level of society. Efforts of aboriginal people to interact as a group with Canadian society or to integrate at a higher level of Canadian society met with suppression. For example, for many years an aboriginal person who graduated from university automatically ceased to be an "Indian" in the eyes of the federal government. The policy of assimilation came to a head in 1969 with the notorious White Paper that called for the termination of Indian status. This document was resoundingly rejected by aboriginal people and in fact became the catalyst for the Canada-wide political organization of First Nations. This policy of assimilation has been a complete and utter failure. The political resistance of First Nations to assimilation into Canadian society has never been stronger. Most aboriginal people, in a fundamental way, view the Canadian government as a foreign government and not one that is "theirs." This should hardly be shocking, since it was only in 1960 that aboriginal people were able to vote in federal elections. Neither have aboriginal communities lost their social, cultural, and economic distinctiveness. The Canadian government has tried long and hard to change this, but it has failed. Its attempts have only created much human misery. The residential school system, where Indian children were separated from their families and forbidden to speak their language and often even sexually abused, is one of those attempts. Another attempt is the criminalizing of traditional native religious ceremonies. Also, the native traditional economy has in many parts of the country been seriously impaired both by the environmental effects of development activities and directly by legislation restricting hunting rights. Yet the attachment of aboriginal people to the land remains unbroken.[2]

So what options are open? The dismal social conditions in which many aboriginal people in Canada live are the results of failed assimilationist policies of the Canadian government. aboriginal people firmly believe that the political key to a better future is the recognition of jurisdiction of First Nations. This must be a jurisdiction that goes well beyond a municipal-government type of jurisdiction, and that would allow and encourage the development of new types of structures that would reflect the distinct cultural, political, economic, and spiritual aspects of aboriginal society. This must be a jurisdiction that is provided with sufficient resources to be viable. It would indeed mean a fundamental restructuring of the institutions of the Canadian state, or perhaps more accurately, a rolling back of the jurisdiction of the Canadian state to allow aboriginal institutions to flourish. It is this approach that could allow for a just and peaceful coexistence of First Nations in the Canadian state.

The defeat of the proposed constitutional amendments in 1992 was a missed opportunity to begin to pursue this path. These amendments were rejected by both the non-aboriginal and the aboriginal people. However, it must be realized that they were rejected for very different reasons. The rejection of the Charlottetown Accord by non-aboriginal people seems to have little to do with the aboriginal proposals in the accord. To the extent that these were a factor, non-aboriginal Canadians were probably disposed to view them as giving too much to First Nations. First Nations, on the other hand, rejected the accord because it was too small a step in the direction they wanted to go.

It is puzzling that the idea of native sovereignty should be so threatening to non-aboriginal people. The very nature of the Canadian political system involves a division of powers between federal and provincial governments. It is but an easy step in theory to implement another order of government and provide for an appropriate division of powers. This would not be a challenge to the very essence of Canada since the sharing of jurisdictional powers between different government institutions is already part of the essence of the Canadian state. Canadian sovereignty is also leaking at the other end with increasing globalization and trade agreements. It becomes confusing, then, why Canada should be unwilling to share jurisdiction with First Nations if it is indeed willing to modify its sovereignty with relation to the provinces and also at the international level. Nor would the idea of native sovereignty within a federal state be an uncharted course. In the United States, a country hardly known for being progressive, it is an established legal doctrine that Indian tribes are "domestic dependent nations." The implementation of this concept extends to separate tribal justice and court systems.

Many non-aboriginal Canadians may be troubled by the idea of native sovereignty since they feel that aboriginal people should be able to achieve their social and economic goals by participation as individuals within Canadian society. This misses the entire point of native difference. Most aboriginal cultures have a distinctive and tangible collective nature that goes well beyond the sum of the individuals that constitute them and that would be destroyed by assimilation on an individual basis. The failure of many non-aboriginal Canadians to appreciate this reflects only that liberal individualism is such a pervasive ideology in Canadian society that it is barely recognizable as an ideology at all and often viewed as ultimate truth. (This appears to be the position taken by Thomas Flanagan in the opposing article.) By definition, a group with a culture that differs at significant points from liberal individualism cannot be accommodated within a purely individualistic framework, particularly when any integration with a larger society can only take place on an individual basis. It is true that a society that permits or encourages interaction on a collective basis is not a "liberal democracy" in the sense of the term used by Flanagan. This is the very point. A "liberal democracy" is not an acceptable political structure for most aboriginal people. Fortunately, Canada has never been a "liberal democracy" in a strong sense, as Flanagan seems to admit. For that matter, whether or not "liberal democracy" is a meaningful term is questionable, since the concepts of liberalism and democracy can come into sharp conflict (for example, when a majority wishes to suppress rights of a minority).

Others may view the kind of structural diversity advocated in this article to be extremely impractical. As Flanagan admits, it is not unprecedented—he cites the Ottoman Empire as an example. There are also analogies less unfamiliar to Canadians—the position of Indian tribes in the U.S. system is one. Another example, in a context without an aboriginal element, is that the social and political structure of the Netherlands permits and encourages structural diversity based on philosophical or confessional communities. But apart from whether operating models exist or not, the alternatives to recognizing aboriginal jurisdiction must be looked at realistically. Flanagan's alternative is to do more consistently what the Canadian government has been trying to do for a century. This has failed utterly, and has created much suffering and resentment in the process. What is there to lose in trying something different? Demands for the recognition of aboriginal jurisdiction are not going to go away. If "legitimate" avenues for advancing these demands are shut down, other means may be sought. The continued peace and security of Canada may well depend on accommodating aboriginal jurisdiction.

Respect for the cultural distinctiveness of aboriginal people requires the recognition of institutional forms of First Nations governments with sufficient resources to exercise jurisdiction meaningfully. The sad history of the treatment of aboriginal people by the Canadian state also cries out for redress in the form of recognition of native sovereignty. Nor should this recognition be viewed as completely impractical or as entailing the very destruction of the Canadian state.

NOTES

1. For more detail on the international law aspects of this, see, for example, O. Dickason, "Concepts of Sovereignty at the Time of First Contact," in Dickason and Green, eds., *The Law of Nations and the New World* (Edmonton: University of Alberta Press, 1989).

2. For more examples of the failure of the policy of assimilation and Native resistance to it, see, for example, Diane Engelstad and John Bird, eds., *Nation to Nation: Aboriginal Sovereignty and the Future of Canada* (Concord: House of Anansi Press, 1992).

✗ **NO**

Native Sovereignty: Does Anyone Really Want an Aboriginal Archipelago?

THOMAS FLANAGAN

"... words are wise men's counters, they do but reckon by them: but they are the money of fools...."

—Thomas Hobbes, *Leviathan* (1651), I, 4

In the spirit of Hobbes, before we can debate native sovereignty, we should be clear on what we are talking about. I have elsewhere defined sovereignty as "the authority to override all other authorities." More specifically, it is

> a bundle of powers associated with the highest authority of government. One is the power to enforce rules of conduct.... Another is the power to make law, [also the power of] raising revenue, maintaining armed forces, minting currency, and providing other services to society. Moreover, in the British tradition sovereignty implies an underlying ownership of all land. Finally, sovereignty always means the power to deal with the sovereigns of other communities as well as the right to exercise domestic rule free from interference by other sovereigns.[1]

That is the abstract meaning of sovereignty in the vocabulary of political science. In this sense, it is a conceptual property of the approximately 190 states that make up the international state system. Most of the entities that possess sovereignty belong to the United Nations or, like Switzerland, could belong if they should decide to apply for membership.

Sovereignty can only pertain to states. It makes no sense to speak of sovereignty unless there is, as in the classical definition of the state, an organized structure of government ruling over a population within defined territorial boundaries. native societies in what is now Canada did not possess sovereignty before the coming of the Europeans; neither the concept nor the underlying institutions were part of the culture of their hunting-gathering societies. Of course, hunting-gathering societies have political processes that assign rank and dominance within communities and involve conflict between communities, but the political processes of stateless societies are not the same thing as statehood and sovereignty.

As a way of increasing their political leverage in contemporary Canada, native political leaders have adopted the classical language of statehood to describe their communities. What used to be called bands or tribes are now called "nations," and these nations are said to have possessed sovereignty from the beginning and to possess it still.[2] This strategic use of language has served native leaders well in their struggle for greater power within the Canadian polity, but politically effective assertions should not be confused with intellectually persuasive analysis.

When native leaders in Canada now claim to possess sovereignty, they typically mean one of three things, each of which is related to a particular political situation. In what follows, I will argue that all three of these meanings are incompatible with the continued existence of Canada and the maintenance of essential Canadian political traditions. It is not that words alone can destroy Canada; words in themselves do not accomplish anything. But words such as "native sovereignty" are the verbal symbols of political projects that cannot be reconciled with Canadian institutions.

1. Some native leaders, for example those from the Mohawk communities of Kahnawake and Kanesatake in Quebec, speak of sovereignty in the robust sense described above, that is, the international sense. They hold that the Mohawks on their territory constitute a sovereign, independent state not part of Canada or the United States. This sovereign state should be admitted to the United Nations and in other respects become part of the international community. A Mohawk elder told the Royal Commission on Aboriginal Peoples in March 1993: "You have no right to legislate any laws over our people whatsoever. Our lands are not yours to be assumed. You are my tenant, whether you like it or not."[3]

While I respect the honesty of this position, I do not take it seriously as a political proposition. In the ten provinces, Canada has over 600 Indian bands living on more than 2200 reserves, plus hundreds of thousands of Métis and nonstatus Indians who do not possess reserves. These scattered pieces of land and disparate peoples are not going to be recognized as independent sovereign states, now or ever. They are simply not viable as sovereign states paying their own way and defending their interests in the international community. Nor is there any practical way to weld them into a single sovereign state. Native peoples are deeply divided by language, religion, customs, and history and in no way constitute a single people. They are not seeking emancipation from the tutelage of Indian Affairs in order to lose their identity in some supratribal bureaucracy.

2. The concept of sovereignty, as originally formulated by the philosophers Jean Bodin and Thomas Hobbes, was thought to be a set of powers located in a single seat of authority—perhaps the monarch, perhaps the parliament, but in any case one sovereign. However, sovereignty can also be divided. Indeed, the classical definition of federalism implies a system of divided sovereignty, in which two levels of government each have shares of sovereign power guaranteed in a constitution that cannot be changed unilaterally by either level of government acting alone. In such a context, it is at least verbally meaningful to speak of giving native peoples a constitutionally entrenched share of sovereign authority.

This is more or less the political theory contained in the Charlottetown Accord. According to that document, "The Constitution should be amended to recognize that the Aboriginal peoples of Canada have the inherent right of self-government within Canada," and aboriginal self-governments should be recognized as "one of the three orders of government in Canada."[4] Although the terms federalism and sovereignty were not used, the most straightforward way to interpret the scheme proposed by the Charlottetown Accord is as an extension of divided sovereignty in a federal system from two to three levels. Although none of the details were worked out, the accord would have endowed aboriginal self-governments with many of the attributes of provinces: an entrenched constitutional basis of authority, participation in constitutional amendment procedures, representation in the Senate, a role in fiscal federalism, broad legislative jurisdiction, and so on.

This proposal cannot be dismissed on a priori grounds. There is no self-evident reason why federalism must be based on only two levels of government. Why not a "third order"? There are in fact many reasons why not, but they are more practical than conceptual.

First, as mentioned above, there are in Canada over half a million status Indians belonging to more than 600 bands on more than 2200 reserves scattered across all 10 provinces. No one has proposed a workable mechanism by which this far-flung archipelago could be knit together into a single political entity, or even a small number of such entities. On the contrary, it was widely assumed in the debate on the Charlottetown Accord that the focus of self-government would be the band, or perhaps small clusters of closely related bands organized into tribal councils. Indeed, one of the widely touted advantages of the third order of government is its alleged flexibility, which would allow different bands or groups of bands to have their own institutions of government, criminal justice systems, schools, and so on.

But surely realism must intervene at some point. We are talking about six hundred bands with an average population of less than a thousand, mostly living on small, remote pieces of land without significant job opportunities, natural resources, or economic prospects. There would be virtually no revenue base, let alone the pool of human skills necessary to operate modern public services. How are such small, isolated, and impoverished groups of people supposed to support and operate an untried system of government incorporating a degree of complexity not seen since the medieval Holy Roman Empire?

However, this is only the initial objection. Hard as it would be to harmonize 2200 reserves into a workable third order of government in a multitiered federal system, the problem is actually much more difficult than that. At any given time, more than half of Canada's status Indians live off reserve. They reside almost everywhere in the rest of Canada, from remote wilderness areas to the city centres of Vancouver, Toronto, and Montreal. Moreover, in addition to status Indians, there are perhaps another half million (the true number is impossible to ascertain) Métis and non-status Indians, that is, people of partly Indian ancestry who are not registered under the Indian Act but have some degree of identity as native people. A small number of Métis live in territorial enclaves (the Métis settlements of northern Alberta), but most are mixed in with the general population of Canada. Again, there is every conceivable kind of social situation. There are Métis hunters, trappers, and fishermen in the northern forests; Métis farmers on the Prairies; and Métis business owners, professionals, and workers in Winnipeg and other major cities.

How could one create a third order of government embracing all aboriginal people, as the Charlottetown Accord purported to do, when most of these people do not live in defined territories? Since no one, thank God, was talking of forcibly relocating populations to create separate territories, the only other approach would be to create a racially defined system of government for aboriginal people no matter where they live.

Now there is a historical model for such a system, namely the Ottoman Empire that ruled the Middle East and southeastern Europe from the fifteenth century until it was dismembered after the First World War. Throughout this immense territory, members of numerous Christian churches (Maronite, Coptic, Chaldean, Greek Orthodox, Armenian Orthodox, etc.) lived alongside the adherents of several Islamic sects (Sunni, Shi'ite, Druze, etc.). There were also important Jewish populations in most parts of the empire. All these ethnoreligious communities were allowed a substantial degree of autonomy, including not only religious freedom but also their own systems of private law, so that matters such as marriage, family, and inheritance were regulated within their separate communities.

It was an admirable system in its way, ruling a colourful, polyglot population for five centuries—no mean achievement in itself. But I doubt it is a model Canadians want to imitate, for it was in no sense a democracy. There were no elections or other institutions of representative government. The sultan was theoretically an autocrat, but in fact rule was carried out by the imperial bureaucracy. The empire existed to collect taxes, keep internal order, and wage war against the neighbouring Persian, Russian, and Austro-Hungarian empires.

Like all liberal democracies, Canada is based on an entirely different set of political principles, most notably the twin concepts of the rule of law and equality under the law. The legal equality of all citizens is what makes democracy possible. As John Stuart Mill argued cogently in his *Considerations on Representative Government,* people cannot participate peacefully and cooperatively in one political system unless they feel themselves part of a single community: "Free institutions are next to impossible in a country made up of different nationalities."[5] A territorial definition of the polity is essential to this system of liberal democracy. Political and civil rights must be contingent on residence within a specific territory, not membership in a specific race or ethnic group.

Admittedly, Canada as a liberal democracy is challenged by the linguistic cleavage between English and French as well as the ethnic diversity of our aboriginal and immigrant population. But, at least prior to the Charlottetown Accord, the solutions toward which we groped were always liberal democratic ones based on legal equality within defined territorial jurisdictions. The French fact in Canada was recognized by creating the province of Quebec, which, although it happens to have a French majority, is a province similar in principle to all the others. Similarly, the contemporary Northwest Territories, although it has a native majority, is a territorial, not an ethnic polity. The same will be true of Nunavut when it comes into being. It will be a territory within which an Inuit majority will control a liberal democratic system of government; it will not be an Inuit ethnic polity.

The aboriginal self-government provisions of the Charlottetown Accord would have changed this by authorizing an ethnically defined third order of government to sprawl across existing territorial jurisdictions. It was a departure from, not an extension of, our federal system of liberal democracy. It is so incompatible with our system that it probably would not have worked at all. But to the extent that it had any effect, it would have encouraged the segmentation of native people. Wherever there were appreciable numbers of Indians and Métis in our cities, they would have been encouraged to develop their own schools, welfare agencies, justice systems, elective assemblies, and other paraphernalia of government. Instead of being encouraged to take advantage of the opportunities of Canada's urban society and economy, as so many immigrants from the Third World are now doing, native people would have been led to withdraw further into a world of imaginary political power and all too real dependence on transfer payments.

Finally, even if they could have been made to work in their own terms, the aboriginal self-government provisions of the Charlottetown Accord would have set up unacceptable pressures to create segmentary arrangements for other groups. In addition to setting up the third order of government across the country, the accord provided for unique aboriginal participation in national political institutions: aboriginal senators, possibly with a "double majority" veto over legislation on aboriginal matters[6]; aboriginal members of the House of Commons[7]; and aboriginal nominations to the Supreme Court, as well as a special advisory role for an aboriginal Council of Elders.[8] It would not have been long before other groups demanded similar treatment: women's organizations, visible minorities, the disabled, gays and lesbians, and so on. Indeed, demands of this type were heard during the referendum on the accord. Reservation of Senate seats for women was a major issue in certain provinces, notably British Columbia; and Joe Clark promised to revisit the situation of the disabled once the accord was passed. Even if Canada's liberal democracy could have survived the distinct society for Quebec and the third order of government for aboriginals, it could not survive if every identifiable group set out to entrench its political power in the Constitution. It would be the end of equality before the law, and ultimately of liberal democracy itself.

3. A third possible meaning of native sovereignty is the assertion that selected aspects of Canadian law, whether federal or provincial, simply do not apply to Indian bands or other native communities. There have now been many incidents of this type, for example, the assertion by Manitoba and Saskatchewan bands

that, regardless of provincial legislation, they can run gambling casinos on their reserves. Now the application of provincial legislation to Indian reserves is a complex and contentious area of the law. The general principle formulated by Douglas Sanders, one of the preeminent experts in the field of native law, is this: "Provincial laws apply to Indian reserve lands if they do not directly affect the use of land, do not discriminate against them and are not in conflict with federal Indian legislation."[9] It may well be that the capricious way in which provinces exploit gambling for their own purposes while forbidding private entrepreneurs to enter the field conflicts with the Indian Act, with Section 91(24) of the Constitution Act, 1867, or some other constitutional protection of Indian rights. But this involves interpretation of the Canadian Constitution; it has nothing to do with assertions of native sovereignty. The appropriate remedy is to seek an interpretation of the Constitution by bringing an action before the courts. Wrapping the issue in declarations of sovereignty only obscures the real question.

It is hardly consistent for Indian bands to continue to receive their full range of governmental benefits, including social assistance from provincial authorities, while maintaining that their "sovereignty" allows them to ignore provincial legislation whenever they choose. This self-contradictory position is an obvious nonstarter.

For the sake of clarity, let me repeat that I am not opposing the desire of Indian bands to open casinos on their reserves. Any form of legal entrepreneurship by anyone in Canada should be applauded (though there are serious concerns that in practice the gambling industry may tend to sprout criminal connections that will be as destructive for natives as for anyone else). My point is simply that, whatever the merits of Indians opening casinos on their reserves, it is not a matter of sovereignty.

Up to this point, the tone of my essay has been unavoidably negative, because I was asked to argue the negative side in a debate about native sovereignty. Let me take the opportunity in closing to state my views in a more positive way.

Status Indians in Canada have suffered terribly under the regime of the Indian Act and the Department of Indian Affairs. Bureaucratic socialism has been a failure wherever it has been tried, whether in Eastern Europe or North America. As quickly as possible, Indian bands should receive full ownership of their reserves, with the right to subdivide, mortgage, sell, and otherwise dispose of their assets, including buildings, lands, and all natural resources. As much as possible, they should assume the self-government responsibilities of small towns or rural municipalities. What happens afterward should be up to them. This kind of devolution of power is already possible under federal legislation; it has taken place in a few cases, such as the Sechelt band of British Columbia, and is being negotiated by other bands across the country. It does not require an elaborate metaphysics of sovereignty.

However, a large and ever-increasing majority of native people do not live on reserves and never will, except for occasional visits. For this majority, neither self-government nor sovereignty can have any meaning except to the extent that they, as Canadian citizens, participate in the government of Canada. For them, the political illusion of self-government is a cruel deception, leading them out of, rather than into, the mainstream of Canadian life. Their future depends on fuller participation in the Canadian society, economy, and polity. They are, to all intents and purposes, internal immigrants, and for purposes of public policy their problems are fundamentally the same as those of other recent immigrants.

It is now twenty-five years since Pierre Trudeau became prime minister of Canada. One of his government's early projects was the famous White Paper on Indian affairs, which articulated an approach similar to the one stated here, namely to encourage the social, economic, and political integration of natives into Canadian society. Sadly (as I see it), native leaders totally rejected the White Paper and set off along the opposite path of emphasizing separate institutions and political power, pursuing the elusive goals of land claims, aboriginal rights, self-government, and sovereignty. As far as I can see, a quarter century of this political approach has produced hardly any beneficial results. There are more native politicians and lawyers than there used to be, but economic and social conditions seem not to have improved at all. We still read every day about unemployment rates of 90 percent on reserves, of Third World standards of housing and health, of endemic alcoholism, drug addiction, violence, and family breakdown.

What the black economist Thomas Sowell has written of the United States is equally true of Canada:

> Political success is not only relatively unrelated to economic advance, those minorities that have pinned their hopes on political action—the Irish and the Negroes, for example—have made some of the slower economic advances. This is in sharp contrast to the Japanese-Americans, whose political powerlessness may have been a blessing in disguise, by preventing the expenditure of much energy in that direction. Perhaps the minority that has depended most on trying to secure justice through political or legal processes has been the American Indian, whose claims for justice are among the most obvious and most readily documented.... In the American context, at least, emphasis on promoting economic advancement has produced far more progress than attempts to redress past wrongs, even when those historic wrongs have been obvious, massive, and indisputable.[10]

In the last analysis, the most harmful thing about the quest for sovereignty is the opportunity cost. The "brightest and best"—the leaders of native communities—are led to devote their talents to a cause that produces nothing except ever-growing levels of discontent and disappointment.

NOTES

1. Mark O. Dickerson and Thomas Flanagan, *An Introduction to Government and Politics: A Conceptual Approach,* 3rd ed. (Scarborough: Nelson, 1990), pp. 35–36.

2. See Menno Boldt and J. Anthony Long, "Tribal Traditions and European-Western Political Ideologies: The Dilemma of Canada's Native Indians," *Canadian Journal of Political Science* 17 (1984): 537–553; Thomas Flanagan, "Indian Sovereignty and Nationhood: A Comment on Boldt and Long," ibid., 18 (1985): 367–374; Boldt and Long, "A Reply to Flanagan's Comments," ibid., 19 (1986): 153.

3. Debbie Hum, "Ottawa Has No Right to Impose Its Law on Natives: Mohawk," *The Gazette* (Montreal), March 18, 1993.

4. Charlottetown Accord, Section 41.

5. John Stuart Mill, *Considerations on Representative Government* (Chicago: Henry Regnery, 1962; first published 1861), p. 309.

6. Charlottetown Accord, Section 9.

7. Section 22.

8. Section 20.

9. Douglas Sanders, "The Application of Provincial Laws," in Bradford W. Morse, ed., *Aboriginal Peoples and Law: Indian, Metis and Inuit Rights in Canada* (Ottawa: Carleton University Press, 1985), p. 453.

10. Thomas Sowell, *Race and Economics* (New York: David McKay, 1983), p. 128.

Postscript

The main purpose of the article by Olthuis and Townshend is to demonstrate that native claims to sovereignty have a strong historical and moral basis. Moreover, the authors argue that there is plenty of room to accommodate broader notions of native sovereignty that would not lead to the destruction of the Canadian state as Flanagan suggests. Nevertheless, even if we accept their argument, there still are a number of nagging practical questions that remain. Would all of the more than six hundred tribal bands in Canada be given equal sovereign status? Or would sovereignty be granted to some kind of pan-Indian confederation? Would such a body constitute a third level of government as envisaged in the Charlottetown Accord? If sovereignty is recognized, and outstanding land claims resolved, would federal and provincial governments, preoccupied with deficit reduction measures, simply withdraw access to all services currently provided? Would small and dispersed Indian bands be able to fund and staff the social, economic, and governmental programs that self-government would necessitate?

One intriguing response to some of these questions has been put forward by Thomas Courchene and Lisa Powell in a volume entitled *A First Nations Province* (Kingston: Institute of Intergovernmental Affairs, 1992). They suggest that instead of creating a third order of government, a First Nations Province could be created that would represent native aspirations, providing the powers, institutions, and ability to carry out intergovernmental relations in largely the same manner as provinces presently do.

The notion of a third level of government was taken up by the Royal Commission of Aboriginal Peoples. In its final report, the commission recommended that an aboriginal order of government be recognized, which would coexist with the federal and provincial orders of government. According to the commissioners, "The governments making up these three orders are sovereign within their own several spheres and hold their powers by virtue of their inherent or constitutional status rather than delegation. They share the sovereign powers of Canada as a whole, powers that represent a pooling of existing sovereignties" (p. 244). Although the commission found that aboriginal communities may choose from one of three different models of aboriginal government, they recommended that a House of First Peoples be created as a third chamber of Parliament. The House of First Peoples would have power to veto certain legislation that "directly affect[s] areas of exclusive Aboriginal jurisdiction ... or where there is a substantial impact of a particular law of Aboriginal peoples" (p. 418). Although aboriginal responses to the report were positive, government complacency and the ongoing preoccupation with unity issues relating to Quebec have ensured that these recommendations have largely been ignored. Some fear that it will take further Oka crises to put the issue of native sovereignty back at the top of the public policy agenda.

Not everyone sympathetic to native concerns feels that these demands should be pressed in terms of claims to sovereign statehood. For example, Menno Boldt and J. Anthony Long point out that sovereignty is really a Western European concept based on notions of territoriality and hierarchical authority that are foreign to traditional native culture. In their article "Tribal Traditions and European-Western Political Ideologies: The Dilemma of Canada's native Indians," *Canadian Journal of Political Science* 17, no. 3 (September 1984): 537–555, Boldt and Long argue that reliance on the concept of sovereignty has led many native leaders to reinterpret their own history in a selective way that actually legitimizes European-Western philosophies and conceptions of authority: "The legal-political struggle for sovereignty could prove to be a Trojan Horse for traditional Indian culture by playing into the hands of the Canadian government's long-standing policy of assimilation" (p. 548).

Although native issues have been ignored for so long, a number of excellent books on the subject have appeared in recent years. *Pathways to Self-Determination: Canadian Indians and the Canadian State,* edited by Leroy Little Bear, Menno Boldt, and J. Anthony Long (Toronto: University of Toronto Press, 1984) is a useful set of essays (many written by native leaders) for beginning to explore these issues. *Nation to Nation: Aboriginal Sovereignty and the Future of Canada,* edited by Diane Englestad and John Bird (Concord: House of Anansi Press, 1992) contains a series of thirty essays that deal with the issues surrounding sovereignty, land claims policy, and native/non-native relations. Also useful are the following volumes: J. Frideres, *Native People in Canada: Contemporary Conflicts,* 3rd ed. (Scarborough: Prentice-Hall, 1988) and B. Morse, *Aboriginal Peoples and the Law: Indian, Metis and the Inuit Rights in Canada* (Don Mills: Oxford, 1984).

Perhaps the most detailed resource on this issue is the five-volume Report of the Royal Commission on Aboriginal Peoples. Especially useful on the issues of sovereignty and self-government is the volume titled *Restructuring the Relationships* (Ottawa: Report of the Royal Commission on Aboriginal Peoples, Volume 2, 1996). For a critical perspective on the issue of native sovereignty, see Melvin Smith, *Our Home and Native Land?* (Victoria: Crown Western, 1995).

Because of the key role of the Oka crisis in focusing Canadian attention on native issues, students will find the following materials useful in exploring some of the issues surrounding the events of the Oka crisis: Robert Campbell and Leslie Pal, *The Real World of Canadian Politics,* 2nd ed. (Peterborough: Broadview Press, 1991), and Geoffrey York and Loreen Pindera, *People of the Pines: The Warriors and the Legacy of Oka* (Toronto: Little, Brown, 1991).

ISSUE**TWO**

Is the Political Culture of Canada Becoming Americanized?

✔ **YES**
PAUL NESBITT-LARKING, "Canadian Political Culture: The Problem of Americanization"

✘ **NO**
ANTHONY A. PEACOCK, "Socialism as Nationalism: Why the Alleged Americanization of Canadian Political Culture Is a Fraud"

In the eyes of the world, Canada and the United States are very much alike. This similarity extends to the beliefs, attitudes, and values that citizens in the two countries hold about government. The *political culture*, in other words, of the two nations is similar; the way Canadians and Americans think about government and politics tends to be the same. They both espouse generally liberal views of government, which translates into a modestly sized public sector and an unwillingness to give elected officials much leeway.

But at the same time it is commonly believed that the two countries are separated by differences in the manner in which they approach political life. Americans have been more suspicious of government than Canadians, seeing it as a threat and not as a benefactor. This view is revealed in the political institutions of the United States, which are structured to ensure that political power is divided and hence difficult to wield. On the other hand, Canadians have been more positively disposed toward government. Since Confederation, when government was crucial to the birth of the nation, Canadians have seen purpose in government. For many Canadians, these differences in political culture are absolutely crucial to the uniqueness of Canada. Inherent in the Canadian political culture is a sense of community and an appreciation of the value of collective efforts and public institutions. Equally important, such an attitude curtails the rapacious individualism found in the purely liberal political cultures, the best example of which is the United States. Canada is the tolerant mosaic, America the unyielding melting pot of assimilation.

For those who see and cherish these differences, there are disturbing changes now taking place in the attitudes of Canadians toward government and public life. There is a declining trust in elected officials, and voters have become less attached to traditional parties and more enamoured of new vehicles of representation. Once valued public policies are now under attack, and the downsizing of government has become the paramount goal. A belief in individual entitlement, fuelled in part by the newly entrenched Charter of Rights and Freedoms, has emerged as well, pushing aside more communitarian sentiments. For many, these and other developments mean only one thing: the Americanization of the Canadian political culture. The toleration, the sense of collective purpose, the respect for authority—all this and more are being lost. The way Canadians think about politics is changing, and it is a change to be regretted, for it threatens to engulf Canada in what has been called the *possessive individualism* of the American political culture.

Not all accept that Canada's political culture is inherently different from that of the United States. From this view, the world's appreciation of the two nations is the correct one: the two are basically the same. Efforts to argue otherwise, to contend that Canada is more community oriented, more caring, distort the basic reality and lead to ill-advised ventures in government policymaking. Moreover, the changes that are taking place in the Canadian political culture hardly amount to an Americanization, for Canada has always been like the United States, but rather reflect the globalizing forces that are transforming all countries. One decidedly beneficial effect of this change is that Canada rids itself of attempts to make it different from its southern neighbour.

A third view of the state of Canada's political culture is possible. Perhaps Canada is different from the United States, though not by much, and this difference still prevails. In politics, it has always been possible to separate Canada and the United States. This was true at Confederation and it remains true today.

In the readings, Paul Nesbitt-Larking argues that indeed the political culture of Canada is being Americanized. He also argues that this offers little cause for celebration, for it spells the end of what it means to be Canadian. Anthony A. Peacock rejects the notion that the political cultures of the two countries are different, and contends that both are now undergoing a transformation wrought by the forces of technology and globalization.

✔ **YES**
Canadian Political Culture: The Problem of Americanization
PAUL NESBITT-LARKING

Living next to you is in some ways like sleeping with an elephant; no matter how friendly and even-tempered the beast, if I may call it that, one is affected by every twitch and grunt. Even a friendly nuzzling can sometimes lead to frightening consequences.

–Pierre Trudeau, speech to the National Press Club, Washington, D.C., March 25, 1969

For a very long time, and certainly since the American Declaration of Independence in 1776, the destiny of Canada has been shaped through its complex interconnections with the political words and deeds of those other European descendants who live to the south of us. Canada is, and always has been, an *American* nation. Carved and crafted from a process of "defensive expansionism,"[1] in which the harsh wilderness of this northern part of the American continent was stitched together in east-to-west chains of settlement, often "in defiance of geography,"[2] Canada, in its very existence and longevity, is a major North American achievement. Less obviously, political and governmental life in Canada reflects two centuries of a love/hate relationship with Americans and their way of life in which Canadians have alternately incorporated and rejected American influences. Americans are a self-confident people who share a common heritage grounded in an evolving covenant among themselves to sustain the most perfect political system of freedom and opportunity. Through their enterprise and determination, Americans have translated the ideals of their founders into enormous economic, cultural, military, and political achievements. It is no idle boast to claim that the United States of America is the greatest nation on Earth.

When Americans are asked to name their "best friends" in the international community, most name the British; when they are asked with whom they conduct the most international trade, Japan is mentioned most often. These responses strike many Canadians as curious. Canada is in fact America's largest single trading partner, and, when probed, a majority of Americans expresses a strong and genuine affinity toward Canadians. What these findings reveal is best expressed by former prime minister Pierre Trudeau in the above quotation: a combination of benign ignorance and careless presumption. Americans do not think much about Canada or Canadians at all, and when they do, they think of Canadians as Americans, with some curious characteristics, who happen to live in another place. Over the past two hundred years, Americans have made gracious and consistent overtures to Canadians to join them in their great republic, and they have never been able to understand the apparent stubbornness with which a succession of Canadian leaders has resisted. American leaders have frequently regarded Canada as an odd little anomaly with its monarchical traditions and its chronic French–English tensions. Such Americans approximate Trudeau's elephants: they do not know their own strength and therefore are often unable to appreciate the damage or the offence they cause. Trudeau's tone is mild in its mockery, and it is possible to argue that his choice of animal attributes too much benevolence to the Americans. The irony of this choice becomes apparent later in his speech, when he praises the United States for not interfering in Canada's decision to trade with communist Cuba or to give diplomatic recognition to communist China. The American approach to Canada, as it has crafted its independent foreign policy throughout the past eighty years, might better be described as "bear-like" in its angry malevolence rather than elephantine in its passive tolerance. Whenever it is hungry, hurt, or under a perceived threat, the bear is prone to attack, lashing out against all who offend it or merely get in its way. While the Americans have uttered no serious threats to invade Canada since the late nineteenth century, they have interfered aggressively in our domestic and foreign affairs and, in so doing, have acted in ways that are at best insulting and undiplomatic and, at worse, in contravention of established international law and precedent.

While it is possible to argue about the extent to which the American impact on Canada has been elephantine, bear-like, or both, it is indisputable that it has been of great magnitude. Our economy is dominated by American capital. American direct investment in Canada is high, and many of Canada's most profitable industries are owned by U.S.-based corporations. Since the 1950s, Canada's military strategy and structure have been shaped in deliberate synchronization with those of the United States through a series of bilateral and multilateral agreements. Whether we refer to it as "culture" or the "entertainment industry," Canada is dominated by American material. The vast majority of the movies or TV shows we watch or the magazines we browse through originate in the United States. In political terms, the American influence has also been profound. Many of our major political institutions have been deliberately shaped to reflect, if not entirely replicate, their American counterparts, including federalism, the Senate, the Supreme Court, and the Charter of Rights and Freedoms. Our political practices and processes have also come to approximate the American pattern in certain ways. In the early twentieth century, Canada adopted the American practice of selecting political leaders through holding large-scale party conventions; in recent decades, commentators have referred to the "presidentialization" of the role of Canada's prime minister. At the deepest level, many Canadians have been enthusiastic followers of the American way of political life and have come to admire American political values and beliefs. These Canadians have attempted to convince other Canadians of the superiority of the American way and to encourage them to incorporate American values into Canadian political parties, institutions, and practices. The struggle between those who value American political ideals and those who wish to preserve a distinctive Canadian set of ideals has been raging since the Declaration of Independence in 1776. In presenting the principal features of this ideological conflict throughout this paper, I shall explain why the Americanizing forces are currently in the ascendancy and why I believe the Americanizing trend is so damaging to Canada and Canadians. I will begin with an introduction to the major concepts.

POLITICAL CULTURE AND IDEOLOGY

Unlike most concepts in political science, "political culture" has a clear and definite beginning. The term was invented by Gabriel Almond and first used in an article in 1956.[3] Like other young American political scientists of his era, Almond was determined to develop political analysis into a more rigorous and scientific discipline than it had been in the early decades of the century. The United States had emerged from the Second World War as the leading military, moral, and economic power in the world, with associated opportunities and dangers. In order to exert a meaningful influence on an unstable and rapidly changing environment, the American state required detailed, accurate, and comprehensive analyses of political character in other parts of the world. Aware of the imprecision and inaccuracy of existing accounts of political life in other countries, Almond adapted the "structural-functionalist" sociological framework of Talcott Parsons as a basis for developing a systematic understanding of political characteristics. Introducing political culture, he said: "Every political system is embedded in a particular pattern of orientations to political action. I have found it useful to refer to this as the *political culture.*"[4] By this, he meant that it is possible to identify coherent and distinctive patterns of beliefs, values, and attitudes toward political institutions and practices among each of the world's political communities. Almond and his colleague Sidney Verba attempted to identify such political orientations among the citizens of England, Mexico, Germany, the United States of America, and Italy in *The Civic Culture.*[5] On the basis of their analyses of responses to survey data, Almond and Verba produced portrayals of the distinctive political cultures of each country based upon rigorous methodological techniques and consistent quantified measures.

Almond and Verba's study generated great interest and admiration and gave rise to over a decade of research based upon their model. The systematic study of political culture was undertaken in many countries, including Canada.[6] Despite its widespread success and acceptability, the approach also attracted its critics. Prominent among the criticisms were the following: that in its assumption of the civic perfection of the United States of America, the political culture approach provided an arrogant, partial, and distorted image of political values, beliefs, and attitudes in other countries; that there were serious methodological flaws inherent in attempting to capture something as deep, nebulous, and "holistic" as culture merely through adding up a series of quick responses to questions by individuals; and, perhaps most damning of all, that in the increasingly turbulent and conflictual years of the 1960s and early 1970s, the approach could offer little to explain mass discontent, institutional paralysis, sudden change, or socioeconomic breakdown. By the mid-1970s, the huge research industry generated by Almond had dwindled to almost nothing and political scholars turned their attention to other matters. In the Canadian case, the decline of interest in political culture was marked by a series of influential anti-American articles, reflecting a more general pro-Canadian assertiveness that was prominent at the time.[7]

Regrettably, in turning away from the "Americanized" version of political culture, the Canadian political science community abandoned a very important subfield of enquiry. With all its faults, the path-breaking work of Almond had alerted us to the importance of how people feel about political issues and how they make sense of their political experiences. In criticizing Almond and others for their failure to achieve the exacting standards of full scientific rigour, it is easy to overlook the obscurity of the concept of culture and the difficulties inherent in working with it. Raymond Williams referred to culture as one of the two or three most difficult words in the English language.[8] Ongoing disputes at the core of political science over the very meaning of "politics" itself attest to the continued controversies surrounding this concept. When politics and culture are put together in a *composite* concept, definitional difficulties are multiplied.

Despite these challenges, it is possible to adapt the core of meaning inherent in Almond's approach, adding to it insights derived from other scholars in the field. The central criticisms of Almond pertain to the manner in which the concept was (ab)used—both methodologically and ethically—rather than to the concept itself. In building on Almond, my own definition of political culture incorporates the following additional insights. First, political cultures should be seen as "events" as well as states of affairs; political cultures are generated, produced, reproduced, modified, and even transformed by people in their daily activities; people are strongly conditioned through their socialization to the symbolic worlds into which they are born and in which they grow up, but they also, in their turn, contribute to the reproduction of those symbolic orders. Second, political cultures are literally "mundane" or everyday; many of the political values, beliefs, attitudes, and symbols that we hold most dearly are so taken for granted and unquestioned that we are often not aware of them. Third, I define politics more broadly than Almond as the manner in which people come to decide on the appropriate distribution of valued resources, as well as on the making of those rules that govern us. The *processes* of politics are both cooperative and conflictual; politics *happens* everywhere there are things to be distributed and rules to be made. To summarize: Political cultures happen as people, operating in an already constituted symbolic field of political cultural concepts and practices, convey to each other conceptions of the distribution and uses of valued resources and of the making of decisions and rules.

As I conceptualize them, political cultures are vague, nebulous, and shifting phenomena, and they are difficult to measure in any precise way. One of the most promising ways in which to explore political cultures is through the employment of the related concept of *ideology*. Political cultures consist of loose and semi-formed ideas, beliefs, and feelings about political institutions and practices. Ideologies are partial appropriations from political cultures, arising from the conscious and deliberate attempts of the intellectual leadership of particular social groups (known as "ideologues") to achieve a definitional monopoly of the political world, which will be accepted by as many people as possible, and which accords with the particular interests of their group. Ignoring the complexities and subtleties of political cultures and focusing on a narrow and self-interested band of values and beliefs, ideologues seek to convince others of the way things are, the way they ought to be, and, less obviously, the way it is *possible* for them to be. In so doing, ideologues hope that their "construction of reality" will convince others sufficiently to effect political change in their favour. Ideologues employ a range of political movements and associations to achieve their ends, including political parties, political institutions, interest groups, the media, the bureaucracy, and the educational system.

Canadian political culture has provided fertile "clay" for a broad range of ideologues, who have attempted to mould and shape it according to their particular interests. Arguably the most important ideological struggle over the past two hundred years has been that between "individualism" and "communitarianism." As will become clear in the next section, another way of saying this is that Canadians have been consistently seduced by the promise of the American dream, but have periodically drawn back in order to develop and sustain distinctive institutions and practices that counter those American values.[9]

INDIVIDUALISM AND COMMUNITARIANISM

The quantitative approach to political culture, developed by Almond and his followers, did not recognize the importance of the ideological opposition between individualism and communitarianism. The reason for this is readily apparent: the model of political reality devised by Almond came from an ideological individualism so profoundly entrenched and successful that it had completely overwhelmed the American political culture. It rarely occurred to American students of political culture to think beyond the limits of their individualistic premises. The entire apparatus of methodology, questions, and comparisons among nations was premised upon this unquestioned individualism. It seems hardly surprising that when Almond and his colleagues applied their benchmarks, the United States routinely emerged as the most "perfect" political culture.

Students of political culture in Canada, however, have enjoyed full access to three other approaches to the study of political culture that have enabled them to reflect upon the Canadian experience of individualism versus communitarianism. These are the "fragments" approach, associated with Louis Hartz, Kenneth McRae, and Gad Horowitz[10]; the "historical–developmental" approach, best expressed in the synthesis offered by Seymour Martin Lipset[11]; and the "political economy" approach manifest in the works of Harold Innis and Janine Brodie, among others.[12]

There are large-scale differences between the three approaches with respect to their theoretical presuppositions and methodological approaches. What unites them is their propensity to portray the evolution of Canadian political culture as an ongoing struggle between the American forces of possessive individualism on the one hand and the European forces of conservative order and socialist collectivism on the other hand. "Possessive individualism" is a phrase originating in the work of C.B. Macpherson, which distils the essence of the pure ideology of individual property rights and freedom from interference, first developed in the work of John Locke.[13] The term "communitarianism" best combines the anti-individualistic impulses of conservatism and socialism. As its name implies, communitarianism is a belief system that stresses both the logical and the moral necessity of thinking about political life in terms of the requirements of the community or the collectivity, rather than in terms of the isolated and abstracted individual. In considering those distinctively Canadian forces that have opposed possessive individualism throughout the past two centuries, communitarianism is best able to convey the alternating right-wing and left-wing critiques of American liberalism.[14]

The fragments approach to political culture argues that the principal "white settler" societies were established by ideologically homogeneous and cohesive colonies of Europeans, whose founding characteristics established the ideological parameters of those societies throughout the succeeding generations. Louis Hartz describes the powerful and pervasive force of liberal individualism in the United States, arguing that even in the twentieth century, its domination of the political culture can explain the early death of American socialism, the reluctant collectivism and populist character of the New Deal era, and the anticommunist vehemence of McCarthyism.[15] Kenneth McRae illuminates the importance of feudalism in the French-Canadian fragment, as well as loyalty to the British crown among the English-Canadian fragment, in the establishment of a society in Canada that, while fundamentally sharing in the liberal individualistic ethos of the American political culture, exhibited elements of a political culture of cautiousness, moderation, gradualism, compromise, and order.[16] McRae also makes reference to the incursion of modest doses of left-wing culture with the settlement of parts of the Canadian west by later European fragments, ideologically committed to socialism.[17] These themes are further amplified by Gad Horowitz in his seminal account of the development of ideologies in Canada. Horowitz goes much further than Hartz and McRae in pointing out the critical importance of the communitarian elements in Canada's historical development.[18] Horowitz also moves his analysis away from the Hartzian notion that the founding ideologies of the fragments "congealed" early and remained unchanged.

The manner in which historical developments, notably major events, shape the emergence of a political culture is explored in detail in the work of Seymour Martin Lipset. Since the early 1960s, Lipset has been developing a comparative analysis of the political cultures of Canada and the United States. On the basis of his understanding of comparative patterns of settlement, formative historical events, such as the American revolution and the Canadian "counterrevolution," and a broad array of sociological data on such matters as crime rates, divorce rates, and church attendance, Lipset comes to concur with Horowitz that differences between the Canadian and American political cultures are profound indeed[19]:

> My central argument is that the two countries differ in their basic organizing principles. Canada has been and is a more class-aware, elitist, law-abiding, statist, collectivity-oriented, and particularistic (group-oriented) society than the United States.... The United States remained throughout the 19th and early 20th centuries the extreme example of a classically liberal or Lockean society, one that rejected the assumptions of the alliance of throne and altar, of ascriptive elitism, of mercantilism, of noblesse oblige, of communitarianism.[20]

While Lipset stresses the fundamentally liberal individualist character of *both* Canada and the United States and argues that, in the *global* context, "the two resemble each other more than either resembles any other nation,"[21] his framework of comparison, like mine, is *between* the two countries, and the distinctions are substantial enough to be noteworthy.

Although scholars in the tradition of political economy employ different theoretical assumptions from the fragments and historical–developmental approaches, their conclusions are often similar. Harold Innis's work analyses the complexity of Canada's improbable and excruciating east-to-west expansion in the creation of a conservative and defensive nation-state, built upon the extraction and export of a series of staple products, notably fish, fur, and wheat. Acutely conscious of the north-to-south pull of the United States with its individualistic ideology and powerful free enterprise economy, as well as of the declining relevance of Great Britain and Europe, particularly in the years following the Second World War, Innis speaks darkly of the domination of American imperialism and of the capacity of its technological, militaristic, and industrial tentacles to overwhelm the less advanced and less aggressive political economies of the world, including that of Canada.[22] From a neo-Marxist perspective, Janine Brodie's work on the political economy of Canadian regionalism explores the historical vulnerability of Canada's political economy to the intrusive force of American capitalism and a series of attempts by the Canadian state to forge a distinctively Canadian economy. Brodie refers to these historical projects as "national policies," each one attempting to sustain a viable, orderly, and humane east-to-west political economy, grounded in possessive individualist principles and designed to create a stable environment for capitalist accumulation, yet balanced with commitments to such communitarian values as social order, interregional equity, and modestly redistributive policies.

As with many other contemporary political economists, Brodie expresses a preference for the communitarian vision of Canada and a concern that the declining relevance of the nation-state to capitalism will be accompanied by a reduction in the quality of democratic life and a decline in the possibility of using the state to achieve collective ends. Despite the historical pervasiveness of communitarian elements in Canada's political culture, and the eloquent passion of many of its supporters in the past, possessive individualistic ideology is currently in the ascendancy.[23] It is quite possible that communitarian tendencies could return to greater prominence in the future, but there are grave dangers to the integrity and continuance of Canada itself as a viable nation-state that attend the continued domination of our political culture by possessive individualism. I now turn my attention to these challenges.

THE PROBLEM OF AMERICANIZATION

To speak of Americanization as a problem is not to adopt a narrowly ethnocentric, anti-American point of view. A few *Americans* have expressed reservations about the consequences of the early and monopolistic domination of individualist liberalism as the American creed. The equation of individualism and libertarian freedom with "Americanism" itself has permitted the ideological intolerances of a variety of "witch hunts" and has discouraged forms of state-led and collectivist solutions to America's problems that have been made possible elsewhere. Globalization, in its economic, cultural, and militaristic forms, represents the universalization of Americanism to some extent. Thus American possessive individualism is not necessarily coterminous with the geographical and sociohistorical entity that we know as the United States of America.

My central point in this concluding section is that the individualistic liberal element of Americanism is rapidly becoming so dominant that communitarian ideological perspectives are in jeopardy. Ideologies in themselves do not die, but given the will and the opportunity, ideologues can so determine and shape political culture that a given people come to believe that only one ideological position is desirable or possible. A political culture can be so imbued with a particular ideological orientation that all others dwindle and fade. Once this is in process, political support for previously existing institutions and practices, which run counter to the interests of the prevailing ideology, falls away. The institutions and practices of the Canadian nation-state have been built on the basis of a political culture characterized by some degree of collectivist logic and communitarianism. Once these diminish beyond a certain point, Canada itself is in question. This point was grasped, in a work of brilliant insight, by conservative scholar George Grant, in 1965. In his *Lament for a Nation*, Grant understood that the uncritical adoption of American technocratic politics and economics, as well as the culture of populist consumerism, would undermine Canada to the point where its continued existence ceased to be relevant. He noted, "The impossibility of conservatism in our era is the impossibility of Canada."24 Put simply, Grant was arguing that if nobody *loves* the country or regards the relationship between the generations as a communitarian trust, then the nation-state itself will become little more than a practical container, governed by the needs of capitalism alone. Grant did not trust Canadian capitalists to care enough to fight for the continuation of the country if such a fight constituted a threat to profitability. To those who reasoned that Americanization (and today we might add "globalization") was "inevitable," Grant made the deceptively simple point that despite its inevitability, it might still be morally wrong and worth contesting, irrespective of the possibility of victory.

The subtitle of Grant's book is "The Defeat of Canadian Nationalism." There has never *been* a massive Canadian nationalism—at least not in English Canada—but there have been assertive moments of resistance to Americanization. The current ideological climate is distinctly unfriendly toward Canadian nationalism, and the signs are that Grant's lament was prescient. For the remainder of this section, I will discuss the principal ideologues of Americanization in contemporary Canada and their impact on the political culture, and specify how their ideological preferences have begun to shape Canada's political institutions and practices.

For nearly two decades, Canada's principal political parties and political leaders have been actively promoting economic policies of Americanized possessive individualism. At the federal level, with the marginal exception of the early 1980s, when the Liberal Party attempted to forge a limited new "national policy," both Liberal and Progressive Conservative governments have driven the ideological agenda toward free-market solutions. As in the construction of any ideological perspectives, the politicians have argued that their proposals are not merely sound, but that "we have no choice." In the 1970s, the Liberals argued that too many demands had been made on the federal system and that it was impossible to continue to provide the kind of extensive and responsive public service that had developed throughout the 1950s and 1960s. They promoted monetary and fiscal policies that increased unemployment, facilitated a decrease in the public sector, and squeezed middle-class incomes through higher interest rates and taxes. In the 1980s, the Progressive Conservative Party pointed out that Canadians had been victims of fiscal irresponsibility, and they began to talk of the need to cut the national deficit. They continued the trend against communitarianism in Canada through their modest attempts at public sector cutbacks, their privatizations and deregulations, but mostly through their two free trade agreements and the introduction of the regressive Goods and Services Tax. The Progressive Conservative government hoped that these policies would stimulate noninflationary growth in the economy. In the 1990s, the emphasis on the national deficit has intensified, and the Liberal Party has perpetuated the trend toward Americanization, with their massive cuts to the federal public sector as well as cuts in transfer payments to the provinces. The radical downsizing of the federal government has inevitably had an impact on the provinces. In some of them, notably Alberta and Ontario, right-wing governments have gone even further than the federal Liberal Party in radical reductions to the size and scope of the public sector on the basis of American-style populist individualism, promoting a generalized distrust of government and large-scale tax cuts designed to curtail redistributive policies. In the 1990s, two new major parties have arisen on the federal scene. One of them, the Reform Party, is a strong proponent of possessive individualism and is committed to further radical cuts in public spending, reductions in existing transfers to individuals and regions, large-scale tax cuts, and the diminution of the power of the federal state to enforce national standards. The Bloc Québécois is the other new party. Its function is to promote the interests of Quebec in the period of transition to that province's independence. This party has no coherent economic ideology, but its former leader, Lucien Bouchard, who is now premier of Quebec, is currently attempting to introduce a modified possessive individualistic ideology into Quebec, based upon his assertion that only by getting the province's debt under control will the province achieve the financial stability upon which the drive to independence can be built. Of all the political parties and politicians in contemporary Canada, very few have been active promoters of policies to enhance the communitarian essence of Canada, or even to slow its decline. To some extent, the New Democratic Party has fulfilled this role, but once in office at the provincial level, New Democrats have been obliged to limit their aspirations and, even if reluctantly, to adopt modified possessive individualistic policies, including cuts to the public sector.

Behind the political parties have been the most important special interest groups. The principal corporations and their associations and organizations, such as the Business Council on National Issues, have actively promoted greater economic integration into the United States as well as policies designed to cut the public sector and reduce taxes on the corporate elite. The corporate elite have been strongly supported by most of Canada's leading journalists, intellectuals, and academics. Some of them have, while attacking collectivism, continued to promote the rhetoric of a united Canada, which cherishes its distinctiveness. In this respect, they have offered some resistance to Americanization in so far as they have advocated the old-style orderly and conservative forms of "elite accommodation" through which Canada's distinctive communities are able to achieve a modus vivendi. In other words, they have advocated the kind of political arrangements that the Progressive Conservatives attempted to promote in the 1980s with the Meech Lake and Charlottetown Accords. The ideals of such accords, based upon bilingualism and multiculturalism in a finely balanced Canada consisting of "a community of communities," continue to be supported at the highest levels. In modified form, such is the agenda of the current Liberal Party, as it is of what is left of the Progressive Conservative Party.

The problem for Canada is that the refined and noble politics of cultural pluralism and mutual respect has been promoted through anachronistic and elitist political practices from which most citizens have felt excluded. The politics of elite accommodation also runs directly counter to the anticollectivist impulses of economic possessive individualism. The cultural message of economic liberalism stresses narrowly defined rights, absolute freedom from restraint and a rejection of those virtues associated with family, community, and society, such as love, tolerance, charity, duty, loyalty, and patriotism. There are signs that the hold of such qualities in the Canadian political culture is diminishing. An angry Canadian public rejected the Charlottetown Accord in 1992. The accord had been designed to provide a new compromise among Canadians in terms of their constitutional rights, as well as to restate the commitment of Canadians to a unified nationhood and distinctive national identity. Canadian voters punished the architects of the plan, the Progressive Conservative Party, by almost completely rejecting them in the federal election of 1993. In their place, English Canadians supported the Reform Party, while many Quebeckers turned to the Bloc Québécois; both political organizations are intolerant of bilingualism and multiculturalism.

The decline in support for the traditional parties, the growing disrespect for politicians, the growth of support for narrowly defined single-issue political movements, and a generalized sense of the atomization of political society all point to a growing Americanization of Canada's political culture.[25] The rapidly declining trust in Canada's political institutions, political parties, and politicians is reported in Nevitte's *The Decline of Deference*.[26] Nevitte's data demonstrate that "confidence in governmental institutions is declining while non-traditional ... forms of political participation are increasing. In political matters, people are becoming less deferential, less compliant, more inclined to speak out...."[27] Similar findings are reported by Clarke and his colleagues in *Absent Mandate*, which also tracks Canadian public opinion in the 1980s and 1990s.[28] Clarke et al. report strong declines in partisan loyalty and attachment over these decades, in conjunction with growing disaffection, detachment, and negativity concerning politicians and parties.[29] Their final chapter is entitled "The Politics of Discontent," and a key feature of that chapter is their characterization of an "angry and cynical" electorate.[30] Concluding their work, Clarke et al. refer to the Canadian political situation as one of "permanent dealignment," by which they mean a consistently fragmented and volatile relationship between citizens and parties.[31] In the context of such permanent dealignment, communitarian attachments to persons and places become strained. While dealignment and disaffection can be dangerous to a political community, blind deference is no better. Deference is always a thin and brittle basis for a political community and is, in the final analysis, as damaging as possessive individualism. Disaffection and the decline of deference are, therefore, in some respects, positive forces and represent an assertive enhancement of political efficacy and political participation. However, in contemporary Canada, the principal ideological forces that have picked up on the mood of popular anger and cynicism offer individuated solutions, which serve to amplify people's negativity, deepening and broadening their defensive possessiveness rather than encouraging their communitarian imaginations to seek new ways in which to invigorate the body politic.

The Canadian public have demonstrated that they are not bound to the traditional political parties and that they are prepared to vote for new "anti-party" parties in numbers large enough to elect entire "Official Oppositions" to the House of Commons. The Reform Party represents an American-style populism that it has made hegemonic in the west of Canada. The Bloc Québécois offers the only true communitarian option in Canada, one that is, of course, grounded in demands for a distinctive and independent Quebec state to reflect the aspirations of the people of Quebec. To some extent, the success of Quebec nationalism is a reflection of the poverty of any true pan-Canadian national vision either inside French Quebec or in the rest of Canada. Current political discourse in Canada is punctuated by the claims and counterclaims of single interest groups, to which citizens are encouraged to adhere on the basis of their narrowly defined personal and individual desires. Among the most recent crop of such groups are gun owners angry about gun control, victims of crime angry about the lack of compensation in the criminal justice system, and noncustodial divorced fathers angry about their lack of parental rights. At present there is little to unite the various single-issue groups other than a shared belief in entitlement based on a conception of the state as a repository of goods and legal precedents that are "up for grabs." Ironically, given its rhetorical opposition to "special interests," it is the Reform Party that most effectively encourages Canadians to adopt the politics of particularistic advantage.

The most recent federal election illustrates these trends. Despite the claims of the Progressive Conservative Party and the New Democratic Party to be truly national parties and to stand for a pan-Canadian vision in which people might again think of themselves as members of a shared political community, these parties were unsuccessful in garnering much support. Where they were successful, largely in the Atlantic provinces, their support base was reflective of a protest against the possessive individualism of both the federal Liberal Party and the Reform Party, and as such represents a small beacon of hope for a renewed politics of community. Jean Charest, the leader of the Progressive Conservative Party, moved many people when, during the English-language debate on television, he talked passionately—in words that might have come from George Grant—of his refusal to permit the legacy of a united Canada to be destroyed before his children could enjoy it. People cheered because Charest's words struck a chord of communitarian consciousness searching for some expression. When Preston Manning, leader of the Reform Party, attempted to replicate the success, he used the Canadian flag as a backdrop and spoke, unconvincingly, of his love of country. Neither Manning's supporters nor his detractors believed in this display. It ran counter to every other liberal-individualistic signal being emitted by the Reform Party throughout the campaign. The most egregious example of this was the infamous "Quebec" politicians advertisement in which the Reform Party employed American-style "attack advertisement" techniques to imply that Canada had had too many prime ministers from Quebec. For many Canadians, the message might simply have read: "My Canada Excludes Quebec." The entire discourse of the Reform Party's campaign was built upon a radical denial of voice to anyone other than "individuals and provinces." By "provinces," the Reform Party was apparently thinking of prominent provincial politicians, and its demand was for the radical decentralization of the Canadian federation.

The impact of the changing composition of Canada's political culture, as well as of the work of the ideologues of possessive individualism, has been acutely felt. Despite the valiant efforts of small Canadian nationalist groups, such as the Action Canada Network, and an assortment of individuals, including some prominent politicians and journalists, the federal state has been radically Americanized in the past decade: NAFTA and the GST are accomplished fact; Air Canada, Canadian National Railways, and Petro Canada, corporations designed with explicit public and nation-building purposes, have been partially or totally privatized; major regulatory agencies, such as the Canadian Radio-television and Telecommunications Commission, have lost many of their regulatory powers; federal crown corporations, notably the CBC, have suffered enormous budget cuts; and there have been radical reductions in the size and scope of the state. The effects of these cuts have reverberated in the quality of life at the provincial level: the "social safety net" has been lowered; universal provision of social services, which nurtures a communitarian ethos, has been rapidly replaced with "means-tested" and limited provision of social services, which targets and stigmatizes the poor; public systems of health care and education are being eroded to the point where partial privatization of so-called core or essential services seems highly probable; the gap between the rich and the poor is increasing as the middle-class, which carried much of the burden of redistribution in the 1980s, becomes increasingly reluctant to share.

In furtherance of these trends, the liberal-individualistic message of radical decentralization is currently being hotly promoted by Canada's richest and most influential special interest group, the Business Council on National Issues. The Business Council and the Reform Party are both promoting a new Canada in which principal socioeconomic and political control is devolved to the provinces and in which there is little more than some vague sentiment to hold the country together. If there is radical decentralization in the future, those ties of common citizenship that bind us will fall away, and the already weak voices for Canada will become even weaker. As the voices for a pan-Canadian vision diminish, so the logic of an independent Quebec state will increase. Once Quebec has gone, the remaining nine provinces and the territories will have very little left to hold them together. As they enter further into the liberal-individualistic ethos of free trade in the North American continent, an ethos buttressed by new World Trade Organization agreements that severely restrict the scope of sovereign states in controlling capital flows, so the patent absurdity of continued independence for a culturally fractured, socioeconomically divided, and geographically split Canada will become increasingly clear. We will have rationalized Canada out of existence.

CONCLUSION

Given the ideological assault of Americanizing possessive individualism on Canada's political culture, and the efficacy of that assault in terms of major changes in public policy, what is the prognosis for Canada? The spirit of self-centred individualism does not bode well for the continued existence of Canada. Traditional conservatives would argue that any nation that has lost its sense of organic connectedness is in poor health. When the phrase "The West wants in" became the rallying cry for the foundation of the Reform Party of Canada, it was taken to mean that the western provinces wished to partake of the benefits and burdens of full and equitable citizenship. Regrettably, the phrase has come to be associated instead with a narrowly focused acquisitiveness, opportunistic rent-seeking, and an unwillingness to share natural advantages with those persons and regions less fortunate in the country. Under such circumstances, it seems improbable that the wealthier provinces, such as British Columbia, Alberta, and Ontario, will be able to see much sense in sustaining Canada as a unified nation-state. The deficit cutting and public-sector gutting economic policies of the Liberal Party and the Progressive Conservative Party are actively promoting this kind of "beggar-thy-neighbour" fragmentation. It is, of course, possible that the decline of public provision, the growing inequality, and the increasing immiseration of the poor will so offend the communitarian impulses of our political culture that Canadians will reject further trends toward possessive individualism.[32]

On the cultural front, there seems to be little patriotism or spontaneous love of country. It simply appears that nobody cares very much. Over a century ago, the French intellectual Ernst de Renan referred to a nation as an act of will, as "a daily plebiscite." There seems to be very little will to sustain Canada. Not only is there an atmosphere of listless apathy about the nation, but also increasing numbers of English Canadians have come to adopt the Reform Party line of "my way or the highway" when it comes to accommodation with Quebec. The unwillingness of a majority of English Canadians to accept even the modest and unexceptional claim of Quebec to be a "distinct society" is perhaps the greatest threat to the future of the nation. Such an uncompromising stance would be welcomed in the radically individualistic melting-pot homogeneity of the United States, but it makes little sense in Canada. It is possible that there are sufficient numbers of French Quebeckers who could be persuaded to remain in a Canada of "two solitudes" united through mutual and distanced respect. The ultimate consequence of the logic of Reform Party ideology on national issues is to drive those moderate Quebeckers into the welcoming arms of the separatists.

Canada is in jeopardy. Our neighbours to the south have consistently stated that they would welcome Canada as a part of their great country. Such a solution might make sense. Here I recall the sarcastic and self-pitying vitriol of George Grant, who said: "Perhaps we should rejoice in the disappearance of Canada. We leave the narrow provincialism and our backwoods culture; we enter the excitement of the United States where all the great things are done."[33] I hear the voice of an idealistic and disillusioned adolescent cry out: "Fine! If you care so little about your country, to hell with you! You *deserve* to lose it." Perhaps something of this defiant spirit will one day provide the wherewithal to sustain Canada for a while longer. Perhaps, given the newfound assertive and anti-elite rebelliousness of Canadians, they will simply reinvent the country and craft something new, authentic, and beautiful. Maybe, in this globalized, postmodern age in which Canada's greatest claim to international distinctiveness is to be a country that is so tolerant of pluralities of differences among its own citizens that it really has no substantive core, Canada will actually become the first "post-nation": an address with no fixed identity, whose very openness will be an exemplar to the remainder of the world, whose new soft tribalisms will gradually infiltrate the remainder of the planet, imbuing them with Canadianism and creating the ultimate global village.

NOTES

1. The phrase comes from H.G.J. Aitken, "Defensive Expansionism: The State and Economic Growth in Canada," in W.T. Easterbrook and M.H. Watkins, eds., *Approaches to Canadian Economic History* (Toronto: McClelland and Stewart, 1967), pp. 183–221.

2. W.A. Mackintosh, "Economic Factors in Canadian History," in Easterbrook and Watkins, eds., *Approaches*, p. 15.

3. Gabriel Almond, "Comparative Political Systems," *World Politics* 18 (1956): 391–409.

4. Ibid., p. 396.

5. Gabriel Almond and Sidney Verba, *The Civic Culture* (Boston: Little Brown, 1963).

6. See Jon Pammett and Michael Whittington, eds., *Foundations of Political Culture: Political Socialization in Canada* (Toronto: Macmillan, 1976); Richard Simeon and David Elkins, "Regional Political Cultures in Canada," *Canadian Journal of Political*

Science 7 (1974): 397–437; John Wilson, "The Canadian Political Cultures: Towards a Redefinition of the Nature of the Canadian Political System," *Canadian Journal of Political Science* 7 (1974): 438–483; Elia Zureik and Robert Pike, eds., *Socialization and Values in Canadian Society: Political Socialization* (Toronto: Macmillan, 1975).

7. Donald Smiley, "Must Canadian Political Science Be a Miniature Replica?" *Journal of Canadian Studies* 9 (1974): 31–42; C.B. Macpherson, "After Strange Gods: Canadian Political Science 1973," in T.N. Guinsberg and G.L. Reuber, eds., *Perspectives on the Social Sciences in Canada* (Toronto: University of Toronto Press, 1974), pp. 52–76; Alan Cairns, "Political Science in Canada and the Americanization Issue," *Canadian Journal of Political Science* 8 (1975): 191–234.

8. Raymond Williams, *Keywords: A Vocabulary of Culture and Society* (London: Fontana, 1976), p. 76.

9. This point is elaborated by Steven Brooks, *Canadian Democracy: An Introduction* (Toronto: Oxford University Press, 1996), p. 38, who attributes a range of economic and cultural policies to a series of deliberate "refusals in the face of Americanizing pressures."

10. Louis Hartz, *The Founding of New Societies* (New York: Harcourt, Brace and World, 1964); Kenneth McRae, "The Structure of Canadian History," in Louis Hartz, *The Founding of New Societies*, pp. 219–274; Gad Horowitz, "Conservatism, Liberalism, and Socialism in Canada: An Interpretation," *Canadian Journal of Economics and Political Science* 32 (1966): 143–171.

11. Seymour Martin Lipset, *Continental Divide: The Values and Institutions of the United States and Canada* (New York: Routledge, 1990).

12. Harold Innis, *Essays in Canadian Economic History* (Toronto: University of Toronto Press, 1962); Janine Brodie, *The Political Economy of Canadian Regionalism* (Toronto: Harcourt, Brace, Jovanovitch, 1990).

13. C.B. Macpherson, *The Political Theory of Possessive Individualism* (London: Oxford University Press, 1962).

14. Sylvia Bashevkin, "The Politics of Canadian Nationalism," in Paul Fox and Graham White, eds., *Politics: Canada* (Toronto: McGraw-Hill, 1995), pp. 40–47.

15. Hartz, *The Founding of New Societies*, pp. 107, 111–112, 119.

16. McRae, "The Structure of Canadian History," p. 239.

17. Ibid., p. 270.

18. Horowitz, "Conservatism, Liberalism and Socialism in Canada," p. 148.

19. General interpretations of the comparatively communitarian character of Canada, proffered by McRae, Horowitz, and Lipset, are rejected by Janet Ajzenstat and Peter J. Smith, "Liberal-Republicanism: The Revisionist Picture of Canada's Founding," in idem., eds, *Canada's Origins: Liberal, Tory, or Republican?* (Ottawa: Carleton University Press, 1995), pp. 1–18. Not only do they claim that there is little Tory conservatism in the Canadian political tradition, but they go further in regarding the Upper and Lower Canadian establishments of the nineteenth century as fundamentally "liberal," and their principal rebel opponents, such as Mackenzie and Papineau, as "civic republican." While this is not the place to engage in detailed debate with Ajzenstat and Smith, I am in fundamental disagreement with their characterizations. Not only do they ignore the abundant evidence of elitist, ascriptive, affective, and particularistic practices on the part of the governing classes, but they also promote

the idea that "civic republicanism" is "antiliberal." The ideology is better interpreted, by Louis Hartz among others, as "left" or radical liberalism. While it is true that Mackenzie and Papineau "scorn ... the nineteenth-century liberal constitution...." (p. 8), the basis of their opposition is not antiliberalism, but antiauthoritarianism. There is little evidence to support the claim that the nineteenth-century rebels were against the basic principles of possessive individualism. Their rallying cry was not for the abolition of capitalism, but for responsible government and genuine democratic rights.

20. Lipset, *Continental Divide*, p. 8.

21. Ibid., pp. 214, 219, 225. Nevitte has recently produced comparative survey data to illustrate the fact that, in the context of the advanced industrial nations, Canada and the United States are often closer to each other than to any other nations. He goes further and argues that Lipset's claims that Canadians are more deferential, law-abiding, and passive than Americans is not supported in his data. See Neil Nevitte, *The Decline of Deference* (Peterborough: Broadview Press, 1996), pp. 105–106.

22. Harold A. Innis, *The Bias of Communication* (Toronto: University of Toronto Press, 1971); Innis, *Canadian Economic History*, pp. 394–412.

23. The historical tradition of communitarianism and collectivism is mentioned in numerous sources, including Rand Dyck, *Canadian Politics: Critical Approaches* (Toronto: Nelson, 1996), p. 286; Michael Whittington and Richard Van Loon, *Canadian Government and Politics: Institutions and Processes* (Toronto: McGraw-Hill Ryerson, 1996), p. 99; and Brooks, *Canadian Democracy*, pp. 56–60.

24. George Grant, *Lament for a Nation* (Toronto: McClelland and Stewart, 1965), p. 68.

25. Peter Dobell and Byron Berry, "Anger at the System: Political Discontent in Canada," in Fox and White, *Politics: Canada*, pp. 4–9; Maclean's/Decima polling data, *Maclean's*, 2 January 1995.

26. Nevitte, *The Decline of Deference*, pp. 56, 79, 267, 291. Nevitte uses his data to interpret recent changes in the Canadian political culture as evidence of a general move toward postindustrial, postmaterialist, and postmodern values, pervasive throughout the West, and he specifically downplays the "Americanization" thesis. Nevitte's method of calculating the degree of "Americanization," outlined in footnote 2 on page 314 of his book, is designed to assess the "cultural lag" thesis that Canadian value changes lag behind those of the United States. Nevitte takes a series of dimensions in which he measures the change in both Canadian and American values from 1981 to 1990. One of these dimensions is "confidence in government institutions." According to Nevitte's data, "confidence in government institutions" declined from 49.6 percent in 1981 to 31.8 percent in 1990 in the United States, a decline of nearly 18 percentage points. In Canada, the comparable change was from 36.9 percent in 1981 to 29.4 percent in 1990, a decline of 7.5 percentage points. Using his calculus of "cultural lag," Nevitte declares *Canada* to be the leader of the trend in 1990. (Table 9–2, p. 292). The fact that the U.S. figure in 1990 more closely approximates the Canadian figure in 1981 than the Canadian 1990 figure approximates the American 1981 figure—Nevitte's criterion for Canada as the cultural leader—is, in my opinion, inadequate as a measure of the degree of Americanization. It is, of course, possible to argue that the Americans are becoming more like Canadians. However, it seems equally plausible to postulate that the profound loss of confidence, tracked in the American data, has a more moderate, yet still substantial, echo effect in Canada.

27. Ibid., p. 267.

28. Harold D. Clarke, Jane Jenson, Lawrence LeDuc, and Jon H. Pammett, *Absent Mandate: Canadian Politics in an Era of Restructuring*, 3rd ed. (Vancouver: Gage, 1996).

29. Ibid., pp. 22, 61, 65, 67.

30. Ibid., pp. 176–180.

31. Ibid., p. 185.

32. For data in support of these claims, refer to Statistics Canada, *Canada at a Glance*, 1995–1996 (www.statcan.ca), "Persons with Low Income" and "Average Income." The average incomes of Canadians decreased from 1988 to 1993 by 3.6 percent in constant dollars, and the percentage of Canadians with low incomes increased from 15.4 percent to 18 percent between 1989 and 1993. The increase was particularly pronounced among children. More detailed—and disturbing—data on child poverty are contained in the Social Planning Council of Metropolitan Toronto's document "Child Poverty in Metropolitan Toronto: Report Card 1996." On the basis of their own data, as well as data derived from the Canadian Council on Social Development, the National Council of Welfare, the Metro Toronto Housing Authority, Metro Community Services, the Children's Aid Society of Metropolitan Toronto, and the Daily Bread Food Bank, the Social Planning Council provides details of the dramatic rise in child poverty in Canada's largest city throughout the 1990s. See also Ann Duffy and Nancy Mandell, "The Widening Gap: Social Inequality and Poverty," in Daniel Glenday and Ann Duffy, eds., *Canadian Society: Understanding and Surviving in the 1990s* (Toronto: McClelland and Stewart, 1994), pp. 49–85.

33. Grant, *Lament*, p. 8.

✗ **NO**
Socialism as Nationalism: Why the Alleged Americanization of Canadian Political Culture Is a Fraud
ANTHONY A. PEACOCK

> Writers on America do not simply speak of the United States; they have also constructed the concept of "Americanism" or "Americanization," which refers to such fundamental developments of modernity as cultural homogenization, democratization, and degeneration. America so conceived may exist outside of the United States and involve no actual Americans. Once this point is reached, it becomes clear that real America is no longer at issue: and idea or symbol called "America" has taken over.
>
> —James W. Ceaser
> *Reconstructing America:*
> *The Symbol of America in Modern Thought*

INTRODUCTION

As my title suggests, the word "nationalism" in Canada has become synonymous with the word "socialism," with the policy preferences of Canada's socialist or social democratic community, a community that prefers public over private enterprise. The proposition, supported by those I will refer to in this chapter as Canadian nationalists, that Canada's political culture is distinguishable from its American counterpart by our greater collectivism or our greater use of public enterprise, is, I submit, a fraud. And it is a dangerous fraud at that.

The nationalist characterization of Canadian–American relations amounts to little more than a caricature, disregarding those fundamental features, including American public enterprise, that identify Canadian and American political culture.[1]

More importantly, the nationalist's argument masks the definitively noncollectivist, noncommunitarian nature of Canadian public enterprise. Not only is Canadian public enterprise divisive, tending to pit one region of the country against another, it also undermines the preconditions of any real Canadian community, surrendering to centralized, bureaucratic authorities the task of self-government that should be left to private individuals and to communities themselves. Having lost sight of the very distinction between community and government, the nationalist advocacy has ironically resulted in the emaciation of Canadian identity rather than its cultivation or clarification. In their simplistic characterization of the alleged conflict between the United States and Canada, a conflict that typically takes shape as one between the "insensitive," "materialistic" individualism of the United States and the more "caring," "compassionate" collectivism of Canada, the nationalists have inadequately explained how American political culture has produced not less, but more, of a sense of community, more of a sense of collective identity, and more of a feeling of national pride than anything produced so far in Canada. There seems to be a connection between individualism and community that the nationalists have to date overlooked.

Since the 1960s, when the social democratic agenda of Canadian nationalism, with its demand for greater protection of Canadian political culture, took hold of Canadian public policy, Quebec nationalism has ballooned, English-speaking Canada has lost whatever semblance of identity it may have enjoyed prior to the 1960s, and cultural relativism has become the mantra of law reform and education. Is this mere coincidence?

In this chapter, I suggest not. What has kept Canadians from realizing or recapturing their identity has little to do with America and much more to do with the destructive policies and disingenuous messages about who they are, perpetuated by Canada's opinion-forming classes: its political elites, its media, its university professors, and other intellectuals.

If we understand political culture in its literal sense as what we have grown in Canada to constitute our politics and our political character, we should see the antisocialistic, free-market movement afoot today as a refreshing attempt to recover a self-reliant, community-oriented individualism, an individualism that provided Canadians a pride and respect before the era of big government and the culture of dependency and entitlements erased what sense of ourselves and self-reliance we had.

NORTH AMERICA: ONE BIG, HAPPY FAMILY, BOURGEOIS, AND LOVING IT

It is a commonplace among advocates of Canadian nationalism that Canadians are culturally distinct from Americans. This, of course, is not true. The differences between Canadians and Americans are ephemeral, not essential. Canadians and Americans prefer the same television, the same music, the same sports, the same magazines, enjoy the same cuisine, and vacation at the same destinations. They seek the same things out of life. As George Grant pointed out a generation ago, the identity shared by Canadians and Americans runs deeper than economics or politics, extending to the very faith that gives purpose and meaning to all who live in the Western world.[2] The tough questions that face Canadians respecting politics and culture are the same tough questions that face Americans. The central issue in both cases is whether anything distinctive about Canada or the United States can survive the universalizing and homogenizing effects of modern technology, which makes people, and the objects they desire in life, more and more the same despite whatever differences in appearance persist. "Lying behind the immediate decisions arising from our status within the [American] empire is the deeper question of the fate of any particularity in the technological age. What happens to nationalist strivings when the societies in question are given over, at the very level of faith, to the realisation of the technological dream?"[3]

The technological dream is what Canadians pursue, just as Americans do. We seek economic growth, take pride in our jobs, our industriousness, and our ingenuity, and measure the success of our politicians by how effectively they manage the debt and the deficit.

Listen to Canadian nationalists and our cultural spokesmen, however, and one gets a different impression. As David Frum has remarked:

> Canada is a big, rich, North American nation, where people live in suburbs, drive to work, shop in malls, invest their money in mutual funds, listen to country music, and resent paying taxes. But watch a Canadian movie, read a Canadian novel, flip through most Canadian magazines, or turn on the news, and you'll see a different country; a poor, struggling hinterland of the American empire, where people live in outposts, work for the government if they work at all, collect groceries from food banks, listen to folk singers, and enjoy paying taxes.[4]

The gap between official Canada and actual Canada[5] has to be maintained by the nationalist community because to do otherwise would undermine the moral and political legitimacy of the protectionist enterprise.

The free trade debate of the late 1980s exemplified nationalist rhetoric, a rhetoric that at the time had little to do either with the stakes at issue or with the nationalists' real concern. The real concern of the nationalists was not the transitory issues of depleted social programs, a tarnished environment, or the loss of water to American farmers free trade might precipitate, although the nationalists protested these issues vociferously. The real concern of the nationalists was that the higher standard of living brought about by more open trade with the United States would cause Canadians to rethink the value of those "nation-building" (read big government) projects that had become the darling objects of cultural protectionism. The wealth and increased freedom free trade would bring might lead Canadians to consign to the dustbin, permanently, those projects that had brought nationalists, and their constituencies, wealth and augmenting, centralized power.[6]

On the other hand, the strong argument for free trade, more than the promise of material prosperity, was precisely the destruction of that official dogma that had become the sine qua non of nationalist indoctrination. Free trade presented Canadians with the opportunity to inaugurate a nationwide self-recognition.[7]

If we were to look for a common thread linking Grant's and Frum's observations, it would be that politics, conceived in any serious sense as a choice between different ends, is over. Modern nations pursue the same ends. This includes Canada and the United States. In the most fundamental respect, Canadian and

American politics are aligned. The only serious question is one of means, of how best to achieve the ends Canadians and Americans tend to agree upon. This means that the respective states in Canada and the United States should not be distinguished by ideological differences, as the cultural protectionists suggest. Rather, if we are to think—and legislate—precisely, we should distinguish the Canadian and American states by their greater or lesser efficacy at resolving the same given problems. This, I believe, is what Canadians are coming to recognize.

The nationalists suggest that the political cultures of Canada and the United States can be distinguished on the basis of the different ends they pursue. If they nationalists are honest enough to concede that the objects of Canadian and American politics are little different, the nationalists will claim that each country pursues these ends by different means. This too, we will see, is a canard.

MULTICULTURALISM, GROUPISM, AND THE POLITICS OF IDENTITY: AMERICAN, NOT CANADIAN, ORTHODOXY

Political commentators in Canada have gone to great lengths trying to establish that Canadians and Americans differ from one another on ideological or cultural grounds, asserting recently, for instance, that our distinctiveness lies in our bilingualism, our multiculturalism, or our greater pluralism. It has also been suggested, as I indicated in the introduction, that Canada's uniqueness lies in its greater collectivist inclinations or its public enterprises, that Canada is more community oriented, less individualistic than the United States, even if we pursue the same political and economic goals.

Again, these ruminations are not only false, but, in the case of multiculturalism and our alleged greater pluralism, reflect the influences of an American phenomenon, the politics of identity, which eventually made significant inroads into Canadian public policy.

Canada is not bicultural or bilingual. French speakers live, for the most part, in Quebec, English speakers in the rest of Canada. There are bilingual Canadians, but they tend to live in bureaucratized Ottawa and slowly unilingualizing Montreal (more and more English speakers are leaving the city every year).[8] As for Canadians whose bilingualism does not involve French and English, they are irrelevant, no different from what we find in the United States.

Canada is, similarly, no more multicultural or pluralist than the United States, nor is it less assimilationist. If statistics count for anything, Canada's population is more uniform than that of the United States, not less. As Peter Brimelow reports, responses to the 1981 census indicated that Canada was ethnically much more homogeneous than the United States, as well as much more British. This was particularly the case when English-speaking Canada was considered apart from French-speaking Canada. Of all Canadians surveyed in 1981, over 40 percent told census-takers that they were British in origin. In addition, nearly 6% more said they were a mixture of British and other ethnic origins. Chinese, Japanese, Indochinese and a large "Indo-Pakistani" group constituted only about 2% of Canada's population, and Latin Americans 0.4%. About 1% were immigrants from Africa and the Caribbean Islands. By contrast, in the U.S. about 14% are of British stock—much less than in Canada, although still the single largest ethnic group. Another 8% are Irish, whom the Canadian census-takers regard as British. Perhaps 12% are black, 6% "Hispanic"—almost all Latin American—and 2% Asian, mostly Chinese, Indochinese and Japanese.[9]

Canadians are no more multicultural or diverse than Americans.

If Canadians believe that their political culture is more tolerant of group politics than that of the United States, that racial and ethnic diversity is better facilitated here through policies of bilingualism and multiculturalism and a constitution that promotes and protects multicultural diversity, again, we might rethink our position. It is true that federal and provincial governments invite racial and ethnic groups to differentiate themselves from other Canadians, in fact, paying these groups to do so. Section 27 of the Charter of Rights and Freedoms also provides that the "Charter shall be interpreted in a manner consistent with the preservation and enhancement of the multicultural heritage of Canadians."

But recent trends in American institutional politics, increasingly tutoring racial and ethnic groups, such as Mexican Americans, to define themselves as racial minority claimants,[10] have encouraged greater differentiation between cultural groups in the United States as well, even if, as in Canada, the differences between these groups are more artificial, more exaggerated, than real. "What is undeniably clear," Peter Skerry has written, "is that contemporary political institutions and culture encourage many Mexican Americans to 'assimilate' precisely by defining themselves as an oppressed racial minority."[11] Mexican Americans, like other ethnic and racial groups in the United States, have been invited by politicians, civil rights legislation, public interest law firms, the academic community, and other powerful groups to distinguish themselves from mainstream America, asserting their ostensible victim status. In doing so, however, Mexican Americans join a host of other groups who have asserted a similar status, if on the basis of other characteristics, such as gender or sexual preference, rather than race or ethnicity.

In short, the politics of differentiation, at work in Canada since the 1970s, has been at work in the United States even longer, since roughly the late 1960s when the civil rights lobby, supported by the United States Supreme Court and others, transformed civil rights initiatives and related public policy into affirmative action for designated classes of citizens.[12] Group identity, group politics, and recognition of group rights have been as prevalent in the United States as in Canada, Canadian policy, in fact, following the American lead. The persistence of opinions north of the border asserting otherwise, even among the most astute observers of Canadian and American politics, is hard to comprehend in light of the significant and mounting evidence to the contrary.[13]

The attempt on the part of the Canadian government, and its intellectual acolytes in the universities and the media, to differentiate Canada from the United States on the basis of our nationwide bilingualism, our greater tolerance for group differentiation, our multiculturalism, or our diversity, is, then, misleading. Official bilingualism does not reflect a greater tolerance for group differentiation in Canada. If anything, it reveals a transparent attempt on the part of the federal government to appease the demands of isolated elements of Quebec nationalism in the face of widespread, vocal opposition to the policy both inside and outside Quebec. Canada's experiment with bilingualism has been an unmitigated exercise in social engineering.[14] And its nationalist ideology has transposed the ethnic reality of Canada and the United States, obscuring the strikingly similar nature of their English-speaking populations.[15]

If we consider, on the one hand, the legacy of American public enterprise[16] and the volume of public interest laws that have been passed in the United States,[17] and, on the other hand, the distinctive nature both of American community and of Canadian and American political and institutional structures, it is also apparent that Canada is no more collectivist than the United States. Like its American counterpart, Canadian collectivism—communitarianism as it is sometimes referred to (I identify the two here)—is both antediluvian and dangerous: antediluvian because it fails to recognize the dynamism and transient quality of modern technological life; dangerous because in failing to recognize reality for what it is, its diagnoses and proposals for reform, when not entirely irrelevant, promote a soft, and more frequently than not, hard, despotism. As David Bercuson and Barry Cooper have pointed out, real communitarians believe in real communities. But real communities have all but disappeared from Canada, as well as from the rest of the modern world. This theme, the subject of volumes of sociological and political commentary, is apparently lost on communitarians who, in their evocations for a more "helping" or "caring" society, work with a romantic vision of a Canadian community that has never existed and likely never will exist.[18]

Canadians are not polis-dwelling pagans. Nor are they the commiserating village people of Rousseau's social contract. They are sophisticated, technological individuals who have come to reject the welfare state and public enterprise in Canada for the same reason Americans have rejected these things in the United States: not because they do not understand their machinations or because they have been duped by a conservative attack on them, but because they see them for what they are—a tax consuming, bureaucratic vortex that costs more and more to provide less and less. Public enterprise, and we might add collectivism in general, in Canada and the United States is on the wane, not because Canadians and Americans have been overtaken by a vulgar, malevolent individualism, but because the welfare state that residents of both countries have generously supported for so long has proven to be enormously inefficient.

Even if we assume that real communities could exist in Canada, nationalist and collectivist prescriptions for such communities would undermine them, as the legacy of such policies since the 1960s demonstrates.

The problem of Quebec nationalism provides a case in point. Charles Taylor has attributed the rise of Quebec nationalism during the Quiet Revolution and after to the emergence in Quebec of a French-speaking business class and political intelligentsia.[19] Another cause, perhaps no less significant, has been the increasing dependency on the federal welfare state that has taken place in Quebec since the 1960s. The growth of federal control in Quebec, as in all provinces, has caused many Quebeckers, like other Canadians, to move to regain their lost autonomy, even if this means resorting to regional or ethnic nationalism. Should we not expect such nationalism to augment as the federal government expands its mandate?

Whatever the relationship between the federal welfare state and Quebec nationalism, it is clear that the collectivist prescriptions of the nationalists have not improved Canadian community. Public enterprise in Canada rarely serves the public because Canada's political and institutional structures, to a much greater extent than similar structures in the United States, seldom work to serve the interests of the whole country. It is difficult, for instance, to explain to an Albertan that Petro Canada was in her best interests[20]; that the CBC has not been preoccupied from its inception with the welfare of Central Canada, treating political issues, not unlike the National Film Board of Canada, from a perspective that is neither right-wing nor middle-of-the-road but definitively left-wing[21]; or that the national policy has not benefited Ontario and Quebec to a greater extent than Canada's "regions." In just what sense are these policies or enterprises "public"? "national"?

Inaugurated in earnest in the 1960s and institutionalized after 1980, when Pierre Trudeau and the Liberal Party unveiled a series of interventionist policies, including the National Energy Program, Canadian nationalism, as I indicated in the introduction, has served as little more than a rhetorical subterfuge for Canada's Left.[22] Under the pretext of "nationalism," Canadian social democrats and their ideological hangers-on have demanded from government, and received, regulation of the economy, education, social programs, medicine, and the media. Champions of communications monoliths, such as the CBC and the NFB, or of regulatory bodies, such as the Canadian Radio-television and Telecommunications Commission, have claimed that these tributaries of government are necessary to preserve the national interest. Canadians, however, have increasingly come to recognize that these entities of state have served as little more than instruments of social democratic indoctrination, more concerned with controlling the future than with preserving the past, with acquiring power than with promoting patriotism.[23] The assumption underlying government regulation of Canada's culture is that

Canadians cannot think on their own. They must be told what to read, what to watch, what to listen to by their nationalist guardians. The same patronizing assumptions have been used by economic nationalists who, in their attacks on foreign investment and free trade during the last thirty years, have claimed to know better than Canadians themselves how they should run their economic and social lives.

INDIVIDUALISM AND COMMUNITY: THE INEXTRICABLE LINK

One reason nationalism has failed to achieve its objectives is the incommensurability of its social democratic policies with the development and maintenance of communities. Communities require individualism—individual autonomy and responsibility—for their generation and maintenance. Cultural protectionists and nationalists tend to assume the opposite: that individualism is incompatible with community, that broad personal autonomy will not result in a strong sense of national or local identity, or a sense of civic pride.

In his contribution to this debate, Professor Nesbitt-Larking remarks that "the cultural message of economic liberalism [meaning America] stresses narrowly defined rights, absolute freedom from restraint and a rejection of those virtues associated with family, community, and society, such as love, tolerance, charity, duty, loyalty, and patriotism." Leaving aside the dubious suggestion that Americans are less loving, tolerant, or charitable than Canadians—the implication here, I believe—one would have to read far and wide among the works of Alexander Hamilton, George Washington, or John Adams, or the icons of economic liberalism—Adam Smith, Friedrich Hayek, or Milton Friedman, for instance—to find any assertion of a connection between economic liberalism and a rejection of those virtues associated with family, community, or society. On the contrary. A central theme running throughout the texts of economic liberals is the impossibility of achieving such virtues without the self-restraint, discipline, and responsibility demanded, and cultivated, by free markets, qualities without which families and communities disintegrate. The mere existence of the United States should be proof enough that duty, loyalty, and patriotism are not incommensurate with economic liberalism or individualism (or their "cultural message"). In fact, individualism would seem to be the necessary precondition for such things.

Presuming individualism and community to be incompatible is an oversight that has led nationalists and collectivists to timeworn interpretations both of Canadian–American relations and of conservatism itself. William Mitchell and Randy Simmons have observed that welfare economists typically view "the unseemly, raucous, and self-interested competition of the market" as debasing individuals. By contrast, they assume that political actors are better informed and less selfish than market actors, and can readily and accurately divine the public interest. "[S]ince the political process is considered costless, the public interest is easily achieved. And political conflict debases no one." As Mitchell and Simmons suggest, however, the welfare economists get things perfectly backwards: it is the political process that is costly and political conflict that tends to be debasing, not the market. The political responses of the welfare economists to perceived market failures generally make things worse, not better. Mitchell and Simmons conclude: "we think [the United States'] chief problems stem not from market difficulties but from political intervention in otherwise robust markets."[24]

So too in Canada. Welfare economists have interfered in the Canadian economy for over a generation, at significant and unnecessary cost to Canadians. Canadians have responded to these problems, attempting to regain control of their lives and communities, with a newfound conservatism. Yet it is a conservatism the meaning of which has been lost among collectivists and nationalists alike. Conservatives have rarely sought the simplistic objectives attributed to them by their welfare economist critics. As Frum notes,

> Conservatives want to roll back the state not because they envision human beings as selfish individualists who must be left alone to make as much money as they can, but because they see the functions of real communities being usurped by overweening governments.[25]

In Canada, our national character and civic community have been undermined as government has expanded. Our understanding of community has been degraded and we take little interest in our surrounding environment. Municipal politics is a low priority for most Canadians and is rarely reported.

> [V]oter turnout in local elections seldom rises much above twenty-five percent. The parent–teacher associations so prevalent in the United States ignite very little enthusiasm here, largely because our schools receive their money from bureaucrats who can ignore parental preferences with impunity. The civic pride that inspired private citizens in the United States and Britain to donate their money and artworks to found great museums, libraries, and universities never seemed to flourish here.... We are *not,* in fact, a highly community-spirited people; we are merely a highly taxed people.[26]

To listen to our political and intellectual elites, however, a different impression of Canada is conveyed, one based, I suggest, not on the real-world, everyday lives of Canadians, but on idealistic, self-flattering visions, on stereotypes and doctrinaire interpretations.

If we are to overcome our misgivings and recapture an identity that for almost a century was a source of significant northern pride, we will have to turn away from the nationalist prescriptions and commonplaces that have comprised the standard version of Canadian political culture presented to us over the last generation.

SOCIALISM, NATIONALISM, AND THE REVOLT OF THE ELITES

Brimelow remarked that "popular journalism has accustomed Canadians to regard a selective cross-section of their business world as 'the Canadian establishment,' imbued with exciting if intangible power and privilege."[27] As Brimelow highlighted, however, the real Canadian establishment was something quite different, an alliance of politicians, bureaucrats, educators, and members of the media that emerged contemporaneously with the development of the welfare state.[28] The real Canadian establishment more closely approximates what Christopher Lasch described in *The Revolt of the Elites and the Betrayal of Democracy* as the emergent thinking classes: well-educated, well-connected individuals who live in a sanitized world of ideas and abstractions, divorced from physical reality and reflecting the experiences of life in an artificial world where everything that resists human manipulation has been excluded. The credo of these new classes is control. "In their drive to insulate themselves against risk and contingency—against the unpredictable hazards that afflict human life—the thinking classes have seceded not just from the common world around them but from reality itself."[29]

Lasch's description comports with Canada's new knowledge class of university professors, journalists, lawyers, and others seeking greater government control over the economy and culture in the name of the national interest. What the advocates of Canadian nationalism and those proclaiming the increasing Americanization of Canadian political culture really lament is not the loss of Canadian identity *per se* but the loss of a *socialist* vision of Canada that demands, as the price of Canadian citizenship, state control over how we should lead our lives, what literature we should read, what programming we should watch, what songs we should listen to, where we should send our children to be nursed and educated, how we should ship our goods, and even what airlines we should fly and where we should buy our gas.

The bankruptcy of this vision, the idea that somehow our collective soul depends on things such as Petro Canada or the CNR, or that our national identity can only be held together by bureaucrats, to say nothing of the expense nationalism has cost, has recently become apparent to Canadians. In the late 1980s and early 1990s, Canadians adopted increasingly expansive free trade, despite the nationalists' misleading, frequently hysterical, protestations. Canadians rejected the pro-Quebec, pro–welfare state Meech Lake and Charlottetown Accords. They displaced—apparently permanently—the federal Progressive Conservative Party with the genuinely conservative Reform Party of Canada. In two of the three most productive provinces in the country, they elected governments that have done more to wean Canadians from bureaucratic largesse and paternalism than any other governments in Canadian history.

These developments have not augured well for the nationalists, who have witnessed their authority over the lives of Canadians dissipate. The response has been predictable enough: intransigence and a denial that Canadians know what they are doing, even that their newfound conservatism is "un-Canadian."

Two things deserve emphasis here. First, although the products of culture—political or otherwise—are by no means matters of indifference, they are seldom matters of national distinction, even if they are at times subjects of national pride. What is unique, for instance, about Margaret Atwood, Michael Ondaatje, or Bryan Adams is not that they are Canadian but that they are excellent at what they do. The crosscultural, transpolitical nature of their work is reflected in how well they sell outside of Canada. That our pride in these artists originates in their recognition outside our borders is proof that Canadians are quite capable of recognizing excellence, even if their government seems intent on blinding them to it.

Related to this observation is a second, more important one: nationalism and the preoccupations of cultural protectionism divert us from the real issues that confront Canadians. As the foregoing analysis suggests, the political movement that purports to protect Canadian culture from Americanization is both misleading and dangerous: misleading because it misrepresents the facts of reality, and dangerous because Canadian culture is not threatened by the United States but, as Grant suggested, by something much more pervasive and elusive, the same thing that threatens American culture. The war of cultures is not between Canada and the United States. It is rather, in Neil Postman's words, "between technology and everybody else."[30]

The dynamism of commercial republics, which both Canada and the United States are, presents problems that governments in both countries must confront: soaring national debts, rising crime, dilapidated educational standards, urban decay, and family disintegration. To the extent that we consume ourselves with affectations over whether the privatization of Petro Canada or the existence of split-run American magazines will lead to a loss of control over Canada's culture—allegations that themselves, ironically, presume that culture to be hopelessly shallow—we divert our attention from the real issues of the day: how we should better manage our economy, deal with our violent criminals and juvenile offenders, reform our schools and universities, redesign our cities, and reunite our families. But diversion, I suggest, is part of the political agenda of cultural protectionism.

The word "culture" fits the moral and political relativism fostered by the politics of identity. An amorphous concept that means many things to many people, "culture" frequently refers to popular culture (music, art, and film) but, at a deeper level, refers to moral and intellectual phenomena, phenomena that are distinct from, sometimes in tension with, or even antithetical to one another.[31]

The indiscriminate use of "culture" to refer to such distinct concepts as justice, truth, morality, virtue, and the like hides from analysis the real issues we should be talking about in Canadian politics. It also serves the political purpose of fortifying the relativism promoted by those on the cultural left who wish to smooth over distinctions in rank and order between individuals and groups, and the moral and political activities they represent. When we describe as irresolvable differences of culture or preference, the distinctions between Quebec nationalism and English-speaking liberal constitutionalism, the relative merits of Aboriginal self-government and other forms of self-government, feminist versus more traditional views of the family, or heterosexual parenting versus homosexual parenting, we dodge admittedly delicate and difficult issues, but we do so at the price of intellectual and moral rigour.

Similarly, when we refuse to discuss issues of privatization, open markets, or government deregulation because they are considered to be antithetical to Canadian political culture, we insulate ourselves from understanding the real issues at stake in the debate over Canada's future, in particular, whether the complex network of rules, content regulations, trade barriers, subsidies, expropriations, and the like, all intended to protect our so-called cultural industries, are really worth supporting or are not just mechanisms for providing pork to a nationalist clientele.

Cultural protectionism serves to immunize the nationalists' projects from the scrutiny they deserve, allowing designated public enterprises to hide behind the mantle of what is alleged to be necessary to protecting Canadian identity, an identity that can only take one shape—social democratic—and that will necessarily create a system of inequality in which certain favoured constituencies will enjoy the spoils of government, while other groups, generally self-sustaining, will remain outside the fold of government largesse.

Some of the dangers presented by Canadian nationalism and the campaign to advance a distinct Canadian culture—political or otherwise—are, then, an unequal distribution of political power, an undermining of the rule of law and equal treatment that the social engineering and redistributive platform of nationalism promotes,[32] an augmenting of bureaucratic waste and coercion, and, ultimately, dishonesty.

To date, the movement in Canada that has sought to free Canadians from the yoke of nationalism has been conservatism. Conservatism has protected Canadians from the indiscriminateness and social and economic levelling of that collectivist ideology that lies at the heart of the nationalist enterprise. If it does not have the answers to all of our moral and political problems, Canadian conservatism has at least diagnosed more accurately, and perhaps less sanctimoniously than its ideological counterparts, the problems that we need to address. If we must choose, we should choose more of it, not less.

NOTES

1. I am following, roughly, Peter Brimelow's characterization. See Peter Brimelow, *The Patriot Game: National Dreams and Political Realities* (Toronto: Key Porter Books, 1986), pp. 136–137:

"[A] common Nationalist misinterpretation of Canada's economic culture.... a carica-ture, ignor[es,] among other things, the American "public enterprise" tradition that produced the Tennessee Valley Authority, the notoriously powerful New York State Parks Commissioner Robert Moses, and—predating the Bank of Canada—the Federal Reserve system."

2. See George Grant, *Technology and Empire: Perspectives on North America* (Toronto: Anansi, 1969), p. 64.

3. George Grant, *Lament for a Nation* (Toronto: Macmillan, 1965), p. ix.

4. David Frum, *What's Right: The New Conservatism and What It Means for Canada* (Toronto: Random House, 1996), pp. 3–4.

5. Ibid., p. 4.

6. Ibid., pp. 200–201.

7. Ibid., pp. 202–204.

8. For an excellent account how the city of Montreal has been changed for the worse by Quebec nationalism, see Mordecai Richler, *Oh Canada! Oh Quebec! Requiem for a Divided Country* (Toronto: Viking, 1992).

9. Brimelow, *The Patriot Game*, p. 138–139.

10. Peter Skerry, *Mexican Americans: The Ambivalent Minority* (Cambridge, MA: Harvard University Press, 1993), p. 7.

11. Ibid., p. 365.

12. See Nathan Glazer, *Affirmative Discrimination: Ethnic Inequality and Public Policy* (New York: Basic Books, 1975); and Herman Belz, *Equality Transformed: A Quarter-Century of Affirmative Action* (New Brunswick, NJ: Transaction Publishers, 1991).

13. See, for instance, Thomas Sowell, *Civil Rights: Rhetoric or Reality?* (New York: William Morrow, 1984); Abigail M. Thernstrom, *Whose Votes Count? Affirmative Action and Minority Voting Rights* (Cambridge, MA: Harvard University Press, 1987); and Terry Eastland, *Ending Affirmative Action: The Case for Colorblind Justice* (New York: Basic Books, 1997).

14. Brimelow, *The Patriot Game*, p. 96.

15. Ibid., p. 139.

16. See note 1.

17. Richard A. Epstein provides a good account of this in *Simple Rules for a Complex World* (Cambridge, MA: Harvard University Press, 1995).

18. See David J. Bercuson and Barry Cooper, *Derailed: The Betrayal of the National Dream* (Toronto: Key Porter Books, 1994), pp. 14–16.

19. See Charles Taylor, *Reconciling the Solitudes: Essays on Canadian Federalism and Nationalism* (Montreal and Kingston: McGill-Queen's University Press, 1993), esp. pp. 3–22, 166–167.

20. For a discussion of the meaning and purpose of Petro Canada, the National Energy Program, and other federal incursions into the Canadian petroleum business, see Peter Foster, *The Sorcerer's Apprentices: Canada's Super-Bureaucrats and the Energy Mess* (Don Mills: Collins, 1982); and *Other People's Money: The Banks, the Government and Dome* (Don Mills, ON: Collins, 1983).

21. See Barry Cooper, *Sins of Omission: Shaping the News at the CBC* (Toronto: University of Toronto Press, 1994).

22. Brimelow, *The Patriot Game*, pp. 18, 132.

23. Ibid., pp. 144, 146.

24. William C. Mitchell and Randy T. Simmons, *Beyond Politics: Markets, Welfare, and the Failure of Bureaucracy* (Boulder, CO: Westview Press, 1994), pp. 3–4.

25. Frum, *What's Right*, p. 5.

26. Ibid., pp. 5–6; emphasis in original.

27. Brimelow, *The Patriot Game*, p. 19.

28. Ibid., p. 18.

29. Christopher Lasch, *The Revolt of the Elites and the Betrayal of Democracy* (New York: W.W. Norton & Company, 1995), p. 20.

30. Neil Postman, *Technopoly: The Surrender of Culture to Technology* (New York: Vintage Books, 1993), p. xii.

31. Mark Blitz, "How to Think about Politics and Culture," *The Political Science Reviewer* 25, no. 5 (1996): 9–11. As Blitz points out (p. 11),

"what we need for a good moral education is not identical to what we need for a good intellectual education. Indeed, they may both conflict. The areas of similarity (the need for 'discipline' in both, for example) should not blind us to the areas of difference—the need, for example in one but not the other, to be unconventional and, even, irreverent."

32. See Friedrich A. Hayek, *The Constitution of Liberty* (Chicago: University of Chicago Press, 1960), p. 232:

"Those who pursue distributive justice will in practice find themselves obstructed at every move by the rule of law. They must, from the very nature of their aim, favor discriminatory and discretionary action. But, as they are usually not aware that their aim and the rule of law are in principle incompatible, they begin by circumventing or disregarding in individual cases a principle which they often would wish to see preserved in general.... [T]he ultimate result of their efforts will necessarily be, not a modification of the existing order, but its complete abandonment and its replacement by an altogether different system—the command economy."

Postscript

In his essay, Nesbitt-Larking paints a picture that must be familiar to many. Government cutbacks, single interest groups, faithless voters, growing public intolerance and anger—these are signs of the times. And Nesbitt-Larking argues, quite convincingly, that these are all manifestations of the growing Americanization of Canadian political life. Canada has always battled the threat of Americanization, and now it faces the prospect of finally losing this protracted war. Yet, it may be possible that Nesbitt-Larking exaggerates his case. Canada still has a national health care program, the United States does not; Canada still has a disciplined political process, the United States does not; and Canada still has a sense of community, the United States does not. One could go on, but this may be enough to throw some doubt on Nesbitt-Larking's basic contention.

Nesbitt-Larking may be challenged in another way. Perhaps the changes taking place are what Canadians want, and they may be considered to be beneficial. One of these changes is a weakening of the deferential attitude Canadians hold toward leaders and political elites. As Nesbitt-Larking himself admits, this development can be seen in a positive light. Perhaps the costs of Americanization are acceptable in view of the development of a more vibrant and democratic polity in Canada. What is happening is not really the Americanization of Canada, but rather the democratization of a nation held back by vestiges of conservatism inherent in predemocratic times.

Peacock has written a very provocative essay. He characterizes any differences in the Canadian and American political cultures as ephemeral, and accuses Canadian nationalists of attempting to graft onto Canada a foreign belief system, namely socialism. Perhaps most arresting is his claim that the United States is at least as caring and community-oriented as Canada, and that individualism and communitarianism go hand in hand. Also interesting is Peacock's argument that the changes now being experienced in Canada, represent an attempt to recover a former self distorted by works of Canadian nationalists.

Peacock is convincing—and refreshing. As he says, Canadians and Americans do tend to enjoy the same things. Furthermore, it does seem that governments in Canada have introduced policies and programs that seem to be some distance from the wishes of ordinary Canadians. But his assertions nevertheless raise some queries. Surely, Peacock misses some important differences between Canadians and Americans; the two are similar, but not the same. Moreover, can the CBC, economic regulations, energy boards, and assorted other government initiatives really be the work of only a handful of socialist-minded nationalists? May they not be true reflections of the political culture of Canada and its inherent collectivism? There may also be some who believe that Peacock's effort is merely a neoconservative's dream of an Americanized Canada.

For students wishing to pursue the debate, it is first necessary to gain a general overview of the Canadian political culture. For this, one would do well to read David Bell's *The Roots of Disunity: A Study of Canadian Political Culture*, 2nd ed. (Toronto: Oxford University Press, 1992). Shorter treatments of Canada's beliefs about politics include David V.J. Bell, "Political Culture in Canada," in Michael S. Whittington and Glen Williams, eds., *Canadian Politics in the 1990s* (Scarborough: Nelson Canada, 1995); and Ian Stewart, "All the King's Horses: The Study of Canadian Political Culture," in James P. Bickerton and Alain-G. Gagnon, eds., *Canadian Politics*, 2nd ed. (Peterborough: Broadview Press, 1994). An examination of the American political culture might also be appropriate, for which Herbert McCloskey and John Zaller's *The American Ethos: Public Attitudes Towards Capitalism and Democracy* (Cambridge: Harvard University Press, 1984) would be appropriate. A text that gives a more nuanced view of the possessive or competitive individualism of Americans is Richard J. Ellis, *American Political Cultures* (New York: Oxford University Press, 1993).

Students might then want to access comparative studies of American and Canadian political cultures. Such studies include: Gad Horowitz, *Canadian Labour in Politics* (Toronto: University of Toronto, 1968), ch. 1; Seymour Martin Lipset, *Continental Divide: The Values and Institutions of the United States and Canada* (New York: Routledge, 1990); Richard M. Merelman, *Partial Visions: Culture and Politics in Britain, Canada, and the United States* (Madison: University of Wisconsin Press, 1991); and George Perlin, "The Constraints of Public Opinion: Diverging or Converging Paths?" in Keith Banting, George Hoberg, and Richard Simeon, eds., *Degrees of Freedom: Canada and the United States in a Changing World* (Montreal and Kingston: McGill-Queen's University Press, 1997).

A large part of the debate revolves around changes in the political culture of Canada. For an important work on this subject, students should consult Neil Nevitte, *The Decline of Deference* (Peterborough: Broadview Press, 1996). As for manifestations of these changes in the operation of the Canadian political system, the following texts and readings are of some relevance: Harold Clarke et al., *Absent Mandate: Canadian Politics in the Era of Restructuring*, 3rd ed. (Toronto: Gage, 1996); Alan Cairns, *Charter Versus Federalism: The Dilemmas of Constitutional Reform* (Montreal and Kingston: McGill-Queen's University Press, 1992); and Reg Whitaker, "Canadian Politics at the End of the Millennium: Old Dreams, New Nightmares," in David Taras and Beverly Rasporich, eds., *A Passion for Identity*, 3rd ed. (Scarborough: Nelson Canada, 1997).

Finally, central to Peacock's essay is Canadian nationalism. For a start on this subject, students might examine Sylvia B. Bashevkin, *True Patriot Love: The Politics of Canadian Nationalism* (Toronto: Oxford University Press, 1991).

ISSUE**THREE**

Should Individual Rights Take Precedence Over Collective Rights?

✔ **YES**
PIERRE TRUDEAU, "Values in a Just Society," in Tom Axworthy
and Pierre Trudeau, eds., *Towards a Just Society* (Toronto:
Penguin, 1990)

✗ **NO**
PAUL MARSHALL, "The Importance of Group Rights"

One of the most significant moments in the 1992 referendum campaign on the Charlottetown Accord took place in a working-class district of Montreal, in a Chinese restaurant with the quaint name "Maison Egg Roll." The journal *Cité Libre* had invited one of its founding editors, Pierre Trudeau, to address its invited guests on the subject of the Charlottetown Accord. As guests munched on Moo Goo Guy Pan, Trudeau launched into a withering critique of the accord, which many feel played a pivotal role in the subsequent defeat of the accord in the October referendum. In the weeks that followed, even those people—particularly in western Canada—who had been bitter critics of Trudeau during his years in government now cited his arguments in making their case against the accord.

What was it that Trudeau said that sparked such a responsive chord in Canadians? His argument was in fact a simple one: the Charlottetown Accord must be defeated because it creates a hierarchy of rights, in which each citizen's rights depend on the group to which he or she belongs and the place that group occupies in the "hierarchy of citizens."

In fact, what Trudeau was arguing against—the recognition of the legitimacy of group, or collective rights—has had a long history in Canada. The British North America Act (now the Constitution Act, 1867) gave special protection to the educational rights of certain denominational groups and to the language rights of the francophone minorities. The distinctive legal traditions of Quebec were recognized and given protection through the composition of the Supreme Court in 1875. Special rights were accorded to the anglophone population of Quebec by entrenching the boundaries of twelve electoral districts with English-speaking majorities at the time of Confederation. (This provision was eliminated only in the 1960s.) When Newfoundland joined Canada in 1949, its denominational school system was given constitutional protection. And even the Constitution Act, 1982, brought in by the Trudeau government retains a recognition of distinct group rights and status. Language rights and the rights of aboriginal peoples were protected in the Canadian Charter of Rights and Freedoms. Section 15(2), the so-called "affirmative action" clause, permits special programs that are of advantage to those groups who have been previously disadvantaged. Even outside the constitutional sphere, Canadian governments have at times accommodated group differences. Quakers and Mennonites have had a long history of being granted an exemption from military service. Tax and educational laws have been modified at times to take into account the special circumstances of groups such as the Hutterites in western Canada who emphasize a collective communal style of life separate from the rest of society. Thus there is a long historical precedence for the kinds of accommodation set out in the Charlottetown Accord.

Despite this historical tradition, the reaction to Trudeau's speech reflects the extent to which the language of individual rights has come to dominate Canadian political discourse. Particularly since the implementation of the Charter of Rights and Freedoms, Canadians have come to see that equality is a fundamental principle of Canadian politics. Equality rights would seem by logical necessity to dictate that no distinctions be made among citizens whether on racial, linguistic, religious, cultural, or socioeconomic background. Thus requests for constitutional protection of certain designated minority groups appear to be nothing more than demands for special group privileges that threaten to undermine the very principle of individual equality.

But is this the case? Do collective rights necessarily threaten to undermine individual rights? In the following excerpts, Pierre Trudeau makes the case for an emphasis on individual rights, arguing that "when each citizen is not equal to all other citizens in the state, we are faced with a dictatorship, which arranges citizens in a hierarchy according to their beliefs." In response, Paul Marshall, a political theorist at the Institute for Christian Studies in Toronto, argues that emphasis on individual rights has been carried too far and that group rights need not necessarily pose a threat to individual rights.

✔ **YES**
Values in a Just Society
PIERRE TRUDEAU

... [I]t is no small matter to know whether we are going to live in a society in which personal rights, individual rights, take precedence over collective rights. It is no minor question of secondary importance to know whether we are going to live in a society in which all citizens are equal before the law and before the State itself. And it is no trivial matter to determine if there will be a spirit of brotherhood and of sharing in the society we are going to live in.

The choice we are going to make in the referendum, the choice of which society we want, has an impact on these three questions. And to know what choice to make, we have to look at the texts. I am not trying to say that those people who give preference to a collective society and collective rights over individual rights, do not have the right to state such a preference. I am saying to them that it is not just an emotional decision they are called on to make. We have to look at history—above all we have to look at contemporary history, the history of yesterday and today.

When collective rights take precedence over individual freedoms—as we see in countries where ideology shapes the collectivity, where race, ethnic origin, language, and religion shape the collectivity—we see what can happen to the people who claim to live freely in such societies. When each citizen is not equal to all other citizens in the state, we are faced with a dictatorship, which arranges citizens in a hierarchy according to their beliefs....*

The Constitution Act of 1982 was proclaimed on April 17. Essentially, it enshrined the values which, back in 1968, I had defined as those that should be respected in the constitution of a Just Society.

First, the principle of equal economic opportunity was stated in Section 36(1), under which "the government of Canada and the provincial governments undertake to promote equal opportunities for the well-being of all Canadians," and in Section 36(2), which guarantees the principle of equalization payments for the redistribution of revenues from wealthy provinces to the less wealthy ones. Further, Section 6 gives all Canadians the right to take up residence and earn their living anywhere in the country. And, of course, the federal government did not give up the powers it possessed under the old constitution concerning redistribution of wealth through subsidies and fiscal measures as well as through its general spending powers....*

---

*Excerpt from Pierre Elliott Trudeau, *A Mess That Deserves a Big "No"* (Toronto: Robert Davies Publishing, 1993), pp. 11–12.

Secondly, the principle of equality of French and English in all domains of federal jurisdiction and in New Brunswick was guaranteed by Sections 16 to 20, while Section 23 guaranteed francophones and anglophones the right to education in their own language anywhere in Canada.

But the Canadian Charter of Rights and Freedoms went much further, of course. In the grand tradition of the 1789 Declaration of the Rights of Man and the Citizen and the 1791 Bill of Rights of the United States of America, it implicitly established the primacy of the individual over the state and all government institutions, and in so doing, recognized that all sovereignty resides in the people. (Provincial charters of rights cannot have this effect because they are simply laws and can be abrogated at any time merely through further legislation.) In this respect, the Canadian Charter was a new beginning for the Canadian nation: it sought to strengthen the country's unity by basing the sovereignty of the Canadian people on a set of values common to all, and in particular on the notion of equality among all Canadians.

Clearly, the very adoption of a constitutional charter is in keeping with the purest liberalism, according to which all members of a civil society enjoy certain fundamental, inalienable rights and cannot be deprived of them by any collectivity (state or government) or on behalf of any collectivity (nation, ethnic group, religious group or other). To use Maritain's phrase, they are "human personalities," they are beings of a moral order—that is, free and equal among themselves, each having absolute dignity and infinite value. As such, they transcend the accidents of place and time, and partake in the essence of universal Humanity. They are therefore not coercible by any ancestral tradition, being vassals neither to their race, nor to their religion, nor to their condition of birth, nor to their collective history.

It follows that only the individual is the possessor of rights. A collectivity can exercise only those rights it has received by delegation from its members; it holds them in trust, so to speak, and on certain conditions. Thus, the state, which is the supreme collectivity for a given territory, and the organs of the state, which are the governments, legislatures and courts, are limited in the exercise of their functions by the Charter and the Constitution in which the Charter is enshrined.

Indeed, the Charter specifies that the governments must meet Parliament or the legislatures at least once a year (Section 5); that Parliament and the legislatures must hold elections at least once every five years (Section 4); and that the courts may act only "in accordance with the principles of fundamental justice" (Sections 7 to 14).

THE ROLE OF THE CHARTER

Thus, the individual is protected from the arbitrary authority of the state. But within a federal or provincial state, individuals may gather together in ethnic, linguistic, religious, professional, political or other collectivities, and delegate to this or that collectivity the task of promoting their collective interests. And since, in a democracy, governments receive their powers from the people by majority vote at elections, what is to prevent a majority from riding roughshod over the rights of a minority?

The answer, of course, is the Charter of Rights and Freedoms and the Constitution. They do this generally, by enshrining the rights of the individual members within minorities; but in certain instances, where the rights of individuals may be indistinct and difficult to define, they also enshrine some collective rights of minorities.

For example, the Canadian Constitution of 1867 provided that in educational matters, Section 93(1) would protect any "*Class* of Persons ... with respect to Denominational Schools," and Section 93(3) would apply to the "Protestant or Roman Catholic Minority."

Similarly, the Charter has clauses to protect certain minority collectivities whose interests could be overlooked in the conduct of the business of the state; this is what Sections 25 and 35 do for the "aboriginal peoples of Canada," and Section 27 for "the preservation and enhancement of the multicultural heritage of Canadians."

Section 93(2) of the 1867 Constitution, on the other hand, addresses individuals as such, in order to protect them: "Protestant and Roman Catholic *Subjects*." Likewise, Section 113 (language before the legislatures and courts) protects "*any* Person."

Except in the two cases I mentioned in the next-to-last paragraph, the Charter always seeks to define rights exclusively as belonging to a person rather than a collectivity: "everyone" (Sections 2, 7, 8, 9, 10, 12, 13), "every citizen of Canada" (Sections 3, 6) "any person charged with an offence" (Section 11), "any party or witness" (Section 14), "every individual" (Section 15), "anyone" (Section 24). It should be noted that this preference holds good even where the official languages are concerned; individuals, not linguistic groups, are ensured of their right to use either language: "everyone" (Section 17), "any person" (Section 19), "any member of the public" (Section 20), "citizens of Canada" (Section 23).

It is clear, then, that the spirit and substance of the Charter is to protect the individual against tyranny—not only that of the state but also any other to which the individual may be subjected by virtue of his belonging to a minority group. Section 15 of the Charter leaves no doubt: all are equal before the law and are entitled to the same protection "without discrimination based on race, national or ethnic origin, colour, religion, sex, age or mental or physical disability."

The reason for this approach is evident. Canada is by nature pluralist—"a mosaic" as Laurier put it—not an American-style melting pot. The Canadian nation is composed of citizens who belong to minorities of many kinds: linguistic, ethnic, racial, religious, regional and so on. Throughout the negotiations leading to the Charter in 1982, our government kept in mind that Canadian history has consisted of a difficult advance toward a national unity that is still fragile and is often threatened by intolerance—the intolerance of the English-speaking majority toward francophones, the intolerance of whites toward the indigenous populations and non-white immigrants, intolerance toward political and religious dissidents such as Communists and Jehovah's Witnesses.

If we had tried to identify each of the minorities in Canada in order to protect all the characteristics that made them different, not only would we have been faced with an impossible task, but we would shortly have been presiding over the balkanization of Canada. The danger inherent in this would have been particularly acute in the case of minorities that are in a position to be identified with a given territory, like the Celts in Nova Scotia, the Acadians in New Brunswick, the French Canadians in Quebec and the Indians and Inuit in the Far North.

This is why Sections 25 and 37 on the aboriginal peoples and Section 27 on multiculturalism avoid any identification of these collectivities with a particular government. Thus, throughout our negotiations with the aboriginal peoples, we refused to talk about "self-determination," and only envisaged the possibility of "self-government" on condition that a heterogeneous population might still live in a given territory.

The case of the collectivity referred to as French Canadians demanded particularly close attention, since the tensions between anglophones and francophones have always been the major source of disunity in Canada. And we were very aware that Quebec nationalist thinking tends both to identify the interests of the French-Canadian collectivity with the province of Quebec and to confuse language with ethnicity, which gives rise to expressions like "the two founding nations of Canada" and "Quebec, the national state of French Canadians." Thus, on May 22, 1963, the Legislative Assembly of Quebec voted unanimously to give itself a mandate to determine "the objectives to be pursued by *French Canada* in the revision of the constitution of Canada, and the best means of obtaining these objectives."

At the time, I was opposed to this approach for several reasons, the most important being that "a state that defined its function essentially in terms of ethnic attributes would inevitably become chauvinistic and intolerant. The state, whether provincial, federal or perhaps later supra-national, must seek the general welfare of all its citizens regardless of sex, colour, race, religious beliefs, or ethnic origin."

Shortly after I wrote this, my friends and I entered federal politics for the precise purpose of proving that French Canadians could be at home in Canada outside Quebec and could exercise their rights in the federal capital and throughout the country. This was also the purpose of the Official Languages Act and of the emergence of what the English-speaking press was soon calling "French power."

The separatists of both Quebec and the West well understood what was happening. Conscious that their ultimate goal presupposed an exclusively English-speaking Canada and an exclusively French-speaking Quebec, they abandoned their minorities in other provinces—French-speaking and English-speaking—and fought tooth and nail against the policy of bilingualism, which in their terms was the work of traitors and double-dealers.

As for the Quebec nationalists, the Quiet Revolution had given them the means to be full-fledged Canadians but also a desire to be not exactly Canadian. Now they were dancing a hesitation waltz, flitting from "special status" to "equality or independence"; from "cultural sovereignty" to "profitable federalism" (profitable or else...).

In answer to our federal law proclaiming English and French to be the official languages everywhere in Canada, Mr. Bourassa saw fit to reply with a provincial law declaring that French alone would be the official language in Quebec—and he observed later that Quebec's self-determination was still an option in his party's platform.

Taking a stand in opposition to the federal policy of bilingualism meant shifting the political debate in Quebec to the only ground on which the separatist party had an advantage over Mr. Bourassa. So, in 1976, a Péquiste government was elected and in due course held a referendum, in which that government asked for a mandate to make Quebec a sovereign country.

Two months after the federalist victory in the referendum, we presented the provinces with a draft charter that would embody a set of values common to all Canadians. Language rights were assigned directly to individuals rather than collectivities. And the reader will understand why, in the lengthy negotiations that followed, we rejected any proposal whose effect would have been to identify a linguistic collectivity (French Canadians) with the government of a province (Quebec).

What we were seeking was the individual himself to have the *right* to demand his choice of French or English in his relationships with the federal government, and the *right* to demand a French or English education for his children from a provincial government. And the individual himself would have access to the courts to enforce these rights.

This is not to say that we were denying the importance of a linguistic community in the defence and advancement of the language spoken by its members. However, it seemed clear to us that these matters would never be settled unless the *individual* language rights of each person were enshrined in the constitution of the country, since the English-speaking community would always outnumber the French-speaking in Canada.

Our approach was indisputably more effective and more respectful of the dignity of Canadians. However, it made things awkward for Quebec nationalist politicians because it made them largely redundant; the moment the survival of "the race" no longer depended on them, their racist preachings became superfluous. So they fought the Charter with much sound and fury and racked their brains for some ploy that would allow Quebec to elude its authority. Years were to pass before they hit upon the "distinct society" formula for interpreting the Charter—and a Canadian prime minister ready to accept it.

But that is another story....

✗ **NO**
The Importance of Group Rights
PAUL MARSHALL

It is common, especially in the United States, to speak about politics largely in terms of "the government and the individual." In the last few decades this way of thinking of people solely as individuals has more and more affected Canada. Indeed, many Canadians have lost the sense that there is any other way to speak about politics. For such people, individuals are all that exist. For them, all groups are really just collections of individuals, and all supposed group rights ultimately boil down to individual rights. The way to protect the culture of French Canada would be by protecting the language rights of individual French Canadians. If francophones were secure in their individual identity, then their language and culture would naturally survive. Similarly if we would protect Native people by protecting the rights of each individual Native person, then Native culture and traditions would be protected. If everyone in the country were able to exercise their rights, then both their own lives and the life of their communities would flourish.

But despite the fact that this way of viewing the world is so widespread, it thrives only by ignoring or denying certain fundamental realities about the world in general and about Canada in particular. One of the most striking examples of this denial occurred early in Mr. Trudeau's tenure as prime minister. In 1969 his Liberal government introduced a White Paper on the treatment of Native peoples. The White Paper sought to treat Native rights in the same way as those of other Canadians. Its ostensible purpose was to liberate Native peoples. It maintained that their desperate situation was due to the fact that they had been victims of discrimination for many years. It proposed to solve this problem by abolishing all such "discrimination." It would abolish their special legal status with the hoped-for result that they would have no more and no fewer rights than any other Canadian. It believed that Native peoples would then be able to take their equal place in Canadian society and so fulfil their destiny.

The Native people's overwhelming and nearly unanimous response was to reject the White Paper. Their rejection was based on the fact that they see themselves not in terms of individual rights, but in terms of community life. Their land-holding is not in terms of individual ownership, but in terms of collective use. Their traditional way of decision making involves reaching consensus rather than counting majorities on one side or another. For the Natives, the key right is self-government, the ability to run their own community life. This is something that cannot be dealt with simply in terms of individual rights: it is something that can only pertain to a people as a whole. Native reaction to the White Paper was so intense that it galvanized them into intensive political action and itself became a major factor in the new drive for self-government. This reaction caused Mr.

Trudeau and the Liberal government to back away from the White Paper. In so doing he said:

> I'm sure we were very naive in some of the statements we made in the paper. We had perhaps the prejudices of small "l" liberals and white men at that time who thought that equality meant the same law for everybody, and that's why as a result of this we said "well let's let Indians dispose of their lands like every other Canadian. And let's make sure that Indians can get their rights, education, health and so on from the governments like every other Canadian." But we have learnt in the process that perhaps we were a bit too theoretical, we were a bit too abstract.[1]

This example illustrates the point that Canada cannot simply be thought of as a collection of individual persons. Rather, it is composed of cultures, groups, associations, and institutions. There is cultural and ethnic diversity, a plurality brought about by French, English, and many other languages, varied subcultures, many Native bands and nations, diverse schools and educational systems, a wide spectrum of religions and denominations. Over two-thirds of Canadians are members of voluntary associations. There are tens of thousands of such associations including churches, political parties, trade unions, cultural groups, cooperatives, academic associations, and public interest organizations. These are not merely private arrangements. They are central to the public life of the country. Indeed, in some ways they are the public life of the country.

This is not only a Canadian phenomenon. Hardly any country in the world is culturally homogeneous. They nearly all encompass a wide variety of language, ethnic, racial, and religious groups and organizations. These groups are not just private arrangements or purely incidental matters. They are important not only for personal lives, but also for public life. They need to be recognized and accommodated in concrete political arrangements. Sometimes the relations between such groups are violent and vicious, as in the breakup of the former Yugoslavia and the subsequent wars in Croatia and Bosnia-Herzegovina. Sometimes group claims and demands are really a cover for racist, fascist, or communist goals. They can produce bigotry and prejudice, persecution and civil war. People's communal life is a dangerous thing and always needs to be treated carefully.

However, the dangers of group identity should not drive us to futile and repressive attempts to eradicate it from politics, but to deal with it responsibly and justly. And, despite tensions, many countries have found creative and tolerant ways of recognizing groups as well as individuals and have thus allowed their diverse communities to live together in comparative peace and respect. One of the principal ways of doing this is by means of group rights. Essentially what this means is that instead of treating every person as if he or she were the same for legal purposes, we should try to develop rights in such a way that we do justice to communal differences. This can happen either by giving rights to members of some groups that are not held by members of other groups, or else by giving rights not just to the members, but to the group itself as a collectivity. Hence, because of the way native people relate to their land and community, they may need rights to the land and to hunt and fish that others need not have, and they may need to exercise collective self-government as a band or tribe.

These types of rights are often viewed with great suspicion, especially by those with an ideological commitment to an individualistic view of the world. In Canada many critics of the Meech Lake Accord of 1987–90 and of the Charlottetown Accord of 1992 believed, like Pierre Trudeau, that the commitment to group rights contained in these proposals necessarily meant that they were unjust and prejudiced. In more extreme instances there has been a tendency to categorize any concern for group rights as a type of incipient fascism that needs to be both rejected and fought.[2]

But both in Canada and throughout the world these types of rights often are means not of exclusion and control, but of mutual respect and harmony. Examples of this can be found all over the world: in Europe and North America as well as in the Third World.[3] For example, the Aaland Islands are a part of Finland, but most of their inhabitants speak only Swedish. The islanders are afraid that since they are a very small minority their language and culture could easily be swamped by the surrounding Finnish speakers. In order to protect the islanders, the government of Finland has passed laws that restrict the ability of nonislanders to buy land or houses in Aaland. Consequently, Swedish speakers are likely to remain a majority in the islands for the foreseeable future, and so their culture is likely to be preserved. Clearly this law makes a distinction between two types of Finns. Some Finns, the islanders, have rights to buy land in Aaland that other Finns do not have. But the purpose and effect of the law is not to maintain a privileged group, but rather to protect a culture that would otherwise be swamped.

The original inhabitants of New Zealand are called Maoris. They often suffered discrimination from the immigrating European population. As more Europeans continued to arrive, the Maoris eventually numbered only about 5 percent of the population. While some of these original inhabitants have assimilated, they still tend to have patterns of life distinct from that of the larger society. Furthermore, since they are not concentrated in any one area of the country, they did not have much weight in the voting system. In a voting system similar to the one in Canada it would be very difficult for a Maori to be elected. In order to combat this problem, New Zealand initiated two separate voter lists: one for Maoris and one for others. Maoris vote for the four seats that have been set aside for them; others vote for the remaining eighty-three seats. In this way Maoris always have seats in Parliament roughly proportional to their numbers in the wider society.

India faces major problems with languages. It has 281 of them, many more if we also count those that are spoken by less than 5,000 people. The government simply cannot provide services in all of these languages. Over the years it has struggled to balance the need to be fair to all the language groups with the need to save costs in a poor country. It has decided to make Hindi (the largest language group) and English the "official languages of the Union" and also to allow each state (province) to choose its own official language or languages. Meanwhile the government commits itself to try to provide basic education in all languages and gives a guarantee to each group that it has the right to "conserve" its language. These seem reasonable and perhaps even the best measures to take in a difficult situation. But we should note that even the best measures necessarily mean that some languages and, of course, those who speak these languages, are being given opportunities denied to others.

In Belgium language rights vary according to which region of the country one is in. Switzerland is similar. The list could go on and on, but the basic point is this: group rights are not some peculiar feature of totalitarian or authoritarian regimes. They are not holdovers from some previous less enlightened age. They are not necessarily expressions of prejudice or bigotry (though, of course, some can be: no part of politics is immune to perversion). They are present in most countries of the world: western as well as eastern, democratic as well as authoritarian. They are widespread and accepted measures to preserve and enhance community life and harmony.

These approaches do not flourish despite international pressure for more uniform human rights. The opposite in fact. The international regime of human rights explicitly recognizes and reinforces many of these approaches.[4] The United Nations itself tries to recognize group rights within its own structure. For example, it gives different status to the different languages of its member countries. Of all the different languages, it selects only some as "official" and some others as "working" languages. The rest do not have official UN status. The organization simply cannot afford to operate in all the languages of the world.

The United Nations recognizes the importance of group rights in its member nations. When it developed its provisions on the treatment of minorities it defined minorities as "non-dominant groups which, while wishing in general for equality of treatment with the majority, wish for a measure of differential treatment in order to preserve basic characteristics which ... distinguish them from the majority of the population."

The major international treaties on human rights give formal recognition to this concern. The Genocide Convention forbids not only actions against individuals *within* a threatened group, but also against the *group itself*. It forbids transferring children out of a threatened group (by adoption, for instance) lest the culture itself be gradually undercut. Hence rights of adoption vary depending on which group one belongs to.

More recently the *International Convention on the Elimination of All Forms of Racial Discrimination* defined racial discrimination as "any discrimination, exclusion, restriction or preference based on race, colour, descent, or national or ethnic origin which has the purpose or effect of nullifying or impairing the recognition, enjoyment or exercise, on an equal footing, of human rights and fundamental freedoms in the political, economic, social, cultural or any other field of public life." It is not the simple fact of discrimination that is crucial. It is the purpose and effect of the discrimination. Any measures that impair the enjoyment of human rights are forbidden; any that enhance the enjoyment of human rights are allowed. *The International Convention on the Elimination of All Forms of Racial Discrimination* makes a similar provision. Racial discrimination does not include "special measures taken for the sole purpose of securing adequate advancement of certain racial or ethnic groups requiring ... protection."

This widespread international pattern is also followed in Canada. Canada's principal constitutional document before the constitutional changes of 1982 was the British North America Act of 1867.[5] Section 93 of this act stipulated that the provinces could not "prejudicially affect any Right or Privilege with respect to Denominational Schools." This meant that Catholics and Protestants had a constitutionally entrenched right to schools reflecting their beliefs. Similarly, when Newfoundland joined Canada in 1949 it had five denominational school systems: Roman Catholic, United Church, Anglican, Pentecostal, and Salvation Army. The arrangements for admitting Newfoundland included guaranteed constitutional protection for this system.

Both of these constitutional guarantees were kept in the new provisions of the Constitution Act, 1982. Nor did this act simply maintain group rights because they were impossible to change. It reaffirmed them and in fact introduced new provisions for group rights. Section 15(2) allows governments to develop programs to help particular disadvantaged groups, even though such programs would treat people in different groups in very different ways. The Constitution Act, 1982, also gives particular language rights to the speakers of two languages—French and English (Sections 16 to 23 of the Charter of Rights and Freedoms). These languages have official status; others do not. The reasons for this are that these are the languages of the founding communities, and moreover, they are the most widespread. These are good reasons and I support the policy. But we should not hide from ourselves the fact that we are giving advantages to some language groups rather than to others. Meanwhile, Sections 25, 35, and 37 recognize the rights of Aboriginal peoples, and Section 27 calls for interpretations consistent with "multiculturalism." In short, Canada is still finding it necessary to establish rights for groups as well as for individuals.

In commenting on this, the majority of the Ontario Court of Appeal said that "the Constitution of Canada ... has from the beginning provided for group collective rights.... As Professor Hogg ... has expressed it: these provisions amount to 'a small bill of rights.' The provisions of this 'small bill of rights,' now expanded as to ... language rights ... constitute a major difference from a bill of rights such as that of the United States, which is based on individual rights. Collective or group rights, such as those concerning language and those concerning certain denominations to separate schools, are asserted by individuals or groups of individuals *because of* their membership in certain ascertainable groups. Individual rights are asserted equally by everyone *despite* membership in certain ascertainable groups."[6]

A common criticism of these types of observations, one offered by Mr. Trudeau himself, is to agree that collective rights are important and should be protected, but to insist that they should never override individual rights. Only if there is no threat to individual rights should collective concerns and collective rights then be considered. While Mr. Trudeau thinks that both types of rights have a place, he asserts that individual rights must always have priority. He believes that unless this happens the result will be oppressive. One of the principal reasons he argued so strenuously against the Meech Lake Accord and the Charlottetown Accord was that he thought each agreement gave some priority to collective rights over individual rights. His criticism was so effective that it actually became a factor in helping to defeat these constitutional proposals.

In many cases, this criticism is undoubtedly correct. Some fundamental rights, such as the right to life, should never be subordinated to any collective interest that does not itself involve protecting someone's life. A group cannot demand that human life be sacrificed to its benefit. But for many other individual rights there is no automatic priority. In most cases there is more than one right at stake, and one does not simply override another. Usually courts have to try to balance them in some way. A famous example of this conflict occurred in Canada in the *Lovelace* case several years ago. The Indian Act, the law governing Indian people in Canada, allowed a form of discrimination against women. If an Indian woman married a non-Indian man then she lost her legal status as an Indian. But this regulation did not apply to Indian men who married non-Indians. Women's groups, including Native women's groups, protested this situation. Many Native leaders acknowledged that there was a problem, but they objected that white people were once again trying to impose their own view from the outside instead of letting Native people work out their own solutions. The result was a conflict of group and individual rights, between the right of Native peoples to govern themselves and the rights of Native women to have an equal status with Native men. As Marc Lalonde put it: "Discrimination against women is a scandal but imposing the cultural standards of white society would be another scandal."[7]

In this instance, it was the individual rights that eventually won out. Nevertheless, this does not support the claim that they should always do so. Rather, it shows that the conflict is very real and that there are two important things that are together being weighed in the balance. In different instances either a group interest or an individual one might win out, depending on how important the particular rights are in the particular instance. In cases such as Native self-government in general, or Native fishing and hunting rights, then the collective rights of Native people have won out. Natives can hunt and fish in ways and at times that non-Natives cannot. They have rights to self-government that others do not. They have rights to land that others do not. In all these cases a group right has won out over various individual claims to nondiscrimination. Similarly, in the case of denominational schools, the collective rights of Catholics to have schools that reflect their religious beliefs have won out over individual claims to have all schools give equal access to people regardless of their beliefs. In these different issues one or the other type of right may legitimately have priority. There is no automatic procedure where one or the other must always necessarily be successful. It is a case of trying to deal with both of them together. But what this means is that we must always be prepared to recognize group rights and when necessary to give them priority over individual rights.

I have argued that Canada must be understood not only in terms of individual people, but also in terms of the groups and communities in which these people live. These groups may need to be protected by recognizing that they have rights as groups. While individual rights can never be ignored or dismissed, at times they may need to be overridden by important group rights. Such recognition is not a violation of human rights, but is an internationally known and respected human rights practice, and one that is also firmly rooted in Canadian history and legal practice. As we consider future constitutional amendments or any other arrangements for our living together in Canada, we cannot assume that all group claims are necessarily valid. But neither can we accept the view that no group right is valid, nor the view that they can never override individual rights. We must be open to either claim, and in the diverse circumstances that our political life produces group rights will often take priority.

NOTES

1. Quoted in Sally M. Weaver, *Making Canadian Indian Policy: The Hidden Agenda, 1968–1970* (Toronto: University of Toronto Press, 1981), p. 185.

2. See, for example, the widely used work by Paul Sieghart, *The Lawful Rights of Mankind: An Introduction to the International Legal Code of Human Rights* (Oxford: Oxford University Press, 1986), pp. 163ff.

3. Most of the following examples are taken from Vernon Van Dyke's *Human Rights, Ethnicity and Discrimination* (Westport: Greenwood Press, 1985).

4. See the examples given in Natan Lerner, *Group Rights and Discrimination in International Law* (Dordrecht: Martinus Nijhoff, 1991).

5. For Canadian examples, see Michael McDonald, "Should Communities Have Rights? Reflections on Liberal Individualism," pp. 133–61 in A.A. An-na'im, *Human Rights in Cross-Cultural Perspective* (Philadelphia: University of Pennsylvania Press, 1992).

6. *Reference Re An Act to Amend the Education Act,* 53 Ontario Reports 566.

7. Quoted in Michael McDonald, "Indian Status: Colonialism or Sexism?" presented to Collective Rights Symposium, University of Ottawa, March 1985, p. 26.

Postscript

For most of us raised in a political culture that emphasizes liberal individualism, the assertion of individual rights and freedoms appears to be a central component of what liberal democracy is all about. Nevertheless, Vernon Van Dyke, in "Justice as Fairness: For Groups?" *American Political Science Review* 69 (1973): 607–614, provides evidence supportive of Marshall's argument that the assertion of individual rights can often undermine and even destroy certain linguistic, ethnic, and religious communities.

The concept of group rights as it relates to liberal democratic traditions can be further explored in Michael McDonald, "Collective Rights and Tyranny," *University of Ottawa Review* 56 (1986): 115–123, and Vernon Van Dyke, "Collective Entities and Moral Rights: Problems in Liberal Democratic Thought," *Journal of Politics* 44 (1982): 21–40.

In the past, before the entrenchment of the Charter of Rights and Freedoms, the task of reconciling the competing claims of individual and group rights was largely the responsibility of the federal and provincial legislatures. As a result, governments were able to pursue a pragmatic mixture of policies designed to mitigate the tensions between the two competing demands. With the adoption of the Charter, and the subsequent emphasis on the language of individual rights, the difficulty in resolving the tensions between individual and collective rights has become more complex. This is especially apparent in regard to the issues of Native rights and language rights. For two essays that deal with these specific issues, see F.L. Morton, "Group Rights Versus Individual Rights in the Charter: The Special Cases of Natives and the Québécois," in Neil Nevitte and Allan Kornberg, eds., *Minorities and the Canadian State* (Oakville: Mosaic Press, 1985) and K.Z. Patel, "Group Rights in the Canadian Constitution and Aboriginal Claims to Self-Determination," in Robert Jackson, Doreen Jackson, and Nicolas Baxter-Moore, eds., *Contemporary Canadian Politics: Readings and Notes* (Scarborough: Prentice-Hall, 1987).

ISSUE**FOUR**

Are Canadians Tory-Touched Liberals?

✔ **YES**
NELSON WISEMAN, "Tory-Touched Liberalism: Political Culture in Canada"

✘ **NO**
JANET AJZENSTAT AND PETER J. SMITH, "The 'Tory Touch' Thesis: Bad History, Poor Political Science"

For many students in introductory courses in Canadian politics, one of the very first things they encounter in class is the claim that the political culture of Canada is tory-touched liberal. A close reading of the assertion shows that it relates largely to English Canada, but this is often not emphasized. What is stressed is that Canadians, historically, have thought about political life in liberal terms, but that this has always been tempered by lingering conservative or *tory* beliefs. This uneven mix of liberal and tory beliefs in turn eventually gives life to socialist ideas, but socialism, like toryism, must bow to the preeminence of liberal ideas. If questioned on the nature of Canada's political culture, the successful student of Canadian politics begins his or her answer with the assertion that Canada is liberal with a tory touch.

To the uninitiated, the need to include a reference to toryism in a description of the Canadian political culture may seem an unnecessary complication, something that serves to confuse rather than inform. But in many minds the inclusion is an absolute necessity, for it helps to explain much about Canadian politics. If Canada were a purely liberal state, one which emphasizes freedom, equality of opportunity, and limited government, then it would be difficult to explain the plethora of Crown corporations, the commitment to national social programs, the deferential quality of political participation, and the trappings of monarchy. But Canada is not a liberal state; it is a *tory-touched* liberal state. By giving Canadians a sense of community and instilling in them as well an acceptance of hierarchy and traditional authority, toryism contributes to developments that appear foreign in most liberal polities. And then there is the presence of socialism. According to those who believe in a Canada that is tory-touched liberal, socialism only becomes possible with a combination of liberalism and conservatism.

later evidence.

The thesis of tory-touched liberalism is an influential one, yet some are not persuaded. There is evidence to suggest that the Canadian political culture is, and always has been, without true toryism. What characterizes Canadian politics is a debate between traditional or constitutional liberalism and what is called *civic republicanism*. The former emphasizes the significance of parliamentary government, a type of rule that relies on political elites and disciplined parties to carry out the responsibilities of government. Constitutional liberalism also recognizes the possibility of corruption in politics, and urges the establishment of political institutions that frustrate those who seek private gain in public life. Alternatively, civic republicanism argues for a politics that is much more participatory and hence more democratic than constitutional liberalism, and condemns the latter's easy acceptance of economic inequality. Above all, civic republicanism champions the idea of the virtuous citizen; in an ideal polity, the individual thinks of the public welfare, not personal profit. What we get in Canadian politics, then, is not a mixture of conservatism, liberalism, and socialism, but rather a tussle between the liberal and the republican.

For support of this alternative view, it is argued that we should look to history. History shows clearly that primary debates in Canadian politics have never been between tories and liberals (and subsequently, socialists) but rather between those content with British parliamentary government and others who wish a more radically democratic type of state. The same holds for politics in the present. What concerns Canadians today are questions of political corruption and participation in political life. The malaise that seems to hang over political life today is the disappointment borne of civic republicanism. Canada is not about socialism versus liberalism, or tradition versus modernity; rather, it is about the populism of the virtuous citizen against the traditional liberal.

In the readings, Nelson Wiseman, a political scientist at the University of Toronto, writes in support of the claim of tory-touched liberalism. Janet Ajzenstat and Peter J. Smith, political scientists at McMaster University and Athabasca University respectively, articulate the case against tory-touched liberalism and in favour of a political culture that reveals the values of liberalism and civic republicanism.

✔ YES
Tory-Touched Liberalism: Political Culture in Canada
NELSON WISEMAN

Canada is a society of immigrants and immigrant ideas. The ideological baggage of different immigrant groups, however, has not counted equally. The works, beliefs, and institutions of pioneers—in the case of English Canada its British American Loyalists, in the case of French Canada its universally Catholic *habitants*—count for more than their children's products and those of later waves of immigrants. The ideas of founding settlers take root and grow unless they are rebelled against or overthrown, but revolution is not part of the Canadian political tradition. Quite the contrary: this country is notable for its counterrevolutionary path. This is quite a contrast to the United States and France, the two societies that made up the earliest Canadians. (Aboriginals, our pre-Canadians, do not reckon here; they were marginalized and treated as inferior or subhuman.) This focus on founding settlers does not deprecate the recent Somali immigrant, her ideas, her contribution, her potential. She can vote and participate in the political system, whereas John A. Macdonald and George-Étienne Cartier no longer do. Nevertheless, Macdonald—an immigrant too—and his contemporaries are more vital than our Somali Canadian to our understanding of Canada's political architecture, its evolution, and its likely future.

Only the parties of Macdonald's era, the Liberals and Conservatives, have ruled Canada (and both still do rule if one lives in Ontario). To understand why these party labels are still current, one must look back to earlier centuries, to Canada's origins as a society and a state. Indeed the Liberal and Conservative parties are older than the Canadian state or Ontario for they predate Confederation. The Canada of 1867 was created as a compact of two unequal peoples, those of British and French stock. That inequality was determined on the Plains of Abraham in 1759: the British beat the French and dictated the rules governing their coexistence. There was virtually no one else on the political landscape: no Arabs, no Africans, no Filipinos, and no Finns. When others arrived, they accommodated themselves to the established British order. That order was cast at the turn of the nineteenth century by America's decamped and expelled Loyalists. It was reinforced by the War of 1812, buttressing an ideological and constitutional continental divide.

IDEOLOGICAL SOURCES

The two prevailing ideologies brought by the French and the Loyalists from their older societies were conservatism and liberalism respectively. Conservative or feudal ideas are the older of the two ideologies and were reflected in the socioeconomic and political structure of France: the seigneurial system, the Catholic Church, and the absolute power of the French gouverneur and his intendant. Pre-Enlightenment conservatism was the reigning ideology of prerevolutionary France. Conservatism continued as French Canada's driving ideology, however, long after the British conquest and mother France's repudiation of it in 1789. French Canada was thus cast adrift, cut off from its parent society, ideologically as well as physically.

Liberalism arose in Europe as the antithetical ideology of conservatism, its philosophically polar opposite. A century before the French Revolution, liberalism had taken centre stage in Britain. It was evident in the Glorious Revolution of 1688 and propelled by the writings of Thomas Hobbes and John Locke. Their ideas were imbued with possessive individualism.[1] Liberalism was the ascendant, dominant ideology of the British and their North American colonists. Nevertheless, discernibly significant traces of older conservative ideas—in the British context we call these "tory"—continued to infect British liberalism. They did so even after the stunning Reform victory in Britain's 1832 election, which promised an extended democratic franchise and a more liberal economy.

Tory-touched or tory-tinged liberalism served as English Canada's founding ideology. To this day it continues to resonate subtly and symbolically in the workings and policies of the Canadian state. In contrast, the American Revolution of 1776 represented the unequivocal, unmitigated triumph of liberalism and republicanism. The Americans rejected British colonial rule, the Crown as a unifying principle, and the rest of the baggage of Old World aristocratic toryism. Whatever vestiges of toryism might have survived in the plantation slave system of the Deep South were expunged in the American Civil War, roughly coterminous with Canada's Confederation in the 1860s.

IDEOLOGICAL CONTENT

Conservatism and liberalism are big, very big, ideas. We must flesh out and simplify what we mean by them here. Always bear in mind that they have variants; different conservatives and liberals stress different ingredients and faces of their ideology. Note too that in popular parlance what is usually labelled today as conservatism—the policies of Mike Harris's Conservatives or Preston Manning's Reformers—is yesterday's liberalism. In Europe, the ideological progression from and clash between classical conservatism and liberalism led to the surfacing of a third ideology, socialism. This newer, largely twentieth-century, ideology combines selective elements of both conservatism (or toryism) and liberalism. Socialism simultaneously rejects some of their other components and the totality of their outlooks. Socialism arose in Europe and Canada as a reaction to these older ideologies. Socialism did not develop in the United States, according to some, because whatever toryism it contained had been liquidated.[2] Conservatism's collectivist, communitarian seeds did not survive to provide the ideological ferment and agitation, the yeast, for a future sprouting of socialism. The relationship of socialism to conservatism and liberalism is like that of a rebellious child to its quarrelling parents. Spawned by them, it both repudiates and embraces them, taking some of what each of them offer.

Ideologies are abstractions, concepts, not things, principles, not concrete blocks. They are philosophies, perspectives, and prescriptions rather than parties, movements, and selective policies. Ideologies are ways of seeing. They tell us how the world is or should be structured, how people relate or should relate to the state and each other. Each of the three ideological constellations in Table 1 have five principle values as their defining features. These ideological constellations are pure types, models, paradigms. All people, all parties, all states, and all organizations exhibit mixtures—in varying proportions and nuance—of these ideologies. Nevertheless, we may think of ideologies as black and white for heuristic purposes, for clarity and analysis. The real people, countries, institutions, and events we describe, however, inevitably have ideological shades of grey in them. No one and no institution is purely conservative, liberal, or socialist. In Table 4.1 we need not refer to any group (e.g., British or French), any country (e.g., Canada or the United States), any political party (e.g., the Liberals or Conservatives), or any government structure (e.g., Parliament or Congress). It is only when we connect ideologies with people and places that we enter the realm of political culture. That is when we move from abstract ideas to the real exhortations of political leaders and the tangible works and behaviour of specific groups.

The five conservative principles in Table 1 hark back to the wisdom (or the curse, depending on your ideology) of the ages. They warn and encourage people to do things the way their ancestors did things. If these principles appear nostalgic or quaint, they are; the age we live in is decidedly not conservative, but is an unabashedly liberal one. Conservatives see society—the family, the church, the corporation, the university, the military—as hierarchically structured and properly

TABLE 4.1

THREE IDEOLOGICAL CONSTELLATIONS		
CONSERVATISM/ TORYISM	**LIBERALISM/ REPUBLICANISM**	**SOCIALISM**
tradition	reason	reason
authority (order)	freedom to have	freedom from want
hierarchy	equality of opportunity	equality of condition
priority of community	priority of the individual	priority of community
cooperation	competition	cooperation

so. Conservatives treasure social order, they fear and loath revolution, chaos, and anarchy. In a conservative society, those with high rank, basking in the privileges of wealth and government, also have a critical duty: to exercise power for the welfare of the whole community. Conservatism thus combines the elitism fostered by hierarchy with collectivist principles. A tory, like a socialist, will justify the restraint of individual conduct in the interests of the community as a whole.[3] Conservatives see humans as innately imperfect, limited, weak. Contrast this to liberalism's ardent faith in the individual's perfectibility and unlimited potential; contrast it too with socialism's passion for equality and for social engineering.

Liberalism is in the triumphant centre of the ideological dialectic depicted in Table 4.1. To counter the conservative's faith in tradition and the ways of old, the liberal offers reason, logic, enlightenment, and the progress associated with science and technology. For the liberal, the state is man's creation. The state exists to serve and protect the individual, not the reverse. The liberal accepts public laws but is ever vigilant that they not abridge private freedoms. He rails against toryism's hierarchies, its landed aristocrats and rigid class divisions. He posits liberty, equality, and fraternity in their stead. In this world view, competition among men and societies is the natural order. This contrasts with conservative and socialist visions of and preferences for cooperative societies. Liberals see man as creative and innovative, as a good and original being who must be permitted to be master of his fate. Conservatives see man in ascriptive, rather than achievement, terms; man is born into, occupies, and pridefully accepts his station in life. To liberals, the conservative understanding of man is anachronistic, undemocratic, stifling, and reactionary. Liberals see man as a rugged individual; he may rise or fall using his skills and wits.

Liberalism has evolved over time. Various faces of it have come to the fore, even competing with one another. Early liberalism bore more of the stamp of preliberalism's or conservatism's elitism. Early liberals sugarcoated their message so as not to suffer derision as revolutionary heretics. They emphasized freedom of religion and negative liberty, loosening the heavy hand of government. Later liberals focused on positive liberty, using the instrumentality of the state to aid man's liberation, to foster equality of opportunity, to break up oligarchies and oligopolies. In brief, welfare liberals, as opposed to business liberals, wanted to help the little guy. They believed that both the newly self-made and privileged (the old privileged were landed tory aristocrats) and the downtrodden should have equal opportunity to reach their liberal aspirations.

It is critical not to confuse ideology with policy. Ideology represents the *rationale* for policy; policy by itself does not necessarily reveal a specific ideological impulse. An example of this is medicare. Liberals, conservatives, and socialists in Canada now all embrace medicare. Does that make it a nonideological policy or a nonpartisan issue? No. All three ideologies may endorse medicare on the basis of three quite different motivations. The conservative underpinning for it might be *noblesse oblige*, a sense that society's privileged classes should underwrite, via the state, universal health care so as to maintain the fabric of the entire community, including its desperately needy classes. A liberal may support medicare based on the belief that all individuals must have an equal opportunity to prove themselves and get ahead, something not possible if one is stricken with an illness beyond one's control. A socialist may embrace medicare because it manifests our care for one another as equal members of a community—medicare is an important aspect of socialist equality of condition. So when a policy is cited as evidence of an ideological inclination or as proof that the "end of ideology" has arrived, be skeptical. Apply the litmus test. Did the governing party nationalize an industry to redistribute wealth (socialism), or to help other industries, private ones, to grow and profit (liberalism), or for the purpose of nation building (possible toryism)?

AN ALTERNATIVE INTERPRETATION AND ITS LIMITS

Janet Ajzenstat and Peter J. Smith have contended that the fundamental divide in Canada's political cultural origins has not been between liberalism and toryism but between liberalism and what they term civic humanism or liberal republicanism.[4] In this revisionist view, Canadian liberalism has represented the high and the mighty in a class-divided society. It has stood for unfettered commerce, a strong state, and the monarchy. Civic republicanism, in contrast, represents small property owners, independent craftsmen, and farmers who reject liberalism's selfish individualism, its corruption, its unsavouriness, and its technology. "Community," to the civic republican, is a shared sense of spirited patriotism, one in which individuals restrain their innate selfishness for the good of the community.

From this vantage point, the underlying philosophical cleavage in Canadian, American, and British politics has revolved around morality and virtue, around a struggle between wealth and virtue (as if the two are mutually exclusive). Civic republicans are the champions of a one-class citizenry whose leaders and members articulate a common sense of the common good and who both embrace participatory democracy. They are true democrats, unlike the sham democratic liberals who manipulate state power for personal self-aggrandizement. Civic republicans collectively define the good life; they endorse and encourage citizens' aspirations to virtuous public service. A twentieth-century version of this dichotomy is the contrast between the liberal aphorism, "What is good for General Motors is good for the United States," and John F. Kennedy's civic republican admonition, "Ask not what your country can do for you; ask what you can do for your country."

From the vantage point of the tory–liberal–socialist paradigm, the distinction between liberalism and republicanism is secondary. The distinction is merely the expression of two variations of liberalism's many facets and is subsumed by the overarching historical and ideological framework of the tory–liberal–socialist dialectic. Ajzenstat and Smith's formulation is subordinate because, on closer examination, both liberalism and republicanism or civic humanism share cardinal liberal assumptions about man and society. Neither tories nor socialists share them. To both liberals and civic republicans, man is a rugged individualist; the former see him as possessive, the latter, as principled. The tory has neither of these views of man. To both liberals and civic republicans, individuals are fully formed and self-sufficient. To both, the state is but the product of its members, a social contract. Both liberals and civic republicans define the common good as the sum of individual good. They both see society atomistically; it is nothing beyond the individuals who make it up. To the archetypical liberal, there is nothing else but individuals: "There is no such thing as society," declared Margaret Thatcher. In dramatic contrast, tories see the individual as a product, as part and parcel, of society. Neither tories nor socialists conceptualize individuals independently of the economic, societal, and institutional structures that form and sustain them. To the tory, state and society represent an ancient bond linking past, present, and future generations. The state is not some constantly renewed arrangement of contemporaries. In this view, society is organic and holistic, its members are integrally integrated components. In its totality, society is greater than the sum of its individuals and has a life and purpose that may be independent of them. Tories, like socialists, are thus willing and prepared to use the state to protect the public good and broad community interests against the private freedoms of individuals.

For toryism, there is no such thing as a fundamentally autonomous individual; the community is prior to the individual; individuals are essentially members of communities, as the limbs are members of the body. On the other hand, the Lockean and civic republican varieties of liberalism agree on the priority of the individual; they differ only on what is the best way for autonomous individuals to govern their common affairs.

THE CANADIAN TORY TRADITION

The difference between toryism and liberalism in Canada is reflected in conceptions of what the country is and how its government works. Tory historian W.L. Morton noted that Canadian government, unlike American government, has possessed an "objective" life of its own despite Canada having steadily become a society of social equals. The law and the state are embodied in the succession of those designated by Parliament and heredity. In the liberal United States, in contrast, government is "subjective." Founded on the principle of a social compact of individuals, it is designed to move on popular impulse. Without it, government falters. American government requires a conforming societal unity in which consensus works to a common end. In contrast, Canada's plural culture, its external dependence and relative economic fragility have meant, according to Morton, that the centre of national unity is the permanent force of its monarchical institutions. Morton saw the principle of allegiance as necessary for Canada's national existence; it was this principle that fed resistance to the insistent lure of republican institutions and republican liberty.[5]

Canadians were never opposed to "life, liberty, and the pursuit of happiness," but they determined early on that "peace, order, and good government" were prerequisites. These two counterpoints in the Declaration of Independence and the British North America Act offer thumbnail sketches of contrasting liberal and tory visions of government. There are others: Compare "All men are created equal" with the prerogatives of the monarch, the governor general, the lieutenant governors, and our unelected senators. Compare the assertive "We the people" with the BNA Act's preamble beseeching the Queen's indulgence for the federal project of her most obedient, humble subjects whom Macdonald described as England's "subordinate" people.[6] The tory principle of common allegiance to the Crown permitted a thousand diversities. Thus, Conservative prime minister Joe Clark could describe his Canada as a "community of communities," a notion that does not gel with America's self-image as a community of rugged individuals. A potent example of the persistent tory strain in Canadian politics and letters in the 1960s was George Grant's *Lament for a Nation*.[7] He bewailed the inexorable power of America's technological liberalism and economic drive, its denial of the good that limits human experimentation, action, and innovation. He compared that U.S. sentiment unfavourably with Canada's once illiberal and old-fashioned ideas of what is good. He was prepared to embrace socialist policies to limit free enterprise ideology for nationalist purposes. That Grant's book was a bestseller attests to Canada's at least modest taste for tory sentiment on an ideological groaning board catering to a liberal appetite.

Canadians' view of how their government should work and be determined has become increasingly liberalized over time. In recent years, liberal republican pressures for referendums and recall elections have reverberated throughout the country, but the status of the Crown as a tory symbol of hierarchy and allegiance has not been modified. Indeed, it has been fortified. The amending formula of the 1982 Constitution requires unanimity of the federal and provincial legislatures to alter the Crown's position in any way. In contrast, virtually the whole Charter of Rights and Freedoms—a liberal and American-patterned insertion into the Constitution—may be repealed by Ottawa and seven provinces representing a bare majority of the population. Fundamental freedoms such as religion, assembly, and speech may be overridden by individual legislatures acting on their own.[8] This emblematic hierarchy of rights and statuses speaks symbolically of Canada's continuing tory constitutional superstructure.

HISTORICAL AND SOCIOLOGICAL PERSPECTIVES

The story of Canadian political culture in the nineteenth and twentieth centuries is one of tension among the uneven weight of conservative, liberal, and socialist ideas. Liberalism and conservatism unfolded differently in two separate arenas:

the *modus vivendi* of primarily English-Canadian liberalism and French-Canadian conservatism was the Canadian compact in Ottawa and in special provisions for majorities and minorities in Quebec. In English Canada, liberalism overshadowed toryism but was influenced by it. The first arena featured physical separation—between Upper Canada and Lower Canada, between English Montreal and rural Quebec—with allowances for the language, religion, civil law, and social institutions of the French. In English Canada, geopolitics and the economic imperatives of a frontier society provided the material context for the struggle between liberal and tory ideas. The French Revolution, followed by the War of 1812, seriously frightened English Canada's elites. "The first imparted to them a 'tory' attitude towards change and reform, the second gave them an acute sense of leadership, loyalty to Britain and a strong anti-Americanism."[9] Thus, in the early nineteenth century colonial administrators pursued rationalized and hardened conservatism. Upper Canada's liberal reformers were denounced as "Jacobins," and whatever Jeffersonian or later Jacksonian democratic murmurings surfaced were vilified as dangerously egalitarian, antiauthoritarian, and anti-British.

Edmund Burke, the British philosopher and economic liberal, provided a political rationale for antidemocratic conservatism. For Canadian purposes, it was Burke's tory notions, rather than the liberal elements in his philosophy, that were pivotal. A continuing reflection of his legacy is that Canadian undergraduate political theory students are more likely to be exposed to him than to Tocqueville. The opposite is true in the United States because Tocqueville was analyzing America's purely liberal democratic blueprint; it had no need or place for Burke. Canada, unlike the United States, would have a balanced Whig constitution; that is, a division of power among distinct and hierarchically ordered estates or classes—the monarch, then a landed gentry or commercial aristocracy, and the masses or the commons on the bottom. This design replicated mother Britain's tory-touched liberal institutional architecture. A Canadian conundrum was this: what was aristocracy or landed gentry in a frontier economy that offered so much land and where cross-generational transfers of estates had not yet occurred? The authorities set out to create such a privileged class by reserving extensive land tracts for the clergy (no liberal American separation of church and state here) and by trying, though failing, to create such a class. Upper Canada's Family Compact and Lower Canada's Château Clique came and went without the tenure and successor rights guaranteed to Britain's House of Lords.

It was the power of the tory streak in English Canada and the feudal mindset in French Canada that contributed to halting and repelling radical liberalism. The liberals leading the 1837 Rebellions—our alleged civic republicans—were neither as radical, nor as weighty intellectually, nor as powerful politically as their American counterparts precisely because toryism in English Canada served as a bulwark for a more moderate, less strident liberalism. In French Canada, *patriote* Louis-Joseph Papineau's economic thinking was guided by "a feudal model";

below the rhetorical liberal façade, his thinking was *ancien, prérévolutionnaire, organiciste.* To stress his liberalism is delusional and erroneous.[10] In Upper Canada, it was the cautiously moderate liberals—Robert Baldwin and George Brown—rather than the radical democratic ones—Robert Gourlay and William Lyon Mackenzie who defined the mainstream of Canadian liberalism. The tory colonial mindset was to imagine that Canada was part of the living body of the metropole. Confederation facilitated nation building via the public works of the newly centralized and executive-driven regime. Peter J. Smith's study "shows how the tory conception of the state predominated in 1867," while Janet Azjenstat somehow simultaneously asserts "there was no significant tory influence in Canada's past."[11]

Toryism has left its imprint on the English-Canadian concept of the state. Toryism has expressed itself in a range of state activities—from the development of private enterprise at public expense, as in the case of the CPR in the 1870s, to the imposition of the illiberal War Measures Act in the 1970s. Along the way, Canadian federal and provincial governments built public enterprises such as hydroelectric, railroad, telephone, airline, mining, and oil companies, as well as a public broadcasting system. The state acquired and disposed of enterprises such as the Grand Trunk Railway and Petro Canada. The dominant pattern has been a liberal bailout or subsidies for business, but Canada has also had the occasional tory or socialist buyout of business and the creation of Crown corporations.

To Gad Horowitz, the presence and relative strength of Canadian socialism is a corollary of the presence and relative strength of Canadian toryism.[12] He argues brilliantly, synthetically, and dialectically that a tory or conservative past contains the seeds—collectivism, cooperation, organic communitarianism—for a socialist future. Although he does not apply his thesis to Quebec, that is where it works particularly well. Its conservative, quasi-feudal ideology finally exploded in the liberal Quiet Revolution of the 1960s. The contradictions between its preliberal ideology, on the one hand, and its new material reality by 1960 could no longer be suppressed. The ideology of Quebec was rural, priest ridden, closed to the world, antidemocratic, antimaterialist, anti–public education, and anti–mass communications; the reality of Quebec was urban, industrial, politically corrupt, and administratively backward, its people relatively poor and uneducated.[13] The inescapable pressures for modernization, that is, liberalism, could no longer be ignored. Quebec emerged from its self-imposed shell, opening itself to the models of political and economic organization of its Anglo-American neighbours. The rapid and heady advances of social democracy in the 1970s—the Parti Québécois's sudden rise and its election—suggest that, indeed, the conservative–liberal–socialist dialectic was at work. Exposed to liberalism, Quebec's intellectual and new middle classes merged their newly acquired rationalism–egalitarianism with their older conservative vision of an organically collectivist society. They described their regime as a "corporatist state" with a social democratic agenda.[14] Quebeckers simultaneously and selectively rejected and celebrated their history, insisting they would be the sovereign masters of their destiny rather than prisoners of their past, but stamping "Je me souviens" on their licence plates. (Contrast that to the Crown on Ontario's plates and the Union Jack on Ontario's flag.)

In English Canada, socialism has developed along a different path. Rather than arising where toryism has been relatively robust—in Atlantic Canada, Quebec's Eastern Townships, and eastern Ontario—socialism has done best where toryism has been weakest—in the West. Socialism's relative strength in English Canada is better explained empirically than as the philosophical collision of liberal and tory ideas. Socialism has been relatively weak in the Loyalist east, especially in the countryside. The West is where large numbers of *British-born* socialists arrived at the beginning of the twentieth century, including figures such as Tommy Douglas, M.J. Coldwell, Harold Winch, and John Queen. The relative numerical impact and political status of these immigrants was substantially greater in the relatively unsettled west than in the East or in the United States. (One could still contend, of course, as Horowitz does, that the very reason socialism was vibrant in Britain a century ago—whereas it was not, relatively, in the United States—was because of the persistence of tory traces in the political culture.) Toryism has been strongest where English Canada is oldest, where the Loyalists settled. Liberalism in the East has been of an older variety, one more influenced by toryism. Eastern liberalism has been more traditional, more elitist, more deferential, more restrained. Western liberalism is of more recent vintage, more modern, more radical, and populist.[15] Contrast the titles of the *Kingston Whig-Standard* and the *Winnipeg Free Press* for ideologically different liberal dispositions. The geographical divide operates within Ontario, too: the eastern part of the province has more of a tory touch than does the western part (the *London Free Press*), which has been more radical and leftist. That is where the 1837 rebels fared best.

Much of the foregoing discussion has been abstract, dealing perhaps more with ideas than behaviour. To be convincing, argument and assertion need description and detail as companions. If Canada on the whole has had a tory-touched liberal political culture and the United States has had one devoid of tory influences, where may we locate some more hard evidence? Turn to the work of the eminent American sociologist Seymour Martin Lipset. In comparing Canadians and Americans on a broad range of values and value-linked behaviours, he has distilled evidence from the fields of literature, religion, and economics, as well as from politics, to argue that "Canadians are more elitist, law-abiding, statist, collectivity oriented and group oriented than Americans."[16] Canadian literature, relatively, has focused more on community survival, American literature, more on personal independence and freedom. Canadians have been more likely to belong to hierarchical churches (Catholic, Anglican); Americans have been more likely to affiliate with egalitarian, fundamentalist ones. Canada has had lower crime rates, higher levels of unionization, more corporate concentration, and more public enterprise. Canadians have been less cynical about their governments, more likely to vote, less likely to participate in riots and protest demonstrations, more likely to trust their police forces, and less concerned with civil liberties. They have also been less likely to insist that new immigrant groups assimilate. Canada has been more of a mosaic and less of a melting pot. Canada's Constitution enshrines group rights (language, religious, multicultural, Aboriginal), while that of the United States shuns them. All these differences suggest a stronger tory and socialist influence in Canada compared with the degree of such influence in the United States.

CANADA'S POLITICAL CULTURE: LOOKING FOR TORYISM AND SOCIALISM

Liberalism in one form or another has always been the pervasive ideology in English Canada. The entrenchment of the Charter of Rights and Freedoms in the 1982 Constitution represented liberalism's formal triumph. Another Americanism was inserted into the Canadian political system and its machinery. Individual liberal rights were declared cherished, protected through the legalization of what had been politics. Parliament and provincial legislatures ceded elements of their sovereignty and supremacy to courts that now spell out the rights of individuals and groups of individuals. Individuals are now parties to the Constitution, as potentially aggrieved litigants, in a way they have never been before. Government has also retreated from national economic development. Crown corporations and public enterprises are being privatized. Policymaking is increasingly shaped by surveys of individuals and less by leaders weighing and harmonizing the competing interests of groups. The historical party of toryism, the Conservatives, opted for right-wing business liberals like Brian Mulroney and Mike Harris, sharp contrasts to more tory-touched predecessors like John Diefenbaker and Bill Davis. The success of the Reform Party, the shift to the right in provincial politics, and the quickening spread of referendums all suggest that even if toryism were a significant force once upon a time, it is surely dead now. No, not at all. Liberalism has been pervasive in Canada but not exclusive as in the United States.

Toryism and socialism are too deeply embedded in Canadian political culture to be written off. As recently as 1995, 77 percent of Canadians were governed by powerful provincial governments that claimed to be social democrats. Neither Lockean liberals nor civic republicans do that. During the Mulroney years, the collectivist nationalism and welfarism of toryism persisted, but it was much stronger relatively in the federal Liberals and the NDP than in the Tories. The lesson is that Canadian toryism is not the preserve of any one party; it may be accessed by all of them and their leaders. They will use the language and principles of toryism when it suits their purposes, when they think it will strike a responsive popular chord. The dichotomization between liberalism and civic republicanism cannot account for toryism, so it insists that it is a figment of imagination. A telling recent link between toryism and socialism is David MacDonald. He calls himself a red tory, someone influenced by working class/socialist forces. (Ajzenstat and Smith will tell him he doesn't know what he's talking about or who he really is.) In the 1980s, MacDonald served as a federal Conservative MP and cabinet minister. In the 1990s he ran for the NDP. Exceptional? Yes, but it does reveal something of Canada's ideological diversity compared with that of the United States, where debates are strictly between different kinds of liberals. Canadians exult in their liberalism, but still stirring among them are distinct tory and socialist murmurs.

NOTES

1. C.B. Macpherson, *The Political Theory of Possessive Individualism* (London: Oxford University Press, 1962).

2. Louis Hartz, *The Liberal Tradition in America* (New York: Harcourt, Brace, 1955).

3. Robert L. Stanfield, "Conservative Principles and Philosophy," in Paul Fox and Graham White, eds., *Politics: Canada*, 8th ed. (Toronto: McGraw-Hill Primus, 1995), pp. 307–311.

4. Janet Ajzenstat and Peter J. Smith, eds., *Canada's Origins: Liberal, Tory, or Republican?* (Ottawa: Carleton University Press, 1995).

5. W.L. Morton, *The Canadian Identity* (Toronto: University of Toronto Press, 1961).

6. Quoted in Edgar McInnis, *The Commonwealth Today* (Saskville, NB: Mount Allison University Publications, 1959), p. 7.

7. George Grant, *Lament for a Nation* (Toronto: McClelland and Stewart, 1965).

8. Constitution Act, 1982, Part V.

9. Robert E. Sanders, "What Was the Family Compact?" in J.K. Johnson, ed., *Historical Essays on Upper Canada* (Toronto: McClelland and Stewart, 1975), p. 136.

10. Denis Monière, *Ideologies in Quebec* (Toronto: University of Toronto Press, 1981), p. 102; and Luis Balthazar, "Les idées politiques de Louis-Joseph Papineau: une étude comparative" (unpublished Ph.D. thesis, Harvard University, 1970).

11. Ajzenstat and Smith, *Canada's Origins*, pp. 48, 265.

12. Gad Horowitz, "Conservatism, Liberalism, and Socialism in Canada: An Interpretation," *Canadian Journal of Economics and Political Science* 32 (1966): 143–171.

13. Marcel Rioux, "The Development of Ideologies in Quebec," in Hugh G. Thorburn, ed., *Party Politics in Canada*, 7th ed. (Scarborough, ON: Prentice-Hall, 1996).

14. Nelson Wiseman, "A Note on 'Hartz–Horowitz at Twenty': The Case of French Canada," *Canadian Journal of Political Science* 21 (1988): 795–806.

15. Nelson Wiseman, "Provincial Political Cultures," in Christopher Dunn, ed., *Provinces* (Peterborough, ON: Broadview, 1996), ch. 1.

16. Seymour Martin Lipset, "Historical Traditions and National Characteristics: A Comparative Analysis of Canada and the United States," *Canadian Journal of Sociology* II (1986): 113. See also Lipset, *Continental Divide* (New York: Routledge, 1990).

✗ NO
The 'Tory Touch' Thesis: Bad History, Poor Political Science
JANET AJZENSTAT AND PETER J. SMITH

I

The "tory touch" thesis gets Canadian history wrong. It cripples Canadians' understanding of Canada's identity, and precludes informed debate about current political issues.

According to the tory touch thesis, the United Empire Loyalists, immigrants to British North America in the late eighteenth century, brought a philosophy of feudal conservatism (toryism) that, in combination with the traditional conservatism of French Canada, left an indelible tory stamp on the Canadian political way of life.[1] It is an important part of the thesis that the influence of Loyalist toryism can still be detected in Canadian politics and political institutions. The suggestion is that Canada takes its identity from habits of feudal conservatism ingrained in the Canadian political character.

Generations of students have been raised on this thesis. It is a staple of Canadian political science and Canadian studies programs. But the fact is that the historical record does not bear it out. Loyalist thought is not imbued with feudal ideas; feudal conservatism is not a feature of political debate at any time in nineteenth-century Canada. In short, there is no toryism in Canadian political history, and none in Canadian politics at present, not even a "touch."[2]

The crucial influence in pre-Confederation years is not that of mythical feudalism, but a vigorous debate between constitutional liberals and "civic republicans" about modern democracy.[3] The constitutional liberals, men like Étienne Parent, Joseph Howe, and Sir John A. Macdonald, argue for parliamentary democracy, in essence not unlike the kind of democracy entrenched in Canadian practice today. The civic republicans, in contrast, men like Louis-Joseph Papineau and William Lyon Mackenzie, argue for a form of democracy that is more participatory and more communal, a "people's" democracy.

Until recently, scholars in general paid little attention to the political ideas of the civic republicans. It is our contention that understanding the republican idea of democracy, and the constitutional liberal response to it, is the key to Canadian political history, the Canadian identity, and Canadian politics today. The quarrels about participatory politics, political community, and nationality that are such a marked feature of Canada's current constitutional reform process have their origins in the nineteenth-century debate about forms of democracy. Ideas that fuelled the British North American Rebellions in the mid-nineteenth century are today transforming Canada, or perhaps, tearing it apart.

II

Advocates of the tory touch thesis admit that liberal ideology was prominent in nineteenth-century Canada. There is supposedly only a touch of feudal toryism in Canada's past; it is not suggested that toryism was the dominant political ideology.[4] Nevertheless the touch is said to be all important. It is commonly argued, for example, that the tory touch is what makes Canada a better place to live than the United States.

To see why the tory touch is believed to be so important, it must be noted that the thesis uses the terms "conservative" and "tory" in a highly distinctive fashion. In ordinary speech, "conservative" has a number of meanings; it is often used, for example, to refer to someone who has doubts about big government and wants to roll back the welfare state, leaving people free to get on with their lives as best they can. But in the tory touch thesis, "conservative" describes a form of elite rule that is far from hostile to big government. The typical characteristic of true-blue tories is said to be readiness to use the power of the state to enact measures for the "common good," at the expense of individual freedoms.[5]

Supposedly then, the tory touch makes Canadians today still more willing than Americans to use the powers of government; hence Canadian welfare programs such as medicare. The magic, feudal touch again is supposed to be responsible for Canada's relative lack of crime and violence. Canadians are presumably more willing than Americans to obey the law because of old tory habits of deference. Canada is the peaceable, caring kingdom! Very flattering. But how credible?

This is not the place to embark on a long comparison of the Canadian and American political cultures. Undoubtedly, most parts of Canada are less violent than most parts of the United States. Undoubtedly, Canada has a more extensive public health system than the United States. But the United States has not always lagged behind Canada in welfare legislation. And although Canadians do like to boast about their health care system, survey data does not suggest that, in general, Canadian support for welfare measures and economic equality is very much deeper than is American support.[6]

The point we wish to emphasize is that it requires a great stretch of the imagination to believe that cultural differences between Canada and the United States, large or small, can be explained by a theory locating the roots of the welfare state in the political thought of the feudal Middle Ages. The tory touch thesis rests on a highly abstract, philosophical argument about the evolution of political ideologies through the centuries.[7] Toryism, originating in the feudal period, is said to be characterized by elitism and a strong sense of community. Liberalism develops next, arising out of rebellions in the seventeenth century against tory autocrats. Rejecting tory elitism and communalism, liberalism adopts egalitarianism and individualism. Socialism follows in the nineteenth century, combining the tory sense of community and liberal ideas of equality. And with socialism the story supposedly comes to an end! Conservatism, liberalism, socialism: this is world history unfolding as it should, according to the tory touch thesis.

What scholars like Gad Horowitz find attractive in this thesis is the idea that a nation with a tory past may have a socialist future. Horowitz is no friend of toryism per se. But he is convinced that a society used to thinking in terms of tory ideas of community will become dissatisfied with liberal individualism, and at some point see the value of socialist community, class consciousness, and collective action. Horowitz's mentor Louis Hartz believed the true flowering of socialism would happen only in Europe; patterns of immigration had brought too little toryism to North America to form a basis for socialism. Horowitz agrees that socialism is an impossibility in the United States, but contends that the lingering Loyalist influence in Canada—the tory touch—will support at least a degree of socialism. This is the crucial point for Horowitz, that the tory touch remains alive in the form of socialism; socialism is a possibility for Canada, and not for the United States.

The thesis makes almost no effort to trace the transmission of ideas from generation to generation. Proponents seldom tell us, for example, that person "C" read the works of "B," who in turn had been influenced by "A." Indeed, the surprising thing is that the scholars who argue so strenuously for Loyalist influence in Canadian history do not appear to have read Loyalist writings. They rely on Hegel, Marx, and Louis Hartz. Note how Horowitz makes his case. He first argues that the existence of socialist parties in Canada in the 1960s (the Cooperative Commonwealth Federation and the New Democratic Party) is evidence of a tory touch in British North America. He then uses the supposed fact of toryism in Canada's past to account for Canada's twentieth-century socialism. Some methodology!

Nowhere do the difficulties of the thesis show up more than in its treatment of the Family Compact and Château Clique, the governing elites of pre-Confederation Canada. The thesis argues that elites in the Family Compact and the Château Clique usurped the right to govern as if they were feudal aristocrats—using their power in projects for the "common good." The colonial oligarchies are proof that the feudal touch continues on!

But there is nothing particularly tory about politicians trying to use public office for party purposes. In fact there is nothing particularly tory about politicians *mis*using public office. Misuse of office can happen in any regime, among politicians of any ideology. What was really going on in those oligarchic governments of pre-Confederation Canada? Nineteenth-century critics of the Family Compact piled up statistics to show that far from acting for the common good, members of the compact were feathering their own nests, siphoning off public money for family and friends. They were abusing the public trust.[8] It is a very odd thesis that takes the actions of petty, greedy politicians as evidence that a political culture inclines toward socialism!

III

A better understanding of Canadian political history results when we focus directly on the Family Compact's critics. New scholarship shows that they fall into two camps: there are liberal critics and republican critics. Both groups oppose the Family Compact and the Château Clique, but they have very different programs for getting the oligarchs out of office, and very different visions of good government.[9]

The constitutional liberals believe the best way to curb greedy politicians is to have a good political constitution, and in their view the best constitution is the British parliamentary system.[10] In short, the liberals emphasize the importance of institutional restraints to moderate human greed and ambition. Throughout the pre-Confederation period, they worked hard to ensure that the colonies adopted British parliamentary practices, especially "responsible government," the parliamentary principle that requires members of the governing party to retain support of the majority of elected representatives in the lower legislative house. In effect, responsible government requires political elites, and thus political parties, to compete for the public's favour. It is designed exactly to prevent the kind of scandalous, self-seeking behaviour that characterized the Family Compact and Château Clique. Responsible government, coupled with a broad electoral franchise, is the constitutional liberal formula for democracy.

The constitutional liberals did not argue that introduction of responsible government would be sufficient. Eternal vigilance is the price of freedom! Judicial independence, the rule of law, the bicameral legislature, and so on are also necessary institutions. The important thing to note about liberal proposals is that they take it as a given that political elites are ambitious and indeed are sometimes, perhaps often, ready to sacrifice public interests to private ends. Instead of trying to change this feature of human nature, constitutional liberals set up the institutions that will turn ambition in the direction of public service. The liberal constitution is meant to make it difficult for politicians to gratify the desire for status and office except by working for the public good. Thus a "responsible" government would favour measures to raise the standard of living for all citizens and not merely the governors. The commercial development of the colonies was a standard item on the liberal agenda.

Civic republicans view politics through a vastly different prism. In contrast to the liberal emphasis on moderation of behaviour through institutional constraints, civic republicans put their trust in social constraints. They argue that democracy requires a particular kind of citizen, and a particular kind of society. What it requires above all is a virtuous citizenry. Civic republicanism depends on civic virtue. Citizens must willingly place the public welfare above individual gain. A crucial element of this philosophy for the civic republicans of British North America was the argument for material equality. In a political society where some are very rich and others poor, civic virtue vanishes. More than this, equal democratic participation in government becomes impossible. Thus the nineteenth-century republicans rejected proposals for commercial development of the kind favoured by the constitutional liberals, arguing that development could only result in the rich becoming richer and the poor poorer. With respect to economic proposals, the republicans indeed saw very little difference between the liberals and the greedy Family Compact politicians the liberals professed to criticize. The argument of the nineteenth-century republicans was that democratic politics would flourish best in a society of small property owners, particularly farmers.

In so far as they had a prescription for institutional reform, the republicans proposed to concentrate power in the hands of the people's elected representatives in the legislative assembly. They argued for an elective upper legislature, and sometimes recommended an elective executive (on the lines of the American presidential system). In short, they opted for all measures that would devolve power to the mass of the people. What is noteworthy is that they had so little confidence in the principle of responsible government. They regarded the vaunted parliamentary system, including responsible government, as merely another means to concentrate elite power. In republican eyes, parliamentary democracy is no democracy at all![11] The important point to note is that they had little respect for the liberal idea that party government and competition of political parties for office restrains ambitious politicians. The republicans argued that the better guarantee is found in the idea of civic virtue. The civic virtue of the people and leaders offers the best assurance of freedom and democracy.

If the republicans believed the constitutional liberal proposals were elitist and antidemocratic, the liberals in turn were convinced that the republican formula was a serious threat to political and individual freedom. Relying on civic virtue would promote a homogeneity of society and politics antithetical to free political speech and the alternation of political parties in office. In brief, the liberals feared republican proposals would lead to popular tyranny.[12]

Civic republicanism declines in importance in the 1840s. The Rebellions are lost. The liberals successfully establish the principle of responsible government. But republican arguments are not forgotten. In particular, the contention that democracy requires civic virtue continues to resonate with Canadians; in the twentieth century, arguments for the kind of democracy fostered by virtue surfaces in populist parties of both the right and left.

It would be wrong to suggest that political debates at the end of the twentieth century reproduce exactly arguments of early nineteenth-century liberals and republicans. Nevertheless we find similar themes. How can we keep elected leaders working for the public good? Is it enough to rely on political institutions, like responsible government, that legitimize criticism of elites? Or must we cultivate a moral climate that militates against elite corruption? If we incline to the former idea, our arguments echo those of the nineteenth-century liberals. If we incline to the later, we are following in the footsteps of the republicans.

Do we put our faith in the rule of law, equality of opportunity, and an expanding economy? That's the liberal answer. Do we rely on social constraints and the good sense of the citizenry expressed in participatory institutions? That's the republican remedy.

Ignoring nineteenth-century republicanism, the tory touch thesis misinterprets nineteenth-century constitutional liberalism, and liberalism's response to republicanism. That crucial nineteenth-century debate between liberal democrats and radical democrats drops out of sight. And Canadians' understanding of present issues in democratic theory is impoverished.

IV

The tory touch thesis militates against clear thinking above all in the very areas it was originally meant to illuminate: political ideology and the Canadian political identity. Even on its own assumption that Canadian political history and current politics can be explained in terms of toryism, liberalism, and socialism, the tory touch thesis is deficient. Consider the following:

- The thesis subordinates the moral dimension of socialism to a jingoistic assertion of Canadian superiority to the United States. And by tying the origins of socialism to an empirically unverifiable tory touch, it plays down Canadian socialism's equalitarian and participatory elements, elements that in our view owe much to the influence of civic republicanism.

- It offers only a caricature of liberal democratic theory. Liberalism is associated with a crass, individualist materialism and is depicted as a mere stepping stone to socialism. The constitutional dimension of liberal democracy (the rule of law, individual and political freedom, representative institutions, responsible and accountable government, toleration of free political speech, etc.) is barely mentioned, except to note the inevitability of its demise.[13]

- It defines conservatism as the ideology of social hierarchy and autocracy, as if conservatives had never emerged from the Middle Ages. It notably excludes from the definition of conservatism political prudence and moderation, principles of political conduct often considered central to a conservative perspective.

- The great strength of the thesis supposedly lies in its definition of the Canadian national identity. But the idea that Canada derives its identity from feudal toryism and a tory-derived socialism can only leave Canadians divided and confused. Can one be a true Canadian without adhering to the tory touch thesis and its highly abstract dialectic of toryism, liberalism, and socialism? Of course!

The most serious charge against the tory touch thesis is that it ignores the historical impact of civic republicanism. It ignores the broad range of political ideas and visions of good government deriving from republicanism that are found sometimes in association with political parties of the left, and sometimes in association with parties of the right. It deprives us as well of the historical liberal response to civic republicanism, and the continuing liberal engagement with republican arguments. How ludicrous is the attempt to squeeze into the straitjacket of toryism–liberalism–socialism today's passionate debates about participatory democracy, populism, public virtue, moral education, and political community!

Until we abandon the tory touch interpretation of Canadian political history and ideology, we will not understand our past, the political culture of French Canada and English Canada, or today's politics. The tory touch thesis is bad history and poor political science.

NOTES

1. Gad Horowitz, "Conservatism, Liberalism, and Socialism in Canada: An Interpretation," *Canadian Journal of Economics and Political Science* 32, no. 1 (1996); George Grant, *Lament for a Nation* (Toronto: McClelland and Stewart, 1965). See the bibliography in Janet Ajzenstat and Peter J. Smith, eds., *Canada's Origins: Liberal, Tory, or Republican?* (Ottawa: Carleton University Press, 1995), pp. 283–288.

2. Janet Ajzenstat and Peter J. Smith "Liberal-Republicanism: The Revisionist Picture of Canada's Founding," in Ajzenstat and Smith, *Canada's Origins* pp. 1–18.

3. The civic republican ideology was a marked feature of political life in eighteenth-century England, France, and the United States. For a fuller picture of the way in which civic republicanism shaped both English and French Canada, see Peter J. Smith, "Civic Humanism Versus Liberalism: Fitting the Loyalists In," *Canadian Journal of Political Science* 26, no. 2 (1991), reprinted in *Canada's Origins*, pp. 119–135. The bibliography in *Canada's Origins* should be consulted for the literature on civic republicanism.

4. Horowitz, "Conservatism, Liberalism, and Socialism."

5. Grant, *Lament*, pp. 69, 71.

6. Paul M. Sniderman, Joseph F. Fletcher, Peter H. Russell, and Philip E. Tetlock, *The Clash of Rights, Liberty, Equality and Legitimacy in Pluralist Democracy* (New Haven: Yale University Press, 1996), pp. 95ff.

7. Louis Hartz, *The Founding of New Societies, Studies in the History of the United States, Latin America, South Africa, Canada, and Australia* (New York: Harcourt, Brace and World, 1964). See especially "Chapter Seven: The Structure of Canadian History," by Kenneth D. McRae, pp. 219–274.

8. See the *Report on Grievances* issued by the House of Assembly in Upper Canada in 1835. (W.P.M. Kennedy, *Statutes, Treaties and Documents of the Canadian Constitution, 1713–1929* (Toronto: Oxford University Press, 1930), pp. 395–407).

9. A longer essay would show the origins of these competing visions in European political thought. Scholars detect the influence of Aristotle, Machiavelli, Locke, Rousseau, Montesquieu, and Burke. But needless to say there is little agreement. Even Ajzenstat and Smith differ!

10. See, for example, Pierre Bédard writing in *Le Canadien,* 1806–1810, Étienne Parent in the same journal in the 1820s, and Joseph Howe's four open letters to Lord John Russell written in 1839 (Kennedy, *Statutes, Treaties and Documents,* pp. 384–414).

11. See the correspondence between Papineau and John Arthur Roebuck, Lower Canada's spokesman in Britain; especially Papineau to Roebuck, October, 1835 (Public Archives of Canada, Roebuck Papers, 1, no. 4).

12. Étienne Parent, *Le Canadien,* 18 February, 1924; John A. Macdonald addressing the legislature of the united Canadas on the subject of Confederation, 6 February, 1865 (Kennedy, *Statutes, Treaties and Documents,* pp. 550–569; see especially p. 569.

13. Grant, *Lament,* p. 63.

Postscript

In his article, Wiseman argues for a tory-touched liberalism, a political culture that gives Canada elements of all three of the major ideologies of modern times. While it is easy to accept the presence of liberalism, the same is not the case for conservatism and socialism. Traditional conservatism, as Wiseman notes, revolves around the values of tradition, authority, hierarchy, and community. But do Canadians truly reflect these values, even if only in the form of a "touch"? Similarly, does socialism really have a place among the political ideas of Canadians? We are, it is granted, sympathetic to the efforts of government in some areas, but this seems a long way from socialism, with its emphasis on equality of condition and public planning. Canadians, it might argued, are simply too liberal to be conservative or socialist.

Ajzenstat and Smith's article, too, raises some questions. As Wiseman says, Ajzenstat and Smith might be accused of reducing Canada's political culture to a struggle between two strains of liberalism; in other words, Canada, like the United States, is basically a one-ideology polity. But surely this misses the richness of political thought in Canada; it also leaves unexplained, it seems, the tolerance that we find in Canada, which many find to be a result of the wide ideological spectrum in the country. Perhaps most important, it makes Canada too much like America, a liberal state with challenges from the populist left. One of the attractive aspects of the tory-touched liberal thesis is that it provides support for what many Canadians instinctively feel: namely, that we *are* different from the Americans. Finally, civic republicanism seems suspiciously like toryism and socialism, for it captures the collective orientation in these two ideologies. Maybe Wiseman, Ajzenstat, and Smith are talking about the same thing, but just using different labels.

Much has been written about tory-touched liberalism and the political culture of Canada. The place to start is Gad Horowitz's initial exposition of the claim, which can be found in Gad Horowitz, *Canadian Labour in Politics* (Toronto: University of Toronto Press, 1968). (Shorter versions are included in numerous readers in Canadian politics.) In this piece, Horowitz also develops a theory—the *fragment thesis*—that endeavours to explain the origins and persistence of tory-touched liberalism. For students who wish to become informed on tory-touched liberalism, an appreciation of the fragment thesis is essential. Other articles and pieces relevant to tory-touched liberalism include Gad Horowitz, "Notes on 'Conservatism, Liberalism, and Socialism in Canada,'" *Canadian Journal of Political Science* 11, no. 2 (1978); Nelson Wiseman, "The Pattern of Prairie Politics," in Hugh G. Thorburn, ed., *Party Politics in Canada,* 7th ed. (Scarborough: Prentice-Hall Canada, 1996); Ian Stewart, "All the King's Horses: The Study of Canadian Political Culture," in James P. Bickerton and Alain-G.

Gagnon, eds., *Canadian Politics,* 2nd ed. (Peterborough: Broadview Press, 1994); H.D. Forbes, "Hartz-Horowitz at Twenty: Nationalism, Toryism and Socialism in Canada and the United States," *Canadian Journal of Political Science* 20, no. 2 (1987); and David Bell, *The Roots of Disunity: A Study of Canadian Political Culture,* 2nd ed. (Toronto: Oxford University Press, 1992).

As for readings that support the other side of the debate, Azjenstat and Smith have edited a collection of articles on this matter entitled *Canada's Origins: Liberal, Tory or Republican?* (Ottawa: Carleton University Press, 1995). Some of these readings will represent a challenge to students, but in the opening and closing chapters Ajzenstat and Smith offer a clear and understandable discussion of their position. Of special interest is the closing chapter, in which the two discuss between themselves the presence of liberal and republican values in Canada today, and do so by comparing Canada with the United States.

PART TWO

THE CONSTITUTION AND FEDERALISM

Is the Canadian Charter of Rights and Freedoms antidemocratic?

Is constitutional reform necessary?

Must national standards be federal standards?

Should Quebec be recognized as a distinct society in the constitution?

Do Canada's tax laws treat women fairly and equally?

Is it time for Canada and Quebec to part?

Is the Canadian Charter of Rights and Freedoms Antidemocratic?

✔ **YES**
ROBERT MARTIN, "The Canadian Charter of Rights and Freedoms Is Antidemocratic and Un-Canadian"

✘ **NO**
PHILIP L. BRYDEN, "The Canadian Charter of Rights and Freedoms Is Antidemocratic and Un-Canadian: An Opposing Point of View"

Do terminally ill patients have the right to a doctor-assisted suicide? Should women have unrestricted access to abortion without fear of criminal penalty? Does freedom of expression include the right to produce and distribute pornography? Are Sunday shopping regulations a violation of freedom of religion? All of these questions raise difficult issues regarding the relationship between individual citizens and their government. In essence they each pose the same questions: What civil rights does an individual have and how are they to be protected from the intrusive arm of the state?

In choosing to establish a system of parliamentary government on the "Westminster model," the founders of Canada adopted a British solution to this problem. Parliament would be supreme and would act as the ultimate guarantor of individual rights and freedoms. This solution reflects an implicit trust in both Parliament and the basic democratic values of civil society. It assumes that civil liberties are so deeply engrained in the national political culture that parliamentarians and citizens alike would never seriously consider using the power of government to infringe upon them. Public opinion and tradition would act as a powerful constraint against any violation of the fundamental civil and political liberties that are considered to be an inherent part of a democratic system. With the establishment of a federal system in Canada, courts were given the task of deciding whether federal and provincial legislatures were acting within their respective jurisdictions, not whether their actions violated civil and political liberties. There was no perceived need to give such rights special judicial protection that put them outside the reach of legislators.

Not everyone was happy with this solution. They pointed to a long history of both provincial and federal governments' trampling of the rights of citizens. In the early part of this century, British Columbia passed laws denying Asians the right to vote in provincial elections. During the Second World War the federal government arbitrarily seized the property of Japanese Canadians and placed them in internment camps without due process of law.

These experiences, and others, convinced many Canadians that greater protection of civil rights was needed. The Americans provided an alternative solution: define the rights of citizens in a written constitutional document that is beyond the reach of the legislature. The courts, through the power of judicial review, can then pass judgment on whether the legislation passed by a government infringes on civil liberties. John Diefenbaker began to move Canada in this direction in 1960, when his government passed the Canadian Bill of Rights. But this bill was simply an act of Parliament and applied only to the federal government. As a result, Canadian courts made only limited use of the Bill of Rights.

With the adoption of the Canadian Charter of Rights and Freedoms as part of a larger constitutional package, the government of Pierre Trudeau brought in a new era in 1982. With the entrenchment of the Charter in the Canadian Constitution, not only were Canadians given an explicit definition of their rights, but also the courts were empowered to rule on the constitutionality of government legislation.

There is little doubt that the adoption of the Charter has significantly transformed the operation of the Canadian political system. Since the adoption of the Charter, the Supreme Court of Canada has been involved in virtually every issue of any great political significance in Canada. As a result, there has been a growing public awareness about the potential "political" role that the Supreme Court now plays in the lives of ordinary Canadians. Increasingly, Canadians define their needs and complaints in the language of rights. More and more, interest groups and minorities are turning to the courts, rather than the usual political processes, to make their grievances heard. Peter Russell has described the dramatic impact of the Charter on Canadian politics as having "judicialized politics and politicized the judiciary."

Has the impact of the Charter been a positive one? Has the Charter lived up to its promise to enhance Canadian democracy through the protection of civil liberties? Robert Martin, a law professor at the University of Western Ontario, feels that the impact of the Charter has been largely a negative one. In particular, he argues that the Charter has had an antidemocratic effect on the country and has accelerated the Americanization of Canada. In contrast, Philip Bryden, Associate Dean of the Faculty of Law at the University of British Columbia, argues that the Charter plays an essential role in protecting and enhancing the quality of Canadian democracy.

✔ YES

The Canadian Charter of Rights and Freedoms Is Antidemocratic and Un-Canadian
ROBERT MARTIN

INTRODUCTION

On April 17, 1982, the Canadian Charter of Rights and Freedoms became part of our Constitution. Everyone who has written about the Charter agrees its effect has been to change profoundly both our politics and the way we think. Most of the commentators have applauded these changes. I do not.

I believe the Charter has had decidedly negative effects on Canada. It has contributed to an erosion of our democracy and of our own sense of ourselves. It is time for a serious and critical stocktaking.

Let me be clear that I am not suggesting the Charter itself has actually *done* any of this. A central problem with the Charter has been its contribution to our growing inability to distinguish between the concrete and the abstract. The Charter is simply words on a piece of paper. What I will be addressing are the uses to which the Charter has been put by human beings. I will look at the antidemocratic effects of the Charter and then turn to an analysis of its un-Canadian character.

THE CHARTER IS ANTIDEMOCRATIC

By their nature, constitutions express a fear of democracy, a horror that the people, if given their head, will quickly become a mindless mob. As a result, constitutions, all constitutions, place enforceable limitations on the powers of the state and, more particularly, on the lawmaking authority of the people's representatives.

Prior to 1982, the Canadian Constitution did contain such limitations. Our central constitutional document, the British North America Act of 1867, divided lawmaking authority between Parliament and the provincial legislatures and, thereby, limited that authority. But these limitations were purely functional. The authority to make laws about education, for example, rested with the provinces. Ottawa could not make laws about education, and if it attempted to do so, the attempt could be struck down by the courts. The courts had no authority to tell the provinces how to exercise their authority over education, to tell them what kind of laws they should make about education.

This is what changed in 1982. The federal division of powers remained, but for the first time substantive limitations were placed on lawmaking authority. The judges were given the power to strike down laws that, in their opinion, were inconsistent with the Charter.

It is crucial to understand basic distinctions between legislators and judges. Any Canadian citizen over the age of eighteen is eligible to be elected to Parliament or a provincial legislature. Elected members are directly accountable to their constituents. They must face reelection at least once every five years. By way of contrast, to become a senior judge in Canada you must be a lawyer and you must have been one for ten years. You are appointed until age seventy-five through a closed process that a former chief justice of Canada described as "mysterious," and you are made constitutionally independent, directly accountable to no one.

The defining feature of representative democracy in Canada has been that it is up to the elected members of our legislatures to resolve issues of social, economic, and political policy, subject, of course, to the approval or disapproval of the people, which is expressed at periodic elections. This has changed since the adoption of the Charter. Judges can now overturn deliberate policy decisions made by the elected representatives of the people where those decisions do not accord with the way the judges interpret the Charter. This is undemocratic. Some of our commentators call this "counter-majoritarian," but the phrase is pure obfuscation.

We seem to be experiencing great difficulty today in grasping this simple truth about the antidemocratic nature of judicial review of legislation. One explanation for our difficulty is that we have forgotten that liberalism and democracy are not the same thing. Liberalism is about individual rights, about the ability of individuals to do as they please without interference from the state. Liberalism makes protection of the autonomy of the individual more important than the promotion of the welfare of the collectivity. Democracy is, and always has been, about the interests of the collectivity, about majority rule, about power to the people.

There is an inherent and irreconcilable tension between liberalism and democracy. This tension has always been built into our political system, a system that is ordinarily described as liberal democracy.

The Charter is a liberal document. It sets out fundamental notions about the rights of the individual that have always been at the core of liberalism. More to the point, the Charter has led to a shift in emphasis in Canadian liberal democracy. The balance has been tilted in favour of liberalism and away from democracy.

Members of the judiciary, led by the Supreme Court of Canada, have shown little restraint in arrogating to themselves a central policymaking role. In 1984 they conferred upon themselves the distinction "guardian of the Constitution." They haven't looked back.

Our judges have not hesitated to substitute their views of acceptable or desirable social policy for those of our legislators. When the judges have not agreed with the policy decisions of our elected representatives, they have invalidated the legislation that expresses those decisions. But the judges have been prepared to go further. They have shown themselves willing to write legislation, to even go to the point of imposing financial obligations on the state.

The willingness to interfere with the traditional policymaking functions of legislatures has not been restricted to the courts. Administrative tribunals now sit in judgment on the validity of legislation, and boards of inquiry set up under human rights acts rewrite legislation and create new legal responsibilities for individuals.

We have become more and more inclined to seek to resolve the central questions agitating our society in the courtroom, rather than through the political process. The result of this is to surrender to lawyers control of the social agenda and of public discourse.

In a similar vein, the Charter has given a great boost to interest group politics. Indeed, an active judicial role and interest group politics seem made for each other.

Interest group politics is antidemocratic in two respects. It erodes citizenship, the essential precondition to democratic politics. People are induced to define themselves according to their race or sex or sexual preference or some other ascriptive criterion, rather than as citizens. And, in practice, interest group politics has meant seeking to use the courts as a means of short-circuiting or bypassing democratic processes.

The Charter has thus, in an institutional sense, had an antidemocratic effect. But it has also reinforced ideological currents that are antidemocratic. The most important of these stem from our growing obsession with "rights."

Our fascination with rights has been central to a process through which we seem to have come to prefer the abstract over the concrete. "Rights" appear to be more attractive than real things such as jobs or pensions or physical security or health care. We have been persuaded that if we have "rights" and these "rights" are enshrined in a constitution, then we need not concern ourselves with anything else. It is difficult to describe as "democratic" a public discourse that avoids addressing actual social and economic conditions.

Rights discourse itself encourages antidemocratic tendencies. The inclination of persons to characterize their desires or preferences as "rights" has two unfortunate results. First, there is an inevitable polarization of opposing positions in any debate. And, second, the possibility of further discussion is precluded. If you assert that something is your "right," my only possible response is, "No, it isn't."

Finally, the interest in rights has done much to promote individualistic and, therefore, antisocial ways of thinking. My impression is that many people view their rights as a quiver of jurisprudential arrows, weapons to be used in waging the ceaseless war of each against all.

THE CHARTER IS UN-CANADIAN

It is difficult to imagine any single event or instrument that has played a more substantial role in Americanizing the way Canadians think than has the Charter. The Charter clearly did not begin this process, but it has, since 1982, been central in it.

The basis for my assertion about the Americanizing effects of the Charter is a recognition that, historically and culturally, the Charter is an American document.

This truth is seldom adverted to. As a technical drafting matter, the Charter, it is true, was the creation of Canadian lawyers. But the document's roots lie elsewhere. The idea of enshrining the rights of the individual in a constitution and then protecting those rights through judicial intervention is uniquely American. It may well be a good idea, but no one who had the slightest acquaintance with our history could call it a Canadian idea.

"Life, liberty, and the pursuit of happiness" are not simply words in the Declaration of Independence, they are essential notions defining the American experience. Up until 1982 the central Canadian notions were profoundly different. Our social and constitutional watchwords were "peace, order, and good government."

That has changed. I now teach students who are convinced that we did not have a Constitution, that we were not a proper country until we adopted the Charter. We have worked diligently to abolish our own history and to forget what was once our uniqueness. We are now told that the Charter is a basic element in defining what it means to be Canadian. And many Canadians do appear to believe that we can understand ourselves through our approach to the constitutional protection of rights.

The Charter has promoted our Americanization in other ways besides helping persuade us that we don't have a history. We have, as has already been noted, become more individualistic in our thinking and in our politics over the last decade. Again, it would be foolish to see the Charter as the only cause of this, but it is noteworthy that the decade of the Charter has seen an increase in the concrete indications of social alienation—crime, marital breakdown—as well as in more subtle forms—incivility, hostility, and so on. There was a time when one had a palpable sense, on crossing the border, of entering a different society. This is no longer true.

The Charter has led us to forget our uniqueness as Canadians and to disregard our history. It has had an incalculable effect in Americanizing both the way we think and the way we see ourselves. We have become incomparably more individualistic. Our collective sense of ourselves, our idea of responsibility for each other and the society we share, has been seriously weakened.

Like Americans, we now believe there must be a legal remedy for every social ill. Like Americans, we put me first.

CONCLUSION

Many Canadians have contrived to forget that most of the things that once made Canada a fine country—physical security, health care for all, reasonably honest and competent government, sound education—came about through the political process, not as gifts from beneficent judges.

The fact is that during the period the Charter has been part of our Constitution, ordinary Canadians have seen a steady erosion of their standard of living.

Unemployment is high and rising. Social services, health care, and pensions are threatened. Not only has the Charter not been of any help in preventing this erosion, it has served to distract our attention from what has been going on.

The great beneficiaries of the Charter have been the lawyers. They are consulted on issues of public policy, they pronounce on the morality or desirability of political and social beliefs and institutions, their advice is sought in a vast array of situations. The number of lawyers grows exponentially as does the cost of retaining their services.

The Charter has, to judge by media commentators, become the basis of our secular religion. And the lawyers are the priests. At some time Canadians will decide to take control of their agenda back from the lawyers. That is when we will begin to give serious thought to repealing the Charter.

✗ **NO**
The Canadian Charter of Rights and Freedoms Is Antidemocratic and Un-Canadian: An Opposing Point of View
PHILIP L. BRYDEN

Robert Martin's essay launches a two-pronged attack on the Canadian Charter of Rights and Freedoms. The Charter is, according to Professor Martin, both antidemocratic and un-Canadian, and the sooner we Canadians come to our senses and realize that our lawyers have hoodwinked us into believing that the Charter is a good thing, the better off all of us (except maybe the lawyers) will be. My own view is that Professor Martin's essay presents a caricature of both the Charter and modern Canadian democracy, and that when we put the Charter in a more realistic light we will see that the Charter can, and does, make a valuable contribution to Canada's democratic system of government.

The more powerful of Professor Martin's criticisms is his argument that we should get rid of the Charter because it is antidemocratic. Its attraction is that it contains a germ of truth. Like most half-truths, however, it hides more than it reveals.

In its simplest terms, the argument that the Charter is anti-democratic rests on the superficially plausible idea that if nonelected judges are empowered to overturn the decisions of elected politicians, the document that gives them this power must be antidemocratic. The usefulness of the argument lies in its reminder to us that the greatest challenge for a court that has the kind of authority granted by our Charter is to interpret the vague but meaningful generalities on which this authority rests—ideas such as freedom of expression, fundamental justice, and equality—in a way that is consistent with our commitment to democratic government. Where the argument begins to mislead is when its proponents assume that because some judges have had difficulty meeting this challenge in the past, the whole enterprise is doomed to failure.

More specifically, two myths that underpin the notion that the kind of judicial review created by our Charter is inherently antidemocratic need to be exposed. The first myth is that the decisions of our elected legislators and the will of the majority of the electorate are one and the same. Democratic government as it is practised in late-twentieth-century Canada bears little resemblance to the workings of the Athenian polis or a New England town meeting. That observation is neither a disavowal of our current system of representative democracy nor an assertion that the way we presently govern ourselves stands in no need of improvement. It is, however, a reminder that when skeptics examine the record of judicial review using our Charter and point out some court decisions that deserve criticism, we should be evaluating that judicial performance against the reality of parliamentary government in Canada today and not against some romanticized portrait of government of the people, by the people, and for the people.

The second (and ultimately more damaging) myth is that majority rule is, or ought to be, all that modern democratic government is about, and it is in perpetuating the myth that "there is an inherent and irreconcilable tension between liberalism and democracy" that Professor Martin makes his most serious error. My point is not simply that we need a Charter to protect us from the tyranny of the majority, though I think it is dangerously naive to believe that our fellow citizens are somehow incapable of tyranny. Rather, I want to suggest that democratic government as we should (and to a significant extent have) come to understand it in Canada consists of a complicated web of commitments to each other, only one of which is the commitment to government that in some meaningful way reflects the will of the people.

A belief that important decisions can only be taken after a free and public discussion of the issues, a willingness to abide by a set of rules that govern the way we make authoritative decisions, an acceptance of significant constraints on the use of force—these and many other commitments, some contained in the Charter and others not, are not mere side effects of modern Canadian democracy. They lie at the very heart of democratic government in Canada. And they are part of the reason why the Canadian system of government—notwithstanding all its shortcomings—is respected by people around the world.

This is, I freely acknowledge, a liberal conception of democratic government. Moreover, I recognize that there are other visions of democracy—the kind of Marxist democracy practised by Chairman Mao's Red Guards during the Cultural Revolution, for example—that leave no room for special protection of those who are not able to identify themselves with the will of the majority. For very good reasons, however, Canadians have accepted a liberal notion of democracy, and our commitment to this version of the democratic ideal was firmly in place long before we adopted the Charter.

The real issue is not whether placing some constraints on our legislators is inherently antidemocratic—it isn't. Instead, we ought to ask whether Canadian judges using the Charter can play a useful role in enhancing the quality of our democracy. The answer to this question is not obvious, but I believe that our judges can play such a role, and that by and large our experience during the first few years of the Charter bears this out.

Robert Martin leaves the impression that the Charter has fundamentally undermined the power of our elected representatives to shape the laws that govern our society. If we take a closer look at both the structure of the Charter and the judicial record in interpreting the Charter, however, I find it very difficult to see how that impression can be substantiated.

Because of the types of rights it does (and does not) guarantee, the Charter has little relevance to large and important areas of our political life, notably economic and foreign policy. The judiciary did not bring us free trade with the United States—our political leaders did. And our elected representatives, not our judges, will decide the shape of any new trade pact we may enter into with the United States and Mexico. Our elected representatives decided to commit our troops in the Persian Gulf War, and they, not our courts, will decide what role we play in other trouble spots around the world.

Where the Charter has had some potential to conflict with social policy, our judges have tended to be rather reluctant to accept claims that individual rights should override important governmental interests. Thus our Supreme Court has decided that provincial Sunday closing laws reasonably limit freedom of religion, that Criminal Code prohibitions on hate speech and obscenity are acceptable constraints on freedom of expression, and that mandatory retirement at age sixty-five reasonably limits our right to equality. We may or may not agree with the wisdom of these and other decisions upholding the right of our politicians to pass laws that place reasonable limits on our constitutionally protected rights and freedoms, but this is certainly not the record of a judiciary that is attempting to undermine democratic government in Canada.

This is not to say that Charter litigation is meaningless because the government always wins. Our courts have made important decisions upholding the rights of refugee claimants, of people accused of crimes, of women, gays and lesbians, and many others. Once again, many of these decisions have been controversial, but I believe they have raised our sensitivity to the concerns of people whose interests are not always well represented through our political process. And in so doing, I would argue, they have enhanced the quality of Canadian democracy.

Professor Martin seems to believe that the Charter has undermined our sense of ourselves as a collectivity and contributed to the rise of a political life that is alternatively characterized by narrow interest group politics or pure selfishness. To the extent that this description of contemporary Canadian politics has an aura of authenticity about it, however, I think it confuses cause and effect. The popularity of the Charter (indeed much of the need for a Charter) arises from the fact that Canadians understand the diversity of their interests and want to incorporate into their democratic system of government a recognition of the vulnerability of some of those interests.

This diversity of interests was not created by the Charter, and getting rid of the Charter is not likely to usher in a return to a mythical golden age of harmony and communitarian spirit. Throughout our history Canadians have recognized and sought to give legal protection to our diversity on regional, linguistic, religious, and other grounds, and I suspect that only someone from Ontario could imagine characterizing this as an erosion of citizenship.

Again, the problem of the fracturing of our sense of ourselves as a political community that Professor Martin identifies is a real one, and it is a challenge for supporters of the kind of political ideals that the Charter represents to realize their goals in a way that does not irreparably undermine other political values that are important to us. What Professor Martin fails to do, in my view, is make a convincing case that it is not possible for us to meet this challenge or that it is not worthwhile for us to try to do so.

Professor Martin's second criticism of the Charter is that it is un-Canadian, by which he seems to mean that the Charter contributes to the "Americanization" of Canadian political life. It would be foolish to deny the influence of the United States Bill of Rights on both the content of the Charter and the political will that animated its adoption. In my view, however, Professor Martin is wrong in his attempt to characterize the Charter as a species of cuckoo in the Canadian political nest that seeks to supplant domestic institutions and traditions with unsavoury ideas from south of the forty-ninth parallel.

In response to Professor Martin I would begin with the rather obvious point that even if some of the important ideas embedded in the Charter were imported into Canada from abroad, so is much of the rest of the apparatus of Canadian government. Canada's parliamentary and common law traditions were imported from England; our federalism was imported (albeit in a substantially altered form) from the United States in 1867; and our civil law traditions were imported from France. In each instance we have made these traditions our own, in some instances by performing major surgery on them in the process.

The Charter itself follows in this tradition of domesticating foreign political ideas and structures. For example, a central element of the American Bill of Rights is the protection of the right to private property. The drafters of the Canadian Charter (wisely in my view) decided that our normal political processes were adequate for the protection of the rights of property owners and that judges should not be given this responsibility under the Charter. In addition, the Charter recognizes certain rights of French and English linguistic minorities, expresses a commitment to our multicultural heritage, and contains approaches to equality and other rights that set it off as a document that is quite distinctive from the American Bill of Rights. The Charter's roots may lie in American soil, but the tree that springs up from those roots is distinctively Canadian.

The more subtle but significant point on which Professor Martin and I disagree is that he seems to use the term "Americanization" as a sort of shorthand for most of what he doesn't like in contemporary Canadian political life. No doubt there are plenty of Canadians who prefer the kind of life we had in the 1970s (or the 1950s for that matter) to the kind of life we have today. What is unclear to me, however, is how unemployment, family breakdown, the consequences of massive public sector debt for our social welfare programs, and the other things that trouble Professor Martin about life in Canada in the 1990s can be laid at the door of the Charter.

In fairness, Professor Martin doesn't ascribe these social ills to the Charter itself, but he says that the Charter has "served to distract our attention from what has been going on." If the Charter has served to distract Canadians from thinking about the problems of high unemployment and threats to the continued viability of our present schemes for delivering social services, universal health care, and pensions, this is certainly news to me. And I dare say it would come as news to those who took part in the 1993 federal election campaign that revolved around these very issues. Professor Martin is probably correct when he states that the Charter is not going to be of much help in addressing these problems, but nobody ever claimed that it would. More important, we shouldn't assume that because the Charter doesn't address these important problems, the issues the Charter does address are somehow insignificant.

The Charter does not represent the sum of Canadian political life, any more than the American Bill of Rights represents the sum of political life in the United States. From a political science standpoint, what the Charter represents is a special way of addressing a limited range of issues that we feel are unlikely to get the kind of attention they deserve in the ordinary process of electoral politics, and a formal commitment to ourselves that the ideals such as freedom, justice, and equality that the Charter enshrines deserve a special place in our democratic political life. I think this was a commitment that it was wise for us to make in 1982, and that Canadians are right to be proud of this new and distinctive feature of our democracy.

Postscript

Robert Martin is not the only one to express serious reservations about the impact of the Charter on Canadian political life. One of the most caustic critiques of the Charter has been written by Michael Mandel. In his book *The Charter of Rights and the Legalization of Politics in Canada* (Toronto: Wall and Thompson, rev. ed. 1994), Mandel argues that the Charter has led to the "legalization of politics in Canada." Because the scope of interpretation of the Charter is very broad, judges make highly political decisions. They are not just interpreting the law according to some technical, objective criteria, but are actually making the law, usurping the role traditionally reserved only for elected legislators. Because of the high cost of litigation, the legalization of politics, according to Mandel, leads to a conservative, class-based politics that works against socially disadvantaged groups.

Like Martin, Seymour Lipset, a noted American sociologist, argues that the Charter threatens to erase the cultural differences between Americans and Canadians by transforming Canada into a "rights-centred" political culture. See his *Continental Divide* (Routledge, 1990). Christopher Manfredi argues that part of this Americanizing influence is reflected in the frequency with which Canadian judges cite American precedents when making their decisions.

Because of the growing importance of the Charter to Canadian politics, there has been a steady flow of books on this subject in recent years. In addition to the works cited above, students will find the following helpful: Rainer Knopff and F.L. Morton, *Charter Politics* (Scarborough: Nelson, 1992); Patrick Monahan, *Politics and the Constitution: The Charter, Federalism and the Supreme Court* (Toronto: Carswell, 1987); and David Beatty, *Putting the Charter to Work* (Montreal and Kingston: McGill-Queen's University Press, 1987). A book written by a civil rights activist who supports Bryden's arguments is Alan Borovoy's *When Freedoms Collide: The Case for Our Civil Liberties* (Toronto: Lester & Orpen Dennys, 1988).

If we accept Martin's argument that we should be concerned about the impact of the Charter, what can be done? Is Martin's closing suggestion that many Canadians may begin thinking about repealing the Charter a likely outcome? Perhaps a more likely development is that Canadians will begin to take a more careful look at the record of individual judges and to demand more say in their appointment. The potential role of Parliament in reviewing the appointment of Supreme Court judges is examined in Issue Fifteen.

ISSUE**SIX**

Is Constitutional Reform Necessary?

✔ **YES**
KATHY L. BROCK, "The Need for Constitutional Reform"

✗ **NO**
MICHAEL LUSZTIG, "Megaconstitutional Reform Is Not Desirable"

Since the 1960s, Canada has been engaged in an almost continuous process of major constitutional reform. A number of forces, including Quebec nationalism, western alienation, special interest groups, and the nation-building drive of the federal government, have made fundamental or *megaconstitutional* change central to Canadian political life. Ironically, these same forces have made agreement on constitutional reform difficult. Though proposals for megaconstitutional change have not been proved wanting, success in this endeavour has been elusive. And even where the level of agreement has made change possible, this has only precipitated the demand for more change.

The process of megaconstitutional reform began over three decades ago with a proposal for a domestic amending formula. The proposal spoke to a general belief that Canadians should be able to reform their own Constitution without the consent of the British parliament, but it nevertheless failed to secure the support of Quebec. In 1971, a more comprehensive set of constitutional proposals emerged, but it, too, failed. A decade later, change was achieved, with the entrenchment of a Charter of Rights and Freedoms and new amending formula in the Constitution. But this has been accomplished only over the objections of the government of Quebec. The Meech Lake Accord, put forward in 1987, represented a set of reforms that attempted to meet the demands of Quebec. However, the accord was rejected, in large part because its focus was too limiting. Finally, in 1992 the Charlottetown Accord, easily the most extensive set of constitutional proposals, sought to meet the varied demands for constitutional change. It seemed that Canada was finally going to put its constitutional house in order. But it was not meant to be, for Canadians rejected the accord in a national referendum.

In some minds, the history of constitutional reform sends a clear message: megaconstitutional change is impossible. The effort to get the Constitution just right assumes a degree of consensus that is absent now and perhaps forever. Some Canadians want a strong national government, others prefer a federal state that empowers the provinces, and still others—Aboriginal peoples, women, gays—demand that their interests be recognized. And, of course, there is Quebec. To satisfy all these elements is a task of Herculean proportions. The problem is that successful constitutional reform takes for granted the existence of a *people*, but that is the very thing that may be missing in Canada.

Others may concede the absence of a people but argue that constitutional reform is the very process that allows Canadians to develop a common purpose and a sense of togetherness. From this perspective, giving up on constitutional reform will most assuredly make matters worse, given that expectations in relation to constitutional change are so high among important elements in the Canadian population. Aboriginal peoples, for instance, came close to achieving their goal of self-government in the Charlottetown Accord, so to ask them to forgo constitutional reform seems unfair and certainly unwise. The same holds for Quebec, the West, and others who have invested so much in the process of constitutional reform.

Constitutional reform has been the Canadian obsession. It has dominated Canadian politics for the past thirty years, and one might say since Confederation. The question is whether this obsession is good for the country. It may be that the goals of constitutional reform can be achieved through other means. Perhaps simple legislative measures might suffice, or even understandings among governments. But sometimes obsessions can be magnificent, the impetus for remarkable achievements. For Canada to thrive and flourish, constitutional reform may be necessary.

Kathy L. Brock, a political scientist and author of numerous articles on the Constitution, puts forward a case for continuing with constitutional reform. Michael Lusztig, who has also written on the Canadian Constitution, argues against further attempts at achieving megaconstitutional change.

✔ **YES**

The Need for Constitutional Reform

KATHY L. BROCK

The anti-climactic failure of the Charlottetown Accord in the 1992 national referendum only fuelled the fires of the critics of constitutional reform who had deplored the thought of another round of constitutional negotiations after the more poignant defeat of the Meech Lake Accord in 1990. The critics of constitutional reform lay the blame for the failure of the two accords at the feet of the "special interest groups," claiming that they had been too self-interested to bargain in good faith and to realize the primacy and urgency of Quebec's need for a newly defined constitutional status. These same critics lamented letting the public into the talks, the demise of executive federalism, and the loss of government control of the Constitution and constitutional agenda. They warned that the 1992 failure would lead only to national disintegration and viewed the results of the 1995 referendum in Quebec as proof positive of their predictions. They cautioned against ever again letting an attempt at constitutional reform become as encompassing as the Charlottetown Accord.

In making these dire pronouncements, the critics overlooked the broken promises emerging from the constitutional processes, as well as the positive results emerging from the constitutional talks, and they failed to see a deeper message that spoke to Canada's changing population and needs. If the constitutional processes of 1980–82, which resulted in patriation of the Constitution and the entrenchment of the Canadian Charter of Rights and Freedoms, 1987–90, and 1990–92 are viewed with an eye to understanding the new tensions and perspectives revealed in these processes, then it becomes evident that megaconstitutional reform is necessary, desirable, and feasible.

Thus, the argument here has three components. First, reform is necessary. A look at the past attempts at constitutional reform reveals the pressures making reform mandatory. Second, reform is desirable because it is through constitutional redefinition that Canada has the brightest prospects for achieving a sense of national unity that will safeguard its existence into the next century. If Canadians try to ignore these pressures, they will fail to realize themselves as diverse peoples with common national objectives. Third, constitutional reform is feasible. That is not to say that it is not very difficult and that the stakes are not high. Let's not kid ourselves, it is and they are. But the costs of failing to meet the challenges posed in the struggle for constitutional redefinition are even higher. Megaconstitutional reform can succeed, but only if it is approached in a carefully devised manner that unites responsible leadership with constructive public consultation. This section concludes with reflections on a workable model of constitutional reform that offers a means of respecting and bridging the differences between Canadians that became disturbingly apparent during the previous constitutional talks. This process builds on the Canadian traits of pragmatism, generosity, and tolerance to maintain the integrity of the national fabric.

REFORM IS NECESSARY

Another attempt at constitutional reform is necessary simply because the constitutional agenda remains unfinished in Canada. The process that culminated in the patriation of the Constitution in 1982 and the entrenchment of a Charter of Rights and Freedoms left three, and some would argue four, items on the agenda for future deliberation. Each is important in its own right.

The most often mentioned item left over from 1982 concerns Quebec's place in the Canadian constitutional family. Despite the fact that Quebec members of parliament both negotiated and voted for the 1982 constitutional amendment package, the legislature of Quebec has not endorsed the amended Constitution. This remains an unforgivable cloud on the Canadian constitutional horizon and one that must be remedied. To have a large province remain a nonsignatory to the Constitution as of 1982 is not acceptable. But there is a further complication. Some constitutional observers and politicians maintain that the federal government never fulfilled its promise to renew federalism, a promise made in the referendum campaign of 1980 to the people of Quebec to accommodate that province's aspirations.[1] This promise was the logical culmination of the intergovernmental negotiations of the 1960s and 1970s, during which the other provinces had acknowledged Quebec as a distinct province, and of the need for reform of the federal division of powers. While other scholars maintain that no promise was made but that the federal government duped the people of Quebec,[2] the constitutional talks of 1987–90 and 1990–92 proceeded on the assumption that reconciliation of Quebec's needs within the Canadian family was a priority. The collapse of those talks means that the promise, whether made in the 1980 campaign or given life and reality in the subsequent negotiations, remains to be honoured.

There was a second piece of unfinished business from 1982. Aboriginal and treaty rights and recognition of Aboriginal peoples were entrenched (Constitution Act, 1982, section 35) but with a provision for a first ministers' conference to be attended by Aboriginal leaders for the purpose of defining those rights (Constitution Act, 1982, s. 37). At that conference held in 1983, the parties agreed to an expansion of Aboriginal rights to apply to land claims agreements and to guarantee all rights to both male and female persons (ss. 35 [3 to 4]). They also entrenched the stipulation that Aboriginal representatives would be consulted regarding any constitutional amendments directly affecting them (s. 35.1). In recognition that the agenda was still not complete, the leaders agreed to hold at least two more conferences on Aboriginal matters by 1987 (s. 37 [1 to 4]). Although three more conferences were held, the leaders bogged down on the issue of Aboriginal self-government, and no further amendments were secured.[3] Aboriginal aspirations went unfulfilled. The seemingly "quick" agreement regarding Quebec, reached by the first ministers at Meech Lake within weeks of the collapse of the Aboriginal talks, and the government of Quebec's decision not to participate fully in the Aboriginal conferences only exacerbated the sense of disappointment and frustration within the Aboriginal community. Aboriginal opposition to Meech Lake resulted in Aboriginal issues being on the agenda during the Charlottetown negotiations. With the controversy over that accord and its demise, the Aboriginal agenda remains incomplete.

A third area of business was dropped from the 1982 constitutional agenda and has returned to haunt the first ministers. Leading into the 1982 constitutional amendment, the western provinces had two demands.[4] The first was for reform of the federal–provincial division of powers to give them more control, particularly with respect to natural resources, in response to Supreme Court decisions in the 1970s that had limited their powers. The more limited version of this demand was met with the amendment giving the provinces more control over resources (Constitution Act, 1867, s. 92A), but the broader concern with the division of powers was not addressed. The second demand was for institutional reform. The underrepresentation and lack of policy influence of the western provinces within the federal government led to calls for reform of the central institutions, especially the Senate. This demand was taken off the table. Subsequently, the wealthier provinces in the west, Alberta and British Columbia, have called for a rebalancing of the division of powers, with more control over local affairs, as well as reform of the central institutions including the Senate, House of Commons, and electoral system.[5] While the less affluent provinces, Manitoba and Saskatchewan, have been wary of the impact of a decentralization of powers on their economic situations, they have supported the suggestions for Senate reform to remedy feelings of political marginalization.[6] This strong desire for more effective inclusion within the central institutions of government has yet to be satisfied. To satisfactorily justify to western citizens the meeting of Quebec's demands within Confederation, it will likely be necessary to meet minimal western demands for reform.

Fourth, the Constitution Act, 1982 mandated a review of the amending procedures set out in Part V of that act after fifteen years (s. 49). Technically this demand was met by the first ministers' brief, or passing, mention of the requirement at their 1996 summit. However, the dissatisfaction with the formula expressed during the Meech Lake and Charlottetown negotiations and the adoption by some provinces of special requirements for amendments may cause the amending formula to resurface as an item in future constitutional negotiations.

The outstanding obligations mean that if constitutional discussions are opened for one of these claimants, the others are likely to expect their considerations to be given due consideration as well. Thus, the pressure is not just for constitutional satisfaction of these legitimate aspirations but for an inclusive set of negotiations. Add to this mixture the interest citizens have in guarding or enhancing their rights as individuals or members of various racial, ethnic, and social communities, and megaconstitutional negotiations seem the logical and necessary outcome.

REFORM IS DESIRABLE

The critics of megaconstitutional reform are correct in deploring the reopening of talks if the process turns out to be a replica of either the Meech Lake or the Charlottetown fiascoes. These types of reform are undesirable and Canadians should put them behind them. The Meech Lake and Charlottetown processes of constitutional reform are undesirable for different reasons. These failings must be avoided in future constitutional negotiations.

The Meech Lake process had four main weaknesses. First, the process was criticized as an attempt by governments to further their agendas at the expense of societal interests by excluding citizen groups such as women, Aboriginal peoples, and various racial and ethnic minorities, among others. This exclusion undercut the legitimacy of the process and of the contents of the accord, leading to the requirement that future processes be more inclusive and representative. Second, the lack of public information and the absence of justificatory papers fuelled suspicions about the accord and spawned the demand for a more accountable process. Third, the process pitted Aboriginal peoples and the less affluent provinces, such as Manitoba and Newfoundland, against Quebec, thus introducing tensions in future relations.[7] Fourth, the political leadership came under attack as pusillanimous, arrogant, and self-interested, thus underscoring the need to reconceptualize their actions and role in future constitutional talks.

The Charlottetown process aimed to correct these failings. It entailed the most extensive consultation process ever held in Canada, employing public hearings at the outset, involving the territorial governments and representatives of Aboriginal peoples at the intergovernmental bargaining table, and culminating in a national referendum. On these points, the political leaders should be commended for their efforts. However, three crucial failings occurred.[8] First, there was limited coordination among the constitutional committees struck nationally and in each province and territory, as well as within the Aboriginal communities, to consult the public. As a result, the public consultations seemed to lack direction and purpose, engendered a sense of constitutional fatigue among Canadians, and resulted in different mandates and objectives for the leaders when they came together to negotiate. Second, the leaders failed to reconcile strong leadership with public input. The various publics felt betrayed when they saw their leaders depart from the committee reports on the hearings without clear justification during the negotiations phase of the accord. The final deal was more representative of societal interests but appeared like a haphazard or poorly crafted bargain between elites that failed to reconcile the diverse elements into a coherent vision of Canada. Thus, the accord failed a basic constitutional test: to provide identity and purpose for the nation. Third, the information on the accord appeared contradictory, confusing, lacking in historical context, and overly complex. This created a suspicion of the accord and the motives of the political negotiators. The desperation of the Mulroney government and the hard-sell tactics employed in the referendum campaign also contributed to the failure of the accord at the polls.

Given the faults of Meech Lake and Charlottetown, why is megaconstitutional reform still desirable? Through the ongoing constitutional debate, Canadians have an opportunity to forge a sense of common purpose, if not a national identity, and to acquit the outstanding obligations. But to do this requires a process that is inclusive and respects differences. Why? Anthony Giddens provides insight into the need for an open debate.

Canada is not unique in its emerging differences among various segments of the population and perceived societal discord. Giddens explains that nation-states are struggling to redefine themselves and their purpose in the face of the challenges posed by globalization. As local communities and the international communities simultaneously become more important to individuals, citizens begin to question and challenge the traditional power structures. The political institutions and social relations cannot be justified by resorting to tradition.9 To restore order and a sense of purpose to their existence, citizens turn to communities and assert their sense of identity or nationalism. They demand that the state recognize and encompass these identities. In Canada, this leads to the fostering of strong provinces and calls for revamping the central institutions and federalism, for revivalism among Aboriginal peoples, and for recognition of their institutions of government, for empowerment of racial and ethnic communities, for fairer representation, and so on.

How can these differences be reconciled? Political leaders must foster an open dialogue that reexamines the relationships and institutions that have governed society. The dialogue must engage the communities that have been privileged in the past and the communities challenging this power structure. Through the dialogue, the groups must strive to achieve new relationships based on trust, mutual accommodation, and respect for differences. Instead of requiring groups to conform to one hegemonic order, the new arrangement would bridge differences and incorporate all groups into the structures on mutually tolerable grounds.10

Why would the current power holders engage in this dialogue? As differences multiply and challenges to the current structures mount, two alternatives to dialogue emerge. The first is exit. If the challenging communities see no hope for accommodation of what they perceive as reasonable demands, then they will shun the traditional order, which has no meaning for them and seek recourse in secession or alienation. For example, in the wake of the Quiet Revolution, the old Canadian accommodation lost its meaning and rationale in Quebec. The province requested changes it deemed reasonable to meet its new requirements within Canada. When its needs were refused, secession became more attractive. Similarly, when the old power structures began to weaken over the Aboriginal communities and their sense of identity began to coalesce at the national and subnational level, those communities began to call for a new relationship.11 If there is no possibility of exit, then the alternative is violence. Traditional communities may try to enforce compliance of the challenging communities with established rules and practices to preserve the integrity of the state, or the challenging communities may resort to acts of violence to assert their identity and compel changes necessary to their autonomy and survival. This threat has been intimated by some extremists in the Quebec nationalist movement, and has been foreshadowed in the Aboriginal community by acts of civil disobedience and standoffs between First Nations and state security forces (at Oka, Ipperwash, and Gustafsen Lake). The choice is obvious: "Difference—whether difference between the sexes, difference in behaviour or personality, cultural or ethnic difference—can become a medium of hostility; but it can also be a medium of creating mutual understanding and sympathy.... Understanding the point of view of the other allows for greater self-understanding which in turn enhances communication with the other."[12] If dialogue is one sided or not managed, then it can magnify differences and beget violence, but if the lines of communication are opened to promote equal respect and tolerance, then dialogue can replace violence. This is a strong incentive for all sides to negotiate.

Constitutional talks promise the most satisfying way of entering into this dialogue and avoiding the alternatives of exit and violence. Unlike legislation, the Constitution gives symbolic status and recognition to communities. It is a powerful means of stating that different groups in society have a place in the future and identity of the nation. Legislation might accommodate particular needs at particular times but does not bestow recognition and acceptance on communities. Only the Constitution can do that. The next section contemplates how constitutional reform can be successful despite (or perhaps because of) the varied and competing agendas brought to the bargaining table.

REFORM IS FEASIBLE

The first ingredient in successful constitutional talks is to avoid the confusion of the past and to clearly distinguish between types of interests and claims in the negotiations. These may be separated into two broad categories, governmental and societal. Governmental interests and claims include those posed by Quebec, the federal government, other provincial governments, territorial governments, and Aboriginal peoples. The aspirations of Aboriginal peoples are included in this category because they involve establishing local governments that are constitutionally protected and recognized within the federal system. In this sense, their claims are most similar to those of Quebec and the western provinces, which are calling for changes within the central institutions of government and the federal division of powers, and to those of the less affluent provinces, which are interested in a strong central government with the power to enforce national standards in social services and to redistribute economic benefits to their regions. The second set of interests, called societal, would include those promoted by citizens and communities within and cutting across the various jurisdictions such as racial and ethnic communities, women, the challenged, gays and lesbians, poverty organizations, labour, business, and so on. These groups have claims that require government recognition and validation through the Constitution (entrenchment in the Charter of a clause protecting sexual orientation), government action to make the political institutions more inclusive and reflective of society, and government protection of their rights and promotion of their equal status in society.

This distinction is important because it situates the two types of claimants in the constitutional negotiating process. Governments and/or their representatives must be at the negotiating table since they have primary responsibility for tending the Constitution. However, their negotiations should be done in full consciousness and view of the second category of claimants. This involves the governments, then, in an ongoing process of consultation with representatives of societal interests who are affected by the proposed changes to the Constitution, whether these effects will be real or perceived. If citizen groups have reservations about the proposed changes, then the governments must be willing to return to the negotiating table and deal with those reservations. The referendum legislation in some provinces and requirement for hearings in others, such as Manitoba, and the precedent of a national referendum on megaconstitutional change offer compelling incentives to governments to bring the people along and win their support before the final package is presented for approval in the legislatures or at the polls. As is recognized within the Aboriginal tradition of consensus government, only changes that are generally accepted and not actively opposed will hold in a society.

How may this be done in practice? The first stage of constitutional talks should have two components. First, the movement of Ontario, Alberta, and the federal government to stimulating debate at the "grassroots" level is a solid start. Governments should make available to all Canadians information on the operation of the Canadian system and the costs of a potential secession. They should also ensure that accurate information is available on the constitutional needs and aspirations of Quebec, Aboriginal peoples, the west, and so on. This will allow for a more informed debate of potential reforms to the political system. Second, the governments should begin a series of public hearings on the Constitution and potential amendments. Governments should encourage Canadians to come forward and discuss the four pieces of unfinished business from the 1982 and subsequent rounds of negotiations. To avoid the pratfalls of Charlottetown, the governments should direct societal groups to provide information and data on how these changes would affect them and require groups to explain how the changes they are advocating or opposing would affect the Canadian union. This data should then become the basis for the committee reports. To further avoid the confusion of Charlottetown, governments should coordinate the work, including the mandates of the committees struck in each jurisdiction, and look for common themes echoed throughout the hearings. If groups in the hearings propose new items for the constitutional agenda and provide clear justifications for their inclusion, then the governments should either include them or find nonconstitutional means of achieving the objective of the groups. The reports, thematic analyses of hearings, and revised agendas should be distributed widely to the public for their consideration. Throughout this phase, the governments should explain that the hearings are a starting point in the discussions and that any subsequent deviations from the reports will be explained and justified in the public ratification phase.

The second stage of the constitutional talks would be the negotiations phase. Negotiations should combine an inclusive, semitransparent, and thorough round of talks at the official and ministerial levels, with first ministers' conferences strategically interspersed to allow for public review of the progress of the talks and to deal with particular topics as they approach resolution. The participants would include representatives from the federal, provincial, and territorial governments, and from the Aboriginal community, including women's organizations.[13] Throughout the negotiations, the executives should inform the legislatures of the progress of the talks, and regular updates should be provided to the media. To aid in the resolution of disagreements between the negotiating bodies, representatives of interest groups or particular communities should be consulted and even brought into the discussions to provide opinions. This would involve making proposals to groups, receiving their feedback, and then revising the proposals in light of any new information. Throughout this phase, the governments must be even stricter with themselves than with the public in the hearings process in requiring that each position and proposed amendment be justified in terms of how it would relate to the other proposals and strengthen the Canadian union. Governments should base their justifications on the needs of their constituents in the context of how suggested changes would affect citizens in other jurisdictions. The negotiations will culminate in a text of proposed amendments, accompanied by an explanatory text that would explain where governments have deviated from the hearings and why, as well as how, each change would strengthen Canada. The governments must not just craft a deal, they must offer a vision of Canada's future.

The third phase involves public ratification and should begin with the release of the text and explanatory documents. Public information sessions could occur through townhall meetings, public forums, televised broadcasts, and media reports. Governments should agree to reconvene after a set period of public debate. If opposition to the text is mounting, then the governments should revise the text to take legitimate criticisms into account. The text should then be presented to the public, and a national referendum should be held. If the results are positive, then the approved document should be introduced into the various legislatures. The governments will have to determine if the vote should be clause by clause or on the whole text, and how to proceed if a split vote occurs in the country. Should the latter occur, then governments would be wise to return to the negotiating table and amend the agreement to deal with the split in support before legislative ratification of the agreement. Adept leadership, marked by responsibility and accountability to the public, should secure a new and more satisfactory ordering of relationships in Canadian society. Platitudes and empty compromises will not suffice—Meech Lake and Charlottetown proved that.

Of course, the alternative to megaconstitutional politics is piecemeal reform. The governments could begin one amendment on Quebec's issues, another on Aboriginal self-government, a third on institutional reform, and so on. However, the possibility arises of governments holding one amendment hostage to secure support for another, or of obstructing one agenda after winning the concessions they desire in another. This is megaconstitutional politics in another form, but it lacks the coordination and imperatives to reach agreement of the process outlined above. It also breeds incoherence as piecemeal reforms are tacked on to the Constitution. Canada would continue to drift rudderless into the future.

CONCLUSION: IS CONSTITUTIONAL REFORM INEVITABLE?

The movement toward constitutional reform has already commenced. The federal government has passed resolutions in the House of Commons recognizing Quebec as a distinct society and its right to a veto on proposed amendments. The federal government, in consultation with Aboriginal communities, has taken measures to give effect to their inherent right to self-government. The federal and provincial governments have been negotiating the transfer of responsibilities from the federal to the provincial level in areas such as labour training and immigration. These actions will reassure Canadians that the proposed amendments to the Constitution in areas such as these will merely entrench practices that have been tested and found to have no ill effects, but some benefits. Critics of constitutional reform argue that these legislative accommodations are sufficient in themselves. No constitutional reform is necessary, they say. However, these reforms are not binding on future governments and may be changed at will, thus offering no permanent reassurance to Quebec or Aboriginal peoples or other Canadians. Only constitutional reform can provide the basis for permanent change and the reordering of relationships required by the groups challenging the status quo.

The stirrings have begun for constitutional reform. At the 1997 premiers' conference, the national unity issue arose again, and the premiers outside Quebec agreed to reconvene to discuss the matter in greater detail in the fall. A volley of open letters between New Brunswick, Quebec, and the federal government in August of 1997 reopened the debate on the effects and legality of secession. The Supreme Court will address this question in 1998. The governments have been negotiating recognition of Quebec in private. Major opinion setters, such as the Business Council on National Issues, have released discussion papers. This is positive in that it may stimulate public interest and debate. However, the federal government has consistently maintained in public over the past two years that constitutional talks should deal with Quebec's issues first and other issues in subsequent rounds. While this is understandable given that a referendum on secession is likely following the pending Quebec election, it is unrealistic. The other constitutional claimants are unlikely to acquiesce and see their needs relegated to the nether world of possible future reforms. Charlottetown and Meech Lake have made the governments timid of grand constitutional reform. But now they must gather their courage, since it is in megaconstitutional reform that the opportunity lies to restructure relations in Canada and to offer the public a clear vision of Canada as a unified nation built on respect and tolerance of all citizens equally. That is true political leadership.

NOTES

1. See Guy Laforest, *Trudeau and the End of a Canadian Dream* (Montreal and Kingston: McGill-Queen's, 1995), pp. 15-34; Peter H. Russell, *Constitutional Odyssey: Can Canadians Become a Sovereign People?* 2nd ed. (Toronto: University of Toronto Press, 1993), pp. 108-110; cf. Andrew Cohen, *A Deal Undone: The Making and Breaking of the Meech Lake Accord* (Vancouver: Douglas & McIntyre, 1990), pp. 62-64.

2. See, for example, Claude Morin, *Lendemains piégés : Du référendum à la "nuit des longs couteaux"* (Montreal: Boréal, 1988), p. 16.

3. K.L. Brock, "The Politics of Aboriginal Self-Government: A Canadian Paradox," *Canadian Public Administration* 34, no. 2 (Summer 1991): 272-285.

4. Peter H. Russell, *Constitutional Odyssey*, pp. 95-97.

5. See, for example, David Elton, "The Reconfederation Challenge," in John H. Trent et al., eds., *Québec-Canada: What Is the Path Ahead?* (Ottawa: University of Ottawa Press, 1996), pp. 304-305.

6. Norman Cameron, Derek Hum, and Wayne Simpson, "The View From the Less Affluent West," in Norman Cameron et al., eds., *From East and West: Regional Views on Reconfederation* (Toronto: C.D. Howe Institute, 1991), pp. 95-99.

7. It is not suprising that tensions ran high during the Oka crisis later in the summer of 1990 following the collapse of the Meech Lake Accord in June.

8. See K.L. Brock, "Learning From Failure: Lessons from Charlottetown," *Constitutional Forum* 4, no. 2 (Winter 1993): 29-33.

9. Anthony Giddens, *Beyond Left and Right: The Future of Radical Politics* (Standford: Standford University Press, 1994), pp. 4-7.

10. Ibid., pp. 104-133, 229-253.

11. Note that this is precisely the language used by national Assembly of First Nations Grand Chief Phil Fontaine and federal Minister for Indian Affairs Jane Stewart at his election to that office in July 1997.

12. Giddens, *Beyond Left and Right*, p. 244.

13. As a result of the constitutional talks and the Supreme Court decisions on representation, Aboriginal women must be represented independent of the general community.

✗ **NO**
Megaconstitutional Reform Is Not Desirable
MICHAEL LUSZTIG

"Megaconstitutional politics" is how one of Canada's foremost constitutional experts has described the so far largely fruitless attempt to reach consensus on the "identity and fundamental principles of the body politic" in Canada.[1] Canadians' first forays into megaconstitutional reform, from the Fulton–Favreau Accord of 1964 through the patriation round (1980–82), entailed a relatively limited set of objectives—an indigenous amending formula and a charter of rights. However, with our lone partial success in 1982, the perceived need emerged to ameliorate the shortcomings of that amendment. This led to the Meech Lake Accord (1987–1990). The failure of the Meech Lake Accord, and the attendant risk of Quebec separatism, created a sense that something (anything?) must be done. The result was the appalling Charlottetown Accord. When, in turn, that accord was decisively rejected, Quebec came within a whisker of voting to separate in the 1995 referendum. The question now is, what should we do next? The answer is, nothing—at least nothing in the megaconstitutional arena.

My argument for stasis in constitutional matters boils down to three points. First, reform is not feasible. We simply cannot reach consensus on the constitutional issues that divide us. We should not, therefore, seek to entrench inflammatory compromises into our national rule book. Second, there is a problem of determinacy. The most controversial parts of the constitutional agenda are made up largely of the quest for what are known as positive rights—claims that some of us make on the rest of us for special treatment. The problem is that there is no well-articulated decision rule to establish who should have these special rights and who should not: positive rights are stubbornly indeterminate. Third and finally, my argument rests on location—that is, megaconstitutional change is an inappropriate means of realizing important objectives. It is certainly not my intention to argue that groups such as Quebeckers, women, Aboriginal people, the disabled, visible minorities, immigrants, and others who have sought input into the constitutional agenda do not have a claim to special or ameliorative treatment. Instead, I believe it is harmful to elevate to the constitutional level those issues that can be considered more appropriately at the legislative or administrative level.

FEASIBILITY

Why can't we all just get along in this country? Is it a matter of ill will or bad faith among the would-be architects of a new constitutional settlement? Is it just a matter of getting to know and understand each other better? Unfortunately, the question is more complicated than that. The problem is that many of us have vastly different conceptions of what this nation is all about. Some want a strong central government to speak for all Canadians and to build a common culture and sense of nationhood. Others see more localized, community rule as the means to ensure that all Canadians are in a position to respect diverse and long-cherished traditions of language, culture, and lifestyle. Some see the individual as the source of political sovereignty; in other words, the individual possesses certain inalienable rights, and these rights are the bedrock upon which liberal democracy is based. Others see groups, such as French-speakers and Natives, as having the collective right to goods like a common language and culture; from this latter perspective, in some cases, the rights of the group might have to take precedence over the rights of the individual. Some see the Constitution as the means to overcome years, even generations, of oppression and discrimination through such programs as affirmative action and special representation in national public institutions. Others see such practices as an assault on the rights of the individual.

Issues like these are extremely divisive. Yet they are at the core of our quest for megaconstitutional change. People tend to hold strong views on such matters and are oftentimes intolerant of opposing opinions. Moreover, these are issues on which compromises are difficult to forge because there is no common ground. (What lies between individual and group rights, for example?) Thus, when compromises are forged they tend to displease proponents from both sides of the debate.

Until the Meech Lake Accord, megaconstitutional reform in Canada took place according to the logic of a process known as elite accommodation or executive federalism. From one perspective, this is a way for government leaders to meet outside the glare of the media's spotlight to discuss critical issues in a forum that encourages compromise and mutual understanding. From another perspective, elite accommodation is the means by which eleven individuals (almost invariably white males) meet in secret to cut deals that affect the lives of all of us. By the time of Meech's failure in June 1990, there was fairly broad sympathy for the latter perspective. It was decided that next time the process would be more inclusive, and would entail popular ratification in the form of a series of provincial referendums. However, making the process more inclusive gave more people a greater stake in the outcome. Thus, not only were passions even more inflamed, but compromise became increasingly elusive.

The Charlottetown Accord is a good illustration of the feasibility problem. On August 28, 1992, the prime minister, provincial premiers, territorial leaders, and representatives of Status and Nonstatus Indians, Métis, and Inuit all agreed on what became known as the Charlottetown Accord. In the two-month campaign leading up to the simultaneous ratification referendums, it rapidly became obvious that the fragile compromise reached at Charlottetown had exposed deep societal divisions. In fact, four distinct and incompatible constitutional worldviews were illuminated and brought to the fore with the Charlottetown Accord.

Let's take a minute to explore these worldviews, or what I have elsewhere called megaconstitutional orientations (MCOs), because they are at the heart of the feasibility issue.[2] The first is Canadian nationalism, whose supporters tend to be wedded to the philosophy of Pierre Trudeau. Canadian nationalists support a strong central government that can provide a generous and uniform set of rights and social programs. Canadian nationalists are distributed throughout Canada, but intuition suggests that they are disproportionately represented in the provinces with the weakest sense of regional grievance and/or strongest reliance on the federal government for financial assistance—the Atlantic provinces and Ontario. Canadian nationalists were committed in their opposition to the Meech Lake Accord, but approached Charlottetown with a great sense of trepidation, which mitigated their hostility to it. Although there was little in the Charlottetown Accord, aside from a "nonjusticiable" social charter, to appeal to Canadian nationalists, and although Trudeau himself blasted the accord,[3] Canadian nationalists appeared most susceptible to the threat that the failure of the Charlottetown Accord might lead to the breakup of Canada. Indeed, in support of this claim Ontario and three of the four Atlantic provinces were the only provinces to vote in favour of the accord.

The second MCO present at Charlottetown was Quebec nationalism, a philosophy that sees Quebec as a distinct society that therefore requires special constitutional status, and the devolution of powers necessary to protect the French language and culture. Unlike most Canadian nationalists, Quebec nationalists were unwilling to hold their noses and vote for the accord. Instead, nationalist opinion leaders in Quebec, including some within Liberal premier Robert Bourassa's own government, argued that while Quebec had received only modest concessions at Charlottetown, other groups had received too many. Quebec nationalists were angered that Aboriginal people, for example, had been granted the kind of powers that are held usually by provinces;[4] these critics were also unhappy that the West's long-standing demand for a Triple-E (elected, effective, and equal) Senate had been included. Finally, the social charter had the potential to centralize even more power in the hands of the federal government. In the end, the perceived concessions outweighed the anticipated benefits for most Quebeckers, who voted to reject the Charlottetown Accord.

Western Canada articulated a third MCO based on the concept of equality of the provinces and devolution of power. While similar in many ways to the Quebec nationalist aspiration of decentralized power in Canada, the West's demand for provincial equality put it in sharp conflict with Quebec. To ensure provincial equality, the West demanded and, had the accord been passed, would have secured a modified Triple-E Senate. However, to offset the effect of this on the sole province with a francophone majority, Quebec was granted in perpetuity no less than 25 percent of the seats in the other parliamentary chamber—the House of Commons—even if its population were to fall below one-quarter of that of the country as a whole. Westerners found this extremely objectionable. They also were concerned with the ambiguity surrounding certain concessions to Aboriginal people, and with the centralizing effect of the social charter. All four western provinces voted convincingly to reject the Charlottetown Accord.

The fourth MCO is known as minoritarianism.[5] Minoritarianism is not so much a cohesive philosophy as an aggregation of nongovernmental[6] interests that traditionally have not fared well in the public policy arena. Major minoritarian groups include Aboriginal people, women, visible minorities, immigrants, homosexuals, and the disabled, but the list of possible new groups is virtually endless. One problem with minoritarianism, as discussed in the next section, is that no determinate criterion is available by which we can decide which groups are deserving of special constitutional status. This created certain problems at Charlottetown, with some minoritarian groups faring much better than others.

As noted, leaders of four Aboriginal groups were invited to the constitutional bargaining table, and the accord included such reforms as the creation of a sovereign level of Aboriginal government in Canada, and guaranteed Aboriginal representation in national institutions such as the Senate. Indeed, roughly one-third of the accord was dedicated to Aboriginal issues. However, in addition to the problems that such concessions posed for adherents of the western and Quebec MCOs, these concessions created internal tensions in the minoritarian camp as well. Even within the Aboriginal community there was opposition to the Charlottetown Accord. Although Aboriginal people voted as residents of their respective provinces and territories, Elections Canada estimates that 62 percent of the Aboriginal community rejected the accord.[7] Native women were especially concerned with the accord, and even sought an injunction to halt the Charlottetown negotiations on the grounds that representatives of the Native Women's Association of Canada were not invited to the bargaining table. Women's groups in general also were displeased with the accord. In large part, women's organizations were unhappy that, while four Aboriginal groups were invited to participate in the constitutional process, the largest feminist organization—the National Action Committee on the Status of Women (NAC)—was excluded. Moreover, there were few specific concessions to women in the accord. The NAC publicly announced that it would not support the accord in the referendum. Similarly, other minoritarian groups were concerned with an emerging "hierarchy of rights" in which some minoritarian groups were perceived to be marginalized in the constitutional process. It was for this reason that the National Organization of Immigrant and Visible Minority Women, the Coalition of Provincial Organizations of the Handicapped, and the Canadian Ethnocultural Council all criticized the accord.

In sum, four MCOs came into conflict at Charlottetown. While Canadian nationalists appeared willing to compromise for the sake of national unity, the others were not. Adherents to each perceived the accord to provide fewer benefits than costs. Indeed, when issues boil down to passionately held convictions over individual versus collective rights, centralization versus decentralization of power, and the entrenchment of special status for some but not all constitutional players, the views held on these issues may be deemed irreconcilable. We should not be surprised that the accord was overwhelmingly defeated in the referendums.

Does the fate of the Charlottetown Accord suggest that future megaconstitutional change is not possible? I think it does for two reasons. First, future megaconstitutional proposals that ignore the aspirations of any of the four (incompatible) MCOs will be condemned as illegitimate. Indeed, this was the fatal flaw of the Meech Lake Accord (which wholly ignored the Canadian nationalist and minoritarian MCOs). Thus, those seeking megaconstitutional change are locked into an agenda that obliges us to find compromises among irreconcilable objectives. Second, the apparent convention (reinforced by law in British Columbia and Alberta) that future megaconstitutional reforms be ratified in referendums has ensured that constitutional change will be characterized by inflamed passions and extremely limited manoeuvrability in terms of compromise.

DETERMINACY

I have already touched briefly on the problem of determinacy, but it is sufficiently important to justify going into the problem in slightly more depth. The problem reduces to the question of who deserves special status?[8] The quest for special status is grounded in the normative demand for protection against repressive policies emanating out of a political process that is deemed insensitive to the special needs of minorities (or, in the case of women, for example, numerical majorities who traditionally have been marginalized). Special status implies rights for one group in society that are not available to all. Thus, whether it takes the form of affirmative action, guaranteed representation in political institutions, or asymmetrical federalism, special status is morally grounded in a sense of grievance—past or future—of the few (or disempowered) against the many.

There is no shortage of groups making claims for special constitutional status in Canada. The list includes, but is not exhausted by, advocates for Aboriginal groups, the disabled, the homeless, homosexuals, immigrants, minority language education groups, the poor, prisoners, Quebec, various religious groups, visible minorities, welfare recipients, and women, to name just some. Brodie goes on to cite the "environmentally sensitive" and even accountants in Prince Edward Island, as other groups that have sought constitutional protection—hence status—under section 15 of the Charter of Rights and Freedoms.[9] Can we articulate a decision rule—short of granting status to every group that asks for it—to determine which groups get status and which do not? Obviously, each of us will be able to determine in our own mind which of these claims are frivolous and which are not. But at least some of us feel sufficiently passionate about each of these groups to undertake costly litigation on their behalf. So how do we determine which claims are valid and which are frivolous?

In Canada, we have tried two different approaches to determining which groups in society should be granted special status through megaconstitutional reform. Neither has been terribly successful. In the rounds of talks on the patriation of the Constitution and on the Meech Lake Accord, we relied on our political elites to act as our moral weathervanes. It was our political leaders who, independent of any publicly articulated decision rule, determined which groups got status (especially under sections 15, 16, 23, 25, 27, and 28 of the Charter, and under the proposed distinct society clause in the Meech Lake Accord), and which did not. When Meech failed, ordinary Canadians vented their frustration over a constitutional process whereby elites cut secretive deals designating the beneficiaries of constitutional status. With the Charlottetown Accord, therefore, although elites determined which groups were allowed at the constitutional bargaining table, the mass public was granted input into the agenda and the power to ratify the agreement. Not surprisingly, judging by how they voted, the people of Canada collectively were unsuccessful in reaching agreement over which groups were deserving of special constitutional status.

Another problem of determinacy is that even if we can decide which groups are to get status, what are we to do when the interests of status-holding groups collide? Imagine a group that has been granted constitutional status for its cultural and/or religious practices. However, these practices involve what some would see as the subjugation of women. What is more important: cultural/religious rights or gender rights?[10] It is easy to see the potential for such rights to come into conflict. Indeed, it was concern about the primacy of gender rights over cultural rights that, as noted, led the Native Women's Association of Canada to seek an injunction to halt the Charlottetown negotiations. The same concern a decade previously caused women's groups to fight for the inclusion, and retention, of section 28 of the Charter.

The problem is that cleavages in our society cut across each other. One can be a member of a number of status-seeking groups at the same time. Since these groups may well have incompatible objectives, the potential—indeed, the likelihood—is always there for status-seeking groups to divide and subdivide along lines of meaningful cleavage.[11] In fact, if we take this logic far enough, and couple it with the fact that we have no articulated decision rule as to which groups deserve status, we are left with the individual as the irreducible core of political life. It appears inevitable, then, that any constitutional principle that grants status according to ascriptive characteristics will be arbitrary and will be be viewed as unfair by large portions of society.

LOCATION

Thus far my argument could be taken to say that since we cannot decide who should get constitutional status (or enhanced constitutional status), there should be no special protection for the most vulnerable or most oppressed in our society; that if the solution is not perfect, we should live with the problem. I don't wish to make this claim, and fortunately I don't need to. Instead, I argue that in some cases special protection may be needed, but that it should be provided at the sub-constitutional level.

To my mind, and to the mind of most liberals, constitutions should be about two things: the basic rules of the political process, and negative liberties. The basic rules of the political process spell out the things that everyone needs to know about the way a nation is to be governed. In short, they describe who does what. Negative liberties are the natural, or inalienable, rights that each of us enjoys. These are our freedoms, our protection against arbitrary action on the part of the state. Because these principles are so important, constitutions are typically very difficult to change. They should be. Political stability dictates that they not be altered at the whim of what might be only temporary popular passion.

However, it is the very impermeability of constitutions that make them so attractive for would-be social engineers. The reason that status-seekers prefer constitutional change to change in the legislative arena is that, unlike the latter, the former is all but permanent. As one prominent American legal scholar, Lino Graglia, has described it:

A constitutional right is a constitutionally protected interest, an interest immune from change through the ordinary political process. A constitutional right in a democracy is, therefore, a restriction on the power of self-government. The difficult and little-discussed question is: Why should a people that enjoys the power of self-government ever deprive itself of or limit that power?[12]

As I have been at pains to point out, there are countless groups with a moral claim to special treatment. Since we cannot decide collectively which of them are most deserving of status, how can we justify privileging some of them with con-stitutional status, while relegating others to outsider status? There is, it seems to me, a better way to provide ameliorative treatment, and that is through the leg-islative process. This is by no means a perfect solution. Legislators can, and often do, make mistakes. But legislative mistakes are far easier to fix than constitutional ones. Of course, one problem with legislation as a remedy to marginalization of certain societal groups is that in many cases the legislative process contributed to their marginalization in the first place. Put differently, it is illogical to rely on the goodwill of the majority to protect the interests of the minority.

To this claim there are two responses. First, it is specious to argue that the leg-islative process is majoritarian while the constitutional process is not. We need look no further than the Charlottetown referendum to refute this point. The Constitution clearly states that all amendments that affect more than one province must be ratified by popular representatives in the federal Parliament and the legislatures of at least seven provinces. Moreover, as noted, popular ratification through referendums appears to have become a constitutional convention. Thus, the only real difference is that the legislative process allows the majority to change its mind, while the constitutional process does not. And this goes back to Graglia's point. Why should a free nation ever limit its freedom to govern itself? Given some of the truly appalling legislative decisions that have been made in our nation's history, it is fortunate indeed that they were not constitutionally frozen in time. Second, given the fact that cleavages in our society cut across various sectors of it, it is not realistic to talk about majorities and minorities within society. Indeed, it requires only two or three divisions cutting across each other to ensure that no subset of society constitutes a majority.[13] Thus, on some issues, each of us will find ourselves in the majority, on others, in the minority. As Manfredi argues:

> Majorities tend to dissolve and must be reconstructed on every issue: today's foe on employment equity policy may be tomorrow's friend on anti-pornography policy. Judicial supremacy cannot be defended by character-izing the legislative process as a continuous attempt by the majority to oppress the minority.[14]

A final point is that the quest for constitutional status is inherently divisive. Constitutional status is by definition a zero-sum game. By contrast, the legislative process is integrative. Groups must form alliances with other groups to construct winning legislative coalitions. This necessarily fosters compromise and the tempering of extreme positions. By contrast, because status-seeking groups have an interest in distancing themselves from other status-seekers, there is no imperative to compromise. Moreover, the incentive is created for group members to view society in "us–them" terms—a socialization process that militates against the creation of a sense of national empathy and community.

CONCLUSION

In this brief discussion, I have attempted to show why megaconstitutional change in Canada is not desirable. I certainly do not base this position on the premise that the Constitution as it stands is perfect. It is not. However, in fixing what is wrong with the current Constitution, we run the risk of making things far worse. I have suggested three reasons why megaconstitutional change is not desirable. First, it is just not feasible. There are at least four conflicting constitutional worldviews in Canada that cannot accommodate compromise. When we add to the mix a divergence between the masses and the elite whereby compromises made at the elite level are not supported by the less accommodating mass constituents—a phenomenon clearly revealed by the Charlottetown Accord—the constitutional process truly can be said to be in a state of paralysis. Attempts to force the issue will only inflame passions to no achievable end. Second, the entrenchment of special constitutional status through megaconstitutional reform is axiomatically arbitrary. Once we deviate from the liberal principle that a person is a person is a person, we run up against the problem of articulating a fair decision rule that establishes who should, and who should not, get special status. Moreover, because cleavages cut across status-seeking groups, we will have to determine a hierarchy of primacy among conflicting status claims. Agreement on such a hierarchy, it seems to me, will not be possible. Third and finally, megaconstitutional reform is simply the wrong means by which to ameliorate the marginalization of certain groups within society. The very permanence that makes the Constitution so attractive to status-seekers is also what makes it so dangerous. Try as we might, we cannot constitutionalize goodwill, tolerance, and mutual respect. All we can do is create institutional structures that facilitate these social goods. Megaconstitutional reform, far from advancing these ends, will work against their realization.

NOTES

I am grateful to Christine Carberry, Doug Long, Chris Manfredi, and Richard Vernon for helpful comments.

1. Peter Russell, *Constitutional Odyssey: Can Canadians Become a Sovereign People?* 2nd ed. (Toronto: University of Toronto Press, 1993), p. 75.

2. A fuller discussion of the megaconstitutional orientation argument can be found in Michael Lusztig, "Constitutional Paralysis: Why Canadian Constitutional Initiatives Are Doomed to Fail," *Canadian Journal of Political Science* 27 (1994): 747–771.

3. See Pierre Trudeau, *A Mess That Deserves a Big No* (Toronto: Robert Davies, 1992).

4. Power is a relative commodity. If someone else has more of it, by definition you have less of it.

5. This term comes from Alan Cairns. See Alan Cairns, "Constitutional Minoritarianism in Canada," in Ronald L. Watts and Douglas M. Brown, eds., *Canada: The State of the Federation 1990* (Kingston: Institute for Intergovernmental Relations, 1990).

6. These interests are nongovernmental in the sense that they are not explicitly represented by either federal or provincial governments.

7. Mary Ellen Turpel, "The Charlottetown Discord and Aboriginal Peoples' Struggle for Fundamental Political Change," in Kenneth McRoberts and Patrick Monahan, eds., *The Charlottetown Accord, the Referendum, and the Future of Canada* (Toronto: University of Toronto Press, 1993).

8. This question has been discussed in greater detail elsewhere. See Rainer Knopff and F.L. Morton, *Charter Politics* (Toronto: Nelson, 1992), ch. 4; Ian Brodie, "The Market for Political Status," *Comparative Politics* 28 (1996): 253–271.

9. Brodie, "The Market for Status," p. 259.

10. An interesting case that explores this issue is *Casagrande* v. *Hinton Roman Catholic Separate School District*, [1987] 4 W.W.R. 167 (Alta. Q.B.): 214, 268.

11. For more on this point with respect to cultural communities, see Chandran Kukathas, "Are There Any Cultural Rights?" in Will Kymlicka, ed., *The Rights of Minority Cultures* (Oxford: Oxford University Press, 1995), esp. pp. 235–236.

12. Lino A. Graglia, "Of Rights and Choices," *National Review*, February 17, 1992, p. 40.

13. This is the logic behind the theory of pluralism. For more on this, see Robert Dahl, *Who Governs? Democracy and Power in an American City* (New Haven: Yale University Press, 1961).

14. Christopher P. Manfredi, *Judicial Power and the Charter: Canada and the Paradox of Liberal Constitutionalism* (Toronto: McClelland and Stewart, 1993), p. 215.

Postscript

There is probably no public issue that Canadians resist more now than constitutional reform. Nevertheless, Brock shows in her essay that we, as Canadians, should at least reconsider our sentiments about major changes in the Constitution. Part of the reason for this lies in the unfinished business of constitutional reform, but a more important reason seems to be the chance to become a true nation through constitutional discussion. The difficulties are many, but the reward is great: Canada finally becomes a sovereign people. Yet, it might be argued that Brock is too optimistic. As many students of Canadian politics have noted, the very thing that makes constitutional reform necessary—the lack of consensus about the present—makes agreement on reform difficult to attain. It seems that Canadians must be a people in order to become a people. We are stuck.

In her paper, Brock also maps out a process of constitutional renewal. She recognizes that *how* constitution making is done is just as important as *what* is done. Brock tries to avoid the failings of the processes associated with the Meech Lake and Charlottetown Accords, and for the most part appears to succeed. But at times her process does appear cluttered and hence somewhat similar to the process that resulted in the ill-fated Charlottetown Accord. The problem with including many interests in the process is that the interests have little in common. The result is either disagreement or a reformed Constitution that lacks coherence.

Lusztig is critical of any further attempts at constitutional reform. He believes that differences separating Canadians are too great to enable successful change in the Constitution. Lusztig also contends that it is difficult and inherently unfair to pick and choose between the competing constitutional interests. If Quebec is recognized as distinct, then why not do the same for the multitude of others who seek special treatment under the Constitution? But Lusztig's rejection of constitutional reform does not mean a total capitulation to the problems facing Canada. Ordinary legislation can do the trick.

As with Brock, Lusztig is persuasive. But here, too, some questions might be asked. At both Meech Lake and Charlottetown, success was so close. It seems rather defeatist to give up when the goal is within reach. Moreover, a rejection of constitutional renewal may exacerbate existing differences, and fortify even further the competing visions of Canada. As for preferring legislative enactments, it can be argued that they are not the same as constitutional change. They are vulnerable to actions of future legislatures, and they do not, as Brock says, "bestow recognition and acceptance on communities." Finally, the results of the Quebec referendum of 1995 seemingly demand a return to the constitutional bargaining table. Without a further attempt to address the issue of constitutional reform, it seems likely that the next referendum in Quebec will be fatal to the unity of Canada.

In September of 1997, the premiers of Canada, except for the leader of Quebec, came up with a new package of constitutional proposals. It includes provisions that recognize the equality of all Canadians and provinces, but that at the same time take note of the "unique character" of Quebec. There are additional sections that endeavour to grapple with the well-known challenges of constitution reform in Canada. The important point, though, for this debate, is whether this new effort in constitution making is a wise one.

It should not be suprising to report that there is a huge literature on constitutional reform in Canada. The place to start is Peter Russell's *Constitutional Odyssey: Can Canadians Become a Sovereign People*, 2nd ed. (Toronto: University of Toronto Press, 1993). This book not only gives the student the necessary background on constitutional renewal, but also provides an excellent analysis of its subject matter. From this point, one might then examine books and articles that treat in some detail particular "rounds" in the constitutional tussle: Roy Romanow, John Whyte, and Howard Leeson, *Canada ... Notwithstanding: The Making of the Constitution 1976–1982* (Toronto: Carswell, 1984); Andrew Coyne, *A Deal Undone: The Making and Breaking of the Meech Lake Accord* (Vancouver/Toronto: Douglas & McIntyre, 1990); Patrick Monahan, *Meech Lake: The Inside Story* (Toronto: University of Toronto Press, 1991); Robert Vipond, "Seeing Canada Through the Referendum: Still a House Divided," *Publius* 23, no. 3 (1993); Leslie A. Pal and F. Leslie Seidle, "Constitutional Politics 1990–1992: The Paradox of Participation," in Susan D. Phillips, ed., *How Ottawa Spends: A More Democratic Canada? 1993–1994* (Ottawa: Carleton University Press, 1994); and Richard Johnston et al., *The Challenge of Direct Democracy: The 1992 Canadian Referendum* (Montreal: McGill-Queen's University Press, 1996).

With a good understanding of the relevant constitutional history, those interested might then focus more directly on the debate question: Michael Lusztig, "Constitutional Paralysis: Why Constitutional Initiatives Are Doomed to Fail," *Canadian Journal of Political Science* 27, no. 4 (1994); Jennifer Smith, "The Unsolvable Constitutional Crisis," in François Rocher and Miriam Smith, eds., *New Trends in Canadian Federalism* (Peterborough: Broadview Press, 1995); Kathy L. Brock, "The End of Executive Federalism?" in Rocher and Smith, eds., *New Trends in Canadian Federalism;* Kathy Brock, "Opening Our Eyes on the Path Ahead," in John E. Trent, Robert Young, and Guy Lachapelle, eds., *Quebec–Canada: What Is the Path Ahead?* (Ottawa: University of Ottawa Press, 1996); and Michael Stein, "Improving the Process of Constitutional Reform in Canada: Lessons from the Meech Lake and Charlottetown Constitutional Rounds," *Canadian Journal of Political Science* 30, no. 2 (1997). Also, Alan Cairns has written a great deal on the topic of constitutional renewal: Alan Cairns, *Disruptions: Constitutional Struggles from the Charter to Meech Lake* (edited by Douglas E. Williams) (Toronto: McClelland and Stewart, 1991); Alan Cairns, *Charter Versus Federalism: The Dilemmas of Constitutional Reform* (Montreal: McGill-Queen's University

Press, 1992); and Alan Cairns, *Reconfigurations: Canadian Citizenship and Constitutional Change* (edited by Douglas E. Williams) (Toronto: McClelland and Stewart, 1995).

For students who wish to examine in more detail some of the specific issues that have emerged in constitutional talks, the following readings are relevant: Keith Banting and Richard Simeon, eds., *And No One Cheered: Federalism, Democracy and the Constitution Act* (Toronto: Methuen, 1983); Michael D. Behiels, *The Meech Lake Primer: Conflicting Views of the 1987 Constitutional Accord* (Ottawa: University of Ottawa Press, 1989); K.E. Swinton and C.J. Rogerson, eds., *Competing Constitutional Visions: The Meech Lake Accord* (Toronto: Carswell, 1988); David E. Smith, Peter MacKinnon, and John C. Courtney, eds., *After Meech Lake: Lessons for the Future* (Saskatoon: Fifth House Publishers, 1991); Kenneth McRoberts and Patrick Monahan, eds., *The Charlottetown Accord, the Referendum, and the Future of Canada* (Toronto: University of Toronto Press, 1993); Curtis Cook, ed., *Constitutional Predicament: Canada After the Referendum of 1992* (Montreal: McGill-Queen's University Press, 1994); and Martin Westmacott, "The Charlottetown Accord: A Retrospective Overview," in Martin Westmacott and Hugh Mellon, eds., *Challenges to Canadian Federalism* (Scarborough: Prentice-Hall, 1998).

ISSUESEVEN

Must National Standards Be *Federal* Standards?

✔ **YES**
ROGER GIBBINS, "Decentralization and the Dilemma of National Standards"

✗ **NO**
RONALD MANZER, "'And Dog Will Have His Day': National Standards in Canadian Social Policy"

In various areas of public policy, the federal government and provinces have entered into joint arrangements that require the provinces to comply with federally set national standards. The best known of these arrangements relate to social and health policy. Under these arrangements, Ottawa transfers to the provinces fiscal support in the form of cash payments and taxing authority. The only condition is that the provinces must observe national standards specified in federal legislation. For example, the Canada Health Act, a federal law, notes that provincial health plans must be universally available to all residents and provide reasonable access to a comprehensive set of health services. If this is done, then the provinces receive financial support from the federal government.

For many, the establishment of national standards has served Canada well. Such standards have made possible programs that are roughly comparable across the nation. Wherever they reside, Canadians can be assured of a basic level of services. This speaks not only to a concern for equity and the treatment of Canadians on an equal basis, but also serves to tie the country together. In a real sense, provincial programs solidified through federally established standards have been the glue that has held this country together. National standards are also good for maximizing efficiency, for they act to limit the distorting effect of the availability of certain services on the allocation of capital and labour. When offered a new job in another province, for instance, one does not want to worry whether health services are available without direct charge.

Not all, however, are swayed by these arguments. Some dispute the value of national standards. But these dissenters tend to be only a handful. What *is* becoming a matter of dispute, though, is whether national standards ought to be federal standards; in other words, standards set by the national government. At a minimum, it is felt that standards should be set jointly by Ottawa and the provinces. More ambitious is the claim that the provinces themselves, through interprovincial agreements, might be able to set and enforce national standards. Under this latter type of arrangement, the federal government would lose its role in shaping provincial programs and policies. It would be up to the provinces alone to ensure that concerns for equity and efficiency in the Canadian federation are addressed.

The decentralizing trend in Canadian federalism is one of the forces behind the challenging of federally set standards. The provinces are becoming more prominent, and they are reluctant to give Ottawa an important say in the operation of their programs. Constitutional purists also applaud the proposed movement away from national standards, for it severely reduces the ability of the national government to intrude into areas of provincial jurisdiction. There is also a belief that present national standards limit the flexibility of the provinces in the management of their programs. When government programs were simple in structure, the imposition of federal standards had the intended effect. But now government programs are complex, and they suffer under the attempt to fit them into an arrangement established by a government that has no direct experience with the affected programs.

The question, though, is whether the provinces by themselves or in conjunction with the national government are capable of providing for national standards. *National* standards require a *national* perspective, something that may be absent in most or even all provinces. The reason the federal government sets the standards is because it alone can see the whole country. Unable to appreciate concerns beyond their immediate borders, the provinces would bicker and compete with one another over the establishment of national standards. The result might be a country without the necessary unifying glue.

Roger Gibbins, a political scientist at the University of Alberta, criticizes the notion that the provinces are capable of establishing standards and by implication argues that only the federal government can ensure the maintenance of national standards. Ronald Manzer, a political scientist at the University of Toronto, offers a contrary opinion.

✔ YES
Decentralization and the Dilemma of National Standards
ROGER GIBBINS

The debate on whether *national* standards should be *federal* standards is taking place within the context of a much broader debate on decentralization. It is the latter debate that is driving, indeed has necessitated, the former. The proponents of decentralization have come up against an awkward reality: most Canadians outside Quebec have an attachment to national standards embedded in and enforced through federal government programs. Thus, if decentralization is to proceed, Canadians must be convinced that it will not threaten national standards. An essential component of the case for decentralization, therefore, is the assertion that national standards need not be federal government standards, and that national standards can be entrusted to the stewardship of provincial governments.

However, this argument is difficult to sustain. Placing national standards in the hands of provincial governments would lead to more cumbersome and less accountable government. It would widen the gulf between electorates and their governments, and intensify regional disparities. It would also make the national unity situation worse rather than better. The problem, it should be stressed, does not lie with decentralization per se. Instead, it lies with trying to graft the maintenance of national standards onto decentralization. As I have argued in an earlier assessment,[1] this particular dog won't hunt. Let me explain.

THE DECENTRALIZATION IMPERATIVE

In the aftermath of the 1995 Quebec referendum, which the federalists won by little more than a handful of votes, there has been a growing political consensus that substantial decentralization is indispensable for any durable solution to the deepening national unity crisis. It is recognized that Quebec federalists, and the so-called soft nationalists in the province to whom most national unity initiatives are directed, will insist on some significant degree of decentralization as a condition for Quebec's continued participation in Canada. Decentralization, therefore, is seen as a necessary condition if the national unity issue is to be put to rest. While for many it is also a sufficient condition, others believe that decentralization alone will not suffice. Thus we saw in the September 1997 Calgary Declaration the expressed intention of the nine non-Quebec premiers to go beyond "rebalancing the federation" and, through a series of legislative proclamations, to recognize Quebec as a "unique society." Yet even this very modest, nonconstitutional attempt to deal with the recognition of duality was tied to a broader decentralization agenda as the acknowledgment that Quebec might eventually need additional powers to protect its uniqueness was linked by the premiers to the principle that any powers flowing to Quebec must be available to all provinces. In this way, the recognition of Quebec's uniqueness is bonded to the equality of the provinces, and enhanced decentralization is the glue holding this unlikely combination together.

A large part of decentralization's appeal as a national unity option stems from the fact that it can be pursued for some considerable distance without formal constitutional change. Most of the perceived targets of decentralization are matters that the Constitution already assigns to the legislative domain of the provincial governments. What is at issue, then, is not the constitutional extension of that domain, although this is proposed by some, but rather the rollback of existing federal intrusions. For example, the Canada Health Act is one such intrusion that imposes conditions the provinces must meet in return for federal funding; failure to meet these conditions can result in "fines" being imposed by the federal government. The repeal of the act and other such legislation would thus deliver greater decentralization in practice without requiring formal constitutional change. In a similar fashion, the federal government could vacate fields that were not explicitly assigned to it in the 1867 Constitution Act, such as manpower training and environmental protection, and the provinces could then occupy these fields without the need for constitutional amendment. Significant steps in these directions have been taken by the federal government since 1995 in an effort to convince Quebeckers that federalism can be renewed to provide greater scope and autonomy for their national assembly *within* Canada.

Decentralization, therefore, is the preferred option for those who want to address the aspirations of soft nationalists and federalists in Quebec without opening the Pandora's box of constitutional change. It is the safe option, and an understandable option, given Canada's recent track record with megaconstitutional change. It is also an option that can be approached in a symmetrical fashion, granting to all provinces what Quebec in particular may need or demand, and thereby tying the recognition of duality to the equality of the provinces. Thus it is hardly surprising to see decentralization being embraced with such enthusiasm in the wake of the 1995 referendum.

Decentralization is also supported for reasons quite apart from a heartfelt desire to address the national unity dilemma and to keep Quebec within Canada. It meshes nicely with the proclivities of many provincial premiers, and particularly those from the wealthier provinces, both to expand the provincial legislative domain and to remove constraints stemming from the federal spending power.[2] Decentralization is supported by many in the business community who believe, perhaps mistakenly, that government decentralized is government shrunk, that ten provincial programs constitute "less government" than one national program. In a similar vein, decentralization would appear to be in line with the populist agenda of bringing government "closer to the people." Furthermore, there is no question that decentralization is essential if meaningful Aboriginal self-government is to become a reality. And, to the extent that the politics of the debt and deficit are still with us, decentralization provides a convenient way to offload expenditures and the responsibilities for expenditure cuts onto the provinces, just as within the provinces decentralization provides the means to pass the buck—actually the responsibility but not the bucks!—to local authorities. Thus there are a number of powerful currents in contemporary Canadian politics that would carry us toward a more decentralized federal state. The national unity impasse may be the principal driver for decentralization, but it is far from alone.

It is also worth noting that support for decentralization is now widespread among the federal political parties. The Liberal Party's national unity agenda has led the party to abandon its traditional defence of a strong central government, and to eschew unilateral federal leadership for diffuse, indirect leadership through partnerships with provincial governments, territorial governments, Aboriginal peoples, the business community, and volunteer groups. Given the mantra of partnership pervading contemporary political discourse in Ottawa, greater decentralization seems inevitable even though the federal government now has more "jingle in its jeans" and is prepared, in a partnership role, to turn on the spending taps. The dominant opposition parties, the Reform Party of Canada and the Bloc Québécois, are both strong supporters of decentralization, albeit for very different reasons; Reform sees decentralization as the solution to the national unity impasse, whereas the Bloc Québécois sees it as a waystation on the road to Québéc sovereignty. The federal NDP, long the strongest supporter of national programs and an activist national government, has been pushed to the wings of Canadian political life, although not off the stage. Its capacity to shape national political debate has been sharply eroded, as has the influence of the federal Progressive Conservatives.

THE DILEMMA OF NATIONAL STANDARDS

It might appear, then, that the momentum in favour of greater decentralization is all but unstoppable. However, there is a troublesome fly in the decentralization ointment. Many Canadians, and quite likely a substantial majority outside Quebec, have a strong attachment to the concept of "national standards."[3] There is a pervasive belief that Canadians, no matter where they live, should have access to roughly the same level of social services and enjoy, for instance, the same standards of environmental protection. There is a complementary belief that federal standards provide an important line of defence for social programs under attack from conservative provincial governments. Whether these beliefs accurately reflect the contemporary reality of "national standards," which vary more across provinces than is generally believed, is beside the point. It is the myth of national standards that threatens to rain on the decentralization parade. This means that the proponents of greater decentralization have been forced to argue that

Canadians can have their cake and eat it too, *that decentralization is compatible with the preservation of national standards.*

As I will go on to illustrate, this argument is wrong. It would be better to admit up front that decentralization will lead to a very different Canada in which standards and conditions will vary substantially from one province to another, a Canada where substantial regional inequalities are the accepted norm. Moreover, it should be acknowledged that efforts to combine decentralization with the preservation of national standards would lead to a loss of democratic accountability and control. Putting national standards in the hands of the provinces would also move government farther from rather than closer to the people. In short, having the provinces set national standards would leave us worse off than the status quo, and even worse off than we would be with decentralization uncoupled from the notion of national standards.

To make the case against placing national standards in the hands of the provinces, six specific points need to be addressed:

- The constitutional case for provincial control is less relevant than we are led to believe.

- Few incentives for provinces to set national standards exist, and any standards that are set will be determined by the lowest common denominator.

- Standards set by the provinces could not be enforced.

- Standards set by provincial governments would increase the complexity of Canadian government and thus move government farther from rather than closer to the people.

- Having national standards set by provincial governments would erode democratic accountability.

- The national unity situation could well become worse, not better.

Let's look at these six points in turn.

The Constitutional Case

The argument that decentralization and the preservation of national standards are compatible often starts with the point that provincial governments are, for the most part, seeking control over matters that are already theirs by virtue of the Constitution. The proponents of decentralization therefore appeal for fidelity to the division of powers established in 1867, one that has been contravened in a multitude of ways stemming primarily from Ottawa's use of its spending powers in areas of provincial responsibility such as health care, social services, and post-secondary education. In this respect, there is little question that the proponents are correct, and that fidelity to the 1867 division of powers would result in greater decentralization than is presently the case. In short, the case for decentralization has a sound constitutional foundation, but it is also one constructed by politicians in the 1860s. It can be argued that the 1867 constitutional division of powers provides a questionable blueprint for federal government in the twentieth century, much less the twenty-first, and that the proponents of decentralization are locked into a constitutional frame of mind badly out of step with the contemporary aspirations of Canadians and the contemporary realities of government. One could argue, furthermore, that the constitutional foundation formally in place provides a better rationale for accepting the differences among provinces than it does for national standards. If we are to step "back to the future" by arguing for fidelity to the 1867 text, we must recognize that we are harkening back to an age when population mobility, and not fiscal transfers, was the solution to regional inequities, and interprovincial collaboration was nonexistent.

The more general point is that any case for having provincial governments set national standards should rest on the challenges of the twenty-first century and not on constitutional blueprints from the nineteenth century. It makes more sense to fix our eyes on the future than on the past. The important question to ask, therefore, is whether Canadians will be better served by national standards set by the provinces than they are by the status quo.

National Standards Need Not Be Federal Government Standards

The argument is often made that *national* standards need not be *federal government* standards, that there are ways of constructing national standards other than through parliamentary initiatives such as the Canada Health Act. National standards could be set by provincial governments acting in concert, with or without the participation of the federal government.[4] In short, intergovernmental agreements could replace unilateral action by the federal government, a change that would be particularly appropriate in program areas falling within the constitutional domain of the provinces.

However, if provinces today are chaffing under the restrictions of national standards imposed through parliamentary legislation, such as the Canada Health Act or federal environmental policy, it is not clear why they would chose to substitute one set of shackles for another. If part of the appeal of decentralization is the elimination of federal constraints on provincial programs, why should provincial governments rush to reinstate national standards through intergovernmental agreements? Why, for instance, would Nova Scotia or Manitoba be better off with intergovernmental constraints than with parliamentary constraints? The answer is not simply that intergovernmental constraints would be self-imposed, nor is it that the people of Nova Scotia or Manitoba could be expected to exert more influence in intergovernmental forums than in the parliamentary arena. The answer must be that standards imposed through intergovernmental agreements would be less restrictive, would accommodate a greater degree of variance among provinces, than would current national standards. If this was not the case, then setting national standards through intergovernmental agreements would lose much of its appeal, particularly for the wealthier provinces. It is hard to imagine, for instance, why the Ontario government would be happy with the standards for its social programs being set, effectively, by the provincial governments from the West and Atlantic Canada.

To illustrate this point, take the ongoing conflict the Alberta government has been having with the constraints imposed by the Canada Health Act, constraints that make it difficult for the province to pursue even limited forms of privatization. If the act should fall as a sacrifice to decentralization, why would the government of Alberta want to resurrect its terms and conditions as an intergovernmental agreement? The answer is straightforward: the only intergovernmental agreement that would be of interest to Alberta would be one that imposed looser constraints on the province's efforts to restructure the financing and delivery of health care. Here I am not suggesting that replacing the Canada Health Act with an intergovernmental agreement would necessarily result in poorer public policy; this is a separate argument that must be judged on its own merits. What I am suggesting is that *decentralization without weaker national standards makes little sense;* it would mean giving provinces greater legislative autonomy, and then having them surrender that autonomy to the constraints of intergovernmental agreements and negotiations.

Alberta provides another useful example. The provincial government has been pursuing economic development and growth through a low-tax regime dubbed "The Alberta Advantage." The province hopes to attract "footloose" Canadian and international investment by offering the lowest corporate tax rates in Canada and by having no sales tax. However, if Alberta is locked into interprovincial agreements on social programs, it would be more difficult to outbid provincial competitors on the tax front. Nor, for that matter, would it be possible to compete with a more favourable regulatory regime on the environmental front if the province was hemmed in by national standards imposed by interprovincial agreements. In more general terms, why would any provincial government want to tie its hands? If national standards imposed by Parliament are deemed to be too restrictive, then national standards imposed by intergovernmental agreements would only be appealing if they were less restrictive.

The logic of the decentralization argument seems inescapable; to be acceptable, intergovernmental agreements must be less constraining than existing national standards. To turn national standards over to the provinces is to weaken them.

The Problem of Enforcement

Intergovernmental agreements on national standards can be set only by unanimous consent; provincial governments have no constitutional power to impose standards on one another, and have no power to police compliance with the standards that are put in place. Newfoundland, for example, cannot force Ontario to accept a majority decision with respect to the establishment of national standards; it cannot impose fines or override Ontario legislation. The logic of unanimous consent therefore means that the standards will be set by the government that is able to pay the least, for other provincial governments cannot force it to pay more than it is able to pay, or by the governments that are the most conservative. If, for example, Ontario insists that national standards with respect to the delivery of health care must be compatible with some significant measure of privatization, this will become the standard. If not, Ontario cannot be forced to comply, and thus the alternative is no national standards. The federal spending power provided a means of enforcing national standards set by Parliament, albeit a means of diminishing force as federal transfers to the provinces are both trimmed and converted to block funding. Intergovernmental agreements, which must be reached through unanimous consent, have no means of enforcement.

But surely, it might be argued, provincial governments will share the beliefs of their electorate in the desirability of national standards of some reasonable character. Well, this argument is far from certain. Take, for example, national standards with respect to welfare payments. Given the mobility of the Canadian population, governments in the wealthier provinces might shy away from relatively high standards for fear of becoming a "welfare haven." Thus the rates and conditions set by the poorest provinces would likely be the rates and conditions accepted as national standards by the wealthiest provinces; to do otherwise would be to encourage welfare-induced migration. While this "race to the bottom" may not be inevitable, it is inherent in the case for national standards set by the provinces. Even if there was a race to the top, the result would be increased regional differences as the wealthier provinces took advantage of low national standards by offering public services well above the national average in order to attract footloose investment.

Now it may be, of course, that enforcement will not be necessary, that voluntary compliance will suffice. This would be particularly so if national standards were set at the lowest common denominator so that even the poorest province, or the ideologically most conservative province, would have no problem with compliance. (In the present environment, national standards would in effect be set by the Mike Harris government in Ontario unless those standards happened to be higher than the poorest province could afford.) But would compliance with such innocuous standards be of any value? Setting a test where everyone is sure to pass might reduce intergovernmental conflict, but this should not be equated with a meaningful sense of shared citizenship stretching from sea to sea to sea.

The Expansion of Intergovernmentalism

The defenders of decentralization often make the observation that intergovernmental agreements are by no means rare in Canada; they exist in the thousands and have been put into place between the federal and provincial governments, among provincial governments, between provincial and local governments, and among federal, provincial, and Aboriginal governments. Intergovernmental agreements range from the training of veterinarians in the western provinces to the Calgary Declaration on national unity; they leave few areas of public policy untouched. Such agreements, moreover, are supported by an extensive infrastructure of intergovernmental relations. It can be argued, therefore, that the establishment of national standards through intergovernmental agreements is consistent with the practice of Canadian government. Adding national standards to the larger intergovernmental stew would not be a radical departure from existing norms; it would be consistent with those norms, and indeed can be seen as their logical consequence.

In light of these arguments, and in light of Canada's vast intergovernmental experience, it may seem small-minded or unduly pessimistic to suggest that national standards could not be set and maintained through intergovernmental agreements. Federal and provincial governments have cooperated in the past, and provincial governments can be expected to cooperate with one another in the future. Indeed, intergovernmentalism has become the defining creed of Canadian federalism, one reflected in the partnership mantra. However, we should also recognize that intergovernmentalism is not without its price. As a mode of governance, intergovernmentalism significantly erodes the importance of legislative assemblies; policy debate takes place in intergovernmental forums rather than within legislatures, and the latter are confronted with the results of intergovernmental negotiations that they have no option but to ratify. Intergovernmentalism tends to take place in forums where political parties play little if any role; certainly the opposition parties are totally excluded. In general, intergovernmentalism tends to minimize the number of policy players, and to take place in an environment that is shielded from public participation and scrutiny.

The proposal to replace federal standards set by Ottawa with national standards set by the provinces is therefore a proposal to move decision making away from legislatures, away from the scrutiny of party competition, and behind the closed doors of intergovernmental negotiations. It would thicken the layer of intergovernmentalism that already lies between the federal and provincial governments, and between those governments and their electorates. For example, health care standards would not be debated in Parliament or in provincial legislatures; they would at the very most be brought to legislative assemblies for rubber-stamp ratification. While perhaps it could be argued that Canadians would be well served by strengthening intergovernmentalism as a mode of government, it must also be acknowledged that the consequence would be to move government farther from the people. Intergovernmentalism as a mode of government is not simply in tension with populism; it is the polar opposite of populism.

The Erosion of Responsible Government

There is a related concern with intergovernmental agreements that may be even more problematic. At present, voters can hold the government of Canada responsible for national standards that it imposes, or fails to impose. In a similar fashion, we can hold provincial governments accountable for the administration of social programs. However, if we shift the setting of national standards to intergovernmental forums and agreements, there is a danger that political accountability will be lost. If voters in Saskatchewan are unhappy with new health care or environmental standards stemming from intergovernmental agreements, who can they hold accountable? Their provincial government can shed responsibility, claiming (correctly) that it was only one of ten or more governments that hammered out an intergovernmental agreement that cannot be altered by Saskatchewan alone. The Saskatchewan government might claim that reduced standards were the consequence of arguments made by other provinces that are beyond the reach of Saskatchewan voters. If, for example, the environmental standards of Saskatchewan residents are out of line with those of conservative governments in other provinces, there is little that can be done. Even if the federal government participates in the framing of intergovernmental agreements, it cannot be held responsible for those agreements if it was only one of many governments at the negotiating table. The risk, then, is that democratic responsibility will be lost. The veil of intergovernmentalism will be drawn across accountable legislative government.

The Erosion of National Unity

Even if all of the above criticisms are accepted, it might still be argued that decentralization and the accompanying relegation of national standards to the provinces might be a price worth paying in order to keep Quebec in Canada. But before accepting this conclusion, we must ask whether this strategy is in fact compatible with national unity over the long run. Unfortunately, here we come to another dilemma. First, it is unlikely that Quebec governments will take part in the setting of national standards through intergovernmental agreements. If Quebec nationalists, or at least those we hope to keep in the federalist fold through decentralization, now chaff under national standards set by a government in which Quebec politicians are the primary actors, why should they be any happier with national standards set largely by the nine English-Canadian premiers? National standards set by intergovernmental agreement would constitute a loss of control for Quebec unless such standards were so innocuous as to be meaningless, or unless Quebec had the right to veto standards it would not accept or to withdraw from any intergovernmental agreement that might infringe on the province's unique character. It is hard to escape the conclusion that Quebec would not participate in the exercise of setting national standards through intergovernmental agreements, for to do so would run against the theme of "masters in our own house" that Quebec governments have pursued since the early 1960s.

This would mean, then, that any "national" standards would be set by the non-Quebec governments acting in concert without Quebec, and the "nation" to which they would apply would not include Quebec. This is a dubious long-term strategy for keeping Quebec in Canada. Instead, it can be seen as setting the preconditions for a Canadian government without Quebec, albeit a Canadian government expressed through intergovernmental agreements. Turning to a greater reliance on intergovernmentalism and a diminished role for Parliament is more likely to be a steppingstone to Quebec's departure than it is to provide a durable solution to the national unity dilemma. Even if Quebec were to participate in intergovernmental agreements, the result would be that the federal government would be less and less relevant to the lives of Quebeckers. But does it make sense to assume that the more irrelevant Ottawa becomes to Quebeckers, the less attractive sovereignty will be? Surely the opposite is a better assumption.

CONCLUSION

The proponents of greater decentralization should be prepared to bite the bullet, and to admit that decentralization is incompatible with the maintenance of national standards. Or, more precisely, it is compatible only if we are prepared to sacrifice democratic accountability, to impose a dense layer of intergovernmental agreements between citizens and the governments they elect, and to run the risk that a new pattern of intergovernmental arrangements will work to disengage Quebec from the rest of Canada. Replacing federal government standards with national standards set by the provinces would not be a constructive step.

There is, however, an alternative to either federal or national standards. Decentralization alone without the window-dressing of national standards set through intergovernmental agreements, in short giving more power to provincial governments who can be held responsible by their electorates, might be a better option. It is clean, accountable, and would facilitate regional differentiation with respect to a wide range of public policy. It is the *combination* of decentralization and national standards that is problematic. Perhaps, then, the debate should shift to decentralization per se. Let the proponents of decentralization make the case for regional differentiation without clouding the issue with the assumption that decentralization is compatible with the retention of national standards. It is not.

NOTES

1. Roger Gibbins, "Decentralization and National Standards: 'This Dog Won't Hunt,'" *Policy Options* (June 1996): 7–10.

2. This comment should not suggest that I am disparaging the motivations of the provincial premiers; it is simply to suggest that, for all kinds of institutional and rational reasons, the premiers can be expected to act in a way that expands provincial jurisdiction.

3. This attachment is likely to be stronger in the "have-not" than in the "have" provinces. Embedding the notion of national standards in federal spending programs provides the mechanism for substantial regional equalization, a mechanism that the "have" provinces want to curtail and the "have-not" provinces to protect.

4. The potential role of the federal government in an intergovernmental process mandated to set national standards is unclear. However, the logic is clear: if the standards are to be set in provincial areas of jurisdiction, and if such national standards are to accommodate a substantial degree of decentralization and the policy diversity that would flow in the wake of decentralization, then Ottawa's role would be minimal.

✗ **NO**
'And Dog Will Have His Day': National Standards in Canadian Social Policy[1]
RONALD MANZER

In an analysis of national standards versus decentralized federalism, Roger Gibbins concludes that "decentralization is incompatible with national standards which are anything more than window-dressing." To be effective, national standards have to be federal standards, set by the Parliament of Canada and enforced by the federal government's willingness to use its spending power in social policy areas that constitutionally are provincial jurisdictions. The alternative, national standards based on interprovincial agreements, is "a dog that just won't hunt."[2]

The metaphor of a dog that hunts, or not, is seductive, but it can also be misleading. Hunting is not the only criterion for judging a dog. In addition to hunting dogs there are guard dogs, show dogs, guide dogs, and family dogs. Even among hunting dogs, there are hounds, pointers, retrievers, and setters. Before acquiring a dog, therefore, we should think about why we want a dog and about which among the many types of dogs is best for us. Similarly with national standards: there are several types of national standards. They differ according to who decides what the national standards are and when and how these decisions are made. As with dogs, so with standards: before getting them, we need to think carefully about what our purposes are in setting standards and, hence, what type of standards is best for us.

In a federal state, who decides national standards is an issue of federal–provincial relations. Four general types of federal–provincial relations can be imagined in theory and found in practice.[3] First, national standards for education, health, and welfare may be determined unilaterally by the federal government. In order to implement federal standards within provincial jurisdictions, federal authorities rely on conditional grants. Provincial authorities that fail to comply with federal standards are penalized by the loss of federal subsidies. If the federal subsidies are large enough, or provincial finances are sufficiently strapped, federal conditional grants become an offer the provincial governments cannot refuse. Second, national standards may be determined voluntarily by interprovincial agreements. Here the constitutional primacy of provincial governments in the policy domains of health, welfare, and education is conceded. If national standards are needed in order to deal with overlapping or joint activities in health, welfare, and education, they are created and enforced by cooperation and consensus among provincial governmental authorities. Third, voluntary federal guidelines assume that the creation of national standards requires the continuing presence and active leadership of the federal government, but discretion over the implementation of national standards within provincial jurisdictions remains with provincial education, health, and welfare authorities. Here there is a vertical division of policymaking functions between the setting of national standards for which the federal government is the lead public authority and the implementation of national standards for which provincial governments adapt the federal government's guidelines to the particularities of regional and local circumstances. Fourth, federal and provincial governments may jointly make national standards in education, health, and welfare. In such cases, it is thought to be infeasible and, in any case, certainly not desirable to divide the functions of setting standards and enforcing them between the two orders of government. Accordingly, joint federal–provincial standards are negotiated through processes of "cooperative federalism" and "executive federalism" that are familiar and well established modes of policy development in the Canadian federal state.

The political issue of who decides national standards is not simply one of federal–provincial relations; it is also an issue of state–societal relations. In addition to state actors–federal, provincial, and perhaps even local public authorities[4]–organized interests commonly are involved in policymaking both as advocates for or against the creation of national standards and as participants in determining the content of standards and carrying out their enforcement. National and provincial organizations of doctors, dentists, nurses, professors, social workers, and teachers, along with many other organized education, health, and welfare workers, are part of the process of policymaking for national standards in social policy. Organized business interests, such as the Business Council on National Issues, the Conference Board of Canada, and Le Conseil du patronat du Québec, become engaged in the politics of national standards, in part because they see that favourable conditions for firms doing business in Canada depend on improving the quality of health care and the supply of skilled workers, in part because national standards for social policy also affect levels of taxation, hence profits and competitiveness. Similarly, the interests of workers are represented by their national and provincial organizations, such as the Canadian Labour Congress, Canadian Auto Workers, Ontario Federation of Labour, and La Confédération des syndicaux nationaux. The Council of Canadians and the Canadian Council on Social Development are examples of citizens' advocacy groups that pay special attention to issues of education, health, and welfare. Relationships among state actors and organized interests vary considerably from one issue of national standards to another, of course, but in general the process of policymaking for national standards in Canada is characterized by an array of competitive organized interests interacting with constitutionally (and organizationally) divided state actors.[5] As a result, even achieving agreement on the need for national standards in principle is always highly conflictual and uncertain, let alone determining the detailed content of standards and enforcing them evenly and equitably across the country.

Beyond the issues of who decides, the politics of national standards involves making choices about the content of standards that range across at least five dimensions of social policy. Standards may be created, in the first place, in order to establish what are unacceptable deficiencies of health, welfare, and education. Here national standards are intended to define citizens' needs for education, health, and welfare and establish criteria to identify social conditions as public problems. Second, national standards may be established by reference to the minimal, adequate, or desirable level of resources required to supply basic needs. The number of hospital beds or the number of doctors per one hundred thousand population, the ratio of students to classroom teachers, the income support levels required to ensure provision of basic needs for food, clothing, and shelter in different parts of Canada—these are typical of social indicators that are used to set standards for the allocation of resources. Third, national standards may be focused on the process of delivering education, health, and welfare services. Standards may specify the types of organizations that are eligible to supply public services, for example, direct agencies of governments only or governmental and voluntary agencies but not profit-making enterprises. Standards may also establish procedures that must be followed in the delivery of services, for example, ensuring informed consent to treatment on the part of patients, ensuring fairness and accuracy in the methods of testing students' achievement, or providing avenues of appeal for people whose applications for social assistance have been turned down.

Fourth, standards may define the content of public services. National standards in primary and secondary education, for example, may specify the basic subjects that will be taught in all schools, the knowledge and skills that students are expected to learn at different stages of their academic careers, specific topics that will have to be included in the curriculum to ensure the desired learning does take place, and even the methods and materials that teachers use each day in their classrooms in pursuit of national educational goals. Fifth, national standards may focus on measuring and evaluating the results of education, health, and welfare policies. This requires decisions about the validity and relevance of various indicators of improvement in social conditions. Incidence of disease and disability and rates of life expectancy may be chosen as standards for measuring improvement in the health of all Canadians or be associated with specific regional or social target groups. Long-term trends in students' scores on standardized tests or rates of secondary school completion, perhaps analyzed in an international comparative perspective, may be adopted as measures of the success of educational programs. The impact of welfare programs may be assessed with reference to changes in the distribution of poverty and the length of time various targeted individuals and families require income support or other forms of social assistance. Obviously, too, the choice of national standards for the measurement of policy results cycles back to the identification of social conditions as public problems.

The politics of national standards inevitably raises questions about when and how decisions about standards ought to be made. One widely held view, not only among professionals working in the areas of education, health, and welfare, but also among the public at large, assumes that setting and implementing standards requires expert knowledge deriving from the theory and practice of scientific and professional disciplines. Here choices about national standards are conceived as rational decisions about what are minimal, adequate, or best standards of practice given existing scientific and professional knowledge and skills. Others contend that citizens, especially those who are the clients of social services, should have a generous opportunity to participate in standards policymaking through such means as public surveys, client interviews, focus groups, and townhall meetings. A third approach insists that, in social policy domains characterized by diverse and conflicting interests, standards policymaking depends on processes of bargaining and negotiation. Realistically, effective national standards can be produced only through the give and take of political exchange among state and societal actors. Otherwise, standards will lack the force that comes from agreements where all the participants have a selfish interest to ensure their implementation. Finally, both setting and implementing national standards may be not so much a matter of expert decisions, public deliberation, or political exchange as a process of adversarial persuasion. In a regime of competitive political parties and pressure groups, where the contest is periodically subject to a vote of the electorate, manipulation by means ranging from partisan propaganda to government advertising may be essential both to get national standards setting on the governmental agenda and to ensure that meeting national standards continues to be a major premise of education, health, and welfare authorities in the delivery of social services.

Given this potential complexity of the politics of national standards and social policy, what can be said about who decides what, when, how in Canada? What have been the experiences in the setting and maintaining of national standards for social policy in Canada from which we might draw lessons about the best type and features of national standards for health, welfare, and education in Canada?

The issue of national health standards in Canada is now quite narrowly circumscribed by the terms of the Canada Health Act. Introduced by the Liberal government of Pierre Trudeau, this legislation was designed with only minimal consultation with provincial governments and passed through the House of Commons in April 1984 with support from both of the opposition parties (Progressive Conservative and New Democratic) during a session in which all parties were staking out their positions for an election later that year. The Canada Health Act requires that to be eligible for federal cash transfers provincial systems of health care have to be universal, comprehensive, accessible, publicly administered, and portable between provinces. These are standards that focus primarily on process. There is no attempt at establishing criteria to identify health deficiencies as public problems, no designation of appropriate levels of resources in the delivery of health services, no specification of social indicators to measure the results of health policies, and only indirect reference to the content of standards in the requirement for comprehensive coverage.

Beyond the original issues of hospital user fees and extra billing by doctors, provincial challenges to unilateral federal standards under the Canada Health Act have involved narrowing the list of medical procedures covered under provincial health care systems by deinsuring such items as cosmetic surgery and newer reproductive technologies, refusing to pay the difference between domestic rates and the cost of medical care incurred by Canadians travelling outside the country, thus forcing travellers to buy expensive private insurance, and proposing to authorize the operation of private hospitals and clinics that would infringe the requirement for public administration. So far these challenges have had no more than a marginal effect on the comprehensiveness or universality of health insurance.[6] Fears have been expressed, however, that under the new arrangements for federal financing (the Canada Health and Social Transfer which came into effect on April 1, 1996) the cash transfer from the federal government to the provinces, which has been stabilized at eleven billion dollars, will gradually erode as an instrument of federal control, and the wealthier provinces in particular will be less inclined to comply with national standards.[7]

Developed by the minority Liberal government of Lester Pearson, the 1966 Canada Assistance Plan (CAP) brought together in a single federal–provincial shared-cost program previously separate provisions for income assistance for the elderly, blind, disabled, or temporarily unemployed, and it extended federal sharing to include one-half of the cost of assistance to needy mothers and widows, and certain welfare services not previously covered.[8] The Canada Assistance Plan was a classic example of the federal–provincial negotiation and bargaining, which also involved major national organized interests, that characterized "cooperative federalism" during the mid-1960s. Under CAP the federal and provincial governments agreed on four national standards that each provincial regime of social assistance would meet in order to qualify for federal transfer payments: financial aid or other assistance would be provided to any person in need, "in an amount and in a manner that takes into account the requirements of that person," without requiring the recipients to meet any other conditions (thus effectively preventing provinces from introducing work-for-welfare programs); the budgetary requirements, income, and available resources of the person in need had to be considered by the province; provinces were required to provide social assistance without setting any minimum residency period as a condition for eligibility; and each province was required to establish a procedure for hearing appeals from individuals whose applications for social assistance had been denied.

These national welfare standards were not immediately affected in 1990 when the Conservative government of Brian Mulroney unilaterally ended equal sharing of the costs by limiting increases of its annual CAP payments to the provinces of

Alberta, British Columbia, and Ontario to 5 percent. National welfare standards were affected, however, when the Liberal government's minister of finance, Paul Martin, announced in his 1995 budget speech that the Canada Assistance Plan would be replaced by the Canada Health and Social Transfer (CHST), a single block funding arrangement covering federal subsidies to the provinces for health, welfare, and higher education.[9] The minister asserted that the federal government would continue to enforce the principles of the Canada Health Act, but, with the exception of the requirement that provinces continue to provide social assistance without setting minimum residency requirements, the national welfare standards under CAP would be dropped. James J. Rice has concluded that merging CAP into the Canada Health and Social Transfer has been fatal for national welfare standards: "No matter how many people were forced onto welfare or for what reasons, CAP ensured the development and existence of a nationwide social welfare system ... With the removal of CAP Canadians are left with a fractured and fragmented welfare system."[10]

In contrast with the unilateral federal standards or joint federal–provincial standards for health and welfare, the approach to developing national standards for public primary and secondary education has been voluntary interprovincial cooperation. The venue has been the Council of Ministers of Education, Canada (CMEC), which was established in July 1967 "to enable the Ministers to consult on such matters as are of common interest, and to provide a means for the fullest possible co-operation among provincial governments in areas of mutual interest and concern in education." The School Achievement Indicators Project (SAIP) was approved by the CMEC in September 1989. Its objective is an annual report on levels of educational achievement in Canada using indicators such as rates of participation, retention, and graduation and scores from tests of literacy and numeracy.[11] In December 1991, based on guidelines negotiated by a committee of deputy ministers, the CMEC agreed that the content and methods of the national tests should reflect differences in provincial curricula, be free of cultural and gender bias and stereotyping, and take account of variations in provincial demography. With half the cost paid by the federal government, the first round of national testing began in April 1993 with a test of mathematics achievement given to forty-seven thousand students aged thirteen and sixteen, and was completed by tests of reading and writing (1994) and science (1996). The second round of national testing in mathematics was held in April 1997, and is to be followed by tests of reading and writing (1998) and science (1999).

The implementation of national testing under SAIP does not represent interprovincial agreement on national educational standards, although the development of a range of social indicators is a crucial step in developing standards to identify problems and assess results. Whether such standards will be formally constructed by interprovincial agreement, emerge incrementally through convergence of provincial policies, or die aborning remains to be seen. Certainly, however, both the process of voluntary interprovincial cooperation and the focus on identifying problems of learning, designing effective curricula, and measuring educational achievement clearly differentiate the politics of national education standards from national standards for health and welfare.

What are the lessons, if any, that can be drawn from these very different experiences in the development of education, health, and welfare policy about who ought to decide national standards, what the standards should be, and when and how they should be determined? Must national standards be set by the federal government? Can provincial governments set and maintain national standards? Are voluntary federal or federal–provincial guidelines effective options? Do we even want to set national standards in education, health, and welfare?

The answer to the first question seems clear: to be generally effective national standards in education, health, and welfare must not be unilateral federal standards. National health standards under the Canada Health Act and national welfare standards under the Canada Health and Social Transfer are unilateral federal standards, and their shortcomings are starkly apparent. National health standards are primarily restricted in their application to the process of health services delivery, leaving unattended the need for standards to identify health deficiencies, allocate resources, specify the content of services, and evaluate policy results. They were conceived and perpetuated in the context of a national party competition for electoral support without reference to provincial interests, and they have become a divisive barrier to federal–provincial cooperation in the development of national health policies. National welfare standards are now even more narrowly restricted to the single criterion of banning provincial residency requirements, the sole survivor of a federal budgetary process that was driven by the Department of Finance's obsession with controlling the federal government's deficit. Unilateral federal standards may be effective in areas of federal jurisdiction; in areas that constitutionally belong to the provinces they are not. As the experience of standards for health and welfare shows, unilateral federal standards are too narrow in their application, they are driven by federal political considerations rather than the needs of national policy, and they persistently offend provincial governments whose willing, not grudging, cooperation is essential for effective national standards.

If unilateral federal standards are too narrowly conceived and aggressively hostile to be effective, are joint federal–provincial standards or voluntary federal guidelines likely to be an improvement? Here the answer appears to be clearly positive in principle but discouraging in practice. National health standards could be created and maintained by federal–provincial negotiations, but federal governments, whether Conservative or Liberal, have shown no inclination to alter the unilateralism of the Canada Health Act. National welfare standards under the Canada Assistance Plan were joint federal–provincial standards, focused on the process of service delivery but also affecting the content of welfare policy, and produced through a process of intergovernmental negotiation and bargaining. By all accounts they represent the most extensive and effective venture into national standards in Canadian social policy, but with the Canada Health and Social Transfer the federal government seems to have abandoned its historical commitment to federal–provincial welfare standards. In the policy domain of public education there are no national standards, but there are strong pressures from major state actors and influential organized interests to develop them. National education standards, if they are achieved, will probably be voluntary interprovincial agreements, but they might take the form of voluntary federal guidelines or federal–provincial agreements (as happened in the 1960s in the case of technical and vocational training and in the 1970s in the case of official languages in education). In the policy domain of public education, however, the federal government's basic capacity to engage in meaningful federal–provincial exchange comprised the Economic Council of Canada and the Science Council of Canada, both agencies that were terminated in the 1992 federal budget cuts and government reorganization.

As an alternative to unilateral federal standards, voluntary federal guidelines, or joint federal–provincial standards, provincial governments could set and maintain national standards for education, health, and welfare through interprovincial agreements. Roger Gibbins has concluded, however, that "standards created and enforced through interprovincial agreements are likely to be pretty pale and insipid things."[12] Without federal fiscal transfers, interprovincial standards will be determined by the poorest provinces, or else by the most ideologically aggressive, and in any case will lack an effective enforcement mechanism. Gibbins seems to assume that the only purpose of national standards is the achievement and enforcement of uniformity in the provision of education, health, and welfare programs across the provinces. This argument forgets the several potential purposes of national standards, and it underestimates both the power of public ideas and the uniformity of policy discourse across provincial social policy communities.

As would be expected in a federal state where education, health, and welfare are provincial jurisdictions, there is considerable territorial diversity in the provision of social programs in Canada, but there is also a remarkable similarity in the construction of issues, formulation of policies, and administration of programs. In each province education, health, and welfare policy communities are organized, as well as divided, by dominant ideas about what social problems are and about how to deal with them. The public ideas that dominate provincial policy communities change over time and at different rates, reflecting the distinctive policy legacies and political conflicts of each province, but provincial policy communities are also interdependent and interactive, affected by common national and international ideological trends.

In Canada national standards appear to thrive during periods of large policy change. National health and welfare standards in Canada originated in the 1960s as part of the expanding welfare state and nationalization of social policy. Similarly, though with more modest goals, the Council of Ministers of Education,

Canada was established in the 1960s to facilitate interprovincial coordination of rapid educational expansion. The revival of the politics of national standards in the 1980s and 1990s has coincided with a contracting welfare state and internationalization of social policy.[13] National standards evidently have the potential to provide a stabilizing frame during critical periods of policy transformation, but this conservative function is less important in coping with social change than the policy learning that results from public deliberation and political negotiation in pursuit of national standards.

National standards mainly are valuable not because they erect controls on the diversity of social programs in Canada, but rather because they focus public debate within and across provincial policy communities. They help us track social problems, decide priorities, think about remedies, and judge results. From this perspective, whether national standards are actually achieved, let alone enforced, through interprovincial agreements is less important than the benefits of policy learning that arise from engagement in the process of interprovincial debate about national standards. Indeed, the imposition of national standards that are narrowly designed for partisan motives will obstruct the very policy learning that is crucial to the ultimate goal of improving Canadian social policy and administration.

The pursuit of national standards ought to be generally inclusive with respect to the participation of state actors and organized interests, take into account the multidimensional content of standards, facilitate the potential for policy learning, and minimize coercion in the process of public decision making. Hence, voluntary interprovincial agreements, as well as voluntary federal guidelines, are generally preferable to joint federal–provincial standards and vastly superior to unilateral federal standards, such as those imposed under the Canada Health Act. Perhaps there are circumstances in which unilateral federal standards can be useful as a short-term policy instrument, but in the long run, improving the quality of education, health, and welfare services for all Canadians requires a sustained interprovincial, federal–provincial, and state–societal dialogue. No doubt such processes are frustratingly slow and uncertain, but they are indispensable for an authentic democratic public life.

To return to the canine metaphor, the policy instrument of unilateral federal standards is really the dog that won't hunt. The reason is that unilateral federal standards are not hunting dogs at all. They are guard dogs kept to protect a politically select few principles of health services delivery, or else show dogs kept as symbols to parade in partisan competition. For the development of social policies in Canada, we need dogs that really will hunt—hounds, pointers, setters, and retrievers that will track social problems, point to priorities, set desirable resource levels, and retrieve results for judgment—and also guide dogs that will help us find new ways of thinking about social problems. Most of all, however, we need friendly family dogs that are companions to, or at least have respect for, all members of our constitutional family. As with dogs, so with standards: in pursuit of national standards that will fit the needs of the Canadian constitutional family, voluntary interprovincial standards now should have their day.

NOTES

1. "What is the reason that you use me thus?/ I loved you ever: but it is no matter;/ Let Hercules himself do what he may,/ The cat will mew and dog will have his day" (William Shakespeare, *Hamlet,* Act V, Scene 1).

2. Roger Gibbins, "Decentralization and National Standards: 'This Dog Won't Hunt,'" *Policy Options* 17 (June 1996): 10.

3. These four types of federal–provincial relations are roughly similar to models of relations between central and local educational authorities that I have elsewhere described as administrative agency, communal autonomy, policy tutelage, and policy interdependence. See Ronald Manzer, *Public Schools and Political Ideas: Canadian Educational Policy in Historical Perspective* (Toronto: University of Toronto Press, 1994), pp. 23–28.

4. The participation of local governments in setting and enforcing national standards may involve a direct relationship with federal authorities, but this is rare in Canada. For local governments in Canada, intergovernmental relations is overwhelmingly provincial–local relations. Whichever is the case, the four general types of federal–provincial relations by extension can also be used to describe federal–local and provincial–local relations.

5. This form of state–societal relationship has been described as a "pressure pluralist policy network" in order to differentiate it from the more institutionalized and less competitive arrangements of corporatism and concertation. See Michael M. Atkinson and William D. Coleman, *The State, Business and Industrial Change in Canada* (Toronto: University of Toronto Press, 1989), pp. 82–87, and also William D. Coleman and Grace Skogstad, "Policy Communities and Policy Networks: A Structural Approach," in William D. Coleman and Grace Skogstad, eds., *Policy Communities and Public Policy in Canada* (Mississauga: Copp Clark Pitman, 1990), pp. 14–33.

6. Carolyn Tuohy, "Health Policy and Fiscal Federalism," in Keith G. Banting, Douglas M. Brown, and Thomas J. Courchene, eds., *The Future of Fiscal Federalism* (Kingston: Queen's University School of Policy Studies, 1994), p. 199.

7. For an assessment of the potential difficulties of the federal government's long-term ability to enforce health care standards under the CHST, see Allan M. Maslove, "The Canada Health and Social Transfer: Forcing Issues," in Gene Swimmer, ed., *How Ottawa Spends 1996-1997: Life Under the Knife* (Ottawa: Carleton University Press, 1996), pp. 288–290.

8. Ronald Manzer, *Public Policies and Political Development in Canada* (Toronto: University of Toronto Press, 1985), p. 62.

9. The unilateral federal action announced in the 1995 budget speech was preceded by a process of public deliberation that was intended to achieve a broad national consensus on the direction of welfare policy reform. Beginning in early 1994, the review of social security involved public hearings and consultations by the House of Commons Standing Committee on Human Resources Development, a discussion paper outlining options for social security programs released by the minister of human

resources development (Lloyd Axworthy) in early October, and a second round of public meetings held by the House of Commons committee. The minister was unable to get partisan unity on welfare policy changes when committee members representing the Bloc Québécois and the Reform Party dissented from the final report, and the minister of finance and his department then bypassed the social security review by introducing the Canada Health and Social Transfer. For an overview of the social security review, see James J. Rice, "Redesigning Welfare: The Abandonment of a National Commitment," in Susan D. Phillips, ed., *How Ottawa Spends 1995–1996: Mid-Life Crises* (Ottawa: Carleton University Press, 1995), pp. 187–189.

10. Ibid., pp. 198–199.

11. Ronald Manzer, *Public Schools and Political Ideas: Canadian Educational Policy in Historical Perspective* (Toronto: University of Toronto Press, 1994), p. 244. Proponents of national testing under SAIP emphasized the need to focus on educational outcomes, the acquisition of basic knowledge and skill, judged against established national standards. According to the president of the Business Council on National Issues, for example, the business community in Canada strongly supports standardized testing because it would improve the quality of high school graduates: "A considerable number of students arriving in the work force are unable to read, write and do their numbers. Standardized tests are one way to introduce excellence into our education systems. The tests set goals for people to shoot at" (Thomas d'Aquino, quoted in *Toronto Star*, September 21, 1991). Opponents of the national tests, which included provincial teachers' unions and the Canadian Teachers' Federation, objected that the proposed national tests were not based on provincial curricula and argued that assessment of even basic knowledge and skills should be based on what is taught in schools, how it is taught, and who the learners are.

12. Gibbins, *Policy Options* 17 (June 1996): 10.

13. See Keith G. Banting, "Social Policy," in G. Bruce Doern, Leslie A. Pal, and Brian W. Tomlin, eds., *Border Crossings: The Internationalization of Canadian Public Policy* (Toronto: Oxford University Press, 1996), pp. 27–54; and also G. Bruce Doern, Leslie A. Pal, and Brian W. Tomlin, "The Internationalization of Canadian Public Policy," ibid., pp. 1–26.

Postscript

The question of whether national standards should be federal standards may soon be put to the test. As mentioned earlier, the Canada Health Act is a piece of federal legislation that outlines various conditions with which the provinces must comply in order to receive federal cash payments. The conditions include universality, portability, comprehensiveness, accessibility, and administration on a non-profit basis. As well, the act effectively prohibits direct charges to patients by physicians and hospitals. At present, the provinces want reforms to this piece of federal legislation. For a start, they want to amend the conditions, with the result that federal standards would become federal–provincial standards. Eventually, some of the provinces, the well-off ones, may want conditions established through interprovincial agreements. If this latter possibility comes to be, then there will be a chance to test the proposition that national standards must be federal standards.

What would happen with these developments? Standards set through federal –provincial negotiation (accompanied still by federal cash transfers) might change the status quo little, aside from the emergence of some standards more in keeping with provincial wishes. But principles set by interprovincial agreement would be more interesting. Clearly, Gibbins feels that such an arrangement would leave standards in a shambles; the central purpose of getting rid of federal standards is to reduce restrictions on individual provinces, so it seems unlikely that the provinces would, as Gibbins says, "choose to substitute one set of shackles for another." Moreover, without the presence of the federal spending power, there would be a problem with the enforcement of interprovincial standards.

Manzer has a different view. He believes that federal standards, and especially those in the Canada Health Act, have very little to do with the quality of services and "are too narrow in their application." Manzer is more optimistic about interprovincial standards, for he believes that there exists a certain similarity in the thinking of provinces when it comes to social policy. He also feels that the very process of setting standards through interprovincial discussions would contribute to the learning process necessary for the making of sound public policy.

The literature on national standards in Canada revolves around major social programs and "associated" federal–provincial arrangements. There are available a number of sources that give a general overview of these arrangements: Michael Whittington and Richard Van Loon, *Canadian Government and Politics: Institutions and Processes* (Toronto: McGraw-Hill Ryerson, 1996), ch. 11; Keith G. Banting, Douglas M. Brown, and Thomas J. Courchene, eds., *The Future of Fiscal Federalism* (Kingston: School of Policy Studies, 1994); Peter M. Leslie, Kenneth Norrie, and Irene K. Ip, *A Partnership in Trouble: Renegotiating Fiscal Federalism* (Toronto: C.D. Howe Institute, 1993); Paul A.R. Hobson and France St-Hilaire, *Reforming Federal-Provincial Fiscal Arrangements: Towards Sustainable Federalism* (Montreal: Institute for Research on Public Policy, 1993); and Martin

Westmacott and Hugh Mellon, eds., *Challenges to Canadian Federalism* (Scarborough: Prentice-Hall, 1998).

For a good look at the question of national standards, students should consult the June 1996 issue of *Policy Options*, which contains a series of pieces on national standards (including a paper by Gibbins). Also, the matter of national standards is intimately linked to recent changes in federal–provincial fiscal arrangements relating to health, welfare, and postsecondary education. The new Canada Health and Social Transfer (CHST) has forced the issue of national standards onto the policy agenda. For more on the CHST, students should consult the following articles: Allan M. Maslove, "The Canada Health and Social Transfer: Forcing Issues," in Gene Swimmer, ed., *How Ottawa Spends 1996–1997: Life Under the Knife* (Ottawa: Carleton University Press, 1996); Odette Madore, *The Canada Health and Social Transfer: Operation and Possible Repercussions on the Health Care Sector* (Ottawa: Library of Parliament, 1996); Thomas J. Courchene and Thomas A. Wilson, eds., *The 1995 Federal Budget: Retrospect and Prospect* (Kingston: John Deutsch Institute for the Study of Economic Policy, 1995); Kenneth J. Boessenkool, *The Illusion of Equality: Provincial Distribution of the Canada Health and Social Transfer* (Toronto: C.D. Howe Institute, June 1996); Thomas J. Courchene, *Redistributing Money and Power: A Guide to the Canada Health and Social Transfer* (Toronto: C.D. Howe Institute, 1995); and Susan D. Phillips, "The Canada Health and Social Transfer: Fiscal Federalism in Search of a Vision," in Douglas M. Brown and Jonathan W. Rose, eds., *Canada: The State of the Federation 1995* (Kingston: Institute of Intergovernmental Relations, 1995).

As might be discerned from the above list of readings, Thomas Courchene is one of the most prolific writers on national standards and federal–provincial arrangements. His work should be carefully noted by those who wish to understand this difficult area of Canadian politics. Students, though, should be forewarned: Courchene has strong views on what should be done, and is no disinterested viewer of the debate over national standards. In 1996, Courchene prepared a working paper for the government of Ontario that endeavoured to show how interprovincial agreements might make possible a strong social union in Canada. The paper is entitled *Access: A Convention on the Canadian Economic and Social Systems,* and can be acquired through the Ontario Ministry of Intergovernmental Affairs and may be available in the government documents section of university libraries. This paper shows a scholar in action, and demonstrates clearly that the debate over national standards is not a mere academic one.

Finally, Manzer has written a book on educational policy in Canada that demonstrates some of the points he makes in his paper. It is a long book, but it richly rewards those seeking to discover how the provinces have gone about making educational policy at the primary and secondary levels without the active involvement of the federal government. The book is Ronald A. Manzer, *Public Schools* and *Political Ideas: Canadian Educational Policy in Historical Perspective* (Toronto: University of Toronto Press, 1994).

ISSUE**EIGHT**

Should Quebec Be Recognized as a *Distinct Society* in the Constitution?

✓ **YES**
PAUL DE VILLERS,"Why We Must Entrench Quebec's Francophone Heritage," in *Canadian Speeches* 11, no. 1 (April 1997)

✗ **NO**
LINE MAHEUX, "Why the Distinct Society Idea Is Tearing Canada Apart," *Canadian Speeches* 11, no. 1 (April 1997)

Easily, the most divisive issue in the realm of constitutional reform is the question of whether Quebec should be recognized as a *distinct society* in the Constitution. Though proposals for such recognition differ in their details, each essentially attempts to state that the Constitution of Canada would be interpreted in a way that takes into consideration the unique character of Quebec and that governments should act in a manner that recognizes the distinctiveness of Quebec. Accordingly, when forced to adjudicate on a matter affecting Quebec, the courts would keep in mind the special quality of Quebec's language, culture, and law. Also, the government of Quebec would act to maintain and build upon the distinctiveness of Quebec.

Attempts have been made to recognize Quebec's distinctiveness in the Constitution. The Meech Lake Accord of 1987 contained a provision that stated, in part, that the Constitution of Canada would "be interpreted in a manner consistent with ... the recognition that Quebec constitutes within Canada a distinct society"; it also indicated that the legislature and government of Quebec were to act in a way to "preserve and promote the distinct identity of Quebec." Similarly, the Charlottetown Accord of 1992 stated that the Constitution would be interpreted in a way consistent with the belief that Quebec, as a distinct society, represented a fundamental characteristic of Canada, and affirmed once again the role of public authorities in Quebec "to preserve and promote" this quality. Both accords fell short of receiving the required level of support, partly because of the rejection of the distinct society provisions.

A more recent attempt to recognize Quebec's distinctiveness was not a constitutional amendment, but rather a motion proposed and accepted in the House of Commons in late 1995. The motion stated that the House of Commons and its representatives recognize "that Quebec is a distinct society within Canada," and that the legislative and executive branches of the national government "take note of this recognition and be guided in their efforts in their conduct accordingly." The drop in status—a parliamentary motion holds much less force than a constitutional provision—reflected the unwillingness of many to concede Quebec's distinctiveness in the Constitution. Most recently, in September 1997, all of the provincial premiers of Canada—except for the premier of Quebec—put forward a new national unity proposal that included a provision noting that the "unique character" of Quebec was "fundamental to the well-being of Canada." But this remains only a proposal and amounts at this time only to a legislative resolution.

For many, the failure to recognize Quebec as a distinct society in the Constitution is unfortunate. Such a recognition would make Quebec feel more certain of the survival of its language and culture, and this in turn would cause its residents to feel less inclined to favour secession from the rest of Canada. Moreover, it would put into the Constitution only what the courts already do, which is to take into account the different nature of Quebec society. In other words, nothing would really change, except that Quebeckers would feel a little more secure in their belief that the French culture and language will prevail. As to the claim that recognition of Quebec's distinctiveness would confer some kind of special benefit upon Quebec, this claim fails to appreciate the fact that *distinct* in this context means only *different,* not *better.*

Many Canadians, though, are not persuaded by these arguments, especially the last. The notion of a distinct society does convey the idea of special treatment or special status. But this clashes with the belief that all Canadians and all regions are equal. No one person or province is better than another in the eye of the law. Moreover, the recognition of Quebec as a distinct society might serve the separatist cause, for it takes very little effort to move from a distinct society to a distinct nation or country. Ironically, those who wish to save Canada by recognizing Quebec's distinctiveness achieve the exact opposite. The distinct society provision is a recipe for the dismemberment of Canada. Finally, there is a fear that the government of Quebec, in promoting the province's distinctiveness, might violate certain individual and collective rights.

Notwithstanding past failures, there is still a movement to entrench a distinct society clause in the Constitution. To some extent, the parliamentary motion of 1995 is a first step, albeit a minor one, toward this aim. The Liberal government of Jean Chrétien is committed to recognizing Quebec's distinctiveness, and so are some of the other federal party leaders. But the leader of the Reform Party, Preston Manning, categorically rejects the idea, and the separatist Bloc Québécois sees it as a futile attempt to hold Canada together. As for the premiers' package of proposals, it, too, shows there is some support for recognizing the distinctiveness of Quebec, though the replacement of "distinct society" with "unique character" reminds us of the objections to any special treatment of Quebec in the Constitution.

Should Quebec Be Recognized as a *Distinct Society* in the Constitution?

The readings are the product of a debate held in April 1997 between Line Maheux and Paul De Villers on whether Quebec should be recognized as a distinct society in the Constitution. The specific debate resolution, which De Villers refers to in his article, is, "It would be in the best interests of all Canadians to entrench recognition of Quebec as a distinct society in the Constitution of Canada." De Villers, an MP and parliamentary secretary to Stephane Dion, the federal cabinet minister responsible for the Constitution, pleads the case for recognizing Quebec's distinctiveness. Line Maheux, a senior advisor to the Reform Party of Quebec, feels differently and states that many problems attend the inclusion of a distinct society clause in the Constitution.

✔ **YES**
Why We Must Entrench Quebec's Francophone Heritage
PAUL DE VILLERS

I know that the resolution deals with the term "distinct society" and the entrenchment of it in the Constitution, but I don't like to use that term. I think it's a term that brings up a lot of baggage from the constitutional wrangling we've been through for many years—the failed Meech Lake Accord, the failed Charlottetown Accord.

When I speak to Canadians in my capacity as parliamentary secretary to Minister Dion, the minute the term "distinct society" is used, immediately all of that baggage is dragged out again and people become very, very suspicious and very apprehensive.

Canadians feel that through all of the constitutional wrangling that we have experienced in this country, that it has been a process that has not involved people, it's been a process that the political elite have been negotiating behind closed doors, coming to agreements and accords and then coming to the people and asking them for their approval, rather than trying to involve the people at the very beginning and having them work on the solutions at the ground level. And I think that is one of the reasons we have so much difficulty in trying to resolve the unity problem.

I like to instead refer to what we sometimes generally think of distinct society, as a recognition of Quebec's distinctive role in protecting and promoting its Francophone heritage. That is a term that was used by Mr. Justice Brian Dickson, the retired chief justice of the Supreme Court of Canada. He was suggesting that this was something we needed to do in order to solve our unity problem. He said that, in fact, and I quote from a *Globe and Mail* article Friday, July 5, 1996, from a speech by Mr. Justice Dickson:

"In fact, the courts are already interpreting the Charter of Rights and the Constitution in a manner that takes into account Quebec's distinctive role in protecting and promoting its Francophone heritage. As a practical matter, therefore, entrenching formal recognition of Quebec's distinctive character in the Constitution would not involve significant departure from the existing practice in our courts."

What the former chief justice of the Supreme Court of Canada is saying is that currently, when the court interprets grey areas of the Constitution it already takes into account that difference that exists in Quebec by reason of the French language, culture, and institutions.... So the courts are already interpreting those grey areas. By entrenching it in the Constitution we would be, in effect, not granting anything more to Quebec than it already has through the constitutional convention of the Supreme Court's interpretations.

So, people then might ask, "Well, what is the benefit if it's not doing anything, not giving to Quebec anything it does not already have? Why would this assist us in trying to resolve the national unity question?"

I think the answer to that is simply that it would be guaranteeing that the constitutional convention which exists would continue because it would then be entrenched in the Constitution.

I know that our premier here in Ontario, Mr. Harris, is quoted last weekend in *The Toronto Star,* from an address to the Fraser Institute in Vancouver, where he talked about the concept of distinct society and he says, to paraphrase him, that it's a past disaster, it's a failure, and we shouldn't be talking about distinct society any longer. Then later on in his address, he talks about "What do they want in Quebec? They want jobs, they want respect, they want prosperity, they want to feel secure in Quebec and they want to know that their French language can thrive into the future. I think we can give them all of those things."

Well, I think that "all of those things" are the same as what I am referring to and what Mr. Justice Dickson was referring to, as the recognition of Quebec's distinctive role in protecting and promoting its Francophone heritage.

The next natural question is, why do they need this? Why should they need this reassurance?

Mr. Stephane Dion, when he is speaking to Canadians outside of Quebec, puts it to them this way. If we here in Ontario were the only predominantly English-speaking jurisdiction in Canada, all other provinces being predominantly French, and all the United States predominantly French, then we would be an island of English in a North American sea of French. And that is exactly the situation that exists in Quebec, except in reverse. They are the French island in the North American sea.

When you look at it that way, there is a natural insecurity that they feel and they are trying to redress that natural insecurity. That's what the separatist movement is playing on—playing on that Francophone insecurity. They fear that the French language will be lost. And it's a fact that all over the world, the French language is on the decline. So it's something they see happening elsewhere, and they are concerned.

What I would like to see, what many of the premiers would like to see, what Stephane Dion is working towards, would be to try to have some form of understanding or consensus built up by the other provinces of Canada to present to Quebec an offer to entrench that recognition into the Constitution.

If that offer were made, we know that the separatists would have to refuse it, because they want nothing but a separate country. So if that offer were made prior to the next Quebec provincial election, that's something that Daniel Johnson, the current leader of the opposition ... could then run on. He could say, "Look, Mr. Bouchard doesn't want to accept this offer. Elect my party and we will accept it." And by doing that, we could then get around what I call the Quebec block on a constitutional matter. With the amending formula as it is in the Constitution, to make significant amendments we need the consent of seven provinces totalling 50% of the population.... That makes it very difficult to get around the fact that Quebec won't agree to anything on the constitutional side. M. Parizeau [former premier of Quebec] wouldn't come to the meetings; M. Bouchard comes, but he won't agree to the time of day. So it's very difficult to make any progress.

In my capacity as the parliamentary secretary to Stephane Dion I've been doing some travelling. He asked me to work with the unity groups that have popped up all over the country as a result of the last referendum where the results were so close. Many Canadians, concerned about the possible breakup of the country, formed unity groups all over and wanted to get involved. They felt that isolation that I described earlier, that the political elites of the country were trying to solve the problem without involving the people. The minister asked me to work with the unity groups, not advise them but to hear them, take their suggestions, and report back to him.

In the course of doing that I travelled to almost every region and province in the country. I found that most Canadians are very proud of the French character within Quebec as part of Canada. And they're prepared to recognize that so long as it's clear that there are no additional rights, powers or privileges that are attached to that recognition. It's not unanimous by any means, but I find very strong support for that concept. People have no difficulty whatsoever with that recognition so long as it is clear that there are no additional rights, powers or privileges.

I think that's something that we need to work on, because Canadian unity is a much bigger question than the Quebec question that most Canadians are very, very tired of having to deal with and very tired of hearing about it. I think we have to get around that, get beyond that.

You might ask, why is Quebec the one jurisdiction that keeps holding referendums when there are separatist sentiments elsewhere? In British Columbia, for example, there is some degree of separatist sentiment that I have experienced in people whom I have spoken to out there. And all of these other regions have very legitimate concerns. Canada has changed. Canada is not the place it was in 1867 when the Constitution was written. The West is far more developed.... B.C., for instance, is the fastest-growing region in the country.

So we need to take all this into account. The present government plans to deal with this one issue at a time, which is a good plan. Because you don't get into the conundrum we were into, for instance, in the Charlottetown Accord where there were so many items that there was no way to determine whether people voted no against distinct society, or because they were against the treatment of women or the lack of provisions for women's rights or the Aboriginal question, or many of the other questions that were contained in this accord. If you approach this on an issue-by-issue basis, then you know exactly—you can get a handle on the consensus. Whether you go the referendum route or not, you can get a handle on the particular question you're trying to deal with.

But that takes an awful long time. And we may not have that much time, if we can't progress this file along much quicker. That's why I think we have to try to get ourselves through this constitutional block that we're in over Quebec. And it's my submission that by the recognition of Quebec's distinctive role in protecting and promoting its French character without granting to it any additional rights, powers or privileges, [this] will help us get there a lot quicker.

✗ NO
Why the Distinct Society Idea Is Tearing Canada Apart
LINE MAHEUX

I'm a Francophone Quebecer. Frankly, I don't feel that the French language in Quebec is threatened. I think it's stronger than ever. I really do. The numbers show that. I would argue differently for the rest of Canada, where the number of Francophones is definitely declining.... But in Quebec, the French language is stronger than ever. In fact, we now know that 90 percent of Quebecers are Francophones as opposed to 80 percent 20 years ago. So that has changed quite a bit.

As for the separatists refusing distinct society, they've already refused it. They opposed it in the House of Commons. So they've already done that. And I didn't really see any benefit for Quebec federalists. I didn't see any change in support for sovereignty. It doesn't seem to prompt federalists into saying that it's the separatists who are not willing to play along with this.

The type of interpretive clause that Daniel Johnson's Quebec Liberals wish to see is one of the Meech Lake type which would, in fact, apply to the entire Charter of Rights and Freedoms. So if you propose that it's merely symbolic—in which case, as a Quebecer, I ask myself why would I want it? what really does it do?— if you propose that, there would be a huge argument between federalists in the national Liberal party and Quebec provincial Liberals.

But I am here tonight to discuss my opposition to the resolution.

I want to affirm the principles of equality, because that is what I believe in. I oppose both the legal and constitutional recognition of Quebec as a distinct society for four different reasons.

The first reason is that I believe in the equality of all individuals, both legal and constitutional.

Secondly, I also believe that the distinct society would foster a debate of divisiveness, pitting one region against another, pitting one group of Canadians against another. I think that the whole debate around distinct society is, in fact, what has divided the country.

Thirdly, I believe that the parties who have proposed it—the Liberals, the Conservatives, and the NDP—have not always viewed distinct society from the best interests of the country, but it has become very political in the same way that the separatists use language in Quebec to make electoral gains.

And finally, my greatest opposition to the distinct society motion is that I really believe it is a two-step strategy toward separation.

I'd like to read to you a resolution that the Parti Quebecois adopted in 1981. The phrase became popular in '82 and onward, but let me tell you about the roots of distinct society. Rene Levesque and his PQ government adopted a motion which stated that "it must be recognized that the two founding peoples of Canada are fundamentally equal and that Quebec, by virtue of its language, culture and institutions, forms a distinct society within the Canadian federal system with all the attributes of a distinct national community."

That sounds awfully familiar. I ask myself, why is it that federalists have now become the greatest salesmen of what began as a separatist motion? That concerns me.

I would also read to you a quote by Jacques Parizeau [former premier of Quebec] when he was interviewed by the late Barbara Frum, about how he would use distinct society. He said:

"I'm going to use the distinct society clause for everything that it is worth. It's remarkable how much one could get through that clause if the courts say, 'Well, yes, in some circumstances it can override certain dispositions of the Charter of Rights.' If the courts say that, my God, what a weapon it could be for the people who have supported, shall we say, political projects that I have."

That is the greatest threat of distinct society. If we concede this, that Quebec is a distinct society, then sovereigntists can say that if we are a distinct society, we ought to be a distinct nation. And if we concede to the first part of that equation, we will [be] moving toward the conclusion of that equation. And that is my greatest opposition to distinct society.

I want to come back to the notion of legal and constitutional equality.

I've always referred to distinct society as affirmative action for Quebec. I'm opposed to affirmative action, quotas, special status of any type. I think that those who advocate it—don't get me wrong, I don't believe Mr. De Villers is wanting to break up Canada by advocating distinct society. Many people who advocate that really think it's going to unify and a lot of people who advocate special status really believe that they're trying to do justice. So I'm not talking about motive here.

But I think it's important to look at the impact, that over time when we see that we start identifying each other on where we come from, what color we are, what gender we are—then what we start to do, is we start pitting one against the other. And I don't think that's right.

Some politicians will do that. Some politicians use that as bait, such as the people who are trying to break up Canada.

Distinct society looks to equality of outcome rather than equality of opportunity. And, of course, equality of outcome is always at the expense of someone else's equality of opportunity. It's essentially an unjust notion.

I compare this to a family situation. If you're from Quebec and you have 10 children—which was once not uncommon—and you decide that one child ought to have special privileges, what do you have end up happening? A family feud. And in Canada, that's what we found. We have a family feud. We didn't have this family feud before.

I remember when this resentment across the country did not exist. It only started flaring up when, in response to the nationalist threat we decided to adopt the nationalist strategy.

Some will say that distinct society won't confer any special rights or privileges to Quebec, that it's purely symbolic, a recognition of what already exists. But there are two problems with this.

One of them was raised by a Quebec lawyer. What he said was that ... if Quebec voted yes in another referendum and then declared UDI, a unilateral declaration of independence, already the fact that we have legally recognized the notion of distinct society in a federal statute would give them an edge in a world court in arguing that, "hey, your country recognizes the distinct society."

The second thing, and again referring to Mr. Justice Dickson, symbolic is only going to be decided by the courts. It is not decided by the politicians. They cannot give any guarantees to that.

In addition to these two points, the legal and constitutional recognition of distinct society, I think, is just a total abdication to the separatists' argument.

This whole idea that it is supposed to be merely symbolic, the whole idea that Quebecers are different, that their language and culture are different—that confirms what is obvious to most people. But to go a step further and say that it requires legal entrenchment, I don't think that Canadians want that. What will end up happening is that we will alienate other Canadians. I don't think that is a good recipe for long-term unity.

That is why I believe in equality. I look at that and I say, "That makes sense." This is a long-term recipe to unity.

I can understand those who have the right intentions to try to keep the country united, but the evidence is to the contrary.

Here we are, we have politicians all over the country saying "We've got to recognize distinct society or Quebec is going to break us up." Well, I'm sorry, but what happened in the last referendum?

It seems that ever since we've had this whole debate on distinct society, the threat of separatism has only grown, it has not waned. The idea of moving toward recognition of distinct society has not united us, it has, in fact, alienated many Canadians.

One thing I do admire about Mr. De Villers is that he showed up tonight to debate this. Others were invited and refused to show up to debate this, because they know, they know that this just doesn't sell. But I respect those who stand for what they believe in and will provide the argument for those beliefs.

The other problem with distinct society is that what I've noticed—I'm bilingual—and when I'm in Quebec and I watch French TV and they talk about distinct society, I'm hearing some very different things from the politicians than when I go to Ontario or out West. What's happening is that in the efforts to try to sell distinct society, people are packaging it differently in different parts of the country to get it through.

If you want to talk about regional divisiveness and pitting one Canadian against another, one region against another, that's the best way to do it: say one thing in French in Quebec and go out West and say another thing in English.

The whole problem with this is that politicians went to Quebec and made promises that they could not reasonably expect to fulfil. It is not the rejection of distinct society that fuels the resentment, it is the fact that the promises were made to begin with and could not be delivered. It is the disappointment of that. If I promised you some chocolate and later said I couldn't deliver, there would be some disappointment. Do it three times and you start to not have credibility.

You can't make promises you can't keep, just to win elections, or form a coalition of people. I don't think that in the long term it's in the best interests of the country.

We create a lot of expectations by doing that, by going into Quebec and saying that we can do something, and then when it can't be delivered, we do something else.

I believe that there is a market for equality in Quebec. In fact—and I'm sure this will surprise many of you—there were three polls that were conducted by Maclean's/Decima. As you know, the distinct society notion is based on the concept that there are two founding peoples in Canada, the English and the French, in a special partnership. That's what the notion of distinct society is based upon. In fact, it was really based on the idea of two founding races.

Obviously that leaves out 11 million Canadians who are of neither French nor English descent. Where does that put them? Where do they fit into the partnership of two founding nations?

When Quebecers are asked, "Do you want distinct society," I don't doubt for a moment that a majority will say yes. But this poll went to Quebecers and said, "Do you favor the two-founding nations constitutional model, or do you favor the 10-equal provinces constitutional model?" Well, in 1992, after the Charlottetown referendum, 52 percent of Quebecers said they favored 10 equal provinces. In 1994, 54 percent said 10 equal provinces. And in 1995, one month after the Quebec referendum 56 percent of Quebecers said they favored 10 equal provinces over the two-founding nations constitutional model.

Now, I'm not a big fan of polls. I don't think that they're gospel. But I do believe this indicates that there is a significant market for the idea of equality. What's great about this is that we know there's a significant market for the idea of equality outside of Quebec.

Now if we can get people in Quebec advocating something that has a significant market, and we can get people outside of Quebec advocating something that has a significant market, I think we may actually have a chance of unifying this country and moving it forward on things such as jobs, economy, taxes, etc.

Why is it that we don't hear about this? I would imagine that for most of you this poll is a bit of a surprise, that you've never heard of it before. But of course, politicians know about these polls, they know that this exists, they know that there's a market in Quebec for equal provinces. So why wouldn't they further it?

This is where it comes down to politics. There are two reasons here. Federally, what has happened with the parties, with the Liberals and the Conservatives, is that it has become a good political strategy to become the unifiers of the country.

But interestingly enough, when we look at the referendum results, neither the prime minister nor the leader of the Conservatives was able to get a No vote in their own ridings. The people closest to them did not believe in their vision. But yet that's what they present themselves as. It is expedient to use it as a strategy. Now I'm not that cynical to say that every Liberal and every Conservative thinks that way. No. But I know a little bit about backroom politics, and I know some of the thinking that goes on.

This thinking is the same strategy that Rene Levesque used in polarizing the French and the English in Quebec and capturing the French vote. Sheer numbers meant that they would win. Sheer numbers of Canadians don't want the country to split up. So if you are going to be the ones who "save the country," then you have a really good chance of winning an election.

On the provincial side of things, you also have the Quebec Liberals, who are in a difficult situation. They need to get the Francophone vote as well as the Allophone and Anglophone vote—they need to get a significant portion of that Francophone vote. The way they have done it is what I object to. They've adopted all the nationalist rhetoric, they've adopted all the separatist terminology. What they have done is in fact supported and echoed the message of the sovereigntists, and used them as a negotiating lever with Ottawa in trying to get a better deal for the provincial government.

So there are many reasons why I am opposed to the notion of distinct society.

Postscript

De Villers and Maheux clearly differ on the question of acknowledging Quebec as a distinct society in the Constitution. In important ways, they mirror the division found among Canadians on this matter. Perhaps these differences could be resolved, though, if a different term were found. De Villers tries his hand at coming up with a new expression, suggesting that "recognition of Quebec's distinctive role in protecting and promoting its francophone heritage" be used instead of "distinct society." But this suggestion is unwieldy, not pithy enough to compete with the present formulation. On becoming the federal minister of intergovernmental affairs, Stephane Dion suggested "special distinction" as a replacement for distinct society. But this seems to indicate preferential treatment even more than the term it seeks to displace. And then there is the premiers' suggestion of "unique character."

It is, of course, possible that no term would be acceptable. Maheux, for one, thinks that this whole effort is wrongheaded. We should abandon the effort to assert Quebec's distinctiveness in the Constitution because doing so inevitably suggests special treatment and encourages separatist efforts. But the results of the 1995 Quebec referendum make some people fearful of such a stance. Surely, it may be argued, something must be offered to the people of Quebec. If not, the next referendum will spell the end of Canada. The response to this is that the distinct society provision does the same to Canada. Clearly, the issue of recognizing Quebec as a distinct society in the Constitution is central to the fate of Canada.

To begin an investigation of this issue, it is prudent to first examine the distinct society proposals found in the Meech Lake and Charlottetown Accords. The Meech Lake Accord (officially known as the 1987 Constitutional Accord) can be found in R.D. Olling and M.W. Westmacott, eds., *Perspectives on Canadian Federalism* (Scarborough: Prentice-Hall, 1988) and the Charlottetown Accord in Kenneth McRoberts and Patrick Monahan, eds., *The Charlottetown Accord, the Referendum and the Future of Canada* (Toronto: University of Toronto Press, 1993). Though not a constitutional amendment, the 1995 motion of the House of Commons dealing with Quebec as a distinct society is also worthy of attention, and it can be found in Jean Chrétien, "Recognition of Quebec's Distinct Society Crucial to Renewing Canada," *Canadian Speeches* 9, no. 8 (December 1995). The premiers' package, sometimes called the Calgary Accord or Calgary Declaration (it was devised in Calgary), can be found in the September 16, 1997, issue of *The Globe and Mail*.

For a history of the constitutional processes and the underlying political context that produced the distinct society proposals, students should consult Peter Russell, *Constitutional Odyssey: Can Canadians Become a Sovereign People?* 2nd ed. (Toronto: University of Toronto Press, 1993). Other useful sources for understanding the historical context of this issue are Kenneth McRoberts, "Quebec: Province, Nation, or 'Distinct Society'?" in Michael Whittington and Glen

Williams, eds., *Canadian Politics in the 1990s* (Scarborough: Nelson Canada, 1995) and Kenneth McRoberts, *Misconceiving Canada: The Struggle for National Unity* (Toronto: Oxford University Press, 1997).

The distinct society proposals in the two constitutional accords have been examined in great detail, especially the one found in the Meech Lake Accord. The relevant readings here include Richard Simeon, "Meech Lake and Shifting Conceptions of Canadian Federalism," *Canadian Public Policy–Analyse de politiques* 14, Supplement (1988); Katherine E. Swinton and Carol J. Rogerson, eds., *Competing Constitutional Visions: The Meech Lake Accord* (Toronto: Carswell, 1988), Part 1; Michael D. Behiels, *The Meech Lake Primer: Conflicting Views on the 1987 Constitutional Accord* (Ottawa: University of Ottawa Press, 1989), ch. 4; Peter Hogg, *Meech Lake Constitutional Accord Annotated* (Toronto: Carswell, 1988), ch. 4; and various articles in Kenneth McRoberts and Patrick Monahan, *The Charlottetown Accord, the Referendum and the Future of Canada* (Toronto: University of Toronto Press, 1993) and Curtis Cook, ed., *Constitutional Predicament: Canada After the Referendum of 1992* (Montreal and Kingston: McGill-Queen's University Press, 1994). Arguably the most influential analysis of the idea of recognizing Quebec as a distinct society in the Constitution has been made by former prime minister Pierre Elliott Trudeau. For his views on this matter, see Donald Johnston, ed., *Pierre Trudeau Speaks Out on Meech Lake* (Toronto: General Paperbacks, 1990) and Pierre Elliott Trudeau, *Against the Current: Selected Writings 1939–1996* (Toronto: McClelland and Stewart, 1996).

The defeat of the Charlottetown Accord seemingly ended any chance for including a distinct society provision in the Constitution. But the razor-thin win of the No forces in the 1995 Quebec referendum renewed efforts to do just that. The aforementioned House of Commons motion constitutes, for the federal government, a first step toward achieving this goal. Not surprisingly, this action has been commented on by the major political actors. For these reactions students might examine the following speeches: Lucien Bouchard, "Why Separatists Reject 'Distinct Society' Status," *Canadian Speeches* 9, no. 8 (December 1995); Preston Manning, "Distinct Society Must Mean Nothing for Quebec," *Canadian Speeches* 9, no. 8 (December 1995); Stephane Dion, "Don't Give Up on the World's Best Hope," *Canadian Speeches* 9, no. 10 (March 1996); and Daniel Johnson, "Change and Recognition Can Avoid Another Quebec Referendum," *Canadian Speeches* 10, no. 2 (May 1996).

ISSUE**NINE**

Do Canada's Tax Laws Treat Women Fairly and Equally?

✔ **YES**
JUSTICE CHARLES GONTHIER, Opinion in *Thibaudeau v. Canada*

✗ **NO**
JUSTICE BEVERLY McLACHLIN, Opinion in *Thibaudeau v. Canada*

On May 25, 1995, the Supreme Court of Canada ruled that certain provisions of the Income Tax Act were not in violation of the Charter of Rights and Freedoms. The provisions at issue stated that a separated or divorced parent with custody of the children must claim as income any support payments from the former spouse. They also stated that the individual making the support payments could claim the payments as an income deduction for tax purposes. Suzanne Thibaudeau, a divorced mother with custody of her two children, had claimed that these provisions violated her equality rights guaranteed under section 15 of the Canadian Charter of Rights and Freedoms. It was unfair, she said, that the custodial parent had to pay tax on the child support payments while the noncustodial parent received a tax break. The Supreme Court of Canada, or at least the majority of the court, respectively disagreed.

Though the case dealt with complex tax matters, it nevertheless attracted a great deal of public attention. One cause for the interest in the case related to the perception that the Income Tax Act discriminated against women and contained outmoded conceptions of the role of women in society. In most situations, the custodial parent is a woman, so for many observers the tax treatment of child support payments favoured men and made an already difficult situation for women even more difficult. Divorce was trying enough, but to create an additional tax burden for the single mother seemed too much.

The genesis of the case lay in actions taken over half a century ago. In the early 1940s, the Parliament of Canada passed legislation that allowed noncustodial parents to deduct child support and spousal payments for the purpose of determining their taxable income. Also, it deemed that the custodial parent would have to include these payments as taxable income. At the time, this arrangement, called the *inclusion/deduction* system, was thought to benefit all concerned. The noncustodial parent, nearly always the father, would be better positioned to make support payments; he would now have to pay fewer taxes. As for the custodial parent, the mother, she would experience little effect because she typically had no job and hence little employment income to tax. As a whole, the couple benefited financially from the legislation, for the tax break offered to the custodial parent exceeded any taxes the custodial parent had to pay on the child support payment. What made the arrangement acceptable then was the traditional family situation: the husband went to work, the wife stayed at home.

By the late 1980s, when Suzanne Thibaudeau faced these provisions as a newly divorced working mother, the traditional family had all but disappeared. Women now participated actively in the labour force, and they had employment income just like men. What had remained the same, though, were the income tax laws affecting child support and spousal payments. Suzanne Thibaudeau was determined to change this. She challenged sections 56(1)(b) and 60(b) of the Income Tax Act on the grounds that they discriminated against the custodial parent. Section 15 of the Canadian Charter of Rights and Freedoms had been interpreted to mean in part that governments could not take actions that placed a burden on a particular group in society. Thibaudeau was convinced that she could use this section of the Constitution to knock down the offending provisions of the tax legislation. What especially irked her was the fact that all of her support payments were in relation to her children, and that she herself had not received any spousal support.

In the Tax Court of Canada, Thibaudeau lost, but on appeal to the Federal Court of Canada she won. But the federal government itself appealed the latter decision to the highest court in the land, the Supreme Court of Canada. At this level, the majority of the justices decided against Thibaudeau. The dominant voice in the majority opinion was Justice Charles Gonthier, who argued that the family—the divorced couple and the children—still benefited from the child support laws. For a law to be in violation of section 15, it had to create a burden, and for Gonthier the laws under review did no such thing; indeed, they provided an advantage for separated and divorced families. A minority, composed of the two women on the Supreme Court, disagreed and found in favour of Thibaudeau. Justice Beverly McLachlin, in one of the two dissenting opinions, contended that the provisions clearly discriminated against the custodial parent, not only in relation to the non-custodial parent but also to others who received child support payments and were without any obligation to pay tax on these payments.

The readings for this debate are abridged versions of the opinions of Justices Gonthier and McLachlin. As might be discerned from this introduction, the opinions require some diligence, and there are terms and concepts with which students may be unfamiliar. One term that is crucial to understanding the case is the notion of a *marginal tax rate*. In basic terms, it refers to the tax bracket in which a taxpayer finds himself or herself. A higher marginal tax rate means that a taxpayer is in a higher tax bracket and hence must pay more taxes than people in a lower tax bracket. It also means that tax deductions are more valuable to those with higher marginal tax rates because they can avoid paying those higher taxes. It should also be noted that in places the readings contain brief editorial summaries of those parts of the opinions that are excluded. These are provided in an effort to increase the readability of the abridged opinions.

✔ **YES**
Opinion in *Thibaudeau v. Canada*
JUSTICE CHARLES GONTHIER

Gonthier J.:—The issue in the instant appeal is whether s. 56(1)(b) of the *Income Tax Act*, S.C. 1970-71-72, c. 63 ("ITA"), which requires a taxpayer to include in computing his or her income any amount received by the taxpayer in the year as alimony, infringes the equality rights guaranteed by s. 15(1) of the *Canadian Charter of Rights and Freedoms*. It should be stressed at the outset that the issue before this court will not be considered from the standpoint of alimony paid to provide for the needs of the recipient parent. The obligation to include is only at issue in the case at bar as it applies to amounts intended to provide *exclusively* for the maintenance of the children of the marriage.

FACTS

The respondent, Suzanne Thibaudeau, married Jacques Chainé on December 23, 1978. There were two children of this marriage, Jean-François and Marie-Christine, born in 1979 and 1981 respectively. On December 1, 1987, the respondent obtained a decree *nisi* of divorce granted pursuant to the old *Divorce Act*, R.S.C. 1970, c. D-8.

Under that decree, which was made absolute on October 22, 1990, the respondent was awarded custody of her two minor children and her ex-husband was ordered to pay her alimony of $1,150 a month for the exclusive benefit of the children, with indexing pursuant to art. 638 of the old *Civil Code of Quebec*, S.Q. 1980, c. 39 (now S.Q. 1991, c. 64, art. 590). No amount was awarded to the respondent for herself as the court was of the view that she had sufficient financial self-sufficiency. In determining the said amount, therefore, account was taken of the cost of maintaining the children, some $900 to $1,000 a month, the tax impact on the former spouses and the respondent's duty also to provide for the maintenance of her children. The court recognized, however, that the amount so determined required a greater contribution from the respondent than would be required by the ratio between the respective incomes of the former spouses.

In 1989, the year at issue here, the respondent received $14,490 for the maintenance of the couple's minor children. For that year she filed three income tax returns: one covered her personal situation and dealt essentially with her employment income; the other two were filed on behalf of the children and reported for each an income totalling half the alimony received by the respondent during the year.

The Minister of National Revenue subsequently reviewed these tax returns and, pursuant to s. 56(1)(b) ITA, included the amounts received as alimony in computing the respondent's income. In a notice of reassessment for 1989, the latter's net federal tax was accordingly increased to $4,042.80.

As the Minister maintained his decision after considering the notice of objection filed by the respondent, the respondent appealed to the Tax Court of Canada, where she argued that s. 56(1)(b) ITA, by imposing a tax burden on her for amounts she was to use solely for the benefit of her children, infringed her equality rights as guaranteed by s. 15(1) of the Charter....

[Before analyzing the case, Justice Gonthier listed the relevant provisions: s. 3 of the Income Tax Act, which enumerated the traditional sources of taxable income; s. 56(1)(b) of the Income Tax Act, which required recipients of child support payments to claim such payments as income; s. 60(b) of the same act, which allowed taxpayers to deduct any child support or alimony payments they may make; and s. 15 of the Charter of Rights and Freedoms, which guaranteed the equality rights of Canadians and protected individuals against discriminatory actions.]

ANALYSIS

Essentially, the respondent's arguments require a review of the separate system created by the combined effect of ss. 56(1)(b) and 60(b) of the ITA, and in particular the question of how the benefit produced by the mechanisms so created is to be distributed between the custodial parent and the non-custodial parent. In this connection, it will thus be useful first to examine the general principles by which we must be guided in formulating a response to the first point at issue. They will be discussed in the next three subsections. The following section then applies these principles to the case at bar.

A. *An infringement of equality rights*

(1) *Background*

In *R. v. Big M Drug Mart Ltd.* (1985), 18 D.L.R. (4th) 321, 18 C.C.C. (3d) 385, [1985] 1 S.C.R. 295, this court *per* Dickson J. (as he then was), at p. 360, indicated the parameters within which a right or freedom protected by the Charter should be analyzed:

... this analysis is to be undertaken, and the purpose of the right or freedom in question is to be sought by reference to the character and the larger objects of the Charter itself, to the language chosen to articulate the specific right or freedom, to the historical origins of the concepts enshrined, and where applicable, to the meaning and purpose of the other specific rights and freedoms with which it is associated within the text of the Charter. The interpretation should be, as the judgment in *Southam* emphasizes, a generous rather than a legalistic one, aimed at fulfilling the purpose of the guarantee and securing for individuals the full benefit of the Charter's protection. At the same time it is important not to overshoot the actual purpose of the right or freedom in question, but to recall that the Charter was not enacted in a vacuum, and must therefore, as this Court's decision in *Law Society of Upper Canada v. Skapinker* (1984), 11 C.C.C. (3d) 481, 9 D.L.R. (4th) 161, [1984] 1 S.C.R. 357, illustrates, be placed in its proper linguistic, philosophic and historical contexts.

There can be no doubt that this passage also applies to the definition and interpretation of the equality rights contained in s. 15(1) of the Charter.

Additionally, the ITA is subject to the application of the Charter just as any other legislation is: the special nature of the former clearly cannot be taken as a basis for maintaining that it is not subject to the latter. This was recently pointed out by my colleague Iacobucci J. in *Symes, supra,* at pp. 550–51. I would add, however, that though it may not be relevant to determining whether the Charter applies to the ITA, the special nature of the latter is none the less a significant factor that must be taken into account in defining the scope of the right relied on, which here as we know is the right to the "equal benefit of the law."

It is of the very essence of the ITA to make distinctions, so as to generate revenue for the government while equitably reconciling a range of necessarily divergent interests. In view of this, the right to the equal benefit of the law cannot mean that each taxpayer has an equal right to receive the same amounts, deductions or benefits, but merely a right to be *equally governed* by the law. The basic purpose of s. 15 of the Charter was explained by McIntyre J. in *Andrews, supra,* at p. 15:

> It is clear that the purpose of s. 15 is to ensure equality in the formulation and application of the law. The promotion of equality entails the promotion of a society in which all are secure in the knowledge that they are recognized at law as human beings equally deserving of concern, respect, and consideration.

That being the case, one should not confuse the concept of fiscal equity, which is concerned with the best distribution of the tax burden in light of the need for revenue, the taxpayers' ability to pay and the economic and social policies of the government, with the concept of the right to equality, which as I shall explain in detail later means that a member of a group shall not be disadvantaged on account of an irrelevant personal characteristic shared by that group.

(2) *The nature and operation of the ITA*

(a) *The general system for taxing individual income*

The basic system of the ITA rests on the principle that a taxpayer's taxable income is computed in accordance with all of his so-called sources of income. Section 3 ITA contains the formula for arriving at a taxpayer's income for a taxation year. It is true that, using wording which is intended to be extremely flexible and all inclusive, the legislature has chosen to refer to the three most important sources of income, namely income from an office or employment, business and property; but this list is not exhaustive. With this in mind, it should not be surprising that certain amounts received by a taxpayer, though they are not on the list of the principal sources of income enumerated in s. 3 ITA, are nevertheless treated as taxable for the person receiving them.

The mechanisms of the ITA are also intended to express another principle, namely that the unit of taxation is the individual. From this principle there follows the rule that the individual is taxed on *the whole* of his income, that he may not, for example, divide it among the members of his family in order to reduce his total tax payable. This is the general prohibition on income splitting. Accordingly, within a married couple each parent has to pay tax on his or her own income; the same applies to the income received by a child of the marriage. There are certainly provisions in the ITA, such as deductions for spouses and dependents, which do take into account the unit represented by the couple, in order to reflect the economic reality peculiar to it. That does not mean they detract from the importance of the rule stated earlier.

(b) *Particular system created by ss. 56(1)(b) and 60(b)*

The legislature has nevertheless sought to deal with the unfavourable economic consequences resulting from the breakup of the family unit. In 1942, it thus created by the combined effect of ss. 56(1)(b) and 60(b) ITA what is commonly referred to as the inclusion/deduction system. This is a system which applies only to separated or divorced spouses and which exceptionally permits income splitting between the latter in order to increase their available resources. This was recognized by Beetz J. in *Gagnon v. The Queen* (1986), 25 D.L.R. (4th) 481 at pp. 483–4, [1986] 1 S.C.R. 264, [1986] 1 C.T.C. 410, where this court had to determine whether certain monthly payments made to an ex-wife to repay charges on her property were deductible under s. 60(b) ITA:

> The purpose of these provisions, by allowing income splitting between former spouses or separated spouses, is to distribute the tax burden between them. As C. Dawe wrote in an article titled "Section 60(b) of the *Income Tax Act:* An Analysis and Some Proposals for Reform" (1979), 5 Queen's L.J. 153 (1980): "[T]his allows the spouses greater financial resources than when living together, compensating in part for the lost economics of maintaining a single household."

For an overall understanding of the inclusion/deduction system we must look at its specific mechanism. Alimony becomes taxable for the treasury by virtue of s. 56(1)(b) ITA. It will be noted that this source of income does not appear in s. 3 ITA. Section 56(1)(b) imposes on a parent who has custody of his or her child an obligation to include in computing income any amounts received as alimony for the maintenance of the child. At the same time, s. 60(b) ITA allows alimony so paid to be deducted in computing the non-custodial parent's income. This is where income splitting comes in: as we know, it is prohibited under the general system of taxation described earlier. A portion of the payor's income, equivalent to the amount of the alimony paid, is taxed in the hands of the recipient. The payor thus has his income split, contrary to the well-settled rule that an individual must be taxed on all his income. It should be noted that the income splitting at issue is not that of the couple but that of an individual, in this case the payor of the alimony. It is my view that this is how the passage by Beetz J. reproduced earlier is to be understood.

It is by means of this income-splitting operation that the legislature has sought to increase the available resources that can be used for the benefit of the children. This measure generally results in a net tax saving, allowing the court which has to set the amount of maintenance to increase the alimony to be paid by an amount equal to the amount thus saved.

The tax savings generated by this system depend, however, on the difference in tax rates between the payor and the recipient of alimony. Accordingly, the more the marginal tax rate of the payor of the alimony exceeds that of the recipient, the greater the tax benefit. If the marginal tax rate is the same for the payor and the recipient, then the effect of the legislation is neutral. On the other hand, if the custodial parent receiving the alimony is taxed at a marginal rate greater than that of the payor, then the tax he or she must pay will be higher than the saving which the non-custodial parent will enjoy. In short, for the deduction provided for in s. 60(b) ITA to produce a benefit for the custodial parent as well, the additional tax which the latter has to pay on account of the inclusion requirement provided for in s. 56(1)(b) must correspondingly be covered by a greater increase in the alimony to be paid by the non-custodial parent.

In fact, although the tax savings generated by the inclusion/deduction system depend on a variable, namely the difference between the tax rates of the members of the couple, the system appears to confer a benefit in most cases: the evidence in the record indicated that recipient parents are generally subject to a tax rate lower than that of parents paying the alimony....

(c) *Section 15(1) of the Charter: some principles of analysis*

In recent years, this court has had occasion to state some of the fundamental principles applicable to an analysis made under s.15(1) of the Charter. *Andrews, supra*, marked the beginning of the effort undertaken by this court to define the content of the right to equality. I note that the essential points in that judgment were recently highlighted by my colleague Iacobucci J. in *Symes, supra*. I again refer to them.

In *Andrews*, at pp. 13–14, McIntyre J. first noted that discrimination will not result from every distinction or difference in treatment. In my view, this observation applies especially to tax legislation, the very essence of which is to create categories (at p. 13):

It is, of course, obvious that legislatures may—and to govern effectively—must treat different individuals and groups in different ways. Indeed, such

distinctions are one of the main preoccupations of legislatures. The classi-
fying of individuals and groups, the making of different provisions
respecting such groups, the application of different rules, regulations,
requirements and qualifications to different persons is necessary for the
governance of modern society.

Section 15(1) of the Charter is thus designed only to eliminate *discriminatory* distinctions. The concept of discrimination was outlined by McIntyre J. as follows, at p. 18:

> ... discrimination may be described as a distinction, whether *intentional or
> not* but based on grounds relating to personal characteristics of the indi-
> vidual or group, *which has the effect* of imposing burdens, obligations, or
> disadvantages on such individual or group not imposed upon others, or
> which withholds or limits access to opportunities, benefits, and advantages
> available to other members of society. Distinctions based on personal char-
> acteristics attributed to an individual solely on the basis of association with
> a group will rarely escape the charge of discrimination, while those based
> on an individual's merits and capacities will rarely be so classed.

(Emphasis added.) These comments make it clear that s. 15(1) of the Charter provides
protection both from direct discrimination and from discrimination by prejudicial
effect. In the words of McIntyre J., at p. 11, equality must be analyzed essentially
according to "the impact of the law on the individual or the group concerned."

These are the basic principles that run through the concept of discrimination. I
note the general nature of the remarks made by McIntyre J. in this connection.
Accordingly, while bearing in mind the analytical framework he has provided us
with, the notion of discrimination requires some further clarification.

The method of analyzing s. 15(1) of the Charter, designed to serve this objective,
is set out in my reasons in *Miron v. Trudel* [Court File No. 22744], rendered con-
currently herewith. As explained in that case, the question is whether the impugned
provision creates a prejudicial distinction affecting the complainant as a member of
a group, based on an irrelevant personal characteristic shared by the group. For the
sake of convenience, this analytical method is divided into three stages.

The first of these involves determining whether the provision in question creates a *distinction* between the individual, as a member of a group, and others....

The second stage involves determining whether this distinction creates *prejudice* in respect of the group in question. This element is essential: discrimination
can only be said to exist if the result of the impugned provision is to impose on
the group a burden, obligation, or disadvantage not imposed on others. I refer in
this regard to what was said by McIntyre J. in *Andrews, supra,* at pp. 22–23:

> The words "without discrimination" require more than a mere finding of
> distinction between treatment of groups or individuals. *Those words are a*

form of qualifier built into s. 15 itself and limit those distinctions which are forbidden by the section to those which involve prejudice or disadvantage.

(Emphasis added.)

Finally, in the third stage it must be determined whether the distinction created is based on an *irrelevant personal characteristic* which is an enumerated or analogous ground under s. 15(1) of the Charter. Relevance is to be determined in light of the underlying objectives of the legislation....

B. *Application to the present case*

(1) *First step: the distinction and the group*

The tax system set out in ss. 56(1)(b) and 60(b) ITA was specifically introduced to alleviate the economic consequences of a breakdown of the family unit. Consequently, it applies only to separated or divorced spouses. That being the case, there is no need to consider further whether the Act creates a distinction.

The group contemplated by the legislation consists of separated or divorced *couples* in which one parent is paying alimony to the other under a judgment or agreement. That is not the group to which the respondent claims to belong: she claims she is a member of the smaller group of custodial parents having some financial self-sufficiency and consequently receiving maintenance solely for the benefit of their children.

With respect, two comments should be made at this point. First, the group cannot be subdivided by income level: this is not a characteristic attaching to the individual. Accepting such a proposition would also mean that the most disadvantaged subgroup would be the group of custodial parents with the highest incomes. Second, it is not possible to consider custodial parents in isolation as a group which would subsequently be compared with that of non-custodial parents, for purposes of determining prejudice; I repeat that in the final analysis the discussion in this court has to do with *distribution* of the obligation to pay taxes within the *couple*. One must not lose sight of the fact that so far as the children of the family unit are concerned, for whose benefit the mechanisms of the ITA seek to free up additional resources, the separated or divorced parents still form an *entity*, ordinarily bound by the support obligation. Accordingly, a single facet of taxation, that of the person receiving the alimony, cannot be isolated and the other aspects disregarded.

This court is also being asked, for the purpose of comparison with the group of which the respondent claims to be a member, to consider the one formed by persons who have custody of children and who as such receive certain amounts needed for the maintenance of the latter though they are not covered by the provisions of s. 56(1)(b) ITA. For example, the respondent mentioned the situation of a parent whose child is receiving business income or income from an estate or trust, of a parent receiving support payments from one of the children's grandparents and of a grandparent receiving support payments from one of the children's parents. The respondent correctly pointed out that none of the members of that group are required to include the support payments received in computing their income.

I note, however, that when she places these persons in the same group for comparison purposes, the respondent is applying two different taxation systems. In the first example cited by the respondent, it is the child himself who is treated like any individual taxpayer and must pay tax on his income, if any. In my opinion, for this very reason this subgroup cannot be validly used as a basis for comparison: the different tax treatment of the children's own income results from the fact that they do not fall either under the system applicable to the income of non-separated couples or under that of separated couples. They are subject to the general system which applies to everyone, including children, regardless of their parents' situation. The situations in which a child has to pay tax reflect a completely different context characterized, _inter alia,_ by the payor being under no obligation to support the child. In that case, I certainly cannot include that category in the group which the respondent seeks to create.

The other examples given by the respondent involve parents to whom the provisions of ss. 56(1)(b) and 60(b) ITA do not apply but who none the less have a support obligation. As they do not fall within the specific ambit of these provisions of the ITA, they are subject to the general taxation system: the payor and the recipient are treated as ordinary taxpayers and amounts which the former pays the latter as support are not classified as income, unless they meet the conditions laid down in ss. 56(1)(b) and 60(b) ITA. The situation of those individuals corresponds to that the respondent's group would be in but for this special system. In order to decide whether there is prejudice, the situation of the respondent's group must be examined depending on whether or not it is subject to the special system.

(2) _Second step: prejudice_

Now that the distinction has been established, it is necessary to determine whether ss. 56(1)(b) and 60(b) ITA, in the context contemplated by them, have a prejudicial effect on separated or divorced parents as members of that group.

The respondent and the intervener SCOPE relied on the evidence in the record as showing that 98 percent of alimony recipients are women. In support of their arguments they also pointed to the recognition by this court, in _Symes, supra,_ of the disproportionate share women bear of the burden of child care and the social costs related to it. They also drew the court's attention to _Moge v. Moge_ (1992), 99 D.L.R. (4th) 456, [1992] 3 S.C.R. 813, 43 R.F.L. (3d) 345, in which this court noted that family breakup had a significant impact on the standard of living of custodial parents.

These are undoubtedly facts which may suggest a need for reform. I would note, however, that the court's function here is first to see whether ss. 56(1)(b) and 60(b) ITA produce a prejudicial effect on the group of separated or divorced couples as identified earlier, and in particular on a custodial parent to whom maintenance is paid for the needs of his or her children.

The respondent and some of the interveners maintained that women in Ms Thibaudeau's situation suffer prejudice which they described in three ways. First, parents who have the custody of children are subject to an obligation not imposed on non-custodial parents, that of including the amount of the alimony in computing their income. This obligation results from the actual wording of s. 56(1)(b) ITA. Then, as a result of this, custodial parents who enjoy a certain amount of financial self-sufficiency are subject to an additional tax burden, that of paying an additional amount in tax. Finally, on account of the very mechanism of the system, custodial parents are denied access to the additional financial resources which the legislature claims to intend for all parents, for the benefit of their children, and not just for non-custodial parents. It should be noted, as Hugessen J.A. [justice in earlier decision] indicated, that the alleged prejudice is of the same kind for all parents in such a situation regardless of sex, although for the most part it is women who are in this situation.

A comparison was made between the respondent's situation, separately, and that of non-separated couples in which each parent is taxed individually on the portion of his or her income intended for a child's needs.

In this connection, I would first note that a valid examination of the situation requires consideration of how the system treats *both* parents, and not only the recipient of the maintenance. As I mentioned earlier, it is the question of distribution which is critical to the discussion, and for it to be meaningful it must be considered from the standpoint of the members of the *couple*. One cannot thus object to taxation in the hands of the recipient of the maintenance without at the same time taking the tax treatment given to the payor into account. To do otherwise would amount to claiming a tax exemption which other parents would not receive. The rule is that the income of parents used for the maintenance of their children shall be taxed in the hands of the parents. This is so for those living together and those who are in single-parent situations. The special system applicable to separated or divorced parents maintains this rule. Where it departs from the general rule is in taxing income intended for the maintenance of children in the hands of the ultimate recipient of the income who disposes of it, rather than in the hands of the parent who earned or received it. There is nothing inequitable in that as such.

As I noted earlier, in order to decide whether the system is prejudicial it must be placed in context by comparing the treatment of parents covered by the special inclusion/deduction system with that which they would receive in the *absence* of such a system, namely that of parents to whom ss. 56(1)(b) and 60(b) ITA do not apply but who nevertheless have a support obligation.

It will be seen from those sections, first, that tax is imposed on the person who can dispose of the income. As I noted above, this measure is not prejudicial in itself. Second, a comparison with non-separated couples indicates that the parents to whom the special inclusion/deduction system applies enjoy an overall lessening of their tax burden. The appellant pointed out that the income splitting allowed by the system gave the parents it covers a tax saving of some $240 million in 1988 alone.

In view of the substantial savings generated by the inclusion/deduction system, it is clear that the group of separated or divorced parents cannot as a whole claim to suffer prejudice associated with the very existence of the system in question. On the contrary, it was shown that *on the whole* members of the group derive a benefit from it: as most of the recipient parents are subject to a marginal tax rate lower than that of the parents paying the maintenance, it can be said that the purposes for which the system was created have been to a large extent achieved.

Additionally, even accepting the respondent's suggestion that a comparison should be made between those who receive and those who pay the maintenance, the foregoing conclusion remains unchanged. In fact, if the recipients of maintenance are taken as a group separate from the payors, on the assumption that as a group the former are likely to be the subject of discrimination, there is no doubt that the Act creates a distinction by making the maintenance taxable in the hands of the recipient alone. However, in the context at issue here, which must always be borne in mind, it was not shown that such a distinction entails a disadvantage: the tax burden of the *couple* is reduced and this has the result of increasing the available resources that can be used for the benefit of the children, in satisfaction of their parents' obligation to support them....

[Justice Gonthier then noted that efforts were made in the family law system to take into consideration the tax treatment of support payments in the determination of the appropriate level of support for custodial parents; in other words, the support payment was increased to pay for the tax on the payment. Following this, Justice Gonthier concluded that s. 56(1)(b) of the Income Tax Act was not in violation of s. 15 of the Charter of Rights and Freedoms.]

✗ **NO**

Opinion in *Thibaudeau v. Canada*
JUSTICE BEVERLY McLACHLIN

McLachlin J. (dissenting):–This appeal requires the court to determine whether the deduction/inclusion scheme for separated or divorced couples set out in s. 56(1)(b) and s. 60(b) of the *Income Tax Act*, S.C. 1970-71-72, c. 63 (hereinafter "ITA"), infringes the equality rights guaranteed by s. 15 of the *Canadian Charter of Rights and Freedoms.*

The scheme taxes Ms Thibaudeau on the amounts paid to her by her ex-husband for the exclusive benefit of the children in her custody through the inclusion requirement contained in s. 56(1)(b) ITA. Her ex-husband, on the other hand, enjoys a deduction benefit contained in s. 60(b) ITA. The inclusion of the children's support payments in Ms Thibaudeau's taxable income increased her federal tax burden by $3,705 for 1989. The divorce decree provided only $1,200 for this additional tax burden. As a result of the application of the ITA deduction/inclusion scheme, Ms Thibaudeau was obliged to pay the difference of $2,505 in federal tax for 1989 out of her own income and resources after considering of all tax credits....

FACTS

As Gonthier J. has already related the principal facts, I need only to refer to certain aspects of the evidence. The evidence established the following facts.

1. The children's support payments in the case at bar are paid and received pursuant to a decree *nisi* of divorced granted on December 1, 1987. By that decree, the judge awarded custody of the two children of the marriage to Ms Thibaudeau. Finding her to be financially self-sufficient, he declined to order her ex-husband to make support payments for her own needs. With respect to support payments for the children, the judge ordered the ex-husband to pay Ms Thibaudeau the sum of $1,150 a month, which included a sum of between $150 and $250 a month to cover the additional tax which Ms Thibaudeau would be paying as a result of including the children's support payments in the computation of her taxable income.

2. The additional amount awarded to Ms Thibaudeau for taxes on the children's support payments was insufficient to cover the increased tax burden resulting from inclusion of their support payments in her income. As a result of the inadequate adjustment of the amount of child support, Ms Thibaudeau was obliged to pay part of her additional tax burden for 1989–$2,505 in federal tax–from her own income and resources....

ANALYSIS

A. *Inequality contrary to s. 15 of the Charter*

(1) *Legislative history*

An analysis of the argument that the ITA treats Ms Thibaudeau unequally as compared with her ex-husband must be conducted against the background of the history of the impugned legislation. This history suggests that Parliament was never concerned with equality of treatment between separated parents, and that the potential for inequality contained in the legislation has been exacerbated during the years following its enactment.

The deduction/inclusion scheme was introduced in 1942. Both the structure of the scheme and the wording of the provisions have essentially remained unchanged since then. The income splitting produced by this system is an exception to the general rule of individual taxation underlying the ITA. The deduction/inclusion scheme does not treat each taxpayer as a separate taxation unit, but treats the non-custodial parents as forming part of a single taxation unit, the family. By a legislative fiction, the deduction/inclusion scheme removes the amount of the support payments paid between former spouses from the non-custodial parent's taxable income, and transfers it to the custodial parent's taxable income.

Parliament created this exception to the general rule of individual taxation in order to ameliorate the situation of separated or divorced couples as well as that of any new family that might result from a new marriage by the non-custodial parent. In 1942, the husband was almost invariably the sole source of financial support for the wife and children. It is thus not surprising that Parliament considered that any improvement in the situation of all concerned—the first wife, the second wife or the children—could best be accomplished by improving the situation of the husband or father. It is also not surprising that Parliament was not concerned with ensuring equal tax treatment for the former spouses. At the time of enactment, women who had custody of children did not work outside the home, rare cases excepted. Thus they very seldom were required to pay tax. The following extract from the *House of Commons Debates*, vol. V, 3rd sess., 19th Parl. (July 17, 1942), indicates the reasoning underlying the establishment of a deduction benefit for the non-custodial parent and reveals the logic which led Parliament in the Mackenzie King era to adopt the system to which Ms Thibaudeau now objects (at pp. 4360–61):

Mr. Hanson (York-Sunbury): Such a man who has married again is in a very tight spot. I think he ought to have a little consideration; that should be allowed as a deduction.

Mr. Bence: I was going to say a word on that point. It seems to me most unfair that when a man is divorced and is supporting his ex-wife by order of the court, he should not be allowed to deduct, for income tax purposes, the amount paid in alimony. If that were done, the ex-wife could be required to file an income tax return as a single women, as she should, and she would have to acknowledge receipt of that income in making up that return. *In many cases the man has married again, but still he must pay a very high tax on the $60, $70 or $80 a month he must pay his former wife. I am not thinking of it so much from the point of view of the husband, though I believe he is in a very bad spot. In the cases with which I have become acquainted, the husband has defaulted in his payments because he has not been able to make them, and in those cases it is the former wife who suffers, and accordingly I believe she should be given as much consideration as the husband.*

Mr. Ilsley: I agree that there is a great deal of injustice to the husband, and perhaps indirectly to the wife, under the law as it stands now, and much consideration has been given some method by which the law might be changed. However, I am not in a position at the moment to say whether or not an amendment to meet the situation will be proposed. The matter is still under consideration.

Mr. Green: I really think it is an impossible situation, with the tax so greatly increased as it has been this year. After all, our law recognizes divorce, and once the parties are divorced they are entitled to marry again. *In some cases that have been brought to my attention the husband has remarried and had children by the second wife, but is forced to pay income tax on the alimony that he pays the first wife, and I suggest that the position is absolutely unfair.*

Mr. Ilsley: *I agree that it is, in a great many cases.*

(Emphasis added.)

Despite its laudable aim of ameliorating the position of all members of the broken family, the method Parliament chose to accomplish this goal contained the seeds of future inequality. It focused solely on improving the financial situation of the non-custodial parent and ignored the tax position of the custodial parent. It contained no provisions to ensure that the custodial parent receiving payments for children would not see her personal tax burden increased, much less share the advantageous tax treatment enjoyed by the non-custodial parent.

At the time, Parliament did not consider the tax impact of the deduction/inclusion scheme on custodial parents (who in the great majority of cases were the mothers). There was no concern with the need to ensure that the latter receive an adequate adjustment of the amount of support payments to offset the additional tax burden they might be required to assume as a result of the inclusion of this amount in computing their taxable income. The fact that most separated women remained in the home, had no income, and paid no tax, suffices to explain why their tax situation received no attention at the time.

These assumptions, however, no longer hold true. The half-century that has passed since the adoption of the tax scheme which Ms Thibaudeau challenges has seen great changes in society and in the family. In the social context of 1942, the inequality inherent in the system was not widely felt; in the modern social context, the same inequality is widely felt. In 1992, 56% of married women held employment (P. La Novara, *A Portrait of Families in Canada* (Ottawa: Statistics Canada, 1993), at p. 21) and there are many more taxpayers today among women than there were in 1942. The negative effect of the inclusion requirement on the custodial parent (women in most cases) has thus become greater over the years.

(2) *Present inequality under s. 15(1) of the Charter*

In *Miron v. Trudel*, S.C.C., No 22744, May 25, 1995, I take the view that an analysis under s. 15(1) of the Charter involves two stages. First, the claimant must show that the impugned legislation treats him or her differently by imposing a burden not imposed on others or denying a benefit granted to others. Second, the claimant must show that this unequal treatment is discriminatory. This requires one to consider whether the impugned legislative distinction is based on one of the grounds of discrimination enumerated in s.15(1) or on an analogous ground. In the great majority of cases, the existence of prejudicial treatment based on an enumerated or analogous ground leads to a conclusion that s. 15(1) has been infringed. Distinctions made on these grounds are typically based on stereotypical attitudes about the presumed characteristics or situations of individuals rather than their true situation or actual ability. Once a breach has been established, it is for the government to justify the inequality under s. 1 of the Charter by showing that the distinction is reasonable and justifiable in a free and democratic society....

(a) *Inequality of protection or benefit of the law and its basis*

The impugned taxation scheme imposes a burden on separated or divorced custodial parents, which it does not impose on separated or divorced non-custodial parents. The custodial parent must include child support payments from which she gains no personal benefit. The non-custodial parent may deduct support payments from his taxable revenue. He is taxed only on his actual personal income less this deduction. On its face, this demonstrates adverse unequal treatment of custodial parents. The evidence in this case suggests that taking into account the amounts from which she benefited in the form of tax credits, Ms Thibaudeau was obliged to pay from her own resources an additional $2,505 in federal tax for 1989 as a result of the inclusion of child support payments in her taxable income: testimony of Jean-François Drouin, a tax lawyer.

The increased tax burden resulting from this artificial inflation of the custodial parent's taxable income may increase the amount of tax payable in two ways.

First, the inclusion increases the amount of taxable income and consequently the amount of tax payable. Second, the inclusion may result in an increase in the marginal tax rate and hence in the tax payable.

The inequality between the custodial and non-custodial spouse is exacerbated by the fact that the latter enjoys an automatic and absolute right of deduction of support payments from personal income, while the former's ability to offset the increase in her taxes by obtaining an adjustment of support is unpredictable. Whether the custodial parent receives such an adjustment or not, the non-custodial parent may reduce his tax burden by deducting the full amount of the child support paid by him in computing his taxable income. On the other hand, not only must the custodial parent request any adjustment from the court, it is not always certain that the court will correctly assess the tax impact or will award a sufficient amount to enable the recipient to discharge her additional tax burden.

Similarly, when the tax cost of child support alters as the result of a change in the circumstances of the parties, it is up to the custodial parent to claim an adjustment of child support. For example, if the custodial parent increases her annual income and her marginal tax rate, she will be obliged to initiate proceedings and show that increase in the tax cost of the child support justifies an adjustment. The economic as well as psychological and practical hardships involved in such proceedings explain why support orders are rarely amended in such cases and why the custodial parent more often than not ends up paying the additional tax burden out of her own resources or those of the children in her custody (Report of the Federal/Provincial/Territorial Family Law Committee, *The Financial Implications of Child Support Guidelines, Research Report* (Ottawa: The Committee, May 1992), at p. 91). The non-custodial parent, for his part, always automatically benefits from the deduction, even if the tax adjustment for the custodial parent is no longer adequate.

The logic of the deduction/inclusion scheme is further called into question by the fact that our society strongly encourages women to attain financial self-sufficiency, and, in pursuit of that essential objective, to increase their income. The higher the income of the custodial parent, the greater will be her tax rate and the more she will be penalized by the requirement of including the amount of child support in computing her own taxable income. Such a mechanism not only does not encourage women to attain financial self-sufficiency, it seems designed in some cases to discourage them from increasing their income. One of the premises on which the logic of the deduction/inclusion scheme rests (that custodial parents are generally subject to a lower tax rate than those who pay the child support) is less and less in accord with present reality and undermines the importance our society places on women attaining financial self-sufficiency. The deduction/inclusion scheme therefore not only presents a problem in the limited context of reviewing the applicable legislation, but also in more general terms.

A further inequality in the deduction/inclusion scheme may be noted. While the non-custodial parent may deduct child support from his taxable income, the custodial parent not only cannot deduct amounts she spends on maintaining the children, but must also pay the tax that the non-custodial parent would ordinarily have had to pay on the income devoted to child support. The deduction/inclusion scheme overlooks the custodial parent's financial contribution to the support of the children. The ITA limits the amounts that may be deducted to child support under a court order or written agreement. Court orders or written agreements never allude to the amounts which the custodial parent personally devotes to supporting the children in his or her custody. Still less do they note the contribution of the custodial parent in terms of services, presence and availability. Standard child deductions and credits claimed by the custodial parent are legislatively capped, and may fall short of her actual expenditure for the child. It need hardly be added that the non-custodial separated or divorced parent has no obligation to include *his or her* taxable income amounts which the custodial parent spends on maintaining the children.

Although a comparison between the tax obligations of the custodial and non-custodial parents seems to me the best means of establishing the existence of prejudicial treatment of the former as compared with the latter, this conclusion can be buttressed by other comparisons.

Apart from s. 56(1)(b) ITA, child support is not included in the taxable income of other persons in situations similar to that of the custodial parent. The general principle of individual taxation applies, and the person having custody is not taxed on amounts which do not personally belong to him or her. For example, if child custody is awarded to a third party to whom the parents pay child support, the principle of individual taxation applies and the third party is not required to include child support in his or her taxable income. The law thus treats a separated custodial parent and a custodial third party receiving child support differently, imposing on the former an obligation to which the latter is not subject. Parliament may have valid reasons for not requiring custodial third parties to include the amount of the children's support payments for their income, for example, a desire not to discourage third parties from accepting child custody. But this does not permit us to infer that it is fair and acceptable to penalize custodial parents by placing an unequal tax burden on them.

The case of a custodial parent who is widowed provides a similar comparison. If one parent dies and leaves money for the child, the surviving parent who retains custody of the child and administers the money for the child is not required to include it in his or her taxable income. The amount bequeathed is intended exclusively for the child, a fact which the tax law recognizes. Again, we see that the law treats widowed custodial parents differently from separated or divorced custodial parents. It may be argued that the different tax treatment results from the fact that the money inherited by the child is the child's property (although the surviving parent administers it), while the child's support paid to a custodial parent for the exclusive benefit of the children is not only administered by the custodial parent but is also part of the latter's property—in short, that the distinction is based not on the status of the person receiving the child support payment but on the nature of the amount paid. But this technical legal distinction must yield to reality. Child support paid to separated or divorced custodial parents is provided exclusively for the child. While the custodial parent is not subject to the obligation of rendering accounts, in reality the money is paid for the exclusive benefit of the child. The fact that in one case the custodial parent holds the property subject to a legal trust and in the other subject to the practical reality of the child's needs, cannot justify imposing a tax burden in one case and none in the other.

I conclude that the deduction/inclusion scheme imposes a burden on the custodial parent which it does not impose on the non-custodial parent or on others who are in similar situations. I turn now to the arguments which are raised against this conclusion. The first argument, adopted by Gonthier J., is that it is wrong to focus the analysis on the individual's tax treatment and that one should consider the fractured family as a unit for taxation purposes. The second argument, adopted by Gonthier J. and by Cory and Iacobucci JJ. [another opinion for the majority], is that there is no inequality if one takes into account the impact of the family law regime on the tax scheme.

With respect to the first argument, Gonthier J. suggests that it is wrong to focus on a comparison of the position of the custodial or non-custodial spouse. This, he contends, distorts the analysis by isolating the component parts of a single system. He argues that the equality analysis must focus on the couple, rather than the individuals who were once members of the couple. With respect, I cannot accept this position.

First, to compare the position of the custodial and non-custodial parent does not, as Gonthier J. suggests, take the matter out of context. Rather, it focuses on the interaction between the various components of the deduction/inclusion scheme. This is to place the analysis in its context and to make a comparison which takes into account the actual situation of the parties affected by the deduction/inclusion scheme.

Second, s. 15(1) is designed to protect individuals from unequal treatment. Its opening words state: "*Every individual* is equal before and under the law and has the right to the equal protection and benefit of the law." Where unequal treatment of one individual as compared with another is established, it is no answer to the inequality to say that a social unit of which the individual is a member has, viewed globally, been fairly treated.

It is true, as Cory and Iacobucci JJ. suggest, that former spouses who are parents of the same children have a joint obligation toward the latter and so may theoretically be regarded as members of a single entity, despite the breakup of the family unit. It can be seen, however, that in practical terms the former spouses conduct their everyday lives much more as individuals than as a couple. As proof of this, Ms Thibaudeau had to pay part of the additional tax resulting from the inclusion requirement ($2,505) out of her own income and resources. Her ex-husband made no contribution to these costs and the law did not require him to make any.

The fact that the deduction/inclusion scheme does not impose prejudicial treatment on the majority of divorced or separated couples as compared with other couples—and even confers a benefit on them in 67 percent of cases (affidavit of Nathalie Martel, an economist in the Personal Income Tax Division of the federal Department of Finance, February 1, 1994, para. 21)—is no bar to concluding that that same system imposes prejudicial treatment within the couple by imposing on one of its members a burden not imposed on the other. Here, s. 56(1)(b) ITA imposes on one member of the separated or divorced couple a burden which does not affect the other member of that couple. The fact that no disadvantage results for *the couple as a whole* in most cases is no bar to concluding that the provision imposes prejudicial treatment on *one of its members,* the custodial parent.

Even if the legislation is viewed from the perspective of the couple, it works significant inequality. Under the deduction/inclusion scheme, the higher the non-custodial parent's marginal tax rate is above that of the custodial parent, the greater is the overall tax benefit. Accordingly, when the custodial parent and non-custodial parent are taxed at the same marginal tax rate, the tax benefit is nil. On the other hand, when the custodial parent's marginal tax rate is higher than that of the non-custodial parent, there is an adverse tax impact since the deduction/inclusion scheme has the effect of increasing the total tax paid by both parents. The result of this is that the deduction/inclusion scheme leads to tax savings for both parents together in about 67 percent of cases, adversely affects separated or divorced couples in about 29 percent of cases and has neutral effects in about 4 percent of cases (affidavit of Nathalie Martel, an economist in the Personal Income Tax Division of the federal Department of Finance, February 1, 1994, para. 21). From the outset, the deduction/inclusion scheme imposes prejudicial treatment on separated or divorced couples in about 30 percent of cases.

The total federal income tax saved by separated parents in 1991 as a result of income splitting under the deduction/inclusion scheme is estimated at $203 million (affidavit of Nathalie Marel, an economist in the Personal Income Tax Division of the federal Department of Finance, June 30, 1994). But this global saving provides no defence to the charge of inequality. The problem is that the overall context in which this scheme is applied does not require, and in some cases prevents, an equitable division of this tax benefit between the separated or divorced parents. In many cases in which a tax benefit results from the application of the deduction/inclusion scheme, the benefit is not passed on to the custodial parent or the children and remains in the possession of the non-custodial parent (Report of the Federal/Provincial/Territorial Family Law Committee, *supra*, at p. 91). The legislation contains nothing to encourage an equitable division between family members of any benefits that may result from tax savings granted to the non-custodial parent by means of the deduction. For example, neither the ITA nor the Divorce Act, R.S.C. 1985, c. 3 (2nd Supp.) (formally R.S.C. 1970, c. D-8) requires the non-custodial parent to share with his former spouse and/or the children the tax savings resulting from the deduction he is allowed. The prejudicial treatment of the custodial parent as compared with the non-custodial parent could scarcely be clearer.

I conclude that the argument that the question of equality must be viewed from the perspective of the couple rather than the individual overlooks individual inequalities which s. 15 of the Charter is designed to redress; and that even if the matter is viewed from the standpoint of the couple, unequal treatment is demonstrated.

Gonthier J., as well as Cory and Iacobucci JJ., argue that the family law regime rectifies the inequality that the legislation creates between custodial and non-custodial parents by allowing the amount of the child support to be adjusted to offset the additional tax burden on the custodial parent. I agree that the s. 15 equality analysis must take into account the rules of family law. I cannot accept, however, the conclusion that the family law regime neutralizes the effects of the inequality created by the deduction/inclusion scheme.

The evidence indicates that in practice the family law regime does not and cannot succeed in rectifying the inequality created by the deduction/inclusion scheme. Tax impact is not always considered by the courts and, when it is, the adjustment is often insufficient to cover the additional tax which the custodial parent must pay as a result of being subject to the deduction/inclusion scheme. A survey of 147 judges conducted by Judge R. James Williams of the Nova Scotia Family Court in 1990 indicates that only a minority of counsel present evidence to the court on the tax impact of the child support and that a majority of judges do not calculate the tax consequences if no evidence is presented to them in this connection (Report of the Federal/Provincial/Territorial Family Law Committee, *supra*, at p. 90, n. 52). The fact that the custodial parent can appeal a judgment which does not adequately take the tax impact into account or apply to the court to increase child support when new circumstances increase the additional tax burden she must bear as a result of including child support in her taxable income, does not answer these practical problems. I cannot accept that the legality of the system is preserved by the existence of corrective mechanisms which, in addition to being illusory, place on the shoulders of one individual—the custodial parent—the psychological and economic burdens inherent in implementing them.

Even when the court considers the tax consequences, complete compensation for the additional tax burden on the recipient is far from certain. Leaving aside the question of the complexity of the calculations required, one cannot ignore the fact that the amount of child support has to be determined in light of several factors—including the child's interests and the duty of both parents to contribute to their children's support in proportion to their means—and leaves room for the exercise of a very wide discretionary judicial power. This precludes complete neutralization of the negative effects that may result from the inclusion requirement provided for in s. 56(1)(b) ITA (Report of the Federal/Provincial/Territorial Family Law Committee, *supra*, at p. 91).

The actual situation of thousands of custodial parents in Canada belies the contention that the family law regime corrects the inequality created by the deduction/inclusion scheme within the couple. In *Willick v. Willick* (1994), 119 D.L.R. (4th) 405 at pp. 431–6, [1994] 3 S.C.R. 670, 6 R.F.L. (4th) 161, L'Heureax-Dubé J. decried the inadequate compensation which the law often provides for the hidden costs associated with the custody of children. To the already difficult task on the custodial parent of proving the true cost to her of raising a child, s. 56(1)(b) ITA adds the additional burden of proving, for the present and the future, what increase in her tax will be as a result of inclusion of child support in her income. It is contradictory to concede on the one hand that family law is able only with difficulty to divide the financial obligations pertaining to the children equally between the former spouses, and at the same time to assert that the same law is able to fully and adequately compensate for the increase in the tax burden which the inclusion requirement imposes on the custodial parent.

The same problems arise where child support is paid pursuant to an agreement between the parties, as opposed to a court order. Once again, full compensation for the additional tax burden imposed on the custodial parent is uncertain and contingent, while the deduction benefit for the non-custodial parent is automatic and absolute. Such agreements are often reached in an informal way and without professional advice. The custodial spouse is placed in the position of demonstrating to the non-custodial spouse the significance of the additional tax burden she must bear on account of the law's inclusion of child support in her taxable income. All this, taken in the emotional, personal and economic context in which such negotiations take place, has as a consequence that the custodial parent often fails to obtain sufficient compensation to indemnify her for the additional tax which the ITA imposes.

In the present case, the judge who set the quantum of the child support expressly considered its tax consequences. Boudreault J. stated that a sum of $900 to $1,000 a month was necessary to maintain the children and thought it advisable to set the amount of child support at $1,150 a month on account of the tax consequences of the latter for the recipient and the payor: *Thibaudeau v. Chainé*, December 1, 1987, Superior Court Montreal, Court File No. 500-12-151837-865. The adjustment made was inadequate, however, forcing Ms Thibaudeau to assume an additional federal tax burden of $2,505 out of her own income for the 1989 taxation year: testimony of Jean-François Drouin. In short, the family law regime failed to rectify the inequality which the tax law imposed on Ms Thibaudeau. Even if she were to seek a variation in child support, there is no assurance that the result would be full indemnity. Ms Thibaudeau's case, far from isolated, negates the notion that the family law regime neutralizes the discriminatory impact of the tax law.

I conclude that the requirement of s. 56(1)(b) ITA that separated or divorced custodial parents include child support in their taxable income imposes obligations on separated or divorced custodial parents that do not apply to others in similar situations and denies benefits which the law accords to others. It denies the right of custodial parents to equal protection and benefit of the law. Unequal treatment under s. 15 is established.

This brings us to the second stage of the analysis under s. 15: an examination of the ground(s) of discrimination.

(b) *Does the status of separated or divorced custodial parent constitute an analogous ground within the meaning of s. 15 of the Charter? If so, is the distinction based on this ground discriminatory?*

The ground on the basis of which the distinction is made here—the status of separated or divorced custodial parent—is not enumerated in s. 15 of the Charter. The question, therefore, is whether it constitutes an analogous ground of discrimination.

In *Miron v. Trudel, supra*, I explained that in order to decide whether a ground of discrimination is an analogous ground within the meaning of s. 15 of the Charter, it is essential to ask whether the characteristic on the basis of which the prejudicial distinction is made may be used to make irrelevant distinctions that are contrary to human dignity. The fact that the group in question has historically been disadvantaged, that it constitutes a discrete and insular minority, that the distinction is based on an immutable personal characteristic rather than on an individual's merit, capacities or circumstances, that the ground under consideration is similar to one of the enumerated grounds, or that the legislatures and the courts have recognized that distinctions based on the ground under consideration are discriminatory, are all factors which may help in deciding whether a ground of discrimination is an analogous ground for the purposes of s. 15 of the Charter.

Is the status of separated or divorced custodial parent an analogous ground within the meaning of s. 15 of the Charter? In my view it is.

First, the imposition of prejudicial treatment solely on the basis of this status may violate the dignity of an individual and his or her personal worth to a degree affecting the individual's personal, social or economic development. One's status vis-à-vis one's former spouse involves the individual's freedom to form family relationships and touches on matters so intrinsically human, personal and relational that a distinction based on this ground must often violate a person's dignity.

Second, separated or divorced custodial parents considered as a group have historically been subject to disadvantageous treatment. The social opprobrium to which this group has been subjected over the years may have lessened with time. Nevertheless, even today evidence of disadvantage suffered by such persons is overwhelming. Separated or divorced custodial parents as heads of single-parent families confront economic, social and personal difficulties not faced by non-custodial parents or those in two-parent families. Several studies in Canada and abroad indicate that the standard of living of the custodial parent and the children is significantly reduced following a divorce, whereas the standard of living of the non-custodial parent increases following the divorce.

Third, the special difficulties with which separated or divorced custodial parents must live and their minority position as compared with Canadian families as a whole justifies viewing them as a discrete and insular minority. In 1991, 13 percent of families were headed by a single parent while in 87 percent of families, the father and mother lived together with the children (La Novara, *supra*, at pp. 10 and 15). Single parents with custody thus constitute a minority. It is, moreover, a disadvantaged minority, confronted with social, personal and emotional challenges unique to its members....

Fourth, classification as a separated or divorced custodial parent may give rise to adverse distinctions on the basis of immutable personal characteristics rather than on the merit and actual circumstances of a particular individual. The status of a divorced parent in respect of children of the dissolved marriage is, for all practical purposes, immutable. The remarriage of the custodial parent does not change the relationship with the children, and the parent still remains a "former spouse" in relation to the first marriage under the Divorce Act. Only if there is remarriage to the former spouse does the status of divorced parent disappear—a possibility so remote that it may safely be ignored. Moreover, the decision to separate or divorce is often far from free. The other party may leave the relationship against the will of the parent who remains with the children. Or the circumstances of the marriage may have left the custodial parent with little choice but to leave it.

Fifth, the status of separated or divorced custodial parents is linked to the enumerated ground of sex given that the great majority of the members of this group are women. In fact, in 1990 the courts awarded custody to women in 73.2 percent of divorce cases while custody was awarded to men in 12.3 percent of the cases and a joint custody order was made in 14.1 percent of the cases (La Novara, *supra*, at pp. 11 and 18).

These considerations lead to a single conclusion: the status of separated or divorced custodial parent constitutes an analogous ground of discrimination within the meaning of s. 15(1) of the Charter.

Unequal treatment by a law on an enumerated or analogous ground ordinarily suffices to establish that s. 56(1)(b) ITA constitutes discrimination and infringes the equality right guaranteed by s. 15(1) of the Charter. The only exceptions are rare cases in which a distinction based on enumerated or analogous ground does not lead to an infringement of s. 15(1) of the Charter: see my reasons in *Miron v.*

Trudel. This is not such as case. The distinction made here on the basis of the status of separated or divorced custodial parent runs directly counter to the values underlying s. 15(1) of the Charter. It increases the disadvantages already suffered by separated or divorced custodial parents based not on their merit or actual situation but solely and arbitrarily by reference to their membership in a group.

I conclude that a violation of s. 15 of the Charter is established.

[Justice McLachlin then addressed the question of whether the violation of s. 15 represented a reasonable limit under s. 1 of the Charter of Rights and Freedoms. She found that s. 56(1)(b) was not a reasonable limit and deemed that the provision was unconstitutional.]

Postscript

Gonthier and McLachlin pursue a fairly similar course of inquiry in determining the existence of discrimination: discover whether a distinction is being made, ask whether this distinction creates a burden for the group that is singled out, and ascertain whether the basis for the distinction is listed in s. 15 or is analogous or similar to those found in the equality rights provision. But they clearly differ in the way they resolve these matters. For Gonthier, the relevant distinction is between separate or divorced couples and other families, whereas McLachlin locates the distinction between custodial and noncustodial parents (plus other nonparental custodians). As to evidence of a burden, Gonthier determines that most couples who fall under the challenged provisions benefit from the differential tax treatment; on the other hand, McLachlin argues that custodial parents in many cases suffer under the Income Tax Act, either because they have higher marginal tax rates or because the family law system fails to ensure the transfer of tax savings to the custodial parent.

Each opinion is convincing in some respects, but questions do emerge. With Gonthier, the major query, voiced by McLachlin, is the focus on the *couple*. As McLachin says, though the two are jointly obliged to care for the children, they do lead separate lives and operate more as individual persons rather than as a couple. And, of course, this is what a separation or a divorce is all about. Moreover, Gonthier appears to have more faith than others in the ability of the family law system to place the tax savings in the pockets of the custodial parents. In determining support payments, judges do try to include the cost of the additional tax, but their calculations are sometimes incorrect. Then there is, of course, the problem of enforcing support orders.

As for McLachlin's opinion, it, too, stimulates some queries. Society has indeed changed, but the fact remains that the majority of separated or divorced couples benefit as a whole from the inclusion/deduction system (to the tune of $203 million). Surely, if the aim is the care of children, then this is not a trifling consideration. Moreover, some lawyers (see the Wolfson citation below) dispute her claims about the inadequacies of the family law system.

Thibaudeau lost in the Supreme Court of Canada, but she won in the court of public opinion. In 1996, the federal government announced the end of the inclusion/deduction system in relation to *child support* payments (but it would remain in effect for *spousal* support payments). Beginning in May 1997, child support payments would no longer be deductible and recipients of such payments would no longer need to claim them. This change was not just a result of the Thibaudeau case. A federal–provincial–territorial committee had found that many Canadians felt uncomfortable with the tax treatment of child support payments. It seems that it was time for a change.

For those wishing to pursue the Thibaudeau case (and the preceding decisions) in more detail, the following articles and documents are worth some consideration: Ellen B. Zweibel, *"Thibaudeau v. R.*: Constitutional Challenge to the Taxation of Child Support Payments," (1994) 4 N.J.C.L.; Lorne H. Wolfson, "Reflections on *R. v. Thibaudeau,"* *Canadian Family Law Quarterly* 13, no. 2 (1995); Department of Justice, *Federal/Provincial/Territorial Family Law Committee's Report and Recommendations on Child Support* (Ottawa: Department of Justice, January 1995), Appendix E; and Claire F.L. Young, "It's All in the Family: Child Support, Tax, and Thibaudeau," *Constitutional Forum* 6, no. 4 (1995). Of course, the full decision of the Supreme Court is available (for example, in 124 D.L.R. (4th)).

The case centres on s. 15 of the Charter of Rights and Freedoms. For more on this important provision, students might consult Peter Hogg, *Constitutional Law of Canada*, 3rd ed. (Toronto: Carswell, 1992), ch. 52, and William Black and Lynn Smith, "Equality, Linguistic, Educational and Aboriginal Rights, and the Multicultural Heritage of Canadians," in Gerald-A. Beaudoin and Errol Mendes, eds., *The Canadian Charter of Rights and Freedoms,* 3rd ed. (Toronto: Carswell, 1996). Also, the case suggests that a gender split might exist on the Supreme Court of Canada. In the case, five male justices all found against Ms Thibaudeau, and the two female justices on the Supreme Court found in her favour. A similar outcome has occurred in other cases dealing with women's rights. For those interested in this line of inquiry, Debra McAllister's, "The Supreme Court in Symes: Two Solitudes," *National Journal of Constitutional Law* 4 might be of interest.

ISSUE**TEN**

Is It Time for Canada and Quebec to Part?

✔ **YES**
DAVID J. BERCUSON, "Why Quebec and Canada Must Part," in
Current History 94 (March 1995): 123–126

✘ **NO**
DAVID T. KOYZIS, "Why Political Divorce Must Be Averted"

In Issue Eight, we wrestled with the question of how the nation should respond to the demands of Quebeckers for constitutional change with the intention of reaching some accommodation that will preserve the nation as a whole. The fractious debates over "distinct society" and recognition of the "unique" character of Quebec have led some to question whether accommodation can ever be reached, or if it can be reached only at an unacceptable cost. These concerns have been voiced in the writing of David Bercuson.

In the following article, "Why Quebec and Canada Must Part," Bercuson gives readers a brief overview of the history of the Quebec–Canada issue. According to Bercuson, Quebec and the rest of Canada have evolved into quite different societies with very different views on the role of the state in society. In reviewing past efforts to reach accommodation, Bercuson finds little evidence to point to a potential resolution in the near future. Instead, he fears that continuation of such efforts will continue to sap the energy and resources of the nation, which could best be focused on other issues. More importantly, each effort at constitutional settlement seems only to drive the wedge still deeper between the "two solitudes."

In making his case, Bercuson reflects a view that has gained strength among those who have become increasingly frustrated with the repeated attempts to reach constitutional accommodation. The argument goes something like this. Preoccupation with the "Quebec issue" has been a drain on Canada's resources and has diverted its attention at a critical time in its history when the nation should be focused on other issues such as how to adapt to an increasingly competitive global economy. The time has come to simply cut our losses and go our own ways. Quebeckers will be happy having achieved their cherished dream of an independent state in which their language and culture is protected. Canada, relieved of the burden of Quebec, will emerge as a stronger nation. It will no longer squander scarce economic resources on misconceived efforts to appease Quebec's demands. And, relieved of its sense of obligation to compete with the

Quebec state to act as protector of the French language and culture, Canadians will be free to develop a stronger sense of national identity and purpose that will help the country prepare for the challenges of the new millennium. Ultimately, letting Quebec go its own way might be a win-win situation for all parties.

Although Bercuson does not deal in this article with what would happen once Quebec left, he has dealt in more detail with this question in a book coauthored with Barry Cooper entitled *Deconfederation: Canada Without Quebec* (Toronto: Key Porter Books, 1991). According to the vision presented in this book, a declaration of independence by Quebec would be followed by a de facto recognition by the federal government of Canada. With the loss of the seventy-five Quebec MPs, a new government would be formed that would enter into negotiations with Quebec. After stripping Quebec of Rupert's Land and the entire south shore of the St. Lawrence River, Canada would then move quickly to adopt a new Constitution. This new Constitution would eliminate many of those features of the current Constitution that are seen as objectionable to many—bilingualism, multiculturalism, collective rights, and the notwithstanding clause. The new Constitution would enshrine a true economic union and institute a genuine triple-E senate. In the end, Canada would emerge "internally more united" and much stronger as a nation.

But, would such a political divorce be so easy and mutually beneficial? In the second article, David Koyzis finds Bercuson's description of an easy divorce troubling. Extending the metaphor of a failed marriage, Koyzis warns that divorce always has its casualties and that these should not be taken lightly. Instead, he argues that a much greater good can be served by making the effort to maintain and renew the federal union.

✔ **YES**
Why Quebec and Canada Must Part
DAVID J. BERCUSON

A house divided against itself cannot stand.

—Abraham Lincoln ⁕

The immortal words of Abraham Lincoln, uttered in the midst of the Lincoln–Douglas debates of 1858, described an America deeply and bitterly divided over the place slavery was to have in the future of the republic. The issues that divide English-speaking from French-speaking Canadians today are not as stark, dramatic, or fraught with the potential for violence as the great issue that inspired Lincoln, but they are as long-standing, and have proven as impervious to solution.

The Canadian nation is as divided today as it has been at any time since its establishment in 1867. It is not divided over the question of whether or not great evil will continue to exist, as the United States was before the Civil War. But it is split by two fundamentally different views of the world—one held by a majority of French Quebecers and the other by a majority of English-speaking Canadians inside and outside Quebec. These divergent worldviews have come to the fore because of major changes in Canadian society since 1945, and they have grown increasingly far apart since the beginning of the Quiet Revolution in Quebec in 1960 and the federal government's adoption of the Charter of Rights and Freedoms in 1982.

Since 1960 Canada's history has essentially been the story of one effort after another to patch over the chasm between English-speaking Canadian and French-speaking Quebecois political culture. The road to the second Quebec referendum on secession from Canada—which may be held this year—is paved with the wreckage of earlier agreements: the 1964 Charlottetown Conference, the 1971 Victoria Conference, the 1981 Ottawa Conference, the 1987 Meech Lake Accord, the 1992 Charlottetown Accord. In each case Canada's leaders tried to square the circle—to reconcile the mounting demands of French Quebecers to create a nation within a nation, and the growing refusal of English-speaking Canadians to make compromises on political principles that they believe constitute the essence of being Canadian.

TWO WORLDS

The men who created Canada in the mid-1860s were well aware that the new country would contain disparate peoples who had different ways of looking at the world. Canada, in other words, would not be held together by a common national heritage, and would not be like the new nationalist states then forming in Germany and Italy. The founders believed, however, that Canada, like the United

Kingdom, would be united by a common allegiance to the monarchy, shared ideals of British constitutionalism (which were strong even in Quebec), and economic self-interest. They were not far wrong, and Canadian unity, though sometimes strained, was for nearly a century never seriously jeopardized.

In June 1960 the Liberal Party came to power in Quebec under the leadership of Jean Lesage. Lesage and his followers took the reins of government from a thoroughly corrupt conservative regime that had held office since 1944. The previous regime had opposed trade unionism, favored foreign capitalists, and supported the Roman Catholic Church's dominant role in education and social services; it did all in its considerable power to keep Quebec rural, Catholic, and conservative. The government refused to cooperate with most federal initiatives in social policy and national economic development, jealously guarding what it believed to be Quebec's constitutional prerogatives.

Lesage's Liberals were determined to move in an entirely different direction. Activists, they believed that if the Quebec government was to succeed in its most important mission—guaranteeing the survival of the province's French-speaking population in a sea of North American "Anglo-Saxondom"—it needed to orchestrate Quebec's development. Thus the Lesage administration launched many new bold new initiatives, from a government-owned electric power monopoly to a provincial pension plan to a government-owned steel complex. It also began to question whether the traditional division of powers between the federal and provincial governments gave Quebec sufficient jurisdiction to carry out its mission. It concluded that it did not, and began a quest for more power that virtually every Quebec government has since continued. This quest has been linked, sometimes subtly, sometimes openly, with the threat that Quebec would secede from Canada if it did not achieve its constitutional goals.

In English-speaking Canada things had been moving in the opposite direction. From 1948 to 1958 Canada had a virtually open door immigration policy. A large number of the immigrants, who arrived at the rate of about 153,000 a year (close to 1 percent of the total population) throughout the decade, were from central, southern, and eastern Europe. The great majority integrated into the English-speaking milieu, but they did not share the British values or loyalty to the monarchy or the Commonwealth that had once formed the bedrock of English Canadian thinking. One sign of the decreased commitment to Britain was the adoption of the Canadian Bill of Rights in 1960; another was the new national flag displaying the maple leaf, first flown in 1964. As a result of these changes in outlook, Quebecois and other Canadians began to look at themselves, their country, and their governments very differently.

THE VIEW FROM QUEBEC

Whatever else Quebecers may desire in the way of forms of government, personal liberty, and social programs, what concerns them first and foremost is their survival as a distinct society in North America. Before World War II it was easy for Quebecers to set themselves apart from other North Americans. They were dominated by the Roman Catholic Church; their values were conservative, religious, and family oriented; and they were discouraged by their religious and political leaders from entering into commerce and constantly lectured about the importance of maintaining ties to the land and rural life, even though Quebec was thoroughly urbanized by 1945. Today the only feature that distinguishes Quebecers from other North Americans is their language—and all that language implies by way of modes of expression, culture, the arts, humor, and so on. Anything perceived as threatening the French language—such as an influx into Quebec of immigrants who choose to integrate into an English-speaking milieu—is seen as dangerous. The role of Quebec governments is to ensure that Quebec's distinct language-based culture survives.

When Canada was founded in 1867, the framers of the country's first constitution believed that if the provinces were given exclusive jurisdiction over education and the French language was afforded special constitutional protections, no other steps were needed to safeguard Quebec's unique heritage. For a generation that view has been rejected by Quebec governments, most intellectuals, a majority of trade unionists, and many journalists in the province. It is now a virtual given for most Quebecers that to safeguard the French language, the government of Quebec must assume powers almost akin to those of a sovereign state (the separatists, of course, want nothing less than full statehood). Since 1960 the province's governments have demanded control over social policy, immigration, investment, communications, broadcasting, manpower training, and other strategic jurisdictions. The government of Premier Robert Bourassa, which preceded the current separatist government, demanded that the Canadian constitution explicitly recognize Quebec as a distinct society, and recognize that the government of Quebec has a specific constitutional obligation to safeguard that status—and the powers that go with it.

The days of the Catholic Church's domination of Quebec's social and educational institutions is long past. Nationalism is the new religion of Quebec, and the state is the new church. In liberal democratic societies such as the United States or the rest of Canada, the state is considered neutral on cultural and religious matters. Not so in Quebec. There, the state is an activist institution charged with the national mission of ensuring the survival of a unique cultural group.

YOU ARE WHAT YOU SPEAK?

In the 1960s and 1970s, more and more English-speaking Canadians demanded a change in their relationship with their government. They began to push for a constitutionally entrenched charter of rights, and consequently, an end to the parliamentary supremacy that is central to the British tradition. Once English-speaking Canadians grew more familiar with the impact of the Bill of Rights on citizenship in the United States, an overwhelming majority of them supported the adoption of the Charter of Rights and Freedoms in 1982.

University of British Columbia political scientist Alan Cairns has written extensively on the growth of what he calls "Charter nationalism" in English-speaking Canada. This is the increasing tendency of English-speaking Canadians to define themselves politically as a people whose rights are embodied in the 1982 Charter, and to ignore the Crown's sovereignty and act as if the people were sovereign.

These tendencies run counter to the Quebec view of the relationship between Quebec's citizens and their government. In the abstract, Quebecers are no less dedicated to the ideal of individual human rights than other North Americans. Quebec has its own provincial charter of rights and freedoms that is as encompassing as the 1982 Canadian Charter. For Quebecers, the key question is not whether they should have a constitutionally entrenched charter, but who will control the enforcement of charter rights. Quebec governments since 1982 have been unremittingly hostile to the Canadian Charter of Rights and Freedoms. This hostility is sparked not by objections to specific charter provisions, but because the ultimate arbiter of the charter is the Supreme Court of Canada, which is appointed by the federal government and will always have a majority of English-speaking Canadians among its judges. For Quebec to accept the charter is to therefore accept a status quo in which the relationship of Quebecers to their government, and the range of options available to the Quebec government to "safeguard" the French language, are subject to the approval of the Supreme Court of Canada.

Why is this a problem for Quebecers and not for other Canadians? It goes back to their view of the confederation agreement of 1867, which they see as a constitutional bargain between what they refer to as "two founding peoples": one English-speaking and Protestant, the other French-speaking and Catholic. Today even Quebecers who consider themselves committed federalists think of Canada as a bicultural state in which the constitutional position of the descendants of the "two founding peoples" must be roughly equal. The country's official dual-language policy rests on this vision.

People who hold this view believe that Canada is not a collection of citizens so much as a partnership of "collectivities," or linguistic communities. This mania to define the nation in terms of collectivities is firmly rooted in Quebec politics. Virtually all Quebecers—even those who are not native French speakers—hold that Quebec society consists of three communities: "francophone," "anglophone," and "allophone," the last composed of immigrants whose mother tongues were neither English nor French.

Similarly, almost all Quebecers see Canada as consisting of French Canadians and English Canadians, the latter everyone not French in origin. English Canadians point out that what the "English Canada" Quebecers see to the east and west of them is actually English-*speaking* Canada, a society made up of people from many ethnic, racial, religious, and cultural backgrounds. Most Quebecers dismiss this as irrelevant.

This difference in the conception of Canada lies at the heart of the current Canadian dilemma. English-speaking Canada is beginning to think of itself as a nation and as a constitutionally defined people. English-speaking Canadians conceive of Canada as a nation of individual citizens who are equal before the law—regardless of the language their forebears spoke—and who live in a federation of provinces with equal constitutional status. English-speaking Canada is diverse, like any society of immigrants; to a considerable degree politically disunited, like any democracy spread out over a large area; and a place of dissonance, like any healthy, vital, creative society.

In English-speaking Canada the state is now almost universally seen as the servant of the individual citizens, charged with ensuring their freedom to develop themselves to the fullest. It is true that the Canada of 1867 was defined as a nation of communities; it is equally true today that that vision of Canada is almost completely dead outside Quebec. Thus very few people in Saskatchewan, for example, would worry much about the prospect of having the province's laws subject to the decisions of a Supreme Court that may or may not have anyone from their province sitting on it.

Quebecers, however, view Canada as a nation of collectivities defined primarily by language. The French collectivity lives primarily in one province (Quebec) and constitutes a majority only in that province; the English collectivity controls nine provinces out of ten, and by virtue of its majority status controls the federal government and all its institutions. This leads directly to the conclusion that Quebec needs special powers to defend itself and cannot be subject to the dictates of institutions representing the collective power of "the English." For Quebecers who hold this view the Canadian Charter of Rights and Freedoms is nothing more than a potential instrument of oppression.

In the summer of 1989 the Supreme Court of Canada declared unconstitutional those portions of Quebec's language law forbidding the use of English on public signs in the province. The court stepped outside its role of strict judicial arbiter to suggest that a fair compromise between constitutional requirements and the desire of the Quebec government to stress the French-speaking nature of the province might be if the law allowed bilingual signs in which the French was made more prominent by appearing in larger letters than the English. Quebec rejected that suggestion, and instead used a loophole in the Canadian Charter of Rights and Freedoms (the so-called notwithstanding clause, which allows a legislature to sidestep a number of Charter provisions for up to five years) to re-pass the original language law. English-speaking Canadians were outraged—the same outrage that was primarily responsible for the death of the Meech Lake constitutional accord. That accord had been arrived at in the spring of 1987 by Prime

Minister Brian Mulroney and all the provincial premiers and was intended to secure Quebec's assent to the constitutional changes of 1982.

AN IMPOSSIBLE IMPASSE?

Are the differences that divide Quebecers from other Canadians serious enough to warrant a division of the country, or can a reasonable compromise be reached that will allow Canada to continue to exist with somewhat the same structure it has had up to now?

Journalist and historian William Johnson, a seasoned observer of Quebec politics, writes in *A Canadian Myth* that Quebec nationalists are driven primarily by demonology, seeing "English-Canada" as mainly malevolent and bent on the destruction of French Quebec. Johnson traces the roots of this to the British conquest of Quebec in 1759 and to the myths nurtured by French Quebecers to sustain their culture in the years following. Generations of Church leaders, writers, journalists, and intellectuals were bent on proving to French Quebecers that they were under siege, and that only a strong sense of communal solidarity would allow them to sustain their distinct way of life. Johnson convincingly shows that when Jean Lesage and his Liberals launched the Quiet Revolution in the early 1960s they used language, the images, and the myths of this demonology—combined with the anticolonialism then virulent in the third world—to convince Quebecers that they had been perpetual victims and that the hour of their liberation was at hand.

If Johnson is correct in his analysis, compromise will not be possible because one party to the dispute sees itself—however wrongly—as battling for survival. Indeed, a dispassionate analysis of the events of the last 35 years reveals the complete unwillingness of any Quebec government to unequivocally declare its support for a perpetually united Canada. From the early 1960s the Canadian federation has been akin to a marriage in which one partner has his or her bags perpetually packed in the vestibule, in full sight of the other partner, as a constant reminder of how tenuous the marriage really is. No marriage can go forward on that basis: nor can a political union.

THE DAMAGE DONE

In the decade between the patriation of the Canadian constitution and the adoption of the Charter of Rights and Freedoms in 1982 and the defeat of the Charlottetown Accord in a national referendum in 1992, untold time, talent, money, and goodwill were squandered in an effort to hammer out a constitutional compromise between Quebec and the rest of Canada. The Quebec question is still unresolved, and Canada faces yet another referendum on secession.

The continuing failure to resolve the conflict, despite repeated reassurances that resolution was just around the corner, has reduced Canadians' faith in their leaders and led to a general sense of malaise. Worse, it has produced government by bribery, under which Ottawa has continually attempted to purchase the loyalty of Quebecers by showing them how profitable their membership in the Canadian nation is. Quebec governments have done their utmost to assist that process. In fact, the cornerstone of federalist Premier Robert Bourassa's so-called commitment to a united Canada was *federalisme rentable*–profitable federalism. He saw Canada purely as a balance sheet exercise, never as a nation in the full sense of the word.

Instead of engendering unity, the constant constitutional tinkering between 1982 and 1992 created greater disunity, as expectations were raised and dashed, and then raised and dashed again. Instead of avoiding the issues that divide Canadians the most, and concentrating on the fiscal and economic matters that divide them the least, leaders poured enormous amounts of salt into Canada's constitutional wounds. The consequent national disunity makes tackling contentious problems such as reform of the social welfare system even more difficult than they would otherwise be. Thus Canada stands at the cusp of a major debt crisis because the national government postponed decisive action in its first budget, in early 1994, for fear that it might alienate Quebecers if it cut programs that historically benefited Quebec more than other sections of the country.

Canada has paid a high price for its fundamental disunity in its inability to focus national energies on the achievement of economic objectives. But it continues to pay a high price in other ways as well–in the more than $160 billion poured into Quebec between 1970 and 1990 (as calculated by University of Calgary economist Robert Mansell) in excess of revenues taken in from the province; and in the dollar/interest rate crises that occur every time support for Quebec separatism increases in public opinion polls. Canada today has the highest real interest rates among developed countries, caused in part by a huge debt load, and in part by the ongoing Quebec crisis.

SO LONG, FAREWELL

It is time for Canadians to recognize that the Quebec question cannot be solved unless one of the competing visions of Canada is subordinated to the other. That is not likely to happen. The proof can be found in the results of the referendum on the Charlottetown Accord, which was a jumble of self-contradictory statements that attempted to accommodate both visions of the country into Canada's constitution. Quebecers overwhelmingly rejected the accord because of its emphasis on individual rights and the equality of the provinces; English-speaking Canadians overwhelmingly rejected the accord because it gave Quebec a special status within Canada and Quebecers a set of constitutional rights different from those of other Canadians.

Some Canadian leaders would have Canadians believe that compromise must always be the ultimate objective in a democratic society and that the art of compromise is an especially Canadian one. But when the principles that are being compromised are fundamental to a society's existence, compromise becomes the lowest form of opportunism. That is the case in Canada today, and that is why it is time for Canadians and Quebecers to go their separate ways.

✗ **NO**
Why Political Divorce Must Be Averted
DAVID T. KOYZIS

A MARRIAGE GONE BAD?

David Bercuson likens English Canada's federal union with Quebec to a failing marriage in which one partner continually threatens to leave unless his or her escalating demands are met by the other. Because neither a marriage nor a political union can long survive on such a flimsy basis, he concludes that it is at last time to call it quits and to allow Quebec to find its own way among the family of sovereign states. Indeed, such a parting of the ways could become inevitable, in which case we shall all simply have to adjust to the new reality as best we can, whatever our respective sentiments and whatever difficulties are involved.

Nevertheless, to extend the marital metaphor further, there are reasons to hope that divorce might be averted and that the partners can be persuaded to work out their differences and seek reconciliation for the sake of everyone involved. These reasons can be grouped into two broad categories: first, to avoid the greater evils that would surely follow such a breakup and, second, to secure the greater good made possible by maintaining and renewing the federal union.

AVOIDING DIVORCE

First, when a marriage ends, there are always casualties, particularly the children who are left with lifelong scars. For this and other reasons, the law, while permitting divorce, places obstacles in the way of those seeking it. However, as Allen Buchanan has pointed out, the whole concept of territorial secession is one for which there is a regrettable lack of theoretical reflection within the several traditions of political thought.[1] International law is generally recognized to favour the territorial integrity of existing states,[2] and even domestic law almost never provides for conditions under which a state will acquiesce in its own dismemberment. The former Soviet constitution of 1977 was one of a very few to provide for the separation of a constituent republic from the union (Art. 72), yet even this document did not bother to set out conditions under which this could take place.

Not surprisingly then, Canada's written Constitution Acts make no provision for the secession of a province from confederation. Nor can an unwritten convention permitting secession be said unquestionably to exist. Thus any attempt to take Quebec out of confederation would move us onto uncertain and potentially dangerous legal ground. Here the analogy to a divorce breaks down, for divorce presupposes a generally recognized legal framework intended to mitigate its negative consequences, while secession does not. In such an ambiguous context, any claim to a unilateral right of self-determination implies an unwillingness to submit to ordinary constitutional or political processes and thus involves considerable risk. In the real world, of course, states do break up. But they do not do so easily. More often than not, bloodshed accompanies their breakup. The list is long: the partition of India and Pakistan in 1947, culminating in severe intercommunal violence and hundreds of thousands of deaths; the three-decades-long Eritrean–Ethiopian war, finally ending in 1993 with Eritrean independence; the failed Biafran war for independence from Nigeria between 1967 and 1970; the breakup of the Soviet Union, which has been accompanied by a series of brush-fire wars along and within the new international boundaries; and, most tragically of all, the shattering of Yugoslavia, with its unleashing of pent-up ethnic hatreds and countless attendant atrocities. Even the peaceful separations of Norway and Sweden in 1905 and of the Czech and Slovak Republics in 1993 involved much rancour if not outright bloodshed.

The principal reason for such violence is that distinct ethnic communities rarely fall within neat geographical boundaries. Once a line is drawn, whether by an invading army, as on Cyprus, or by a colonial power, as in India, or even by mutual agreement, as in the former Soviet Union, people are inevitably left on the wrong side of seemingly arbitrary borders. The number of ethnic Russians living outside Russia proper is nearly as large as the population of Canada, and they undoubtedly have difficulty comprehending why their previous loyalty to Moscow should now be replaced by allegiance to Almaty, Bishkek, Kiev, or Riga. The existence of such a sizable diaspora population is an obstacle to political stability in the region. Even here in Canada the two founding peoples do not neatly separate themselves along provincial boundaries.

An attempted secession by Quebec would meet with domestic opposition on at least three fronts: (1) from profederalist francophones, (2) from anglophones and allophones who have assimilated into the English-speaking community, and (3) from aboriginal peoples who claim the northern two-thirds of the province as their own. Members of these communities have made it clear that they do not wish to be part of an independent Quebec. It will be difficult, if not impossible, to convince such groups that, if Quebec has the right to leave Canada, they do not have a similar right to leave Quebec. This indicates that the logic of secession is difficult to limit once it has come to be accepted in some form. Indeed the only effective way to stop it going too far is by brute force, the use of which most people, even Quebec separatists, would prefer to avoid. Yet one cannot will the end without also willing the means.

Bernard Crick has observed that politics is the ongoing task of peacefully conciliating diversity, which entails a minimal willingness on the part of all parties to compromise and to accept less than ideal solutions to potential conflict.[3] But it is difficult to imagine a possible compromise that will satisfy separatists, on the one side, and the Cree and Inuit, on the other. This is due to the simple fact that their respective claims are mutually incompatible and that one of the parties wants no part of the very conciliating institutions that might make such a peaceful settlement possible. Irreconcilable claims coupled with an unwillingness to abide by an authoritative settlement of such claims is a recipe for trouble, at the very least, and possibly much worse. For all the headaches entailed in maintaining Canadian unity, it is nevertheless preferable to the likely alternatives.

THE FAULT IS NOT WITH FEDERALISM

But to underscore the dangers of *dis*unity, as we have done above, is to tell only half the story. There are also positive reasons for maintaining a united Canada and the federal system on which it is based. To begin with, the federal government is legally and constitutionally obligated to protect the rights of all Canadians, whatever their mother tongue and wherever their residence. Furthermore, Ottawa is under special obligations towards certain linguistic and religious minorities, as well as towards Aboriginal communities, as prescribed in the Constitution Act, 1867, and the Constitution Act, 1982. The federal government cannot simply wash its hands of such obligations through bilateral negotiations with a single province.

But even if it could do so, there are other, larger reasons to defend Canada's federal union with Quebec. We Canadians tend to assume erroneously that our country is one of a very few encompassing more than one dominant culture and language. In fact, homogeneous states such as Sweden and Japan are the exception rather than the rule,[4] while the vast majority of states throughout the world contain two or more geographically delimited cultural or "national" communities. In such diverse polities the normal political process demands that justice be done to these communities and that their respective interests be harmonized to the extent possible. Where this is successful, as for example in Switzerland, mechanisms have evolved enabling potentially antagonistic communities to live together under a common legal and political framework.

Canada has admittedly had a spotty record with respect to working out such mechanisms of accommodation between English and French. From the time of the conquest of the French in 1759 up to Confederation in 1867, British policy vacillated between attempted assimilation and accommodation, the latter being made necessary by an understandable refusal of French Canadians to disappear into a dominant anglophone population and by their dogged determination to preserve their unique culture in North America. After 1867 the creation of a federal system offered a promising way of allowing French and English to live side by side by recognizing the majority status of French Canadians within a single territorial entity while protecting minority francophone communities outside Quebec and anglophone communities within Quebec.

Once again, relations between the two founding communities were sometimes strained, and francophones were often made to feel like second-class citizens in their own country, particularly in those provinces with anglophone majorities. Nevertheless, such strained relations cannot be attributed to Canada's federal system as such, which in fact served to mitigate some of the negative effects of the old anglophone–francophone rivalry. Canada's misfortune is that the principle of power-sharing across linguistic lines, which has normally functioned on the federal level, did not always filter down to the provincial level, where the British constitutional tradition of unconstrained, single-party majority rule was more likely to make itself felt. Nor did it significantly affect Canada's one-time imperial connection with Britain, which necessitated the pursuit of policies, such as conscription in 1917 and 1944, that clashed with francophone sensibilities.

Moreover, Canada has been saddled with an electoral system that effectively discourages principled parties or parties with national aspirations and instead encourages regionally based parties. In the federal elections of 1993 and 1997, under our current first-past-the-post system, the Progressive Conservative and New Democratic parties were severely underrepresented in the House of Commons, simply because their popular support was not sufficiently concentrated to enable them to win more than a handful of seats. On the other hand, the Bloc Québécois was overrepresented in the Commons after both elections, because this same system places a premium on geographically concentrated voter support. In such a context, recent elections have artificially accentuated rather than bridged Canada's regional cleavages. The electoral map of Canada makes the country look more divided than it actually is.

To summarize, despite the shortcomings of several facets of our political system, federalism, with its principle of unity amid diversity, nevertheless remains basically sound and ought not to be abandoned. It is well suited to a polity characterized by cultural duality or plurality insofar as it enables geographically defined communities—some of which might call themselves "nations"—to govern themselves in those fields relevant to their own regional and local needs, while also providing for the common defence and central coordination of economic and other policy areas of shared concern. If separatist sentiment has grown among the people of Quebec in the past thirty years, it is not because of the failure of federalism, but because of the inadequacy of those very elements in our system most antithetical to federalism, such as our electoral system, our one-party governments, our unrepresentative Senate, and our executive-dominated parliamentary bodies. If reform is to take place, it should start with these latter institutions and then move on to federalism.

MAKING ROOM FOR GREATER DIVERSITY

At least two basic reforms would seem to be in order, one of which would affect directly the workings of our federal system and the other indirectly. We begin with the latter.

The first necessary reform would be to change our electoral system before it destroys Canada. The first-past-the-post system, also known as winner-take-all or single-member plurality (SMP), divides a country into a number of territorial constituencies, or ridings, with roughly equal population. Canada now has 301 such ridings. Each riding elects a single member to Parliament on the basis of plurality and not absolute majority. In other words, in a closely contested three-way race, the winning candidate could win the seat with as little as 34 percent of the popular vote, meaning that most citizens would have opposed the "winning" candidate. Taken together, these outcomes badly distort representation in the House of Commons as a whole, sometimes resulting in governments with inadequate representation from Quebec (e.g., Joe Clark's Progressive Conservative government in 1979–80) or from the west (e.g., Pierre Trudeau's Liberal government from 1980 to 1984). Thus an increasing number of Canadians believe it is time for a change. Short of this, the merits of federalism will continue to be eclipsed by those elements of our political system least capable of accommodating diversity.

Most European countries operate with some form of proportional representation (PR), which ensures that a party's true popular support is reflected fairly accurately in the parliamentary body. If, say, a socialist party received 37 percent of the popular vote, then under pure PR it would be given 37 percent of the seats in Parliament. In this way Parliament becomes a genuine microcosm of public opinion. Many Canadians believe it is time for this country to discard SMP, which distorts representation and creates artificial majority governments, and to adopt some form of PR. Nick Loenen, a former MLA from British Columbia, has recently argued in favour of the single transferable vote (STV), a form of PR that allows voters to rank candidates in order of preference in multimember ridings.[5] Even *The Globe and Mail*, which styles itself "Canada's National Newspaper," has published more than one editorial in favour of abandoning our current antiquated and divisive electoral system and adopting some form of PR.[6]

Perhaps the most appropriate electoral system for Canada would combine the best features of both PR and SMP. The German system gives citizens two votes, one for a local candidate elected on the basis of SMP, and another for a party list elected according to a modified PR. This mixed member system has worked well in that country for nearly half a century and has been adopted by several other countries since then. Although the partisan composition of the German Bundestag (the lower chamber of parliament) does not reflect true popular support as accurately as does pure PR, the results are nevertheless more proportional than unadulterated SMP would be. Some variant of this mixed system could well be put to use here in Canada.

A second major reform would see us alter radically the way we have come to conceive our federal system. Many of the strains on this system originate in clashing visions over the nature of Canada. Is Canada a compact between two founding peoples, as many Québécois believe? Is it a partnership among ten provinces, as westerners tend to hold? Or is it a community of citizens, as traditional liberals would have it? Canada can plausibly claim to be any and all of these, and none of these visions is necessarily incompatible with the others—*unless, that is, the language of equality is brought into the picture.* Here again we run up against the limits of the marital metaphor. Canada cannot simultaneously be a community of two equal partners *and* of ten equal provinces *and* of thirty million equal citizens. To speak of equality in this context forces us to try to quantify that which cannot easily be quantified. Moreover, because equality is so often confused with sameness, the use of this term tempts us to overlook the considerable differences separating the two linguistic and several provincial communities making up Canada.

For purposes of renewing our federal system then, we Canadians would do well to abandon the language of equality. We might better speak of equity or justice, which would avoid inflexible abstractions and recognize the unique needs and characteristics of each of these communities. With this change in language and the worldview that flows out of it, we should be able to accept that not every province need have the same relationship to Ottawa and that our federal arrangement can be *asymmetrical.* As journalist Michel Auger has pointed out, the Scots were able to vote to revive their own parliament without Britons automatically assuming that every other constituent part of the United Kingdom needed its own assembly too. In similar fashion, Spain has gradually devolved power from the centre to seventeen autonomous communities, not all of which relate to Madrid in exactly the same way.[7] If Europe is able to experiment with asymmetrical federalism, there is in principle no insurmountable obstacle to its implementation here in Canada.

Quebec *is* different, and it is time for all Canadians to recognize this obvious reality once again, as we have always done in some fashion throughout our history. With its French language and its unique civil law code, Quebec has a strong case for seeking greater autonomy over its own affairs. Contrary to the fears of some, granting this autonomy need not harm the interests of other provinces, and it might even allow the west a greater voice in those issues on which Quebec has opted out. Ultimately, then, with a little imagination and a willingness to compromise, we might yet succeed in saving Canadian unity and thereby securing the future for our children.

NOTES

1. Allen Buchanan, *Secession: The Morality of Political Divorce from Fort Sumter to Lithuania and Quebec* (Boulder: Westview Press, 1991).

2. See Gerhart von Glahn, *Law Among Nations: An Introduction to Public International Law,* 7th ed. (Needham Heights, MA: Allyn & Bacon, 1995), especially pp. 104–105, 106–107. Von Glahn points out the disagreement among legal writers concerning the extent, applicability, and even the validity of a right to self-determination. Moreover, there is an apparent contradiction within the Charter of the United Nations between the right of a state to territorial integrity (Article 2(4)) and the right to self-determi-

nation (Article 1). In practice, the UN's promotion of self-determination has tended to be applied largely, if not exclusively, to colonial situations.

3. Bernard Crick, *In Defence of Politics,* 4th ed. (London: Weidenfeld & Nicolson, 1992).

4. Even Sweden has its Finno–Ugric-speaking Saami minority in the north, and Japan has the Ainu residing on the northern island of Hokkaido.

5. Nick Loenen, *Citizenship and Democracy: A Case for Proportional Representation* (Toronto: Dundurn Press, 1997).

6. See, for example, the issues dated Monday, January 27, 1997, and Saturday, March 15, 1997.

7. Michel C. Auger, "No thanks to equality of provinces," *The Globe and Mail,* Tuesday, September 16, 1997, p. A17.

Postscript

While Bercuson argues that letting Quebec go its way would be beneficial for Canada, he provides little discussion of the process by which this would be achieved. Koyzis warns us of the potential dangers for violence that such a breakup would entail. The process by which Quebec would separate and Canada would reconstitute itself has received little attention until recently. One scholar who has studied this in detail is Robert A. Young. He has carried out an exhaustive study of the potential scenarios surrounding the secession of Quebec and the major issues that must be negotiated such as citizenship, national debt, borders, armed forces, economic relations, currency, First Nations, and mobility, to name only a few of the myriad issues. Robert A. Young, *The Secession of Quebec and the Future of Canada* (Montreal: McGill-Queen's University Press, 1995) is perhaps the most comprehensive guide available to the many questions surrounding Quebec secession.

Young reminds readers that secessions are rarely peaceful. He notes: "Most secessionist movements are violent, and most secessions are contested" (p. 291). Even though some cases of peaceful secession can be found, such as the dissolution of Czechoslovakia, Young notes that these may be the result of unique historical circumstances that are not easily replicated elsewhere. However, Young does see a peaceful secession as a possibility if certain preconditions are met. Thus, he notes: "There must be a clear referendum question, a fair campaign, a Quebec commitment to economic and social policies that are not highly offensive or costly to Canadians, and a sense among people in ROC [rest of Canada] that the separation would not very much threaten their collective future. Similarly, Quebecers must not feel deeply threatened or oppressed ..." (p. 290). While Young thinks that such a scenario is not out of the realm of the possible, he warns that any move to contest Quebec's existing borders, as Bercuson and Cooper suggest in their book, "could quickly lead to organized violence" (p. 290).

While arguing that the dangers of secession should not be taken lightly, Koyzis does not believe that another round of constitutional discussions will necessarily solve the problem. He argues instead for greater attention to electoral reform, which he sees as holding greater potential for reducing some of the current discontent in Canada. The issues that he raises here will be examined in more detail in Issue Nineteen.

PART THREE

INSTITUTIONS

*Is the doctrine of individual
ministerial responsibility workable?*

*Does the institutionalized cabinet
provide for good government?*

Should party discipline be relaxed?

*Do the courts practise judicial
self-restraint?*

*Should Parliament review Supreme
Court nominees?*

ISSUE**ELEVEN**

Is the Doctrine of Individual Ministerial Responsibility Workable?

✔ **YES**
KENNETH KERNAGHAN, "Is the Doctrine of Ministerial Responsibility Workable?"

✘ **NO**
HUGH SEGAL, "Ministerial Accountability: Confronting the Myth"

An important element of government in Canada is the doctrine of individual ministerial responsibility and accountability. This constitutional convention stipulates that a minister must answer all questions in relation to the actions of his or her department and resign in the event of serious administrative error. Accordingly, when something goes wrong in a department, it is the minister who takes *full* responsibility. The minister responds to queries made in the legislature and elsewhere about the matter, and in theory resigns if it attains serious proportions. The doctrine ensures that public servants are accountable to the public through the responsible minister. The doctrine also establishes a clear, direct locus of responsibility. There is no need to track down the person who literally committed the act under review. One has only to approach the relevant minister.

In recent years, a number of highly publicized events have led to a questioning of the doctrine of individual ministerial responsibility. In 1991, the former Iraqi ambassador to the United States, a man who had staunchly defended the aggressive actions of his country in the Persian Gulf War, suddenly was admitted to Canada as a landed immigrant. A few years later, a young Somalian boy was tortured to death by some Canadian soldiers, an event that the Defence Department allegedly tried to cover up. In the 1980s, the government-regulated blood supply system purportedly failed to institute tests for HIV, with the result that some Canadians became afflicted with the virus through blood transfusions. Finally, in 1995 a senior official in the Department of Justice wrote a letter, which became public, that accused former prime minister Brian Mulroney of engaging in criminal activities.

In all of these occurrences, appointed officials had seemingly made serious mistakes. At a minimum, the hope was for a thorough consideration of the matters and for appropriate action to be taken. The minister would answer the questions relating to these issues, and those responsible would suffer the consequences. But that did not happen, at least not to a sufficient extent for some. Instead, these and other matters became highly politicized—making it difficult to discern the truth—and seemingly no one wanted to take responsibility. The doctrine promised accountability, but in the minds of many people this was not achieved.

For critics of the doctrine of individual ministerial responsibility, this outcome is to be expected. By placing the full responsibility with *political* officials, the doctrine guarantees an environment hostile to the truth; here, politics becomes paramount. A more sensible doctrine might endeavour to locate responsibility for administrative or operational mistakes with those who actually committed them, namely the appointed officials. Ministers cannot possibly know all that goes on in their departments, so it seems pure folly to act as if they do. Without the presence of high-profile ministers, it might be possible to conduct a more disinterested review of the matter, and a greater sense of responsibility would probably develop among the ranks of appointed officials.

But this, too, has its problems. Looking for the official responsible for the act might amount to an attempt to find a needle in a haystack. More seriously, it might hurt the nonpartisan nature of the civil service, for public servants now would be more clearly identified with certain operations and policies. The attractiveness of the doctrine of individual ministerial responsibility is that it ensures that elected officials—political officials—are the ones accountable for the behaviour of government, something that seems consonant with a democratic form of government.

In the readings, Kenneth Kernaghan, who has authored many articles on individual ministerial responsibility, argues that the doctrine is workable. Hugh Segal, who served as a senior political advisor in various governments, contends that the doctrine is fatally flawed and changes must be made to ensure greater accountability in government.

✔ YES
Is the Doctrine of Ministerial Responsibility Workable?
KENNETH KERNAGHAN

THE IMPORTANCE OF MINISTERIAL RESPONSIBILITY

The doctrine of ministerial responsibility is the cornerstone of Canada's parliamentary democracy. This doctrine (sometimes called a convention or principle) has worked well since Canada's founding and it continues to work well. Understanding its purposes and requirements is essential to understanding the way in which our political system should, and does, operate. The doctrine prescribes the nature of the relationships that should exist among politicians, public servants, and the public. We must be careful, therefore, that reforms in the machinery and culture of government do not unduly weaken this fundamental doctrine of our Constitution; reforms should be made within the general framework of the doctrine's central requirements. It is notable, however, that the doctrine is not inflexible or unchanging. Indeed, its meaning and application have gradually evolved over time.

Ministerial responsibility is a constitutional convention, that is, it is an essential element of the Constitution but it is not specified in written law. The major purpose of the convention is to ensure that someone in government is answerable for each government action, regardless of whether it is possible to pinpoint the person(s) who actually took the action. The convention does this by protecting the authority and accountability of elected officials, namely cabinet ministers, for government decisions. Appointed officials (generally known as public servants) provide policy advice to ministers and make many decisions under authority delegated to them by ministers and by the legislature. However, ministers alone answer to the legislature, and through the legislature to the public, for their own actions and for the actions of public servants.

Historically, there has been considerable debate over the appropriate interpretation and application of the doctrine of ministerial responsibility in particular cases of real or alleged government wrongdoing. This debate has been heightened in recent years by such events as the Al-Mashat affair in which public servants were named and blamed in public; the decision in the Krever Inquiry on tainted blood not to name or blame either ministers or senior public servants; and the allegations made by public servants against former prime minister Mulroney in the Airbus affair. Increasingly also, questions have been raised as to whether the doctrine is compatible with certain reforms in the structures and processes of government. As explained later in this essay, analysis of these developments suggests that much of the criticism of the doctrine results from misunderstanding of its requirements or from manipulative interpretation of these requirements for partisan purposes.

The doctrine of ministerial responsibility does not always work perfectly, in part because the manner in which it is interpreted and applied has significant consequences for the electoral fortunes of political parties. It is both entertaining and disquieting to see the different ways political parties interpret the doctrine, depending on whether they are the governing party or an opposition party. Occasionally, there are fierce political debates about ministerial responsibility that almost invariably involve calls for a minister's resignation. These well-publicized and highly partisan events tend to obscure the fact that, in general, *the doctrine works quietly, steadily, and successfully each day as a framework for the exercise of power and responsibility in the political system.* It "involves the daily provision of information and explanations, to Parliament and the public, about the activities of the minister's department, and conversely a daily sensitization of the department to the views and concerns of Parliament and the people. It involves day-to-day direction to departments and the correction of problems that may arise."[1]

Criticisms of ministerial responsibility typically have one or more of the following deficiencies. They neglect the doctrine's important links to other elements of the political system; they misinterpret or misrepresent the purpose and operation of the doctrine; and they fail to provide a workable alternative. Nevertheless, given the importance of the doctrine and concerns about its viability, it is sensible to ask whether the traditional doctrine[2] can simply be reaffirmed or whether it needs to be reformulated—or even replaced.

The second section of this essay explains the meaning of ministerial responsibility and the third section examines its relationship to the constitutional conventions of political neutrality and public service anonymity. This is followed in the fourth section by an examination of recent developments that have put the doctrine under stress, and in the fifth section by an explanation of the considerations that must be taken into account for a full understanding of its meaning and implications.

THE MEANING OF MINISTERIAL RESPONSIBILITY

While the focus of this essay is on *individual* ministerial responsibility, it is important to explain the closely related concept of *collective* ministerial responsibility (often referred to as cabinet responsibility or cabinet solidarity). Collective ministerial responsibility has implications for the cabinet as a whole, as well as for individual ministers. It requires that the prime minister and the cabinet must resign if the House of Commons passes a vote of no confidence in the government. It requires also that individual ministers must support cabinet decisions in public or submit their resignation. Throughout the rest of this essay, the term ministerial responsibility refers to individual, rather than collective, responsibility.

Individual ministerial responsibility has two related components—the resignation component and the answerability component. According to *the resignation component*, ministers must answer to the legislature (and legislative committees) for their own acts and those of administrative subordinates. In the event of serious departmental error or serious personal misconduct, answerability takes the form of ministerial resignation. According to *the answerability component*, where the gravity of the error does not warrant ministerial resignation and where the error was made by administrative subordinates, ministers must explain to the legislature what occurred, take appropriate disciplinary action within the department against the public servant(s) who made the mistake, and adopt measures to ensure that the error does not happen again.

Critics of ministerial responsibility often describe the doctrine as a myth because ministers do not adhere fully to its resignation component. These critics note that no minister in Canada has ever resigned on account of mistakes made by his or her administrative subordinates. Indeed, it is generally agreed that it is unreasonable to hold ministers accountable, in the form of resignation, for the acts of administrative subordinates about which ministers could not be expected to have personal knowledge. But the critics see only part of the picture. They ignore the fact that ministers often do resign when they have been personally involved in wrongdoing (e.g., breaking the law) or when they have personally directed public servants to take a specific action that turns out to be a serious mistake. More importantly, however, these critics ignore the fact that ministers usually fulfil the answerability requirement of the doctrine. Ministers routinely answer questions in the legislature about actual or alleged governmental or departmental mistakes. A *"fundamental principle of responsible government"* is *"that it is Ministers and not public servants who are accountable to the House of Commons for what is done by the Government."*[3]

The answerability component of individual ministerial responsibility has three additional requirements that further reinforce its importance as a mechanism for ensuring government accountability to the legislature and the public. These requirements are as follows:

1. Ministers answer to the legislature, in the form of *explanation,* for the acts of their predecessors.

2. On behalf of their ministers, public servants answer to legislative committees for administrative matters, but not for policy or politically controversial matters; this answerability takes the form of explanation, not defence, of departmental actions.

3. Ministers answer publicly for the acts of their administrative subordinates so as to protect public servants' political neutrality and anonymity.

Ministerial responsibility can usefully be viewed along a continuum where the extent of the minister's responsibility depends on the extent to which he or she was personally involved in taking or directing a particular action. At one extreme, the minister may be required to resign for a personal violation of the law; at the other extreme, the minister may simply be required to provide information to the legislature on an error made by a public servant well down in the administrative hierarchy. Just because ministers must answer for the mistakes of their departmental subordinates does not mean that they are to blame for the mistakes.

POLITICAL NEUTRALITY AND PUBLIC SERVICE ANONYMITY

Critics of ministerial responsibility often ignore or downplay its close links to two other constitutional conventions, namely those of political neutrality and public service anonymity. Changes in one of these conventions can have important consequences for the others. This interdependent relationship can easily be demonstrated by reference to the convention of political neutrality, which requires that public servants not engage in activities that impair—or seem to impair—their political impartiality.[4] Taken together, the conventions of political neutrality and ministerial responsibility require, among other things, that "public servants execute policy decisions loyally, irrespective of the philosophy and programs of the party in power and regardless of their personal opinions; as a result, public servants enjoy security of tenure during good behaviour and satisfactory performance."[5] If responsibility for the public defence of certain government decisions is shifted from ministers to public servants, there is considerable danger that public servants will become involved in partisan political debate as they try to defend these decisions. If they engage in public controversy, including possible clashes with their ministers as to who is responsible for what, their loyalty will come into question and ministers will be tempted to appoint senior-level public servants on the basis of partisanship rather than merit. One result would be the replacement of such political appointees with each change of government and a consequent loss in the continuity and expertise provided by professional public servants.

Similarly, the conventions of public service anonymity and ministerial responsibility require that public servants "provide forthright and objective advice to ministers in private and in confidence" and "ministers protect the anonymity of public servants by publicly accepting responsibility for departmental decisions."[6] Ministers are unlikely to take responsibility for the actions of public servants who become involved in public controversy, especially if this involvement embarrasses the minister or the government.

Some of the critics of ministerial responsibility, far from being concerned about a decline in political neutrality or public service anonymity, favour the "politicization" of the senior levels of the public service, that is, they support the appointment of senior officials on partisan grounds and their replacement with new partisan appointees in the event of a change of government. This "patronage" system would be similar to the system in the United States, which has in recent years been compared unfavourably to our own system because of our emphasis on merit, rather than partisanship, in senior appointments. Those in favour of political appointments argue that the appointees will be more dedicated to carrying out the government's policies and more attuned to the political implications of these policies. It is understandable that ministers should sometimes be frustrated by the advice of public servants who carry out their duty to explain the negative as well as the positive implications of policies that ministers want to pursue. But few Canadians would want government decisions to be made largely on partisan political grounds, in ignorance of some of the probable social, economic, or financial consequences.

Another common argument for political appointments is that long-serving public servants are too resistant to change and must, therefore, be regularly replaced by "fresh blood" with new ideas from outside government. This argument ignores the enormous changes that have recently been made with the loyal and creative assistance of public servants in governments across the country, most notably in Alberta and Ontario. It also ignores the loyal and effective implementation of such major federal government initiatives as the dismantling of the National Energy Program and the introduction of NAFTA and the GST. It is especially notable that the Harris government in Ontario carried out massive reforms while expounding and following the traditional requirements of ministerial responsibility and political neutrality. Moreover, many public servants have responded positively to the encouragement of politicians that they be more innovative and take more risks.

The general view, which has been reinforced rather than weakened by recent practice, is that ministers and, indeed, all Canadians are best served by public servants who help to ensure continuity and a smooth transition from one governing party to another and who provide professional, nonpartisan advice and management based on experience and expertise. There is at the same time continuing support for the practice of having ministers make political appointments to their own offices, as opposed to the public service, to provide them with partisan political advice.

Proponents of political appointments also ignore the fact that several other forces are moving the public service toward greater politicization, including the expansion of political rights for public servants and the decline in public service anonymity. We must recognize the systemic effects of these changes and the fact that, taken together, these changes will lead to much greater politicization than any one change considered by itself. This increased involvement of public servants in partisan politics and public controversy tends to undermine the ministers' authority and accountability for government decisions.

LESSONS FROM RECENT EVENTS

As noted earlier, debate over the meaning of ministerial responsibility arises in large part from insufficient understanding of its requirements and attempts to use it for partisan or personal advantage. Consider the following two cases by way of example.

In 1991, considerable public controversy arose from the news that government officials in Canada had expedited the admission of Mohammed Al-Mashat, the Iraqi ambassador to the United States and his country's spokesperson during the Gulf War, as a landed immigrant to Canada. Canadians were treated to the spectacle of public servants being called before a parliamentary committee of inquiry during which ministers blamed public servants, politicians blamed one another, public servants took different positions from one another, and a senior public servant and an opposition member of Parliament engaged in a remarkably undiplomatic exchange. Several politicians tried either to lay blame or to avoid blame by providing creative interpretations of the doctrine of ministerial responsibility. Most, but not all, public servants acted in accordance with the doctrine's formal requirements and the conduct of one public servant was "text-book perfection" in its conformity to these requirements.[7]

The second case involves the Krever commission, which was established in 1993 to inquire into events surrounding the infection of as many as three thousand Canadians by tainted blood. A considerable number of groups and individuals, both within and outside government, argued vigorously that they should not be named or blamed in the commission's report. The Federal Court gave the commission the right to blame certain federal officials and volunteers but prohibited the blaming of former ministers and senior public servants who headed the federal and provincial Departments of Health during the time the problem occurred. Monique Bégin, who had been the federal minister of Health at the time, wrote to the commission to request that she be included among those persons named to appear before the commission to answer questions. She said that her action was "a matter of personal morality and integrity" and that "ministerial responsibility is the cornerstone of our executive government.... Politicians must definitely be accountable and I am therefore prepared to join the 'named' people to answer the inquiries of your commission."[8] Ironically and coincidentally, on the same day, General Jean Boyle, chief of the Defence staff, in an appearance before the Somalia Inquiry into military misconduct during the 1993 peacekeeping mission, refused to take responsibility for improper conduct in the Department of Defence and accused certain senior officers of a lack of integrity and moral fibre.[9]

Several learning points emerge from these cases. First, no constitutional doctrine, whether it is ministerial responsibility or some alternative, will work well if those who know, or should know, its requirements do not fulfil them. Personal integrity and commitment to preserving the integrity of our system of parliamentary democracy are essential to the doctrine's workability. Second, despite efforts to interpret the doctrine for personal and partisan purposes, it *did* serve, even in these highly politicized cases, as the framework for determining the responsibilities of the politicians and public servants involved. The central question was not whether ministerial responsibility was a myth, but what it required of government officials in these particular cases. Third, there is a need for a comprehensive and comprehensible statement of the doctrine's requirements.

THE DIRECT ACCOUNTABILITY OF PUBLIC SERVANTS

As explained above, ministerial responsibility protects the authority and accountability of ministers. However, critics of the doctrine and of the related notions of political neutrality and public service anonymity often argue that the doctrine permits public servants to avoid public accountability for their actions. It is true that public servants are not held *publicly* accountable in the sense of having to defend their decisions in public; they are, however, subject to administrative sanctions within their department. It is true also that the public is not informed as to the nature and severity of these sanctions; the public is obliged to take the word of ministers that, to the extent that public servants are to blame, they will be appropriately disciplined. However, if the names of public servants who were disciplined were made public, they would suffer double discipline, once by internal penalties and a second time by public notoriety.

There is considerable support for a system of direct public service accountability, according to which public servants would answer directly to legislative committees. Having public servants answer directly for a modest number of specifically assigned administrative matters might not cause undue harm to the doctrine of ministerial responsibility. However, direct accountability for a substantial number of *administrative* matters would require a careful separation of policy matters from administrative matters so that ministers and public servants would be clear as to who is to be held accountable for what. Making such a separation would not be easy. Holding public servants accountable for *policy* recommendations and decisions would be even more problematic. The potential consequences would be as follows:

> Relations between ministers and public servants would be complicated by the difficulty of distinguishing their respective contributions to the development of specific policies. The answerability of public servants to Parliament would compete with their accountability and loyalty to their minister. The remaining healthy component of ministerial responsibility—the answerability of ministers—would be severely weakened.... There would be a dramatic decline in public service anonymity and the senior echelons of the public service would be politicized. Public servants would be compelled to defend their policy recommendations before parliamentary committees and the public. Officials would become personally associated with

particular policies and would, therefore, become involved in political controversy. Security of tenure for senior officials would be replaced by a system of political appointments and a consequent turnover of public servants with a change in government.[10]

The issue of direct accountability has arisen recently in the context of proposals to create agencies within government that would be separate from government departments and that would operate in a more "business-like" fashion. These agencies would implement policies formulated by departments and, according to some proponents of this agency approach, should answer directly to legislative committees. Experience with Crown corporations and regulatory agencies suggests, however, that the opposition parties, the media, and the general public would try to hold ministers "politically accountable" for these new agencies. To protect both the authority and the accountability of ministers, the heads of these agencies could be required to answer directly to a minister on the basis of a contractual agreement specifying the performance levels the agencies would be expected to achieve. Ministers would in turn answer to the legislature for the agencies' performance. It is extremely important that decisions to adopt new forms of organization be made in full awareness of the implications for ministerial responsibility and, indeed, for democratic accountability in general.

CONCLUSION

A more practicable objective than seeking an alternative to ministerial responsibility is to specify its meaning and requirements—and to help politicians, public servants, the media, and the citizenry understand them. We should apply the doctrine in accordance with its central requirements, but we should keep in mind that the doctrine is a constitutional convention capable of gradual evolution to cope with major changes in our political or bureaucratic systems.

A clear statement of the doctrine's requirements would provide a valuable basis for their proper application. The explanation of the requirements set out earlier in this essay provides a partial basis for developing such a statement. But there is a need for elaboration on the subtleties and complexities of the doctrine. A full statement of the meaning and application of the doctrine should take account of at least the considerations shown below. These considerations also provide a summary of the main arguments presented in this essay.

1. The doctrine of ministerial responsibility is the cornerstone of democratic governance. It is intended to protect the authority and accountability of ministers for government decisions.

2. The doctrine is a positive and pervasive force for accountability in the myriad day-to-day operations of government.

3. The meaning and application of the doctrine are often distorted by undue emphasis on ministerial blame and resignation. While ministers are responsible for answering to the legislature for the errors of administrative subordinates, they do not thereby accept personal blame for these errors.

4. Similarly, while ministers are responsible for answering to the legislature for errors committed during the tenure of their predecessors, they do not thereby accept personal blame for these errors.

5. It is generally recognized that it is unreasonable to hold a minister personally responsible in the form of resignation for the errors of administrative subordinates.

6. Ministers usually resign in the event of serious personal misconduct or in cases where they have directed public servants to take a specific action that turns out to be a serious mistake.

7. On behalf of their ministers, public servants answer to legislative committees for administrative matters, but not for policy or politically controversial matters; this answerability takes the form of explanation, not defence, of departmental actions.

8. Ministers are responsible for answering to the legislature for policy directives given to nondepartmental bodies (e.g., Crown corporations, regulatory agencies) but not for the day-to-day administration of these bodies.

9. Ministers have a commitment to protect the conventions of political neutrality and public service anonymity.

A carefully crafted—and widely accepted—statement on ministerial responsibility that takes careful account of these considerations would help to ensure that the doctrine continues to work well.

NOTES

1. Government of Canada, Privy Council Office, Deputy Minister's Task Force, *Discussion Paper on Values and Ethics in the Public Service* (Ottawa: Privy Council Office, 1996), p. 12.

2. For more comprehensive explanations of the doctrine, see Government of Canada, Privy Council Office, *Responsibility in the Constitution*, prepared in 1977 and published in 1979 as part of a submission by the Privy Council Office to the Royal Commission on Financial Management and Accountability; Kenneth Kernaghan, "Power, Parliament and Public Servants in Canada: Ministerial Responsibility Reexamined," *Canadian Public Policy–Analyse de politiques* 3 (1979): 383–396; and S.L. Sutherland, "Responsible Government and Ministerial Responsibility: Every Reform Is Its Own Problem," *Canadian Journal of Political Science* 24, no. 1 (1991): 91–120.

3. Government of Canada, Privy Council Office, *Notes on the Responsibilities of Public Servants in Relation to Parliamentary Committees* (Ottawa: Privy Council Office, 1990), p. 3, emphasis in original.

4. For elaboration on this convention, see Kenneth Kernaghan, "Politics, Policy and Public Servants: Political Neutrality Revisited," *Canadian Public Administration* 19 (Fall 1976): 432–456.

5. Ibid., p. 433.

6. Ibid., p. 433.

7. S.L. Sutherland, "The Al-Mashat Affair: Administrative Accountability in Parliamentary Institutions," *Canadian Public Administration* 34, no. 4 (1991): 600.

8. André Picard, "Blame Me for the Blood Scandal, Bégin Says," *The Globe and Mail,* August 21, 1996, pp. A1, A7.

9. Paul Koring, "Boyle Blames His Subordinates," *The Globe and Mail,* August 21, 1996, pp. A1, A4.

10. Kenneth Kernaghan, "Power, Parliament and Public Servants in Canada," p. 394.

✗ NO
Ministerial Accountability: Confronting the Myth
HUGH SEGAL

The evolution from absolutist monarchical government to responsible democracy had a series of milestones beyond the Magna Carta itself. The notion of an elected assembly, popularly chosen, to which the treasury benches are responsible is one of the crowning achievements of the Westminster model.

The notion of ministerial accountability emerges from that model and history in a way that is equally emblematic of the evolution from the rule of one to a parliament of the people.

As with many great ideas and important principles, their continued and constructive relevance requires a careful eye to the negative effects distortion can bring to the original principle. In Canada, the principle of ministerial accountability has produced some serious problems that work against the ability of the public sector in general and departmental operations in particular to adapt to and better serve the public interest as their statutory mandate directs. When a principle of ministerial accountability to Parliament can be deployed both aggressively and passively to frustrate the core mandate of serving the public required by Parliament, surely it is time to reflect carefully on the operation of the principle.

In my experience in both provincial and federal government, and in opposition legislative work, the inappropriately applied principle of ministerial accountability has produced a series of negative results.

These impacts tend to subvert rather than enhance accountability; depress rather than encourage innovation and improvement in public service; dilute rather than enhance the clarity of information coming both to the minister, his or her staff, or Parliament itself; promote the "gotcha phenomenon" of mindless media coverage of the legislative process; diminish rather than encourage the need for an opposition to be well prepared and studied on specific issues; depress rather than encourage media competence on specific issues; oppress rather than liberate creative and thoughtful capacities in the public service; and dilute rather than enhance other statutory responsibilities. (But aside from these the effect is rather benign!)

Let us begin with the core hypocrisy and charade associated with the ultimate reality of ministerial accountability. It is revealing even in its simplest and most flatly stated form. The simple notion that a minister of a department is directly responsible for everything that happens in that department is a corrosive and unhelpful proposition. It implies that in some way he or she must know or be advised of all that is transpiring in every detailed aspect of a ministry's operations. Let's follow this through.

Let us assume that a corrupt junior retail sales tax auditor seeks a bribe while auditing a retail business, a bar, in British Columbia. Initially no one complains. The auditor's supervisor has no idea of the corrupt practice. The regional director has no idea because the local supervisor has no idea. Because the regional director does not know, she has not told her director general of audit services. Because the director general does not know, he has not informed the assistant deputy minister. The ADM does not tell the deputy minister, nor is the matter discussed at the executive management committee of the ministry, because no one knows about the corrupt practice. Consequently, the minister has not been informed of anything untoward by her deputy minister.

But the parliamentary assumption is that the minister ought to know. How do we know that this is the parliamentary assumption? Well, because after hearing the bar owner boast about how he was able to reduce his true tax bill through a small understanding with a local retail sales tax auditor, one of the bar owner's suppliers, who was sitting in the bar with the owner, remembered that his sister-in-law was heavily fined recently for not paying retail sales tax. The supplier found the boasts of his customer quite troubling and made an anonymous call to the local RCMP detachment, which began an investigation. Within days of the beginning of this investigation, a newspaper got wind of the affair and began asking questions at the local level. An opposition MLA heard about the investigation, now several weeks old, and raised the question in the legislature.

Now in this context, we should be clear about one thing. The opposition MLA knows there is no way the minister can know about a single auditor who decides to take the wrong course in life. The media know that the minister could not possibly know. The bureaucracy, which itself may not know, does not believe that the minister knows. And, it is highly unlikely that the public would expect that the minister would or could know about this level of detail. But the parliamentary assumption is the opposite!

Similarly, the minister of Justice or the solicitor general should not know because the RCMP should be conducting their investigation without informing their ministers, just in case there is a broad conspiracy that spreads beyond one single auditor acting alone. Premature disclosure in the House of Commons or a legislature of an investigation could imperil the investigation.

When the question is asked in the House, the minister of Revenue can say that she is not aware of any specific investigation but would take the question under advisement. Her department checks frantically all the way down the line to try to find out what is happening. Essentially no one knows. A question goes across to the law officers of the Crown in the Justice Department, who have been advised by the police that confirming or denying an investigation could assist in the tampering with evidence or even in its destruction. By the second day in the legislature, the opposition MLA is alleging cover-up. The head of the provincial RCMP detachment issues a nonstatement saying that investigations of allegations of many kinds are discussed all the time and are not disclosed so as to protect both the rights of the Crown and the rights of the innocent, and to assist in gathering evidence.

If the deputy minister of Revenue is able to find out through formal or informal sources what is going on, the doctrine of ministerial accountability says that the minister must be informed. If the minister is informed, the question becomes, what is she doing about it? If the minister is not informed, she does not know. If the deputy minister of Justice speaks to her colleague the deputy minister of Revenue and says that the RCMP are close to laying charges, but that confirmation of the investigation could result in the evidence, for which the RCMP is seeking a seizure warrant, being destroyed in the Kamloops area—an area that may have several occurrences of similar crimes—then the deputy minister of Revenue is torn between duty to the administration of justice and the duty to inform ministerial accountability. If the minister is informed by the deputy, and then is asked questions the next day in the House, the minister's choices are to respond honestly to the questions, to obfuscate and wiggle waggle, or to avoid the truth and lie. She will then face the risk of being in contempt of the legislature, of having lied to the opposition or, in the minds of the press, of having been part of some sort of cover-up.

Not one person in the department, except the allegedly corrupt low-level auditor, knows much or anything about this. The minister has yet to be informed. The deputy has been cautioned by a colleague of equal rank in the Justice Department not to do anything that could jeopardize the investigation.

The public interest here is quite clear. The police should be allowed to continue their investigation. If evidence warrants it, the auditor should be charged. The due process of the law should determine guilt or innocence. The Department of Revenue should then conduct an investigation, which should perhaps be done by an outsider, to see if there is any systemic problem. Once charges are laid, a full statement, which does not refer to the matter now directly before the courts, should be made to the legislature concerning what the Revenue Department knew, how it assisted with the investigation, and what it now intends to do about the problem.

Chances of any of this happening are slim. The doctrinal application of ministerial accountability would force a feeding frenzy in the legislature and in the legislative press gallery, which is tied to the fiction that the minister should know and that she should have acted with dispatch as soon as she knew. Who knew what when, and what they did about what they knew, is far more important than the substance of the matter. And, however trivial all of this might be, and however marginal the matter is, these matters become even more removed from any focused pursuit of the public interest by a minister and her senior officials.

We should consider the culture this breeds in terms of the relationship between the bureaucracy at all its levels, the minister, and Parliament.

Does the doctrine of ministerial accountability mean that the minister must defend the activities of her department at all times because when she is unable to do so she must accept personal blame? Should, as some have argued relative to the Al-Mashat case, the minister or ministers accept responsibility for things they did not know anything about or in which they were not involved? Purists on the issue would argue in the affirmative, saying that what the minister of Immigration knew at the time is essentially irrelevant, and that the minister has a duty to accept responsibility in order to sustain the principle of ministerial accountability. By definition this is to diminish the concept of public service accountability, which is surely an undesired outcome from the point of view of responsible ministerial and public service conduct.

The culture of accountability, which is a desirable context for the able, competent, and focused public servant, is not advanced when all the accountability rests in practical terms in only one place. The political price will be paid by the elected politician at the political level. But that price should not absolve other competent and responsible players from their own duty.

There is no path of innovation in public service that does not carry with it some meaningful risk. New approaches to contracting out, new relationships with public sector unions, new approaches to job sharing or ensuring a more representative public service all require senior managers to take risks and try new approaches and procedures. The notion that every mistake, misstep, or experiment gone awry may plunge the minister and or government into some hot water is surely less than a liberating framework for innovation and growth. The hard truth of the matter is that the doctrine of ministerial accountability, applied as it is in Canada today, only serves to suppress innovation and discourage any risk taking within the public service culture. Often it is the very same opposition that decries less than up-to-date approaches to the administration of the public's affairs that are the first to, with allies in the media, seize on any chance to use ministerial responsibility to end a career rather than improve government. New governments faced with this reality often use different approaches to both keep their electoral promises yet avoid the daily melodrama of feigned horror at marginal events the minister could not possibly know much about.

Whenever elected officials say they want to take politics out of an issue, it usually means that there is absolutely no way they can reasonably be accountable for the details of how that particular issue is addressed. The Health Restructuring Commission in Ontario is a classic example of a government having to hand over to an extraparliamentary organization the actual implementation of the government's publicly and electorally mandated restructuring of the health care system. No minister of Health, however brilliant, articulate, well informed, balanced, and thoughtful, could have dealt on a day-to-day basis with the detailed calculations that saw decisions in any community made relative to health care rationalization in support of more appropriate and efficient care. Often, therefore, the purpose of ministerial accountability—namely, having a minister held accountable by Parliament for the actions of his or her department—produces just the opposite effect—namely, giving nonparliamentary bodies a statutory mandate to perform functions that might otherwise have been performed in a more direct legislative context. This will tend over time to diminish the role of Parliament rather than enhance it.

The effect of ministerial accountability on the media is equally perverse. The media assess issues in terms of their capacity to trip up a minister, show the government to be incompetent, or, the media hope, end a minister's career, which is all fair enough in a competitive political environment. But the media (and they too have competitive survival pressures) are reduced to focusing on ministerial foul-ups, parliamentary peccadilloes, and feeding frenzies, rather than on any sustained consideration of the larger issues at play. The result is media coverage that stresses minutiae and personalities rather than substance, making all politics seem petty, small-minded, and ritualized. There are consequences to continued and sustained pettiness.

Beyond the politics of legislative competition, there is also the reality of the larger competitive framework within which governments must contribute to, rather than dilute, national productivity. That reality clearly implies that a wide range of service delivery options be deployed to ensure both value for money and adequate resources for those services that truly matter.

The minute one moves to alternative forms of service delivery, from special operating agencies to Crown corporations to models of codetermination or commercialization, one moves beyond the realm of simple vertical function of ministerial responsibility. Are we not to let government structure services in innovative ways simply because some of those innovations, however cost efficient or more citizen friendly, may not facilitate direct vertical accountability through the minister to Parliament? Surely this is using ministerial accountability to diminish effective service to citizens rather than advance it.

The nature of our parliamentary democracy requires that Parliament give approval for estimates, budget bills, and appropriate ways and means motions, and that members of the cabinet generally be responsible to the House for the conduct of their departments. But using the narrow doctrine of an all-inclusive ministerial accountability constricts the flow of information and legitimacy to and from the legislative chamber. Instead, we should be looking for a way of articulating more carefully the underlying themes of that accountability in a fashion that enables creative and capable ministers, empowers the legitimate supremacy of the parliamentary part of the governance process, and diminishes the mindless ritual that serves no purpose other than to promote mockery and contrived outrage in the House at Question Period. We should be looking for a compelling definition of accountability that allows a culture of market sensitivity, citizen friendly program design, and risk taking, and that leads to better ways of serving the public.

How might this broader and more articulated definition move forward, and on what basis? Well, we might begin with the truth, however unappetizing it may be to proponents of a more traditional view of ministerial accountability.

Truth number one: A minister can only be responsible to Parliament for the broad policies that govern his or her department's goals, purposes, and operations and that determine how the ministry's act is actually put into effect. This must include specifically all those matters that fall, by virtue of any legislation, within the precise discretion of the minister or that of those staff members the minister has hired at the political level.

Truth number two: The deputy minister is appointed by the cabinet as a whole through an order-in-council whose content is determined by the cabinet or Privy Council Office with the express approval of the first minister. Deputy ministerial conduct is the responsibility of the government as a whole. Direct reports to the deputy are the responsibility of the deputy minister who is accountable to the secretary of the cabinet and the first minister.

Truth number three: No public service that is asked to perform effectively in a fast-paced and competitive environment can do so unless there is a legitimate tolerance for mistakes made and risks taken in good faith within existing statutory mandates. Ministers must not be accountable for these mistakes unless they are the product of explicit policy direction given by them or their political staff, or explicitly approved by them.

A clear division must be maintained between the role of policy in the department, for which the minister is responsible to Parliament, and the operational side of the department. This division will encourage deputies and bureaucracies to be less risk averse and more adventuresome within existing statutory mandates (which were and are approved by Parliament in the normal legislative way). This division will also promote a clear and liberating operational mandate for the department and its officials.

The constructive use of these truths, while not in any way limiting the range of questions that can be asked in Parliament or at committee, will provide some discipline around the more excessive misuses of parliamentary ritual that showboat and overdramatize rather than seek information and hold governments accountable. Holding a minister accountable for a deputy the minister did not appoint or who in essence does not truly report to the minister only sustains a charade that dilutes the first minister's responsibility for those matters a prime minister or premier is genuinely able to control. Accepting the difference between operations and policy allows deputies and public servants to speak more frankly at committee and when questioned about matters clearly within their purview. This division would in fact promote more information flow to our elected parliamentarians and the media than is now the case. Today, the need to protect the minister because of the doctrine of ministerial accountability produces a "need to know" hierarchy in most departments that operate on the premise that a minister cannot be held accountable for that which he or she does not know. This fails both to assist Parliament in doing its job and to provide transparency for the public or the media. A ritualistic assumption about a mythological accountability based on a false capacity to know everything actually works to constrain information flow and diminish parliamentary accountability in any real sense.

Public information, more dialogue between Parliament and the bureaucracy, more freedom for the bureaucracy to innovate in serving the public, and less of a culture of information management and control would be among the very first benefits of this more modern and realistic approach to ministerial accountability. Over time there would be others. The role of central agencies, like the Treasury Board, the Finance Department, and the cabinet office, would no longer be obscured by a focus on ministerial accountability that takes the legislative eye off these other seminal forces. Key decisions about staffing levels, levels of remuneration, extent of departmental field service, and administrative accountabilities are usually made outside the ministry involved. There are a host of statutory accountabilities around hiring practices, financial practices, expenses, facilities, and purchasing that are determined outside most line departments. The narrow focus of ministerial accountability often obscures the importance and impact of these accountabilities. A broader approach that allowed a clear distinction between policy issues within the minister's realm and administrative accountabilities quite outside that realm would facilitate a broader debate on and understanding of those other accountabilities. While it would end up being more substantive and less dramatic than simple "good cop–bad cop" rituals, it would also produce a far broader and more widespread understanding of the ways in which government actually works.

From the point of view of the serious parliamentarian and the opposition research offices, the separation of policy from operations and the more clear definition of ministers' responsibilities to Parliament would result in better use of research facilities, resources, and House time. Ministers could be questioned on policy matters in great detail. At estimates hearings and committee hearings, deputies would be more closely examined on administrative and operational issues. At estimates hearings, the long, time-wasting, and drawn-out ministers' statements about the full and detailed nature of their departments' operations could well be done away with. A closer and more detailed analysis of administrative and operational issues with the deputies would be far more revealing. The deputies' appointment by the first minister's office would make that discussion as politically salient as any. The accountability of the public service, as well as the understanding of its role and function, would increase. Government as a shared responsibility between Parliament, the cabinet as a whole, the prime minister or premier, and the minister would no longer exclude the public service from accountability.

A minister and government today do not decide whether to support a public servant who has made a controversial or understandable mistake in good faith.

Today what is decided is whether the doctrine of ministerial accountability can include supporting a public servant who has taken a risk or made an honest mistake. This forces the public servant and the parliamentarian into a Catch-22 circumstance. True oversight and questioning is dealt with only in the context of the ministers' responsibility. The minister faces the task of standing by his department to the last point of minutiae whatever the facts may suggest in terms of right and wrong. The parliamentarian's capacity to generate any change for the better is tied utterly to his or her capacity to embarrass or catch the minister. The public servants who share precisely the same interest in good government as do the other players are largely prevented from interacting with the system because of the almost coercive doctrine of ministerial accountability.

None of this conspires to produce any real opportunities for a broad national debate through Parliament about how government can be improved, or how government can be used either sparingly or otherwise to strengthen our way of life, our society, our compassion, our effectiveness, or our competence in the way we govern ourselves. In a sense, ministerial accountability is a shield that protects any government from any real discussion of how it manages its internal affairs while protecting the opposition parties from any real duty to deal with the issues at hand in a serious, researched, and informed way. Ministerial accountability acts, no doubt unwittingly from the perspective of those who fought for responsible government centuries ago, to actually diminish the real responsibility of many of the players in the system.

Like so much of our parliamentary heritage that is of value, our challenge is to save the best. We should be speaking instead about an updating that would not only strengthen the role of minister and public servant but also, and more importantly, increase the relevance, impact, and capacity to influence events of the people we elect to Parliament and legislatures.

Which, in terms of democracy and genuine accountability, would make a very significant difference indeed. It is a difference that would revitalize the parliamentary process and expand its genuine reach. It would help the process of public understanding of our governing realities and processes.

And it would represent the setting aside of mythology for reality, which is often a step in the right direction.

Postscript

In his article, Kernaghan offers a set of convincing arguments. On the whole, he contends, the doctrine of individual ministerial responsibility works well and offers a coherent framework for understanding relations between elected and appointed officials. He also asserts, convincingly, that ministers can hardly be blamed for actions of which they have little knowledge; they can investigate the matter and answer any questions, but resignation seems unfair and unrealistic. Yet, some questions remain. If it is unrealistic to blame ministers, then who is to take the responsibility? Perhaps the responsible parties in the public service are sanctioned, but the public never sees this. All they see is the evasion of responsibility. Also, if the bureaucracy is too large for ministers to control, then maybe it is time to make public servants more directly accountable. For some, it may seem curious to rely on a doctrine that is ill-suited to the age of big government.

Segal's article points to an important flaw in the doctrine of individual ministerial responsibility: it is impossible for the minister to know all. Nevertheless, as Segal says, we persist in this belief. The result is that not only is a hypocrisy foisted upon the people of Canada, but also the dynamics of individual ministerial responsibility lead to a sacrifice of the public interest; "who knew what when," contends Segal, takes precedence over the "substance of the matter." But it may be argued that Segal is being too harsh, and that he underestimates the value of accountability resting with a single person. His preference is the one mentioned above, that public servants begin to share some of the responsibility; yet, if everyone becomes responsible for an action, then no one in particular is responsible. Passing the buck becomes a real possibility. What might also be questioned is Segal's convenient division of duties into policy and administration. It is not always easy to make this distinction, with the result that appointed officials operating under Segal's recommended system may find themselves dealing with political issues. The transformation of the appointed official from disinterested advisor to de facto politician becomes complete.

Kenneth Kernaghan has written a number of articles and chapters on the issue of individual ministerial responsibility: Kenneth Kernaghan, "Power, Parliament and Public Servants in Canada: Ministerial Responsibility Reexamined," *Canadian Public Policy–Analyse de politiques* 3 (1979); Kenneth Kernaghan and David Siegel, *Public Administration in Canada: A Text*, 3rd ed. (Scarborough: Nelson Canada, 1994), ch. 17; and Kenneth Kernaghan and John Langford, *The Responsible Public Servant* (Halifax: Institute for Research on Public Policy, 1990). Though somewhat dated, the collection entitled *The Future Public Service* (Halifax: Institute for Research on Public Policy, n.d.) contains some useful articles on bureaucratic accountability (including articles by Kernaghan and Segal). Sharon Sutherland's article "Responsible Government and Ministerial Responsibility: Every Reform Is Its Own Problem," *Canadian Journal of Political*

Science 24, no.1 (1991) offers an excellent overview of the practice of individual ministerial responsibility and an analysis of some of the recommended changes to the doctrine.

The readings suggest that examining case studies is an important way of gaining an appreciation of individual ministerial responsibility. One pertinent case study involving the doctrine is Sharon Sutherland, "The Al-Mashat Affair: Administrative Accountability in Parliamentary Institutions," *Canadian Public Administration* 34, no. 4 (1991). Scholarly articles on some of the cases mentioned in the introduction (the Airbus affair, the Krever Commission [blood supply], the Somalia affair) have yet to appear, but newspapers and magazines have dealt with all of them in some detail. As well, government reports relating to some of them have been released, including House of Commons, Standing Committee on External Affairs and International Trade, *Minutes of Proceedings and Evidence of the Standing Committee on External Affairs and International Trade, Final Report on Consideration of the Immigration to Canada of Mohammed Al-Mashat*, 13 June 1991; Committee of Inquiry into the Deployment of Canadian Forces to Somalia, *Dishonoured Legacy: The Lessons of the Somalia Affair* (Ottawa: Minister of Public Works and Government Services Canada, 1997)); and the soon to be released report of the Commission of Inquiry on the Blood System in Canada.

Another useful source on ministerial responsibility is Geoffrey Marshall, ed., *Ministerial Responsibility* (Oxford: Oxford University Press, 1989). The text contains articles on the theory of individual ministerial responsibility and the practice of the doctrine in relation to political life in Great Britain.

Notwithstanding the support in some circles for individual ministerial responsibility, it is under pressure. Two publications that address this (and related matters) are Donald J. Savoie, *Thatcher, Reagan and Mulroney: In Search of a New Bureaucracy* (Toronto: University of Toronto Press, 1994) and G. Guy Peter and Donald J. Savoie, eds., *Governance in a Changing Environment* (Montreal and Kingston: McGill-Queen's University Press, 1995) (especially the article by Phillip J. Cooper). These studies reveal that the movement toward "managerialism" in government—giving public servants more autonomy and responsibility—is calling into question the doctrine of individual responsibility. It appears that public servants will indeed be forced to become more directly accountable for their actions.

ISSUE**TWELVE**

Does the Institutionalized Cabinet Provide for Good Government?

✔ **YES**
CHRISTOPHER DUNN, "The Utility of the Institutionalized Cabinet"

✗ **NO**
PAUL BARKER, "Problems with the Institutionalized Cabinet"

The cabinet is the single most important body in Canadian politics. It is the entity that outlines the overall direction of government and makes the important decisions that form the basis of the public agenda. At the head of the cabinet is the prime minister, who chooses elected members from his or her party to sit in cabinet as responsible ministers. In light of the centrality of the cabinet, the issue of the structure and operation of the cabinet assumes critical proportions. How the cabinet performs, how it carries out its duties, depends in part on how it is structured to make decisions. The manner of cabinet decision making may not guarantee good government, but it certainty assists senior elected officials in their attempt to deal with the challenges of governing.

In the past, the decision-making structure of cabinets in Canada was relatively simple. The relevant minister, with the aid of departmental officials, would develop policy in response to an issue, and then bring it to the cabinet's attention. The cabinet would examine the proposed policy, but not in great detail, for it would rely on the minister's good judgment. In such a cabinet system, the individual minister and the relevant department played a dominant role. Accordingly, this type of arrangement came to be known as the *departmentalized cabinet* (or *unaided cabinet*).

For a period of time, the departmentalized cabinet performed well. It helped governments to make decisions in an effective and timely way, and it contributed to the overall goal of good government. In the 1960s, this opinion of the departmentalized cabinet began to change. It was felt that a different structure was needed. Individual ministers and their officials seemed to have *too* much influence, and policies went without extensive analysis. Perhaps more important, the growing size of government required a cabinet able to coordinate the multifaceted offerings of government, yet this was missing: cabinet decision making was just the sum of its individual ministerial parts.

Because of these perceived failings, a new framework for cabinet decision making began to emerge. It came to be known as the *institutionalized cabinet.*

This new structure provided for stronger committees of cabinet, in which ministerial proposals would be given closer consideration than before. To assist these committees in their work, bodies called central agencies were given the authority to closely review policy initiatives and report their opinions to the committees. More generally, the institutionalized cabinet offered a forum for the collective consideration of government policies. No longer would the cabinet be the sum of its parts. There would now be a cabinet view on the policies and programs of government.

Governments throughout Canada adopted one or more of the features of the institutionalized cabinet. It seemed that the cabinet had made the adjustments necessary to accommodate the greater role of government. But soon dissatisfaction with the new cabinet structure began to emerge. Individual ministers felt slighted, the empowered central agencies appeared too empowered, and the decision making at times was slow and sluggish. Consequently, some have suggested that the institutionalized cabinet has gone too far in its changes, and that it would be prudent to return to a departmentalized cabinet. Supporters of the institutionalized cabinet concede its weaknesses, but contend that these failings can be fixed without abandoning the new style of cabinet decision making.

In the readings, Christopher Dunn, a political scientist and author of a major study of institutionalized cabinets in the western provinces, argues that the institutionalized cabinet provides for good government. Paul Barker contends that governments would benefit if they structured their cabinets in a way that reflected the main working principles of the departmentalized cabinet.

✔ YES
The Utility of the Institutionalized Cabinet
CHRISTOPHER DUNN

The institutionalized cabinet provides for good government. At least, that's what the vast majority of first ministers think, and they count. They are the ones whose prerogative it is, in the Westminster tradition, to design governments. As any cabinet secretary will testify, the major criterion for design of the machinery of government is whether it meets the needs of the prime minister or premier. The fact that the institutionalized (structured) cabinet has persisted in most governments in the Canadian political system is telling testimony. The sign of "good government," in other words, is utility. That is the primary point this essay makes. It makes two other points. One concerns international practice: most developed nations are oriented toward institutionalization, and one is never a structural heretic for long in this context. The other is that the criticisms of the structured cabinet implicitly refer to various pathologies that have occurred, but that could and should be averted with better organizational design. Institutionalization properly practised is about balance, not top-down control.

Since the term institutionalized cabinet is likely to be misunderstood by many, we have included here a table outlining its major characteristics.[1] This type of cabinet is actually a conglomeration of characteristics, and cannot easily be reduced to a few pithy comments. Because of its variegated nature, it tends to be a more flexible instrument than many think. I noted this in my book on western provincial governments, saying that "there are no facile generalizations about who are the focal decision-makers in unaided and institutionalized cabinets. What can be offered instead are statements of tendency.... [and a constant difference between the two being] in an institutionalized cabinet [the first minister] is the architect not only of personnel choice but of cabinet structure as well."[2] The statements of tendency can be reduced in shorthand to the characteristics in Table 12.1. They are contrasted with the earlier unaided (departmentalized or unstructured) cabinet, historically the pattern followed until the sixties and seventies in the federal and provincial governments.

CANADIAN EXPERIENCES

It is true, of course, that the federal cabinet has in part moved away from the institutionalized model. Rand Dyck says that the Chrétien government has "reverted to the St. Laurent model of a departmental cabinet in which individual ministers and departments were allowed to look after their own affairs. The maze of cabinet committees was reduced, as was the scope of many other coordinating central agencies. Departments were allowed more leeway in moving funds from one program to another as long as they did not exceed their overall allotment."[3] Similarly, Peter

TABLE 12.1
UNAIDED AND INSTITUTIONALIZED CABINET MODELS

UNAIDED CABINET	INSTITUTIONALIZED CABINET
CABINET	
• personnel choice by first minister	• personnel choice plus cabinet organization job
• dominant first minister, restricted collegiality	• greater collegiality
• simple cabinet structure	• complex cabinet structure
CENTRAL AGENCIES	
• central departments	• central agencies as well as central departments
• fewer cabinet staff	• more cabinet staff
• little cabinet-level analysis	• extensive cabinet-level analysis
BUDGETING AND PLANNING	
• budgeting centralized: major role played by first minister	• budgeting collegial
• budgeting aim: mostly control	• budgeting aim: broader than control
• budgeting means: traditional (annual budget cycle)	• budgeting means: both traditional and political/off-budget controls
• planning: optional, but either project oriented or indicative if practised	• planning: still optional, but collective and comprehensive where practised
• short-term coordination by first minister or finance minister is usually all that can be expected	• planning–budgeting nexus (balance, complementarity of the two functions)
DECISION-MAKING MODES	
• hierarchical channels of policy advice, from senior officials to the cabinet with no competing sources	• alternative channels of policy advice for cabinet and committees
• decentralized decision making: departmental autonomy favoured over power of the central executive	• centralized decision making: power of the central executive favoured over departmental autonomy

Source: Abstracted from Christopher Dunn, *The Institutionalized Cabinet: Governing the Western Provinces* (Montreal and Kingston: McGill-Queen's University Press, 1995).

Aucoin sees traces of most of the earlier phases of cabinet development (collegial, conglomerate, command, and corporate) in the current Liberal government, but says that the clear choice of the prime minister—to judge from the cabinet/ministry differentiation he introduced—is toward the conglomerate model.[4] This model is essentially the same as the departmentalized cabinet as described by J. Stefan Dupré,[5] which pertained from the 1920s to the 1950s. "The modern equivalent of this mode of cabinet government finds expression in efforts since the mid-1980s to decentralize decision making from cabinet and cabinet committees (and thus the central policy and management agencies of government) to individual ministers and their operational departments."[6] Cabinet appears relegated to performing strategic planning and resolving interministerial conflicts.

However, important qualifications are necessary. One is that the federal cabinet is only one of eleven in Canada, and the institutionalized cabinet is still a staple of most governments in Canada. Kernaghan and Siegel note that "in most provinces, the functions of the PMO, the PCO, and sometimes the TB are all carried out in the premier's office. However, there is a general movement toward the establishment of what is commonly described as an institutionalized cabinet, i.e., a cabinet with a formal committee structure and supporting agencies."[7] They also noted that the "reforms in general to the structures and processes of provincial cabinet decision-making systems followed a pattern similar to the federal reforms ... and aimed to achieve the same objectives of cabinet coordination and control of policy-making."[8]

When surveyed in 1995, provincial cabinets revealed a fairly common tendency toward hierarchy and/or coordination, as well as multiple cabinet committees. All provinces except Manitoba had some version of the planning and priorities type of cabinet committee. British Columbia had four committees and four "policy working groups" reporting to the planning board of cabinet. Alberta had eight, Saskatchewan six, Manitoba twelve, Ontario eight with two subcommittees, Quebec four, Nova Scotia five, and Newfoundland six. Only two provinces, New Brunswick and Prince Edward Island, made do with two committees of cabinet, a policy/priorities committee and a treasury board. Of course, not all of the provinces retained these numbers of committees (Ontario under Mike Harris's Conservatives reduced them to three), but it is instructive to note that two years after the federal cabinet's downsizing there was still a preoccupation with this kind of structural differentiation of provincial cabinets.[9]

Moreover, a quick look through available provincial public accounts figures for the late eighties to the late nineties for selected provinces (see Appendix 12.1.) shows that the central agencies and central departments that attend the institutionalized cabinet have not withered away, in terms of funding levels, as one might expect if the policy coordination role were switching to the departmental level. Many have remained in a steady state; some have even grown substantially. Perhaps most suggestive are the figures for budget analysis agencies, which have gone up substantially in Saskatchewan, Manitoba, Quebec, Newfoundland, and New Brunswick. If there had been a massive shift of financial decision-making power to the departments, as one theme of the New Public Management goes, one might expect that treasury board staffs would be smaller. This shift can only be determined, of course, by empirical research on each provincial administration.

Another qualification concerns historical parallels. Reversing history, moving from an institutionalized format to an earlier historical version like the unaided or departmentalized cabinet, is not without parallel. It has happened at the provincial level. What is useful to contemplate is that in those cases, the move was incomplete, was inconvenient, and ultimately was abandoned. Premiers who follow those who have partially deinstitutionalized cabinets (like Blakeney after Thatcher, Pawley after Lyon) have found the results constricting and unsatisfactory and have moved to reinstitutionalize: more committees, more central officials, more planning, and so forth.[10] Could the same happen at the federal level? Most conceivably.

Still another qualification to note is that, like our preceding provincial examples, only partial deinstitutionalization has taken place. The prime minister is still the architect of central government organization. There are still two cabinet committees with corporate responsibilities, namely the treasury board and the Special Committee of Council. There are still central agencies and central departments. There is still a balance between the partisan (PMO) and policy (PCO) functions. Strategic planning is still a collegial cabinet responsibility. Budgeting and planning are made to correspond. The agencies that serve the cabinet seem fairly substantial as well. The Public Accounts of Canada reveal that in 1995–96 the federal taxpayer paid $5.6 million for the Prime Minister's Office, $29.6 million for the Privy Council Office, and $88.5 million for the Treasury Board Secretariat. Appendix 12.1 shows approximate full-time equivalencies (employee numbers) in the central agencies (PCO and PMO) and in the central departments (Treasury Board Secretariat and Finance) for the last decade. The numbers have not dropped, the apparent decentralization of their function notwithstanding. One can be forgiven for thinking that this is not quite a decentralized, departmentalized cabinet and its attendant skeletal assemblages of officials, but a reluctant and only partially deinstitutionalized cabinet. A partially deinstitutionalized cabinet is obviously easier to return to than a fully deinstitutionalized cabinet.

The last qualification to note is that although the first minister's views on government organization are the ones that count in modern government, first ministers come and go. In Chrétien's case, we have the example of a politician whose character is not sympathetic to the institutionalized mode at a basic, visceral level. Trudeau's motto was "reason before passion," but Mr. Chrétien's heart is at the centre of his discourse, to judge from his self-titled autobiography. As he noted there, "I've always been more comfortable making decisions than engaging in long and intellectually satisfying discourses, perhaps because I'm an impatient person."[11] Long discourses were, of course, what the Trudeau committee system engendered. Another shot at the committee system of the sixties and seventies comes later in the book, when Chrétien both criticizes the system and implicitly lays out criteria for a workable cabinet system. "The committee reforms initiated by Gordon Robertson and carried on by Michael Pitfield [successively, the clerks of the Privy Council] were both complex and controversial. They took up too much of the ministers' time and energy; they produced too much paper work; and they resulted in weaker decisions, because even the strong ministers had to submit to collective decisions."[12] There is a subtheme to the Chrétien autobiography; one comes to realize that he saw himself as a strong minister whose important initiatives were often watered down—or at the very least were in constant danger of reversal—in the collegial settings of the institutionalized cabinet.

Yet the day may come when the government is again led by a first minister more sympathetic to institutionalization. Promoting the return to a more structured approach is likely to result in a different view of rationalism in government and a dissatisfaction with the "superminister" concept.

SECTORAL RATIONALITY AND SUPERMINISTERS

One problem with the current Chrétien cabinet organization is its implied model of rationality. As Gustafsson and Richardson have noted, there are three "locations of rationality," that is, three conceptions of the appropriate scale on which to conduct rational deliberations ("rational" meaning decision making that aims at increasing the likelihood of policies meeting objectives or goals).[13] These locations of rationality are sector rationality, coordinated rationality, and decentralized rationality. Sector rationality occurs in policymaking systems that are divided into relatively autonomous policy segments, each having a policy community that operates independently of the other policy communities, and within which goal achievement is independently established and measured. Coordinated rationality occurs in policy systems where interrelationships are established between policy sectors in order to mitigate against serious goal conflicts, and in which there are strategic (overriding) objectives that cabinets—the usual mechanism for achieving coordinated rationality—use to resolve those goal conflicts that do arise. Decentralized rationality is a special kind of coordinated rationality that occurs when the connections between apparently separate problems become more transparent because they are viewed from a local perspective, and when coordination overcomes the usual boundaries between policy segments. One of the difficulties in designing the machinery of government is to establish at what level one does rationalist calculation, and for what policy areas.[14]

The Chrétien government seems dependent on sector rationality. The main evidence of this is the reliance on superministries like Human Resources Development (HRD), Canadian Heritage, and Industry, where parts of previously separate departments are fitted together to facilitate coordinated in-department policy development and simultaneously reduce overhead costs that would have been associated with central agency coordination.

The government's focus may be too narrow. One result of weakened cabinet-level policy coordination is the tendency to rely on other horizontal mechanisms, such as ad hoc deputy ministerial task forces and interdepartmental committees of assistant deputy ministers whose principal focus is policy development. Between 1994 and 1996 there were several of these task forces, covering such varied matters as the future of the public service, service delivery models, federal presence, federal presence abroad, overhead services, values and ethics, policy planning, and horizontal policy issues. Two of the task forces—the Task Force on Strengthening Our Policy Capacity and the Task Force on Managing Horizontal Policy Issues—focused on policy advice in the public service. They led the clerk of the Privy Council, in her fourth annual report, tabled in 1997, to concede:

> Many of today's principal policy issues are horizontal in nature. Horizontality requires *corporate rather than departmental action* [emphasis in the original], a characteristic which is placing new demands on traditional Public Service decision-making structures and culture. The public service must expand its knowledge base and increase interorganizational collaboration to tackle the growing number of crosscutting policy issues that defy the authority and expertise of any single department or even, in a globalized world, any single government.[15]

Yet the solution offered—in essence, more deputy ministerial committees—is not realistic, given the analysis. It is appropriate to advocate the various bureaucratic mechanisms to achieve coordination, but past "corporate" decision making and activity has incorporated significant cabinet committee elements, as well. Surely policy coordination is essentially a ministerial function, to be performed by cabinet and its committees, the annual cabinet "strategic policy cycle" notwithstanding. The report also mentions the need to be more diligent in responding to the growing demands of citizens for increased access to information and participation, perhaps an indication that the decentralized variant of rationality was, like coordinated rationality, undervalued and overlooked.

Another closely related problem with the Chrétien model is its dependence on the superministries concept. An OECD report, which did in fact take notice of the Chrétien use of superministries, offered a pithy comment on the main problem with the concept:

> While it is logical to locate similar programmes within a single ministry, the co-ordination gains may be more apparent than real. A large ministry might engender its own co-ordination problems. A minister who has too large an organisation, with many internal divisions, may encounter the same span-of-control problems as a prime minister with an equal number of ministries to co-ordinate. Also, by placing the main co-ordination responsibility within a ministry, decisions tend to be taken more by officials than by ministers, who would have to debate those issues in the council of ministers if the programmes were in different ministries.[16]

It is ironic that the government party that introduced the institutionalized cabinet system in order to wrest control of government from the nonelected officials should now be returning control to them.

INTERNATIONAL EXPERIENCES

Some international experiences are relevant when discussing institutionalization. They demonstrate that the weight of opinion in developed countries is toward a more structured, collegial central executive. They also suggest that new developments in public management, surprisingly, may be hastening the return to institutionalization.

A recent (1996) report by the OECD is heavily oriented to a structured central executive. It is a review of the experience of practitioners involved in the design and operation of the "centre of government," that is, those bodies that assist and advise the head of government and council of ministers such as Prime Ministers' Offices, Cabinet Secretariats, and Offices of the Presidency. The report was engendered by a concern that "policy coherence" was declining due to the "hollowing out" of the state brought about by globalization and public sector reforms.[17] While the report took care not to recommend specific models, it did proffer some "practical lessons" or commonalities that had been judged successful in most OECD countries. (In applying them, of course, countries had to adjust such lessons to the legal, administrative, and political requirements of the nation, by means of careful experimentation.) The report does not pretend that the systems it suggests putting in place will rid the government of policy incoherence (policy conflicts or countervailing effects). It accepts some incoherence as inevitable, but insists that the policymakers should, as far as possible, be made aware of it.

This OECD report is relevant here for a number of reasons. It implicitly criticizes the preoccupation with decentralized policymaking that seems at the heart of much of the New Public Management literature and that has given rise to many of Chrétien's structural reforms.[18] The report stresses that a major problem of modern government is how to deal with cross-cutting policy issues, which are a central concern of the institutionalized cabinet. In addition, many of the "lessons" of governance are lessons Canadians already know and have learned by the simple expedient of having a structured cabinet. Consider the suggestions the OECD report makes (summarized at the end of this paper in Appendix 12.3), stating that there should be senior officials attending ministerial meetings; comprehensive central gathering and analysis of information; an organizationally separate central planning capacity; comprehensive planning promoted by less differentiated central policy units; ministerial committees for policy coordination; a resistance to superministries as a general organizational design feature; higher level arbitration mechanisms; an effective interface between the setting of policy priorities and budgeting; formalized (institutionalized?) forced points of passage at the centre of government; and systematic dialogue between policy communities. Even a casual comparison of Table 12.1 and Appendix 12.3 will reveal a striking similarity. Governments have a tendency to copy institutional designs from one another. Canada may one day be borrowing from OECD nations who, ironically, have borrowed the new institutionalization from Canada. International commentators are of like mind. Examining cabinet experiences in Australia, Canada, and the United Kingdom by the early nineties, Patrick Weller noted the following:

> The lessons that emerge from these descriptions are that a range of alternatives are possible. There is an accepted need for a nonpolitically based support for cabinet, although as that becomes more complex, so the service is provided more for a prime minister than for cabinet collectively. There is a need for partisan assistance in party and media matters. In policy concerns— usually short-term and crisis-management—a combination of career and partisan advisors can work together to provide the support the prime ministers need. Prime ministers have all assured that they receive advice from several channels. Ministers are not prevented from being their chief's main advisors, if they have the ability. Supporting institutions may be as flexible and responsive as the leaders require. The name of the support services is not too important: the functions delivered by No. 10 and the Cabinet Office in Britain, by the PCO and PMO in Canada, by PMC and PMO in Australia are beginning to look increasingly similar. They are all compatible with collective cabinet decision making and with parliamentary government.[19]

They are also, of course, compatible with institutionalization.

REBALANCING THE INSTITUTIONALIZED CABINET

The institutionalized cabinet can, but does not always, provide for good government. It does not always function smoothly. Its potential pitfalls are indeed daunting. Premiers may not consider the structure of the central executive a burning issue until their existing institutional arrangements go awry. Cabinets may have difficulty defining their roles. Central departments often have trouble establishing appropriate working relationships with departments. Planning and budgeting processes at times have appeared gripped by pathological complexity and detail. These are examples of the institutionalized cabinet gone astray, and the traits its opponents will characterize as endemic to it.

No decision-making structure is perfect, but if organizational design is pursued with adherence to some basic principles, such as balance, the institutionalized cabinet can still be a vital element of government. The centre and the departments, the political and the bureaucratic, the collegial and the individual, prime ministerial government and cabinet government—these are the elements that must be balanced in order for government decision making to work.

Perhaps the most important immediate need, given the bad press that the structured cabinet has had,[20] is to achieve balance between the centre and the departments. Departments have long ceased to consider themselves the passive receptacles of cabinet direction. Premiers and the central executive in general would do well to assure them of an important role in the decision-making structure. The reason for this is not charitable, but political. The government of the day depends on the bureaucracy to implement its program with enthusiasm, but the bureaucracy will not do so if excluded from decision making. As well, there has to be a sphere of independent influence for ministers if collective cabinet instruments are not to become too overloaded.

A caveat is appropriate here. One has to be respectful of departmental autonomy, but not to the extent of weakening the collective cabinet's program. The same with the political and the bureaucratic, the collective and the individual: these are not dichotomous choices but elements to be melded when designing the machinery of government. Such a melding may yield reforms such as the following, which aim at achieving balance in the decision-making process:

- Delete the "control orientation" and replace it with management systems and standards that require only occasional monitoring.
- Emphasize flexibility for line managers in program implementation.
- Establish specialized mandates for central agencies to leave lead responsibility for important functions (e.g., specific intergovernmental matters, or merit principle protection) in departmental hands.
- Allow departments to provide the secretaries for some committees of cabinet.
- Keep personnel numbers low in central agencies so that leadership perforce often falls to departments.
- Pursue a conscious strategy of "spinning-off" personnel from central agencies to departmental posts in order to build a nondichotomous corporate consciousness for government.
- Enhance departmental training and expertise.

The institutionalized cabinet will work if the various parts of government have basic philosophies to guide them. Let us, therefore, suggest some. Cabinet should be organized according to its main responsibilities, the "five Cs": control, coordination, communication, compromise, and counsel. Within each of these categories can be organized subduties (see Appendix 12.4). As well, first ministers and cabinets should know what is appropriate to expect from central agencies. Central agencies, in fact, exist to protect cabinet authority and prerogatives. Accordingly, their duties are to help cabinet perform those duties already listed for cabinet in this paper. Clinton Rossiter is helpful to Canadian analysts when he discusses the role of the U.S. president's intimate advisors:

It is their unrelenting duty to protect the President against all but the most essential problems in their designated areas, to present these in such form that they can be readily mastered, and to especially preserve [sic] the President's freedom of choice among competing alternatives.

We might nickname these duties "the three Ps": protect, present, and preserve. Substitute "first minister and cabinet" for "President" and one has as concise a prescription for central agency responsibilities as it is possible to get. Certainly these are honourable—and indeed vital—functions in our modern complex government. The political and the bureaucratic aspects of the budgetary process also need balancing. This is, as ever, an ongoing need, and one that is acknowledged by the experimentation that governments have done in this regard in the last two decades.

There is a certain amount of irony surrounding this essay. In my book *The Institutionalized Cabinet*,[21] I advised against seeing the institutionalized cabinet as the product of a teleological process, as a natural end to which cabinets evolved, as a form that would never change. I even hinted that we may be on the dawn of a "post-institutionalized cabinet" because of a different set of determinants facing decision makers in the nineties. However, I must conclude that that time has not yet come, and we will have the institutionalized cabinet for some time yet. It is the cabinet of choice nationally and internationally, and its ills are, for the time being, fixable.

APPENDIX 12.1

Amounts Expended on Central Agencies, by Province

AMOUNTS EXPENDED, BRITISH COLUMBIA PUBLIC ACCOUNTS (000s of Dollars)

Department Name and/ or Specific Section	1989/90	1990/91	1991/2	1992/3	1993/4	1994/5	1995/6	1996/7
Office of the Premier	1 390	1 339	1 525	1 590	1 750	1 879	1 904	2 408
Cabinet Office[a]	1 956	2 319	3 078	2 580	2 344	2 316	2 154	2 566
Treasury Board Staff	5 233	5 771	3 240	3 578	7 703	7 876	7 068	6 495

[a]Also called "Executive Council Operations" earlier in the decade.

APPENDIX 12.1 (CONT.)

AMOUNTS EXPENDED, ALBERTA PUBLIC ACCOUNTS (000s of Dollars)

Department Name and/ or Specific Section	1989/90	1990/91	1991/2	1992/3	1993/4	1994/5	1995/6	1996/7
Department of Executive Council[a]	105 547	137 273	296 235	183 456	142 126	24 003	22 684	20 819
Treasury Board	b	b	b	b	b	b	b	b

[a]Figures include both voted appropriations and statutory appropriations.
[b]In the Government of Alberta, the Treasury Board is structured as a Provincial committee with no staff and expenditure budget. Accordingly, the Treasury Board incurs no expenditures. Expenditures incurred as a result of the existence of Treasury Board are absorbed by the programs of the departments incurring the expenditures.

AMOUNTS EXPENDED, SASKATCHEWAN PUBLIC ACCOUNTS (000s of Dollars)

Department Name and/or Specific Section	1989/90	1990/1	1991/2	1992/3	1993/4	1994/5	1995/6	1996/7
ECO Cabinet Secretariat/Policy and Planning Secretariat	837	772[a]	728[a]	1345[a]	957	883	849	920
Finance: Budget Analysis	2 012	1 992[b]	2 504[b]	3 843	3 818	3 945	3 822	3 550
Intergovernmental Relations	765	736[c]	805[c]	654	779	845	1 088	647

[a]The single Cabinet Secretariat (called the "Policy Secretariat" in 1989–90) entries in the Public Accounts were split into "Cabinet Secretariat" and "Policy and Planning Secretariat" from 1993–94 on. Here combined.
[b]Called Treasury Board Division.
[c]In the ECO this year, alternately called Intergovernmental Affairs.

APPENDIX 12.1 (CONT.)

AMOUNTS EXPENDED, MANITOBA PUBLIC ACCOUNTS (000s of Dollars)

Department Name and/or Specific Section	1989/90	1990/1	1991/2	1992/3	1993/4	1994/5	1995/6	1996/7
Finance: Federal-Provincial Relations and Research	1 395	1 331	1 329	1 376	1 458	1 587	1 587	1 587
Treasury Board Secretariat	2 012	2 428	2 444	2 289	2 713	2 941	2 990	2 997
Executive Council[a]	2 954	2 939	2 840	2 863	2 648	2 793[b]	2 738[b]	2 981[b]

[a]Breakdown of appropriation not available.
[b]When a breakdown is provided here, it is line item, rather than program, oriented.

AMOUNTS EXPENDED, ONTARIO PUBLIC ACCOUNTS (000s of Dollars)

Department Name and/or Specific Section	1988/9	1989/90	1990/1	1991/2	1992/3	1993/4	1994/5	1995/6	1996/7
Office of the Premier	2 225	2 251	3 611	2 636	2 593	2 261	2 001	2 130	2 610
Cabinet Office	4 835	5 368	6 758	6 182	5 687	5 649	5 105	7 868	9 968
Ministry of Finance: Treasury Board	N/A	N/A	N/A	10 806	10 119	6 115	14 157	12 740	N.A.[a]
Management Board Secretariat	38 233	40 577	56 124	68 741	560 239	636 758	564 885	737 884	591 070
Ministry of IGA[b]	9 129	8 159	9 810	7 296	8 807	6 969	5 692	5 097	4 370

APPENDIX 12.1 (CONT.)

AMOUNTS EXPENDED, QUEBEC PUBLIC ACCOUNTS (000s of Dollars)

Department Name and/ or Specific Section	1989/90	1990/1	1991/2	1992/3	1993/4	1994/5	1995/6	1996/7
Conseil exécutif (Executive Council)	25 281	27 685	28 601	30 668	32 234	49 081	48 417	42 451
Affaires internationales (International Affairs)	84 304	101 287	109 496	117 709	115 915	109 846	117 088	81 095
Conseil du trésor (Treasury Board)	20 262	21 685	21 893	23 806	23 442	27 875	25 316	26 000

AMOUNTS EXPENDED, NEW BRUNSWICK PUBLIC ACCOUNTS (000s of Dollars)

Department Name and/ or Specific Section	1989/90	1990/1	1991/2	1992/3	1993/4	1994/5	1995/6	1996/7
Executive Council Office: Executive Council Secretariat	576	590	600	547	604	953	1 043	1 120
Department of Finance: Budget and Financial Management Division	293[a]	364[b]	357[b]	891	866	873	826	902
Office of the Premier	817	871	916	1 097	1 121	953	1 022	1 147

[a]Called Budget Secretariat in 1989–90.
[b]Called the "Budget Secretariat" this year.

APPENDIX 12.1 (CONT.)

AMOUNTS EXPENDED, PRINCE EDWARD ISLAND PUBLIC ACCOUNTS
(000s of Dollars)

Department Name and/ or Specific Section	1988/9	1989/90	1990/1	1991/2	1992/3	1993/4	1994/5	1995/6
Executive Council	1 756	1 915	2 009	2 175	2 284	1 949	1 816	1 811
Premier's Office[a]	418	484	461	441	486	496	466	432
Treasury Board	585	900	761	N/A	N/A	N/A	N/A	N/A

[a]Premier's Office found under/within Executive Council.

AMOUNTS EXPENDED, NOVA SCOTIA PUBLIC ACCOUNTS (000s of Dollars)

Department Name and/ or Specific Section	1989/90	1990/1	1991/2	1992/3	1993/4	1994/5	1995/6	1996/7
Executive Council Office	460	395	433	326	370	307	287	325
Intergovernmental Affairs			318[a]	456	392	383	350	286
Office of the Premier	428	480	759	526	782	702	707	702
Priorities and Planning Secretariat			466[b]	c	c	1 077	1 094	1 116

[a]Part of the Premier's Office this year; figures adjusted accordingly.
[b]Policy Board.
[c]Not included this year.

APPENDIX 12.1 (CONT.)

AMOUNTS EXPENDED, NEWFOUNDLAND AND LABRADOR PUBLIC ACCOUNTS
(000s of Dollars)

Department Name and/ or Specific Section	1989/90	1990/1	1991/2	1992/3	1993/4	1994/5	1995/6	1996/7
Premier's Office	1 373	1 090	1 115	1 034	1 009	1 015	1 177	962
Cabinet Secretariat	2 751	2 570a	3 089	3 879	3 332	2 601	3 155	1 939
Treasury Board Secretariat	4 777	5 025	4 441	4 179	8 113	11 902	8 444	12 708
Intergovernmental Affairs Secretariat	2 975	3 960	2 298	2490	1 842	2 293	1 120	904

APPENDIX 12.2
Full-Time Equivalents [FTEs], Federal Central Agencies

AGENCY	1985– –86	1986– –87	1987– –88	1988– –89	1989– – 90	1990– –91	1991– –92	1992– –93	1993– –94	1994– –95	1995– –96	1996– –97	1997– –98
PCO	117	99	182	182	174	177	185	195	288	289b	310b	322b	328b
PMO	120	107	90	89	a	a	a	a	68	68	78	85	85
TBS	777	762	754	749	798	800	799	820	781	939	886	837	801
FIN	811	788	788	784	679	695	695	760	721	694	651	601	–

aNot available.
bThe increase in these years is due to the absorption of the FPRO [Federal–Provincial Relations Office] into the PCO staff.
cThe relevant definitions have changed over the years. Until 1992–93, Treasury Board counted human resources as person-years. It switched to "full-time equivalents" (FTEs) in 1993–94.

PCO=Privy Council Office, PMO=Prime Minister's Office,
TBS=Treasury Board Secretariat, FIN=Department of Finance.

Source: Canada, *Estimates: Part III*, Minister of Supply and Services, 1985–86 to 1997–98.

APPENDIX 12.3

The OECD Tools for Building Policy Coherence (1996)

PRACTICAL LESSONS IN THE TOOLS OF GOVERNANCE AND POLICYMAKING	ELABORATION
1. Commitment by the political leadership is a necessary precondition to coherence, and a tool for enhancing it.	• The centre builds up coherence as a positive value. • There is a political-administrative interface: senior officials attend meetings of the council of ministers in order to broaden ministerial views.
2. Establishing a strategic policy framework helps to ensure that individual policies are consistent with the government's goals and priorities.	• While ministers do policy planning for their own portfolios, the centre needs to perform comprehensive, multisectoral information gathering and analysis. • An organizationally separate planning capacity is needed within the centre to assure a long-term perspective and to shelter it from lesser operational issues. • Strategic advisors perform a gate-keeper function for the centre's policy units.
3. Decision makers need advice based on a clear definition and good analysis of issues, with explicit indications of possible inconsistencies.	• Less compartmentalization of central policy units assures that information flows. • Competitive policy roles between ministries assure a creative tension between them, a pattern that is needed in turbulent times.
4. The existence of a central overview and coordination capacity is essential to ensure horizontal consistency among policies.	• A variety of coordinating mechanisms can be useful in the face of cross-cutting policy issues: ministerial committees, superministries, ministries centred on client groups, lead ministers, junior ministers, advisory committees, interministerial committees, and a matrix management model.

(continued)

APPENDIX 12.3 (CONT.)

PRACTICAL LESSONS IN THE TOOLS OF GOVERNANCE AND POLICYMAKING	ELABORATION
5. Mechanisms that anticipate, detect, and resolve policy conflicts early in the process help to identify inconsistencies and reduce incoherence.	• Governments should resist wide restructuring into superministries or, alternatively, into small ministries. Interministerial conflicts are inevitable whatever the scale, and excessive largeness or smallness may both lead to serious coordination problems. • Complexes of programs should be evaluated, rather than single programs. • There should be "forced points of passage" [mandatory decision points] established to encourage the effected ministries to offer comments on cross-cutting issues and policies. • A higher-level arbitration mechanism should be created. • The coordination system should systematically flag, for higher-level arbitration, items on which negotiation has failed. • Consultation should be sought with "multiple voices" rather than with groups oriented toward a single narrow cause.
6. The decision-making process must be organized to achieve an effective reconciliation between policy priorities and budgetary imperatives.	• The budget should be seen as a tool of coherence. • The budget ministry should both coordinate and prioritize programs. • There should be symmetry between the policy agenda and budgetary imperatives. • Policy–budget linkage mechanisms, such as bilateral negotiation or consultation, should be established. • The centre should exercise an independent advisory and arbitration capacity on budgetary issues (special advisors or units).

(continued)

APPENDIX 12.3 (CONT.)

PRACTICAL LESSONS IN THE TOOLS OF GOVERNANCE AND POLICYMAKING	ELABORATION
7. Implementation procedures and monitoring mechanisms must be designed to ensure that policies can be adjusted in the light of progress, new information, and changing circumstances.	• The centre should ensure that ministers implement the intended policies. • Monitoring procedures should be put in place. • Circulation of draft decisions ensures that there are few remaining outstanding issues. • Formalization of decision making is important and is achieved by a single decision-making forum, a forced point of passage at the centre of government, and by systematic documentation of decisions.
8. An administrative culture that promotes cross-sectoral cooperation and a systematic dialogue between different policy communities contributes to the strengthening of policy coherence.	• Consultation should be a regular practice. • Personnel management policies should promote cooperative networking. • Policy communities [groups of actors sharing an interest in particular policies or policy areas] promote greater coherence the more they are interdisciplinary in nature. • Shared frameworks of understanding aid horizontality.

APPENDIX 12.4

Modern Duties and Subduties of Cabinets: "The Five Cs"

Control	Coordination
• of public expenditures in line with available revenues • of the size of the bureaucracy • of the policy development process • of information to the public	• of planning and budgeting • of interdepartmental working groups on planning • of public input into policy formation • of governmental priority setting

(continued)

APPENDIX 12. 4 (CONT.)

Modern Duties and Subduties of Cabinets: "The Five Cs"

Communication	Compromise
• of priorities and goals to the bureaucracy and to the public • of standards, where appropriate, for financial management, planning, personnel matters and auditing • of the need for the bureaucracy to be productive and innovative Counsel • on public needs • on priorities • on political strategies and tactics	• between departments on their competing demands for resources • between the needs of departmental managers for authority, accountability, and flexibility, and the needs of the central agency for standardization and predictability • on controversial issues, to be achieved either by keeping an uncommitted majority in cabinet or by instituting a hierarchy of cabinet committee authority in cabinet

NOTES

I am grateful to my research assistant, Steven Noel, for the professional work he has done in this and other projects. I also thank the staff of the MUCEP program at Memorial University of Newfoundland for student research funding.

1. The term *institutionalized cabinet* derives from J. Stefan Dupré, who contrasted it with the traditional and departmentalized cabinets that pertained at both the federal and provincial levels before and during the rise of the modern administrative state in Canada. See J. Stefan Dupré, "Reflections on the Workability of Executive Federalism," in *Intergovernmental Relations,* coordinated by Richard Simeon, Study 63 of the Macdonald Royal Commission (Toronto: University of Toronto Press, 1985), pp. 3–4.

2. Christopher Dunn, *The Institutionalized Cabinet: Governing the Western Provinces* (Montreal and Kingston: McGill-Queen's University Press, 1995), pp. 11–12.

3. Rand Dyck, *Canadian Politics: Critical Approaches,* 2nd ed. (Toronto: Nelson Canada, 1996), pp. 493–494.

4. Peter Aucoin, "The Prime Minister and Cabinet," in Robert M. Krause and R.H. Wagenberg, eds., *Introductory Readings in Canadian Government and Politics* (Toronto: Copp Clark Ltd., 1995), p. 189.

5. J. Stefan Dupré, "Reflections on the Workability of Executive Federalism."

6. Peter Aucoin, "The Prime Minister and Cabinet," p. 183.

7. Kenneth Kernaghan and David Siegel, *Public Administration in Canada: A Text*, 3rd ed. (Scarborough: Nelson Canada, 1995), p. 203.

8. Kernaghan and Siegel, p. 390.

9. Christopher Dunn, "Premiers and Cabinets," in Christopher Dunn, ed., *Provinces: Canadian Provincial Politics* (Peterborough: Broadview Press, 1996), esp. pp. 180–181.

10. Christopher Dunn, "Changing the Design: Cabinet Decision-Making in Three Provincial Governments," *Canadian Public Administration* 34, no. 4 (Winter 1991): 629.

11. Jean Chrétien, *Straight from the Heart*, 2nd ed. (Toronto: Key Porter Books Limited, 1994), p. 73.

12. Jean Chrétien, *Straight from the Heart*, p. 84.

13. Gunnel Gustafsson and J.J. Richardson, "Concepts of Rationality and the Policy Process," *European Journal of Political Research* 7 (1979): 415–436.

14. Gustafsson and Richardson, "Concepts of Rationality and the Policy Process," p. 430.

15. Canada, Privy Council Office, *Fourth Annual Report to the Prime Minister on the Public Service of Canada*, by Jocelyn Bourgon, Clerk of the Privy Council and Secretary to the Cabinet (Ottawa, February 3, 1997), ch. 5.

16. Organization for Economic Cooperation and Development, Public Management Occasional Papers, No. 12, *Building Policy Coherence: Tools and Tensions* (Paris: OECD Publications Service, 1996), p. 17.

17. Organization for Economic Cooperation and Development, *Building Policy Coherence: Tools and Tensions*, p. 3.

18. Peter Aucoin, *The New Public Management: Canada in Comparative Perspective* (Montreal: Institute for Research on Public Policy, 1995).

19. Patrick Weller, "Support for Prime Ministers: A Comparative Perspective," in Colin Campbell and Margaret Jane Wyszomirski, eds., *Executive Leadership in Anglo-American Systems* (Pittsburgh: University of Pittsburgh Press, 1991), pp. 377–378.

20. See, for example, the PS2000 Report and its condemnation of the control orientation and high overhead costs associated with the traditional central agencies of the federal government.

21. Christopher Dunn, *The Institutionalized Cabinet: Governing the Western Provinces*, p. 292.

✗ **NO**

Problems with the Institutionalized Cabinet

PAUL BARKER

In the last three decades, governments in Canada and elsewhere have changed the structure and operation of cabinets in similar ways. The *departmentalized* or *unaided cabinet* of the past has come to be replaced by the *institutionalized cabinet*. In the former type of cabinet, the responsible minister and his or her department would forward a proposal for the cabinet's consideration, and the cabinet as a whole would in most instances accept the proposal with little serious review. There existed entities, called central agencies, whose job was to provide the overall cabinet with some analysis of departmental initiatives, but the role of theses agencies was relatively small. With the advent of the institutionalized cabinet, this manner of executive decision making changed. Department proposals now received close scrutiny in newly established cabinet committees, which would be assisted in their review by greatly strengthened central agencies. Under the old system, a great deal of the power resided with the individual ministers. Under the new system, the collective cabinet, acting as a whole, assumed much more responsibility.

The shift in the operation of the cabinet revealed a belief that the institutionalized cabinet would provide for better government. The departmental cabinet had been found wanting in its ability to deal with the increasing interrelatedness of government policy. What was required was a structure capable of ensuring that government was not working at cross-purposes or in different directions, and that demanded a cabinet capable of examining the full scope of government activities. Related to this, it was felt that the cabinet has to be more rigorous in its analysis of policy proposals; simply relying on departmental expertise was not sufficient. Additionally, the departmentalized cabinet, with its emphasis on the offerings of departments, placed too much power in the hands of appointed officials. Accordingly, it was thought that the cabinet had to be restructured to give elected officials greater control so as to make governments more sensitive to the political winds of the day. The traditional cabinet had given nations, including Canada, "neutral competence," or government that was efficient but not attentive enough to the wishes of the public and its elected representatives. Ideally, what was wanted was "responsive competence," government that was both efficient and politically sensitive.[1]

These and other factors resulted in the emergence of the institutionalized cabinet. In Canada, it might be said that the institutionalized cabinet took its greatest hold, especially at the federal level. Cabinet committees proliferated, central agencies loomed much larger, formal procedures were specified, and the cabinet took on a more much collegial or collective orientation. No longer would individual ministers and their officials dictate the direction of government. The question, though, is whether this has made for good government in Canada. Has government become more responsive, more analytical, and better able to handle the interrelatedness of government activities? An examination of the experience of the institutionalized cabinet in Canada suggests a negative answer. Though the indictment against the institutionalized cabinet is a long one, this paper will focus on four problems. The implication of this analysis is that governments would be better off returning to the departmentalized cabinet, albeit one that has been adjusted to meet the modern challenges of governing.

DISSATISFIED MINISTERS

A certain amount of ministerial dissatisfaction is expected and desired in the institutionalized cabinet, for one of the aims of the new system is to shift some of the responsibility to the collective cabinet. But the degree of unhappiness among senior ministers with the institutionalized cabinet goes beyond what is consistent with good government. In the new cabinet, ministers more often than not find themselves involved in innumerable cabinet committee meetings endeavouring to review the proposals of others. Successful politicians, ones who are responsive to the public interest, do not spend much of their day poring over memorandums and coming together in closed-door meetings. Yet, that is what happens frequently in the institutionalized cabinet. As a deputy minister observes of the institutionalized cabinet, "Ministers did not enter political life in order to undertake a career in management."[2] Even those generally supportive of the institutionalized cabinet concede that ministers " could become exhausted if they were too conscientious" in the reading of cabinet documents and memorandums.[3]

Other aspects of the institutionalized cabinet also frustrate ministers. Collegiality, or joint decision making, is a big part of the institutionalized cabinet. Not surprisingly, it sometimes turns out that proposals are modified just to incorporate the view of others even if this leads to inferior policy. In other words, the tail wags the dog: the cabinet structure and its committees become the end, public policy the means. For strong ministers, eager to move ahead with their agendas, this becomes almost intolerable. In his reflections on his time as a minister, Prime Minister Chrétien comments critically on this element of the institutionalized cabinet, saying that cabinet committee reforms "resulted in weaker decisions, because even the strong ministers had to submit to collective judgements."[4] The fact that Chrétien as prime minister has downgraded the significance of cabinet committees and reduced their numbers suggests the intensity of his belief about this particular failing of the institutionalized cabinet.

In the institutionalized cabinet, ministers also find themselves increasingly challenged by *appointed* officials located in central agencies. This, too, is to be expected, for the central agencies are supposed to offer their advice to cabinet committees on departmental proposals. But this particular practice of the institutionalized cabinet is unsettling to ministers who come to office believing that elected officials, not appointed officials, determine the course of government.[5] The intrusiveness of committees and central agencies is also evident to individual ministers when they attempt to deal with counterparts in the other order of government. Under the departmentalized cabinet, federal ministers and their provincial counterparts established relations that were conducive to the development of important federal–provincial arrangements. For example, federal and provincial welfare ministers met to provide for social assistance programs, and health ministers did the same. Out of this emerged crucial "trust ties"–bonds of confidence–that were considered essential to workability in federal–provincial relations.[6] But the institutionalized cabinet ended this situation; individual ministers no longer could be trusted to represent federal or provincial interests. In their place emerged the collective cabinet and central agencies, and with this came the breaking of the trust ties and a decline in civility between federal and provincial governments.

Finally, the institutionalized cabinet saps the creativity of individual departments and their ministers. In the traditional cabinet, departments probably did have too much power, but they also provided governments with new and exciting proposals at times. This was in large part because the departments were able to work on their own and were not restricted by the participation of others. That has now changed, and policymaking under the institutionalized cabinet comes closer to policymaking by committee. As most familiar with decision making appreciate, this is an arrangement that hardly fosters innovation and creative decision making. Indeed, it is usually "hostile" to such attributes in policy, and often the result is government action that represents the "lowest common denominator" or policy that is acceptable to all interests.[7]

The institutionalized cabinet promises more responsive government. The latter is greatly dependent on individual ministers able to pursue their mandates, but this is exactly what the modern cabinet denies. Some defend the treatment of ministers under the institutionalized cabinet by claiming it is necessary to wrest political power from departments and to save ministers from becoming captives of their departmental officials. But good governments, ones with strong leadership, have never had a real problem with departments and ministers. Prime ministers and premiers ensure through constant reiteration–preaching, one might even say–that ministers are cognizant of the fact that their basic duty "is not to carry the views and interests of the department to the cabinet table ... [but] to carry the views and interests of the Cabinet to the departments."[8] What is needed to ensure good government is not elaborate institutional arrangements, but strong direction from the first minister. As with corporate heads in the private sector, a primary responsibility of the prime minister or premier "is to continuously articulate the essential values of the organization."[9]

TROUBLESOME CENTRAL AGENCIES

Generally defined, central agencies are staff entities that seek to monitor and coordinate the efforts of departments. In the departmentalized cabinet, this responsibility took on rather limited proportions, but this situation changes with the institutionalized cabinet. As indicated already, central agencies now rigorously analyze the offerings of departments, and they also aggressively endeavour to ensure that government policies complement one another and refrain from working in a contradictory fashion. Though well intentioned, these efforts have had detrimental effects. One is in relation to the pursuit of coordinated policies, or the problem of interrelatedness. The complaint here is that the cabinet decision-making system quickly gets clogged with coordination exercises. A department presents a proposal, and is told by central agencies that the department must wait until it is determined how the proposal fits into the overall scheme of things. This is a laudable aim, but the fact remains that it takes time, the result of which is that government is perceived as slow-moving and unresponsive. It has also been observed that central agencies effectively acquire a taste for coordination, and engage in coordination exercises when the need for them is difficult to discern.[10]

A second effect is that in the institutionalized cabinet the world of central agencies inevitably becomes crowded. At the federal level in Canada, the departmentalized cabinet had three central agencies, the Prime Minister's Office, the Privy Council Office, and the Department of Finance. With the institutionalized cabinet, the number of central agencies grew to include, in addition to the established agencies, the Treasury Board Secretariat, the Federal–Provincial Relations Office, and the Ministries of State of Social and Economic Development. As well, the number of personnel in these agencies increased. With the greater emphasis on coordination and analysis, the demand for central agencies increases, with the result that cabinet decision making becomes more bureaucratic and weighted down with formal procedures and red tape. Moreover, with the greater number of central agencies, competition among them begins to emerge. Not only do central agencies contest the offerings of departments, but also they argue over and criticize their own analyses.[11] This, too, makes little contribution to a process that tries to provide responsive and effective public policy.

Another effect relates to the expertise of central agencies. Those who inhabit these structures have been called "superbureaucrats,"[12] and are recognized as the best and the brightest in the public service. The high flyers of public administration usually find themselves in a central agency. All this recognizes that central agency officials are intelligent individuals. However, this does not mean that they have the requisite expertise on substantive matters. Most of this kind of expertise is located in departments, with senior appointed officials who have spent a career developing their knowledge and appreciation of the concerns of the department. But sometimes in the institutionalized cabinet this expertise is displaced by the analyses of central agencies. When a departmental proposal, in the form of a cabinet memorandum, reaches a cabinet committee, the proposal is always assessed by a central agency, and this practice affords central agencies an opportunity to displace the views of department officials with their own. If good government is in part about engaging the machinery of government for the purpose of ensuring competent government, then this practice, if observed on a widespread basis, is to be discouraged.

Lastly, there is the sheer power of central agencies in institutionalized cabinet. In some reports of the workings of the institutionalized cabinet in Canada, concern has been expressed about the influence of central agencies. For example, interest groups that are eager to comment on the decisions of government find it difficult to gain access to central agencies. In the past, interest groups advised government through individual line departments, but the emergence of the institutionalized cabinet has forced groups to focus on central agencies because of the latter's ascendancy. But central agencies have proved resistant to the approaches of interest groups.[13] The senior line officials in departments, deputy ministers, have also experienced the enhanced power of central agencies. Deputy ministers find that they have to spend more time responding to the demands of central agencies, and, more generally, they have experienced a loss of influence as the centre of the institutionalized cabinet draws power to itself. Then there are the ministers. The power of central agencies in relation to ministers has been touched upon already. As noted, ministers expect to play a major role in respect to their area, but find this role usurped at times by central agencies. Relating to his own experience, one minister in the Trudeau cabinet reports that central agencies "did not hesitate to interfere with ministerial authority, often to the point of killing ministerial initiatives." He also notes that the influence of central agencies "had grown far beyond anything reasonable in a parliamentary democracy."[14] The minister may exaggerate, but this kind of comment from a senior elected official is disturbing.

NEW PUBLIC MANAGEMENT

Though it was not greatly emphasized, one of the reasons for implementing the institutionalized cabinet was to deal with calcified or rigid line departments. In the minds of some, departments were incapable of providing resourceful responses to social problems. The bureaucracy had become bureaucratic. Under the institutionalized cabinet, the collective cabinet could, if necessary, take the policymaking responsibility away from the individual minister and his or her department. Of course, the cabinet committee that undertook such action could not literally assume this responsibility; a central agency would have to do it. There is some evidence to support such a dynamic, that the institutionalized cabinet was right to allow central agencies to become policymaking bodies. Line departments *had* become too bureaucratic, too set in their ways, too unwilling to entertain new ways of doing things. For example, in the early 1980s the federal government searched for ways to dissuade the provinces from introducing direct patient charges for health services, but the responsible line department proved unable to come up with appropriate policy on its own. It was only through the diligence of central agencies that Ottawa managed to secure its goal through the introduction of the Canada Health Act.[15]

But now the incentives and environment facing departments are changing. Whereas in earlier years little was done to address the slothfulness of departments, at the present there is a concerted attack on old departmental practices and their replacement with a new management philosophy. In this new world of public administration, which is often called the New Public Management (NPM), bureaucrats are to be given more freedom and autonomy to deal with departmental responsibilities.[16] They are expected to behave like private sector entrepreneurs, searching out creative means of meeting the wishes of their "customers." Along with this new responsibility is a new accountability mechanism, which takes the form of performance measures that evaluate the actions of the newly minted policy and managerial entrepreneurs. The hope, and initial results provide some grounds for this hope, is that departments will do a better job, that they will become as effective as the best private sector firms in meeting the needs of their clients, the electorate.[17] Accordingly, the need for the institutionalized cabinet and its concern over lethargic departments becomes less apparent.

The New Public Management also makes the institutionalized cabinet unnecessary in another sense. Inherent in the institutionalized cabinet is the belief that the departments must be better controlled. If government is to provide for more effective and better coordinated public policy, then central agencies and cabinet committees must be established to ensure that line departments toe the line. But this approach reflects the old belief that the best way to make appointed officials accountable is by stipulating rules and making certain that these rules are followed. But the NPM dispenses with this perspective, and asserts that accountability can be achieved through a combination of greater freedom and solid performance measures. When it is clear to all what is required, then there is little real need for monitoring agencies anxious about whether a particular rule is being followed. Ideally, what is desired under the NPM is simultaneous "loose-tight controls," in which the centre—cabinet—posits a few, clear objectives and then gives departments the leeway to achieve these aims with means they deem to be the most effective.[18]

It should be noted that not all are convinced of the value of the New Public Management. It may fail to work, and it may not even be appropriate for government, given that it borrows heavily from the private sector.[19] From this perspective, the trappings of the institutionalized cabinet may still be necessary. But the very pervasiveness of the NPM philosophy across governments in various countries suggest that many believe it to be suitable for government. As well, the practices underlying NPM—empowerment, decentralization, focus on the client, autonomy, entrepreneurialism—seem to inform organizational change in all walks of life. The hierarchical world of the past, complete with controls and rules, is to be replaced by one that emphasizes participation, partnership, and performance. In a way, the institutionalized cabinet is out of date, wedded to values that are increasingly discarded by a new age in government and management.[20]

UNWORKABLE AND UNNATURAL

Perhaps the most damning argument against the institutionalized cabinet is that it fails to work in many instances. For every minister who is forced to bend to the collective will of the institutionalized cabinet, there is another who escapes the collegial clutches of the institutionalized cabinet. Writing of the institutionalized cabinet operating in Canada at the federal level during the 1970s and 1980s, Aucoin says that the supporters of the cabinet were "too optimistic about the collegiality of ministers," that ministers were unwilling "to compromise their personal objectives and departmental ambitions in pursuit of coherent corporate policies." The result, says Aucoin, was that "substantive priorities and policies proposed to give effect to them were too often driven by individual ministerial and departmental ambitions."[21] Along the same lines, there are reports of "end runs" on the institutionalized cabinet. Instead of navigating the labyrinth of committees, agencies, and other entities, ministers and their officials bypass the process and deal directly with the major decision makers.[22] Perhaps more dispiriting, sometimes the major issues are simply pulled from the institutionalized cabinet and dealt with through separate channels. In this case, there is no end run, but rather a formal decision to handle an issue, a significant one, elsewhere. The institutionalized cabinet handles matters, but not the important ones.

Each of these failings can be interpreted as reflections of contests of power within cabinet. A minister, jealous of his or her prerogatives, resists the collective quality of the institutionalized cabinet; another minister, desperate for a quick decision, simply skirts the cabinet; and a prime minister and his senior officials believe that their interests can be better served by constructing a decision-making process outside the institutionalized cabinet. But it might also be suggested that the unworkability of the institutionalized cabinet relates to a certain *unnatural* quality. In other words, the institutionalized cabinet simply does not fit into a normal governing process, for it upsets too many of the traditional dynamics of political life.

At first, the institutionalized cabinet *does* appear as a natural component of the modern governing apparatus. The demands of the political process require responsive governments able to coordinate complex policy offerings, and the institutionalized cabinet seems ideally suited to this challenge. The fact that so many democratic polities have embraced one aspect or another of the institutionalized cabinet also suggests that this type of cabinet system is entirely appropriate. Yet, there is great resistance, in Canada and elsewhere, to the institutionalized cabinet, with various attempts made to distort the operations of the cabinet or even to circumvent it. This hardly seems indicative of anything natural to the political system. The lack of collegiality, the end runs, the hivening off of the significant issues—all this and more points to the unnaturalness of the institutionalized cabinet. For further support of this claim, one need only look at some of the descriptions of the operation of the institutionalized cabinet. Here is one such description:

> Overall the sheer complexity of the system meant that the process was time consuming, confusing, and frustrating to both insiders and outsiders who wished to gain access to the policy process.[23]

And another, this time from an active participant in the institutionalized cabinet:

> [I]t was completely rational but deeply impractical. It was based on the belief that you could construct a system and then force not only people but events to fit themselves into it. It required a breed of supermen, and a universe unfolding as it should. Instead, it produced a world that was an administrative nightmare, and it drove able people out of public life.[24]

These are not votes of confidence in the institutionalized cabinet. Indeed, they suggest that there is a fundamental discordance between the institutionalized cabinet and good government.

WHAT TO DO?

In light of the failings of the institutionalized cabinet, one is tempted to recommend a return to the departmentalized or unaided cabinet. This has been essentially the reaction of the Chrétien government at the federal level in Canada. This government has reduced the number of cabinet committees, curtailed the power of central agencies, and given influence and authority back to the individual ministers. But this reaction to the institutionalized cabinet probably constitutes an overreaction, and fails to recognize that there were problems with the departmentalized cabinet. In the unaided cabinet, at times departments did wield too much power, and government did act at cross-purposes, and sometimes overall direction was lacking. It is not surprising, then, to hear reports of poor coordination and too powerful ministers in the Chrétien government.[25]

A more prudent response to the failings of the institutionalized cabinet might be to make adjustments that are in keeping with the basic logic and operation of the departmentalized cabinet.[26] For example, instead of using powerful central agencies to ensure coordinated policy, the cabinet system could rely more heavily on interdepartmental efforts. Coordination is achieved, not through the introduction of new bodies, but rather through existing structures. Similarly, ad hoc task forces, consisting of interested ministers and officials seconded from line departments, might be employed to provide sufficient analysis of important matters; if bad analysis is the problem, then bring together, *temporarily*, the best in the departments. These same task forces could also be used in coordination efforts. Again, the attraction here is the reliance on the structures of the traditional cabinet. There is no need for aggressive central agencies or a complex network of cabinet committees, but only for reforms to the way the departmentalized cabinet has always worked.

There are other reforms that might be suggested, but the key point is that any changes should be consistent with the workings of the traditional cabinet. There were problems with the operation of the traditional cabinet, but the institutionalized cabinet goes too far in responding to these problems. The trick is to ensure that a similarly overaggressive response does not take place in relation to the shortcomings of the institutionalized cabinet.

CONCLUSION

Over the past half century, government in Canada and other countries has assumed a much more important place in society. It is no longer concerned solely with services relating to the maintenance of order and the assurance of external security. The electorate now expects government to take an active role in many areas. In such a setting, it is not surprising that some would find it necessary to change the operation of cabinet, to make it better equipped to handle the new challenges of governing. As a result, the institutionalized cabinet arose to displace the departmentalized cabinet. But the contention of this essay is that this particular change has produced some major problems, which strongly suggest that the institutionalized cabinet does not provide for good government. Ministers feel, under the institutionalized cabinet, that they are unable to properly represent the interests of their constituents, so responsive government becomes difficult to achieve. Central agencies flourish under the modern cabinet, a development that leads to a cabinet process that, among things, becomes sluggish, formalistic, and, paradoxically, less expert than before. And the institutionalized cabinet as a whole hinders efforts at making government more innovative through new modes of departmental management, and goes against the natural flow of the governmental process.

All of this is not to mean that a simple return to the departmentalized cabinet of yesteryear is called for. What it does mean is that any structuring of the cabinet should seek to remain as close as possible to the practices of the traditional cabinet. The traditional cabinet has its weaknesses, but the institutionalized cabinet is not the solution. To ensure good government, cabinet makers in Canada should be more willing to learn from the past.

NOTES

1. Terry M. Moe, "The Politicized Presidency," in John Chubb and Paul Peterson, eds., *The New Direction in American Politics* (Washington DC: Brookings Institution, 1985), p. 239.

2. Richard Van Loon, "The Policy and Expenditure Management System in the Federal Government: The First Three Years," *Canadian Public Administration* 26, no. 2 (1983): 287.

3. Mitchell Sharp, *Which Reminds Me ... A Memoir* (Toronto: University of Toronto Press, 1994), p. 166.

4. Jean Chrétien, *Straight from the Heart*, 2nd ed. (Toronto: Key Porter Books, 1994), p. 84.

5. Colin Campbell, *Governments Under Stress: Political Executives and Key Bureaucrats in Washington, London, and Ottawa* (Toronto: University of Toronto Press, 1983), p. 351.

6. J. Stefan Dupré, "Reflections on the Workability of Executive Federalism," in R.D. Olling and M.W. Westmacott, eds., *Perspectives on Canadian Federalism* (Scarborough, ON: Prentice-Hall, 1988), p. 236.

7. A.W. Johnson, "Public Policy: Creativity and Bureaucracy," *Canadian Public Administration* 21, no. 1 (1978): 9, 11.

8. Allan Blakeney and Sanford Borins, *Political Management in Canada* (Toronto: McGraw-Hill Ryerson, 1992), p. 5.

9. Ibid., p. 11.

10. Peter Aucoin and Herman Bakvis, *The Centralization-Decentralization Conundrum: Organization and Management in the Canadian Government* (Halifax: Institute for Research on Public Policy, 1988), p. 45.

11. Peter Aucoin, "Organizational Change in the Machinery of Canadian Government: From Rational Management to Brokerage Politics," *Canadian Journal of Political Science* 19, no. 1 (1986): 16.

12. Colin Campbell and George Szablowski, *The Superbureaucrats: Structure and Behaviour in Central Agencies* (Toronto: Macmillan of Canada, 1979).

13. James Gillies and Jean Pigott, "Participation in the Legislative Process," *Canadian Public Administration* 25, no. 2 (1982): 263.

14. Donald Johnston, *Up the Hill* (Montreal: Optimum Publishing, 1986), p. 69.

15. Paul Barker, "The Canada Health Act and the Cabinet Decision-Making System of Pierre Elliott Trudeau," *Canadian Public Administration* 32, no. 1 (1989): 84–103.

16. Christopher Hood, "A Public Management for All Seasons," *Public Administration* 69 (1991); and Peter Aucoin, *The New Public Management: Canada in Comparative Perspective* (Montreal: Institute for Research on Public Policy, 1995).

17. Sanford Borins, "The New Public Management Is Here to Stay," *Canadian Public Administration* 38, no. 1 (1995): 122–132.

18. Aucoin and Bakvis, *The Centralization-Decentralization Conundrum*, p. 5.

19. Donald J. Savoie, "What Is Wrong with the New Public Management?" *Canadian Public Administration* 38, no. 1 (1995): 112–121.

20. Neil Nevitte, *The Decline of Deference* (Peterborough, ON: Broadview Press, 1996).

21. Peter Aucoin, "Organizational Change in the Machinery of Canadian Government: From Rational Management to Brokerage Politics," 14–15.

22. Peter Aucoin and Herman Bakvis, *The Centralization-Decentralization Conundrum*, p. 39.

23. Paul B. Thomas, "Central Agencies: Making a Mesh of Things," in James P. Bickerton and Alain-G. Gagnon, eds., *Canadian Politics*, 2nd ed. (Peterborough, ON: Broadview Press, 1994), p. 293.

24. Christina McCall-Newman, *Grits: An Intimate Portrait of the Liberal Party* (Toronto: Macmillan of Canada, 1982), p. 213.

25. Edward Greenspon and Anthony Wilson-Smith, *Double Vision: The Inside Story of the Liberals in Power* (Toronto: Doubleday Canada Ltd., 1996), pp. 249–250.

26. For more on this theme, see Blakeney and Borins, *Political Management in Canada*.

Postscript

Dunn makes a convincing case for the institutionalized cabinet. He notes its wide-spread use, and shows that it tends to persist even when governments seek a return to the unaided cabinet. At present, the Chrétien government is attempting such a return, but Dunn intimates that this effort will suffer the same fate as other attempts. Indeed, Dunn presents evidence that the trappings of the institutionalized cabinet are still visible in the Chrétien cabinet. Notwithstanding all this, though, a few questions emerge on examining Dunn's analysis. Does the fact that governments around the world embrace the institutionalized cabinet necessarily mean that it is good for government? It may be that the institutionalized cabinet is a fad in government, that its popularity stems from the fact that others are adopting it rather than from a prudent consideration of its utility. Also, Dunn admits to some failings of the institutionalized cabinet, and urges a rebalancing of the cabinet in a way that makes it appear suspiciously like the departmental-ized cabinet. Take his recommendation for an end to the "control orientation" of the institutionalized cabinet: some might say that control is at the centre of the institutionalized cabinet, and to make this change is to pronounce a death sentence on the institutionalized cabinet.

In his paper, Barker outlines some purported shortcomings of the institutional-ized cabinet, and concludes that a reformed departmentalized cabinet would be in the best interests of governments. On the surface, the analysis here is persuasive in spots, but a closer look suggests some problems. For one, he notes that the institutionalized cabinet drains the creativity out of departments, but then later admits that departments under the departmentalized cabinet suffered from a severe case of lethargy. He also downplays some of the problems of the depart-mentalized cabinet. According to most studies, appointed officials in departments did have too much influence in the departmentalized cabinet, but Barker takes little heed of this. Perhaps most important, he fails to recognize that the increasing size of government requires a forum that can tackle the interrelated-ness of government policy. If he did recognize this, he would be less willing to ask for a return to the departmentalized cabinet.

Though Dunn and Barker are on opposite sides of the debate, their recommen-dations bring them closer together. Dunn recognizes that the institutionalized cabinet should become less institutionalized, and similarly Barker concedes that the departmentalized cabinet must become less departmentalized. One challenge for the student would be to see whether some hybrid format might represent the best cabinet structure for facilitating good government.

There are many relevant articles on the topic of cabinet structure, but probably the place to start is Dupré's article on the effect of the changing nature of cabinet structure on federal–provincial relations: J. Stefan Dupré, "Reflections on the

Workability of Executive Federalism," in Richard Simeon, ed., *Intergovernmental Relations*, Study 63 of the Macdonald Royal Commission (Toronto: University of Toronto Press, 1985). The article is challenging, but it is where the term "institutionalized cabinet" was first coined, and Dupré gives pithy definitions of the possible types of cabinet arrangements. Another source that outlines the features of the institutionalized and departmentalized (or unaided) cabinet structures is Christopher Dunn's *The Institutionalized Cabinet: Governing the Western Provinces* (Montreal and Kingston: McGill-Queen's University Press, 1995). This text also provides a rich discussion of the evolution of cabinet toward an institutionalized form in the provinces of Manitoba, Saskatchewan, and British Columbia. Dunn also provides a summary of his major findings in "Cabinet Decision-Making in Three Provincial Governments," *Canadian Public Administration* 34, no. 4 (1991). Students might also be advised to become familiar with the basic institution of cabinet. The following provide some guidance on this: Peter Aucoin, "Prime Minister and Cabinet," in James P. Bickerton and Alain-G. Gagnon, eds., *Canadian Politics*, 2nd ed. (Peterborough, ON: Broadview Press, 1994); Herman Bakvis and David MacDonald, "The Canadian Cabinet: Organization, Decision-Rules, and Policy Impact," in Michael M. Atkinson, ed., *Governing Canada: Institutions and Public Policy* (Toronto: Harcourt Brace Jovanovich Canada Inc., 1993); and Norman Ward, *Dawson's The Government of Canada*, 6th ed. (Toronto: University of Toronto Press, 1990).

For appraisals of the institutionalized cabinet, there are a number of publications that might be reviewed. Most deal with the operation of the institutionalized cabinet at the federal level, and many of these document the experience of the Trudeau government with cabinet decision making. The articles and books include Richard D. French, *How Ottawa Decides: Planning and Policy Making 1968–1984* (Toronto: James Lorimer and Co., 1984); Richard Van Loon, "The Policy and Expenditure Management System in the Federal Government: The First Three Years," *Canadian Public Administration* 26, no. 2 (1983); Peter Aucoin, "Organizational Change in the Machinery of Canadian Government: From Rational Management to Brokerage Politics," *Canadian Journal of Political Science* 19, no. 1 (1986); Paul Barker, "The Canada Health Act and the Cabinet Decision-Making System of Pierre Elliott Trudeau," *Canadian Public Administration* 32, no. 1 (1989); and Christopher Dunn, "Premiers and Cabinets," in Christopher Dunn, ed., *Provinces: Canadian Provincial Politics* (Peterborough, ON: Broadview Press, 1996).

As Dunn says in his article, the trappings of the institutionalized cabinet are not limited to Canada. For more on the institutionalized cabinet in other countries, students might consult the following: D.A. Kemp, "The Recent Evolution of Central Policy Control Mechanisms in Parliamentary Systems," *International Political Science Review* 7, no. 1 (1986); Roger Porter, *Presidential Decision-Making: The Economic Policy Board* (New York: Cambridge University Press,

1982); and Colin Campbell and B. Guy Peters, eds., *Organizing Governance: Governing Organizations* (Pittsburgh, PA: University of Pittsburgh Press, 1988). It should be noted that the institutionalized cabinet does not go by this name in other states, but the keen observer will be able to recognize it.

Lastly, other analyses and frameworks have been developed to deal with the evolution of the cabinet. One such framework can be found in the work of Colin Campbell, who has written widely on the issue of cabinet organization. His publications present a relatively complicated picture of cabinet changes, but they are certainly worth considering by the student who wishes to pursue this subject area in detail. In addition to those already noted, Campbell's publications include *Governments Under Stress: Political Executives and Key Bureaucrats in Washington, London, and Ottawa* (Toronto: University of Toronto Press, 1983); "Administration and Politics: The State Apparatus and Political Responsiveness," *Comparative Politics* 19 (1987); *Managing the Presidency: Carter, Reagan, and the Search for Executive Harmony* (Pittsburgh, PA: University of Pittsburgh Press, 1986); and (with John Halligan) *Political Leadership in the Age of Constraint: The Australian Experience* (Pittsburgh, PA: University of Pittsburgh Press, 1992).

ISSUE**THIRTEEN**

Should Party Discipline Be Relaxed?

✔ **YES**
DAVID KILGOUR, JOHN KIRSNER, AND KENNETH McCONNELL,
"Discipline versus Democracy: Party Discipline in Canadian
Politics"

✘ **NO**
ROBERT J. JACKSON AND PAUL CONLIN, "The Imperative of Party
Discipline in the Canadian Political System"

David Kilgour, a member of Parliament from Alberta, has had a rocky relationship with the Progressive Conservative Party over the years. Elected to Parliament in 1979 as a member of the Conservative Party, Kilgour quit the party caucus in April 1987 in protest over the Conservative government's policies for the west and its failure to develop adequate ethical guidelines for elected representatives. Kilgour rejoined the Tory caucus in February 1988, but soon became critical of his party's proposed Goods and Services Tax (GST). On April 10, 1990, he voted against the government's bill authorizing the GST, and as a consequence was expelled from the caucus of the Progressive Conservative Party. Kilgour subsequently crossed the floor to sit as a member of the Liberal Party. He has subsequently been reelected twice as a Liberal member of Parliament.

David Kilgour's troubles with his party stem from the well-known tradition of party discipline, which requires members of Parliament to vote according to their party's position. Clearly, the member from Alberta has some difficulty with this tradition, and he is not alone. In 1983, a Gallup poll showed that only 7.9 percent of respondents believed that the first priority should be loyalty to his or her party.

Despite this, political leaders have long felt that the principle of party discipline was vital to the functioning of parliamentary government in Canada. When necessary, as in the case of David Kilgour, party officials have shown that they are willing to take strong measures to enforce party discipline—by withholding support for a candidate at election time, by denying parliamentary appointments, or even by expelling a recalcitrant MP from the party caucus.

The rationale for discipline in political parties is a simple one. Canada has a parliamentary system of government that requires that the party in power maintain the support and confidence of the majority of the members of the legislative branch. Without this support, the government would find it difficult to carry out the mandate on which it is elected and, more important, to remain in power. Party discipline is a means of preventing these occurrences.

For many Canadians, as reflected in the following two readings, the debate over party discipline hinges largely on whether or not Canada should move closer to an American model, where members of Congress are seen as being relatively free to vote according to personal conscience and constituency interest. David Kilgour, John Kirsner, and Kenneth McConnell argue that relaxed party discipline would advance the cause of democracy and provide better representation for individual constituents. Robert Jackson and Paul Conlin counter that the weakening of party discipline would give Canada an American-style system in which special interest groups, not elected officials, would control our legislative representatives.

✔ YES

Discipline versus Democracy: Party Discipline in Canadian Politics

DAVID KILGOUR, JOHN KIRSNER, AND KENNETH McCONNELL

Representative democracy in Canada is so dominated by political parties that some experts believe the party discipline exerted on most votes in our House of Commons and provincial legislatures is the tightest in the democratic world. Defenders of our model argue that many Canadians prefer it this way because each party's candidates can be assumed at election time to share the party's position on every issue. Others contend our executive democracy, patterned on a system prevailing in Great Britain about three centuries ago, requires iron party discipline if our fused legislative and executive branches of government are to function effectively. Another reason, probably the most important, is that our practice makes life easier for leaders of both government and opposition parties.

Unlike parliamentary systems in places such as Great Britain and Germany, virtually every vote in Canadian legislatures is considered potentially one of non-confidence in the government. Even a frivolous opposition motion to adjourn for the day, if lost, can be deemed by a cabinet to have been one of nonconfidence. The whips of government parties have for decades used the possibility of an early election to push their members into voting the party line. The opposition attitude is so similar that we had a few years ago the spectacle of both opposition parties in our House of Commons arguing that a free vote on an abortion resolution would "rip out the heart" of our parliamentary system of government. The constituents of both provincial and federal legislators would be the real winners if party discipline is loosened. Private members from both government and opposition benches could then take positions on government bills and other matters based on assisting their constituents instead of their respective party hierarchies.

PARTY DISCIPLINE IN CANADA

W.S. Gilbert put the present Canadian political reality succinctly: "I always voted at my party's call and I never thought of thinking for myself at all." Canadian members of Parliament are essentially passive observers in the formulation and administration of most national policy. Indeed, Sean Moore, editor of the Ottawa lobbyist magazine *The Lobby Digest*, told a committee of MPs in early 1993 that they are rarely lobbied by the almost three thousand reported lobbyists in the capital because "elected officials play a very minor role in governing."

MPs from all parties vote in solid blocs on almost every issue. Government members do so from a fear that a lost vote on a measure will be deemed by their prime minister as a loss of confidence. This stems from the early to mid-19th-century British concept that a government falls if it loses the support of a majority in the Commons on any vote.

Besides the threat of parliamentary dissolution, private members are also subject to rewards and punishments from party leadership, depending on how they vote. A "loyal" MP who votes the party line will be a candidate for promotion (if in the government party, perhaps to cabinet), or other benefits from the party, such as interesting trips or appointment to an interesting House committee. A "disloyal" MP who votes against the party leadership may be prevented from ascending the political ladder and could ultimately be thrown out of the party caucus. In light of this, "caucus solidarity and my constituents be damned" might be the real oath of office for most honourable members in all political parties.

Reg Stackhouse, a former Tory MP for Scarborough West, in a submission to the Task Force on Reform of the House of Commons in 1985, commented on the discipline imposed on private members of the government party:

> Not only is it demanded that [the member] vote with the government on crucial matters such as the Speech from the Throne or the budget, but also that he vote, speak or remain silent according to the dictate of the government. Even though a government may be at no risk of falling, it requires this all but unconditional commitment, and renders the member a seeming robot, at least imaginatively replaceable by a voting machine.

This is the major defect in Canadian parliamentary democracy: most MPs are essentially brute voters who submit to any demand from their respective party whips. In Canada's current political culture, a prime minister or premier could in practice on all confidence votes cast proxy votes on behalf of all government members. The same practice prevails in the opposition parties because they think themselves obliged to vote in uniform party blocs virtually always. If not, some of our media, apparently unaware that parliamentary democracy has evolved elsewhere, including in the matters of the parliamentary system in the United Kingdom, report that the opposition leaders cannot control their caucuses. This status quo has persisted for so long primarily because party leaders and policy mandarins obviously prefer it. Measures going into the House of Commons where one party has a majority usually emerge essentially unscathed. Everything follows a highly predictable script: obedient government members praise it; opposition parties rail against it; and plenty of bad measures become law essentially unamended.

The present regional differences and priorities require much better public expression in Parliament, at least if one central institution of our national government is to reflect adequately all parts of the country. Regional voices are frequently suffocated by rigid party discipline and the entrenched habit of the national caucuses to maintain a close eye on what opinion leaders, particularly columnists in Toronto–Ottawa–Montreal, regard as the national interest on any issue. Therefore, reforming the role of MPs is not only essential for parliamentary legitimacy in post-modern Canada, but is vital to "nationalizing Ottawa."

ELIMINATING EXCESSES

A report by the late Eugene Forsey and Graham Eglington *(The Question of Confidence in Responsible Government)* lists a large number of measures defeated in the Westminster Parliament. On most, the cabinet of the day simply carried on, presumably either dropping the failed proposal or seeking majority support for a different measure. For tax bills, the list of such defeats begins in 1834. During 1975, for example, a financial bill of the Harold Wilson cabinet dealing with their value-added tax rate was defeated, but the ministry carried on in office, treating it not as a confidence vote.

The Forsey-Eglington Report also emphasizes that in earlier years, government MPs in Canada were permitted to vote against cabinet measures. For example, between 1867 and 1872, their study lists fully eighteen pages of cases in which Conservative MPs voted against measures of John A. Macdonald's government. The sky did not fall; Macdonald's government was able to function effectively; government MPs could keep both their self-respect and their membership in the government caucus.

The study also provides interesting data about voting in our House of Commons during other periods: in 1896, fully sixteen Conservative MPs voted with Laurier's Liberals to adjourn a Conservative measure intended to restore Catholic schools in Manitoba; in 1981, sixteen Conservative MPs, including three who later became ministers, voted against the final resolution patriating our Constitution.

The all-party McGrath Report on parliamentary reform came to the conclusion that the role of the individual member must be enhanced. As James McGrath himself said in 1985, "I wanted to put into place a system where being a member of Parliament would be seen to be an end to itself and not a means to an end." On the question of nonconfidence, McGrath recommended the following:

- A government should be careful before it designates a vote as one of confidence. It should confine such declarations to measures central to its administration.

- While a defeat on supply is a serious matter, elimination or reduction of an estimate can be accepted.

- In a Parliament with a government in command of a majority, the matter of confidence has really been settled by the electorate.

- Government should therefore have the wisdom to permit members to decide many matters in their own personal judgments.

Reg Stackhouse agrees that party discipline must have limits: "Tight party lines need be drawn only when the government's confidence is at stake, i.e., when the government decides the fate of a bill is absolutely essential to its objectives."

One way to reduce party discipline in the interest of greater fairness for every province would be to write into our Constitution, as the West Germans did in their

Basic Law, that MPs and senators shall "not [be] bound by orders and instructions and shall be subject only to their conscience." Party discipline diluted this principle in West Germany, but when combined with another feature of their Constitution—that no chancellor can be defeated in their equivalent of our House of Commons unless a majority of members simultaneously agree on a new person to become chancellor—there now appears to be a more independent role for members of the Bundestag than for Canadian members of Parliament. For example, in the case of the defeat of the minority Clark government in 1979 on its budget, the West German rule would have kept Clark in office unless the Liberals, New Democrats, and Social Credit MPs had agreed simultaneously on a new prime minister who could hold the confidence of a majority of MPs. A similar rule, if adopted by the House of Commons, would inevitably weaken our party discipline significantly because MPs from all parties could vote on the merits of issues, knowing that defeat would bring down only the measure and not the government.

Another approach would be for each new federal or provincial cabinet to specify at the start of their mandate which matters at the heart of their program will be confidence issues. The Mulroney government, for example, might have spelled out in late 1988 that the Canada–U.S. Free Trade Agreement would be a confidence issue. In those situations, party discipline would be justifiable. Otherwise, its backbenchers would be free to vote for their constituents' interests at all times. This restored independence for legislators would lead to better representation for all regions of Canada and much more occupational credibility for Canadian legislators.

A study of the 32nd Legislative Assembly of Ontario (1981–85) indicated that its members voted in uniform party blocs about 95 percent of the time. The same pattern has applied in at least the past four Parliaments in Ottawa. The Canadian pattern indicates that all of the various party leaders could cast a proxy vote on behalf of all their followers without even bothering to have them physically present. It also overlooks that a majority or even a minority government can function effectively without our present stratospheric levels of party solidarity.

THE AMERICAN WAY

In the United States Congress, where admittedly there is a strict separation of powers between the executive and the legislative branches of government, legislation does get passed with far less party loyalty. The constitutional separation of powers and the weakness of party discipline in congressional voting behaviour greatly facilitate effective regional representation in Washington. Unlike the situation in Canada where a government falls if it loses the support of a majority in the House of Commons on a confidence vote, United States presidents and Congress are elected for fixed terms. Neither resigns if a particular measure is voted down in either the Senate or the House of Representatives.

The practices in our two countries are so different that *The Congressional Quarterly* defines party unity votes there as those in which at least 51 percent of members of one party vote against 51 percent of the other party. Under this definition, itself astonishing to Canadian legislators, the *Quarterly* notes that for the years 1975 to 1982 party unity votes occurred in only 44.2 percent of the 4,417 recorded Senate votes and in only 39.8 percent of those in the House of Representatives. This sample, moreover, includes the years 1977 to 1980, the last period before 1993 to 1996 when Democrats controlled the White House and both branches of Congress.

Another feature of the congressional system that fosters effective regional input in national policymaking is territorial bloc voting—something quite unknown in Canada's House of Commons. Representatives from the two political parties of the Mountain states, Sun Belt states, New England states, and others vote en bloc or work together in committees to advance common interests.

A good example of how effective regional representatives can influence the geographic location of federal government procurement, which affects the geographic distribution of the manufacturing sector, is the Southern congressional influence. It played a major role in the postwar concentration of federal military and space expenditures in the South and in the general economic revival and growth of the Sun Belt. And during 1981–82, the height of the "boll-weevil era," the longtime legislative coalition of Southern Democrats and Republicans was successful more than 85 percent of the time, due to mutual areas of agreement and interest.

The point of this comparison is only to emphasize that, unlike the American Congress, Canadian bloc voting makes bipartisan or tripartisan agreement on anything in our legislatures exceedingly rare. In our current political culture, if a government or opposition MP's loyalty to his or her province clashes with the instruction of the party whip, putting constituents' or regional considerations first in his or her way of voting implies considerable risk to one's prospects for party advancement. Backbench MPs in Canada are thus far less able to represent regional interests effectively than are their counterparts in Washington where the congressional system provides the freedom for effective regional representation when an issue has clear regional implications. This, of course, is not to suggest that Canada should duplicate the American congressional style of government. Rather, it is to point out that the best solution to ongoing problems of representative democracy in Canada might be to adopt attractive features from various systems, including the American one.

PUTTING CONSTITUENTS FIRST

Canada is a federal state and federalism means that on some issues the will of the popular majority will be frustrated. If the biggest battalions of voters are to prevail over smaller ones under any circumstances, we should drop the charade that we have a federal system of government that respects minorities in times of stress. The notion that the largest group of Canadians, that is, southern Ontarians and metropolitan Quebeckers, must be accommodated always has resulted in discontent everywhere and accompanying feelings of regional irrelevancy.

In an increasingly interdependent world, many Canadians in our outer eight provinces and the territories at least want new or altered institutions that will represent the interest of both "inner Canadians" (those who live in the Toronto–Ottawa–Montreal corridor) and "outer Canadians" effectively. Unless we move away from the notion that "the national interest" is merely a code phrase for the most populous region dominating all corners of the country, frictions between inner and outer Canada are likely to worsen.

If party discipline in Canada were relaxed, representation for all areas of Canada would be improved. It would be easier for, say, western MPs to defy their party establishments, if need be, in support of western issues. Coalitions composed of members of all parties could exist for the purpose of working together on issues of common regional or other concern. The present adversarial attitudes and structures of Parliament or legislatures in which opposition parties oppose virtually anything a government proposes might well change in the direction of parties working together for the common good.

Members of Parliament today represent an average of about eighty-seven thousand voters. At present, few government and opposition MPs have any real opportunity to put their constituents first in votes in the House of Commons. Real power is concentrated in the hands of the party leaderships. Canadian democracy itself would benefit if we put our present mind-numbing party discipline where it belongs—in the history books.

✗ **NO**
The Imperative of Party Discipline in the Canadian Political System
ROBERT J. JACKSON AND PAUL CONLIN

The fact that Canada has been successful as a state leaves some observers perplexed. The Canadian border encases the second-largest geographic land mass in the world under the authority of one Constitution. At the same time, the country is sparsely populated by a narrow ribbon of inhabitants stretched along the forty-ninth parallel. This widely dispersed population is subject to the pull of global economics dominated by its American neighbour to the south. From its genesis, Canada has been a linguistically and culturally heterogeneous society, and is becoming more so with each successive year. Despite the existence of all these centrifugal pressures, what we know today as Canada has existed and thrived for over a century and a quarter.

It is not by historical accident that Canada occupies the position it does today. On the contrary, the fact that Canada exists is the result of deliberate measures taken by Canadian leaders to establish policies and institutions that transcend diversity and bind the country together. Examples include national economic and social policies, a responsible cabinet/parliamentary system of government, and in particular, the establishment of broadly based and national political parties. Institutional structures, such as political parties, can transcend Canadian diversity and provide poles of allegiance against centrifugal influences. In order to fulfil this function effectively, the parties themselves must act as cohesive units and strive for party solidarity. Strong parties, based on a broad consensus, are thus vital to the effective functioning of responsible government and the Canadian state. Party solidarity, the apex of which is party discipline, is the guiding principle of the party system in Canada.[1]

Party discipline refers to the ability of the leader in a democratic state to enforce obedience on his or her followers in the legislature and in the party organization. The argument for relaxing party discipline is that MPs should not be "trained sheep," but should be free to represent the views of their constituents. Members are, after all, elected by their constituents and should be responsible to them. But the issue is not that simple; the Canadian form of government relies on cohesive political parties. In the responsible government model, the party in power is awarded an electoral mandate to enact a legislative program, and its members must support the cabinet and prime minister in order to accomplish this. An MP is not primarily a delegate of his or her constituents. Rather, an MP is elected to serve as a member of a particular party. Within that party, the MP is called upon to deliberate and participate in formulating policies, and then to accept and support the majority decision. The government will not be made more responsive if its members make it more difficult to pass legislation. The prime minister and government must have the means of achieving their objectives.

The Canadian system is premised on the idea that reason and judgment are to be respected in the field of policymaking. Parties must be entrusted to deliberate, decide, and then be judged by the electorate. Otherwise MPs would be elected to deliberate, but constituents, who have not participated in the deliberations, would retain the right to decide. Such a procedure would be ludicrous. MPs do not and should not directly represent their individual constituencies, provinces, or even regions, polling on every issue to see how they should vote. Rather, they are members of a particular party that provides broad perspectives on national issues. They run under the banner of that particular party and seek the privileges offered by it because they are in general agreement with its broad base of national policy directions, directions that can be influenced and adjusted in caucus.

As a British politician pointed out more than a century ago, "Combinations there must be—the only question is, whether they shall be broad parties, based on comprehensive ideas, and guided by men who have a name to stake on the wisdom of their course, or obscure cliques, with some narrow crotchet for a policy, and some paltry yelping shibboleth for a cry." After all, if MPs do not accept the decision arrived at by their executives and party, which groups will they represent? The special pleading of a particular pressure group that has a narrower conception of the national interest?

Party discipline is a feature inherent in the Canadian model of Parliament, and is inextricably linked to the concept of responsible government and the confidence convention. The Constitution Act, 1867, established that Canada would have a responsible cabinet/parliamentary system of government. This is the basis of our current system whereby the cabinet, as selected by the prime minister, is composed of members of the legislature and must keep the confidence of the House of Commons. The system also presupposes an opposition party or parties that are ready and willing to attack the government in an attempt to alter or reject its legislation. The government must therefore enforce party discipline not only to enact its legislative program, but also for the sake of its own self-preservation.

The United States congressional system of government differs from the parliamentary system in several key areas. Rather than fusing the executive and legislative branches of government, the American system is based on the separation of powers. The president and all of his or her cabinet members are prohibited by the Constitution from simultaneously sitting in the executive and legislative branches. The absence of responsible government and the corresponding absence of confidence convention allows the congressional system to function without party discipline.[2]

Calls for the relaxation of party discipline in Canada are not a recent phenomenon. Like the perennial cure for the common cold, the topic of parliamentary reform provides exaggerated hopes for optimists, then later gives way to despair when it fails. As early as 1923, for example, the MP from Calgary, William Irving, introduced a motion in the House of Commons that would have allowed for the relaxation of party discipline by reducing the number of votes considered to be votes of confidence. The motion was defeated, but to this day "reformers" still look to the United States and see the relaxation of party discipline as the panacea for perceived parliamentary inadequacies. Simplistic prescriptions such as the relaxation of party discipline, while seductive, fail to take into account the complexity of the parliamentary system. It is fallacious to assume that certain selected features of the congressional system can be appended to the parliamentary system without seriously affecting the functioning of the entire system.

Imagine a scenario where party discipline in Canada was significantly relaxed. Issues formerly resolved along party lines, based on consensual lines and accommodation in caucus, would be decided on much narrower grounds. Regionalism and special interests would dominate decision making in the House of Commons, and political parties would cease to serve their function as institutions that bind the country together. The decision-making model now in place, which requires political parties to produce nationally acceptable compromises, would be replaced by an increase in confrontation. MPs liberated from the yoke of party discipline would be saddled by the demands of lobbyists and others representing narrow special interests and regional interests. This scenario is especially disquieting when taken in conjunction with the fact that there are now five and possibly six parties legitimately competing for seats in the House of Commons, instead of only two or three. The prospect of minority governments has been greatly enhanced following the growth of the Reform Party and the Bloc Québécois. In the context of this development, the importance of party discipline increases exponentially. A lack of party discipline during a minority government would result in a chaotic situation where no prime minister could maintain the confidence of the House.

Many of the arguments against party discipline are founded on misconceptions about the practice. The very term "whip," the name given to the party member charged with the task of enforcing party discipline, conjures up images of a menacing disciplinarian imposing the will of the party on recalcitrant MPs. This is not the case, however. While there are instances where MPs have been coerced or even threatened with sanctions if they do not conform, party discipline is largely self-imposed. Because the majority of MPs enjoy relatively little job security, they do not relish the prospect of facing reelection. Consequently, never in Canadian history has a government been toppled by a breach in party discipline. Furthermore, recent studies indicate that since 1940, no MP from the governing party has ever broken party ranks during a minority government. Nor has any MP ever left the government side with a majority of fewer than nine seats.[3] This indicates that MPs, at least for the sake of their own self-preservation, are willing to tolerate party discipline.

Another misconception is that constituents do not want their MPs to toe the party line. This is a somewhat complex issue owing to the fact that the vote for the executive and legislative representative is fused into the same ballot in parliamentary systems. While it is impossible to determine the exact weight voters give to the individual candidate and the party label, several studies indicate that the determining factor is the party label. One report found that shortly after an election, fewer than two-thirds of respondents could correctly give the name of their recently elected MP.4 More specifically, from 1940 to 1988, thirty-one MPs ran for reelection in the general election following the parliamentary session in which they revolted against their parliamentary caucus and crossed the floor. Only twelve of them were successful in the election, and three were forced to run under their former party banner. These figures contrast with the argument that the voters will reward an MP for acting independently.

The most recent substantive recommendations for reforming party discipline are embodied in the so-called McGrath Report, released in June 1985. The report had three basic conclusions:

1. There should be attitudinal changes.

2. The parties should relax their discipline.

3. There should be organizational reform.

The committee reported: "We believe the country would be better served if members had more freedom to play an active role in the debate on public policy, even if it meant disagreeing with their parties from time to time." The report then called for an "attitudinal change" by backbenchers and asked the prime minister to accept more dissension and defeat of government measures without recourse to the threat or use of dissolution of the House.

Unfortunately, this part of the report is romantic nonsense for the following reasons:

1. Calls for an attitudinal change are unlikely to be effective. The only practicable reform is one that changes the organization around members.

2. There never was a Golden Age of Parliament, as the report implies. In the period before parties, when Canadian MPs were "loose fish," MPs were not free of financial and other social ties that constrained their voting behaviour.

3. The question should not be whether MPs are free to vote against their parties, but rather, whose interests or groups are they adopting when they do so? Free voting does not mean that MPs are free of pressures to conform with other groups' positions.5 Is it better to have MPs' behaviour determined by widely based cohesive political parties or narrower interest groups?

The facts also belie the utopian assumptions of the McGrath Report. Since 1985, there has been no relaxation of party discipline in the House of Commons. The urging cries of "reformers" have had no effect: the reality is that MPs are already free to vote as they wish. The point is that they do not choose to exercise their liberty by taking stands against their parties. They will always be subject to constituents, interest groups, and financial pressures: the only question is whether they will follow the dictates of a broadly based party or those of another group with a narrower conception of the national interest. Those who choose wisely stand solidly with their parties, helping to protect the system of government and providing a counterpoint to the centrifugal influences of our geography and society.

NOTES

1. Robert J. Jackson and Doreen Jackson, *Politics in Canada,* 2nd ed. (Scarborough: Prentice-Hall, 1990).

2. Robert J. Jackson and Doreen Jackson, *Contemporary Government and Politics: Democracy and Authoritarianism* (Scarborough: Prentice-Hall, 1993).

3. Paul Conlin, "Floor Crossing in the Canadian House of Commons, 1940–1992" (Carleton University: Unpublished B.A. (Hons.) research paper, 1993).

4. William Irvine, "Does the Candidate Make a Difference? The Macro-politics and Micro-politics of Getting Elected," *Canadian Journal of Political Science* 15, no. 4 (December 1982).

5. Robert J. Jackson, "Executive–Legislative Relations in Canada," in Jackson et al., *Contemporary Canadian Politics* (Scarborough: Prentice-Hall, 1987), pp. 111–125.

Postscript

One's stance on the issue of party discipline depends in part on how one interprets the experience of other countries, particularly the United States. Kilgour, Kirsner, and McConnell like the freedom that the relaxed party discipline of the American system gives members of Congress to represent their constituents, especially their regional concerns. But Jackson and Conlin are skeptical–they fear that an American-style system of lax discipline leaves the door open to the excessive influence of special interests on members' voting decisions.

But is there another model that could be followed? As Kilgour, Kirsner, and McConnell note, in Great Britain, members of the House of Commons may vote against their party without fear of recrimination on issues that are understood by all not to constitute a vote of confidence. Accordingly, a government may be defeated on a particular bill and still survive. It is suggested that such a practice allows MPs some independence in the legislature without putting at risk the life of a government.

Those wishing to understand how Britain has dealt with the issue of party discipline should read John Schwarz, "Exploring a New Role in Policymaking: The British House of Commons in the 1970s," *American Political Science Review* 74, no. 1 (March 1980): 23–37. Schwarz examines the changes made to British parliamentary traditions to permit a greater amount of "cross-voting." He argues that these changes have greatly strengthened the role of the House of Commons in the legislative process.

Not everyone is convinced that the British experience can be readily adapted to Canada. C.E.S. Franks, in *The Parliament of Canada* (Toronto: University of Toronto Press, 1987), notes that there are a number of factors that make the British experience unique. Because of the much larger number of members in the British House of Commons, party discipline is much harder to enforce. A large number of safe seats make MPs less dependent on party patronage for their postparliamentary livelihood. The cabinet in Britain is much smaller. Long-serving MPs from safe seats, who are not obsessed with promotion to the cabinet, are much less likely to succumb to the brandishments of their leader, as both Margaret Thatcher and John Major have learned to their chagrin. In contrast, there is a much higher turnover among Canadian MPs, who generally do not feel secure enough to challenge a leader they feel is necessary to their own reelection chances.

The applicability of the British experience to Canada is also explored in Peter Dobell, "Some Comments on Party Reform," in Peter Aucoin, ed., *Institutional Reforms for Representative Government* (Toronto: University of Toronto Press, 1985). Dobell is not optimistic about the prospect of Canadian party leaders relinquishing their strong control over party discipline in the near future. However, he does propose some minor modifications that would give some flexibility to individual MPs.

ISSUE**FOURTEEN**

Do the Courts Practise Judicial Self-Restraint?

✔ **YES**
PETER H. RUSSELL, "Canadian Constraints on Judicialization from Without"

✘ **NO**
F.L. MORTON, "Judicial Policymaking Under the Charter"

The entrenchment of the Canadian Charter of Rights and Freedoms into the Canadian Constitution in 1982 raised many questions. One was whether the Charter might lead to a greatly empowered judiciary. At the time, there was a belief that the country would witness a transfer of power from elected officials in the executive and legislative branches of government to appointed judges sitting on the Supreme Court of Canada and the lower courts. Until 1982, Canadian courts had been fairly restrained in their decisions, resisting any concerted attempt to challenge the laws and actions of government. But the appearance of a charter of rights increased the chances of a much more activist court, one that might be more willing and able to find government behaviour in violation of the Constitution.

In the past decade and a half, the Supreme Court and other judicial bodies have made numerous Charter decisions. Some of these decisions have made front-page news, in part because they involved the courts deciding against government. In 1988, the Supreme Court declared Canada's abortion law to be in violation of the Charter. A few years earlier, the same court ruled unconstitutional legislation that prohibited Sunday shopping in the province of Alberta. At about the same time, Canada's highest court found that aspects of Quebec's language laws clashed with provisions in the Charter that protected minority language education rights. However, not all of the decisions of the courts have gone against government. In many cases, the courts quietly noted that no Charter violation had taken place, or that an infringement of one freedom or another was reasonable.

In light of the performance of the courts, it is at first difficult to determine if the Charter of Rights has ushered in an age of judicial activism or left Canada still with a rather restrained set of courts. In some minds, though, a closer look at the evidence suggests that the earlier fears of an imperial judiciary were largely unfounded. In relation to constitutional law, *judicial self-restraint* refers to an orientation on the part of the courts to find government policies consistent with the Constitution, and for some this is largely what one still finds in the courtrooms of Canada. The Supreme Court has, among other decisions, said no to a right to strike, declared Sunday shopping laws in Ontario to be valid, and limited the reach of the equality rights section in the Charter. The court also found itself agreeing that some violations of rights could be considered reasonable in light of the importance of the underlying aim of the legislation at issue and the means chosen to pursue that aim. To be sure, instances of a less restrained court could be found, but they were few in number. As well, the absence of any legitimacy crisis facing the courts—something that one might expect with a strengthened court system—has failed to emerge. Surely, if the courts had indeed experienced a substantial change in their power, Canadians might have begun to question the acceptability of appointed officials making major policy decisions.

There are grounds, however, for a different view. It may be argued that the courts have engaged in *judicial activism*, which refers to a tendency on the part of the judiciary to find unconstitutional the actions of the other branches of government. Thanks to the courts' interpretation of the Charter, the rights of criminal suspects have greatly broadened as elements in the criminal justice system have been found in conflict with one right or another. The Supreme Court has also declared unconstitutional language laws in Quebec, an action that has done little to abate the national unity crisis, and it has as well found fault with important procedures relating to immigration. For still another example of judicial activism, the courts have struck down a number of family laws that limit benefits solely to heterosexual couples. Homosexual couples, too, must be included in these laws.

In the readings, Peter Russell, author of numerous articles on the courts in Canada, contends that the courts still practise judicial self-restraint in their interpretation of the Charter. The appearance of the Charter, suggests Russell, has not greatly changed the orientation of Canada's courts. F.L. Morton, also author of many essays on the judiciary, argues that Russell is mistaken. For Morton, judicial activism, not judicial restraint, best describes the behaviour of the Supreme Court of Canada and other judicial bodies. Incidentally, Russell refers to "judicialization from without" in both the title and in the body of his paper. This term is simply another way of describing the process by which bodies in the judiciary review the actions of the executive and legislative branches.

✔ **YES**
Canadian Constraints on Judicialization from Without
PETER H. RUSSELL

INTRODUCTION

This paper focuses on Canada's recent experience with what Torbjörn Vallinder (1992) terms "judicialization from without," even though "judicialization from within" in Canada as elsewhere may be the more pervasive, though less spectacular, aspect of expanded judicial power. As an example of judicialization from within, Vallinder refers to the judicialization of decision-making within Britain's administrative tribunals. There has certainly been plenty of that in Canada. The insistence on judicial due process in ever widening realms of public administration is part and parcel of the expanding catalogue of justiciable rights that has been a hallmark of modernizing societies as they moved from *Gemeinschaft* to *Gesellschaft*. (Tonnies, 1965). The adoption of national and international bills of rights, the primary foundation of judicialization from without, reflects and reinforces this tendency.

IMPACT OF THE CHARTER OF RIGHTS

Since 1982, when Canada adopted a constitutional bill of rights called the Canadian Charter of Rights and Freedoms, the nation has experienced a heavy new dose of judicialization from without. Charter-based judicial review of legislation and executive acts has undoubtedly expanded the Canadian judiciary's sphere of activity, and in that sense has increased the judiciary's power. However, this expansion of judicial power has not necessarily been "at the expense" (to use Vallinder's phrase) of the legislative or executive branches. The main impact of a constitutional bill of rights on the political system, if Canada's experience is a guide, may be less a transfer of power to the judiciary than a general transformation of the nature of political life. That transformation might be better summed up by the phrase "juridicialization," as used in Professor Shapiro's paper (1992), than by the term "judicialization."

When Canadians were debating whether to adopt a comprehensive constitutional bill of rights, a few academics and politicians drew attention to such a measure's tendency to expand judicial power. Indeed, at the time the Charter was adopted the present writer stated that its main effect on the governmental process in Canada would be "a tendency to judicialize politics and politicize the judiciary" (Russell, 1983: 50–51). It may seem ironic that ten years after the Canadian Charter came into force we find the same person presenting a paper on the limits to judicialization in Canada. The purpose in doing so is not to recant the earlier prediction but to illuminate some of the key factors that shape and limit the consequences of the judicialization process.

Constraints on Use of the Legislative Override

how effective is it?
not very beyond Quebec

A constraint on judicialization which has *not* been very effective is one built right into the Canadian Charter—Section 33, the legislative override clause. Canada's constitutional bill of rights is one of the few in the world that expressly permits legislatures (federal or provincial) to pass legislation notwithstanding certain specific rights.[1] The rights against which the override can be used include virtually all of the Charter's universal rights—political freedoms, due process rights, and protection against discrimination. Its use requires only a majority vote of the legislature. An override dies after five years but can be renewed.

The legislative override was inserted in the Charter at the insistence of politicians, mainly provincial premiers, who wanted an accountable, democratic check on judicial review (Weiler, 1984). To those who believe fundamental, constitutional rights are being taken seriously only when the judiciary can uphold them against the majoritarian decisions of the political branches, the legislative override contradicts the very purpose of the Charter (Whyte, 1990). For those who see judicial review as another form of fallible policy-making, the override is a prudent fail-safe device (Russell, 1991). In practice, the legislative override is hardly ever used. The fact that outside of Quebec the legislative override, politically speaking, is almost unusable tells us much about how constitutionalizing rights can affect the nature of politics.

The override has been used only once outside of Quebec—that was in the Charter's early years, when Saskatchewan's legislature attached the override to legislation ordering striking civil servants back to work. As it turned out there is no need to immunize that kind of legislation from judicial review because in subsequent cases the Supreme Court of Canada ruled that the Charter's right to "freedom of association" does not embrace the right to strike (Russell, Knopff and Morton, 1989: 5). Quebec, however, used the legislative override in a massive way, applying it to all past legislation and all new legislation. It did this for symbolic reasons, as a way of protesting the fact that the Charter and the other 1982 constitutional changes were imposed on Quebec without the consent of its National Assembly. But in 1988, after a Liberal government led by Robert Bourassa had replaced a separatist government, and after the override's five-year period had run out, Quebec's National Assembly used the override clause to counter a Supreme Court decision. The Court had ruled that a section of Bill 101, Quebec's Charter of the French language, requiring French-only advertising signs, violated the Charter's guarantee of "freedom of expression" (*Quebec v. Ford* 1988, 2 SCR 712). The Court's decision provoked the largest nationalist rallies in Quebec since the 1980 referendum. "Ne toucher pas la loi 101" was their slogan. Responding to this pressure the Bourassa government, which in its election campaign had promised to restore bilingual signs, decided now to use the override to restore French-only commercial signs outdoors but to allow multilingual signs indoors.

All this occurred during a major round of constitutional politics based on the Meech Lake Accord, a set of constitutional proposals primarily designed to win

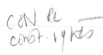

Quebec's support for the constitutional changes imposed on the province in 1982. By December 1988, when the Supreme Court rendered its decision, ratification of the Meech Lake Accord was almost complete—the federal Parliament, Quebec's National Assembly, and the legislatures of all but two of the other provinces had approved the Accord. But so great was English Canada's furore over Quebec's use of the override to protect its "visage linguistique" that from this point on "there was virtually no chance that the Meech Lake Accord would be ratified" (Monahan, 1991: 164). The Meech Lake Accord indeed died, and with it, perhaps, the chance of maintaining the unity of the Canadian federation. A constitutional bill of rights designed to unify the country may turn out to be the final instrument of the country's break-up.

That this could happen shows, at least in the Canadian case, that the impact of constitutionalizing rights on civic consciousness can be far more significant than any shifts it brings about in the balance of power between the judiciary and the other branches of government. For opinion-leaders in English Canada the Charter had become an icon, its rights fundamental and absolute. The episode demonstrated the extent to which the rhetoric of constitutional rights invests political discourse with a deep sense of moral rectitude. English Canadians had never cared very much for the French-only sign policy which had been in place since 1977, but now that this policy could be impugned as a violation of a fundamental constitutional right, opposition to it could be mounted on a high moral plane. No longer was there any need to consider French Quebecers' beliefs about what was necessary to ensure the survival of a French-speaking community on a continent dominated by the English language. The individual's freedom to advertise in the language of choice was so fundamental that it should not make room for any other value or interest.

After the Quebec sign-law incident, the legislative override became, from a political standpoint, virtually unusable outside of Quebec. Even before the signs case, the popularity of the concept of a Charter of Rights made legislators reluctant to use the override. Now the override was tainted in English Canada by its use to secure the language policy of Quebec's French majority. Normally politicians are not reluctant to use constitutional powers that are important to them. The key to understanding the willingness of Canadian governments—other than Quebec's—to forsake use of the override power is that the Charter, as it was being interpreted and applied by the courts, did not threaten their vital policy interests.

The Limited Policy Scope of the Charter of Rights

Here we encounter the most important constraint on the Canadian Charter's tendency to promote "judicialization from without": the limited policy scope of Canada's Charter of Rights and Freedoms. The policy area most frequently affected by Charter litigation is criminal justice. At least 80 percent of court cases involving Charter-based judicial review fall in that area. Criminal justice is undoubtedly an important field of state policy, but it is a field in which the judiciary, throughout the common law world, has always been an active policy-maker. Also, criminal justice is not normally a high priority policy area for governments in Canada. Outside of criminal justice only one program of major importance to a government has been mauled by Charter-based judicial review, and that is Quebec's language policy. At the federal level, the most important Charter hit is the Supreme Court's ruling in the *Singh* case requiring judicial type hearings (that is, judicialization from without forcing judicialization within) in settling claims for refugee status (*Singh v. Minister of Immigration* 1985, 1 SCR 177). Even here, the government quite independently of the *Singh* case was already planning to introduce such a change in refugee proceedings. None of the key economic and social policy interests of governments—monetary and fiscal policy, international trade, resource development, social welfare, education, labour relations, environmental protection—have been significantly encroached upon by judicial enforcement of the Charter.

The limitations on the Charter's policy impact stem both from the Charter itself and from its interpretation by the judiciary. Although the list of rights and freedoms included in the Canadian Charter is relatively comprehensive, one notable omission is property rights. This omission is no accidental oversight. The omission of property rights was insisted upon by Canada's social democratic party, the NDP, as a condition for its support of the Charter.[2] The absence of property rights reduces the Charter's impact, especially its due process of law guarantees, on social, economic, and environmental regulation. Of more fundamental importance is the fact that the Charter applies only to governments and legislatures. Charter rights and Charter freedoms can be claimed only against actions of governments or legislatures. But the main barrier to full enjoyment or exercise of some rights, particularly equality rights, is not government action but government inaction in responding to problems emanating from the private sector and the very structure of society. This, I believe, is the main reason the Charter has been a disappointment to those who expected it to be a major vehicle for social reform.

The Charter's limited scope has not deterred lawyers representing social action groups from trying to use the Charter as a vehicle for social change. This has aroused the ire of critics on the right who fear that a "court party" of Charterphile lawyers will use Charter advocacy as an undemocratic means of advancing the objectives of special interest groups (Knopff and Morton, 1992). Meanwhile critics on the left fear that Charter litigation will fritter away the resources available to progressive social forces (Mandel, 1989). There is not much empirical evidence to support either of these concerns (Sigurdson, 1992). The right-wing critics can point to few instances where judicial review under the Charter has forced elected politicians to initiate policies or spend money against their wishes. Nor is there any evidence that feminists, anti-racists, the labour movement, environmentalists, and other groups working for social reform in Canada have decided to forsake *this is my biggest for !*

direct political action while some of their lawyer-members flail about in the courts with the Charter.

THE CHARTER'S IMPACT ON POLITICAL CULTURE

Although the Charter has not judicialized Canadian politics in the sense of bringing about a major transfer of policy-making power to the courts, it could have a long-term impact on policy by shaping how Canadians think about political values. I have already commented on the Charter's highly divisive influence on attitudes to constitutional politics in Canada.

The Charter could also have a potent effect on policies concerned with the distribution of wealth and power in the Canadian variant of welfare-capitalism if its concern about restricting government activities came to be identified in the public mind with social progress. In other words, if most Canadians in English Canada come to believe that their Charter rights are more fundamental than any other rights or interests they might have, then the direction of policy and the entire political spectrum might well shift to the right. Some would argue that the emergence of a new right-wing Reform Party in Canada, with policies resembling those of the American Republican Party, is evidence that this shift is occurring.

Judicial Restraint in Charter Interpretation

The Charter's built-in limitations have been augmented by a cautious performance on the part of its most authoritative interpreter, the Supreme Court of Canada. After a rollicking barrage of initial decisions in which the Court, citing John Marshall, expressed its determination to take Charter rights seriously, and upheld three-quarters of the Charter claims brought before it, it settled down to a relatively moderate approach (Russell, 1988). In its first 100 Charter decisions, the percentage of successful Charter claims—35 percent—was just 1 percent below the success rate of Bill of Rights claims in the United States Supreme Court during the same period (Morton, Russell and Withey, 1992). The Canadian Supreme Court's moderate performance has not been well received in the academy—it is far too restrained for proponents of judicial activism and not nearly deferential enough for advocates of judicial self-restraint. But is has probably kept the Court in line with the mainstream of political opinion in the country. That, it has been argued, may be the underlying, if somewhat instinctive, rationale of the Court's Charter performance (Pond, 1992).

Whatever the motive, there can be no doubt that the Supreme Court's jurisprudence has significantly restricted the scope of the Charter's impact and thus the ambit of judicialization. In a 1986 case, *Dolphin Delivery* (1986, 2 SCR 573), the Court narrowed the realm of state action to which the Charter applies by removing from that realm judicial decisions applying common law (in this case a common law rule against secondary picketing) in actions involving private parties. In a trio of 1987 cases, the Court denied that the right to strike and other collective bargaining rights could be included within the Charter's guarantee of "freedom of association" (*Alberta Labour Reference* 1987, 1 SCR 313). Having rebuffed organized labour's efforts to use the Charter to expand its power, the Supreme Court was at pains to rebuff parallel efforts of the business class. In *Edwards Books*, the Court upheld Ontario Sunday-closing legislation designed to give retail workers a common day of rest. Chief Justice Dickson justified this decision by arguing that in interpreting the Charter "the courts must be cautious to ensure that it does not become an instrument of better situated individuals to roll back legislation which has as its object the improvement of the condition of less advantaged persons" (1986, 2 SCR 713, 779). In *Irwin Toy*, Dickson made it clear that the right of liberty guaranteed in Section 7 was not to be used to protect corporate commercial rights (1989, 1 SCR 927).

The Supreme Court's treatment of the Charter's Section 15, which sets out equality rights, has shown a similar limiting tendency. That Section, as written, was potentially wide open. It inscribes general right to equality "before and under the law" as well as "equal protection and equal benefit of the law without discrimination" and then gives as particular examples of unconstitutional discrimination, "discrimination based on race, national or ethnic origin, colour, religion, sex, age or mental or physical disability." In interpreting this Section, the Supreme Court has in effect reduced Section 15's coverage to laws that harm or prejudice groups covered by or that are analogous to the Section's enumerated categories (*Andrews v. Law Society of B.C.* 1989, 1 SCR 143). This immunizes a great many discriminatory laws—for instance most areas of business regulation—from judicial review. And even to laws that discriminate on the explicitly prohibited grounds, the Court applies no doctrine of "strict scrutiny." Under the Charter's "reasonable limits" clause, the Court can defer to legislative judgment on the balance to strike between constitutional equality rights and other important societal interests. It did just that, for instance, in dismissing a challenge by university professors to policies requiring mandatory retirement at age 65 (*McKinney v. Univ. of Guelph* 1990, 3 SCR 229). Most recently, the Supreme Court has ruled that where a social welfare law is found to be unconstitutional because of its under-inclusiveness the courts must not extend the law's coverage if doing so would have major budgetary consequences.[3]

THE CHARTER'S IMPACT ON CRIMINAL JUSTICE POLICY

The targets of most of the Supreme Court's Charter activism have been criminal law and police practices. In a number of areas of criminal justice the Court's treatment of due process rights has been more liberal even than the Warren court in the United States. Examples are extending the right to counsel to non-custodial situations and excluding evidence based on a non-consensual blood sample as a violation of a right to privacy (Harvie and Foster, 1990).

But even in the criminal justice field where the courts have always been relatively active, constrains on judicialization are operative. Enunciating liberal rules of criminal procedure is one thing—securing police compliance with these rules is another matter. Until the appropriate kind of empirical research is carried out, we will not know the extent to which the Supreme Court's Charter jurisprudence is actually modifying police behaviour, particularly in the treatment of suspects. Even at the level of constitutional doctrine, the Court has not pushed its activism so far in the criminal justice field as to overturn highly popular law enforcement programs. For example, it invoked the reasonable limits clause to uphold gun control provisions of the Criminal Code (*R. v. Schwartz* 1988, 2 SCR 443), and random roadside tests aimed at apprehending drunk drivers (*R. v. Hufsky* 1988 1 SCR 621 and *R. v. Thomsen* 1988, 1 SCR 640).

So far the Court's Charter activism has not undermined criminal justice policies to which elected governments are strongly attached. A major exception would seem to be the Court's decision in *Askov* which, through its interpretation of the Charter's speedy trial rule, put at risk thousands of criminal charges in Ontario (*R. v. Askov* 1990, 2 SCR 1199). The principal policy impact of this decision was the strengthening of the position of Ontario's Attorney General in securing more resources for the province's justice system and the implementation of management changes in a very badly administered judicial region. Besides, when the media made a hullabaloo about dangerous criminals going free because they were not brought to trial within eight months, the Supreme Court justice who authored the opinion was moved to comment (off the bench) that he had not meant his judgment to be interpreted so rigidly. In a subsequent decision the Court clarified its *Askov* ruling to make it clear that it did not support a rigid eight-month rule.[4]

What we see then in the Canadian experience with a new constitutional bill of rights is a judiciary constraining the growth of its power. Most of the members of the country's highest court are conscious of the political reasons for exercising this constraint. This consciousness is evident in the following passage from an interview with the current Chief Justice, Antonio Lamer, published in a leading national newspaper on the tenth anniversary of the Charter of Rights:

> In 1982 when the Charter came in, governments were watching the courts to see what they would do. I think now they realize we haven't gone berserk with the Charter and we aren't striking down laws right and left. They know how far we'll go and how far we're not going to go because we've said so ... (Lamer, 1992).

Lamer reflects the desire of most members of the Court not to push their power of judicial review so far as to antagonize leaders in other branches of government or the mainstream of public opinion.

JUDICIAL PROCESSING OF MORAL ISSUES

Of course sometimes it is impossible to avoid controversial outcomes. Some Charter cases raise "moral issues" around which there are sharply opposed political interest groups and no strong or clear public consensus. Abortion, Sunday-closing, anti-hate propaganda, prostitution, and pornography are examples. These are issues most politicians are happy to off-load onto the courts. A legislative override could really be an embarrassment here if it encouraged those who lost in the courts to bring the issue back to the legislature.

The clearest examples of this pattern of judicial interaction with the legislative process are the Supreme Court's decisions on abortion and sexual assault. In *Morgentaler* (1988, 1 SCR 30), the Court struck down restrictions on abortion in Canada's national criminal code, and in *Seaboyer* (1991, 2 SCR 577) it struck down "rape-shield" provisions of the criminal code, which in sexual assault cases had prevented the use of evidence of a complainant's sexual history. *Morgentaler* aroused the right-to-life movement, while *Seaboyer* aroused feminists—evidence in itself of the Court's weaving down the centre lane in areas of social controversy. In both cases, the aroused and losing group went immediately to the parliamentary lobby to press for legislative redress. In neither case was there any inclination on the part of the politicians to use the override, but in both cases the government agreed to bring in new legislation designed to accommodate the Supreme Court's jurisprudence.[5]

In cases dealing with anti-hate propaganda (*R. v. Keegstra* 1990, 3 SCR 697), restrictions on Sunday shopping (*Edwards Books v. R.* 1986, 2 SCR 713), prostitution (*R. v. Skinner* 1990, 1 SCR 1235), and pornography,[6] the Supreme Court invoked the Charter's reasonable limits clause to uphold legislation encroaching on Charter freedoms. Here, as with cases where it overturned legislation, the Court's decisions did not remove the issues from politics. Judicialization in these cases is best analyzed not as transferring decision-making authority from one branch of government to another but as judicial processing of social controversy. We should trace the political consequences of this judicial processing along two lines: its effect on the political resources of the contending sides and its tendency to inject a rights discourse into the political debate.

Though a court decision upholding legislation against a constitutional challenge may increase the legislation's legitimacy, and thereby enhance the resources of those interested in maintaining the legislative policy, it will not make legislation invulnerable to a determined political attack. A good example is the provincial Sunday-closing legislation upheld by the Supreme Court. Sunday-closing has continued to be under siege by commercial interests and the strength of consumerism. These political and societal forces, in one way or another, will bring about a different outcome from that sanctified by the Supreme Court. There are clear examples of judicial decisions injecting a rights discourse into disputes. I have already commented on that consequence of the Supreme Court's decision in the Quebec signs case. The passionate sense of righteousness which characterizes both sides of the abortion issue in Canada (and in the United States) has been intensified by judicial processing. To the extent that judicialization has this effect it may make social consensus on such issues more difficult to obtain.

THE ABSENCE OF A LEGITIMACY CRISIS

As Canada has settled into life under a constitutional bill of rights, judicial review has not provoked a legitimacy crisis. There is no popular hue and cry—even in Quebec where Charter decisions appear to be most obviously counter-majoritarian—against appointed judges making decisions on important questions of public policy. The constraints flowing from the structure of the Canadian Charter of Rights and Freedoms plus the self-imposed constraints of the Canadian judiciary, especially the country's highest court, partially account for the absence of a legitimacy crisis. Even more fundamental is a general disillusionment with representative democracy. The *Citizens' Forum* which in 1990–91 heard from over 400 000 Canadians on their concerns about the country, reported that the most common concern of forum participants was that they "have lost faith in both the political process and political leadership" (Canada, 1991). In Canada, as in other liberal democracies, it is the elected politicians, not the judges, who are experiencing a legitimacy crisis.

Even though judges are in better odour in Canada than politicians, there is, nonetheless, a good deal of resistance to giving the judiciary a major role in applying some new constitutional provisions that are now being considered in Canada. Among the constitutional provisions under discussion in the current round of constitutional politics are a stronger guarantee of free trade within the Canadian federation and a social charter establishing social policy and environmental standards to be maintained by all governments in the federation (Russell, 1992). The supporters of both proposals are of the opinion that "the courts are not the appropriate forum in which to settle disputes on such complex issues of law and public policy" (Canada, 1992: 87). Non-judicial monitoring agencies are proposed for these constitutional policy objectives.

It is, of course, politicians in the elected branches of government who favour these constraints on the growth of judicial power in Canada. Nonetheless the reluctance of political leaders to deal the judiciary into a vast expansion of discretionary decision-making in the field of socio-economic policy has not stirred up much public controversy. There are some on the left who say that they would like to see the courts enforcing positive entitlements to such things as "comprehensive health care," "high quality education," "adequate social service and benefits," "the integrity of the environment," "full employment," and a "reasonable standard of living."[7] But it is most doubtful if a majority of Canadians—left, right, or centre—could come to believe in such judicial fairy tales. In Canada, judicialization of politics from without is not likely to exceed its modest expansion under the Charter of Rights.

CONCLUSIONS

This brief overview of Canada's ten-year experience with a new constitutional bill of rights suggests three general conclusions about the judicialization of politics stemming from such a constitutional change.

First, the main impact of a bill of rights is not so much a transfer of power to the judiciary as a more general judicialization of politics, in which the language and norms of constitutional rights, to use Alec Stone's phrase, "permeate and are absorbed by, political discourse" (Stone, 1992). In the Canadian case, this process of judicialization would seem to be the principal outcome of those situations in which the Charter of Rights has dealt the courts into controversial public issues. Court decisions on language rights and abortion, for instance, rather than removing these issues from the political realm, returned them to political contention recast in less compromising and more strident terms—making consensual resolution of the issues more difficult than before.

Second, a constitutional bill of rights codifying what government must abstain from doing to its citizens has a limited impact on public policy. The policy field that has felt the greatest impact of Canada's Charter is criminal justice. With the exception of Quebec's language policy, social and economic policies of central importance to elected governments have not been significantly affected by the Charter. Judicialization resulting from the Charter has not led to a power struggle between the judiciary and the political branches. On the contrary, politicians are happy to off-load on to the courts responsibility for making decisions on divisive moral issues such as abortion, pornography, and Sunday-closing.

Third, the judiciary itself can limit the scope of judicialization by decision-making strategies that confine the impact of a constitutional charter to policy fields where judges believe they have competence and legitimacy. This has certainly happened in the Canadian case. Although the Supreme Court of Canada has set a fairly activist standard in applying the Charter to criminal law and procedure, the Court has minimized the Charter's impact on issues involving the interests of business and labour, and is very cautious about making decisions that impose fiscal burdens on government. Ironically, Canadian judges may underestimate their own legitimacy and overestimate the legitimacy of elected politicians. In an age that has become so cynical about representative democracy, the same may be true of judges in other countries.

Finally, the inclination of Canada's constitution makers to adopt a "Social Charter," establishing positive constitutional rights to social benefits, raises an important question for the future. The demand for the constitutionalization of such positive entitlements is a product of the juridicalization of politics fostered by the Charter of Rights. Still, if the Social Charter is detached from judicial review as its sponsors propose, it will be interesting to see if it can be as potent an instrument for juridicalization as the Charter of Rights has been. If Canada's Social Charter does nothing else, it will at least test whether judicialization is a necessary dimension of juridicalization.

NOTES

1. The other constitution with a clause most resembling Canada's is that of Jamaica. However, it requires a two-thirds majority of both Houses of Jamaica's Parliament. For further comparisons see Letourneau, 1991.

2. In the round of constitutional politics that followed defeat of the Meech Lake Accord, the Conservative federal government proposed inserting property rights in the Charter but found insufficient support to continue with this proposal.

3. The judgment was given in *The Queen v. Schachter* on July 9, 1992. The case has not yet been reported in the *Supreme Court Reports*.

4. The judgment was given in *Deepak Kumar Sharma v. The Queen* on March 26, 1992. The decision has not yet been reported in the *Supreme Court Reports*.

5. The new criminal code provisions on abortion were blocked by the Senate. The new "rape-shield" law, at the time of writing, is still at the drafting stage.

6. The judgment was given in *Butler v. The Queen* on February 27, 1992. The decision is not yet reported in the *Supreme Court Reports*.

7. These are some of the social policy standards to be included in the social covenant and economic declaration proposed in the *Report on a Renewed Canada* (Canada, 1992). For an attack on the social charter proposal for its failure to empower judges to help the disadvantaged, see Jackman, 1992.

REFERENCES

Canada, *Supreme Court Reports* (SCR).

Canada (1991). *Citizens' Forum on Canada's Future.* Condensed version, *Globe & Mail,* p. A9. 2 July 1991.

Canada (1992). *Report of the Special Joint Committee of the Senate and the House of Commons on a Renewed Canada.*

Harvie, R. and H. Foster (1990). "Ties that Bind: The Supreme Court of Canada, American Jurisprudence and the Revision of Canadian Criminal Law Under the Charter." *Osgoode Hall Law Journal* 28: 729–788.

Jackman, M. (1992). "When a Social Charter Isn't." *Canadian Forum,* (April) 8.

Knopff, R. and F.L. Morton (1992). *Charter Politics.* Toronto: Nelson.

Lamer, A. (1992). "Interview with Chief Justice of Canada on Tenth Anniversary of the Charter of Rights." *Globe & Mail* Toronto, 17 April.

Letourneau, S. (1991). "The Legislative Override Power: Section 33 of the Canadian Charter of Rights and Freedoms." M.Litt. thesis, University of Oxford.

Mandel, M. (1989). *The Charter and the Legalization of Politics in Canada.* Toronto: Wall & Thompson.

Monahan, P. (1991). *Meech Lake: The Inside Story.* Toronto: University of Toronto Press.

Morton, F. L., P.H. Russell and M.J. Withey (1992). "The Supreme Court of Canada's First One Hundred Charter of Rights Decisions." *Osgoode Hall Law Journal* 30: 1–56.

Pond, D. (1992). "The Supreme Court of Canada and the Politics of Public Law." Ph.D. dissertation, University of Toronto.

Russell, P.H. (1983). "Political Purposes of the Canadian Charter of Rights and Freedoms." *Canadian Bar Review* 61: 30.

Russell, P.H. (1988). "Canada's Charter: A Political Report." *Public Law* 385–401.

Russell, P.H. (1991). "Standing Up for Notwithstanding." *Alberta Law Review,* 293–309.

Russell, P.H. (1992). *Constitutional Odyssey: Can Canadians Become a Sovereign People?* Toronto: University of Toronto Press.

Russell, P.H., R. Knopff and F.L. Morton (1989). *Federalism and The Charter: Leading Constitutional Decisions.* Ottawa: Carleton University Press.

Shapiro, M. (1992). "Judicialization in the United States." Paper presented to Interim Meeting of the International Political Science Association Research Committee on Comparative Judicial Studies, University of Bologna, Forli, 14–17 June.

Sigurdson, R. (1992). "Leaf and Right-wing Charterphobia in Canada." Paper presented to Annual Meeting of the Canadian Political Science Association, University of Prince Edward Island, Charlottetown, 31 May.

Stone, A. (1992). "The Politics of Complex Coordinate Construction: Judicialization and Constitutional Development in France and Germany." Paper presented to Interim Meeting of the International Political Science Association Research Committee on Comparative Judicial Studies, University of Bologna, Forli, 14–17 June.

Tonnies, F. (1965). *Community and Association* (C. Loomis, ed.). New York: Barnes and Noble.

Vallinder, T. (1992). "The Judicialization of Politics: Meaning, Forms, Background, Prospects." *Festskrift tillägnad Hakan Strömberg på 75-årsdagen den 18 februari 1992.* 267–278. Lund: Juristförlaget.

Weiler, P.C. (1984). "Rights and Judges in a Democracy: A New Canadian Version." *University of Michigan Journal of Law Reform,* 18: 51–92.

Whyte, J.D. (1990). "On Not Standing for Notwithstanding." *Alberta Law Review,* 347–357.

X NO
Judicial Policymaking Under the Charter
F.L. MORTON

Peter Russell has argued that the Charter of Rights has had a minimal impact on Canadian public policy.[1] I disagree, and will present evidence that the courts' activist interpretation of the Charter has affected a broad range of government policies and spending priorities.

Russell's claim that the Charter has had only a minimal policy impact begs the question: minimal compared to what? An obvious and relevant point of comparison is pre-Charter Canadian practice. By this standard, there has clearly been change. In twenty-two years under the 1960 Bill of Rights, rights claimants won only 14 percent (five) of thirty-five cases and only one statute was declared invalid. In the first decade under the Charter, the Supreme Court ruled in favour of rights claimants in 33 percent (65) of 195 Charter decisions and declared 41 statutes invalid. In purely quantitative terms, the Charter has clearly had more policy impact than its predecessor. But what about qualitative impact?

Russell's claim of minimal policy impact is correct if we look only at one sector of public policy—the perennial struggles between business and labour and the corollary politics of economic redistribution—health, education, and social welfare. At least until recently (see the important recent exceptions noted below), the courts have interpreted the Charter in a fashion that minimizes judicial oversight and intervention in these important policy fields.

The verdict changes, however, when we look in other policy fields: criminal law, official minority language (OML) education, aboriginal issues, immigration, electoral distribution, and the so-called social issues such as abortion, gay rights, school prayer, and prisoner voting. Here the Supreme Court has used the Charter to effect real and significant policy changes, almost all to the applause of the political left and to the chagrin of the right.

Russell concedes that Supreme Court initiated reform of the criminal law is an exception to his more general claim, but still minimizes the extent of this change. Prior to the Charter, Canadian criminal law enforcement (like its British and Australian common law counterparts) was clearly distinguished from American practice on such issues as the exclusion of illegally obtained evidence, right to counsel, police search and seizure procedures, and rules governing police questioning of suspects. This pre-Charter Canadian practice conformed to the "crime-control" model of criminal law that stresses efficiency in the detection and punishment of criminal activity.

This has changed dramatically under the Supreme Court's interpretation of the Charter. Two major studies by Harvie and Foster[2] have concluded that in a number of areas—exclusion of evidence, blood samples, lineups, fingerprints, and arrest—criminal suspects in Canada now enjoy more rights than their American counterparts.[3] While there has been no empirical study of the street-level effect of these judicial reforms, law enforcement authorities are clearly unhappy with them. In the 1993 federal election, the Canadian Police Association abandoned its historical policy of nonpartisanship and endorsed and opposed various candidates based on their law enforcement positions.

A veteran prosecutor recently described the Charter as a defense lawyer's dream and a police officer's nightmare. Another observed sarcastically: "What is on trial is no longer the evidence respecting the guilt of the accused, but the procedures used to collect the evidence."[4] These are the effects not of the Charter, but of the Supreme Court's interpretation of the Charter. Because of the Supreme Court's increasingly broad interpretation of the exclusionary rule, for example, trial courts across the country have been forced to exclude reliable evidence in thousands of cases, leading to acquittals or the dropping of charges against defendants who otherwise would have been convicted, including at least two self-confessed and convicted murderers. In response to this, the Attorney General of Canada, joined by six other provincial attorneys-general, recently petitioned the Supreme Court to soften its rules on the exclusion of evidence such as blood and hair samples. The Supreme Court refused (*Stillman* 1997,1 SCR, 607).

In another set of criminal law rulings, the Supreme Court has frustrated Parliament's efforts to craft a new sexual assault law that protects the privacy of victims by prohibiting irrelevant questioning by defence lawyers about the victim's past. The Supreme Court struck down this law in 1991 (*Seaboyer* 1991, 2 SCR, 577). The government then re-enacted new legislation that narrowed the kind of information that was to be protected. In 1995, the Supreme Court struck down a section of the revised law that protected victims' prior medical records. The government then spent another one and a half years studying how best to balance the victim's right to privacy with the accused's right to a fair trial, before putting in effect a second revised law in May 1997. Since then, this revised law has been declared invalid by judges in both Ontario and Alberta.

In May 1997, the Supreme Court ruled that police could not enter a private residence to arrest a suspect without first obtaining an arrest warrant (*Feeney* 1997, 2 SCR, 13). When police arrested the accused in his home, he was dressed in blood-splattered clothes and was in possession of money stolen from the eighty-five-year-old victim. The Supreme Court ordered the evidence excluded and threw out Feeney's conviction. The *Feeney* decision created a public uproar and a serious gap in the authority of the police to make timely arrests. In October 1997, the government introduced legislation to limit the effect of *Feeney* by authorizing a new type of warrant that can be obtained by telephone from the scene of the crime. Taken together, these developments challenge Russell's assessment that "the Court's Charter activism has not undermined criminal justice policies to which elected governments are strongly attached."

OML EDUCATION

A second area in which the Supreme Court has decisively changed public policy is OML education. Russell acknowledges the Supreme Court's Charter interventions to protect English-language education in Quebec, decisions that have antagonized Quebec nationalists and contributed to the national unity crisis. However, Russell is silent about significantly greater judicial activism in the expansion of French-language education in the rest of Canada. In Quebec, the Supreme Court has simply been asked to restore the old policy status quo, something it can achieve through the use of its traditional constitutional veto. In the English-speaking provinces, by contrast, francophone groups are using section 23 of the Charter to invite judges to design and administer *new* French-language education instruction and facilities.

In its landmark ruling in *Mahé v. Alberta* (1990, 1 SCR, 342), the Supreme Court accepted this invitation. Contrary to the intent of the Framers, the Supreme Court interpreted section 23 as requiring some degree of management and control over OML education. Since the degree of management and control will vary depending on the size of the francophone student population, the Supreme Court in effect made itself the OML school board (of last resort) for the nation. Since *Mahé*, the courts have become involved in the design and management of OML education programs in Alberta, Saskatchewan, Manitoba, Ontario, and Nova Scotia. *ABORIGINAL*

The courts have also had a significant impact on public policies affecting aboriginal issues. Section 35 of the Constitution Act, 1982, declares: "The existing aboriginal and treaty rights of the aboriginal peoples of Canada are hereby recognized and confirmed." In 1981 there was no consensus on what practical meaning "Aboriginal rights" might have. Provincial premiers, led by Peter Lougheed of Alberta (himself part Indian), prudently wished to limit the recognition of aboriginal and treaty rights to those "existing" at the time. They demanded that the government amend the wording by adding the qualifier "existing." The then current legal understanding was that proof of prior government regulation (federal or provincial) would be sufficient to prove extinguishment of an aboriginal right, that is, that it no longer existed. The narrowing intent of this qualification was so clear that three of the four major Canadian aboriginal groups opposed it.

Notwithstanding such intent, the Supreme Court effectively removed this explicit limitation by announcing an unprecedented and generous definition of "existing" in its 1990 *Sparrow* (1990, 1 SCR, 1075) decision. The Supreme Court gave such strict rules for determining the "extinguishment" of an aboriginal right that it "found" that the Nishga'a band's aboriginal right to fish for food in the Fraser River was not extinguished, despite almost one hundred years of government regulation. The judges justified their new invention by declaring that section 35 invokes "the honour of the Crown" and thus imposes a "fiduciary obligation" on all government dealings with native people—with the courts to judge whether this duty has been met. Aboriginal advocates have complained that more recent Supreme Court rulings have failed to live up to the "spirit" of

Sparrow. While 1996 did witness several legal defeats for Aboriginal rights claimants (*Van der Peet* 1996, 2 SCR, 507, *Gladstone* 1996, 2 SCR, 723, *Pamajewon* 1996, 2 SCR, 821), most observers would not see judicial rejection of an alleged aboriginal right to run gambling casinos as either surprising or unfair. Nor has the Court.

Law professor Hamar Foster has described the effect of *Sparrow* as contributing to "a virtual revolution in consciousness ... a sea change in Canadian law ... kick-started to a large degree by the courts."[5] Russell himself has observed that while "native peoples in ... Canada historically lacked the support of a judicial protector, ironically the late intervention of the courts ... may provoke constitutional adjustments in the position of native peoples that are more radical and far-reaching than anything now in prospect for American Indians."[6] Foster concurs: "*Sparrow* provides a much stronger protection for aboriginal rights than presently exists in the United States."[7] There can be no doubt, Russell has written, "that court decisions supporting aboriginal rights claims have provided a major political resource to Aboriginal peoples."

The courts have also used the Charter to change public policy in a variety of other fields. The Supreme Court's ruling in *Singh* (1985, 1 SCR, 177) struck down the procedures for hearing applications for refugee status under the Immigration Act and forced the government to provide a mandatory oral hearing for refugee applicants. This decision had the consequences of creating a backlog of 124,000 refugee claimants, an amnesty for 15,000 claimants already in Canada, $179 million in additional costs, and a new refugee law. The new law took effect January 1, 1989. Eighteen months later, the government announced that the "new" Immigration and Refugee Board would quadruple its capacity to keep up with applications. This meant hiring an additional 280 personnel, in addition to the 496 already on staff, and bringing the budget of the new board to $80 million annually. This was all to replace a refugee determination process that, prior to *Singh*, the United Nations had commended for its fairness and recommended to other nations as a model to be copied.

The Supreme Court has directly contributed to the demise of Sunday-closing policies across Canada. In *Big M Drug Mart* (1985, 1 SCR, 295), the Court struck down the Lord's Day Act as a violation of the Charter right to freedom of religion. Under the 1960 Bill of Rights, the Supreme Court had upheld this same legislation as not violating freedom of religion. While the Supreme Court eventually upheld Ontario's secular Sunday-closing law, it was too late. The wave of litigation induced by its first ruling, and the resulting policy uncertainties, eventually swamped government attempts to preserve a common day of rest. On a related issue, the courts have interpreted freedom of religion to prohibit voluntary school prayer and Bible reading in public schools (*Zylberburg* 1988, 65 O.R. (2d), 641).

The Supreme Court's decision to interpret the section 3 "right to vote" as a right to an "equal vote" has propelled judges into the political swamp of electoral distribution (*Carter*, 1991, 2 SCR, 158). While the Supreme Court refused to endorse the American principle of "one person, one vote," its ruling stimulated additional litigation that has led to the redrawing of electoral boundary maps in Saskatchewan, Alberta, British Columbia, and Prince Edward Island. The courts have also used section 3 to strike down long-standing policies denying prison inmates the right to vote in both federal and provincial elections. Parliament subsequently revised the federal Elections Act to limit disenfranchisement to only those prisoners serving terms of two or more years. The courts then struck down this revised law.

The courts have been even more activist in policy fields affecting "social issues" raised by the feminist and gay rights movements. Abortion is the pre-eminent example. The Supreme Court began by striking down the abortion law in its 1988 *Morgentaler* ruling. It then threw out the *Borowski* (1989, 1 SCR, 342) "pro-life" case on the grounds that the Supreme Court's own *Morgentaler* (1988, 1 SCR, 30) ruling had rendered Borowski's claim "moot." The following year, however, the Supreme Court took the opportunity to reject rights claims on behalf of the unborn child in *Daigle* (1989, 2 SCR, 530), a case that was equally moot. When Nova Scotia tried to restrict the impact of the *Morgentaler* decision by enacting a law that restricted the performance of abortions to certified hospitals, the Supreme Court struck down this law as an invasion of the federal government's jurisdiction over criminal law. When British Columbia adopted a policy that would have restricted public funding of abortions, a B.C. court struck it down. When Saskatchewan was on the verge of adopting an "informed consent" law, the Saskatchewan Court of Appeal declared such a policy a covert form of criminal law and thus beyond the jurisdiction of the province. In 1997 the Supreme Court ruled (in *Winnipeg Child Services v. G. (D.F.)*, Supreme Court of Canada, Oct. 31, unreported) that the fetus has no rights independent of the mother, and that Winnipeg social workers had acted illegally in hospitalizing a glue-sniffing pregnant woman in an attempt to protect her unborn child, which she intended to carry to term (and did). In sum, the courts have played a major policy role in helping pro-choice advocates make Canada the only Western democracy with no abortion law and no legal protection for the unborn, a policy that is supported by less than one-third of Canadians.

Abortion policy is just the leading example of judicial activism on behalf of feminist policy objectives. A recent study of forty-five appeal court rulings involving feminist issues found that the feminist position had been successful in 70 percent. More significantly, the decisions had changed the policy status quo in a direction favoured by feminists in seventeen cases, while only three resulted in new policy opposed by feminists. Of these three, two were subsequently reversed by new legislation. Feminist success has been highest in the fields of abortion, family law/divorce (division of property, support payments, and child custody), immigration, private sector discrimination, and pornography, and lowest in sexual assault and income tax cases. The latter two, however, were instances of legislative reversal of court losses.

The significance of the courts' activism on behalf of feminist goals is heightened by several comparisons. In the decade prior to the Charter, feminists did not win any of five cases before the Supreme Court. South of the border, American feminists saw their success rate in court drop from 70 percent during the 1970s to 37 percent during the 1980s. The decline in litigation success for American feminists is attributed to a conservative reaction against feminism during the 1980s. But there has been a similar decline in public support for organized feminism in Canada. In surveys done in the past decade, only a third of Canadian women identify themselves as "feminists." But while Canadians were electing neoconservative governments—Mulroney at the federal level, Klein in Alberta, Harris in Ontario—the courts have continued to use judicial activism to advance a variety of feminist policy goals.

The courts have also been active in the field of gay rights. Despite the fact that the Framers explicitly excluded sexual orientation from the list of prohibited grounds of discrimination in section 15 (the equality rights section), the Supreme Court has added it as an "analogous, non-enumerated" form of discrimination (*Egan*, 1995, 2 SCR, 513). In that case, a sharply divided (5 to 4) Supreme Court ruled that it was still a "reasonable limitation" for Parliament to restrict pension and OAS benefits to partners of the opposite sex. However, lower courts have used the *Egan* precedent to strike down dozens of laws that restrict a variety of benefits to heterosexual couples—adoption, family support obligations, conjugal visits for inmates, income tax, death benefits, dental and medical benefit programs, and private pension and insurance programs. The Ontario Court of Appeal also lowered the age of legal consent for anal intercourse from eighteen to fourteen, claiming that it was discriminatory to have a higher age of consent for anal intercourse (eighteen) than for vaginal intercourse (fourteen). In perhaps the most activist ruling, a trial judge ruled that the Alberta government's refusal to add sexual orientation to its provincial antidiscrimination law was itself an unconstitutional discrimination against gays (*Vriend*). Previously, there was a widely shared understanding that the Charter applied only to government action, not "inaction." This ruling was overruled by the Alberta Court of Appeal, but it is now on appeal to the Supreme Court of Canada, where it is widely expected to be restored.

The cost of a public policy is often an indication of its importance. Russell enlists this standard to de-emphasize the importance of whatever judge-initiated policy reform has occurred under the Charter: "The right-wing critics [of the court party] can point to few instances where judicial review under the Charter has forced elected politicians to initiate policies or spend money against their wishes." What constitutes a few instances? Russell himself acknowledges that compliance with the *Singh* (1985, 1 SCR, 177) immigration ruling has cost Ottawa hundreds of millions of dollars. He also acknowledges that compliance with *Askov* (1990, 2

SCR, 1199) forced Ontario to hire dozens of new judges. Elsewhere he points out that the Court's ruling in *Guerin* (1984, 2 SCR, 335) forced Ottawa to pay "millions of dollars" to compensate the Musqueam band for the government's commercial mismanagement of their land.

On the other hand, Russell doesn't mention the effect of the Charter on legal aid spending. This effect is illustrated by the growth rates in the Legal Aid Plan of Ontario (LAPO). Between 1967, the year it started, and 1982, the year the Charter was adopted, LAPO's cost doubled from $27 million to $56.2 million. Once the Charter was in place, the LAPO budget doubled again in only six years—to $113.5 million in 1988—and then doubled again in the next six—to over $200 million in 1994. These increases cannot be attributed to similar increases in population, crime, or economic growth. By 1993, the total bill to Canadian taxpayers for legal aid programs was $603 million per year, double the amount only five years earlier.

One of the most dramatic instances of a Charter-driven explosion of legal aid costs has been outside the area of criminal law—immigration. In the Ontario legal aid plan for 1994–95, immigration and refugee lawyers received $29.5 million. In 1989, Ontario legal aid issued only 1,610 certificates for immigration and refugee cases. The following year, that figure rose to 15,247, a whopping 950 percent increase in one year. The reason was the new Federal Immigration Act requirement for additional oral hearings, an amendment that was forced on the government by the Supreme Court's 1985 ruling in *Singh v. Canada*.

While expenditures of these magnitudes are not peanuts, Russell is—or was—still right in saying that none of the Supreme Court's decisions directly challenged government spending priorities, and, more importantly, that they did not address the issue of government inaction. So long as the Supreme Court accepted the liberal tradition of rights as a "state-limiting" doctrine (i.e., "more freedom through less government"), inequalities that existed in the private sphere would be beyond the reach of the Charter. Since Russell penned this assessment, however, the situation has changed.

In 1994, the gay rights activists succeeded in persuading a trial judge to declare that Alberta's refusal to add sexual orientation to its provincial antidiscrimination act was a violation of the Charter's equality guarantee. Stripped of the homosexual issue, the *Vriend* (1996, 132 D.L.R. (4th) 595) trial ruling stands for the new and revolutionary principle that section 15 can be used to compel governments to undertake regulatory policies that they oppose. In September 1997, while the *Vriend* appeal was waiting to be heard by the Supreme Court, an Ontario judge ruled that the Ontario government's legislation cancelling future payments in a pay equity program also violated section 15. Ontario voters had elected the Harris government in large part to do something about the deficits run up by the spending habits of the previous NDP government, from which the pay equity program was a legacy. The cost of *not* cancelling the remaining payments on the Ontario NDP's pay equity legislation is estimated at $418 million.

One might have concluded that the Ontario pay equity ruling was, like *Vriend*, a trial court aberration with a short life expectancy on appeal. This was not to be. Several weeks later in *Eldridge v. British Columbia* (Supreme Court of Canada, Oct. 9, 1997, unreported), the Supreme Court of Canada declared that the failure of a provincially funded hospital to provide an interpreter for deaf patients constituted discrimination against the handicapped and a violation of section 15. The annual cost of providing interpreters for deaf people is put at a modest $150,000 per hospital. But this is just the tip of the iceberg. The principle embraced by the Supreme Court is that under section 15 of the Charter, *all* governments have a *positive* obligation to accommodate *all* disabled persons in *all* government services— health, education, transportation, and so on. Treating them the same or ignoring requests for special accommodation will no longer be acceptable. (This is the connection to *Vriend*.) When the costs of this are added up—in a decade or three— they may make Ontario's pay equity bill look small by comparison.

To conclude, the Charter has affected a much broader range of government policies than Russell suggests. With few exceptions, it has been the Supreme Court's activist interpretation of the Charter, not the rights themselves, that have had this effect. Again, with few exceptions, the direction of these judge-ordered policy changes has pleased the social left and upset social conservatives. Cases decided since Russell wrote challenge his earlier claim that judges are not using and cannot use the Charter to redirect government spending priorities. Read together, these more recent cases have the potential to transform the Charter from a state-limiting instrument to a state-expanding instrument. If the Supreme Court remains committed to the underlying principle of *Vriend, Eldridge*, and the Ontario pay equity ruling, this opens the door to interest group use of Charter litigation to challenge government cutbacks of entitlements or social programs and even to order the addition of new ones.

Russell observes, correctly, that to date, the Supreme Court has not experienced a legitimacy crisis. That is, there has not been a sustained attempt to curb the Supreme Court's new power through the appointment of new judges committed to a more self-restrained exercise of judicial review—the American approach—or through the repeated use of the section 33 notwithstanding clause—a uniquely Canadian procedure that allows governments to set aside temporarily a judicial Charter ruling.[2] However, if the Supreme Court continues the trajectory described above, it is inevitable that its authority will be challenged. One of the "iron laws" of democratic politics is that "Where power rests, there influence will be brought to bear." Courts that act politically will come to be treated politically. There is no reason to believe that Canada is exempt from this law.

NOTES

1. The Russell arguments to which I am responding are "Canadian Constraints on Judicialization from Without," *International Political Science Review* 15, no. 2 (1994): 165–175; and "The Political Purposes of the Charter: Have They Been Fulfilled? An Agnostic's Report Card," in Philip Bryden, Steven Davis, and John Russell, eds., *Protecting Rights and Freedoms: Essays on the Charter's Place in Canada's Political, Legal and Intellectual Life* (Toronto: University of Toronto Press, 1994), pp. 33–51.

2. R. Harvie and H. Foster, "Different Drummers, Different Drums: The Supreme Court, American Jurisprudence and the Revision of Canadian Criminal Law Under the Charter" (1990), 24:1 *Ottawa Law Review*, pp. 39–115; and R. Harvie and H. Foster, "Ties That Bind: The Supreme Court of Canada, American Jurisprudence, and the Revision of Canadian Criminal Law Under the Charter" (1990), *Osgoode Hall Law Journal* 28, no. 4, pp. 788–789.

3. The exception is in Quebec, where between 1982 and 1985 the Parti Québécois government of René Lévesque routinely attached the notwithstanding clause to every piece of provincial legislation.

4. Mr. John Petch, Milner Fenerty, Calgary. Comment to author.

5. Hamer Foster, "Canadian Indians, Time and the Law: What Happened North of 49," paper presented at the Interim Meeting of the Research Committee on Comparative Judicial Studies, August 1–4, 1998, Sante Fe, N.M., pp. 46–47.

6. Peter H. Russell, "The Catalytic Role of Courts in Aboriginal Constitutional Politics: Canada in Comparative Perspective," paper presented at the Interim Meeting of the Research Committee on Comparative Judicial Studies, Université de Sherbrooke, Que., August 21, 1995, p. 21.

Postscript

Peter Russell is *the* leading authority on the Canadian judiciary. Accordingly, any questioning of his thoughts on the courts is fraught with danger. Nevertheless, his article does raise some questions. Despite his argument against the notion of a more powerful Supreme Court, Russell seems to admit the existence of an activist court in the field of criminal justice. But he saves his argument by saying that compliance with these rulings by the police should not be assumed. Yet, as Morton reveals, there appears to be evidence of compliance, for the Charter has been described as "a law enforcement officer's nightmare." Russell also admits that controversy has arisen over Supreme Court decisions relating to abortion, Sunday-closing, prostitution, and pornography, but responds that these are matters that politicians are more than happy to leave to the courts. This may be true, but the fact remains that it is appointed members of the court—not elected officials in the other branches of government—who are dealing with important issues. Some might conclude that this amounts to a transfer of power to the judiciary. More generally, Russell thinks that instances of an activist court relate to areas that are of minor importance to government and its citizenry; alternatively, the more important areas of health, education, welfare, and economic policy have remained relatively untouched by Charter litigation. However, one might argue that, as Canada becomes a more liberal polity, issues relating to abortion, crime, pornography, and sexual orientation assume greater salience. The liberal is less concerned with government efforts that impinge upon the collective whole and more attuned to policies that directly affect the individual.

Morton has written a very persuasive paper. His listing of court decisions seems to provide a full-proof case against the claim of judicial self-restraint. Still, a few queries may be made about Morton's effort. For evidence of an activist court, Morton compares the record of the Supreme Court in relation to the Canadian Bill of Rights and the Charter of Rights and Freedoms respectively, and finds the court to be much more willing to strike down statutes under the Charter. But one might argue that this is an instance of comparing apples and oranges, that the Bill of Rights was a mere statute and applied only to the federal government while the Charter is entrenched in the Canadian Constitution and affects both orders of government. With a statute, the courts might be reluctant to question government legislation, but the situation changes with an entrenched charter of rights in hand. Also, Morton argues that feminists have greatly benefited from an activist Supreme Court. Yet, there have been some fairly high-profile cases in which the Supreme Court has supported government legislation against feminist claims (e.g., *Symes*, *Thibaudeau*). However, as Morton says, some of these cases have been reversed through legislative amendment. Lastly, Morton may exaggerate the impact of Charter decisions on public policy. According to Russell, immigration procedures were already planned, so the *Singh* case may not be that important, and the emergence of Sunday shopping may have more to do with an increasingly liberal political culture than Supreme Court decision making. Similarly, one might wonder whether court rulings on minority language education rights have been decisive in fomenting the crisis of national unity.

To understand the issue contained in this debate, one might first endeavour to acquire an appreciation of the meaning of *judicial self-restraint* and *judicial activism* in the context of Charter litigation. The following two publications are helpful in this regard: Rainer Knopff and F.L. Morton, *Charter Politics* (Scarborough: Nelson Canada, 1992), ch. 2; and the introductory essay in Peter H. Russell, Rainer Knopff, and Ted Morton, eds., *Federalism and the Charter: Leading Constitutional Decisions*, new ed. (Ottawa: Carleton University Press, 1989). As for readings on the courts' interpretation of the Charter, a number of articles, chapters, and books have been written on this matter: F.L. Morton, "Courts," in Mark Dickerson, Thomas Flanagan, and Neil Nevitte, eds., *Introductory Readings in Government and Politics* (Scarborough: Nelson Canada, 1995); F.L. Morton, "The Effect of the Charter of Rights on Canadian Federalism," *Publius: The Journal of Federalism* 25, no. 3 (1995); Peter H. Russell, "The Political Purposes of the Charter: Have They Been Fulfilled? An Agnostic's Report Card," in Philip Bryden, Steven Davis, and John Russell, eds., *Protecting Rights and Freedoms: Essays on the Charter's Place in Canada's Political, Legal and Intellectual Life* (Toronto: University of Toronto Press, 1994); Peter H. Russell, "The Three Dimensions of Charter Politics," in James P. Bickerton and Alain-G. Gagnon, eds., *Canadian Politics*, 2nd ed. (Peterborough: Broadview Press, 1994); Radha Jhappan, "The Charter and the Courts," in Michael Whittington and Glen Williams, eds., *Canadian Politics in the 1990s* (Scarborough: Nelson Canada, 1995); Michael Mandel, *The Charter of Rights and the Legalization of Politics in Canada*, 2nd ed. (Toronto: Wall and Thompson, 1993); Joel Bakan, *Just Words: Constitutional Rights and Social Wrongs* (Toronto: University of Toronto Press, 1997); and Peter W. Hogg and Allison A. Bushell, "The Charter Dialogue between Courts and Legislatures" (or "Perhaps the Charter Isn't Such a Bad Thing After All"), (1995) *Osgoode Hall Law Journal* 35: 1, 75–124. As can be seen, many of the readings continue the debate between Morton and Russell.

The truly diligent student should also examine Peter Hogg's *The Constitutional Law of Canada*, 3rd ed. (Toronto: Carswell, 1992). This wonderfully rich text, which is now coming out in student editions, offers a thorough and well-organized review of Charter decisions. Unlike some of the other readings, Hogg's primary purpose is not to determine whether the courts are becoming more powerful, but rather to delineate carefully the decisions of the courts. Still, no student can afford to miss the thoughts of Peter Hogg on the Charter and its implications for Canada.

For a more quantitative review of Charter decisions than that obtained in the aforementioned readings, students may once again turn to Russell and Morton for assistance: F.L. Morton, Peter H. Russell, and Troy Riddell, "The Canadian Charter of Rights and Freedoms: A Descriptive Analysis of the First Decade, 1982–1992," 5 *National Journal of Constitutional Law.* A more recent quantitative analysis and one directly related to the question of judicial activism is Patrick J. Monahan and Michael J. Bryant, "The Supreme Court of Canada's 1996 Constitutional Cases: The End of Charter Activism?" *Canada Watch* 5, no. 3–4 (March–April 1997): 41, 43–49. Also, students should consult *Canada Watch* regularly, for it often has timely articles on the Charter.

ISSUE**FIFTEEN**

Should Parliament Review Supreme Court Nominees?

✔ **YES**
F.L. MORTON, "Why the Judicial Appointment Process Must Be Reformed"

✘ **NO**
H. PATRICK GLENN, "Parliamentary Hearings for Supreme Court of Canada Appointments?"

In late August of 1997, Justice Gérard La Forest announced his decision to retire from the Supreme Court of Canada. The decision precipitated a flurry of activities, all of which related to the question who would become the new member of Canada's highest court. Convention dictated that the new justice would be from Atlantic Canada, so members of legal communities in the four eastern provinces urged that one of their own be selected. Pressure groups, too, joined in, arguing that the new appointee reflect their particular interests. Governments also seemed concerned about the decision. The federal Department of Justice reportedly wished for someone less sympathetic to the rights and freedoms of alleged criminals. More important, senior federal officials wanted in place someone who could adjudicate on a forthcoming reference case dealing with the secession of Quebec.

Finally, on the first day of October, a month after Justice La Forest's announcement, Prime Minister Chrétien revealed that Michel Bastarache, a senior judge from New Brunswick, would sit on the Supreme Court of Canada. The selection seemed to satisfy many within the legal world, for the new justice had impeccable professional credentials. Moreover, he was bilingual, and had a keen grasp of the important issues of language and rights. On the whole, the process of appointing Supreme Court justices had apparently worked. The legal community had offered its input, interested groups had expressed their preferences, and other concerned parties, too, had had their say. With this all in hand, the prime minister, who has the authority to make the final decision, had come up with an excellent choice.

For some, though, the appointment of Justice Bastarache was just further evidence of what was wrong with the appointment process: it is too closed, too secretive. Only those able to break into the closed decision-making process of appointing Supreme Court juctices have an impact, which means only a handful of lawyers, judges, and leaders of powerful groups. The rest of the country, the majority of Canadians, can only stand by and watch. In previous times, when the Supreme Court had only a minimal impact on the daily lives of Canadians, this was not a serious concern. But the advent of the Canadian Charter of Rights and Freedoms had changed that. With its interpretations of the Charter, the Supreme Court now *does* have an impact on the lives of Canadians, yet Canadians have no direct role in the selection of the increasingly influential members of the Supreme Court. This set of facts, for some, cried out for a change in the appointment process, one that gave Canadians a chance to become acquainted with justices of the Supreme Court of Canada.

One such change is the holding of parliamentary hearings on Supreme Court nominees. Under this arrangement, nominees would appear before a parliamentary committee, at which time the people's representatives would ask various questions of the candidates. With this, the nation would become more informed about the men and women who sit on the Supreme Court. The qualifications, past decisions, and judicial philosophy of the nominees would see the light of day. But some are less than enamoured of this proposal. Canada's present minister of Justice, Anne McLellan, fears that parliamentary hearings present the "possibility of a circus and sideshow." Her evidence for this? The American experience with legislative hearings for judicial appointments. These hearings sometimes turn into events that have little to do with the capabilities of the candidates. The present system, it is argued, avoids the excesses of the American system while providing Canada with capable justices. Furthermore, hearings might politicize the appointment process, making the courts more vulnerable to prevailing political winds. Clearly, then, the proposal for parliamentary hearings is controversial.

In the readings, F.L. Morton, a political scientist who specializes in judicial politics, argues for parliamentary hearings. H. Patrick Glenn, a professor of law at McGill University, contends that Canada should resist the temptation to adopt hearings for Supreme Court appointments.

✔ YES
Why the Judicial Appointment Process Must Be Reformed
F.L. MORTON

It is time to reform the appointment process for Supreme Court judges. Since the adoption of the Charter of Rights and Freedoms in 1982, the Supreme Court has become a powerful actor in Canadian politics. Yet the appointment of our new constitutional masters remains unchanged, shielded from any public review or comment. Like the selection of a new Pope, Canadians learn who has been chosen as one of their new constitutional priests only after the decision has been made. This closed system was appropriate to the important but secondary role played by judges under Canada's old regime of parliamentary supremacy. It is completely inconsistent with the powerful new role of judges under the Charter. In a properly organized democracy, the exercise of political power must be ultimately accountable. Under the new regime ushered in by the Charter, this is no longer the case. If we are to prevent constitutional supremacy from degenerating into judicial supremacy, we must amend the appointment process to include some form of public review of the candidates.

There can be no questioning the fact that the Charter has fundamentally altered the role of the Supreme Court in Canadian politics. Prior to 1982, the court rarely obstructed the policy choices of Parliament or provincial legislatures. During this era, most of the Supreme Court's decisions dealt with civil (private) law disputes. Legislatures made these laws and courts applied and interpreted them. If a government believed the court had misinterpreted a statute, this mistake could be quickly reversed by legislative amendment. During the 1950s and 1960s, the court averaged less than three constitutional decisions per year, almost all in the field of federalism. Impact studies found that even a negative division of powers decision rarely prevented a determined government from achieving the same policy objective through alternative legislative means.

The adoption of the Canadian Bill of Rights in 1960 did not change the court's low political profile. In keeping with the then strong British influence in Canadian legal culture, the court interpreted the Bill of Rights in a traditional and deferential manner. In thirty-five decisions over twenty years, the individual rights-claimant won only five cases. In only one case did the Supreme Court declare a federal statute invalid. Writing in the late 1960s, one expert accurately described the Supreme Court as "the quiet court in an unquiet country."[1]

The "Charter Revolution" of the 1980s brought this era to an abrupt end.[2] In the first decade following its adoption, the Supreme Court made over 200 Charter decisions. The court now averages close to twenty-five Charter decisions a year, about 20 percent of its total case load. In these first 200 decisions, the court ruled in favour of the rights-claimant sixty-seven times, in the process striking down portions of twenty-seven federal and fourteen provincial statutes. These statistics, as impressive as they are, still fail to capture the extent of the court's new influence over public policy—of who gets what, when, and how.

The court has virtually rewritten the law of Canadian criminal process, reversing many of its earlier precedents along the way. The court has adopted an exclusionary rule that is at least as rigorous as the American practice.[3] The right to counsel has been interpreted to discourage almost any police questioning of suspects in the absence of counsel[4] and to preclude judicial use of almost any form of self-incrimination at any stage in the investigative process.[5] A recent comparative study concluded that the accused in Canadian criminal cases now enjoy more rights than in the United States.[6] As a consequence of these decisions, the cost of publicly funded legal aid has skyrocketed. In Ontario, legal-aid costs rose from $56 million in 1982 to $213 million in 1992. In Alberta, legal-aid costs grew 42 percent in 1992 alone. As predicted by constitutional expert Eugene Forsey in 1982, the Charter has indeed proven to be a gold mine for lawyers.

The court struck down Canada's abortion law in its 1988 *Morgentaler* ruling, notwithstanding the fact that any reference to abortion—pro or con—had been intentionally excluded from the Charter. In a similar vein, lower courts have added homosexuality to the list of forms of discrimination prohibited by the Charter, again despite clear evidence that this option was explicitly rejected when the Charter was being drafted.[7] The court also struck down the federal Sunday-closing law (which it had upheld under the 1960 Bill of Rights), paving the way for wide-open Sunday shopping in most provinces. In the politically sensitive area of language rights, the court has also been active. It struck down several sections of Quebec's Bill 101, the Charter of the French Language, contributing to Quebec's sense of alienation from English Canada and the failed attempts at constitutional reconciliation in the Meech Lake and Charlottetown Accords. The court has aggressively interpreted the official minority language education rights provisions, requiring provinces not just to provide minority-language education services, but in some cases separate facilities and even specially designated "minority-only" seats on school boards. The court's decision in the *Singh* case forced Ottawa to revamp its refugee determination process, at a cost of over $200 million. In addition to such indirect costs of compliance with Charter decisions, the court recently ruled that judges have the authority to order "affirmative remedies" such as the expansion of social benefit programs that unfairly exclude (i.e., discriminate against) a disadvantaged group.[8] While the court stressed such remedies could only be used in rare circumstances, within a month lower courts had ordered a costly extension of spousal benefit plans in the homosexual rights cases mentioned above.

Despite the broad sweep of the Charter's impact on Canadian public policy, no one could reasonably object to these decisions if they were simply dictated by the text of the Charter. In other words, if the Supreme Court has simply been giving effect to the clear or intended meaning of the Charter, any critics would have to direct their ire at the Charter itself and not the judges. But as anyone familiar with Charter decisions knows, the opposite is much more often the case. There have been only one or two cases involving clear-cut violations of the central meaning of Charter rights. The overwhelming number of Charter claims involve activities that fall on the periphery of the meaning of rights, issues over which reasonable citizens can and do disagree. The court's free speech cases, for example, have dealt not with core issues of political speech, but with questions such as whether types of commercial speech—television advertising or on-street soliciting for purposes of prostitution—are constitutionally protected forms of expression. Judicial answers to questions such as these are purely discretionary, and vary from one judge to another, depending on their judicial philosophy and personal judgments. In other words, different judges find different rights.

This was clearly evident in the four different judgments delivered in the Supreme Court's *Morgentaler* abortion decision. Only one justice out of seven—Justice Wilson—declared a constitutional right to abortion. The other four members of the majority coalition found only procedural violations of the Charter, and were further divided on their seriousness. The two dissenters said there was no constitutional violation.

This division of the court was not caused by technical legal disagreements. Rather it reflected two different theories of Charter review, two different conceptions of the proper role of the judge. The fractured *Morgentaler* decision accurately reflected the growing division of the court: more than a third of its Charter decisions now contain dissenting votes. One wing of the court, as exemplified by Justice Wilson, has adopted an activist approach to applying the Charter. These judges are more inclined to read in new and even unintended meaning to the broadly worded principles of the Charter, and are not reluctant to strike down legislative decisions with which they disagree. The other wing of the court, exemplified by Justice McIntyre, attempts to minimize judicial discretion by limiting Charter rights to their "original meaning," as disclosed (when possible) by the intent of the framers, and as a result is usually more deferential to Parliament's policy decisions.

These two different approaches to interpreting the Charter lead to very different results. A study of the Supreme Court's first 100 Charter decisions revealed that Justice Wilson supported individuals' Charter claims in 53 percent of her decisions, while Justice McIntyre upheld Charter claims in only 23 percent. The court average was 35 percent.[9] Wilson and McIntyre wrote the most dissenting opinions, yet never dissented together. Not only did they depart from the majority most frequently, but they did so in opposite directions. In each of her thirteen dissents, Wilson supported the individual's Charter claim, while McIntyre supported the crown in ten of his eleven dissents.

These statistics confirm that the meaning of the Charter, and thus the "existence" of a right, can vary from one judge to another. In most Charter cases, it is the judges who drive the Charter, not vice versa. The policy preferences (conscious or otherwise) of a judge, combined with judicial philosophy, are more likely to determine the outcome than the text of the Charter. Different judges "find" different rights.

Well-intentioned traditionalists have argued that even if all of the above is true, requiring public parliamentary hearings would still do more harm than good, that the cure would be worse than the disease. This analysis is usually premised on recent U.S. experience, most notably the Robert Bork and Clarence Thomas hearings before the Senate Judiciary Committee. These media-circus events featured aggressive interest group lobbying, strong ideological overtones, and character assassination. Most Canadians were repulsed by these transparent "court packing" attempts and thus sympathetic to the argument that this is one American institution that we definitely do not want to import into Canada. If we tease out the different strands of this argument, however, we find that none are conclusive.

The most obvious criticism of confirmation hearings is that they would politicize the process. Special interest groups would leap at the opportunity to influence the choice of the next Supreme Court judge, promoting candidates sympathetic to their objectives and opposing those who are not. This criticism assumes that the current practice is not politicized. In fact, there is growing evidence to the contrary. When Justice Estey retired shortly after the 1988 *Morgentaler* decision, *The Globe and Mail* reported that "activists in the abortion debate and representatives of ethnic communities are lobbying hard.... Many members of the ruling PC Party's right-wing ... are putting pressure on PM Mulroney to appoint a conservative judge." Member of Parliament James Jepson, one of the most outspoken pro-life Tory backbenchers, explained the importance of the new Supreme Court appointment:

> Unfortunately, with the Charter that Trudeau left us, we legislators do not have final power. It rests with the courts.... You have seen the battling in the United States for the [most recent] Supreme Court nominee. Well, it doesn't take a rocket scientist to see we have the same situation here now.[10]

The same kind of pressure is coming from the political left. At a 1991 conference on the Charter and Public Policy, Marilou McPhedran, a leading feminist legal activist in Ontario, challenged several speakers who spoke as if there were no politics in the appointment process. "We're not being completely honest about the present appointment process," she declared. "We've all been involved in judicial appointments."[11] Other sources confirm that feminist organizations such as LEAF and NAC have privately lobbied the government on judicial appointments.[12]

It is hardly surprising that the new role of the court under the Charter has stimulated behind-the-scenes manoeuvring to influence the appointment of ideologically friendly judges. Indeed, it would be more surprising if it had not. It is an axiom of political science that "where power rests, there influence will be brought to bear."[13] The new Supreme Court is no exception. The appointment process has already been politicized. A confirmation hearing would simply bring these politics out into the open.

A related criticism is that the political lobbying that would inevitably accompany confirmation hearings would undermine the rule of law by making the personal preferences of judges more decisive than the content of the law they are supposed to interpret. Once again, this criticism comes too late. As noted above, the approach to interpreting the Charter chosen by the majority of judges has maximized judicial discretion by minimizing the value of the actual text and its intended meaning. This previously heretical view was actually voiced by Justice Estey, after he retired from the court, in an interview with *The Globe and Mail:*

> Justice Estey said it worries him that Canadians still do not realize how decisions vary according to the personality of each judge. As the misconception is gradually corrected, he said, people may lose respect and faith in the institution.... People think a court is a court is a court. But it is elastic. It is always sliding.[14]

Another variation on this criticism is that public hearings for judicial nominees will inevitably lead to American-style judicial activism. This view is wrong on two counts. First, American-style activism is already here. The argument that the Section 1 "reasonable limits" provision makes judicial review under the Charter qualitatively distinct from U.S. judicial review—an opinion very much in vogue in judicial circles—is just legalistic myopia. Section 1 simply gives Canadian judges even more discretion than they already had. True, judges can use Section 1 as a vehicle of self-restraint. But they can just as easily use it in an activist fashion, and that is what they have done. Section 1 has become just another path to the same end.

Second, public hearings could also encourage the appointment of more judges who believe in judicial self-restraint. This is what has happened in the United States over the past two decades. As a conservative public reaction set in against the liberal activism of the Warren court of the 1960s, a series of Republican presidential candidates—Nixon, Reagan, and Bush—successfully campaigned on the promise to appoint "strict constructionists" to the Supreme Court. By the late 1980s, these new appointments had made the court much less interventionist and more deferential to the policy decisions of both Congress and state governments. While some would argue the Republican appointments pushed the court too far in the direction of self-restraint, the newly elected Democratic president, Bill Clinton, now has the opportunity to try to redress the balance.

This last aspect of American experience provides the rebuttal for yet another argument against public hearings: that they are inconsistent with the Canadian convention of "ministerial responsibility"—that the justice minister and the prime minister must be "responsible" to the House of Commons for their judicial appointments. Again, this criticism is wrong on two counts. First, the simple fact of holding public parliamentary committee hearings for judicial candidates does not mean that the committee (or the House of Commons) will have a "veto" power, analogous to the U.S. Senate. Presumably this committee, like all parliamentary committees, would be struck in a fashion that reflects the government's majority in the House of Commons. In the final analysis, a government would always have the votes to push through a positive committee recommendation, no matter how badly its nominee had performed.

In this sense, committee hearings would actually strengthen ministerial responsibility, because a government would have something to be responsible for! That is, for the first time, the opposition and the Canadian people would have the opportunity to learn what kind of judge the government was appointing: an activist or an apostle of judicial self-restraint, a conservative or a liberal. What it means is that prior to final appointment, a government's candidate for the Supreme Court will be expected to field responsible questions about his or her judicial philosophy from a multiparty committee. The purpose of the hearings is not to prevent a government from making appointments to the Supreme Court, but to make it clear—and public—what kind of criteria the government is using.

As U.S. experience indicates, a government's judicial appointments can become an issue at election time. With the adoption of parliamentary committee hearings, an incumbent government could be challenged to defend its appointment record. Whatever else might be said of this, it certainly does not offend any of the tenets of responsible government.

The last criticism is perhaps the most serious and difficult to meet: that public hearings will deter qualified men and women from seeking or accepting appointments to the Supreme Court. There is no denying that many qualified candidates would refuse to submit themselves and their families to the kind of dissection and inspection of their private and professional lives—not to mention slander and innuendo—that both Robert Bork and Clarence Thomas had to endure.

My response is twofold. First, the same thing could be said of democratic politics in general. For generations, many of our most qualified citizens have refused to enter electoral politics because they do not have the stomach or the patience for the public scrutiny that comes with the job. Yet even as we acknowledge the seriousness of this problem, we would not for a minute consider abandoning the free elections, freedom of speech, and independent press that can make political life so uncomfortable. To speak bluntly, having decided to share some of the privileges of elected lawmakers, Canadian judges must also be prepared to share some of the disadvantages that come with the exercise of power.

The second reason is more cheerful: adopting the practice of judicial nomination hearings need not mean adopting the way Americans conduct theirs. Canadians have always prided themselves on conducting politics in a more civil and professional manner than their American neighbours. There is no reason this tradition cannot be extended to judicial nomination hearings. If professional norms and courtesy are observed, there is no reason that Canada cannot reap the advantages of this system while minimizing its potential negatives.

To conclude, those who defend the status quo would have us believe that in preserving a British-style judicial selection process with the new U.S.-style judicial review of constitutional rights, Canadians can have the best of both worlds. In fact, this combination can just as easily produce the worst of both worlds—judicial lawmaking with no accountability. The solution to this problem is public hearings for Supreme Court nominees before a parliamentary committee.

NOTES

1. R.I. Cheffins, "The Supreme Court of Canada: The Quiet Court in an Unquiet Country," *Osgoode Hall Law Journal* 4 (1966): 259–360.

2. F.L. Morton, "The Charter Revolution and the Court Party," *Osgoode Hall Law Journal* 30, no. 3 (1992): 627–53.

3. *R. v. Collins*, [1987] 1 S.C.R. 265.

4. *R. v. Manninen*, [1987] 1 S.C.R. 1233.

5. *R. v. Hebert*, [1990] 2 S.C.R. 151.

6. R. Harvie and H. Foster, "Different Drummers, Different Drums: The Supreme Court, American Jurisprudence and the Revision of Canadian Criminal Law under the Charter," (1990) 24 *Ottawa Law Review* 39.

7. *Haig (and Birch) v. Canada* (1992), 5 O.R. (3d) 245; and *Leshner v. Ministry of the Attorney-General* (1992), 10 O.R. (3d) 732 (Ont. C.A.).

8. *Schachter v. Canada*, [1992] 2 S.C.R. 679.

9. F.L. Morton, Peter H. Russell, and M.J. Withey, "The Supreme Court's First One Hundred Charter Decisions: A Statistical Analysis," (1992) *Osgoode Hall Law Journal* 30, no. 1.

10. "Reduced Role for Politicians Urged in Naming of Judges," *The Globe and Mail*, May 16, 1988, p. A1.

11. Morton, "The Charter Revolution and the Court Party," p. 638.

12. Ibid. Also see Sherene Razack, *Canadian Feminism and the Law: The Women's Legal Education and Action Fund and the Pursuit of Equality* (Toronto: Second Story Press, 1991), pp. 36–63.

13. V.O. Key, *Politics, Parties, and Pressure Groups* (Thomas Y. Crowell, 1958), p. 154.

14. *The Globe and Mail*, April 27, 1988, p. A5

✗ **NO**

Parliamentary Hearings for Supreme Court of Canada Appointments?

H. PATRICK GLENN

Should there be parliamentary confirmation hearings for Supreme Court of Canada appointments? There has been only limited discussion of the question in Canada, though a number of themes have emerged. Proponents of hearings have said that the Supreme Court, particularly since the enactment of the Canadian Charter of Rights and Freedoms, exercises important political responsibilities, and that a more openly political appointment process is therefore appropriate. The larger role of the Supreme Court is also said to require increased public knowledge of judges and of judicial aspirants. Confirmation hearings are therefore urged as a means of facilitating public awareness and debate. A further argument, more rooted in a particular philosophy of judicial activity, is to the effect that judges are free to decide cases as they wish and that such unlimited discretion requires political surveillance, at least at the stage of appointment.

Since there have never been confirmation hearings of judicial appointments in Canada, few people have tried to explain or justify their absence. Recently, however, in response to arguments in favour of confirmation hearings, it has been said that the existing process has served Canada well ("if it ain't broke, don't fix it"); that changes to the existing process would be difficult to implement and not likely to yield better results; that confirmation hearings would give rise to unseemly and inappropriate attacks on appointees while provoking no meaningful response from them; and that the public ordeal of hearings would deter good candidates from seeking judicial office.

A contemporary observer of this debate would probably come to the conclusion that confirmation hearings should be held. They accord with democratic theory; it is true that the judges of the Supreme Court of Canada, who are accountable to no one for their decisions, render judgments that have major political importance; the arguments against hearings seem both undemocratic and elitist, in seeking to protect important people from public scrutiny. Shouldn't we just get on with it?

There may be more to be said. In particular it seems worthwhile to ask some further questions as to the compatibility of confirmation hearings with existing Canadian institutions, and as to the relations between law and politics.

CONFIRMATION HEARINGS AND CANADIAN INSTITUTIONS

The creation of confirmation hearings for Supreme Court of Canada appointments is related to the existing political institutions of the House of Commons and the Senate, where the hearings would take place, to the Supreme Court itself, whose composition might be affected, and more generally to the Canadian judiciary, for the model of judicial appointment procedure that would be created. In each case, it will be suggested, confirmation hearings are incompatible with existing Canadian institutions and the philosophy that underlies them.

What is the significance of confirmation hearings for the House of Commons and the Senate? In the U.S. model, hearings of Supreme Court nominees are conducted by a committee of the Senate, in execution of the Senate's mandate to confirm or reject all nominations. The hearings are part of the system of checks and balances written into the U.S. Constitution. The executive, in the person of the president, cannot abuse the appointment process and the Senate holds in effect a veto power over presidential nominees. Moreover, the Senate majority is frequently of a different political allegiance than that of the president. However, neither the Canadian House of Commons nor the Canadian Senate plays the same role as the U.S. Senate. The Canadian parliamentary system is one of responsible government. The government, or the executive, is responsible to the House of Commons in the sense that it can be defeated by it and turned out of office. The result, however, is that the party that obtains the majority of seats will form the government and also control the House. Canada does not have a system of checks and balances. One may agree or disagree on types of government, but ours is unlikely to change in the foreseeable future, at least in this respect. There are, moreover, reasons for systems of responsible government. They have to do with entrusting government to those who have democratically won it, and requiring them to act ethically and responsibly for the public good, or be voted out. Checks and balances are not seen as useful or efficient devices to ensure this outcome. Hearings before a House of Commons committee would therefore not serve the primary purpose of nomination hearings in the United States, that of allowing partisan control to be exercised on governmental nominations.

Some recent constitutional proposals have therefore called for confirmation hearings before a Senate (rather than a House of Commons) committee, but the committee would have been one of a radically reformed Senate. There appear to be no proposals to allow a committee of the present Senate to hold confirmation hearings and vote conclusively on Supreme Court nominations. There are good reasons for the absence of such proposals, given the status of the existing Senate.

There remain the possibilities of hearings before a joint House of Commons/Senate committee, which would then vote conclusively on the nomination, or a simple hearing before a House of Commons committee, with no conclusive vote. No one has suggested how such a joint House of Commons/Senate committee should be composed or the degree of governmental control over it, and this is not a question of simple plumbing or technique. It is a fundamental question of whether an institution other than Parliament itself is to control the government and if so in what circumstances. Adoption of such a committee, with such powers, would constitute a radical change to the system of parliamentary responsible government. The advantages and disadvantages of doing so have yet to be raised in the context of the debate on confirmation hearings.

Should there then be public hearings before a House of Commons committee, with no conclusive vote? This would be in a sense a reversal of the U.S. model, which until the twentieth century consisted of a Senate vote with no hearings. Is it publicity alone that is sought? This may depend ultimately on our concept of the relations between law and politics (more on that below).

Parliamentary confirmation hearings therefore do not sit well with our political institutions. What about the Supreme Court itself? Does its mandate require appointments only after hearings and the exercise of some form of political control? Here the importance of the Charter and the intermittent activism of the U.S. Supreme Court have dominated the discussion. What is the nature, however, of the Supreme Court of Canada? In the Western legal tradition it has become a unique type of court, unlike the highest courts of the United Kingdom, the United States, or France. In each of those countries the jurisdiction of the highest court is more specialized than that of the Supreme Court of Canada. In the United States, the Supreme Court is a court essentially for federal and constitutional matters only; its constitutional responsibilities dominate its workload. In the United Kingdom, the House of Lords has no constitutional responsibilities similar to those exercised by the Supreme Court of Canada in application of the Charter. In France, there are three separate high courts, one for constitutional law, one for administrative law, and one for private law.

The Supreme Court of Canada is the only generalist court among these courts. A large part of its docket is given over to criminal appeals, and it continues to hear appeals in all other areas of private and public law. Charter cases occupy only some 25 to 30 percent of its case load. The Supreme Court is very much a court of law in the traditional sense, deciding individual cases involving individual litigants. Its decisions have important precedential value, but this is true of the decisions of all high courts. It is therefore incorrect to treat the Supreme Court as a fundamentally political institution simply because it has begun to decide Charter cases. It certainly does decide Charter cases, and they are important cases. It is not, however, a court dominated by a political workload, a political agenda, and politically motivated judges. This too is related ultimately to our views concerning law and politics. Do we wish to give dominance to the overtly political part of the court's workload? The present structure and jurisdiction of the court does not indicate that this need be done.

Finally, what is the relation of confirmation hearings at the level of the Supreme Court to our entire system of judicial appointments? Would hearings be compatible with the system or constitute a useful model for its reform? Canada originally inherited the British system of appointment of judges, which relies on the professional opinion of a very small number of judges, including the Lord Chancellor, to inform the government's choice of members of the judiciary. As well, judges are chosen from a very small and select group of professionals, those barristers who have become Queen's Counsel. This system of appointment was of course appropriate for the British judiciary, which has historically been very small, with much adjudication being left to lay magistrates (the local notables). The Canadian judiciary, however, has become quite unlike the British judiciary. It is much larger; it is composed almost entirely of professional judges; and its members are generally drawn from a very large, unified legal profession (and not from a very small corps of professional pleaders or barristers). In keeping with these changes to the judiciary, the Canadian system of appointment has changed considerably from the British model. At the provincial level judicial nominating commissions are becoming the rule. These commissions receive applications and nominations for judicial positions, assess qualifications, and make recommendations for appointment (often in the form of short lists) to provincial authorities. At the federal level the process of screening and recommending judicial candidates has become a major activity of the Ministry of Justice, involving consultation with a committee of the Canadian Bar Association that provides formal evaluations of all candidates. The process is neither secretive nor internal to the government. It is simply not conducted in a public forum.

These changes in the process of appointing Canadian judges have been occurring gradually, and the process of change is certainly not complete. One result of change has been a decline in the importance of political patronage in the appointment process. It is reasonable to think that the quality of the bench has also been reinforced, since the procedures allow much more information to be processed about a larger number of judicial candidates than would otherwise be the case. Appointments to the Supreme Court of Canada go through this process, and to this writer's knowledge, there is no criticism of the quality of appointments to the Supreme Court of Canada. It is evident that successive governments have taken the task very seriously and that the visibility of the court has enhanced the likelihood of high-quality appointments.

The underlying political ethic of this appointment process is that of responsible government, i.e., that it is the task of the government to act, as government, in the public interest. The underlying judicial ethic of the process is that of obtaining a judiciary of the highest quality. Quite absent from the process have been the ideas of checks and balances on government action and of democratic approval of the judiciary. Discussion of the existing judicial appointment process in Canada thus provides little or no support for judicial confirmation hearings, given the underlying principles of responsible government and a judiciary of the highest quality. This conclusion in no way prejudices the current movement toward judicial nominating commissions, which have as their task the searching out of the best candidates, as opposed to merely eliminating allegedly bad governmental nominations.

It has not been possible in discussing Canadian institutions to ignore entirely the relations between law and politics. What more must be briefly said on this large subject?

LAW, POLITICS, AND CONFIRMATION HEARINGS

The relations between law and politics have already been mentioned, in discussing whether confirmation hearings should be held before a House of Commons committee for reasons of publicity alone (with no vote to be taken) and whether judicial appointments and activity should receive some form of democratic approval (notably through election of judges). Since democracy has been a relatively successful form of government, its extension to the judiciary appears to be a good thing. Democracy is a form of politics, however, and its application to law means politicizing the legal process in an explicit manner. Do we want to do this?

One of the most frequently made criticisms of the legal order is that it is ultimately political. Since it is ultimately political we should do away with the legal charade and apply to the legal process the same methods and techniques that are used elsewhere in politics. Law should be the object of public and transparent political debate and be subject to democratic institutions. The notion of the "political" is here very large and appears to extend to most forms of human interaction. Such an attitude underlay the adoption of systems of election of judges in both the former Soviet Union (implementing socialist legality) and the United States (implementing Jeffersonian democracy). We have now had substantial modern experience with the notion of democratizing the legal process in such a direct way. The problems with this are both theoretical and practical.

Ultimately our view of judicial activity may be driven by our view of law itself. Is there such a thing, for example, as a natural legal order? The Aboriginal population of this country tells us there is. It teaches respect for the natural environment. We should continue to act in traditional ways since these ways do least violence to the world. If there is such a natural legal order, it does not require elected judges or a democratic legal process. It requires the legal process that will ensure respect for the natural legal order, and in the Aboriginal legal order this meant adherence to the wisdom of people recognized as elders. Nor do religiously inspired legal traditions insist on democratic legitimation; legal authority is derived from religious learning and some form of official recognition of such acquired authority. In the Western, secular world these ancient traditions have had and continue to have great influence. The Western legal tradition is remarkable, however, for its insistence that law is presently made by those entrusted with the task. This philosophical attitude emerged with the Renaissance, but the Renaissance did not lead to a radical democratization of the legal process. Something else was also at work.

In contemporary liberal societies people are entitled to different views and different ways of life. Law is used to regulate and conciliate the conflicts that inevitably arise. Since there is no consistently imposed social fabric, law must do more than it does in a society in which common forms of life are accepted by all concerned. In the inevitable turmoil of social relations, the major teaching of the Renaissance was that law had to be separated from politics. Politics would, of course, continue to exist and would give the major forms of direction to society. At the level of daily life, however, where decisions are made that affect the individual, it was felt that the political process was too large, too biased, and too crude to regulate the minutiae of social existence. The person charged with social deviance could not be judged, for example, by those who had made the rules. From the seventeenth century the notion of an independent judiciary emerged, one that was not subject to the political process and that was given remarkable institutional liberty to pursue justice in the individual case. This is why Canada has professionalized its judiciary. No one wishes to be judged by those controlled by someone else, or by those fearing sanctions for the decision they reach, or by those biased by social position or attitude. In short, most of our present legal institutions have been developed, not because it is felt that law is somehow inevitably different from politics—more scientific, more technical, or more neutral—but because it has been felt that every possible effort should be made to provide institutional protection to individuals—in liberal, democratic states—from the brute forces of politics. The separation of law and politics does not deny the political character of law, but assumes it. It then seeks to control and limit the influence of politics through institutional guarantees of fair process, independent decision makers, and application of established rules.

The notion of an independent judiciary, one that is not democratically elected and not subject to democratic recall, is thus parallel to and consistent with the political ethic of responsible government. Those entrusted with authority are expected to exercise it in the public interest. There can be no guardians of the guardians, at least in any immediate and direct way. The independence of the judiciary takes the ethic a step further, however, in awarding tenure for life (or its statutory equivalent, the seventy-fifth birthday) to those judged best qualified to have it. Since our judiciary is now a large one, there are judicial councils that have been established to discipline judges for nonjudicial conduct, but no political authority can interfere in the judicial decision-making process and no judge need fear official or popular sanction for unpopular decisions. Most of our legal institutions today thus represent efforts to separate law from politics, because their confusion has been recognized by most people at most times to be highly undesirable.

Efforts to democratize and politicize the legal process are visible today because they have been so consistently rejected in the past, and because our existing institutions translate this rejection. It is not that no one thought of parliamentary confirmation hearings before the Charter. It is rather that institutions were created that would, as much as possible, free the legal process from the political one. Judges *are* free to decide as they wish, and this freedom is given to them because you would not want *your* case to be decided on majoritarian political grounds. Creating judicial confirmation hearings would not change a great deal in the unfolding of history. It would be a small, further step in the politicization of law, however, and as such there should be a presumption against such hearings, as indeed there is in this country.

The practical difficulties in democratizing the legal process have been more significant than the theoretical ones, however, in the jurisdictions that have attempted the process. In the former Soviet Union the process of election of judges was party controlled and the result was the opposite of democratic control. In the United States the election of judges at state levels has been the object of ongoing reforms designed to eliminate party influence and corruption while reinforcing the quality of judges. The democratic control has been largely illusory and voter influence, never strong, has been declining steadily in favour of various forms of judicial nominating commissions. There has, however, been a politicization of the role of the Supreme Court of the United States, and judicial nomination hearings have become a very visible political phenomenon at this level of the judicial process. What should we make of the U.S. experience?

As mentioned above, confirmation hearings are a relatively recent phenomenon in the United States, beginning only in this century, shortly before the First World War. Why did they come about? Why was the presumption against politicization (federal U.S. judges are appointed and not elected) here reversed? It does not appear to have been the role of the U.S. Supreme Court in deciding Bill of Rights cases that caused the change, since this had been going on for a long time prior to the introduction of confirmation hearings. What appears to have brought about the change, according to U.S. writers, was the process by which appointments to the court became to be seen as further means of advancing political goals. Today in the United States there is talk of "transformative appointments," in the sense of appointments that would change the course of decisions of the court, in a broad, political sense. The judges are expected to decide according to a broad, personal political philosophy. Very recently, there has thus been surprise at the emergence of a group of "legal conservatives" on the court, those who refuse to overrule prior decisions with which they disagree because of the need for legal stability. Yet if governments are entitled to use the Supreme Court for political objectives, and its judges are expected to act as majoritarian political appointees, then it is normal that the process of appointment be politicized and even radically so. It is also normal that the process be subject to the full range of political debate and struggle, as unedifying and inefficient as it frequently is. There is no practical means of ensuring only serene and enlightened democratic participation in the nomination process. Most important, there appears to be no means of politicizing the appointment process without also politicizing the court itself.

The Supreme Court has not become a political battleground in Canada. If we are to struggle toward a rule of law rather than a rule of political power, it is undesirable that it become a political battleground. Its present role as a court of law should remind us of why it is there. Let's leave it alone. One day it may have to decide my case, or yours.

Postscript

In his article, Morton makes a forceful case for parliamentary hearings. If the Supreme Court is now much more powerful than before, then it seems only sensible to make it more accountable to the public. His contention that the present appointment process is already politicized—but only behind the scenes—is also disturbing. It appears that some Canadians get to influence who sits on the Supreme Court, but not others. Yet, some lingering doubts remain about parliamentary hearings. Morton is confident that the basic civility of Canadians would preclude any of the excesses associated with American hearings. But scholarly studies suggest that Canadians are losing this civility (or deferential attitude), and are becoming more like their neighbours to the south. Also, it is unsettling to think that the country could lose some very capable jurists just because of the wish to ask nominees a few questions. For some, this might be too high a price to pay.

There is also the concern about the impact of hearings on the public perception of judicial decision making. At present, most citizens believe that justices offer disinterested interpretations of the law. As Morton shows, this is not an entirely accurate conception of how judges decide—indeed, for Morton, it is patently false. But one might argue, as Glenn seems to, that adjudication of conflicts over the law does involve the application of judicial expertise and wisdom, and that the spectacle of hearings might undermine public confidence in the judiciary. If the electorate believes that judges are merely imposing their own preferences on society, then the legitimacy of the judicial branch of government may be in jeopardy.

Obviously, Glenn is much happier with the present appointment process. He also finds little good to say about public hearings—and seemingly for good reason. If one looks to the American experience, the presence of hearings seems to be sign of a highly politicized court system, one in which the rule of law takes a back seat to the rule of political power. However, Glenn's arguments, like Morton's, are not entirely convincing. He contends that the appointment process in Canada *is* open and nonsecretive; it is simply not carried out full view of the public. But surely the absence of a public forum turns the process into what Glenn denies it to be: a closed process. Glenn makes the important point that the present appointment practice helps to shield the judicial process from the intrusiveness of politics and majoritarian thinking. But it might be argued that allowing public hearings would not put a large dent in the shield that protects the independence of the judiciary. Glenn concedes as much, but nevertheless seems to argue that hearings go against basic principles regarding judicial appointments. There also appears here to be a fear of the slippery slope, that the small steps toward a more politicized system encourage the taking of larger steps.

In his book *The Judiciary in Canada: The Third Branch of Government* (Toronto: McGraw-Hill Ryerson, 1987), Peter Russell presents a good discussion of the judicial appointment process in Canada and ways of reforming this process. Students might also consult Peter McCormick and Ian Greene's *Judges and Judging: Inside the Canadian Judicial System* (Toronto: James Lorimer, 1990). As well, Morton has edited an excellent collection of articles on the judicial process entitled *Law, Politics and the Judicial Process*, 2nd ed. (Calgary: University of Calgary Press, 1992). Finally, Martin Friedland has published a text entitled *A Place Apart: Judicial Independence and Accountability in Canada* (Ottawa: Canadian Communications Group–Publishing, 1995) that offers ways of reforming the appointment process without adopting public hearings.

Clearly, an understanding of judicial interpretation of the Charter of Rights is crucial to the issue of parliamentary hearings. On this issue, one might examine Christopher P. Manfredi, *Judicial Power and the Charter: Canada and the Paradox of Liberal Constitutionalism* (Toronto: McClelland and Stewart, 1993) and Rainer Knopff and F.L. Morton, *Charter Politics* (Scarborough, ON: Nelson Canada, 1992). Also Issue Fourteen in this text is pertinent to this matter.

On the American appointment process, which is relevant to the issue at hand, Henry Abraham's two texts, *The Judicial Process: An Introductory Analysis of the Courts of the United States, England, and France,* 6th ed. (New York: Oxford University Press, 1993) and *Justices and Presidents: A Political History of Appointments to the Supreme Court,* 3rd ed. (Toronto: Oxford University Press, 1992), as well as David Rohde and Harold Spaeth's *Supreme Court Decision-Making* (San Francisco: W.H. Freeman, 1976) and David M. O'Brien's *Storm Center: The Supreme Court in American Politics,* 3rd ed. (New York: W.W. Norton, 1993), are useful.

Lastly, the American appointment process has in the past decade generated a great deal of controversy. In 1987, president Ronald Reagan nominated Robert Bork for the U.S. Supreme Court, but he was rejected by the Senate after a long and acrimonious set of hearings. Four years later, president George Bush put forward Clarence Thomas, who was subsequently accused during the hearings of acts of sexual harassment. Eventually, the Senate accepted the Thomas nomination, but the effect of the hearings still reverberates through American political life. Two accounts of these events are Ethan Bronner, *Battle for Justice: How the Bork Nomination Shook America* (New York: W.W. Norton, 1989) and Timothy M. Phelps and Helen Winternitz, *Capitol Games: Clarence Thomas, Anita Hill, and the Story of a Supreme Court Nomination* (New York: Hyperion, 1992).

PART FOUR

POLITICAL BEHAVIOUR

Are political parties necessary?

Should representation in Parliament mirror Canada's social diversity?

Do referendums enrich democracy?

Should Canada adopt proportional representation?

ISSUE**SIXTEEN**

Are Political Parties Necessary?

✔ **YES**

G. GRANT AMYOT, "Democracy Without Parties: A New Politics?"
in A. Brian Tanguay and Alain-G. Gagnon, eds., *Canadian Parties
in Transition*, 2nd ed. (Scarborough: Nelson Canada, 1996)

✗ **NO**

VAUGHAN LYON, "Parties and Democracy: A Critical View," in
A. Brian Tanguay and Alain-G. Gagnon, eds., *Canadian Parties in
Transition,* 2nd ed. (Scarborough: Nelson Canada, 1996)

In recent years, Canadian political life has witnessed a near rash of new political parties. The Reform Party of Canada, the Bloc Québécois, and the National Party of Canada have all emerged relatively recently. Although some, like the National Party, have been shortlived, the Reform Party and Bloc Québécois have both emerged as major players in Parliament, each taking the role of Official Opposition in the last two Parliaments. A country accustomed to three federal parties must now adjust itself to a new reality—a Parliament composed of five political parties. It seems that political parties are in strong demand. It would appear that democracy is alive and well in Canada.

Yet, appearances can be deceiving. Some serious observers of Canadian politics claim that parties are actually in decline. Typically, parties have performed functions critical to the operation of democratic governments. They structure the vote, offer alternatives at election time, mobilize participation in politics, and effectively fuse the legislative and executive branches of government through the exercise of party discipline. But increasingly there is evidence that parties are no longer crucial to the political process. Interest groups, television, and polling, among other things, have arisen to compete with parties in the performance of the functions of government. The fact that a similar development seems to be taking place in the United States also suggests that parties may be past their prime.

Of special interest is the role of parties in providing information on the attitudes and preferences of voters. Thirty years ago, parties represented the best way of finding out what people wanted from government. Party members would become immersed in community life and develop a picture of voter likes and dislikes. Today, however, the parties' hold on this particular function has been greatly weakened—polls do a much better job.

G. Grant Amyot is one analyst who argues that these and other trends over the past quarter of a century are undermining the role of parties. For Amyot, this is a troubling trend, which threatens to impoverish the quality of democracy. Only parties are capable of performing many key functions, such as aggregating interests around a common public interest and providing a vehicle for ordinary citizens to influence public policy.

Vaughan Lyon provides us with an alternative view of the role of political parties in a democratic system. Lyon argues that the way parties have come to dominate our political life "denies people the rights and responsibilities of full citizenship." Rather than a genuinely responsive democratic government, Lyon fears that we have been left with government by "partycracy"—rule by competitive elites governing in their own interest. However, while Lyon might welcome talk of the demise of parties, he is not anxious to have decision-making power shift to some anonymous bureaucracy that is even further removed from the public. Instead he proposes a more radical idea—the creation of an elected "community Parliament" in each of Canada's constituencies, which would define the local community's position on issues and give clear guidance to their MPs. Only such an institution, according to Lyon, would take decision-making power out of the hands of the partycracy and return it to the common citizen.

✔ YES
Democracy Without Parties: A New Politics?
G. GRANT AMYOT

Are political parties necessary? While they are still a fact of life in Western democracies, there are clear signs of their decline, which have led many to question their role and effectiveness. Party loyalties among voters are weakening, as more and more voters take up an independent stance among parties. Policies seem to emanate from the bureaucracy and increasingly lack real alternatives. Major interests have their own pressure groups to represent their points of view. Most recently, the party organizations have lost even a large part of their prominence in fighting elections to staffs of pollsters, fundraisers, and strategists. These professionals serve the leaders, who have upstaged their parties in media and seem to dominate them as never before.

Furthermore, many citizens are not just disaffected from the existing parties, but criticize parties as such. Suggestions for more free votes in the House of Commons, greater accountability of individual MPs to their constituents, or the use of referenda on major issues all recall turn-of-the-century populist attacks on party government as corrupt and unresponsive to the will of the people. Have parties in fact outlived their usefulness? Are they destined to be replaced by a new politics, a nonparty form of democracy characterized by independent voters, charismatic leaders, and opinion polling?

PARTIES IN DEMOCRATIC THEORY

The preceding notion is not as outlandish as it may seem; in spite of the major role that parties have played in democratic politics, they do not have a firm footing in the liberal-democratic tradition of political thought that has underpinned it. For classical liberal thinkers, party in the modern sense was unnecessary and indeed harmful. Politics was about the rational pursuit of the public interest, and liberals believed that all citizens, if they used their faculty of reason, would arrive at roughly similar conceptions of that interest. Correct reasoning would tend to create unity in the polity, rather than division. Not all classical liberals, of course, went as far as Rousseau in his antipathy to factions that would distract the citizenry from the search for the general will, but his thought illustrates this facet of their views in an extreme form. Generally speaking, reason would dictate a framework of human laws, reflecting natural law, that would preserve the rights of the citizens vis-à-vis the state, and legislators were meant to work together to formulate this framework.

At any rate, politics for classical liberals was *not* primarily about the struggle of conflicting interests, for the public interest was beyond particular concerns. Therefore legislators were to be chosen for their highly developed powers of reason and their *dis*interestedness, rather than as delegates or representatives of their constituents. As Burke said in his often-quoted speech to the electors of Bristol: "Parliament is a *deliberative* assembly of *one* nation, with *one* interest, that of the whole; where, not local purposes, not local prejudices ought to guide, but the general good, resulting from the general reason of the whole" (1826, 335; Beer, 1969, 20–22).

While Burke defended the embryonic parties of his day—the Whig "connexions"—his conception of politics does not allow for strong party discipline. In his view, each individual member of Parliament (and each citizen) had to be free to follow his own reason in the pursuit of the public interest, although the ideal situation would be one of unanimity around a conception of that interest. Burke's famous definition of party—"a body of men united for promoting by their joint endeavours the national interest upon some particular principle in which they are all agreed" (1826, 335)—suggests something quite different from the disciplined parties of today, which are held together by more substantial and complex links than principle alone. When only principle binds a group of citizens together, there is always the potential for differing individual interpretations of that principle; indeed, individual freedom is necessary to the search for the true common good.

One of the greatest principles which early liberals thought a fit and noble basis for the organization of party was the struggle against "tyranny." In Burke's case, this meant the attempts of the ministers of George III to rule in disregard of constitutional traditions: "When bad men combine, the good must associate" (Burke, 1826, 336ff.). Later, Utilitarians such as Bentham viewed democracy itself principally as a means of controlling the government, which otherwise might use its powers to oppress the people. While the common good remained the goal, they recognized that both reason and desire inhabit human nature, particularly when men and women are placed in positions of power. These conceptions are difficult to apply to the present-day situation, however, when all parties accept the democratic basis of the constitution and when, in an era of positive government, Opposition parties have a role that goes far beyond checking governmental "tyranny."

Other liberal-democratic thinkers, such as John Stuart Mill, shared these views but at the same time laid a greater emphasis on citizen participation as a goal in itself. However, Mill's favoured locales for this participation were the workplace and local government, which could, in many cases, allow for direct democracy. It is only in the work of 20th-century scholars such as C.B. Macpherson that parties are seen as the principal vehicles for citizen participation.[1]

In the 20th century, the politics of interest achieved primacy over the politics of principle, in theory as well as in practice. Pluralist writers, such as Arthur Bentley, began to argue that politics was the struggle of a multiplicity of different interest groups, each striving to attain its goals in bargaining with the others. The pure pluralist scheme replaces parties almost completely with interest groups, and in the weak party discipline of the United States Congress we can see this tendency at work: senators and members of the House of Representatives vote in response to the pressures of the various lobbies rather than in accordance with party line, and certain key interests have captured the parts of government that are supposed to be regulating them. What seems to keep the parties alive are institutional mechanisms such as the direct election of the president and the legislative framework of party registration, primaries, etc. For pluralists, parties are supposed to perform a "brokerage" function, mediating between the various interests and presenting policy packages which they hope will maximize their appeal to the voters by skilfully combining as many different group demands as possible. Nevertheless, the tendency of pluralist thought is to depreciate the role of parties and privilege that of interest groups.

Only if we accept the Marxist thesis that there are only two fundamental interests, that of the workers and that of the capitalists, can the politics of interests produce a system of stable, disciplined parties. Marxism, having no belief that a "common good" can be attained in a capitalist society, can embrace the idea of the political party and partisanship without reservations. For Gramsci (1971, 227), parties are "the nomenclature for classes," and all Marxists believe that the working class has particular need of a strong party: "In its struggle for power the proletariat has no other weapon but organization" (Lenin, 1967, 440).

Marxism, however, is not part of the mainstream of liberal-democratic theory that has historically justified our contemporary democracy (although in Italy, for instance, it was one of the ideological influences on the Constitution). Nor, as Marxists would admit, do all parties in democracies represent distinct social classes in a clearcut fashion. Of all the other varieties of democratic theory, the only one that gives parties a key role is Schumpeter's "competitive elitist" theory—arguably one of the most impoverished from a normative point of view, though it claims for itself the virtue of a greater correspondence with empirical reality. For Schumpeter, the mass of citizenry are uninformed and irrational, and elites must rule, but party competition within the elite is necessary to simplify the electorate's decision, to prevent tyranny, and to legitimate the system by giving the voters the illusion of consumer choice (Schumpeter, 1950, 269–283). Competitive elitism is a far from morally compelling form of democracy, and the role it reserves for parties, while necessary, is not particularly noble.

Given the lack of a strong justification for parties in liberal-democratic theory, what accounts for their ubiquity in modern democracies? Most simply, in any representative system association provides such a powerful advantage that parties inevitably form. The "justification" for parties, then, stems not from principal, or from the need to fashion compromises between interests, or from their utility as a barrier to tyranny, but rather from the more mundane functional characteristics of our political systems. Even where a popular assembly rather than a parliament ruled, as in ancient Rome, the election of magistrates led to the formation of parties; indeed, parties would have advantages even in a system with no election of representatives (e.g., a popular assembly with magistrates chosen by lot).

A party of some sort has been seen as a virtual necessity if one is to contest the U.S. presidency seriously, or aim at a majority in the House of Commons, and even at a purely local level it offers a considerable edge. Only a party can provide the money and the organization needed to win. In playing this key role of aggregating individuals into election-fighting coalitions, ideally parties also organize the alternatives offered to voters into a small number of well-publicized, coherent packages; they are valuable in reducing the voter's "information costs," especially since they tend to adhere to similar programs over time. Once an auto worker has identified the NDP, for instance, as the party most favourable to unionized workers, the worker may rationally vote for that party without troubling to find out its positions on each issue in each election. This simplifying role of parties is especially useful in allowing voters to assign responsibility for governmental policies and performance: where there is no party discipline, it is too easy for representatives to excuse themselves for failing to carry out their promises by citing the absence of majority support; individual voters have difficulty determining the truth of the matter.

At the same time, parties do from time to time perform the tasks indicated by liberal-democratic theory—advocating competing principles, representing and aggregating interests, and checking governmental high-handedness. They may also provide a useful way for citizens to participate in politics, thereby achieving another of the classical goals of democracy. From the point of view of competitive elitism, parties are also valuable because they recruit, select, and train leaders; the selection of the best leaders is a key function for Schumpeter and his followers.[2]

Historically, however, many political parties have been formed from the top down, so to speak, in a manner which reflects much more their functional utility or necessity *for government* than the opinions or interests of the people. In the British tradition this is expressed in the maxim, "The Queen's government must be carried on." This means that a majority must be found in the House of Commons to support the government, and some form of party organization is required to ensure this, particularly when members are elected by universal suffrage. In the 18th century, the cabinet, chosen in name and sometimes in fact by the king, was able to create a majority for itself using various forms of patronage and influence, giving rise to the court "party," and the raison d'être of opposition groups was often largely to gain a share of the spoils of office. The general election of 1832 was the first the cabinet "lost." Similarly, in many other countries party organization proceeded from government to Parliament to the country, giving rise to what Duverger has dubbed the "cadre party." Even in the postwar period, in countries such as Italy or Japan, the occupation of government has given longtime ruling parties considerable resources with which to maintain their electoral positions. More generally, institutional arrangements have either strongly encouraged the formation of parties (e.g., the election of the U.S. president) or directly enshrined them in law (e.g., U.S. laws regulating primaries, list systems of proportional representation, or public funding of parties). In Canada, the cabinet system has stimulated party formation, while provisions for the assignment of broadcasting time and funding elections and political activity led in the 1970s to the institutionalization of parties, which had previously been only informal entities with no precise legal status (Courtney, 1978, 34, 36).

THE DECLINE OF PARTIES

That parties lack a strong theoretical justification, owing their existence instead to more practical factors, simply reinforces other tendencies at work that seem to be dissolving parties as we know them. These tendencies interact, but one of the most powerful is a growing sense that parties do not matter, that whichever party wins the election, the actual range of choice open to government is small. This is more than the often-lamented narrowness of the range of choice offered by parties. Such a convergence has occurred in many countries, most notably the U.S., but by no means everywhere; elections are often fought with clear and distinct alternatives before the voters. However, other factors have intervened to make it difficult for the winning party to deflect policy in any significant way from the logic seemingly imposed by the situation. It is forced to abandon election promises and yield to the "necessary" solutions proposed by its officials. The governing party then becomes, as Poulantzas suggested (1980, 232–240), more a public-relations agency for the bureaucracy's policies rather than an independent source of ideas and initiatives.

Of course, there have always been limits to the ability of governments to effect fundamental change. The constraints of the capitalist economy often seem to impose certain kinds of solutions, or severely narrow the range of choice, unless the government is prepared and has sufficient popular backing to institute a virtual war economy. These constraints, however, have become much tighter and more evident in the past 20 years, since the end of the long postwar boom. Governments simply have less money with which to embark on new policies; they now also have less room to maneuver because of budget deficits. Also, the internationalization of the economy makes traditional Keynesian demand-stimulus measures less effective, as the Mitterrand government in France found out in 1981–82. Balance-of-payments crises and runs on the currency await any government that overstimulates the economy or undermines the confidence of international investors. International agreements, such as the European Monetary System, and the end of capital and exchange controls have deprived governments of many policy instruments. They are therefore less able to deal with the root problems of slower economic growth and rising unemployment. These, rather than so-called "overload," provide the real explanation for the relative ineffectiveness of government action, but governing parties are the nearest and most obvious targets for disappointed voters.[3]

Another more tangible direction in which power has shifted from elected governments is toward independent bodies such as central banks and supranational institutions. Central banks, such as the Bank of Canada, have varying degrees of legal autonomy, but the real basis of their independence is the investment community, at home and abroad. It favours independent agencies rather than political control over currencies, which it considers less conducive to monetary stability and a positive climate for investment. Central banks' autonomy has been increasing in the past 20 years, with the adoption of monetarist policies in the late 1970s throughout the developed world and a massive shift in power to the holders of financial assets. The German Bundesbank is particularly powerful: the overriding goal of its policies has remained, controlling inflation at the expense, if necessary, of full employment and growth. The European Monetary System, dominated by the German mark, has forced Germany's partners to pursue similarly restrictive (or often more restrictive) policies in order to defend the parity of their currencies. The point is that the Bundesbank, and the other central banks to varying degrees, enjoy considerable autonomy and that their policies are not affected by changes in the make-up of the government. Even in the economically strong countries, those which have not had International Monetary Fund teams impose conditions for loans, the maneuvering room of the government is limited.

In some countries, of course, the regular bureaucracy has traditionally been the major source of ideas and policies, and this naturally diminishes the role of the parties. France and Japan are perhaps the strongest cases. In Japan in particular, the interlocking network of bureaucrats, business leaders, and political bosses constitutes a power structure that prevents any one person from making fundamental changes; this is what van Wolferen (1989) means by the "enigma" of Japanese power. The system seems to be directed by an impersonal guiding hand, and the Liberal Democratic Party's function has been chiefly to provide democratic legitimacy for this power structure, making liberal use of the state's resources and the privileges of office in the process. It is not clear that any radical changes will follow the Liberal Democrats' loss of their majority in 1993; after a brief period in opposition, they have returned to power in coalition with their erstwhile antagonists, the Socialists.

In Canada, as well, the bureaucracy is highly professional (in spite of a few politically motivated appointments at the top) and has generated many policy innovations, which have been adopted by the party in power as its own. Though not part of the bureaucracy, royal commissions also have been a common source of nonpartisan policy advice and innovation.[4] But while a certain amount of interchange of personnel between the civil service, the ruling party, and business has occurred, especially in the last years of the long Liberal reign before 1957, there is not the same close and ongoing relationship in Canada as has evolved in Japan. Relations between elected politicians and bureaucrats may be close or strained, depending on the circumstances, though even in the latter case the power of the civil service in framing policy alternatives is considerable.

All these influences conspire to limit the room elected governments have to maneuver. There have been numerous examples of governments severely limited by economic circumstances that have reacted by reversing their original policies and long-standing commitments to their constituencies. A spectacular Canadian example was the Trudeau government's introduction of wage-and-price controls in the fall of 1975, after it had just won election the previous year by campaigning against the Conservatives' proposal of just such a plan (Meisel, 1979, 130). The Mitterrand government found it impossible to pursue "Keynesianism in one country" when other major economies were being squeezed by harsh monetarist measures. In 1976 the British Labour government was forced by International Monetary Fund (IMF) loan conditions to institute public-sector cuts that foreshadowed Thatcherism. In 1993, the Ontario NDP government, in response to a mounting deficit caused by the economic downturn, introduced a series of harsh cuts in public spending, including imposed cuts in public-sector pay. Even the Swedish Social Democrats in 1990 abandoned de facto the goal of full employment in their pursuit of monetary stability. In Canada, during the 1993 federal election campaign, few believed the Liberals were serious in their promise to refuse ratification of the North American Free Trade Agreement unless their conditions on matters such as labour and the environment were met; as it turned out, they did in fact ratify it, although they received few concessions.

There were alternatives in each of these cases, but the governments were genuinely under tremendous pressure to renege on their previous policy commitments. The "logic of the situation," as interpreted by policy advisors and powerful lobbies, seemed to point in a single direction. It would have taken considerable courage and commitment, and solid popular backing, to defy it. In some cases (e.g., the Mitterrand government), the only alternative might have been some measure of isolation from the international economy, with very serious consequences. Human agency has its limits. Nonetheless, it would perhaps be most accurate to say that these severe economic tests have revealed the latent weaknesses of many of these parties: their unresponsiveness to their members, their leaders' absorption into the existing networks of power, the degeneration of the parties from movements into simple electoral machines.

The result, of course, of government "U-turns" with respect to announced policies, or of the simple inability to fulfil promises to create jobs, to reduce the deficit, or to improve social services, is increased public disenchantment with the governing parties. These disappointments fuel cynicism about the democratic process itself, and often about parties as such. Party loyalties are strained—citizens become floating voters, and often angry protest voters, available for recruitment by new movements. These strains have affected parties of the left more seriously than those of the right, but the latter have also failed to deliver economic prosperity and have suffered in their turn.

Another factor, in addition to the narrowing of policy alternatives and the growing role of the bureaucracy, that has contributed to the decline of parties is the increased importance of interest groups and social movements. In some political systems, parties themselves have been at the centre of subcultural networks of associations. Citizens are now more mobile and less likely to be part of tightly knit communities that reinforce party loyalties. In Europe, for instance, the destruction of traditional working-class neighbourhoods has undermined the socialist and labour parties, while the traditional religious subcultural networks are being weakened by secularization.

The fading of traditional cleavages and subcultures is viewed by social theorists such as Jürgen Habermas as resulting from an inevitable destructive process of rationalistic criticism of premodern values and patterns of behaviour. As these are subjected to public scrutiny, their weak intellectual foundations become apparent.[5] Many politically active citizens have broken with these "churches" and their world views and are bypassing the parties to express their opinion. Grassroots social movements, such as environmentalism and feminism, have generally chosen to act outside established parties (though they have occasionally founded parties of their own, such as the Green Party in Germany). They have typically been unable to stomach the fact that established parties which have recognized their concerns have had to compromise them because of conflicting demands from other segments of their constituency. The party organizations have often appeared unwelcoming, already in the hands of other groups, and unable to offer the type of participatory politics the new social movements have sought. While the movements are also attempts to affirm new identities, the older parties have on the whole failed to provide either the symbols or the forum for such affirmations.

In Canada, this pattern has been evident as groups such as women's organizations (e.g., the National Action Committee on the Status of Women) or environmental groups (e.g., Greenpeace) have acted outside the parties. The parties too have been influenced by feminism and environmentalism, but have also seen major conflicts between these movements and other interests. The British Columbia NDP, which has been divided in recent years between supporters of logging, especially the forest unions, and conservationists, provides a textbook case of such conflict. As a result, the movements cannot fully identify with the parties, while some of their attempts to become parties themselves, such as the Canadian Green Party, are short-lived.

Of course, business interests have always exercised considerable power in all capitalist countries; sometimes this manifests itself as direct economic power (e.g., threats, open or implicit, to close factories, invest elsewhere, etc.), and in other situations it is wielded by interest groups. In Canada, the Business Council on

National Issues (BCNI), founded in 1976, greatly enhanced the ability of business to engage in lobbying activity. It has been described as "the most powerful and effective interest group in Canada" (Langille, 1987, 70); its main objective has been to limit state intervention in the economy.

Other conventional interest groups, such as trade unions, have in some countries taken up issues like economic planning, social policy, or taxation that were previously the domain of the parties. In Sweden, for instance, the Landsorganisation (LO) union confederation is widely recognized as the source of innovative thinking for the Social Democratic Party, rather than the reverse. Liberal corporatist arrangements provide the greatest opportunity for this sort of expansion of union functions. Once again, the role of parties can be diminished.

Even in the absence of corporatist arrangements, interest groups have been able to exercise considerable influence in many Western democracies. For instance, the well-known phenomenon that Lowi (1967) dubbed "interest group liberalism" gives certain groups in the United States virtual control over the congressional committees and executive agencies which oversee their members' activities (the so-called "iron triangles"). This situation goes well beyond the interplay of different groups envisioned by pluralist theory. These entrenched interests make change very difficult, even if the "logic of the situation" dictates it (another demonstration that it is not truly ineluctable). Party allegiances are less relevant here than the strength of the interest group in the legislator's district, especially since the presidential system removes the incentives for tight party discipline.

The role of interest groups as opposed to parties is further enhanced by their importance as sources of campaign finance. American political action committees, furthermore, finance the campaigns of individual members of Congress: most funds are not channelled through the parties. Individual businesses, too, often exercise their own pull on politicians by contributing directly to their campaigns— in Japan and Italy, where recent scandals have revealed the extent of kickbacks and influence peddling, the bribes have generally gone to parliamentarians themselves or to factional leaders, not to the parties.

Moreover, the greater economic challenges facing governments during the past 20 years have created conditions favourable to powerful, charismatic leaders, who have often overshadowed their parties. Inflation, unemployment, deficits, and major industrial restructuring all have required stronger governments, able to take on vested interests in the name of their visions of the national good. The decline of parties has meant that they could not provide the fund of legitimacy and support governments needed for these actions. Instead, strong leaders, of whom Ronald Reagan in the U.S. and Margaret Thatcher in Great Britain were the prototypes, took over the function of gathering public support for new and wrenching policy shifts designed to respond to the radically changed climate of the late 1970s and 1980s. Both were able to garner votes beyond their parties' traditional constituencies on the basis of their own personal appeal and their own perception of the public mood. Both could be viewed as examples of "Bonapartism."

This term refers to the rule of leaders who are able to override even dominant interests in the name of their particular vision of the long-term national good. They generally come to power in times of acute conflict between dominant groups, or with the subordinate classes, or when the country is faced with extraordinary challenges; they typically have the charisma that allows them to appeal for support directly to the masses. They rise above parties, replacing them as sources of policy formation and political legitimacy. General de Gaulle, for example, made no secret of his contempt for partisan politics.

Reagan and Thatcher are less extreme cases of Bonapartism. Both, however, received mandates not only to attack the working class and the poor, though these were prime targets for both, but also to ignore the interests of many segments of business and industry. Thatcher came to power when Britain's economic decline had reached an acute stage, and when the working class appeared to be in need of a short, sharp lesson, having brought down the Heath government in 1974 and undone Callaghan's attempts to create an incomes policy. Her monetarism also imposed real hardship on many sectors of British manufacturing; the deindustrialization of Britain has hit some sectors of British business very hard. She dominated the Conservative party, as its constitution allowed her to do, and placed her own supporters in key positions of power. When she came into acute and open conflict with the dominant segment of business—the City of London—over European integration, however, she fell from power. Reagan, similarly, was deaf to the cries of many segments of the U.S. manufacturing industry for protection, pursuing instead a policy of trade liberalization, and ignored business opposition to his deficit spending.

Both leaders had forged a direct link to the electorate, based on an appeal to traditional values and racial insecurity. Reagan drew heavily on the support of the Christian Right, while Thatcher stressed the Protestant virtues of hard work and self-reliance; both combined these with strident patriotism, an aggressive posture in foreign policy, and support for strengthening the state against criminals and internal disorder.

In Canada as well, more and more leaders have come to overshadow their parties, not only in campaign appeals but also in policy formation (Carty, 1988, 24–28). John Diefenbaker may have initiated the trend, but Pierre Elliott Trudeau illustrated it more completely. Trudeau had had no connection with the Liberal party until his election to Parliament in 1965; yet three years later he was party leader and prime minister, winning an election with a highly personalized campaign. In power, he showed little interest in party affairs or in Parliament, formulating policy with the aid of the civil service and a few trusted political advisors (Meisel, 1979, 129). It was after his return to office in 1980 that "Bonapartist" tendencies became most pronounced, as initiatives such as the

National Energy Policy (NEP) alienated the most important sectors of Canadian business.

At the provincial level, too, leaders who are fresh recruits to the party and can put their stamp on it have been quite numerous in recent years (e.g., Ralph Klein in Alberta, Mike Harcourt in British Columbia). In addition, election campaigns are increasingly leader-centred. The electronic media, with their tendency to personalize the political struggle, seek out and focus on the leaders as symbols and spokespersons of their parties. Voters tend to pay greater attention to the leaders in making their electoral choices; this development has been reinforced by the importance of televised leaders' debates, which have played crucial roles in swinging the voters in at least three of the last four Canadian federal elections.

A well-known example of the predominance of leaders over parties is the candidacy of Ross Perot for the U.S. presidency in 1992. A billionaire, he was able to purchase the services of experienced political consultants, including the manager of Reagan's 1984 campaign, and large blocks of media time. In the end, in spite of his temporary absence from the race, he captured 19 percent of the popular vote. Most noteworthy is that he did this without the support of any existing political party, while his own organization, United We Stand America, was less a party than an ad hoc collection of personal supporters.

An even more extreme case of a leader creating a "party" around himself is the 1994 campaign of Italian media magnate Silvio Berlusconi, who in roughly three months organized a grouping known as Forza Italia ("Go Italy") that emerged from the election as the largest single party and catapulted him into the prime ministership. Berlusconi's personal motives for entering politics aside—his financial empire was in difficulty and threatened by antimonopoly legislation—his campaign carried Perot's method to the nth degree. No fundraising was necessary, as his companies and his three television networks provided money and media time; Forza Italia is a network of supporters' clubs modelled on those of Berlusconi's soccer club, AC Milan; they were set up by employees detailed from his companies, especially his television-advertising sales network. "There are no policy committees, elected leaderships, or votes. Policy is decided from on high and fine-tuned through extensive market research" (Jacques, 1994, 4.1). While Berlusconi's success was made possible by the collapse of the Italian governing parties in the wake of massive corruption scandals, it is nonetheless symptomatic of trends in all advanced democracies, where disenchantment with parties and politicians has become widespread.

The trend toward stronger, more charismatic leaders, not all of the right, has been seen too in the already established parties: Craxi in Italy, Hawke in Australia, Nakasone in Japan, and Gonzalez in Spain, though in the event Craxi and Nakasone were unable to stave off the serious crises their parties were approaching. While technological developments and the personalizing effect of the mass media have contributed to the increased emphasis on party leaders, especially in the two-party systems, more important have been the new challenges and more difficult tasks that have faced governments over the past 15 years, which have created a need for reinforced support for state policies. One important channel through which this increased support has been generated is the selection of leaders with wide popular appeal.

All of these factors—the narrower room for maneuver available to governments and parties, the greater importance of interest groups, and more leader-centred politics—have combined to weaken parties' bases of support among the people. Whereas in the past, parties could rely on a large group of traditional supporters who had absorbed their politics with their mothers' milk, or at least from their families, today voters are much less firmly attached to one party and more likely to switch votes from one election to the next. In part this is because the issues and cleavages that gave rise to our party systems are now less relevant: for instance, few remember the events that made the Liberals in Canada the party of the great majority of Catholics and the Conservatives the party favoured by most Protestants. In part it is because of the erosion of traditional cleavages and subcultures. However, the rise of working-class subcultures over the past century-and-a-half demonstrates that, beside these processes of destruction, new traditions can also be created. Similarly, in our day the new social movements have given rise in some countries to new parties and world views (e.g., the German Green Party); anti-authoritarian, less materialist values have taken root in large segments of the population, particularly well-educated young people. These trends have been felt in Canada as well, but have lacked a clear national focus because of the regional fragmentation of the country and the persistence of ethnic and linguistic cleavages as major factors in politics. Since most parties remain wedded to their original subcultures, the new social movements, as mentioned above, have often chosen to operate outside of them. Some older cleavages inevitably lose their salience for voters, but parties, being complex organizations, often lag in adjusting to these changes. Their caution is understandable. Attempts by parties to "renew" themselves may succeed (e.g., the French Socialists in 1971, though the new party was more leader-centred than the old Section Française de l'Internationale Ouvrière [SFIO]), but there is always the risk of losing traditional supporters while failing to attract new followers (e.g., the Italian Communists' transformation into the Democratic Party of the Left in 1991 led to the splitting off of a sizable left wing).

As the bases of parties are being eroded, they are tempted to resort increasingly to the perquisites of office to maintain themselves in power. However, in a climate of growing cynicism and hostility toward parties, these expedients can be counterproductive, as the recent events in Italy and Japan demonstrate. Corruption discredits the entire party system and makes the electorate yet more volatile.

The upshot of these trends is a decline in stable partisan allegiance and increased electoral volatility. The 1993 Canadian federal election is a striking illustration of this volatility: the Conservatives fell from 43 to 16 percent of the popular vote and the NDP from 20 to 7 percent, while the new Bloc Québécois received 14 percent, and the Reform Party rose from barely 2 to 19 percent. But instability is also evident in other major democracies. Italy had seen the sudden rise of the Northern League even before the appearance of Forza Italia on the scene, Sweden that of the New Democracy party, and Japan [that] of a series of reforming parties. All of these new formations, and the Canadian Reform Party, have as part of their appeal a rejection of party politics as it has been conducted, and of party politicians as well. They are also markedly leader-centred. Beyond these immediately visible phenomena, the number of voters reporting that they have no party identification has been rising. Such increased electoral volatility *might* be interpreted as evidence of greater political knowledge and sophistication on the part of the citizenry, but in many cases it stems from a simple, often emotive reaction against the existing parties and their ability to solve the pressing problems besetting the country.

CONCLUSION

The prospect is one of continued decline for political parties, as leaders take on increasing prominence. Yet this decline is not inevitable, and the disappearance of parties would impoverish our democracy. Without strong parties, democracies are subject to the seemingly ineluctable imperatives of the market economy and the soulless struggle for power of mighty interest groups.

Experiments with nonparty democracy have shown its weaknesses. At the turn of the century, American Progressives advocated "nonpartisan" city government in reaction to corrupt political machines. They saw local government in largely technocratic terms, and their attempt to depoliticize it served to mask underlying conflict of interests rather than to eliminate it. Well-organized interest groups were able to impose their agendas with relatively little competition or scrutiny. Depoliticization and nonparty councillors meant citizens had to work harder to inform themselves about the councillors' records, which resulted in lower voter turnout; elected officials became less, rather than more, responsible to the electorate. In most Canadian municipalities, the same defects can be seen to this day. The strongly technocratic flavour of Ross Perot's message is of a piece with this nonpartisan syndrome.

Parties are not only necessary to organize choice in a representative system; they can also play a positive role in enhancing democracy. They can provide the vehicle through which ordinary citizens can affect the course of policy; they can be agencies for political participation, leadership recruitment and selection, and political mobilization. Only parties can aggregate disparate interests around common purposes, forcing single-issue groups to take into account other viewpoints and considerations. They are not simply passive aggregators and brokers of existing interests; parties can also create new interests and world views, and shape existing ones. Only parties can, in this way, inject even a modicum of principle into public life. In the end, the new politics may have only its novelty to recommend it.

NOTES

1. See Macpherson (1977, 112–114). Macpherson's work also contains many acute observations on liberal-democratic theory in general.

2. See King (1969) for a good summary of the functions parties are held to perform in liberal democracies.

3. I am indebted for these ideas to Clarke et al. (1984), chs. 1 and 2.

4. Royal commissions are formed to deal with particularly knotty policy issues, and when innovative solutions may be required. A notable example was the commission chaired by Justice Emmett Hall which laid the foundation for universal medicare in Canada (though it had been pioneered by the CCF in Saskatchewan). The Macdonald Royal Commission's 1985 report was arguably even more influential in opening the way for freer trade and a series of neoconservative policy initiatives. The point is that royal commissions are generally nonpartisan, relying primarily on expert opinion, supplemented at times by submissions from interest groups.

5. See Habermas (1975), esp. Part II, ch. 7, and MacIntyre (1981).

REFERENCES

Beer, S. 1969 (1965). *British Politics in the Collectivist Age.* New York: Vintage.

Burke, E. 1826. *The Works of the Right Honourable Edmund Burke,* Volume 2. London: C. & J. Rivington.

Carty, R.K. 1988. "Three Canadian Party Systems." In *Party Democracy in Canada,* edited by G. Perlin, 15–30. Scarborough: Prentice-Hall.

Clarke, H., J. Jenson, L. LeDuc, and J.H. Pammett. 1984. *Absent Mandate: The Politics of Discontent in Canada.* Toronto: Gage.

Courtney, J.C. 1978. "Recognition of Canadian Political Parties in Parliament and in Law" *Canadian Journal of Political Science* XI, 1: 34–60.

Gramsci, A. 1971. *Selections from the Prison Notebooks,* edited by Q. Hoare and G. Nowell Smith. London: Lawerence and Wishart.

Habermas, J. 1975 (1973). *Legitimation Crisis.* Boston: Beacon.

Jacques, Martin. 1994. "Big Brother." *The Sunday Times* (April 3): 4.1–4.2.

King, A. 1969. "Political Parties in Western Democracies." *Polity* II, 2: 111–141.

Langille, D. 1987. "The Business Council on National Issues and the Canadian State." *Studies in Political Economy* 24 (Autumn): 41–85.

Lenin, V.I. 1967 (1904). "One Step Forward, Two Steps Back." In *Selected Works,* Volume I. New York: International Publishers.

Lowi, T. 1967. "The Public Philosophy: Interest Group Liberalism." *American Political Science Review* 61, 1: 5–24.

MacIntyre, A. 1981. *After Virtue: A Study in Moral Theory.* Notre Dame, Ill.: University of Notre Dame Press.

Macpherson, C.B. 1977. *The Life and Times of Liberal Democracy.* Oxford: Oxford University Press.

Meisel, J. 1979. "The Decline of Party in Canada." In *Party Politics in Canada,* 4th ed., edited by H. Thorburn, 119–135. Scarborough: Prentice-Hall.

Poulantzas, N. 1980 (1978). *State, Power, Socialism.* London: Verso.

Schumpeter, J. 1950 (1942). *Capitalism, Socialism, and Democracy,* 3rd ed. New York and Evanston: Harper & Row.

van Wolferen, K. 1989. *The Enigma of Japanese Power: People and Politics in a Stateless Nation.* New York: Knopf.

✗ **NO**
Parties and Democracy: A Critical View
VAUGHAN LYON

SYSTEM ORIGINS: ACCOMMODATING PARTIES, REPRESSING DEMOCRACY

"... parties are inevitable. No one has shown how representative government ⚡
could be worked without them."
(Byrce, 1921, 119)
"... parties have consistently and universally been accepted as the only
tenable alternative, as a working system, to tyranny."
(Goodman, 1960, 607)

Claims that democracy must be based on a system of competing parties abound
in the literature of political science. While parties have eased the transition from
autocratic government to the form we have today, they are now blocking progress
toward a more democratic and responsive political system. Viable alternatives to
parties could be developed if the elites controlling our political life were to act on ⚡
the aspirations of their constituents.

"Democracy" is the people's ideology. Individuals must be persuaded to accept
the ideologies of liberalism, conservatism, and socialism. Each rationalizes a form
of elite rule and the interests of a particular class. Democracy, however, springs
virtually unprompted from people's hearts and minds, reflecting their desire for
dignity, security, and self-realization. Translated into a political system, democracy is "government by the people."[1]

To be realized, this form of government requires political institutions that
encourage citizen participation. But political parties frustrate rather than support
"citizen" politics. They are "fighting" organizations that exist to advance the
interests of certain segments of society in electoral politics. A party seeks to mobilize the citizenry to march to the party's tune, not to help people recognize and
realize the aspirations they have in common.[2] As Max Weber wrote, "The management of politics through parties simply means management through interest
groups" (Gerth and Mills, 1958, 94).[3]

The domination of political life by parties denies people the rights and responsibilities of full citizenship and the responsive government that can only flow
from their exercise. If we are to break free from "partyology," we must see organizations and the role they play in our political system realistically. We must see
through, or past, the theorizing which asks us to accept the oxymoron, "party
democracy."

Responsible Government: Rule by Competitive Elites[4]

The fundamental character of Canadian politics was established in the mid-19th century. To deal with instability in its colony, the British bowed to pressure for responsible cabinet government. This proved to be a form of government that the rival factions, the conservative "ins" and the restive liberal "outs," could both support. With responsible government, an elected prime minister and party leader replaced the British governor as the central figure in the network of power. The prime minister inherited virtually all the powers of the British governor. These were reinforced by the ability of the new "monarch" to claim a popular mandate and by his control of the governing party team.[5] The reformers who pressed for responsible government "... did not wish to reduce executive power; they wished to take it over and exercise it" (Stewart, 1986, 30). Responsible government empowered Canadian elites; it did little to change the power relationship between those elites and the citizenry.

The new form of government established a relatively level playing field on which Tories and Grits could compete for control of the state. Citizens who already had the right to elect the assembly, or were later to get the vote, would decide only the outcome of the party competition. The citizens' electoral participation would be used by the winning party to support its largely mythical claim to have a popular mandate to implement its program. In office, a party would have the opportunity to impose its visions of society, to maintain the political order that had rewarded it, and, most important from its perspective, to reward its supporters with patronage of various kinds (Simpson, 1988).

The democratic values held by many Canadians were exploited by the liberals who demanded responsible government in their name, but those values were not reflected in the new institutional arrangements. As S.D. Clark observed,

> What has been thought of in Canada as an orderly process of adapting political institutions to changing circumstances has actually represented an effort to hold in check the kind of democratic forces which were growing up from within the Canadian community. Responsible government developed in reaction rather than in response to the true democratic spirit of the Canadian people. (1962, 208)

Those "democratic forces," championed in Upper Canada by William Lyon Mackenzie and others, had been repressed by force in 1837 and discredited. The political leaders of the time made no claim that the system was democratic (Stewart, 1986, 30; Hodgins, 1967, 83–91).[6] Indeed, they saw democracy—"mobocracy"—as a dangerous Americanism only supported by the unpatriotic. Elites, organized in factions that evolved into parties, were, from the beginning, formally in control of the new system and have remained so. With the franchise extended to include all Canadians over 18, and some minor changes, this 19th-century predemocratic political model remains in place.

Responsible government was a step toward popular rule in that it put control of politics in the hands of Canadians and established a political structure that might someday house a popular democracy. But at the same time, this step forward was offset by legitimating and reinforcing a system of executive/party dominance and continuing to restrict the role of citizen to choosing between candidates (soon party candidates) for office.

THE REMARKABLE TRANSFORMATION: PARTY-PARLIAMENTARY GOVERNMENT BECOMES 'DEMOCRACY'

"You can't put a sign on a pig and say it's a horse," claims an old Czech aphorism. But posted often enough such misleading signs will, at the very least, confuse people.

Relabelling 19th-century elitist parliamentary government as parliamentary "democracy" or, on the hustings, as simply "democracy," took place at the end of World War I.[7] During the war, the masses were called on to sacrifice—many to make the ultimate sacrifice—with the promise of a democratic social order once the war was won.[8] As the war came to an end, however, political leaders would agree only to extend the franchise to women—even that required much public pressure. Rhetoric was proffered as a substitute for the democracy promised during the wartime crisis. The word "democracy" was now to trip lightly from the tongues of politicians.

A great deal of effort is required to promote and maintain even a weakly held belief that a pig (the existing political system) is a horse (democracy). Many political scientists have helped by qualifying, distinguishing, and stretching the concept of democracy. A host of terms—liberal, pluralist, procedural, etc.—has been developed to describe what are alleged to be different forms of democracy.

These terms and concepts do make important theoretical distinctions that facilitate a serious discussion of political systems. At the same time, however, they tend to obfuscate and even trivialize essential democratic values. It is made to seem that with the appropriate modifier almost any system can be "democratic." Parties are easily made "inevitable" in a democracy by simply defining "democracy" as a political system characterized by competing parties. Those objecting to this depreciation of the democratic ideal are themselves depreciated.[9]

The cause of democratic development (and clear thinking) would be better served, as Charles Lindblom advises, by "not confusing hope with fact" (1977, 131). To refer to the system as "democracy" or even "liberal democracy" is to "confuse hope with fact." Both "competitive party model" and, Sartori's term, "partycracy" are used here to refer to the Canadian political system. Let us turn now to an examination of why parties and democracy are incompatible.

PARTIES: AGENTS OF MISREPRESENTATION

Ideally, in a democratic system citizens, individually and collectively, would speak for themselves. However, in large states it was impossible even to imagine all citizens meeting together to discuss their common interests—at least until recent developments in communications technology raised that possibility. Citizens would have to depend on a few representatives to act for them in the political arena. How this representation is organized is of crucial importance. If it is done in such a way that the "authentic" voice of the people is heard clearly and authoritatively where public policy is made, then, despite its representative character, the system could properly be called a democracy. The government would be the agent of the people carrying out its wishes. One could expect to find politicians and citizens working closely together to accomplish shared goals.

When, however, the system of parliamentary government based on competing parties was relabelled "democracy," those dominating political life gave no thought to reorganizing the system of representation along democratic lines. The elite who controlled the parties had no intention of sharing power more widely with the citizenry and reforming the representative system to make this possible. However, more emphasis would now have to be placed on the parties' claims to represent the public in order to legitimate the system.

How could parties, the means that elites developed to mobilize support in their struggle for power, possibly be "passed off" as agencies that represented the people? The finesse was made easier because virtually all the means of communication were controlled by elites, and no serious effort had been made to raise the political consciousness of the public.

Political leaders insisted that competitive party elections allowed ample opportunity for democratic expression. Through elections citizens could choose directly a constituency representative from candidates nominated by parties and, indirectly, as a result of that choice, a party team to form the government and its program. No further public input was needed or desired.

The citizen's position was seen as analogous to that of the consumer who, on entering a supermarket, was faced with two or three shopping carts full of groceries. She could choose only one and was asked to believe that on the basis of this choice she was, indirectly, controlling the grocery industry. It takes only a little thought to realize that while the consumer is not without some power in this commercial interaction, far more control rests with those who determine what products will be put in the carts.

This analogy has some explanatory value but it exaggerates the power of the citizen/voter who is in an even weaker position than the consumer. To mention just two of several ways why this is the case: the voter is "buying" promises that are difficult to assess, and the "store" has a policy of no refunds.

Allowing parties to continue to dominate the representative system—to fill the carts—frustrates genuine democratic representation in several important ways.

Forming Citizen Interests

Before their interests can be properly represented, citizens must comprehend them. They then must be motivated to contribute their understanding to the community's pool of ideas. It is easy for the average person to identify most pressing personal needs. It is, however, very complex and challenging to consider those needs and others in a broad social context. An individual's knowledge and social awareness is always incomplete. However, a central feature of a democratic system must be to enhance the citizens' political sophistication to the greatest degree possible. This is the only way to guarantee that the interests they want represented are their own.[10]

Is the development of aware, articulate citizens a fundamental concern of the parties? Hardly. They exist to persuade people to accept their definition of what is good for the community. As Maurice Duverger puts it, "Parties create opinion as much as they represent it; they form it by propaganda; they impose a prefabricated mould upon it ..." (1962, 422).[11] It is consistent with their indifference to the ideas of their constituents that parties as government devote few resources to political education.[12]

This lack of party interest in discovering the real needs and aspirations of those they purport to represent is obscured since, in order to win votes, they must make an effort to appear sympathetic to whatever concerns citizens do have. A host of "motherhood" issues will be supported rhetorically by all parties in order to get into office and implement as much of their own agenda as they can. The public's ability to hold the parties to these commitments is minimal. Frequently, parties will not even mention publicly the causes that are of primary importance to them. Supporters of the party know where it is coming from. It may be counterproductive, in terms of mobilizing electoral support, to advertise the party's priorities to others.

This lack of party interest in helping citizens discover and articulate their own interests may be admitted. Supporters of partycracy argue, however, that interparty and intraparty debates and discussions do help the citizens who listen to them get a better fix on their own interests. This might be the case were it not for two features of that debate.

First, party battles on the hustings and in the legislature—just different phases of never-ending party warfare—are generally uninformative to the point where they even disgust the players.[13] The parties must pitch their message to the "audience" they do so little to inform, i.e., they must pitch it low. There are often more votes to be obtained by unrealistic promises, appeals to ignorance and cupidity, and the exploitation of social divisions and prejudice, than by a balanced presentation of issues.

While elitists insist that this audience should leave "acting" on the political stage to the qualified few, it has never been made clear how this poorly informed mass can be expected to identify quality political leadership.

Second, the parties fail to raise many socially important issues. We do know a little more about the strengths and weaknesses of market systems because of the debates of the parties. It has been economic interests—establishment and counter-establishment—that have had the resources and incentive to support successful parties. But on a whole range of vital community interests the parties have been silent until interest groups have, usually very belatedly, forced them to at least show concern.[14]

Native issues were neglected for so long that aboriginal peoples have given up on the system and want self-government. Further, the problems of abuse, domination, and lack of opportunity for a group comprising over 50 per cent of the population have only been discovered by the parties in the last 30 years; the female franchise, no more empowering than the male, was insufficient to force the parties to address the particular concerns of women. The environmental movement is still working intensely to persuade the parties to heed ecological problems (Lyon, 1992). No party presses strongly for the development of a more effective world authority to regulate conflict between and within states. The public wants a more participatory political system (Canada, 1991). Parties scarcely want to discuss the matter.[15]

According to theory supporting partycracy, when the main parties ignore the concerns of enormous numbers of people, new parties will emerge to represent them. The dominant parties, however, use their power to prevent that happening.

Listening to the rhetoric of competing parties will do little to help citizens determine their own interests. The parties also interfere with political learning and expression by inhibiting political participation. They encourage people to be politically lazy and irresponsible. The fundamental conflict between parties and democratic citizenship was clear to M. Ostrogorski, one of their earliest critics.

> The first problem ... which arises in democratic practice is the following: how to so organize political action as to develop spontaneous and regular impulse, to stimulate individual energies and not let them fall asleep. The party system offered its solution: Let the citizens choose a party, let them enlist in it for good and all, let them give it full powers, and it will undertake to supply the required impetus. Put forward with every semblance of political piety, this solution found favor with the citizens, and enabled them to sink, with an untroubled conscience, into their habitual apathy.... They raised political indifferentism to the level of a virtue, and this aloofness has combined with ignorance of the masses to repress public spirit. (1964 [1902]: II, 332–333)

Accepting the beguiling party invitation—"leave it to us"—has harmful consequences since most people learn much of what they know through doing. In addition, only by participating can citizens express those views they do have so that they can be represented. Further, people come to care about the polity, to be motivated to learn about its needs, through active participation. As de Tocqueville wrote: "I maintain that the most powerful and perhaps the only means that we still possess of interesting men in the welfare of their country is to make them partakers in the government" (in Broder, 1972, 262–263).

Ignoring demands for a more participatory system, the parties insist that voting occasionally for one of them is all the formal, public political input that is desirable.[16] For those who insist on being more involved, party leaders recommend joining a party, equating such membership with good citizenship. Only a tiny portion of Canadians accept the invitation, and, for some of us who do, it is a less-than-satisfying experience. For principled, practical, and power reasons, party leaders pay little attention to the policy ideas of members of their party—especially when they are in office. Party members are primarily involved in choosing leaders, nominating candidates, and running campaigns. There is a significant qualitative difference between these activities and the exercise of democratic citizenship. One is devoted to defeating "the enemy," the other to building a vital community.

Recognizing the limitations of party membership, citizens determined to share in making public policy, or merely to find a better way to protect and advance their political interests, join interest groups or adopt other means of influencing policy from the "outside." Dalton Camp, a man with vast party experience, supports their decision.

> There remains ... some primordial ambition that lurks in the heart of a few citizens to participate in the formulation of policy through the party apparatus. I would advise them that if they insist on doing so, not to join a political party. The very least they should do is join a parapolitical pressure group. The very best thing they could do is join the civil service. (1981, 150)

These nonparty forms of participation are not a good substitute for democratic citizenship either. They have some of the same drawbacks as party activity, and others. At most they can only give the person using them influence rather than power and responsibility. The insiders, elected politicians and bureaucrats, may or may not choose to listen to them.

Parties are, then, a major barrier to representative democracy because their desire to dominate and control leads them to discourage thoughtful responsible citizenship. Without such citizenship there can be little of substance to represent. In summarizing empirical studies of the politics of the people who are, in one dimension, the product of partycracy, John Wahlke concludes:

1. Few citizens entertain interests that clearly represent "policy demands" or "policy expectations," or wishes and desires that are readily convertible into them.

2. Few people have thought-out, consistent, and firmly held positions on most matters of public policy.

3. It is highly doubtful that policy demands are entertained even in the form of broad orientations, outlooks, or belief systems.

4. Large proportions of citizens lack the instrumental knowledge about political structures, processes, and actors that they would need to communicate policy demands or expectations if they had any (1978, 75).

Articulating the Views of Citizens

The major parties compound the damage they do to a system of democratic representation by supporting institutional arrangements that permit the citizenry only the most narrowly circumscribed formal opportunity to express its demands. The 19th-century first-past-the-post electoral system continued, after the "relabelling," to be the only formal means of public political expression. But since "free and open elections" were now the main support for the system's claim to be democratic, their importance as a means of citizen empowerment had to be vastly inflated, if not misrepresented.

Politicians frequently infer in their speeches that voters have the opportunity in periodic elections to express themselves on a variety of issues. But their claim does not hold up to even the most cursory examination. Citizens are supposed to be able to:

1. choose the best candidate to represent the constituency,

2. choose the party that will best govern the country,

3. indicate which of the party leaders would make the best prime minister,

4. hold the local MP, government, and Opposition accountable for their respective performances during the years between elections,

5. pass judgment on the program of the parties,

6. use the election as a kind of referendum on highly salient issues like free trade, and so on.

Use of the ballot to make a statement on any one of these issues usually makes it impossible to express an opinion on others that are equally important. The conscientious citizen is so constrained that, frustrated, she tends to vote more out of a sense of duty than any expectation of influencing policy outcomes (Edelman, 1964, 2–3). Political pundits have a field day after the election trying to interpret the results because, inevitably, voters were "saying" widely different things with their ballots. The parties' freedom to put their interpretation on the voters' behaviour is a major source of power for them.[17]

In theory, partycracy should not constrict the ability of citizens to express themselves as much as it does. As already noted, where existing parties fail to articulate effectively a strongly held body of opinion, a new party should form to do so—just as new companies emerge to exploit overlooked market opportunities. Parties and businesses, however, have a strong vested interest in restricting competition. In the case of business, government regulations limit the ability of corporations to choke off competition. But parties control the only body—the government—that can regulate them. The major parties tacitly agree to maintain a system that restricts competition (voter choice) and distorts that choice.

The party oligopoly is maintained in part through the first-past-the-post or plurality system. It discriminates in favour of the dominant party and against minor parties that do not have geographically concentrated support. This feature of the system makes it extremely difficult for new parties with fresh and widely supported ideas, like the Greens, to become credible competitors. The public resents the limited choice.18

With enormous consequences in terms of public alienation from government, the same electoral system seriously distorts the already limited and confused message that can be drawn from election results. For example, a majority, neoconservative government was elected in Ottawa in 1988 with 43 percent of the popular vote in a contest billed as a referendum on the Canada–U.S. Free Trade Agreement or, more extravagantly, on the future of Canada. The opposition Liberal and NDP parties, holding down the centre-left on the ideological spectrum and strongly opposed to free trade, won a majority of the popular vote.19 However, these opposition parties, longtime supporters of the system, could not seriously challenge the Conservatives' claim to have a mandate to enact free trade and impose a neoconservative agenda on the country. When they formed governments they made similar claims and expected the opposition parties to accept them.

Not content with the advantages meted out to them by the biases built into the electoral system, the main parties have found a further means of reinforcing their competitive advantage. Over the last 20 years they have provided themselves with more and more funds from the public treasury through grants and tax deductions for people contributing to them. But they have made it difficult for the candidates of minor parties to secure the partial reimbursement of election expenses available to the "majors" by requiring that a candidate first get more than 15 percent of the popular vote in order to qualify.

As presently organized, elections are, as Michael Parenti states,

> ... more a surrender than an assertion of popular power, a gathering up of empowering responses by the elites who have the resources for such periodic harvestings, an institutionalized mechanism providing for the regulated flow of power from the many to the few in order to legitimize the rule of the few in the name of the many. (1978, 201)

These criticisms of our electoral arrangements from a democratic perspective are commonplace. What needs to be emphasized, however, is that the parties' support of them is totally consistent with their basic function. While the aim of a genuine representative democracy would be to see that the authentic views of citizens were articulated, parties want to muffle those views so that their own can dominate. In allowing parties to dominate the representative system, we virtually ensure that government will be unresponsive and weak.

PARTYCRACY AND RESPONSIVE DEMOCRATIC GOVERNMENT

Limited Authority: Pusillanimous Government

We are encouraged to blame the party and individual office-holders when we object to particular government policies. Part of the responsibility does belong there. But here we want to investigate what there is about the competitive party model that results in unresponsive government regardless of which party is in office. The power of systems to determine behaviour, because it is somewhat abstract, is too often neglected.

To be responsive to the citizenry a government must have authority.[20] Only with authority can government meet its responsibilities in the face of opposition from powerful vested interests and survive at the polls.[21] Without it, governing parties, fearful of the electoral consequences of coercing compliance, will be pusillanimous where they should be strong. The major source of government authority is the people, and its strength varies with how they feel about the legitimacy of the political system. As David Easton writes,

> ... if demands are to be processed into binding decisions ... without the extensive use of coercion, solidarity must be developed not only around some set of authorities themselves, but around the major aspects of the system within which the authorities operate. (1965, 157–158)

Signs that the system is not vesting government decisions with adequate authority are everywhere—from widespread smuggling of cigarettes to rejection of constitutional proposals, to the NIMBY (not-in-my-backyard) phenomenon.

Supporters of partycracy urge public support for the major aspects of the system. But it is crucial to note that these vest government with only limited authority. In other words, even if we were all enthusiastic boosters of the political status quo, of partycracy, that would not necessarily ensure the governing party politicians the authority they need to discharge their responsibilities. They would have more authority than they do now when support for the system is so low, but their clout would still be limited.

We have already discussed how the representative system as presently constituted ensures that government cannot be experienced as a collaborative venture of citizens and their elected leaders. The agenda of government is that of a party, not the people. That limits the authority of government. The structure of party government reduces it still further.

The small-"l" liberal elites of the 19th century compromised on a political arrangement that assured each a chance to compete for power and to protect its supporters while out of office. Weak government was a requisite of such an arrangement. Competition could not be maintained if, for example, the Conservatives could hold office for four years and during that time promote their supporters' interests so vigorously that it would then be impossible for any other party to challenge them at the polls.

The desire to limit government power and keep the system competitive was, of course, consistent with the dominant political ideology of the 19th century. Both Liberals and Conservatives believed in small government where most public policy was made by "private" interests.22 At the time, the power of those private interests was not as great as it is today, and the government's need for authority to control them was, therefore, less.

Institutional arrangements were biased in several ways in favour of keeping competition open and government limited. The party in office would only hold power temporarily. It would have to give the other party an opportunity to replace it every five years at the latest. While it waited its chance, it would be seated across from the governing party and enjoy the special status of his (or her) majesty's loyal Opposition. The system legitimated questioning, debating, challenging, posing alternatives, and, generally, weakening the legitimacy and authority of the government. The incumbents were further restrained by the knowledge that what they did to their opponents might later be done to them, and that their policies might well be reversed after the next election.23

The social and economic world has changed dramatically since the 19th century, putting heavy new demands on government and creating blocs of private power well able to resist state direction. These limiting 19th-century liberal institutional arrangements have remained in place, however. No other large organization in modern society has chosen to govern or manage its activities in the way that partycratic government does. Imagine how much careful long-term planning would be done, and how much authority would be exercised, in a major corporation if the management's jobs were subject to renewal every fours years and in between the executives were subject to constant heckling, challenge, and obstruction from a paid opposition determined to replace them.

Partycracy and Pluralist Ad Hockery

Partycratic governments have a number of characteristic weaknesses. They have difficulty planning or even coordinating the work of their various departments and agencies. Policy-making is usually ad hoc and often driven by partisan considerations. Organized interests are given disproportionate power. Response to public needs is usually tardy and inadequate. There is a tendency to abdicate or delegate responsibilities. The interests of bureaucrats and politicians are too often placed ahead of those they are supposed to serve. This list is far from exhaustive.

These weaknesses result in large part from both the failure of the representative system to deliver a clear public mandate to policy-makers and the tentative hold on power of the governing party. Without "instructions" from the citizenry that all the participants in government respect, including interest groups, policy-making becomes a pluralist power game. It is legitimate for every interest in and outside government to fight for policies that benefit it or its clients, all the while claiming to be acting for the public. The governing party brokers these competing interests using the power of the state to advance those it supports. Policy outputs command limited support because the policy-making process through which they are developed is so lacking in democratic credibility.

The absence of a binding public mandate enables the parties and party leaders to "do what comes naturally." Decisions on whether to tackle problems, and how, are heavily influenced by prospective short-term party gains or losses in the ongoing partisan struggle. These are normally calculated in terms of the response of powerful organized interests and their ability to mobilize resources in support of or against the party in office.

The personal values of the prime minister/party leader are strongly reflected in public policy. A case can be made for the proposition that the government is more responsive to the prime minister than to the millions it claims to represent. Brian Mulroney, for example, was able to recast the Progressive Conservative party to reflect his neoconservative and continentalist values despite widespread public hostility.

The apparatus of the modern state is vast, encompassing innumerable power centres, each of which enjoys some, and in many instances considerable, autonomy. Partycratic government's authority and management abilities, weakened by continuous party conflict, are insufficient to get this far-flung bureaucracy to pursue common objectives with commitment.

With the example before them of the nation's leaders engaged in constant competition to maximize their interests, all other participants in the policy-making process, including individual civil servants and branches of government, feel justified in doing the same.

Working for party government is like employment in the private sector, with employees exhibiting roughly the same mix of conscientiousness and self-seeking. Would it be otherwise if civil servants were implementing an agenda that they and other citizens had drawn up?

The argument that the present system produces weak government seems to be refuted by the fact that occasionally governments take very strong actions. Analyzed carefully, however, these actions support the weakness thesis. For example, governments are now taking strong action on debt reduction. But they are only able to do so because, after failing to check the dramatic growth in public debt in a timely fashion, they have allowed a fiscal crisis to develop. Now they can appeal for support from a wide range of interests, who would usually withhold it, to buttress their normally weak position.[24]

Crisis management of this sort is, of course, very costly in human and economic terms. It may, however, appeal to some politicians because it allows them to cast themselves as heroic—standing fearlessly between the public and disaster. It is more exciting than the hard work of analyzing problems and building a consensus behind long-term solutions to them.

Consider another, somewhat different, example. The government acted decisively/authoritatively in implementing free trade. But note that here the government was able to add the authority of the business community, which may exceed that of government, to its own. There is no question that when this uniquely powerful special interest and the government team up, the concentration of authority is substantial. But what of situations where the government ought to challenge the business agenda?

Considering what might reasonably be expected of democratic government, we find partycracy a weak "underachiever." Others, using softer standards, would be more charitable. However, the assessment that really matters is not that of academics but of the general public whom the system exists to serve. Its support for the system is vital if government is to function effectively.

Instead of support/authority, interacting features of partycracy—the representative system, the structures and output of government—produce high levels of public alienation.

Attempts are often made to present this alienation as a passing phenomenon related to the recession, the mishandling of constitutional issues, the insecurities surrounding globalization, and so on. All feed it, but dissatisfaction with the competitive-party model and the government policies it produces has been present (and successfully repressed) throughout Canadian history.[25] As Parenti notes: "It is time to consider the possibility that if millions are disillusioned with conventional politics, it is because conventional politics are disillusioning" (1978, 204).

Can there be a more damning indictment of the system than the ability of neoconservative politicians and business leaders to convince millions that an amoral, impersonal market, that has failed spectacularly in the past to advance many vital human needs, is more worthy of their trust than their "democratic" government?[26] The cycle of alienation leading to an erosion of government authority, weaker government, more public disillusionment, and further erosion is likely to continue until the system is reformed.

A DEMOCRATIC ALTERNATIVE TO PARTYCRACY

Do Canadians have to put up with partycracy, as elites who equate it with "democracy" insist? The amorphous public cannot itself articulate clearly an alternative political order. When citizens do manage to make themselves heard, however, they show that they are not taken in by claims that party MPs speak, in a roundabout way, for their constituents. Overwhelmingly, citizens demand that the person they elect to represent them do so.[27] Isn't this a reasonable request, one that is totally consistent with the democratic values virtually all of us endorse?

There are, however, two major but rather easily resolved problems that must be tackled if the public is to be represented as it wishes. First, the majority viewpoint of the MP's constituents must be clearly established. Second, if that opinion is to be worthy of representation and respect, it must be informed and socially responsible.

Currently, it is impossible for the MP to reflect community opinion, even if the MP wants to do so, because on almost every issue this opinion is diverse and dis-aggregated. Scientific polling or referenda could overcome this difficulty and determine what the majority believes. That would not resolve a second more significant difficulty, however. Democratic representation must involve far more than just carrying forward the off-the-cuff, out-of-context, policy reaction of the majority.[28] As Joseph Tussman observes, such representation means bringing to bear on public policy the best advice of the citizen acting as "... agent of the body politic, a ruler, ... with all of the duties, obligations, and responsibilities that go with that role" (1960, 118).

For citizens to assume the role of "rulers" they must have the information and stimulation needed to think clearly and reach socially responsible decisions. A new institution, specifically designed to accommodate the democratic aspirations of citizens, must be established to provide these. The most suitable, we believe, would be an elected part-time assembly or "community Parliament" in every one of Canada's 295 constituencies. Its members would participate in regular, ongoing deliberations with their MP on all the major political issues of the day. The local assembly would define the community's position on public questions. The MP would then be faced with the clear choice between representing constituency or party when the two differed on issues. Few ridings would continue to elect MPs who consistently ignored those they professed to represent.

With community Parliaments operating, political life would focus on the continuous consideration of public issues at the national and local levels. No longer would there be any pretence that elections were the means by which citizens offered an opinion on issues or were empowered. They would merely be a rather low-profile opportunity for people to pass judgment occasionally on the calibre of the representation they were receiving from their MP.

A network of community Parliaments would allow the government and citizens to talk directly to one another, bypassing the mass media. They would jointly draw up and share responsibility for implementing a national program. "Self-government" would be a giant step closer. A major source of political alienation would be removed, as the system functioned more as its democratic rhetoric suggested it should.

Citizens acting through their community Parliaments could consider what further political reforms were needed. They would have a rational, orderly process through which to decide constitutional questions, whether to change the electoral system, how Parliament should be reformed, whether and on what issues referenda should be held, if political parties should be publicly financed, whether there should be a recall procedure, and other issues.

It seems likely that in the new (community Parliament) order, MPs would elect and dismiss the executive—the cabinet and prime minister—as most democratically structured organizations now do. If so, the current myth that the cabinet is responsible to the House would become reality.

Even with community Parliaments, the system would remain dependent on representatives. The number of citizens directly involved in the political process would, however, be dramatically increased.[29] Power would be shifted from remote party elites to easily accessible representatives—members of the community and national Parliaments. Those who might be alarmed at the prospect that community Parliaments would significantly expand citizen participation in policymaking might find it more reassuring to see them as a vehicle to enlarge the elite running the country. Both perceptions are defensible.

Community Parliaments are a natural and logical step toward a fuller form of democracy and more effective government. They are not a political panacea. They would, however, break the current political stalemate by meeting the long-ignored demands of 20th-century Canadians that those purporting to represent them actually do so. Further, they would provide a means through which a close working relationship between citizens and their government could develop. Politicians and citizens would be able to work together on an agenda they jointly authored.

Where would parties fit into this more democratic model? Perhaps they would retain a place.[30] Perhaps they would prove redundant and atrophy, going down in history as a useful organization that served, for a time, to facilitate the transition from autocracy to a closer approximation of popular democracy.

A FINAL WORD: LIBERALISM AND DEMOCRACY

Max Weber wrote: "Certainly all historical experience confirms the truth that man would not have attained the possible unless time and again he had reached out for the impossible" (Gerth and Mills, 1958, 128). Our forebears reached out once, and the present system, the best yet devised but very far from what we need or are capable of today, was the result. It is time, past time, that we pressed on.

Yet there is a significant concern that may inhibit even strong democrats from promoting change. If empowered, will the masses curb the liberal freedoms that are the essential foundation of the democratic project?

It was, in part, the denial of individual liberties by autocratic regimes that led to the liberal revolutions of the 18th and 19th centuries. Liberals came to defend a system of fragmented and contained public authority as necessary to guarantee those rights against either a renewed autocracy or the intolerant masses. In the 20th century, when democratic values also came to command the loyalty of liberals, they argued that these guarantees were essential to democracy. Partycracy, which in one century was a bulwark against mass power, was represented as its friend and guarantor in the next.

But supporting a competitive-party model of politics that blocks democratic progress to protect liberal freedoms is a fundamentally misguided approach. It is an orderly, responsible expansion of democracy, not its containment, that is the best guarantee of political liberties. Containment, and the poor quality of both government and citizenship it requires, may cause an outpouring of public frustration and anger that will sweep aside essential liberties. However, movement toward a more democratic polity has, historically, been accompanied by an ever stronger commitment to individual rights. Involvement in political life strengthens the individual's commitment to the rights and liberties that make possible meaningful political involvement in a peaceful community (Pateman, 1970, 105; McClosky and Zaller, 1984, 48).

While, ultimately, it is the politically active citizens' support that is the crucial guarantor of political freedoms, additional "backup" support, not present in the 19th century, is now available through the legal system. Rights are protected by the Canadian Charter of Rights and Freedoms and provincial rights codes. Such limited and costly guarantees as partycracy offers are increasingly redundant. From liberal, as well as from democratic and responsive government perspectives, the competitive party model is archaic, not inevitable.

NOTES

1. Democratic ideology prescribes a particular kind of political organization: "The essential feature of a democratic polity is its concern for the participation of the member in the process by which the community is governed. It goes beyond the insistence that politics or government be included among the careers open to talent. It gives to each citizen a public office, a place in the sovereign tribunal and, unless it is a sham, it places its destiny in the hands of that tribunal. Here is the ultimate decision-maker, the court of last appeal, the guardian of the guardians, government 'by the people'" (Tussman, 1960, 105–106).

2. As Kay Lawson describes them, "Parties ... are agencies for the acquisition of power, not selfless political versions of the Red Cross, to whom citizens may go crying in time of need." (1980, 23).

3. Gerth and Mills, 1958, 94. For a discussion of parties as interest groups, see Lyon (1983–1984).

4. By "elite" we are referring to a "minority of individuals whose preferences regularly prevail in cases of differences in preferences on key political issues" (Dahl, 1958, 464). The dominant political elite includes more than professional politicians, although they are its core. The elitist nature of Canadian politics is commonly accepted. Manzer writes, "An upper-status group possessing position, expertise, and wealth is firmly in control of economic and political power, lessening the potential for an authentically democratic polity" (1985, 3).

5. The Governor General retains only some discretion in deciding who shall be asked to form a government when no party has a majority in the House of Commons.

6. There was substantial practical justification for elitism when this style of politics was established—lack of communication, striking differences in mass and elite education, deferential mass attitudes.

7. Typically, politicians now only emphasize that we still have a system of parliamentary rather than democratic government when there are demands for public involvement in policy-making, by means of a referendum, for example. Then the parliamentary character of the system is used to rationalize rejecting such demands. See Boyer (1992, 40–45).

8. See Naylor (1991) for a full discussion of this promise and betrayal.

9. As Robert Dahl states: "As long as the professionals remain substantially legitimist in outlook ... the critic is likely to make little headway. Indeed, the chances are that anyone who advocates extensive changes in the prevailing democratic norms is likely to be treated by the professionals, and even by a fair share of the political stratum, as an outsider, possibly even as a crackpot whose views need not be seriously debated" (1962, 320).

10. The inability of citizens to sort out their own interests in the present political system is widely acknowledged. "It is one of the world's most extraordinary social phenomena that masses of voters vote very much like their elites. They demand very little for themselves" (Lindblom, 1977, 209).

11. For a Canadian elaboration of this point, see Brodie and Jenson (1980, 1).

12. For a series of articles discussing this point, see Pamment and Pepin (1988).

13. See, for example, Walter Pitman, "It's time to end insulting campaign," *The Toronto Star* (April 21, 1972), 9; Bob Rae, Premier of Ontario, assesses the process more generally, "Politics is a tough business. People have to be prepared to live with it. Everybody who goes into public life knows it's going to be tough. All kinds of allegations get made, many and most of which are completely unfounded." Richard Mackie, "Rae tastes his own medicine," *The Globe and Mail* (April 20, 1992).

14. The "belatedness" is not the fault of the interest groups. Having elected representatives and financed the political system, citizens are entitled to expect that important issues will be raised in the political arena by the politicians. It should not be necessary for people to form interest groups to pressure representatives to do their job.

15. These criticisms of the parties are shared by the majority of the public. When political life is dominated by agencies that the public sees as performing badly, alienation from the system and the governments it produces is the inevitable result. See Clarke and Kornberg, 1993.

16. Is this conviction weakening or is it merely that party rhetoric is adjusting to public demands? In a response to a question about whether his attitude toward referenda had changed, former prime minister Mulroney replied: "... it has changed from some years ago. I always thought, quite frankly, that under the British parliamentary system that a referendum was a kind of abdication of responsibility. I've changed my mind over the years. I've come to recognize that in a modern, pluralistic society like ours, people do indeed require a much greater degree of participation than a kick at the can every four years. And they have proprietary rights in respect to the constitutional document.

And that indeed there should be public consultation, and the ultimate is that in a referendum." Edited transcript of interview with editors, *The Globe and Mail* (October 23, 1992).

17. For a discussion of the obstacles standing in the way of generating a clear mandate, see Clarke et al., 1984, 181–182.

18. "Canadians just do not have much confidence in those whom they elect. One source of this dissatisfaction appeared to be the feeling that they simply do not have enough of a choice. Political parties are perceived to engage in too much unproductive squabbling and to confuse the issues rather than provide a clear choice on them. Along with stricter regulation of electoral finances, the findings suggested that a party system which posed fewer barriers to new political parties could help restore some degree of confidence." André Blais and Elizabeth Gidengil, "Making Representative Democracy Work," Institute for Social Research, *Newsletter* 8, 1 (Winter 1993): 1.

19. For a full discussion of the results of the "free trade election" and whether it produced a mandate, see Doern and Tomlin, 1991, 238–242.

20. "It [authority] exists whenever one, several, or many people explicitly or tacitly permit someone else to make decisions for them for some category of acts. Once I give permission to someone else to make decisions for me, then all that he need do in order to control me is to make his wishes known (Lindblom, 1977, 17–18). The possession of authority is of crucial importance to partycratic government because parties cannot rely on coercion and power to govern and win popular elections. If they do not have authority, dysfunctional behaviour results.

21. Dealing with the powerful business community is, of course, the primary challenge to government authority. For a full discussion of this, see Lindblom (1977).

22. Public policy can be defined as policy that has an impact on the community, whatever its source, e.g., government, private business, professional organizations or, more narrowly, as policy made by public (government) agencies.

23. Lindblom summarizes the evolution this way: "... all historical and contemporary examples [of partycracies] are, in their anxiety over the conventional liberties, marked by a separation of powers and other devices to prevent a great mobilization of authority in one person or organization, even for what might be thought to be legitimate national purposes. Polyarchies [partycracies] are systems of rules for constraining rather than mobilizing authority. They grow out of a struggle to control authority rather than to create it or make it more effective.... They practice decentralization, diffusion of influence and power, and mutual adjustment so that individuals and small groups rather than national collectivities can strive for whatever they wish" (1977, 165). Words in brackets have been added.

24. A long-time Swedish minister of finance summed up the problem of trying to make economic policy in a partycracy this way: "In economic policy, I've learned, when things are due to be done for economic reasons, it's very often too early for political reasons. The crisis is not manifest, not obvious. When the crisis is there, the things you have to do come at the wrong time." Cited in David Crane, "Sweden at the Crossroads," *The Toronto Star* (May 16, 1993), A12.

25. Long before the recession in the early 1990s and the constitutional crisis, we find reports like this one common: "The political process does not seem to be, in the public's mind, a satisfactory way of resolving the many problems and conflicts in the country today.... In general, the parties and politicians are regarded with distaste by

most of the public ... we are ... struck by the tendency to turn away from the political process, its methods, and its practitioners" (Clark et al., 1980, 29–30).

26. Polling regularly indicates the lack of confidence in government. For example, a Gallup poll found: "Fifty-one per cent of Canadians look upon big government as a greater threat in the years to come than either big business or big labor. Twenty-one per cent thought big business was the biggest threat and 17 per cent thought big labor was the top threat. Eleven per cent said they didn't know which was the greatest threat." *The Toronto Star* (September 10, 1990).

27. Asked "How should your member of parliament vote on major issues?" Canadians responded: according to the majority view in your riding, 71 percent; according to his or her own conscience and beliefs, 21 percent; according to the policies of his or her party, 7 percent, *Maclean's* (January 4, 1993), p. 19. This is only the latest expression of a popular demand dating back to World War I, if not earlier. Representations to the Citizens' Forum on Canada's Future (the Spicer Commission) supported this poll result and carried it further, stating, "... since election campaigns do not constitute a vote by the people on these policies, and since elected representatives seem to have little or no influence or freedom to represent constituents' views, there is a perceived need for mechanisms which will (a) require members of parliament to consult their constituents on major issues; and, (b) either give them more freedom, or require them to vote according to their constituents' wishes" (1991, 21).

28. Joseph Schumpeter, no friend of participatory democracy, set out the challenge that must be met: "If we are to argue that the will of the citizens per se is a political factor entitled to respect, it must first exist. That is to say, it must be something more than an indeterminate bundle of value impulses loosely playing about given slogans and mistaken impressions" (1950, 253).

29. I propose that one community Parliament member be elected for each 1000 voters. This would mean that, across Canada, 18 500 "junior parliamentarians" would be actively involved in governing. For a somewhat more detailed sketch of the community Parliament model, see Lyon, 1984, 43–45.

30. For a discussion of this point, see Macpherson (1977, 112–115).

REFERENCES

Boyer, P. 1992. *The People's Mandate*. Toronto: Dundurn.

Broder, D. 1972. *The Party's Over*. New York: Harper and Row.

Brodie, M.J., and Jenson, J. 1980. *Crisis, Challenge and Change: Party and Class in Canada*. Toronto: Methuen.

Bryce, James. 1921. *Modern Democracies*, Volume I. New York: Macmillan.

Camp, D. 1981. "The Limits of Political Parties." In *Sovereign People or Sovereign Governments*, edited by H.V. Kroeker, 147–155. Montreal: Institute for Research on Public Policy.

Canada. 1991. *Citizens' Forum on Canada's Future*. Ottawa: Minister of Supply and Services.

Clark, S.D. 1962. *The Developing Canadian Community*. Toronto: University of Toronto Press.

Clarke, H., J. Jenson, L. LeDuc, and J. Pammett. 1980. *Political Choice in Canada*, abridged edition. Toronto: McGraw-Hill Ryerson.

———. 1984. *Absent Mandate*. Toronto: Gage.

Clarke, H.D., and Allan Kornberg. 1993. "Evaluations and Evolution: Public Attitudes toward Canada's Federal Political Parties, 1965–1991." *Canadian Journal of Political Science* XXVI, 2: 287–312.

Dahl, R. 1958. "A Critique for the Ruling Elite Model." *American Political Science Review* 52: 464.

———. 1962. *Who Governs*. New Haven: Yale University Press.

Doern, G.B., and B.W. Tomlin. 1991. *Faith and Fear*. Toronto: Stoddart.

Duverger, M. 1962. *Political Parties*. New York: John Wiley and Sons.

Easton, D. 1965. *A System Analysis of Political Life*. New York: Wiley.

Edelman, M. 1964. *The Symbolic Uses of Politics*. Urbana: University of Illinois Press.

Gerth, H.H., and C.W. Mills, eds. 1958. *From Max Weber: Essays in Sociology*. New York: Galaxy Paper.

Goodman, William. 1960. *The Two-Party System in the United States*, 2nd ed. Princeton: D. Van Nostrand.

Hodgins, Bruce W. 1967. "Democracy and the Ontario Fathers of Confederation." In *Profiles of a Province*, edited by Edith G. Frith, 83–91. Toronto: Ontario Historical Society.

Lawson, Kay, ed. 1980. *Political Parties and Linkage*. New Haven: Yale University Press.

Lindblom, C.E. 1977. *Politics and Markets*. New York: Basic Books.

Lyon, V. 1983–84. "The Future of Parties—Inevitable ... Obsolete?" *Journal of Canadian Studies* 4 (Winter), 108–131.

———. 1984. "House of Citizens." *Policy Options* 5, 2: 43.

———. 1992. "Green Politics: Parties, Elections, and Environmental Policy." In *Canadian Environmental Policy: Ecosystems, Politics, and Process*, edited by R. Boardman, 126–143. Toronto: Oxford.

Macpherson, C.B. 1977. *The Life and Times of Liberal Democracy*. Oxford: Oxford University Press.

McClosky, Herbert, and John Zaller. 1984. *The American Ethos*. Cambridge: Harvard University Press.

Manzer, Ronald. 1985. *Public Policies and Political Development in Canada*. Toronto: University of Toronto Press.

Naylor, J. 1991. *The New Democracy*. Toronto: University of Toronto Press.

Ostrogorski, M. 1964 (1902). *Democracy and the Organization of Political Parties II*. Chicago: Quadrangle Books.

Pammett, J.H., and J.L. Pepin, eds. 1988. *Political Education in Canada*. Halifax: The Institute for Research on Public Policy.

Parenti, M. 1978. *Power and the Powerless*. New York: St. Martin's Press.

Pateman, Carole. 1970. *Participation and Democratic Theory*. Cambridge: Cambridge University Press.

Sartori, Giovanni, 1965. *Democratic Theory.* New York: Praeger.

Schumpeter, Joseph A. 1950. *Capitalism, Socialism and Democracy,* 3rd ed. New York: Harper and Row.

Simpson, J. 1988. *The Spoils of Power.* Toronto: Collins.

Stewart, Gordon T. 1986. The *Origins of Canadian Politics.* Vancouver: University of British Columbia Press.

Tussman, Joseph. 1960. *Obligation and the Body Politic.* New York: Oxford University Press.

Wahlke, J.C. 1978. "Policy Demands and System Support: The Role of the Represented." In *The Politics of Representation,* edited by Heinz Eulau and J.C. Wahlke, 73–90. Beverly Hills: Sage Publishing.

Postscript

Amyot's article raises some disturbing questions. Parties and elected representatives are typically thought to be at the centre of the democratic process, yet Amyot suggests that nonelected elements especially (bureaucrats, central banks, and corporations) are now assuming greater importance. If so, does this mean that democratic polities are witnessing the triumph of the unelected over the elected? Amyot writes that responsibility for mobilizing and aggregating the citizenry is increasingly in the hands of pressure groups and the like. Again, if so, does this mean that parties are no longer the essential link between the people and their governments? Furthermore, Amyot notes how charismatic leaders, sometimes using their considerable personal wealth, have created a "party" around themselves thereby bypassing traditional party channels. In this leader-centred system, do physical appearance and personality become all important determinants of voter decisions?

Amyot's article provides an eloquent statement of the "decline of parties" thesis. For an article supportive of Amyot's argument, see John Meisel, "Decline of Party in Canada," in Hugh Thorburn, ed., *Party Politics in Canada,* 6th ed. (Scarborough: Prentice-Hall, 1991). A critique of the "decline of parties thesis" can be found in Ronald Landes, "In Defence of Canadian Political Parties," in Mark Charlton and Paul Barker, *Crosscurrents: Contemporary Political Issues,* 2nd ed. (Scarborough: Nelson Canada, 1994).

The article by Lyon takes a different tack and in doing so raises some equally disturbing questions. Lyon is less concerned with the question of the demise of parties and whether they contribute positively to the enhancement of democracy. In fact, for Lyon the existence of a strong party system is just as much a threat to real democratic participation as would be its demise in favour of unelected bureaucratic elites. In this respect, Lyon stands in a tradition of thinking that has long questioned whether party politics is compatible with a healthy democracy. For a sense of these historic debates, students should consult two classic works, M.I. Ostrogorski, *Democracy and the Organization of Political Parties,* 2 vols. (New York: McMillan, 1902) and Robert Michels, *Political Parties: A Sociological Study of Oligarchical Tendencies of Modern Democracy* (New York: The Free Press, 1966). While intriguing, Lyon's article does leave the reader with further questions: Would a "community Parliament" be able to avoid party identities and loyalties? To answer this question, students may wish to examine the experience of cities where an effort has been made to establish "nonpartisan" elections in which candidates would not run as official party candidates. How successful have they been in eliminating the influence of parties and party labels at the municipal level?

ISSUE**SEVENTEEN**

Should Representation in Parliament Mirror Canada's Social Diversity?

✔ **YES**

TIM SCHOULS, "Why Group Representation in Parliament Is Important"

✗ **NO**

JOHN H. REDEKOP, "Group Representation in Parliament Would Be Dysfunctional for Canada"

Canada is a representative democracy in which, every four or five years, we choose certain individuals (members of Parliament) to act on our behalf. As our representatives, we empower them to act as our agents and to represent our interests in the national decision-making process. As long as representative democracy has existed there has been debate over the exact nature that representation should take.[1] [1]

Much of this debate has focused on how the representative is expected to carry out his or her duties. Traditionally three different views of representation have been put forward. First, there are those who argue that the representative is to act as a *trustee*. That is, members of Parliament are given a mandate to act as they best see fit on behalf of the interests of the electors. MPs are given considerable leeway to exercise their personal judgment in balancing the interests of their constituents with those of the broader community and in coming up with a policy that best serves the common good. While the representatives can exercise wide latitude in making decisions, the voter will hold them accountable by removing them from office at the end of their term if they are perceived to have failed in adequately representing the voter's interests.

Second, there are those who argue that the representative is to act primarily as a *delegate*. According to this view, members of Parliament are to act primarily as they have been instructed to by the voters rather than trusting their own judgment as a guide. Representatives should not stray too far from the explicit wishes of their constituents. In the 1996 federal election campaign, Preston Manning often emphasized this theme, arguing that the seats in Parliament belong to the voters and they should elect only those candidates who promise to vote as the constituents have instructed them to do. A variety of techniques such as constituent surveys, public hall meetings, and telephone referendums have been used in recent years by MPs, especially those from the Reform Party, before voting on a particular issue in an attempt to ascertain what the "instructions" of the electorate were.

Third, representatives have been seen as first and foremost *party members* who act and vote primarily according to the dictates of the party leadership. This perspective assumes that the representatives in a party act as a team and that the electorate chooses which team they feel best represents their interests. Like the trustee model, the voters must wait until the next election to render a judgment on the success of the representative in representing their interests. The debates that follow in Issues Eighteen and Nineteen address weaknesses of the party model of representation and ways that these deficiencies in representative government can be addressed.

In recent years, the debate over representation has shifted toward a more fundamental question—to what extent do the representatives in Parliament reflect the characteristics of ethnicity, language, and gender that are found in the population at large. On one level, this argument suggests that to be truly "representative," Parliament should be composed of the same proportion of social groups as is Canadian society at large. Parliament, in other words, should be a microcosm of Canadian society. If the population is composed of 51 percent women, 6 percent visible minorities, and 4 percent Aboriginal people, then there should be at least the same proportion of representatives elected to Parliament from each of these groups. A basic premise of this argument is that voters, especially those from minority and marginalized groups within society, will not see the decisions of Parliament as being fully legitimate unless the voters see themselves reflected in the social makeup of the legislature. As the social and cultural makeup of Canada changes, our political institutions could increasingly lose credibility if their composition does not adequately reflect the changing face of the country.

However, this argument goes beyond the question simply of increasing the numerical representation of certain social groups, such as women, in Parliament. It argues that representation is important because, once elected, women will act in the interests of women. They will interpret issues and respond to them differently than a male representative would. Thus, the election of women and minority groups to Parliament would result in substantive changes in the content of public policy, as the views of groups once marginalized and unrepresented in the political system are now given voice within the corridors of power. Only those who truly know from experience what it is to be a woman, an Aboriginal person, or a member of a visible minority can truly represent other members of the groups to which they belong in Parliament.

In the essays below we examine in greater depth this view of representation. Tim Schouls sets out the philosophical case for ensuring that the social diversity of Canada is represented in the Canadian legislature. In response, John Redekop examines the implications of this move away from more traditional definitions of representation and questions both the wisdom and practicality of such an approach.

✔ **YES**
Why Group Representation in Parliament Is Important
TIM SCHOULS

An increasing number of Canadians are convinced that the system of parliamentary representation in Canada is unfair because it is seen as unrepresentative of Canada's social diversity as a whole. Parliament has long reflected the regional and linguistic composition of Canada by allocating seats in the House of Commons and Senate in a manner that ensures adequate representation of provincial interests at the national level. But this exclusive concern for provincial and regional representation is now being challenged by nonterritorial groups who demand representation on the basis of characteristics that are not tied to geography. These groups argue that if the full diversity of Canada's population is to be reflected in Parliament, its representative character must be expanded beyond that of territory to include guaranteed seats for disadvantaged groups such as women, Aboriginal peoples, ethnic and visible minorities, and people with disabilities. The belief here is that parliamentary representatives must share central experiences and assumptions with those they represent if those representatives are to understand their constituents' needs and interests. Conversely, these groups believe that they cannot be adequately represented if their needs and interests are not advanced by those who share their gender, Aboriginal status, ethnicity, race, or disability.

The conventional Canadian approach to representative democracy, as represented in the article that follows by John Redekop, is generally hostile to claims for guaranteed group-based representation. According to Redekop's view, effective representation does not depend upon representatives and constituents sharing the same personal attributes. Instead, the effectiveness of representatives is measured by the degree to which they are able to present and advance the concerns and claims of their constituents. According to his line of argument, just as lawyers can represent clients who are very different from them, so too can representatives protect the interests of those whose lives have little in common with their own.

While this article will not take direct issue with this more traditional understanding of democratic representation, it will argue that democracy in Canada can be considerably deepened and enhanced when the composition of the House of Commons substantially reflects the social diversity of the Canadian population.[1] No doubt, MPs can represent constituents who are very different from them, but at the same time it is not always obvious that this representation has been effective in cases where the constituents in question have been subject to historical disadvantage and marginalization. Of course, not all groups in Canadian society have been marginalized or have suffered disadvantage, but for those that have, their argument that seats in the House of Commons be guaranteed to them is worthy of serious examination. For democracy implies equality, but, where conditions of marginalization and disadvantage exist, it necessarily follows that some groups possess greater opportunity, and thus privileges and powers that others do not. In the Canadian parliamentary setting, white males from professional and business backgrounds have historically dominated the House of Commons and Senate, and, as a result, it is they who have traditionally held a monopoly upon the political reigns of power. Conversely, many women, Aboriginal peoples, certain ethnic and visible minorities, and people with disabilities claim that they have been marginalized, which means, among other things, that they have been minimally represented in parliamentary discussions and decision-making processes. This article will argue that where political marginalization of groups has historically existed, active reform to secure these groups seats in the House of Commons is a healthy democratic response. Not only will such reform ensure marginalized groups a greater presence and thus a voice in the parliamentary process, but also such reform may encourage the development of legislation and laws that take more fully into account the views of marginalized groups. In short, an active reform process will counteract the current imbalance in political power and so promote greater democratic equality of opportunity and participation in the House of Commons for Canada's socially diverse groups.

GROUP IDENTITY IN CANADA

It could be argued that to focus exclusively upon demands by marginalized groups for political inclusion within the House of Commons is to largely miss the point of group identity politics in Canada. The range of political differences and objectives represented by Canada's diverse population is extensive, pushing far beyond the kinds of solutions that a politics of inclusion within the House of Commons can offer. To be sure, over the last twenty-five years or so Canadians have begun to define themselves in new ways, and the politics of parliamentary inclusion is in large part an initiative that attempts to address those changes. For political purposes, Canadians used to identify themselves largely with their provinces of origin, with their use of French or English as their first language, and with their Catholic or Protestant religion. In response, the House of Commons was set up, both in terms of its allocation of seats and in terms of representation within cabinet, to reflect this geographic, linguistic, and religious diversity. In recent years, however, a new set of identity categories has become increasingly salient for many Canadians, categories associated primarily with changing conceptions of ethnicity and with the newfound political relevance of gender. Immigration and demographic trends of the 1970s to the 1990s have made Canada a far more multiethnic and multicultural country, while strong feminist initiatives during this same time frame have elevated the political status of women. New Canadians with origins in the Caribbean, Africa, Middle East, Central and South America, and Asia identify themselves not simply as provincial residents speaking either English or French, but more importantly as members of ethnic groups with distinctive perspectives and interests to offer to the broader Canadian political agenda. Feminists, meanwhile, point out that the social and political structures of Canada reinforce men's power to the detriment of women. In response, redress of the current structural imbalance of power between men and women constitutes a central component of the feminist political agenda. In short, attachments to geography, language, and religion are receding in their overall political importance. At the same time, attachments to ethnicity and gender are becoming more significant politically. Against these shifting demographic trends, it is therefore not surprising that the conventional geography-based strategy for allocating House of Commons seats is coming under increasing attack.

However, despite the need to address the challenge of representation in the House of Commons for the marginally represented categories of women and ethnic groups, Canadian identity politics is more typically driven by demands for Aboriginal self-government and the recognition of Quebec's "distinct society." Like women and ethnic minorities, Aboriginal peoples and the citizens of Quebec argue that the existing conventions of representation do not grant them standing that is proportional to their numbers in Canada. From the perspectives of their leaders, however, greater representation in Parliament will not guarantee Aboriginal peoples and the citizens of Quebec the kind of legislative power they need to secure their political objectives within Canada. Their numbers are simply too small and their influence too weak to counteract the legislative priorities of the non-Aboriginal, non-Québécois parliamentary majority. Hence, Aboriginal peoples demand an equal partnership with federal and provincial governments based upon the recognition of their inherent right to self-government, while Quebeckers demand at minimum an expansion of their powers within the federal system of government so as to increase their provincial autonomy within Canada. Thus, when Aboriginal peoples and Quebeckers claim that they do not enjoy equal powers within Canada, they typically seek solutions within the realm of intergovernmental affairs rather than parliamentary representation.

When considering the arguments for greater parliamentary representation for disadvantaged or marginalized groups within Canada, it is important to realize from the outset, then, that the demands for political inclusion by Aboriginal peoples, the citizens of Quebec, women, and ethnic and visible minorities are not naturally all of one piece. Aboriginal peoples and Quebeckers demand more autonomy *from* Parliament through self-government and special provincial status (or secession), while women and ethnic and visible minorities demand more autonomy *within* Parliament through elevated levels of representation. In fact in many respects, the demands of the former two groups are mirror images of those of the latter groups. Be that as it may, the demands for equal representation within Parliament remain an important concern for some groups. The intent of this article is to draw attention to only this very small piece of the larger, often poorly interlocking, Canadian identity puzzle.

REPRESENTATIONAL DEFICITS

On the surface, there is an undeniable, indeed, almost irrefutable, logic attached to the demand that the House of Commons reflect the diversity of the Canadian population. At present, for example, electoral mechanisms organize Canadians into geographically bound constituencies. While Redekop is quite right to point out that dividing voters into constituency groups makes sense from a practical point of view, such a division also carries with it the assumption that voters' primary political identity flows from their attachment to territory. MPs are thus linked to their constituents in geographic terms. The geographical division of the electorate encourages voters to think of their varied interests (whether relating to jobs, social security, the environment, etc.) largely in terms of where they live.

Now, while features associated with geography may well shape citizens' identities in some respects, Canadians also possess diverse identities by virtue of their cultural, gender, ethnic, and religious differences, which have very little to do with geography. It therefore stands to reason that along with geographic affiliation, Canadians may want to be represented by those who share their Aboriginal status, gender, ethnicity, or religious identity. There is an intuitive logic attached to the idea, for example, that when legislative initiatives dealing with abortion, childcare, or pay equity are before the House of Commons, female constituents may want to be represented by women who can identify with these issues because they are women. Similarly, when legislative initiatives dealing with reserve-based economic ventures or housing starts are before the House, it makes sense that Aboriginal constituents may want to have Aboriginal people representing their interests. According to this line of reasoning then, there is clearly something amiss when representation within the House is monopolized by a single group (upper and middle-class males, for example), a group, moreover, that most likely possesses a relatively limited range of perspectives. Indeed, most well-intentioned Canadians would probably readily admit that where underrepresentation of certain groups exists, reforms ought to be encouraged to stimulate a more proportional balance of representation in the House.

While there have been a few improvements, it is undeniably the case that the composition of the House of Commons is only a very pale reflection of the diverse social characteristics of the Canadian population, as can be seen in the following three examples. In the 1988 federal election, 39, or 13.2 percent, of the MPs elected were women; in the 1993 election, 54, or 18.3 percent, were women; while in the 1997 election, 61, or 20.2 percent, were women. Given that women constitute 51 percent of Canada's population, the severity of their underrepresentation in the House is hard to miss.[2] In the case of Aboriginal peoples and visible minorities, underrepresentation in the House is even more striking.[3] Aboriginal peoples constitute approximately 4 percent of Canada's population, yet they were able to capture only 1 percent of the seats (3 of a total 295) in each of the 1988 and 1993 elections.[4] Visible minorities, meanwhile, while constituting 6.3 percent of Canada's population, captured only 2 percent of the seats (6 out of 295) in 1988, though they improved their fortunes slightly by increasing their share to 3 percent (9 out of 295) in the election of 1993.[5] Compare these lean numbers to the following scenario. If a proportional share of seats were given to each of the three groups mentioned above, women would be entitled to 153 seats, Aboriginal peoples to 12 seats, and visible minorities to 19 seats out of the total 301.[6]

The obvious question here is why do women, Aboriginal peoples, and visible minorities persist in being so severely underrepresented in the House of Commons? There is no short answer to this question, for the barriers that inhibit each group from entering electoral politics are numerous and in many respects different from one another. Women, for example, have traditionally avoided political life at the national level because the heavy demands of family life and a political career often strain significantly against one another. Moreover, the challenge associated with securing financing to contest constituency nominations and run campaigns, coupled with the perception that the fierce competition associated with politics is symptomatic of a male domain, has made the political arena at the national level minimally appealing for many women.[7] Aboriginal candidates share with women the structural barrier of limited financing. In addition, as the Committee for Aboriginal Electoral Reform argues, "Canada's history of assimilationist policies have had an adverse impact on Aboriginal perceptions of Parliament and the value of participating within it."[8] The negative feelings Aboriginal peoples hold against Parliament as a colonial instrument of oppression means that many Aboriginal people are inclined not to vote in federal elections. This in turn discourages parties from fielding Aboriginal candidates as there is little incentive for them to use such Aboriginal candidates, in attempts to win a largely apathetic Aboriginal vote. Barriers inhibiting the participation of visible minorities are also readily identifiable. For example, Daiva Stasiulis argues that for many recent immigrants a significant barrier exists in the form of lack of familiarity with Canada's two official languages and with the customs of the British parliamentary tradition.[9] This barrier is compounded in turn by party politics that tend to identify the issues of Canadian politics along a French–English continuum and to engage in the recruitment of candidates by using old, well-established networks that have little, if any, connections to the immigrant community.

Given these structural barriers, it seems but a small step to justify reforms aimed at securing a proportional number of women, Aboriginal peoples, and ethnic and visible minorities in the House of Commons. Moreover, the case for inclusion only gathers strength when we recognize that the primary reason why women, Aboriginal peoples, and ethnic and visible minorities are absent from the House of Commons is because they have been ignored and marginalized by the male hierarchy that holds power. Given that men dominate the House of Commons, it only stands to reason that they will have greater opportunity and power to advance their perspectives and legislate their preferences. Conversely, it has been well documented that, relative to men, women suffer greater social and economic disadvantage, a condition that in turn means that women have fewer political resources than men. Aboriginal peoples and ethnic and visible minorities, meanwhile, have long struggled against what Iris Marion Young calls cultural imperialism.[10] In the Canadian setting, cultural imperialism has typically manifested itself in the form of English and French cultures establishing society-wide norms. Aboriginal, ethnic, and visible minority cultures, conversely, were traditionally stigmatized as being inferior and in need of transformation to align them more closely with the perspectives and worldviews of the two dominant cultures.

THEORIES OF REPRESENTATION

It is largely in reaction to these structural barriers that numerous calls for reform leading to a more proportional balance of representation in Parliament have been issued over the years. In essence, calls for proportional representation constitute a claim to tip the scales of the currently imbalanced composition of the House of Commons toward a more balanced representation of Canada's social diversity. If the political assumptions associated with white male privilege hamper the capacity of minorities to gain access to the House of Commons, then on democratic grounds surely no effort should be spared to get more minority representatives into the House. Moreover, the urgency that many marginalized groups attach to their claims for inclusion flows directly from the fact that the House of Commons lies at the symbolic heart of representative government in Canada. It is with this state institution more than any other that the primary qualification to become an MP is purely and simply the ability to represent. No doubt, as Redekop points out, many MPs get elected simply because they are better than their opponents in capturing the vote. But in the end, the test of good service is established by the degree to which constituents judge their MP to have been an effective representative on their behalf. This stands in sharp contrast to employment within the judiciary or bureaucracy, for example, where professional expertise and academic qualifications are of first importance. Simply put, legislatures exist to represent the population they serve; this is their central function. It is therefore imperative from the point of view of numerous marginalized groups that, if they are to achieve social and political equality in any meaningful sense, they simply must achieve proportional standing in the parliamentary domain where many of their interests are so regularly considered and debated.

If the case for more proportional inclusion in the House of Commons is so compelling, then why do so many Canadians accept with little trouble the prevailing patterns of white, male-dominated representation? In order to get a handle on this question, it is important that we step back for a moment and examine with some care the conflicting understandings that lie behind the idea of representation itself. To date, there has been significant agreement in Canada that the practice of parliamentary democracy ought to adhere to a liberal conception of representation. From a liberal point of view, it is the individual who is to be treated as the most important of all political entities. This means that when it comes to representation, each individual is to count equally as one, and no one as more than one. In the context of elections, moreover, this concern for individual equality translates into the well-known slogan One Person, One Vote. What is of principal importance from the liberal point of view, then, is that while group interests can be advanced (given that it is individuals who form groups for the deliberate purpose of promoting common interests), individual interests must not be ignored in the process. Indeed, for liberals, to represent groups exclusively potentially poses two immediate dangers to the individual. First, when MPs represent group interests they tend to regard those interests as held by all members of the group. However, not all group members may hold the same interests. For example, some women may dissent from a particular daycare strategy, yet if women are treated as a group, MPs may be tempted to regard the endorsement of the strategy by some women as an endorsement by all. Focusing upon the interests of each and every individual gets around this problem of universalizing interests. Second, to focus upon the interests of groups brings with it the possibility that MPs will privilege some groups over others. Under this scenario, not only are dissenting individuals within privileged groups left unrepresented, but so too are all members of groups who are not fortunate enough to gain the attention of MPs in the first place.

In the interests of equality of representation, then, representatives are elected to advance the individual interests of their individual constituents. To be sure, the interests of constituents will regularly conflict, and so the MP will be forced to make compromises and secure tradeoffs. The measure of effective representation is determined when, despite being faced by the challenge of conflicting interests, MPs are nevertheless able to take appropriate positions demonstrating that in doing so they have taken the interests of all their constituents into account. The issue, then, is not who is in the House of Commons doing the representing, but rather whether the MP, regardless of personal characteristics, is able to get the job done on behalf of his or her constituents. In short, MPs may well possess different social, ethnic, or sexual characteristics from those they represent, but this should not matter if MPs demonstrate a constant readiness to respond in helpful ways to their constituents' needs.

This liberal argument of representation is certainly a very powerful one. But on its own, this liberal theory simply does not do full justice to the political marginalization and exclusion that many women, Aboriginal peoples, and ethnic and visible minorities experience. As Redekop so powerfully argues, men can represent women (much as a male lawyer can represent a female client) if the issue in question is a legislative initiative to which both men and women agree. But what Redekop fails to take seriously is that with respect to many issues, women, Aboriginal peoples, and visible and ethnic minorities will want to be represented by those who are like them because they believe that their identities carry with them distinctive experiences that white male MPs will be hard-pressed to understand. Women, for example, may possess experiences and consequently perspectives that are distinct from those of men with respect to the issues of childbearing and childcare, sexual harassment and violence, the division of paid and unpaid labour, and the matter of women's exclusion from significant portions of the economic and political world.[11] Furthermore, with respect to Aboriginal peoples, Ovide Mercredi and Mary Ellen Turpel argue, "As Peoples with distinct cultures, languages, governments, territories and populations in Canada, we must be recognized as full and equal participants in the Canadian political system. We can speak for ourselves and no one else has the political or spiritual authority to speak for us. Canadians cannot speak for us because Canadians are different."[12] What is at issue here is not so much the capacity of MPs to advocate on behalf of their female, Aboriginal, or ethnic and visible minority candidates per se; minorities would certainly endorse any initiative that sees MPs support and advance their political agendas. More directly, what is at issue is the desire of women, Aboriginal peoples, and ethnic and visible minorities to gain a more proportional balance in the House of Commons on the grounds that they have been marginalized and excluded from representing themselves in the past.

At the same time, it is critical to underscore the point that the leaders of marginalized groups do not generally stake their claim for greater inclusion on the grounds that they share common interests, interests, moreover, that they believe only their own representatives are capable of putting before the House of Commons. Such an argument cannot provide the moral foundation for a claim to greater inclusion because the experiences of marginalized groups are normally too varied to be contained within a single common interest. Women have different perspectives on abortion, childcare, and pay equity, for example, while Aboriginal peoples have different perspectives on economic development, land claims, and self-government. Within their respective communities, women and Aboriginal peoples may thus share common policy concerns, but this does not mean that they will also share the same views on how those concerns ought to be handled. Minority groups are not homogeneous, possessing single, distinct policy perspectives. Such images portray far too simplistic a view of the world. Because minority groups do not by definition possess common policy interests, the strength of the argument for greater inclusion in the House of Commons necessarily lies elsewhere.

The argument for greater inclusion in the House of Commons gathers far more strength when considered within the framework of political marginalization or exclusion. The representational claim of marginalized groups is a forceful one because groups want to overcome the barriers of domination that have excluded them from participating in an equitable way in the House in the past. As the argument goes, if the distinct voices and (internally multiple) perspectives of marginalized social groups are not represented in the House, then it is almost certainly the case that the legislative initiatives and policy outcomes of the dominant white male majority will (continue to) prevail. In essence, what marginalized groups are saying is that they have a right to participate in these parliamentary discussions whatever their opinion may be on the matter under consideration. In this sense, the demands for parliamentary inclusion put forward by women, Aboriginal people, and visible and ethnic minorities flow from their common experiences of exclusion as groups, and from their mutual desire to engage more directly in parliamentary debate and decision making. To be sure, as Redekop points out, inclusion in parliamentary debate is not in and of itself enough to guarantee satisfactory legislative outcomes for marginalized groups. Influence can be effective only to the degree that marginalized groups can make their presence felt where power in parliamentary government is exercised—by the majority party and, more particularly, by the prime minister and cabinet drawn from the majority party. At the same time, however, without presence in the House of Commons there is little opportunity for marginalized groups to exercise any influence at all.

The larger point that the leaders of marginalized groups seek to establish, however, is that because white males have traditionally monopolized parliamentary power, they cannot at this juncture in history take the place of the very groups they have marginalized by standing in as their representatives. As social groups, women, Aboriginal peoples, and visible and ethnic minorities need to be represented by other women, Aboriginal peoples, and visible and ethnic minorities because they share identities, which goes along with having been historically excluded. Thus, for example, men may be able to advance women's interests, but what men cannot do is stand in for women when women want to have all their diversity *as women* represented in the House of Commons. This is a task that only women can perform for themselves. Against historical patterns of exclusion, the presence of women in the House of Commons ensures that all the diverse and quite possibly conflicting interests of women will actually be heard and debated in Canada's central representative political arena.[13]

In sum, the proportional presence of women, Aboriginal peoples, and visible and ethnic minorities in the House of Commons matters because this presence would have the effect of counteracting the current hierarchy of white male power. A more sustained and numerically balanced presence would help to raise the profile of marginalized groups and thereby possibly place their multiple issues more regularly before the House. In this vein, Young argues, "The principle of group representation calls for some means by which the needs, interests, knowledge, and social perspective of oppressed or disadvantaged groups receive explicit and formal representation in political discussions and decision-making. The primary argument for such group representation is that where there are social group differences and some groups are privileged and others oppressed, group representation is necessary to produce a legitimate communicative forum."[14] Proportional representation of marginalized groups in the House of Commons would ensure that the full range of views represented by Canada's diverse population would have the opportunity for expression on a consistent and ongoing basis. This may in turn encourage a situation in which "those who had previously monopolized positions of power and influence might be equally encouraged to recognize their partiality and bias."[15]

OBJECTIONS

In the article following, Redekop raises a number of objections against the arguments put forward thus far. Let me conclude by addressing the three that are most significant.

First, Redekop argues that a politics of parliamentary inclusion based on gender, ethnic, or other minority identities introduces or possibly intensifies divisions between Canadian citizens, divisions, moreover, that arguably may not be of the first importance in the public eye. He points out that Canada has enough trouble as it is building points of commonality between Canadians in Parliament, so why should Canadians further fuel the fire of divisions by paying attention to gender- and ethnicity-based claims to inclusion? Indeed, would it not be far better to encourage citizens to focus on matters of policy instead and try to build alliances across identity differences in support of policy initiatives that all groups can support? To cede to demands for parliamentary inclusion by marginalized groups, argues Redekop, would seem only to add additional stress to an already severely stretched Canadian unity fabric.

There is no easy answer to this objection, for Redekop is undoubtedly right that the demand for inclusion by women, Aboriginal peoples, and visible and ethnic minorities would add a new and potentially divisive dimension to parliamentary politics. However, one way to partly allay these fears of division is to recognize that what marginalized groups are asking for is not to be separated from the structures of Canadian democracy, but rather to be more fully included within them. Contrast, for example, the demands of Quebec separatists with the demands of marginalized groups and consider which is the more divisive force within Canadian politics. Quebec separatists threaten political unity within Canada because they question the credentials of the Canadian government to exercise any authority over them. Marginalized groups, on the other hand, have drawn attention to their identities only because they want to be more fully included in the political discussions that shape the political identity of Canada as a whole. Thus, although marginalized groups may focus upon the political importance of their social differences, what they are actually doing, as Will Kymlicka puts it, is trying to find avenues for "full membership in the larger society."[16] Seen from this perspective, the demand for greater inclusion by marginalized groups can be seen as an important endorsement of the Canadian parliamentary system.

Redekop's second objection relates to who potentially qualifies for distinct representation within Parliament. If Parliament is to be considered truly representative of Canada's social diversity, Redekop asks, then does this mean that all sectors of the Canadian population should be represented, including, for example, the aged, teachers, students, factory workers, retail sales workers, parents, athletes, and environmentalists? Once we accept the view that the characteristics of people play a role in determining whether they feel adequately represented in Parliament, then we seem to be in the absurd position of having to consider the claims for inclusion by a potentially endless list of groups. Moreover, even if we can establish which groups might qualify for guaranteed representation, Redekop asks further, how do we go about establishing who legitimately belongs to which group? Is the attempt to establish boundaries simply too difficult, given so many people now have what might be called "hybrid" identities (e.g., a person may be both female and Aboriginal)? In other words, on what basis do we distinguish legitimate claims by groups for parliamentary inclusion from those that are not legitimate?

Again, there is no straightforward answer to Redekop's objection, though Anne Phillips points us in a helpful direction. She argues that the case for greater inclusion of women, ethnic groups, and ethnic and visible minorities rests upon "an analysis of the existing structures of exclusion."[17] That is, a system of fair representation does not mean that any or all groups are entitled to specific representation on the basis of some purported principle of equality or fairness. Instead, what we must do is focus upon those particularly urgent instances where the oppression of groups has led to those same groups experiencing a profound degree of marginalization and exclusion from the political process. Proportional representation of groups is thus never simply required, but must be determined on a case-by-case basis in reference to these questions: Has this group been historically oppressed? Will proportional representation in Parliament constitute a significant step in overcoming those conditions of oppression? In other words, what qualifies groups for greater inclusion is the likelihood that without guaranteed access to the arena of policymaking they will be unable to overcome their current experiences of exclusion and marginalization. While this approach does not get around the difficulties associated with defining who is and who is not a member of a disadvantaged group, it at least narrows the field of potential candidates who may be eligible for guaranteed representation. Against these more restrictive criteria, women, Aboriginal peoples, and numerous visible and ethnic groups in Canada are able to put forward a very strong case.

Third, Redekop argues that the proposal to move to identity-based representation is condescending toward those groups that would benefit from guaranteed seats because, among other things, such representation would relegate them to the status of second-class MPs. If groups can't make it to the House of Commons on their own, in other words, and are thereby "reduced" to relying upon special governmental facilitation to get them there, they will undoubtedly lack credibility.

No doubt, securing seats through special guarantees does constitute a significant departure from standard electoral practice in Canada. But though a departure, these reform proposals are not in and of themselves condescending to disadvantaged and marginalized groups. Here everything depends on one's perspective. Despite what Redekop says, disadvantaged and marginalized groups are not after guaranteed seats because the dominant male hierarchy has told them that such a course of action would be good for them. To accept the directives of the dominant male hierarchy on these grounds would indeed be condescending. On the contrary, disadvantaged and marginalized groups who make the point are saying that they are after guaranteed seats because this is the only way they will be able to break the stranglehold upon power that the dominant male hierarchy now exercises over them. They would stand for office and get elected through conventional channels, in other words, if they could reasonably expect to be successful in this way. The trouble is that their success is minimized because the dominant male hierarchy (which constitutes a minority in demographic terms) has been very effective at retaining its vast majority of seats in the House since it has at its disposal a disproportional share of the party and electoral machinery needed to win elections. From this perspective, the only way to break this cycle of dominance is to make structural changes that directly challenge the male hierarchy. One way to mount this challenge is through a system of guaranteed seats.

CONCLUSION

Redekop is quite right to point out that the practical complications associated with getting a system of guaranteed seats off the ground are considerable. I have no easy solutions to offer. However, simply because there are practical difficulties associated with reform should not lead us to abandon the project. Advocates of reform tell us that a system of guaranteed seats is an integral component of their larger project to overcome the debilitating cycle of political marginalization and exclusion they now experience. The question is, what is the best route to heeding this call for justice? There is, of course, safety to be had in steering the ship of democratic practice in Canada into the tranquil waters of the status quo rather than into the rocky waters of reform. The latter route may well lead to significant structural damage to the parliamentary ship as we know it. However, avoiding rocky waters also means that those who now hold power will continue to pilot the ship. The message that the marginalized and disadvantaged in Canada draw to our attention is that this inclination toward "safety" may be less than desirable.

NOTES

1. I will leave aside the question of representation in the Senate as this would raise issues that lie beyond the scope of this paper.

2. See Jane Arscott and Linda Trimble, "In the Presence of Women: Representation and Political Power," in Jane Arscott and Linda Trimble, eds., *In the Presence of Women: Representation in Canadian Governments* (Toronto: Harcourt Brace & Company, Canada, 1997), pp. 1–17.

3. At the time this article went to press, the official number of Aboriginal and visible minority MPs elected federally in June 1997 was unavailable.

4. See Committee for Aboriginal Electoral Reform, *The Path to Electoral Equality* (Ottawa: Committee for Aboriginal Electoral Reform, 1991), p. 2.

5. See Daiva Stasiulis, "Deep Diversity: Race and Ethnicity in Canadian Politics," in Michael S. Whittington and Glen Williams, eds., *Canadian Politics in the 1990s* (Toronto: Nelson Canada, 1995), pp. 199–200.

6. In the June 1997 federal election, the number of House of Commons seats contested was raised from 295 to 301.

7. On this point, see Lisa Young, "Fulfilling the Mandate of Difference: Women in the Canadian House of Commons," in Jane Arscott and Linda Trimble, *In the Presence of Women: Representation in Canadian Governments*, pp. 85–86.

8. Committee for Aboriginal Electoral Reform, *The Path to Electoral Equality*, pp. 7–12.

9. Daiva Stasiulis, "Deep Diversity: Race and Ethnicity in Canadian Politics," pp. 200–204.

10. Iris Marion Young, "Justice and Communicative Democracy," in Roger S. Gottlieb, ed., *Radical Philosophy: Tradition, Counter-Tradition Politics* (Philadelphia: Temple University Press, 1993), p. 133.

11. Anne Phillips, *The Politics of Presence* (Oxford: Clarendon Press, 1995), pp. 67–68.

12. Ovide Mercredi and Mary Ellen Turpel, *In the Rapids: Navigating the Future of First Nations* (Toronto: Penguin, 1993), p. 36.

13. For an extensive discussion of this point, see Anne Phillips, *The Politics of Presence*, ch. 2.

14. Iris Marion Young, "Justice and Communicative Democracy," p. 136.

15. Anne Phillips, *The Politics of Presence*, p. 152.

16. Will Kymlicka, *Multicultural Citizenship: A Liberal Theory of Minority Rights* (Oxford: Clarendon Press, 1995), p. 192.

17. Anne Phillips, *The Politics of Presence*, p. 47.

✗ **NO**
Group Representation in Parliament Would Be Dysfunctional for Canada
JOHN H. REDEKOP

A. INTRODUCTION

Various critics rightly assert that the Canadian Parliament does not accurately reflect Canada's social diversity. They are also correct when they say that Canada's electoral system plays a major role in producing unrepresentative legislatures. What is at issue in the present discussion is not whether the Canadian Parliament, specifically the House of Commons, should be reformed and the electoral system improved but whether the proposal to adopt group representation, as explained by Tim Schouls, constitutes a desirable and workable change.

As I understand it, the proposal under consideration seeks to remedy the alleged major flaw in Canada's electoral system by guaranteeing parliamentary seats for "disadvantaged groups such as women, Aboriginal peoples, ethnic and visible minorities, and people with disabilities." While additional categories are suggested by the phrasing, we will limit this discussion to these five groups; they encompass about 75 percent of Canada's population. We will also limit this analysis to the House of Commons. Senate reform needs to be discussed in its own right.

It should be noted that the proposal emphasizes the need for "political equality," which apparently means "equal representation" or mathematical proportionality. Thus, since females constitute about 51 percent of the population, they would, in the proposed scheme of "proportional parliamentary inclusion" and "proportional presence," be guaranteed 51 percent of the seats in the elected House of Commons. The other four groups would similarly be guaranteed a percentage of seats in this "identity-based" system of representation.

This essay will demonstrate that identity-based group representation in Parliament, with guaranteed seats, as described by Tim Schouls, is neither desirable nor workable in Canada. On balance, I believe, it would not be an improvement over our present single-member plurality electoral system.

One can think of several reasonable and democratic ways in which our present system could be reformed. One way would be to have half of the House of Commons seats filled by our present form of election—which would enable all Canadians to retain the benefits of having their own MP—with the other half being filled by a proportional representation system as is presently practised in Germany, Japan, and New Zealand. Having half of the MPs elected according to the second system would promote unity and goodwill, for example, by allowing a nationally victorious party to have at least some representation from a province where it got a large number of votes but did not come first in any riding. Such was the situation for the Liberals in the general election of 1980, for example, when they received 24 percent of the popular vote in Saskatchewan and 22 percent in each of Alberta and British Columbia but failed to elect even one member in those three provinces. In those three provinces, thus, the Liberals were unrepresented in the national cabinet.

B. ARGUMENTS BASED ON IDEOLOGICAL CONSIDERATIONS

In part the case for group representation, as presented in the preceding article, rests on faulty assumptions; we will review seven.

1. **The five groups under consideration are all definable entities with basically clear boundaries.** This assumption is important because we would need to be clear about who belongs to a particular group if we want to assign guaranteed seats to that group. While there is no difficulty in identifying the women in Canada, the situation is problematic for the other four groups. Who should be in the Aboriginal group? Would a person who is one-eighth Aboriginal and seven-eighths French-Canadian—and there are many such people—be part of the Aboriginal group or the French-Canadian group or both? What fraction of Aboriginal blood would be required? Would Aboriginal people be allowed to decide on fractions for themselves? Such kinds of problems are legion. The actual membership and boundary problems boggle the mind. Also, should we include in the Aboriginal group those Aboriginal people who don't want to be part of this racially segregated group but would rather participate in the category of general voters? Would we force them to be racially categorized?

Similarly, who would belong to a given ethnic minority? Would we require some racial tests? And what about the millions of Canadians who identify with more than one ethnic group? To ask the question is to think of enough problems to keep a small army of bureaucrats happy for years. Further, would a Chinese-Canadian husband and his Jamaican-Canadian wife vote for different slates of candidates, and would their twenty-year-old daughter living at home vote for a third slate of candidates? Would she have a choice?

Moreover, which ethnic groups and which visible minorities would qualify for separate and guaranteed representation? If we want to accommodate all organized ethnic groups in Canada, we would have to deal with at least 160 of them. If they each got even one seat—and the larger groups would insist on getting more—then more than half of the seats in the House of Commons would be assigned to these ethnic groups. And let us not wiggle out of this dilemma by suggesting that only the larger ethnic groups would be assigned seats. They already tend to win seats on their own. It's the scores of smaller groups that systematically and regularly get no representation. Perhaps one could argue that ethnic groups could be lumped together, for example, East Europeans, people from the Middle East, Blacks from Africa, and so on. But often the greatest animosities exist between neighbouring groups, such as Serbs and Croats, Jews and Arabs, Taiwanese and mainland Chinese, and so on.

Even agreeing on who in Canada should belong to the group termed "disabled" would be very difficult. Are we thinking only of paraplegics or quadraplegics? Do we include the blind? What about the hearing impaired? What about the visually impaired? What about the mentally impaired? What about those with perpetually sore backs? Do we include those who have AIDS? Would people with chronic fatigue syndrome qualify? And what about the thousands who are terminally ill with cancer or some other disease? They are certainly disabled and permanently so. Should these and others who could be listed all be included? They certainly all have disabilities. Furthermore, how much impairment creates disability? Who would decide? And would it be logical to assume that this diverse spectrum of groups would have a common political agenda?

2. Voters can be represented well only by representatives who share their social traits. Schouls states that "parliamentary representatives must share central experiences and assumptions with those they represent if those representatives are to understand their constituents' needs and interests." I find his argument unconvincing.

If we look at the professions of teaching, medicine, and law, for example, we find that effective representation and service do not require social similarity. I am confident that if members of the five identity-based groups were given the choice, the vast majority would rank competence as more important than social similarity. When people are sick, it is more important that they have a competent physician than that they have one from their own ethnic group. Similarly, people generally look for competent teachers, lawyers, mechanics, accountants, photographers, and other professionals and tradespeople. Why should we assume that it would be different when we turn to the profession of politics? Granted, social similarity is a significant asset, but it is not the most important criterion.

3. Parliamentary input will shape parliamentary output. The Canadian political system grants power and authority to a majority party or coalition, not to minority groups whose support is not needed by governments in order to retain office. Clearly, identity-based minorities would influence what is said in legislative debate, but why should we assume that such minority voices would affect legislative output, the policy decisions? (The special situation with the majority composed of women will be discussed later.) In fact, it would likely be the case that the majority rulers, either one party or a coalition, would be inclined to discount and marginalize the input of identity-based MPs with their narrow agenda because the rulers cannot realistically hope to win them over to the perspective of the governing majority. There is nothing to be gained by acceding to the requests of opposition minorities. Majorities can safely ignore such minorities.

Conversely, if these same identity-based MPs were members of the governing party, or even of the official opposition, they would have some hope of influencing policies and platforms, but only if they were prepared to accept substantial compromises.

As I see it, the error in Schouls' apparent assumptions in this regard is that voice equals influence. A second apparent assumption is that representation in itself, even having one or a few MPs advocating a certain perspective, constitutes power. Both assumptions, in my view, are faulty. All the eloquence one can imagine and a total sharing of social traits with one's constituents carry virtually no weight in legislative debate if there is not a political reason for the decision makers, generally the cabinet, to take such input seriously. A few eloquent MPs may achieve publicity, even popularity, but generally do not have significant influence on legislative output.

4. Political decisions grow out of parliamentary debate. In earlier times, generations ago, public policies may actually have had their genesis in parliamentary debate, but those days have passed. It is now erroneous to assume that important public policies, the type that the five identity-based groups would like to see enacted, are actually shaped in Parliament and are the result of MPs' input and debate. It seems safe to say that at least 98 percent of public policies in Canada are generated by the cabinet—which may get its ideas from many sources including pressure groups—and are not formed or changed to any significant extent by parliamentary debate. Just because an identity-based group has 5 or 10 percent of the MPs does not mean that it has 5 or 10 percent of the influence on public policies.

Schouls states that "marginalized groups," including the five we are considering, "want to be more fully included in the political discussions that shape the political identity of Canada as a whole." I seriously question whether parliamentary debates play a significant role in shaping Canada's political identity. It seems more accurate to say that these five groups would achieve more success in influencing Canada's political identity if they contributed informed input to cabinet members and senior officials before cabinet decisions are made. In this way they could also, with greater credibility, threaten voter retaliation, if need be, a tactic they cannot employ if the constituency they represent votes in its own elections or at least for its own set of candidates and the decision makers have nothing to gain by accommodating them. A group that is electorally hived off by itself should not expect to gain concessions from decision makers who have nothing to gain by making such concessions.

It could be that MPs who represent identity-based groups would become part of a governing coalition. In such a situation they might be able to influence policy decision but in virtually all cases only by making compromises, which is exactly what we have under our present system. In rare instances, such MPs might actually be able to topple a government. Such action would perhaps give the key MPs a sense of power, but it would not bring about the implementation of their political agenda.

5. **Women do not participate in politics as much as men do because the women "have been ignored and marginalized by the male hierarchy."** In earlier times this assumption was valid, but today it has little validity. My experience and observation lead me to conclude that in most situations, political parties, still dominated by males, bend over backwards to get qualified women to stand as candidates. They do so for the same reason that they often seek out ethnic and other minority people to stand as candidates—they believe that having such candidates increases their chances of victory.

If we want to find out why women remain relatively underrepresented in Parliament (although the situation is gradually improving), we must probe more deeply. Simply blaming men will not do. Electoral results and various studies have shown, as former prime minister Kim Campbell and many others could verify, that women do not necessarily or even disproportionally vote for women. Most female voters, just like most male voters, tend to vote for the candidate or party that they believe to be the best of the options. People are more sophisticated than to vote, blindly, for a candidate on the basis of which bathroom that candidate uses.

It is also the case, of course, that most of society, including many women, still believes that women can make their greatest contribution by providing a strong home setting. As long as that view is dominant there is likely to be a relative shortage of qualified women standing for office and being elected. This point ties in with another important reality, namely, that women have babies and men don't.

Any remaining societal barriers hindering political success by women should, of course, be removed. These barriers may include inadequate childcare in Parliament, inadequate leave policies for pregnancy, or inappropriate financial policies. We should not delude ourselves, however, by assuming that if we guarantee women a certain number of seats in Parliament we are thereby eliminating barriers.

6. **"The primary qualification to become an MP is purely and simply the ability to represent."** This assumption strikes me as being false. The primary qualification, in our electoral system, to become an MP is to find a way to get more people to vote for you than for any other candidate. Often the person who appears to have the greatest "ability to represent" is not elected. Many explanations come to mind as to why such an outcome is commonplace. For a variety of reasons, a candidate may get a huge sympathy vote. The strongest candidate may not belong to the most popular party or even to a credible party. The incumbent may have done so many favours and created so many IOUs that he can defeat all other candidates even if they are obviously more capable. And a certain party or party leader may sweep a lamentably weak candidate into office by promising major benefits to the candidate's constituency.

Once we acknowledge the fact that "simply the ability to represent" is not the primary qualification to become an MP, then we realize that there are key factors other than sharing social traits that shape political outcomes and that we should not concentrate primarily on social traits.

7. **"The presence of women in Parliament ensures that all the diverse and quite possibly conflicting interests of women will actually be heard and debated in Canada's central representative political arena."** For better or worse, such an assumption does not bear up under scrutiny. For one thing, no one can ensure that "all" interests will be presented. The significant subgroups of women, as well as of many other groups, are far too numerous to allow us to accept such an assertion as valid. In our parliamentary system, debate in Parliament will continue to be dominated by differences between government and opposition agendas, not by diverse values and perspectives among men or among women or among Aboriginal people or among ethnic groups. Those differences will, in the main, need to be debated elsewhere.

Moving beyond these ideological assumptions, we need to consider **several basic ideological issues.**

1. **Identity-based representation would increase social fragmentation in Canada.** That's exactly the opposite of what Canada needs at present. The biggest question we face is whether we have enough commonality to remain united. The country may not survive the injection of additional cleavages that pit some Canadians against other Canadians. In a free society, having a plethora of organized groups—religious, social, ethnic, economic, athletic, professional, and so on—is a sign of political health. But if these groups are elevated to the point of formal and official electoral competition, then differences tend to overwhelm commonalities.

This country would be dangerously weakened if social differences were incorporated into electoral struggles. We do not need the religious animosities that dominate Irish or Israeli party politics, the ethnic tensions that destroyed Yugoslavia and that perennially threaten Belgium and various other countries, the race-based policies that have bedevilled South Africa and other countries, or a parliamentary division that pits women against men simply because some MPs are women and some MPs are men.

Indeed, I would go so far as to argue that Canada has evolved into a stable, free, and tolerant country largely because our national legislature has not reflected the major cleavages in society and has not let these divisions become dominant in our national political agenda.

2. **Identity-based group representation raises insoluble problems of boundary and number.** Once we start categorizing people according to their personal traits instead of their possession of citizenship, where do we stop? Groups will quickly

realize that to be assigned guaranteed seats is the easiest, indeed, for some the only, way for them to be assured of gaining representation in Parliament. If we guarantee seats for women, we can safely assume that soon homosexual women will want to have the authorities guarantee them a quota of seats because as a small minority group among women, they probably would otherwise not get any.

Quite apart from the long list of groups, especially ethnic groups, that would quickly clamour for guaranteed seats, we would soon see a series of divisions and further divisions within the groups initially assigned seats. This problem raises another key question. Who would decide which groups and subgroups would be guaranteed seats? And would the same authority or authorities decide how many seats each group would get? The whole exercise would undoubtedly generate widespread disappointment, resentment, frustration, and anger.

3. The proposal to move to identity-based representation is condescending toward the five groups under consideration. Today, members of all of these five groups have the right to stand for office and to vote. Increasing numbers do, in fact, stand for office, vote, and win seats. Now, with progress well under way, we are being told that these groups are not good enough to make it on their own.

This proposal is condescending in that it assumes that women, who constitute 51 percent of Canadian society, do not know their own best interests or are too incompetent to vote according to their own best interests. They cannot be trusted to decide which candidates, be they male or female, will be the best representatives for them. They need to be told by the dominant male "hierarchy," to use Tim Schouls' term, that they should vote only for women. That's an insult. Why don't we let them decide for themselves who can best represent their interests? If they want to organize a women's party or if they want to vote for women, let them do so. But surely they do not have to be instructed by men or by our mostly male Parliament what they should do.

The same line of reasoning can be applied to the other groups. It may well be that some categories of voters in some parts of the country will not elect people who are their best advocates. But that's how democracy works. Democracy does not ensure that the wisest and most competent and the most effective representatives will be elected; it can only ensure, generally speaking, that the truly uninformed and the seriously incompetent and the utterly ineffective and those who would seek to destroy freedom do not become representatives in our legislatures.

4. The proposal would create first-class and second-class MPs. Presumably, in an electoral system that incorporates identity-based group representation, some women, some Aboriginal people, some visible minorities, some members of ethnic groups, and some disabled people would still be elected in the open segment of the electoral process in the way that they are elected now. Others would be elected by their own kind to fill guaranteed seats. It seems to me that very quickly a situation would develop in which those who were elected to guaranteed seats would be deemed to be second-class MPs because they were elected with special governmental facilitation. They could not make it on their own the way the others did.

One result of such a development would likely be that those who were elected to guaranteed seats would have less credibility in Parliament. Such a result would, of course, undermine the whole reason for embarking on the exercise in the first place.

5. To a significant extent immigrants should be assimilated into Canadian society; Canada should not serve only as a receptacle for transplanted societies from around the globe and should not tolerate the transplanting of tensions and animosities that exist in many of those societies. Generally speaking, ethnic groups in Canada should not expect governmental assistance in the perpetuation of their ethnic communities. Analogous to the shifting popularity of religious groups, the survival or disappearance of ethnic groups in Canada is properly the concern of the private sector.

This is, after all, Canada, not the immigrants' former country. Ethnic groups should, as I see it, expect gradual assimilation. In any event, they should not expect the Canadian Parliament to make provision for their segregated survival. Above all, we do not want ethnic cleavages and rivalries built into our Parliament. Guaranteeing ethnic seats would, in my view, seriously increase ethnic antagonisms. Let us assume, for example, that the responsible authorities would guarantee two seats to Indo-Canadians; it could hardly be more, given that half of the total seats would be assigned to women and many other groups would need to be accommodated. Immediately there would be fierce rivalries concerning who should be selected. Should Indo-Canadian Hindus, Buddhists, Sikhs, Muslims, and Christians all be given seats, with the groups taking turns electing their MPs? And what about the growing nonreligious subset?

Would the Canadian government, in trying to be fair, undertake to count the members of the various Indo-Canadian subgroups? It would be a mammoth task to decide which Indo-Canadian groups would get the assigned seats.

Surely it would be much wiser to let Indo-Canadians take their place as Canadians and eventually make their political contributions the way the majority of Canadians do. As a matter of fact, Indo-Canadians have already made important political contributions in various jurisdictions in Canada, even at the cabinet level. The same situation prevails for many other ethnic groups, including Chinese-Canadians and other visible minorities.

What multiethnic Canadian society and its government should promote is the identification and strengthening of areas of commonality. We need all the glue we can find to keep this country united. We do not need an electoral system that emphasizes and reinforces ethnic cleavages and thus also ethnic tensions and rivalries. To put it very candidly, Canadian multicultural policies, in electoral matters and in other areas, should guarantee freedom, tolerance, and respect, but in a truly free society these policies should not underwrite the political costs of ethnic group perpetuation, and they certainly should not undermine democracy in a futile attempt to guarantee ethnic group survival.

6. It would be very unwise to agree with the proposal that "no effort should be spared to get more minority representatives into the House. "No effort spared" means exactly that. These words may be a popular slogan, but the fundamental idea they convey is a great threat to democracy. Do we want the effort made to ban the nomination of nonminority candidates so that the minorities can win? Do we want quotas applied along racial and ethnic lines for the general elections? These and numerous other efforts should not be undertaken.

7. The term "political equality" needs to be clarified and then to be understood and applied appropriately. I have difficulty understanding what Schouls means by this term, one which seems to be central to his thesis. If he means equality of opportunity, then he is on solid philosophical and political footing. If, on the other hand, he means equality of influence or, even worse, equality of political outcome, then we have a serious problem.

Democracy cannot guarantee ideal outcomes. Freedom of choice means choice, including the right to make unwise or less than ideal decisions. It includes the right to make choices—in politics, religion, economics, and so on—that are not the most advantageous to oneself. It includes the right to make illogical choices. In the area of religion, for example, freedom does not ensure even the survival, let alone the good health or expansion, of any one faith. Concerning ethnic group survival in Canada, guarantees of freedom should only provide a climate of opportunity and perhaps some general tax and other minor concessions. They should not attempt to ensure or guarantee anything more.

With reference to the proposal for identity-based group representation, one needs to ask in what way would minority representation create political equality? It would create minority representation and not much more than that. It certainly would not create equality of influence on legislative outcomes.

8. The liberal approach to representation does not insist that MPs ought to represent individuals only. I question the statement that in the liberal perspective "representatives are elected to advance the individual interests of their individual constituents." Liberalism assumes more than that. Certainly Canadian MPs do more than represent individual interests. Even a brief reading of *Hansard* should correct such a misconception. Individual MPs from both sides of the House and from all parties frequently urge policy changes or initiatives to assist companies, towns and cities, ethnic and other groups, categoric groups such as families, women, taxpayers, or the unemployed, and, of course, the country as a whole.

For me, however, the main issue in this regard is not whether individuals or groups should be represented and promoted—clearly the interests of both categories must be upheld—but whether national well-being is being advanced. With Edmund Burke I believe that though individual representatives have specific responsibilities to their own constituencies, they should always balance constituency well-being with national well-being.

9. The election of MPs representing identity-based groups would likely produce chronic governmental instability. Most proportional electoral systems have some means, usually a 1 percent or a 5 percent clause, as in Japan and Germany respectively, to prevent the appearance of numerous one-person, two-person, or three-person parties in the legislature. Under the proposal advocated by Schouls, there could be no threshold exclusion clause. In fact, the whole intent would be to have a series of mostly small, special interest groups in Parliament that would be likely soon to become special interest political parties.

Such a situation would, of course, almost certainly produce a series of Parliaments without a majority party, and, therefore, a sequence of shaky and short-lived governments, unless the 153 or more women decided to govern as a bloc. Thus, in trying to address a problem of underrepresentation we would, in fact, be creating much more serious problems for Canadians.

One of the major reasons for general Canadian political and economic stability, even when separatists threaten to break up the country, is our majority cabinet system with its stability and predictability between elections. If no one party is permitted to field its own slate of candidates in all constituencies in an effort to form a majority government, we might well regularly produce minority governments consisting of numerous groups and parties and, therefore, vulnerable to disintegration in the face of separatist threats or various economic and political crises. We should not toy with such risks.

In passing, we should also note that small ethnic or other groups invited to join coalitions should not expect to make substantial headway with their particular agendas. The larger party or parties leading the coalition would likely have at least several small groups to appease, as best they could, so that each small group would likely get very little of what it wanted.

Such a situation reminds us again that in a democracy compromise is a crucial ingredient. The desire to implement narrow, doctrinaire agendas is not an important component.

10. Political accountability is greater when half or more of the members in a legislature are elected in single-member districts. Single-member districts, as in Canada's present electoral system, tend to create majority governments by disproportionally rewarding that party or those parties that are the most popular. While this system tends thus to distort public preferences, it also tends to produce governmental accountability.

If one believes, as I do, that an effective system of political accountability is a very important factor, then one is prepared to accept the distortion that the system creates. The distortion can, of course, be greatly reduced by the adoption of the dual German electoral system.

Given the broad economic and social scope of governmental activity in our day, it is surely important to know whom to thank and whom to blame. It is much easier to do so if a majority government is in place than if a broad coalition governs. Since most governments tend not to change greatly the general political direction and policies that they inherit when they take office, it seems more important that we should be able to hold governments accountable than that the composition of a legislature accurately reflect the social composition of society.

Furthermore, in the identity-based system of representation being advocated, it is not clear how voters could identify the official loyal opposition, that is, a "government in waiting," the likely alternative to the government of the day. The important distinction between two relatively clear sets of policies and politicians, offering clear alternatives to voters, would become very blurred or even disappear. That would be a serious loss.

11. Social, religious, or racial fragmentation of society probably constitutes a greater threat to political stability than does the geographical division of the electorate for purposes of electing a legislature. The proposal makes much of the supposed division of the electorate into geography-based constituencies. Schouls suggests that such a method of dividing voters "rests on the assumption that voters' primary political identity flows from their attachment to geography." As I see it, such an assertion misstates the point. The division of voters into constituency groups is a pragmatic and utilitarian means of getting MPs elected by approximately the same number of potential voters per riding with special provisions made for sparsely inhabited regions. As I see it, this system does not imply primary attachment of voters to territory or to anything else, although in some cases there is considerable racial or religious homogeneity. It is only a convenient way to divide voters, most of whom likely have nongeographic primary attachments, into groups of the desired size.

Above all, these constituency groupings are not based on social, religious, or other social tests, do not reinforce cleavages or animosities, and do not exacerbate tensions.

C. ARGUMENTS BASED ON PRACTICAL CONSIDERATIONS

1. The categories and percentages presented in the proposal raise numerous important problems and dilemmas. In the early sections of the article, Schouls emphasizes the importance of the "New Canadians with origins in the Caribbean, Africa, Middle East, Central and South America, and Asia." If, in his ethnic categories, he includes, as he logically should, all ethnic groups, including those not part of the visible minorities, that come from these regions, then the total becomes considerably greater than the 6.3 percent that he cites. Further, when he introduced his five categories he listed "ethnic and visible minorities" as two groups. What has happened to the ethnic groups that are not visible minorities? Having

acknowledged that "numerous visible and ethnic groups in Canada are able to put forward a very strong case," Schouls seems to have forgotten about the nonvisible ethnic minorities.

In the scheme before us, 153 seats in the current 301-seat House of Commons would be assigned to women. An additional 12 seats would be assigned to Aboriginal people. Given Schouls' strong commitment to equality, one must conclude that 6 of these 12 would be given to Aboriginal women. Of the 19 seats he would guarantee to visible minorities, we ought to conclude that at least 9 would be given to women. The result would be that 168 seats would be assigned to women, which means that the male voters, with 133 seats, would be seriously underrepresented. Or maybe the 6 aboriginal females would be part of the 153.

The situation becomes additionally complicated if we factor in the people with disabilities, who seem also to have been forgotten somewhere along the way, and, of course, the large groups of ethnic minorities who belong to distinct and cohesive ethnic groups but who, in most cases, are not physically recognizable.

Other complicating factors come to mind. Where would one place an MP, elected to a nonguaranteed seat, who is female, disabled, and Aboriginal? Would she be counted in one or all of those categories, or in none? Even more important, who would decide? And would the number of guaranteed seats be reduced if significant numbers of women and several Aboriginal people and members of visible minorities, or even any of them, managed to get elected to nonguaranteed seats? Surely the authorities could not simply let the number of seats allocated to the "others," the presumably nonvisible minority males, be markedly reduced or the whole scheme would go out of whack in that direction.

The assigning of individuals to the several voting groups would be a national nightmare. How would one categorize spouses in mixed marriages? How would the authorities categorize the children of these marriages? Would every Canadian have to carry a racial or ethnic identity card, a Canadianized version of apartheid? Presumably so, or the overall registering of voters could not be carried out in a way to facilitate the achievement of the stated percentage goals.

Additional major problems would involve the allocation of the twelve Aboriginal seats to the numerous competing groups, the allocation of the nineteen visible minority seats to at least twenty-five visible minority groups, and the allocation of whatever the appropriate number of seats is to people with disabilities. The challenges and problems boggle the mind.

2. We are not told how the electoral system would be altered to ensure that the guaranteed seats would be filled as intended. This is no small matter. Since relatively well-paid, high-status positions as members of Parliament are at issue, we can be assured that there would be a great clamouring for the occupancy and control of these seats. Who would handle the nominations? For example, concerning the women, would various organizations each be assigned certain seats? Would the National Action Committee on the Status of Women be given a bloc? Would Real Women be assigned a large segment, since they seem to represent a high percentage of nonorganized women? Would the women's organizations be allowed to nominate candidates who would compete against one another? Would there be primary elections? If so, who would pay for the costs? What about all of the other women's organizations? Would the guaranteed women's seats be spread across all of the provinces?

And what happens if most of the voters in a given riding don't want to be part of such a guaranteed constituency? Will they simply be told by whoever has the authority to tell them that their MP will be a woman, like it or not? What happens if all of the established parties in one of these ridings refuse to nominate anybody in such an authoritarian situation but a small women's pressure group manages to nominate a woman? Would that female candidate automatically become that riding's "elected" MP?

And what happens if, in a guaranteed woman's riding, a party nominates a male? Would the sex (or gender) police declare the nomination invalid on account of a candidate being the wrong sex? How would such a ruling be upheld given Canada's commitment to equality? How could such a ruling or policy be justified given all of the official legislative and judicial decisions, not to mention constitutional provisions, spelling out equality of the sexes?

If, perchance, the assumption is that the guaranteed women MPs, more than half of the House of Commons, would not be elected in existing ridings, then how would they be chosen? Would they be selected by women's groups, or one women's group, such as the National Action Committee on the Status of Women, without any connection to a given territory such as a riding? And how could this be seen as fair in that the women get to vote twice, once in the general election and, presumably, once in a women's election? Or are the 153 "guaranteed" female MPs not even going to be elected? If that is the intent, then how could this be done given the stipulations in the Elections Act and the relevant equality provisions of the Charter of Rights and Freedoms?

Furthermore, if it is fair to guarantee a specified number of seats to women, why is it not fair also to specify a number of seats for men? Surely that would be more equitable than giving special guarantees to members of only one sex. Would men be allowed to vote in the women's elections? Would parties still be allowed to nominate women in all of the nonwomen's seats? And what happens if, after all of the ballots are counted, the total number of female MPs comes to 60 or 65 or 70 percent of the House of Commons? That would be a distinct possibility. Would that constitute equality? Would that be more democratic than what we have now?

3. Who will administer the incredibly complex and probably unworkable scheme advocated in the proposal? Somebody will have to make many very controversial, often very unpopular, decisions. Some of the dilemmas would involve policy and others would involve implementation and administration. Is it assumed that the last freely elected House of Commons would try to implement this Orwellian manipulation? Is it assumed that the cabinet would issue an order-in-council or that the legislature would enact a statute, perhaps relying on article 33 of the Charter, the notwithstanding clause, to get this whole venture under way without having it aborted by the courts?

D. CONCLUSION

Tim Schouls is to be commended for urging that the barriers that many women and other groups face in politics should be removed. Unfortunately, guaranteeing seats does not in itself remove barriers. In fact, the proposal being advanced as a remedy creates more barriers than it removes.

Perhaps the major flaw in the proposed scheme is that it fails to accommodate the fundamental principle that democracy cannot, and should not attempt to, guarantee outcomes. Democracy cannot ensure that the ideal will be realized or even that the best option will be chosen. Freedom of political choice, like freedom of religion, includes the right to make wrong choices, wrong as some people or even the majority might define wrong. It includes the right to make choices that are not self-serving, self-advancing, or even well informed.

Throughout history, ideologues have tried to combine idealistic outcomes with democratic means—to do so cannot be ensured and no coercive attempt should be undertaken to try to achieve that goal. Political leaders and common citizens alike must rely on education and persuasion. Either the voters have free choice, within very broad and reasonable limits, or they do not. All else is undemocratic manipulation even if done in the name of democracy and equality. The French Revolution bears solemn witness to that fact. The proposed plan for representation based on group identity ultimately takes away choice, specifically the option to choose that which ideologues and true believers of various sorts deem to be improper and unwise.

The proposed plan, however laudable its genesis and honourable its intent, must be rejected as both undemocratic and unworkable. It risks the achievements that have been made in assisting the politically marginalized groups, and it undermines the prospect for further democratic progress. We must look elsewhere for the agenda for further success.

Postscript

In reading this debate, it is interesting to note the absence of discussion of class issues, especially in the article by Schouls. While he is concerned about increasing the representation of those marginalized in society, marginalization is identified primarily with the identity politics of ethnicity and gender. What role does class play in this analysis? Is the issue of class merely subsumed or transcended by issues of ethnicity and gender? What relevance, if any, does class analysis have to this debate?

Will Kymlicka is one theorist who Schouls uses to develop the philosophical basis for his argument. See Kymlicka's *Multicultural Citizenship: A Liberal Theory of Minority Rights* (Oxford: Clarendon Press, 1995) for a defence of granting differentiated rights to ethnic groups based on their vulnerability. For an interesting critique of this position, see Brian Walker, "Plural Cultures, Contested Territories: A Critique of Kymlicka," *Canadian Journal of Political Science* 30, no. 2 (June 1997): 211–234.

A number of good references are useful for pursuing this issue further. For two books that deal with the philosophical dimensions of this debate, see Jane Arscott and Linda Trimble, eds., *In the Presence of Women: Representation in Canadian Governments* (Toronto: Harcourt, Brace & Company, 1997) and Anne Phillips, *The Politics of Presence* (Oxford: Clarendon Press, 1995). For a book that tackles some of the practical difficulties of implementing proportional representation for social groups, see Committee for Aboriginal Electoral Reform, *The Path to Electoral Equality* (Ottawa: Committee for Aboriginal Electoral Reform, 1991).

It might be useful to consider the debate over proportional representation for social groups in the context of Issue Nineteen. There the argument is made in favour of granting proportional representation to parties on the basis of their share of the popular vote. If, as Redekop points out, there are a number of practical difficulties in implementing proportional representation for social groups, would a better approach be to emphasize proportional representation for parties? In this way, rather than being guaranteed a certain number of seats in the legislature, minority groups, women, Aboriginal people, and others could form their own parties that, under a system of proportional representation, would have a chance of winning seats and gaining representation in the House of Commons. Would this approach address some of the objections raised by Redekop?

ISSUE**EIGHTEEN**

Do Referendums Enrich Democracy?

✔ **YES**

BRIAN NEEDHAM, "A Better Way to Vote: Why Letting the People Themselves Take the Decisions Is the Logical Next Step for the West," in *The Economist,* September 11, 1993

✘ **NO**

MARK CHARLTON, "The Limits of Direct Democracy"

In recent years, the number of Canadians feeling a sense of frustration and disillusionment with Canada's political system has steadily increased. This discontent is rooted in the perception that Canada's political institutions are less responsive and less representative of the public's true interests. New political parties and special interest groups have emerged as alternative vehicles for political expression.

As more Canadians become disenchanted with Canada's system of representative government, they argue that simply voting for public officials is no longer enough. Canadians need to have the opportunity to participate directly in making their own laws. As a result, there has been a renewed interest in the instruments of direct democracy, especially the use of referendums, initiatives, and recall.

This wave of populist sentiment is reflected in a number of recent developments. The Reform Party of Canada has made direct democracy an important part of its party platform. It argues that citizens should be able to make use of citizen initiatives and referendums to give clear instruction to Parliament regarding the laws that should be passed. In addition, the Reform Party endorses the use of a recall procedure, which would enable voters to unseat members of Parliament who appear to be acting against their wishes. For Reformers, the October 1992 referendum on the Charlottetown Accord was a healthy lesson in the kind of direct democracy that should become more commonplace in Canada.

What is direct democracy? The concept of direct democracy is rooted in the notion that all citizens should have the opportunity to participate personally and directly in collective decision making about how they should be governed. Direct democracy may take a number of different forms. In a *referendum,* a policy question or proposed law is submitted directly to the electorate for approval or rejection, rather than being dealt with exclusively through the legislature. Referendums may be merely *consultative,* in which case they are intended to serve as a guide to politicians in their decision making on an issue. In Canada, these are generally referred to as *plebiscites.* Or, referendums may be *binding,* in which case politicians are required to enact the legislation that has been approved, whether or not the government agrees with the outcome.

Another common variation of direct democracy is the *initiative*, which is common in many American states. This method allows citizens to propose new laws that are then submitted to voters for approval. Each proposal requires a petition with a certain number of signatures before it can be added to the ballot. The procedure in effect shifts the whole referendum process into the hands of citizens, bypassing elected officials altogether.

A third technique of direct democracy is the *recall,* which allows citizens to remove a public official from office by filing a petition that demands a vote on the official's continued tenure in office. This technique enables voters to discipline elected officials who are not performing adequately.

The current wave of populist sentiment reflects an anti-party, anticabinet feeling that is impatient with the compromises and delays inherent in the parliamentary system of representative government. Our political institutions are rapidly losing their legitimacy, it is argued, because Canadians no longer sense that they truly represent our needs. Only by moving swiftly to give citizens more direct say in decision making will a profound crisis of legitimacy be avoided and confidence in government be restored. The Citizens' Forum on Canada's Future, chaired by Keith Spicer, found that what Canadians wanted most was a "more responsive and open political system, whose leaders—they think—are not merely accountable at election time but should be disciplined swiftly if they transgress greatly."[1]

In the following article, Brian Needham argues that the growing interest in direct democracy is a worldwide pheonomen and is a development whose time has come. Using the Swiss experience as a model, he suggests that the growing interest in direct democracy is a healthy sign of a populist revolution that promises to revitalize and strengthen democracies everywhere. In contrast, Mark Charlton argues that, despite their promises, referendums pose a number of serious problems that could undermine our system of representative government and further shift power away from elected officials to unelected and unaccountable special interest groups.

NOTES

1. Canada, *Citizens' Forum on Canada's Future: Report to the People and the Government of Canada* (Ottawa: Minister of Supply and Services, 1991), p. 135.

✔ YES
A Better Way to Vote: Why Letting the People Themselves Take the Decisions Is the Logical Next Step for the West
BRIAN NEEDHAM

The difference between today's politics and the politics of the coming century is likely to be a change in what people mean by "democracy": to be precise, a radical change in the process by which the democratic idea is put into practice.

The collapse of communism, everybody agrees, removes the ideological framework that has shaped the politics of the 20th century. One of the two great rival bodies of ideas has been defeated, and the other will be transformed by the consequences of its victory. This does not mean that the world is now wholly non-ideological; there will be other ideas in the name of which politicians will call upon people to follow them into the good fight. But the end of communism, and of the special sort of confrontation it produced, both reinforces the need for a change in the way democracy works and, at the same time, gets rid of a large obstacle in the path to that change.

In crude terms, this overdue change is a shift from "representative democracy" to "direct democracy." The basis of modern democracy is the proposition that every adult person's judgment about the conduct of public affairs is entitled to be given equal weight with every other person's. However different they are from each other—financially, intellectually, in their preference between Schubert and Sting—all men and women have an equal right to say how they wish to be governed. The concept sprang originally from the Protestant Reformation, which declared that everybody was equal in his dealings with God. The political offspring of that religious declaration is now accepted everywhere in the world, at least in principle, except among diehard Leninists and conservative Muslims. (The Muslim exception could be the cause of the world's next great ideological confrontation.)

In most places where it is practised, however, democracy is in a condition of arrested development. Every adult person exercises his or her political right every few years, in elections by which the voters send their representatives to an elected assembly; but in the intervals between elections—which can mean for anything up to about seven years—it is these representatives who take all the decisions. This is not what ancient Athenians meant by democracy.

Some countries do it differently. The most clear-cut example is Switzerland's system of direct democracy. In Switzerland it is possible to insist, by collecting a modest number of signatures, that any law proposed by the government must be submitted to a vote of the whole people. Even better, you can also insist (by getting more signatures) that a brand-new idea for a law must be put to the people even if government and parliament are against the idea.

Australia and some of the western parts of the United States also now use referendums in a fairly regular way. There have even started to be referendums in Europe outside Switzerland—the politicians in Italy, France, Denmark and Ireland have all consulted their people within the past year or so—though only on subjects of the government's choice, and when the government thinks it dare not deny the people the final word. But elsewhere democracy is still stuck at a halfway house, as it were, in which the final word is delegated to the chosen few.

THE DO-IT-YOURSELF WAY

There are three reasons for thinking that this is going to change. One is the growing inadequacy of representative democracy. It has long been pointed out that to hold an election every few years is not only a highly imprecise way of expressing the voter's wishes (because on these rare election days he has to consider a large number of issues, and his chosen "representative" will in fact not represent him on several of them) but is also notably loose-wristed (because the voter has little control over his representative between elections). Now the end of the battle between communism and pluralism will make representative democracy look more unsatisfactory than ever.

This is because the removal of the ideological component has changed the agenda of politics, in a way that has a worrying consequence. The old central question that is asked at election-time—Which of these two incompatible systems of politics and economics do you prefer, and how does your preference bear upon the decisions that must now be taken?—has disappeared. What is left of the agenda of politics is, by comparison, pretty humdrum. It deals for the most part with relatively minor differences of opinion over economic management, relatively small altercations over the amount and direction of public spending, and so on. The old war of principle, the contest between grand ideas, is over. The new politics is full of dull detail.

It is therefore ideal ground for that freebooter of the modern political world—the lobbyist. The two most dramatic things that have happened to the developed world since the end of the Second World War—its huge increase in wealth, and its explosion of information technology—have had as big an effect on politics as they have had on everything else. The lobbyists, the people who want to influence governments and parliaments on behalf of special interests, now command more money than they ever did before. They also have at their disposal a new armoury of persuasion in the computer, the fax machine, and the rest of it.

In the new agenda of politics, where so much depends upon decisions of detail, the power of the lobbyist can produce striking results. It will at times be, literally, corrupting. But even when it is not as bad as that it will make representative democracy seem increasingly inadequate. The voter, already irritated at having so little control over his representatives between elections, will be even angrier when he discovers how much influence the special-interest propagandists are now able to wield over those representatives. An interloper, it will seem, has inserted himself into the democratic process. The result is not hard to guess. The voter is liable to conclude that direct democracy, in which decisions are taken by the whole people, is better than representative democracy, because the many are harder to diddle—or to bribe—than the few.

This conclusion will be reinforced by the second reason for thinking there is going to be a change in the way democracy works. This is that there is no longer so much difference, in wealth or education, between voters and their elected representatives as there was in the 19th century, when democracy first took widespread root. It used to be argued that the ordinary man's role in politics had to be confined to the periodic election of representatives whose views he broadly agreed with, because the ordinary man was not equipped to take the hard, practical decisions of government (as those representatives, it was blithely assumed, were). A century ago there was something in this. There is far less now.

A hundred years ago fewer than 2% of Americans aged between 18 and 24 went to university; now more than a quarter do. The share of the British population that stayed in education beyond the age of 15 rose sevenfold between 1921 and 1991; in the western part of Germany, between 1955 (when the country was still recovering from Hitler's war) and today, the increase has been almost double that. The spread of education has been accompanied by an equally dramatic increase in wealth. In 1893 American GNP per head was $4,000 at today's prices; a century later it is $24,000. The average Briton's income has quintupled in real terms since the beginning of the century. The average West German's has more than quadrupled in the past half-century alone. Bigger incomes bring bigger savings, so more people own houses or shares or whatever. And the rising totals have been accompanied by a more even distribution of prosperity. "We are all middle-class now." Not quite; but we are surely heading that way.

The democracies must therefore apply to themselves the argument they used to direct against the communists. As people get richer and better educated, a democrat would admonishingly tell a communist, they will no longer be willing to let a handful of men in the Politburo take all the decisions that govern a country's life. The same must now be said, with adjustment for scale, about the workings of democracy. As the old differences of wealth, education and social condition blur, it will be increasingly hard to go on persuading people that most of them are fit only to put a tick on a ballot paper every few years, and that the handful of men and women they thereby send to parliament must be left to take all the other decisions.

People are better equipped for direct democracy than they used to be. The altered character of post-cold-war politics increases the need for direct democracy. And then comes the third reason for believing that change is on the way. The waning of ideology weakens the chief source of opposition to the new sort of democracy.

WHEN THE PARTY'S OVER

This opposition comes from the political parties that have grown up under representative democracy, since these have most to lose from changing to a different system. Parties are almost indispensable for the holding of elections, and they are the building-blocks of the parliaments chosen by elections. The introduction of direct democracy would instantly diminish the importance both of elections and of parliaments, since most big decisions would be taken by referendum, in a vote of the whole people. Parliaments and parties would not cease to exist; even in the fairly thoroughgoing "Swiss" form of direct democracy, they survive as partners of the referendum. But they would lose much of their old grandeur. The "representatives of the people" would perform that function only on the people's daily sufferance. This is why most political parties do not like direct democracy.

But they now have less power to resist it, because the end of the cold war has taken away part of the authority they possessed in the old era of ideological confrontation. Then, parties were the spokesmen of one or other of the two grand ideas, or of some variant of one of those ideas. They could also claim to or were accused of being, the instrument of a social class, a subdivision of mankind easily recognisable (it was thought) to those who belonged to it. It was in large part these things that gave parties their sense of identity, and enabled them to demand the loyalty of their supporters.

Now, in post-cold-war politics, much of this is disappearing. There are no longer heroic banners to be borne aloft in the name of ideology. In the wealthier parts of the world, at any rate, class divisions are steadily losing their meaning. In the prosaic new politics, many of the issues that have to be decided are matter-of-fact ones, requiring little excitement. In these conditions fewer people will feel the need to belong to parties, and people will more easily shift from one party, to another. This will make the parties weaker. And that will make it harder for them to oppose radical innovations—such as the bold step forward to direct democracy.

Politics is not about to become utterly homogeneous. In the luckier parts of the world, there will still be a difference between people who think that the most important thing is to make the economy work as efficiently as possible (who will tend to band together) and people who prefer to concentrate on looking after the unfortunates who get least benefit from this efficiency (who will form another band). In unluckier places, nationalism and religion will continue to provide the driving-force of political parties. The survival of religious politics, for instance in the Islamic world, will remind us that ideology has not been abolished; the fact that one ideological beast has just died, in Moscow, does not mean the breed is globally extinct. But, where nationalism and religion are not the dominant issues, it should be possible to reorganise politics in a less party-controlled, less vote-once-every-x-years, way: in short, in a more directly democratic way.

Of course, the move from a looser form of democracy to this more developed variety has to be made with care. It requires the ordinary voter to become more knowledgeable about a wide variety of subjects, and to use his judgment responsibly. It will take time for him to learn how to do it well. But a look at Switzerland, the country with the most systematic experience of direct democracy, suggests that the change presents no insuperable difficulty. The best subjects on which to start mass voting are, oddly, those at opposite ends of the spectrum of possibilities. At one end, broad questions about a country's future course of development —constitutional issues—are manifestly the sort of thing to be decided by universal vote. The governments of France, Denmark and Ireland correctly allowed their people to decide by referendum whether they approved of the Maastricht treaty on European union; the other members of the EC should have done the same, as a majority of voters in most of them plainly wished. Constitutional amendments in the United States could in future be made, or rejected, by referendum.

At the other end of the spectrum, the small, specific decisions of local government—Do you want to add a wing to the local school, or should the money go on road improvement instead?—are equally suitable for direct vote. In both cases, the voter can almost certainly understand the question that is laid before him, and answer it competently.

The difficult area lies in between. Opponents of direct democracy argue that the ordinary voter should not be asked to decide about matters which either (a) have a large emotional content or (b) are too intellectually complex for "ordinary people," especially if the complexity is of the financial sort. For both of those purposes, they say, the people's elected representatives can be trusted to do the job better. In fact, the Swiss experience tends to contradict this cynicism about the potential sophistication of the voters. In the 1960s the Swiss had an attack of the xenophobia that has since affected so many other Europeans. Strong passions were aroused. There were too many foreign workers in the country; jobs were being taken away from honest Swiss. And yet, after a long battle involving several referendums, the result was surprisingly restrained. A limit was set on the total number of foreigners who could come to work in Switzerland, but the limit was only a little below the number actually in the country at the time. Even more strikingly, the measure was framed so as to permit a subsequent rise in the total. Today, a quarter of a century later, almost 27% of the country's workforce, and more than a sixth of the total population, is non-Swiss.

More hesitantly, Switzerland has also pushed direct democracy into the field of taxation and public spending. The Swiss system does not in theory provide for referendums on financial matters. But it has been possible to get around this difficulty by the device known as the "initiative." In Switzerland, if you can get 100,000 signatures on a petition, you can insist that any proposal you feel strongly about must be put to the people's vote.

It was by this means that, in June this year, a group of Swiss took to the country their proposal that the country's armed forces should be denied authority to buy any new military aircraft for the rest of the century. The proposal had the double attraction of saving a large amount of public money and of appealing to post-cold-war anti-militarism; nevertheless, it was defeated. It was also this year that the Swiss agreed, by referendum, to an increase in Switzerland's petrol tax. These two recent examples make the point. Direct democracy can deal with complex matters responsibly, even when they affect the voter's pocket.

Deciding things by vote of the whole people is not, to be sure, a flawless process. The voter in a referendum will find some of the questions put to him dismayingly abstruse (but then so do many members of parliament). He will be rather bored by a lot of the issues of post-ideological politics (but then he can leave them for parliament to deal with, if he is not interested enough to call for a referendum). He will be subjected, via television, to a propaganda barrage from the rich, high-tech special-interest lobbies (but he is in one way less vulnerable to the lobbyists' pressure than members of parliament are, because lobbyists cannot bribe the whole adult population).

On the other hand, direct democracy has two great advantages. It leaves no ambiguity about the answer to the question: What did the people want? The decisions of parliament are ambiguous because nobody can be sure, on any given issue, whether a parliamentary majority really does represent the wishes of a majority of the people. When the whole people does the deciding, the answer is there for all to see.

Second, direct democracy sharpens the ordinary man's sense of political responsibility. When he has to make up his own mind on a wide variety of specific issues—the Swiss tackled 66 federal questions by general vote in the 1980s, hundreds of cantonal ones and an unknown number (nobody added them up) of local-community matters—he learns to take politics seriously. Since the voter is the foundation-stone of any sort of democracy, representative or direct, anything that raises his level of political efficiency is profoundly to be desired.

This move forward by democracy will not happen at the same speed all over the world. It is certainly not yet feasible in the new democracies of Africa and southern Asia. The new system requires the voters not only to be fairly well-educated and reasonably well-informed, but also to have a big enough share of material prosperity to understand why they are responsible for their country's future. Those conditions do not yet apply in much of Africa and Asia. Nor, quite possibly, will it happen very quickly in the Confucian region of eastern Asia. There the local 20th-century experiments with democracy still operate in a culture that pays great respect to the idea of authority, and respect for authority does not sit easily with the general sense of individual self-sufficiency required by direct democracy.

But in the heartland of democracy—meaning in North America and in Europe at least as far east as Budapest, Warsaw and Tallinn—the move should now be possible. Here, at any rate, the least bad form of government yet invented by man can advance from its present half-way house to something more like full application of the democratic principle.

NO
The Limits of Direct Democracy
MARK CHARLTON

In the current climate of cynicism and disillusionment with Canadian political institutions, reform-minded citizens argue that Canada needs a more participatory form of democracy that gives citizens the right to vote directly on critical issues. For many populist supporters of direct democracy, the use of referendums, citizen initiatives, and recall are seen as important steps toward the implementation of a more genuine form of democracy in Canada, giving Canadians renewed hope and confidence in their political system.

Despite these noble aspirations, the concept of direct democracy is not without serious shortcomings. Referendums and initiatives, especially if combined with other techniques such as recall, could ultimately prove to be disruptive, expensive, and damaging to the structure of government decision making without measurably increasing the quality of democracy in Canada. In fact, the experience of American states shows that direct democracy may simply represent a shift of power from one elite to another, without really giving effective voice to the aspirations of the "common" voter. Canadians should be aware of these shortcomings and potential dangers before pressing forward with this latest "democratic reformation." In order to make this case, we will critically examine the major claims that are generally made in support of referendums and initiatives.

REFERENDUMS ENHANCE CITIZEN PARTICIPATION

Proponents of direct democracy claim that it "empowers" the voter by transforming Canadians from passive spectators into active participants. Whereas citizens may ignore issues because they feel the outcomes are already decided by others, referendums stimulate citizens to take up their responsibilities, become informed on the issues that they must vote on, and voice their opinions. In short, referendums overcome voter apathy.

On the surface this claim is logical and straightforward. Citizens are cynical and turned off the political process because they feel voiceless and alienated. Citizens feel a greater sense of efficacy when they have a voice. As they feel more confident of influencing the political system, they become more active participants in the political process.

Unfortunately, the empirical evidence does not provide clear support for such claims. Certainly, in the case of Canada's national referendum in 1992, voter turnout and interest was high. However, this may have been a reflection of the uniqueness of the event and the sense of its historical importance. In countries, such as Switzerland and the United States, where direct democracy is a common feature, voter turnout is actually lower than in most other Western liberal democracies. In Switzerland more than 350 national referendums have been held since

1848. But compared with other Western European democracies, voter turnout is very low, dropping to 35 percent for referendums and initiatives in recent years. Many Swiss voters choose not to vote because of a widespread feeling of helplessness and a lack of political efficacy.[1]

This phenomenon has also been found in some American states where legislative proposals appear on virtually every election ballot. In examining the level of voter turnout in these states, David Magleby found that there is no strong correlation to the use of direct legislation. When voters were asked what brought them out to vote, only 2 percent named a specific proposition as the main reason.[2] In cases where referendums and elections are held separately, there are generally lower turnouts for the referendums. Thomas Cronin, a leading American authority on direct democracy, reports that in states where initiatives appear on the regular election ballot, as many of 15 percent of voters do not even bother to vote for them.[3] Such empirical evidence suggests that referendums are not any more likely to transform a spectator into a participant than the normal election process itself.

REFERENDUMS ALLOW THE COMMON PERSON TO BE HEARD

A second claim made for direct democracy is that the "average" voter has a stronger voice in government. This argument in part reflects a populist discontent with the "professionalization" of elections in which the citizen's role as participant seems to be usurped by professional party organizers, public relations firms, media pundits, and "expert" pollsters. In the process of creating "sound bites" and "photo ops," the needs and aspirations voiced by the alienated and marginalized voter are drowned out. In bypassing these intermediaries, direct democracy affords the common citizen the opportunity to be heard without distortion and reinterpretation by professional politicos.

A careful examination of the experience of direct democracy in other constituencies does not support this argument. In fact, the empirical evidence suggests that those taking advantage of the opportunities of direct democracy are generally unrepresentative of the general population. Studies in Switzerland show that most voters in referendums are between the ages of forty and sixty and are male, well educated, and affluent.[4]

The American experience also provides a lesson. In California, it is common for every election ballot to contain citizen-initiated proposals. An issue is placed on the ballot only after it receives a required number of signatures. In many cases, the proposal may be binding on the legislature if passed, thus letting voters write the legislation themselves. Surely, this system would seem to give the greatest opportunity for the marginalized to have their voice heard.

However, a closer look at the evidence is hardly reassuring. Political scientists have found that, in the beginning, civic groups and volunteer organizations took the lead role in gathering signatures for the petition process. But increasingly this task has been turned over to professional firms who pay petitioners for each signature gathered. In many cases, those who sign the petitions have little under-standing of what they are signing.[5] Over time the petition process has come to be dominated by special interest groups who can afford the expensive petition gath-ering process.

Special interest groups have come to dominate the entire referendum campaign process. Since the American Supreme Court struck down efforts to restrict cam-paign spending by interest groups, they may spend as much as they want on their campaigns, limited only by their ability to raise funds. Referendums have become big business, with professional public relations firms, media consultants, direct-mail specialists, and pollsters dominating every phase of the referendum process.

Interest groups now dominate the California referendum process because they use citizen-initiated referendums to advance their own special interests rejected or ignored by the state legislature. Thus, direct democracy can be a powerful instrument in the hands of special interests to circumvent the legislative process.

As in Switzerland, direct democracy in America does not seem any more suc-cessful in drawing those with lower educational levels and socioeconomic status into the political process. As David Magleby has found, those who benefit the most from referendums are those "who can understand and use the process."[6] In partic-ular, he found that the "less educated, poorer, and nonwhite citizens" failed to ben-efit because they lacked organizational and financial resources to have their voices effectively heard in referendum campaigns.[7] Those who dominate the whole direct democracy process, whether it be in initiating legislative proposals, campaigning for support, or actually voting, are no more representative of the population at large than is the case in other traditional forms of political participation.

Patrick Boyer, perhaps Canada's leading student of referendums, believes that "special interest democracy represents one of the most important challenges to Parliament and the Canadian people."[8] This is because "their recommendations and criticisms are seldom filtered through a broader consideration for the good of Canada as a whole."[9] Thus, Boyer defends the use of referendums because "any direct link that reconnects citizens and their elected representatives is valuable in part because it goes over the heads of those who speak on behalf of partial and vested interests."[10]

But, as the extensive involvement of interest groups in the 1992 federal refer-endum on the Charlottetown Accord demonstrated, such groups are unlikely to pass up the opportunity to have their voice heard. After the recent Canadian court decision to strike down federal restrictions on interest group spending during election campaigns, Canadians should not be so naive as to believe that California-style referendums, dominated by powerful, big-spending interest groups, would not come to Canada. Thus, rather than empowering the average cit-izen and giving voice to the marginal and alienated in society, referendums may simply mean the transfer of power and influence from one group of elites to another.

REFERENDUMS PROVIDE A BETTER FORUM FOR DEBATING NATIONAL ISSUES THAN DO ELECTIONS

Supporters of direct democracy generally argue that the referendum process, with full debate and consideration of an issue, provides the best forum for considering issues of national importance. They criticize their opponents for taking a condescending view of voters, feeling perhaps that contemporary national issues are far too complex for the average voter to understand. Many advocates of direct democracy argue that referendums fulfil an educative function, prodding voters out of their apathy and forcing them to define themselves. Thus, a national referendum is a civics lessons writ large, which can drive citizens to new levels of understanding by forcing them to concentrate on the "real" issues. Referendums are assumed to fulfil this function because they are qualitatively different from elections that are alleged to be "about people and personalities as much as they are about policy."

Nevertheless, there are serious doubts whether referendums do enable the citizenry to come to some new level of national enlightenment. In cases where referendums are used frequently, citizens are often overwhelmed by the plethora of issues. In many American states it is not uncommon for voters to be faced with a dozen or more referendum questions on the ballot. In the November 1990 mid-term elections in the state of California, there were twenty questions on the voter's ballot. The electoral guide explaining the questions for the voters took up 144 pages! Needless to say, even a well-educated voter can soon feel a sense of overload in facing such a daunting list of questions. Even when voters may have only one question before them, as in the 1992 national referendum, pollsters still found that a majority of voters complained that they did not know enough about the issue just days before voting. Thomas Cronin notes that the notion that direct democracy serves an educative function "was plainly overstated from the start."[11] In his studies of American voters, Cronin found that most voters do not make up their mind until the very end of the campaign, and that "as many as a quarter of those polled at the time of voting state that they could have used more information."[12]

But, the issue is not so much whether voters are competent or overloaded, but whether referendums provide a better forum for resolving national issues than election campaigns. Populists, like Boyer, rightly note that voters are tired of slick media campaigns and staged political events that give little opportunity for genuine debate and discussion. But, this assumes that referendums would be unencumbered by party partisanship, preoccupation with the personality of the party leaders, sound bites, targeted direct mailing, and the media's traditional obsession with horse race style reporting.

Nevertheless, there is little reason to suggest that modern referendum campaigns do not take on all of the modern accoutrements of election campaigns. In Canada, the 1992 federal referendum campaign provides some troubling evidence.

Although the campaign was unique in the way that political leaders from competing parties came together to support a common position, the actual conduct and reporting of the campaign were very similar to that of an election campaign. Political leaders staked out their positions, putting their political reputations on the line and feeling compelled to "win the vote." This ran against the expectations of many voters who complained frequently that the politicians were telling them how to vote rather than simply giving them neutral information on which to base a decision. The media reported the referendum much like any election campaign, focusing on the latest developments in the polls and on which leader had performed the best in a particular debate. Even the strongest proponent of direct democracy, the Reform Party, could not resist the temptation to launch an election style, personality-oriented campaign against the "Mulroney deal" in an attempt to capitalize on voter animosity toward the prime minister. Certainly this does not suggest, as referendum advocates would have us believe, that referendum campaigns are any freer of people and personality issues than traditional election campaigns.

REFERENDUMS ARE NOT DIVISIVE

A common concern about referendums is that they cause division and confrontation rather that lead to consensus and accord on an issue. Butler and Ranney contend, "referendums by their very nature set up confrontations rather than encourage compromises."[13] Concern about the divisive impact of referendums is especially relevant in Canada's case, where regional and linguistic cleavages have always made national unity a fragile thing at best.

In his book, *Direct Democracy in Canada,* Patrick Boyer argues that referendums will not unleash greater disintegrative tendencies in Canada. But a closer examination of the historical cases seems to undercut this position.[14] Boyer himself notes, for example, that Prime Minister Laurier responded to the referendum on prohibition by simply deciding not to adopt a single Canada-wide policy and by leaving the matter to provincial and municipal decisions. He also notes that Prime Minister King chose to delay the implementation of conscription for as long as possible because Quebeckers had voted so strongly against it. Thus, both referendums actually threatened to produce greater levels of conflict and division, which were avoided only by delaying implementation of the results of the referendums. This undercuts the more general populist argument that referendums are a more effective vehicle for national decision making because they avoid unnecessary delays.

However, Boyer seems to argue it both ways. On the one hand, he argues that referendums do not create divisions, they merely reflect them. On the other hand, he notes later that "of course, it is divisive; that is its purpose: to divide us up into those who favour a particular course of action and those who oppose it...."[15] But, as Butler and Ranney note, referendums "divide the populace into victors and vanquished."[16] Losers in a passionate referendum campaign feel a sense of betrayal and alienation. One has only to remember the bitter words of Ovide Mercredi on the evening of the October 1992 referendum to realize how deep these wounds can be. This is especially dangerous in Canada, where a majority of voters in one region of the country can be within a particular linguistic or ethnic group (francophones or Native people). The entire region may vote on the losing side of a referendum that vitally affects its interests. Such defeats can easily enter into the political mythology as yet another injustice forced on a dissenting group within society. Although Quebec voted against the Charlottetown Accord, along with most of the rest of Canada, many Quebec nationalists nevertheless interpret the defeat as another demonstration of English Canada's rejection.

A complicating factor here is that simple yes-no votes can in no way measure the level of intensity behind the votes. A small majority of voters who are largely indifferent to the issue or who have little understanding of it may vote in a measure. At the same time, a large minority of voters may have an intensely passionate commitment to its position. This is a sure recipe for producing an alienated and bitter minority that feels even more betrayed by the democratic process.

Defenders of referendums have proposed ways of avoiding this. For example, David MacDonald has recommended that a formula similar to that in the Constitution Act, 1982, could be used. Thus, for any national referendum proposal to pass, it would need the endorsement of seven out of ten provinces, making up at least 50 percent of the population. But recent constitutional experience has amply demonstrated that this formula has not worked well in permitting compromise on sensitive constitutional issues. It is unlikely to work any better in diminishing regional conflict over other sensitive national issues.

Part of the drive behind populist sentiment is an impatience with the delays and frustrations involved in the parliamentary system's reliance on compromise and brokerage. Referendums offer the opportunity of resolving in a relatively short time a controversial and sensitive issue that may have nagged at the country for years. It is often argued that by forcing people to stake out positions and resolve the issue in a final vote, referendums can have a cathartic effect on the body politic. This position overlooks the fact that referendums rarely ever represent the last word on the issue. Ireland has gone through three referendums on the abortion issue, and there is still heated controversy over legalizing some abortions.

MAJORITIES WILL ALWAYS MAKE THE RIGHT CHOICE

The populist sentiment that underlies the proreferendum movement reflects an impatience with the bargaining, compromises, and log-rolling that often appear to be a central part of representative government. Referendums are a way of short-circuiting that painstakingly slow process by directly asserting the will of the majority, without the mediation and reinterpretation of too many intermediaries.

However, there are real dangers in identifying democracy simply with the will of the majority. The whole history of liberal democracy has been an effort to come to some balance between the principle of majoritarianism and the rights of individuals and groups outside of the majority. One hazard of referendums is that they might easily be used as an instrument of one group to attack and undermine the rights and interests of other smaller groups. In the United States, citizen-initiated proposals have been used for just such purposes. In some southwestern states where the Spanish-speaking population has been growing rapidly, propositions have been put forward promoting the establishment of English-only laws. Similar efforts have been made to strike down legislation that prohibits discrimination against gays. These uses of direct democracy have led some minority groups to feel increasingly under assault at the ballot box and have exasperated tensions between various segments of society.

REFERENDUMS WILL NOT UNDERMINE REPRESENTATIVE GOVERNMENT

The populist argument for direct democracy reflects a pervasive frustration with the system of representative government found in a parliamentary system. Populists argue that their legislators are so heavily influenced by party policy and discipline that they can hardly be said to truly "represent" those that elected them to office. Direct democracy is thus seen as a way of making elected officials more directly accountable to the wishes of the voter.[17]

Is there a fundamental contradiction between direct democracy and representative government? Defenders of direct democracy argue its usage can actually strengthen the confidence and trust that we place in our representative system.

Despite this contention, there are three areas—accountability, leadership, and consensus building—in which direct democracy does threaten to undermine representative government.

(1) *Diminished accountability.* Representative government provides a clear means of identifying those who are responsible for public policies. A group of individuals are chosen by the electors and given a mandate to carry out the functions of government. We expect that at election time we will be given an opportunity to hold these members of government responsible for policies that they have produced.

In cases where referendums and initiatives are used on a regular basis, some studies suggest that "voters increasingly will bypass the legislative process, especially on issues that generate intense feelings."[18] But, this poses a problem in identifying who is actually responsible for the policies that are passed. As Neil Johnson notes, the "striking thing about consultation and the right to vote on this or that is that the person consulted or voting bears no responsibility for the decision and what follows."[19] If the voter has no real duties in carrying out the decision, is not held accountable for the results, and may not even be affected by the consequences, have we really moved toward a more responsible form of democracy?

It is easy for voters to make decisions that satisfy some short-term interest but for which they do not have to take any responsibility for the consequences. Elected officials realize that each time that they make a public decision, they will be held accountable for its results at the next election. This is not true for those making decisions in a referendum. Voters in Victoria, B.C., rejected a referendum proposal to build new sewage treatment facilities that would end the dumping of raw sewage into the ocean, a practice that has irritated not only environmentalists but also the thousands of Americans living south of Vancouver Island. While voters may have avoided the immediate problem of additional tax increases needed to finance the project, they have merely shifted the responsibility to future taxpayers who may also have to pay for the ongoing environmental damage. Businesses, facing a threatened tourist boycott by Washingtonians, will be left to cope with the economic costs of lost revenues.

(2) *Weaker leadership.* When voters themselves do not bear direct responsibility for their decisions, elected officials become more reluctant to make difficult decisions. Politicians may become apprehensive about making decisions that may be unpopular or deemed illegitimate if not referred directly to the public for a vote. As Thomas Cronin states, referendums, especially those on a national level, could "reduce some aspects of political leadership and policymaking in a large and diverse nation to a Gallup-poll approach to public policy."[20] David MacDonald notes that the danger referendums pose to representative government is especially potent if they are held at the same time as elections. The result, he argues, is "that a certain symbolic threshold would be crossed, and elected representatives would have limited legitimacy to manage critical issues of the day without direct endorsement from a majority of voters. Under such circumstances, governments would have insufficient discretion to establish priorities, to make choices, to affirm the value of minority interests, and to respond to changing political and economic events—in short to do what governments are supposed to do."[21] A wider use of referendums is unlikely to give disillusioned voters the stronger leadership they desire.

(3) *Lack of consensus building.* A vital function of representative government is to reconcile the various competing interests among citizens. Governments are most effective when they can develop a broad consensus regarding the major problems they are facing. However, Joseph Zimmerman concludes that "popular decision making in the form of the direct initiative and the referendum is incapable of developing such a consensus."[22] In Canada, the Royal Commission on Electoral Reform and Party Financing, in reviewing the evidence on referendums, also concluded that while they provide "citizens with more opportunities to express their policy preferences or to pass judgment on their elected representatives outside of general elections, they are less well suited to accommodating and representing the many different interests of citizens."[23] The commission felt this was a critical weakness in referendums since "effective reconciliation of these interests is crucial for any democratic government."[24]

CONCLUSION

Historical experience with direct democracy has several telling lessons for us. Referendums have not been very effective in addressing the grievances of disillusioned citizens. Referendums cannot ensure that voters do not feel alienated, nor do they guarantee that powerful interests will not continue to dominate contemporary political life. Referendums cannot provide a basis for creative and balanced consensus building. They do not accurately reflect the intensity of feelings on an issue. When voters realize that direct democracy cannot possibility deliver on all that it promises, they may feel even more alienated and disillusioned from the political process than before.

Direct democracy is not the path toward democratic renewal in this country. In his study of direct democracy in America, Thomas Cronin concludes that nationwide use of referendums is undesirable. Instead, he notes that "those who are dissatisfied with Congress should find ways to make it more responsive, accountable, and effective rather than inventing ways to bypass or supplement it with these potentially dangerous devices."[25] The recent Royal Commission on Electoral Reform and Party Financing sounds a similar note, arguing that the referendum issue actually detracts attention from the real issue—the need to strengthen the institutions of representative government. Many of the current concerns about the unresponsiveness of Canadian political institutions are really rooted in deeper concerns about the functioning of the present electoral system and the credibility of political parties. As the commission argues, "Strengthening representative government will ensure that individual citizens are provided with political institutions that reconcile conflicting views and interests."[26] This is clearly the direction that we need to take to achieve true democratic reform.

NOTES

1. Oswald Sigg, *Switzerland's Political Institutions* (Zurich: Pro Helvetia Division Documentation-Information-Press, 1987), p. 25.

2. David B. Magleby, *Direct Legislation: Voting on Ballot Propositions in the United States* (Baltimore: Johns Hopkins University Press, 1984), p. 127.

3. Thomas Cronin, *Direct Democracy: The Politics of Initiative, Referendum, and Recall* (Cambridge: Harvard University Press, 1989), p. 67.

4. Sigg, *Switzerland's Political Institutions*, p. 25.

5. Magleby, *Direct Legislation*, p. 62.

6. Ibid., pp. 183–184.

7. Ibid.

8. Patrick Boyer, *Direct Democracy in Canada: The History and Future of Referendums* (Toronto: Dundurn Press, 1992), p. 242.

9. Ibid.

10. Ibid.

11. Cronin, *Direct Democracy.*

12. Ibid.

13. Ibid.

14. Boyer, *Direct Democracy in Canada,* p. 250.

15. Ibid., p. 251.

16. Ibid.

17. It should not be surprising that those who argue for direct democracy are also generally strong advocates for relaxing party discipline in the House of Commons as well.

18. Joseph Zimmerman, *Participatory Democracy: Populism Revived* (New York: Praeger, 1986), p. 170.

19. Neil Johnson, "Types of Referendums," in Austin Ranney, ed., *The Referendum Device* (Washington, DC: American Enterprise Institute for Public Policy Research, 1981), p. 32.

20. Cronin, *Direct Democracy,* p. 194.

21. David MacDonald, "Referendums and Federal General Elections in Canada," in Michael Cassidy, ed., *Democratic Rights and Electoral Reform in Canada, Volume 10,* Royal Commission on Electoral Reform and Party Financing (Ottawa: Minister of Supply and Services, 1991), p. 331.

22. Zimmerman, *Participatory Democracy,* p. 172.

23. Royal Commission on Electoral Reform and Party Financing, *Reforming Electoral Democracy: Final Report, Volume 2* (Ottawa: Minister of Supply and Services, 1991), p. 229.

24. Ibid.

25. Cronin, *Direct Democracy,* p. 195.

26. Royal Commission on Electoral Reform and Party Financing, *Reforming Electoral Democracy,* p. 229.

Postscript

The current wave of populist interest in direct democracy is not new to Canada. In the 1920s and 1930s, there was a similar wave of populist, anti-party sentiment. Taking their cue from the progressive movements in the United States, Canadian agrarian movements organized themselves to challenge the two major parties, the Liberals and the Conservatives. Both parties, the populists charged, catered too much to the interests of economic elites in eastern Canada while ignoring the needs of farmers and workers. Because of party discipline, elected representatives were unable to represent the interests of their constituents. In the period following the First World War, these populist groups gained strength. The Progressive Party, after winning sixty-five federal seats in 1921, displaced the Conservatives as the second-largest party in Parliament. In Alberta, the United Farmers of Alberta (UFA) and the Social Credit Party came to power in 1919 and 1935 respectively, both selling themselves as parties committed to implementing a plebiscitarian democracy. However, once in power, both parties eventually backtracked on their commitment to govern by direct democracy and functioned much like any other parliamentary government. Despite their changed views, both parties also governed for long periods of time, using the traditional instruments of representative government.

A good place to begin examining the issue of direct democracy in detail is in the writings of Patrick Boyer. His book, *The People's Mandate: Referendums and a More Democratic Canada* (Toronto: Dundurn Press, 1992), provides a good overview of the issues relevant to the debate on direct democracy. Boyer's *Direct Democracy in Canada: The History and Future of Referendums* (Toronto: Dundurn Press, 1992) presents extensive historical information on the role of direct democracy in Canada.

In the two preceding articles, both authors make allusions to the experiences of other countries with direct democracy. The most authoritative and comprehensive source on the American experience is Thomas Cronin's *Direct Democracy: The Politics of Initiative, Referendum, and Recall* (Cambridge: Harvard University Press, 1989). A useful set of essays that compares the experiences of a number of countries can be found in David Butler and Austin Ranney, eds., *Referendums: A Comparative Study of Practice and Theory* (Washington, DC: American Enterprise Institute for Public Policy Research, 1987). David Pond's "Direct Democracy: The Wave of the Future?" *Canadian Parliamentary Review* 15, no. 1 (Winter 1991–92): 11–14, provides a useful review of the lessons that Canadians may draw from the American and Swiss experiences.

Charlton makes a number of references to the negative lessons that can be drawn from the American experience with direct democracy. Matthew Mendelsohn, in "Introducing Deliberative Direct Democracy in Canada: Learning from the American Experience," *American Review of Canadian Studies* 26, no. 3 (Autumn 1996): 449–468, agrees that the American experience "has only served to further entrench the power of well-financed interest groups and to professionalize the political process" (p. 463). However, he does not believe that this should be the basis for rejecting direct democracy in Canada. Instead, his article outlines some unique ways he believes direct democracy can be adapted to Canadian political culture to help revitalize Canadian political institutions.

One of the most thorough studies of a referendum carried out in Canada can be found in Richard Johnston, Andre Blais, Elisabeth Gidengil, and Neil Nevitte, *The Challenge of Direct Democracy: The 1992 Canadian Referendum* (McGill-Queen's University Press, 1996). They explore in depth the various reasons why people voted the way they did and how issues were perceived and understood by voters.

ISSUE**NINETEEN**

Should Canada Adopt Proportional Representation?

✔ **YES**
JOHN L. HIEMSTRA AND HAROLD JANSEN, "Getting What You Vote For"

✗ **NO**
PAUL BARKER, "Voting for Trouble"

In recent years, elections in Canada have led to some rather curious results. In the last provincial election in Alberta, the triumphant Progressive Conservative Party won over three-quarters of the seats but needed only one-half of the popular vote to do so. At the federal level, the Liberal Party secured a majority government in 1997 with only a minority of the votes, while Canada's other traditional party—the Progressive Conservatives—attracted the support of nearly 20 percent of all Canadians, yet won only 7 percent of the seats in the House of Commons. Perhaps most perplexing, the latest election in British Columbia saw the party with the *minority* of votes win the electoral contest and the party with the *majority* of votes lose.

On viewing these outcomes, one might be tempted to conclude that the Canadian electoral process had succumbed to a new system of mathematics. Surely, the degree of success enjoyed by a party in an election should be a direct reflection of the number of votes it receives. But that is not how the electoral system usually works in Canada. Instead, the system divides the country into a number of constituencies or ridings, and then declares the winner in each riding to be the one who receives the most votes. With these rules, a party may win many seats by relatively small margins, with the result that a disjunction between the distribution of seats and votes emerges. In this system, there is no reward for coming in second or third place. Only the first place finisher, the candidate with the greatest number of votes, gets to sit in legislative assemblies, and this is what leads to the sometimes unsettling results of Canadian elections.

An explanation, of course, is not a defence. For many, the single-member plurality system is unacceptable. As can be seen, it plainly distorts the preferences of voters, since it gives some parties too many seats and other too few. In a democracy, it might be argued, an electoral system should strive to represent the true wishes of the people, but this fails to occur in Canada. Accordingly, some have proposed a system of proportional representation for Canada. Though proportional representation comes in many variations, it basically allocates seats in proportion to the number of votes received. If a party obtains 50 percent of the votes, then it obtains 50 percent of the seats. With this system, the electoral oddities in Canadian politics would vanish, to be replaced by a more richly democratic result.

The case for proportional representation seems so solid that it is a wonder that the plurality system remains intact in Canada. Yet, there are points in favour of the status quo. Because of its structure, the plurality system increases the chances of electing majority governments, which are considered important to a stable governing process; on the other hand, proportional representation, because of *its* structure, ensures in most cases a string of minority governments. Stated differently, the plurality system reminds us of the adage that a "government must *govern* as well as represent." Another benefit of the current system, with its single-member constituencies, is that it forges a link between the voters and their representatives. Also, the present manner of electing officials is familiar to Canadians and easy to comprehend. Alternatively, arrangements for proportional representation can be difficult to explain and understand.

At various times, the matter of electoral reform has become an item on the public agenda. Now seems to be one such time. The results of recent elections have led to a questioning of the plurality system. The fact that Canada is one of the few nations that still uses the single-member system has also encouraged a debate on the nature of this country's electoral system. Eventually, Canada may join other countries in embracing one form or another of proportional representation. In the past, political interests—those who benefit from the plurality system—have helped to stymie reform, but they may not be enough this time to ward off the forces of change.

In the articles, John L. Hiemstra, Harold Jansen, and Paul Barker debate the merits of introducing a system of proportional representation in Canada.

✔ **YES**

Getting What You Vote For
JOHN L. HIEMSTRA AND HAROLD JANSEN

A commonly accepted principle of democracy is that governments should make decisions by majority rule. While a majority of the Progressive Conservative members of Parliament (MPs) passed the Goods and Services Tax in 1992, these MPs represented only 43 percent of the Canadian voters. This is only one of many problems caused by Canada's plurality electoral system. The plurality system fails to reflect Canadians' political opinions in the House of Commons. Using plurality to elect the House deepens divisions within Canada, weakens the accountability of MPs to electors, and undermines representative democracy.

This essay argues that the plurality method for electing MPs to the House of Commons should be replaced with list system proportional representation (PR). Both the plurality and PR systems have had mixed records in other countries, sometimes producing excellent and sometimes poor results. For Canada's distinct needs, however, PR is the best electoral system. PR would make every vote count, enhance national unity, give an accurate reflection of the political opinions of Canadians in the House, and strengthen the MPs' sense of obligation to the voters. This essay draws on national and provincial examples to make this case since both levels use the plurality electoral system.

A MODEST REFORM

In Canada, we use the single-member plurality electoral system to decide who will be our representatives in the House of Commons. The country is divided into 301 single-member districts, each of which elects one MP to the House. The winner in each district is decided by the plurality formula. Simply put, the candidate in a riding who wins more votes than the other candidates—even if less than 50 percent—is the winner and takes a seat as an MP in the House of Commons.

Adopting the widely used PR system would require only modest reforms to our current system. While it may be difficult to secure a parliamentary majority in support of these reforms, they can be brought about by a simple act of Parliament and without a constitutional amendment. The number of federal MPs per province is determined by several factors, of which population is the most important. Under the plurality system, the provinces are carved into geographical electoral districts with one MP elected in each district. For example, under the current formula, New Brunswick is entitled to ten seats in the House of Commons. To change this to list system PR, the provinces would not be divided into districts, but each province would remain a single district with multiple members. Thus, New Brunswick would be one district that sends ten representatives to the House.

Voting in a federal election under PR would be straightforward. In the New Brunswick district, for example, voters would receive a ballot featuring lists of ten candidates for each political party contesting the election. Voters would place an "x" above the list they support. The ten seats in New Brunswick would be divided among the parties based on the percentage of the popular vote that each party won. If the federal Liberal Party won 30 percent of the popular vote, it would receive 30 percent, or three seats. The three candidates at the top of the Liberal list would be declared elected. If the Tories won 40 percent of the vote, they would get four of New Brunswick's seats in the House of Commons. Thus, PR ensures that the MPs sent to the House from each provincial district would closely mirror the preferences of Canadian voters.

MAKING EVERY VOTE COUNT

As a democratic state, all Canadians should have a say in the composition of the House of Commons, since it deliberates on and approves the laws that govern us all. Sadly, Canada's plurality electoral system repeatedly fails to deliver just and equitable representation when it allows the "winner to take all."

The plurality system is often unjust when it fails to give each vote its "due." In the 1984 federal election, for example, less than 50 percent of the voters supported the Conservatives, yet they won 75 percent of the seats. That means one-quarter of Canadian voters did not get their "due" because they were represented by an MP from a party they did not vote for. The plurality system effectively disenfranchises these voters.

The injustice done by plurality is illustrated even better in two recent provincial elections. In the 1993 Prince Edward Island election, Catherine Callbeck's Liberal Party won 97 percent of the seats (thirty-one of thirty-two) with only 55 percent of the vote. This left 40 percent of the voters who voted Tory with one MLA and the 5 percent who voted NDP with none. More dramatically, in the 1987 New Brunswick election, Frank McKenna's Liberal Party won 100 percent of the seats with 60 percent of the popular vote. This left the other 40 percent of the voters unrepresented by the party they supported.

The other serious defect in the plurality electoral system is its inequity, that is, it often makes your vote count for less than others. For example, in the 1997 federal election, eight hundred eighty-six thousand voters in Ontario supported the Reform Party but the plurality system did not give Reform any seats in Ontario. Whereas in Alberta, the plurality system rewarded the five hundred seventy-seven thousand Reform supporters in that province with twenty-four seats. Clearly, a Reform vote in Alberta was worth a lot more than a Reform vote in Ontario.

Plurality is a "winner takes all" system that almost always overrewards the winning party. In contrast, PR is widely recognized as a just and equitable system that accurately translates the percentage of the vote each party wins into a proportionate percentage of seats in the House of Commons. PR greatly reduces the injustice and inequity that is so common in the plurality system. In short, PR gives you what you vote for, which is reason enough to adopt the system in Canada.

PROPORTIONAL REPRESENTATION AND GOVERNMENT EFFECTIVENESS

Proportional representation is almost always acknowledged as the fairest electoral system. Yet some still reject PR for Canada because they fear it would make the government ineffective. They argue that the plurality method produces stable and effective majority governments out of minority electoral returns, while PR would produce unstable and ineffective minority governments. This implies that Canadians must make an unacceptable choice between the value of effectiveness and the values of justice and equity. Fortunately, the facts show that we do not have to make this decision.

The experiences of other countries indicate that the improved representation provided by PR need not come at the expense of effective government. Arend Lijphart, a noted expert on electoral systems, found in a comparative study of established democracies that countries using PR maintain public order and manage the economy as well as countries that use majoritarian electoral systems, such as plurality.[1]

Besides this comparative evidence, we can look at Canada's experience with minority governments. Canada has had effective government since well before Confederation. Yet there does not seem to be any connection between this effectiveness and the plurality electoral system being able to produce majority governments. Between 1962 and 1992, Canada's plurality system produced six minority and six majority governments, which is not exactly a stellar record.[2] In spite of these minority governments, Canada's governments have generally been effective. In his seminal study of Canada's Parliament, Franks concludes that "there is no evidence that minority parliaments are less efficient than majorities."[3]

It is true that minority governments have tended to fall more quickly than majority governments in Canada. However, this is less due to the inherent instability of minority governments and more to the incentive the plurality system gives to some parties to collapse minority governments. The large parties know that a small shift in the vote toward their party will often be translated by the plurality system into a majority government for them.

If Canada adopted PR, minority and coalition governments would be more common. But we have already seen that the frequent minority governments under the plurality system in the past did not render the government ineffective. Nor is it the case that coalition governments are automatically weak or unstable. In PR systems, political parties normally win a steady percentage of the vote in each election. This neutralizes the incentive plurality gives to parties to collapse minority or coalition governments. Since forcing an election under PR will not dramatically alter party strengths, parties are encouraged to work for just policy compromises within Parliament. Thus, coalition governments will be able to "get things done" for Canada. The improvement is that coalitions get things done while involving a majority of the MPs who truly represent a majority of Canadians. PR gets rid of artificial-majority governments that make decisions on issues such as the deficit and reform to the health care system with support from less than half of the voters.

Critics also suggest that PR causes unstable governments by promoting too many small parties. Under plurality, however, Canada has already produced many small parties, a contradiction of "Duverger's law," which asserts that a plurality electoral system tends to produce a two-party system. This diversity of smaller parties should not be denied since it reflects the views of Canadians. Moreover, except for Ontario and Quebec, the provincial electoral districts proposed here would have relatively few MPs. Parties would still require a significant proportion of the vote to earn representation in the House of Commons.

PROPORTIONAL REPRESENTATION CAN INCREASE NATIONAL UNITY

Some critics also argue that PR would be detrimental to national unity. They charge that it would magnify divisions between regions and between English and French cultures. While the plurality electoral system has treated this diversity unfairly, some claim that at least plurality has kept our country stable and united. The facts show, however, that quirks in plurality actually serve to worsen these divisions in Canada.

One tendency of the plurality system is to "reward" small, regionally concentrated parties. For example, the federal Social Credit Party regularly won more seats in Quebec than its popular vote justified. In 1968, Social Credit won 4.4 percent of the popular vote but took 20 percent of the Quebec seats. PR would give small parties their electoral due, without allowing them an unfair number of seats.

A particularly troublesome feature of plurality's tendency to reward regionally concentrated parties is that some regional parties have promoted separatism or a sectional view of Canada. The plurality system has multiplied the negative impact of these regional parties by rewarding them with far more seats than their electoral support warrants. In the 1993 election, for example, the separatist Bloc Québécois won 72 percent of the seats in Quebec with the support of only 49.2 percent of Quebec voters. In 1997, the party won 59 percent of the seats with 38 percent of the vote. This also occurred in several Quebec provincial elections where the plurality system allowed the separatist Parti Québécois to win majority governments with only a minority of the provincial vote. For example, in 1994, the PQ won 77 of 125 seats in Quebec's National Assembly with 44.8 percent of the vote, while the provincial Liberal Party won only 47 seats with 44.4 percent of the vote.[4]

Another bias of the plurality electoral system is that it hurts small national parties with supporters dispersed across the country. For example, the NDP is a national party with a democratic socialist vision that has some support in all regions of the country. Yet, under the plurality system it always receives fewer seats in the House of Commons than its support would justify. In the 1993 federal election, for example, the NDP was reduced to nine seats (3.1 percent) in the House of Commons, even though the party earned 6.9 percent of the vote. In

— not proportional.

1997, the NDP won more votes than the Bloc Québécois but earned less than half as many seats. Unfortunately, the plurality system hurts small parties with regionally dispersed support even when they promote a unifying national vision.

The plurality system is also predisposed to overreward large parties in regions where they have strong support while underrewarding them where their support is weak. Thus, Canada often lacks truly national parties in the House. When large parties win the majority of the seats, in one region but none in another region, divisions in Canada are perpetuated and worsened. For example, in the 1980 federal election, the Liberal Party formed the government but did not win a single seat in British Columbia, Alberta, or Saskatchewan, although it won over 20 percent of the vote in these provinces. Meanwhile, the Liberals won 74 of 75 seats, or 99 percent of the seats in Quebec, with 68 percent of the popular vote. In 1997, the Reform Party won almost 20 percent of the vote in Ontario but did not elect any MPs. This flaw leads voters to develop a regionally skewed perception of the parties' support. It also handicaps the governing and opposition parties' ability to include regional viewpoints in their caucus discussions. In fact, plurality gives parties an incentive to favour regions where they might receive large electoral payoffs, while ignoring other regions.

The weaknesses of the plurality system, Alan Cairns concludes, make Canada's electoral system "divisive and detrimental to national unity."[5] PR is a better way to handle Canada's regional divisions since it gives seats to national parties in direct proportion to the percentage of the popular vote they win in the election. Since every vote counts in PR, parties have a strong incentive to take a national viewpoint on issues and to search for votes in all regions. PR encourages the growth of parties that will integrate the regions of Canada. PR also gives party caucuses representation from each region of Canada, thus allowing parties to more fully understand the needs of all regions. At the same time, PR still permits small parties to form in response to the genuine regional needs, but without overrewarding these parties.

Why does Canada remain stable even though the plurality system produces minority governments and encourages destabilizing regional parties? Much of the answer lies in Canada's strong, democratic, and tolerant political culture. Adopting PR would not suddenly change this. Nor would PR transform Canada into an unstable regime like pre–Second World War "Weimar Germany."[6] Canada's strong, democratic political culture has kept and will continue to keep our system stable. Canada with PR would more likely resemble the Netherlands, which has used PR for seven decades and remains eminently stable and unified in spite of its serious societal divisions.

PROPORTIONAL REPRESENTATION IS EASY TO USE

It is often claimed that the plurality electoral system is the simplest and thus the best electoral system. The plurality system is certainly simple. The candidate who wins more votes than the other candidates—even if it is less than 50 percent of the total popular vote—wins the riding. The calculations are straightforward. Plurality, however, also requires the drawing and redrawing of district boundaries every time the population grows or shifts. This complex and time-consuming process encourages corrupt practices such as malapportionment and gerrymandering.[7] In the last few years alone, Alberta, Saskatchewan, and British Columbia have all faced major court challenges over the fairness of their electoral boundaries.

List system PR is easy to understand and use.[8] While the calculations are more complicated, PR does not require any more from the voter than does plurality. As stated above, using list system PR is simple. The ballot for each provincial district contains as many lists of candidates as there are parties contesting the election. You vote by marking your preferred list. The percentage of the vote each party won is counted, and the same percentage of candidates from the top of each party's list are declared elected. Since PR would treat provinces as districts, it would be immune to malapportionment or gerrymandering of riding boundaries.

FIRST-PAST-THE-POST PRODUCES FALSE MAJORITY GOVERNMENTS

Another claim for the plurality electoral system is that it allows voters to select a government at the same time as they elect their representatives. Indeed, forming a cabinet is largely routine in Canada's parliamentary system, where the party winning the most seats usually forms the government. But it is an illusion to suggest that voters purposefully or automatically select a government. In fact, the majority of Canadians have not been involved in selecting most of Canada's governments. Since the Second World War, only two of our national governments have been formed by a party that won a majority of the popular vote in an election (in 1958 and 1984).

The plurality system actually allows a minority of voters to select the majority of the seats, and thus to select the government. This problem with plurality is closely related to Canada's multiparty system. In the 1997 federal election, when five major parties contested the election, the plurality system translated the Liberals' 38 percent of the vote into a majority government. These results were not an anomaly; such distortions occur repeatedly in federal and provincial elections.

The plurality electoral system frequently magnifies a small shift in the vote to determine who will form the next government. In the 1979 election, Joe Clark's Conservatives were supported by 36 percent of Canadians and took 48 percent of the seats to form a minority government. The Liberals gathered 40 percent of the vote and took 40 percent of the seats. In the 1980 election, the Liberals increased their share of the vote by only 4 percent, but won a clear majority government with 52 percent of the seats. And in the following election of 1984, a shift of 17 percent of the vote to the Mulroney-led Tories allowed them to increase their seats by 38 percent, from 37 percent to 75 percent of the seats.

This type of chancy outcome in the formation of governments under plurality is illustrated even more pointedly in two provincial elections in British Columbia. The NDP failed to form the government in 1986 when their 42.6 percent of the vote translated into 31.9 percent of the seats. In the 1991 election, however, the NDP's popular support dropped to 41 percent of the vote, yet the party took 68 percent of the seats and formed the new government. Sometimes, plurality allows a party to win more seats and form the government with fewer votes than the main opposition party. In the 1979 federal election, for example, the Conservatives formed the government when they won 36 percent of the vote and 136 seats, while the Liberals won 40 percent of the vote and only 114 seats.

Selecting a government through the plurality electoral system has the further side effect of distorting the public's perception of the parties' strengths. A month after the 1988 federal election, nobody remembered that the Tories won 57 percent of the seats with only 43 percent of the vote. The public is constantly reminded of the percentage of seats a party won, but not the percentage of the vote it won. Yet Mulroney used his minority electoral support to pass the highly unpopular Goods and Services Tax as well as the controversial free trade agreement with the United States. Governments should make dramatic policy changes only if they are selected and supported by the majority of Canadians.

It is a mistake to think that we can solve the problems created by the plurality system by abolishing Canada's multiparty system rather than by reforming the electoral system itself. We must accept that Canadians have deeply held political views and choose different parties to express these views. The democratic answer is to amend our electoral system so that it responds to the beliefs and actions of Canadians, and not to force the system to produce the result the critics want. The real challenge is to allow the deeply held political views of Canadians to be properly, safely, and fairly expressed in politics. People with different ethnic, religious, or ideological views often arrive at, or endorse, a particular policy for their own distinct reasons. A PR system will give no viewpoint a hegemonic grip on the system but will force all parties to discuss their real differences as a means of arriving at mutually acceptable policies.

Since PR would make the House of Commons accurately reflect the opinions and views of Canadians, it would be better to shift the duty of forming governments away from "chance" and to our MPs. This would give the majority of voters a stronger say in the creation of government. It would place the task of forming governments in the hands of our MPs, who currently hold the power of dissolving governments. This conforms with and develops Canada's parliamentary theory.

FIRST-PAST-THE-POST WEAKENS REPRESENTATIVE DEMOCRACY

Indeed, voters would have a greater say over all aspects of their MPs' actions if MPs were obliged to represent their supporting voters. The plurality electoral system, however, is weakening representative democracy in Canada.

Representative democracy was created in response to the increasing number of citizens entitled to be involved in politics, but who lacked the time or energy to study political issues and devise fitting solutions. Most Canadians expect their representatives to engage actively in policymaking for them. Even so, plurality fails to give representatives a clear mandate from the voters and does not allow voters to hold MPs responsible for their actions.

Instead, the plurality system is increasingly encouraging Canadians to weaken or even bypass representative democracy. The weakening of the relationship between voters and representatives occurs because plurality requires politicians and parties to compromise too early in the process. Before an election, politicians are forced to develop lowest common denominator policies that will appeal to a plurality of voters in each riding. For example, some voters believe the state should strongly intervene to protect the environment while others believe market forces will correct environmental problems. In response to this spectrum of opinions, political parties develop a compromised platform that homogenizes the environmental views of Canadians. This is done to attract the widest range of voters necessary to win a plurality of votes in a single district.

Early compromises on policy produce pragmatic, look-alike parties. Election campaigns increasingly focus on party leaders and image and downplay principles, policy platforms, and the teams of politicians behind the leaders. Pragmatic parties make principled discussion rare in the House of Commons and foreclose the opportunity for compromise between principled party platforms. Consequently, voters seldom know what their MPs and parties stand for and find it difficult to hold them accountable. At the same time, MPs do not receive clear mandates from voters. In these and other respects, plurality weakens the relationship between voters and representatives.

The much vaunted "close contact" between a representative and a voter in the plurality electoral system is largely illusory. Certainly, if a voter has trouble with Revenue Canada, his or her MP will help. But should you want your MP to represent your principles in a debate on major taxation legislation, he or she will refuse for fear of offending other voters who the MP needs in order to gain reelection. The plurality system encourages MPs and political parties to reflect some limited concerns of their geographic districts while ignoring the deeply held principles of the voters. MPs seem to feel very little moral obligation to act for their voters on matters of principle, except when necessary for reelection.

Increasingly, voters are turning away from these indistinct parties and turning to interest groups for better representation. Political parties are responding to this challenge to their representative role by merely becoming brokers for the interest groups. Other voters are pushing reforms such as recall, referendums, and initiatives, which bypass representative democracy.[9] Thus, the dynamic set in motion by plurality actually encourages voters to bypass their representatives, a process that is undermining the very essence of representative democracy.

INCREASING THE REPRESENTATIVES' OBLIGATIONS TO VOTERS

In opposition to plurality, a PR electoral system would strengthen Canada's political system by encouraging a new dynamic. PR encourages strong political parties, but would force them to define how they are distinct from the others in order to attract votes. To compete effectively, parties would need to develop clearer principles and to define their policy platforms. This would allow political parties to become vehicles for voters to give mandates to MPs and to hold them accountable between elections. MPs would clearly be obliged to act in accordance with the principles and policies that they agreed to with supporters. This would include serving the individual voters according to these principles, if the parties want to maintain electoral support. MPs with a sense of obligation to voters would be a clear advance over the plurality system, which limits voters to rubber-stamping or jettisoning representatives at election time.

While PR would encourage a sense of obligation between representatives and their supporters, it would not guarantee this outcome. However, evidence from other countries shows that PR has been superior to plurality in bringing in minority parties. It has also increased the parliamentary representation of women, ethnic groups, and cultural minorities.[10] Significantly, PR has done so without extensive affirmative action programs. PR has also allowed parties to increase the overall quality of individual MPs on their lists. PR also allows citizens to be free to join the political party of their choice and to decide whether their party's MPs will be "trustees" who will deliberate independently on issues, "delegates" who mechanically reflect their views, "mirrors" that reflect their gender, age, ethnic, or other characteristics, or defenders of their party's interests and positions.[11] If "party bosses" dominate under PR, it will be the fault of those who create parties that tolerate them.

PR allows parties and governments to be as good or as flawed as the people they represent. It leaves the public free to decide which groups or principles or approaches they want represented, by creating parties to reflect these concerns. PR ultimately leaves the voters to decide which parties they want to be represented by in the House of Commons. For example, if 7 percent of Canadians support the Green Party's approach to environmental issues, PR will give it 7 percent of the seats, no more and no less.

CONCLUSION

Democratic principles are the foundation upon which political life in Canada rests. The plurality and PR electoral systems are structures through which Canadians can exercise their democratic choices. But structures are not neutral. They reflect values that the people in a society want the system to advance, and thus encourage citizens to act in a certain way. The dominant value of the plurality system is stability—which it is supposed to achieve by translating a minority of votes into a majority government. In spite of the plurality electoral system, however, Canada has frequently produced minority governments. The plurality system also produces electoral outcomes that aggravate and intensify Canada's regional and nationalist divisions. Too many outcomes of the plurality electoral system have been chancy, unfair, and inequitable. Also, plurality has encouraged the growth of pragmatic and brokerage parties that weaken the incentives of MPs to represent their voters. In spite of these problems, Canada's remains a stable, democratic political system.

Since Canada is stable in spite of the plurality system, it has ample room to add the values of justice and equity to stability by adopting a PR electoral system. PR makes every vote count and produces results that are proportionate to what voters desire. Canada's distinctive needs would also be best served by PR. It would increase Canada's stability by improving regional representation in major parties, while reducing the unjustified strength of small divisive parties that happen to have regionally concentrated support.

The biggest asset of PR, however, is that it enhances representative democracy by encouraging MPs and parties to develop a clearer profile on principles and policies. Voters will have a better idea of the mandate they are giving to MPs and thus be able to hold MPs accountable for their principles, policies, and political actions. A PR electoral system should be adopted in Canada, since it is the fairest and most effective way to involve Canadians in their representative democracy.

NOTES

1. Arend Lijphart, "Democracies: Forms, Performance, and Constitutional Engineering," *European Journal of Political Research* 25 (1994): 1–17.

2. The plurality system not only fails to produce regular majority governments but frequently fails to produce the strong oppositions needed to effectively run a parliamentary system. See Alan C. Cairns, "The Electoral System and Party System in Canada, 1921–1965," *Canadian Journal of Political Science* 1 (1968): 55–80.

3. C.E.S. Franks, *The Parliament of Canada* (Toronto: University of Toronto Press, 1987), p. 50.

4. In 1976, the Parti Québécois formed the provincial government with 71 of 110 seats but only 40 percent of the popular vote. In 1981, it won 80 of 122 seats with 49 percent of the vote.

5. Cairns, p. 92.

6. Enid Lakeman reports that if Weimar Germany had used plurality, the Nazis would likely have won all the seats; cited in Michael Lind, "A Radical Plan to Change American Politics," *The Atlantic Monthly*, 270, no. 2 (August 1992), pp. 73–83.

7. Malapportionment is the practice of skewing the number of voters in each riding so that the electoral outcome favours one of the political parties. Gerrymandering involves reshaping districts to alter their partisan composition so the electoral outcome favours one party.

8. Other types of PR, such as the single transferable vote, are more complicated, but, as *The Economist* states, "the Irish can work it, so why not others?" "Electoral Reform," May 1, 1993, p. 21.

9. See Nick Loenen, *Citizenship and Democracy: A Case for Proportional Representation* (Toronto: Dundurn, 1997), ch. 5, for a comparison of PR with these other reforms.

10. Arend Lijphart and Bernard Grofman, *Choosing an Electoral System: Issues and Alternatives* (New York: Praeger, 1984), p. 7.

11. Several conflicting definitions of representation confuse this debate; see Hanna Fenichel Pitkin, *The Concept of Representation* (Los Angeles: University of California Press, 1967).

✗ **NO**
Voting for Trouble
PAUL BARKER

At first glance, proportional representation (PR) is an attractive proposal for reforming Canada's electoral system. It promises to make the House of Commons more representative of the population and in so doing enhance the legitimacy of public authorities. It also speaks to our concern for fairness and equity through its impartial treatment of both parties and voters. Perhaps most important, PR replaces an electoral system that aggravates regional tensions in this country with one that lessens them.

On close inspection, though, the shortcomings of PR become evident. PR creates new problems, the most important of which is weak and unstable government. It also underestimates the advantages of the present way we elect members, and falls well short of delivering on its own promises. Finally, it exaggerates the importance of the electoral system. On certain matters of significance, proponents of PR believe—mistakenly—that adjusting electoral rules will make a major difference.

BACKGROUND

Democracies all have their own set of rules for structuring the electoral process. In Canada, the rules in most instances stipulate the existence of geographically based constituencies or ridings in which parties present their candidates for election. Persons residing in these constituencies consider the candidates and make a choice. The candidate with the greatest number of votes—which may not be a majority of the votes—wins the constituency and the right to represent the riding in the House of Commons. Usually, the party that prevails in the greatest number of constituencies forms the government.

Canada's electoral process thus has two major features. First is the single-member constituency. One and only one member may be elected. Some electoral systems allow for multimember constituencies, but not Canada's. The second feature is that the winner need only secure a plurality of the votes, which means that he or she only has to finish first. A majority of the votes, a requirement of some systems, is not necessary. These two features combine to create an electoral system that is commonly called either the first-past-the-post or the single-member plurality system.

Though the plurality system is used by many jurisdictions in Canada, it has been heavily criticized, so much so that some have advocated its replacement by PR. The indictment against the plurality system is long and detailed.[1] It supposedly misrepresents the wishes of the people because of its failure to translate accurately the popular vote into legislative seats. It also plays favourites, rewarding parties that finish first in the popular vote and punishing third parties with diffuse support. It treats voters differently—in some ridings, it takes a relative few to elect a member of a particular party, in others it takes a great many. This electoral system facilitates, as well, the formation of majority governments, even when the government party fails to convince one-half of the electorate to vote for it. Lastly, the plurality system makes it difficult, if not impossible, for governments and parties at the national level to receive representation in all parts of the country. In Canada's electoral history, many national governments have failed to achieve legislative representation in crucial areas of the nation. Sometimes Quebec goes unrepresented, other times it is the West. In a country with strong regional and language differences, the absence of truly national parties is of some concern. Political parties are meant to integrate this country, to pull all Canadians together, but parties can hardly accomplish this without seats in the major regions.

The purported failings of the plurality system have spawned a large number of proposals for reforms, one of which is list system proportional representation.[2] Under this particular version of PR, each province would constitute a single riding with multiple members. So, for example, Ontario might be one constituency with one hundred members. For each province, parties would place before voters a list of candidates corresponding to the number of seats available. Voters would then vote for one of the lists, and the resulting distribution of vote would determine what percentage of the candidates on a party's list would be elected. For instance, in a province with one hundred seats, a party that secured 50 percent of the vote would see its first fifty members on the list elected.

PR is supposed to deal with the failings of the single-member system. It provides for a more accurate matching of votes and seats, it affects all parties and voters fairly, and it offers the prospect of a national government with backing in all regions of the country. Canada, say proponents of PR, can only benefit. The reality, however, is quite different. There are many arguments against PR, and the following pages outline them. These arguments demonstrate that adoption of PR is not in Canada's interest.

WEAK AND UNSTABLE GOVERNMENT

A major argument against PR is that it would produce weak and unstable governments. For a government to rule effectively, it must have the support of the legislature, but PR—unlike the plurality system—would make this impossible. The result in most cases would be minority governments. Under these circumstances, the party in power could never be assured of passage of its policies, and accordingly would find it difficult to respond to the issues of the day. A government might want to change the workings of the education system or institute measures for reducing the public debt, but it would almost certainly be forced at a minimum to alter its plans to suit the wishes of the opposition. Forceful and coherent rule would become a relic of the past, replaced by desultory and tentative rule.

Weak government would also entail unstable government. The prospect facing every minority government is defeat. Each time a minority government submits a bill for consideration by the legislature, there exists the chance the government will fall. That is how our system works. The survival of any government under PR would be a day-to-day affair. To be sure, in some cases, a party facing a minority government situation might ally itself with another to form a coalition government. A coalition would provide the seats necessary for majority support in the House of Commons. But this solution would only transfer the problem from the legislature to the government. Now, the lack of support would be found within the government itself. The haggling and the disagreements would be centred in the cabinet, and the same forces that frustrate minority government in the legislature would emerge in the executive.

Proponents of PR are sensitive to these criticisms. They respond that the plurality system is no guarantee of majority governments, and point to the minority governments that have been elected at the national level in the last three decades. What they do not mention, however, is that these minority governments lasted at most one or two years—the plurality system acts to correct its mistakes. The short life of minority governments also directs our attention to a point already made, namely, the instability of minority governments.[3] When this general line of defence fails, advocates of PR suggest that minority governments have no real effect on stability. Canada has had many minority governments throughout its history, they say, and yet it has remained a stable democracy. It is also argued that coalition governments might actually be beneficial. The present complexity of public policy supposedly requires more than one voice. For example, the increasing impact of the international economic order demands the participation of all major parties.[4]

These latter claims, too, are without much support. Imagine a coalition government at the bargaining table with other countries discussing international trade policies. It would be difficult enough trying to represent Canada's interest without having Canada's own representatives fighting among themselves and being unable to agree on what to do. As for the claim that minority governments have no impact on stability, it is true that they have not undermined the democratic nature of government in Canada. But stability is more than the preservation of democracy. It also suggests governments with the time and support to make sound, coherent public policies. But minority governments have neither time nor support. They are here today and gone tomorrow.

DECLINE OF RESPONSIBLE GOVERNMENT

The system of government we have in Canada is called responsible government. If PR were to be implemented, responsible government would be undermined. Responsible government means that the government, in the form of the cabinet, must maintain the confidence of the legislative branch—it requires a majority in the House of Commons. But repeated government defeats in the legislature, which PR almost guarantees, would force a reform of this practice. If not, Canada would experience frequent elections. Somehow the government in a PR system would have to become less dependent or even separate from the legislature. Even PR proponents admit this eventually.[5]

Responsible government also means that the government is expected to look after the welfare of the country.[6] Under responsible government, a party is charged with the task of tending to the public interest. It formulates policies, administers programs, makes laws, submits budgets—the list is almost endless. All of this requires strong and confident government, something that PR denies. Another element of responsible government would thus have to be abandoned. More generally, responsible government is at the heart of government in Canada. It *is* our system of government. In trying to make government more representative, PR weakens responsible government. If Canadians truly want a different system of government, then this should be addressed head on. It should not occur as a byproduct of electoral reform.

SEVERS TIES BETWEEN CONSTITUENT AND MP

A valuable part of the present electoral system is the relationship between constituent and representative. A member of Parliament represents the views of constituents in the legislature and tries to deal with any specific problems in the riding. An MP also reports the viewpoints of his constituents to the major policymakers in the cabinet. In exchange for these services, the constituent supports the MP and provides the *raison d'être* for most elected representatives. Without the constituent, the MP has little to do. He or she becomes an ornament of democracy, nice to look at but with no real purpose.

PR would cripple this relationship. No longer would one MP be responsible for the concerns of a specific constituency. Instead, there would be one large constituency and a multitude of MPs. The intimacy and direct nature of the relationship between voter and MP would be lost. At present, if a person has a problem receiving, say, a pension benefit, that person can contact his or her MP and expect some action. With PR, the very size of the constituency might prove daunting to the voter, and there would be some uncertainty over whom to call. Should the first person on the Liberals' list be contacted, or the second one, or perhaps the first one on the Conservatives' list? There is also the possibility that no one would respond to the call. If everyone is responsible for the constituents, which is the case with PR, then no one is really responsible. The potential for "passing the buck" becomes real.

The cutting of the ties between voter and MP is not only damaging to the voter. MPs would be hard pressed to become familiar with their constituencies. Do they consider the entire provincial population to be their constituents? Campaigning would also be difficult. Furthermore, MPs would find themselves beholden to party leaders with the power to put them on the party list. MPs would spend more time courting party bosses than talking to voters.

PR proponents disagree with these points. They show, correctly, that the way we vote and our general orientation to the political system is determined largely by party labels.[7] When we come to vote, we tend not to look at the name on the ballot, but rather to the party affiliation. Moreover, the only thing an MP can really do is address minor concerns. Due to the operation of party discipline, individual MPs have little way to affect party policy. They must adhere to the party line. All of this is true, but it does not follow that the relationship between voter and MP is without value. Parties and leaders are the most significant short-term factors affecting our voting behaviour, but studies also show that MPs still matter.[8] It is also true that MPs (unless they are ministers) can at best deal with small issues, but for many voters that is all they really care about. Free trade, the environment, and the Constitution are important, but getting one's child tax credit or student grant also counts.

One final point needs to be made regarding the symbolic value of individual MPs. MPs may not have much of a voice in the inner sanctums of government. Nevertheless, it is still comforting to know there is at least one person in government whose job it is to look after your interests. In a country as large as Canada, there is the very real possibility of losing touch with the political system.

PLURALITY DOES NOT PRECLUDE NATIONAL PARTIES

One of the most damning charges made against the plurality system is its alleged bias against the emergence of parties with representation across the country. The regional divisions present in Canada and the splits between English- and French-speaking Canadians demand parties that can integrate the country, and this in turn requires parties with nationwide representation. But the electoral system supposedly works against this. In 1980, the Liberals won 24 percent of the vote in Saskatchewan, 21 percent in Alberta, and 22 percent in B.C., but won no seats in any of these provinces; for their part, the Conservatives won nearly 15 percent of the vote in Quebec, but no seats. The major parties had support—the votes clearly showed this—but the electoral system denied them legislative representation. The electoral system, it seems, works against the unity of the country.

And this is not all. The absence of national parties supposedly feeds perceptions that Canada is indeed rife with division—the Liberals represent the east, the Conservatives the west, or the Liberals are to be found in Quebec and the Conservatives in Ontario. Also, the failure of parties to secure representation in certain areas gives them little incentive to change this situation. Parties are much like investors. They only invest in areas that provide a good return, and investing in areas that produce little hope of seats is a bad investment. Parties are doomed to be regional entities, forever incapable of integrating the country.

It is this alleged effect of the electoral system that has precipitated many attacks against the single-member system. Canadian politics is concerned, some would say obsessed, with unity. Anything that works against unity receives much critical attention. The problem with this charge, though, is its inconsistency with the facts. In 1984, a Conservative government won seats in all provinces. To be sure, for the previous two decades the Tories had almost no representation in Quebec, a product in part of the electoral system. But in 1984, it won fifty-eight of the seventy-five seats. And it still managed to hold on to its support in traditional areas of strength. The same thing happened in 1988. The Conservatives achieved support in all major regions. Canada had a genuinely national government. In the next election, in 1993, the triumphant Liberal Party also secured seats in each of the provinces, and it was only in the 1997 election that the winning party secured rather meagre representation in some of the regions (though seats were won in all of them).

What happened? One response is that nothing happened. These elections were aberrations, and the results of the 1997 election foreshadow a return to regionalized governments. This is, however, an answer of convenience. A better answer is that the critics of the plurality system misunderstood the interaction between the system and party behaviour. Parties were indeed investors, but the bad investments were the areas already under control. What was the sense of putting additional resources into areas in which a party already had support? Alternatively, the unrepresented areas constituted a benefit of some magnitude. The risk of no return was there, but unlike in the controlled areas, there was a promise of a windfall.[9]

A more straightforward version of this argument is that the electoral system presented a challenge to parties. If you could win all the regions, power was almost guaranteed. The plurality system made this difficult, but this very difficulty caused parties to make the kind of effort necessary for success. The electoral process, seen this way, is a kind of test that only committed parties can pass.[10]

Whatever the reason, the fact is that the last two decades have seen elections return governments with countrywide support in the House of Commons. As we shall see, this has not meant an end to regional conflict, but it has dampened the enthusiasm for electoral reform.[11] This lack of support is evidenced most vividly in the fact that a recent federal royal commission on elections found no reason to consider seriously PR.[12]

LIMITED IMPACT OF ELECTORAL SYSTEMS

Underlying the push for PR is an unexamined assumption: electoral systems have an important impact. On some matters, they do. In this paper, it has been argued that a shift to PR would exert a negative effect on some aspects of Canadian politics. It would limit the ability of governments to govern, challenge the practices of responsible government, and weaken the link between voter and MP. But on other issues, some might say the truly important ones, electoral systems have no real impact. Arguably, the two issues central to discussion of electoral systems in Canada are *representation* and *regional conflict*. Changes in electoral systems, as we will now see, would have little effect on either.

Let us take representation first. PR supposedly provides for government whose makeup mirrors the wishes of the electorate. But does it? It would certainly do so in the legislature, but government in Canada is executive dominated. What counts, ultimately, is representation in the cabinet. Would the composition of the legislative branch be reflected in the cabinet? Not necessarily. Assume in a federal election with 301 ridings that the Conservatives win 130 seats, the Liberals 120, and the NDP 51. One possible scenario would be for the Liberals and the NDP to enter into some kind of implicit coalition government. Would this arrangement mirror representation in the House of Commons? No. What about all those who voted PC? Furthermore, the NDP, given that it allowed the Liberals to form a government, would wield a great deal of power even though it had only paltry representation in the House of Commons. It must be recognized, then, "that achievement of fairness in the allocation of seats is no guarantee of fairness in the allocation of power."13

The negligible impact of the electoral system on representativeness can be seen in another way. Critics of the plurality system note that it punishes the NDP. The NDP is the classic third party with diffuse support. From this fact, many jump to the conclusion that the NDP is without representation or has little effect on public affairs. But most students of Canadian politics know this to be untrue. The ideas of the NDP, and its predecessor the CCF, have had a profound impact on political life, especially in the area of social policy. This influence has just not been exercised through NDP members in legislative assemblies. As Wiseman says, "The NDP may not get its 'fair share' of the seats, but it has its 'fair share' (and perhaps more) of influence in fashioning the public policy arena."14

The minor effect of electoral systems also emerges when we examine the way the plurality system exacerbates regional divisions. PR promises to diminish this problem by facilitating representation of all regions in governing parties. The belief is that a national government with nationwide representation would contribute to national unity. In the 1980s, Canada achieved the former, albeit not through PR. But the point is that we had a government capable of integrating the country. But did it? The tussles over Meech Lake, the Charlottetown Accord, free trade, and regional development policy suggest not. And this should not be surprising. The deep divisions within Canada are unlikely to be papered over by a shift in the electoral map.15 The differences that divide Canadians are much more deeply rooted.

FRAGMENTED POLITICAL SYSTEM

Proportional representation would enrich, its supporters say, the quality of representative democracy in Canada. The single-member system leads to bland or "lowest common denominator" policies because of the need to appeal to as many voters as possible. The fact that there can be only one winner forces parties to act in this manner. Consequently, many views in society go unrepresented, and voters are faced with little choice. Alternatively, PR would permit a full flowering of parties representing varied perspectives and outlooks. The diversity found in a society would be reflected in its legislative bodies.

This line of argument is premised on the belief that PR would lead to more representative government. As shown in the previous section, this is a dubious proposition. But let us assume for the sake of argument that it is true, or that Canadians would be content with a representative House of Commons. Would the resulting diversity in the political system be beneficial? Admittedly, this is a difficult question to decide. Faithful representation of different societal beliefs is an important goal in a democracy. But so is order. Indeed, the key function of government is the preservation of peaceful relations, and this is accomplished by the integration of competing views. Giving voice to many divergent positions may make integration a feat of Herculean proportions. There might be a party for the environmentalists, for women, for the West, for separatists, for industry, and so on. The political system could fragment into many parts, and it is not clear that it could be put back together. This, of course, brings us back to a point already made. PR fosters instability. In its zeal to achieve representation, PR neglects the need for a stable governing authority.

CONCLUSION

To the unwary, PR is appealing. It lists the perceived inequities and failings of the plurality system, and puts in its place a system that leads to unity, fairness, and representativeness in politics. But in truth, PR does none of these latter things. It does not provide for representative government, and is helpless against the forces that divide this country. As for its impact on the actual machinery and operation of government, it reduces the influence of our public decision makers and eliminates the one direct tie each of us has with government. Canada would be unwise in adopting PR.

NOTES

1. For the classic critique of the plurality system in relation to Canada, see Alan C. Cairns, "The Electoral System and the Party System in Canada, 1921–1965," in J. Paul Johnston and Harvey E. Pasis, eds., *Representation and Electoral Systems: Canadian Perspectives* (Scarborough: Prentice-Hall, 1990).

2. For a discussion of the various reform proposals, including list system PR, see William P. Irvine, "A Review and Evaluation of Electoral Reform Proposals," in *Institutional Reforms for Representative Government*, Vol. 38, prepared for the Royal Commission on the Economic Union and Development Prospects for Canada (Toronto: University of Toronto Press, 1985).

3. For those who doubt the more general point about the relationship between minority governments and PR, the following article is recommended: A. Blais and R.K. Carty, "The Impact of Electoral Formulae on the Creation of Majority Governments," *Electoral Studies* 6 (1987). The two authors show a definite correlation between minority governments and PR.

4. William P. Irvine, "'Additional Member' Electoral Systems," in Arend Lijphart and Bernard Grofman, eds., *Choosing an Electoral System: Issues and Alternatives* (New York: Praeger, 1984), p. 71.

5. Tom Kent, *Getting Ready for 1999: Ideas for Canada's Politics and Government* (Halifax: Institute for Research on Public Policy), pp. 44–45.

6. C.E.S. Franks, *The Parliament of Canada* (Toronto: University of Toronto Press, 1987), p. 11.

7. William P. Irvine, "Does the Candidate Make a Difference? The Macro-Politics and Micro-Politics of Getting Elected," *Canadian Journal of Political Science* 15, no. 4 (December 1982).

8. Harold D. Clarke et al., *Absent Mandate: Interpreting Change in Canadian Elections*, 2nd ed. (Toronto: Gage Educational Publishing Co., 1991), p. 115.

9. J.A.A. Lovink, "On Analyzing the Impact of the Electoral System on the Party System," in Johnston and Pasis, eds., *Representation and Electoral Systems*, p. 342.

10. John C. Courtney, "Reflections on Reforming the Canadian Electoral System," in ibid., pp. 377–378.

11. F. Leslie Seidle, "The Canadian Electoral System and Prospects for Its Reform," in Alain-G. Gagnon and A. Brian Tanguay, eds., *Canadian Parties in Transition: Discourse, Organization, and Representation* (Scarborough: Nelson Canada, 1989), pp. 252, 265.

12. Royal Commission on Electoral Reform and Party Financing, *Final Report*, Vol. 1 (Ottawa: Minister of Supply and Services, 1991), pp. 18–21.

13. R.J. Johnston, "Seats, Votes, Redistricting, and the Allocation of Power in Electoral Systems," in Lijphart and Grofman, eds., *Choosing an Electoral System*, p. 69.

14. Nelson Wiseman, "Cairns Revisited–The Electoral and Party System in Canada," in Paul W. Fox and Graham White, eds., *Politics: Canada*, 7th ed. (Toronto: McGraw-Hill Ryerson, 1991), p. 270.

15. Ibid., p. 273.

Postscript

The two articles present some good arguments, but they also leave some questions unanswered. Hiemstra and Jansen believe, correctly, that PR would allow for the emergence of a wide range of parties and give the voters greater choice. They applaud this development, but one has to wonder whether this development would make Canada almost ungovernable. Would not a true expression of the differences separating Canadians prove fatal to the country's unity? As well, the two authors make much of the representation in the House of Commons, but say little of the executive branch, where the true power lies and where accurate replication of the popular vote is not guaranteed under PR. Their argument here appears to presume an American-style government in which the legislative branch has real policymaking power. At a minimum, their argument requires an important change in the operation of parliamentary government in Canada. Finally, Hiemstra and Jansen seem to ignore or understate the problems that may arise with coalition governments. Would not this type of government be held hostage by small parties crucial to the survival of the coalition? Would coalition governments not be difficult to form? Would the formation of coalitions not require the kind of backroom dealing now so detested in Canadian politics?

For his part, Barker seems unnecessarily harsh on minority governments. At times, they have worked well. Could not the past repeat itself? In their article, Hiemstra and Jansen also point to an article by Arend Lijphart that suggests that the tradeoff between *representation* and *effectiveness* may be illusory, that the plurality system does not produce more effective government than PR. Barker notes as well that the plurality method can produce parties with nationwide support in the House of Commons—but only with great difficulty. Is it not safer to proceed with a system such as PR that makes fully national parties more probable? The emergence of two highly regionalized parties in the 1993 election certainly suggests so. As for Barker's claim that national parties have no impact on regional conflict, the claim seems rather premature. More study is required. Barker may also exaggerate the close relations between MP and constituent. To test his claim here, ask yourself whether you know your MP's name. If you do, then Barker may have a point; if not, then students should lean toward Hiemstra and Jansen.

The debate contained in the two articles revolves around one type of PR. But other proposed reforms of the electoral system have been forwarded. A particularly popular one is a combination of plurality and PR. Some MPs would be elected by the plurality method, others under PR. The House of Commons would have two types—or classes, some say—of MPs. Another reform is called the *single transferable vote*, a version of PR in which voters have a greater voice in determining who would be elected from party lists. It is, however, complex in its structure.

Students wishing to pursue the subject of electoral reform might begin with F. Leslie Seidle, "The Canadian Electoral System and Proposals for Reform," in A. Brian Tanguay and Alain-G. Gagnon, eds., *Canadian Parties in Transition*, 2nd ed. (Scarborough: Nelson Canada, 1996). Another useful introductory article on electoral reform is Roger Gibbins and Loleen Youngman, "The Institutional Expression of Multiple Identities: The Electoral Reform Debate," in Thomas M.J. Bateman, Manuel Mertin, and David M. Thomas, eds., *Braving the New World: Readings in Contemporary Politics* (Scarborough: Nelson Canada, 1995). For detailed analyses, students should consult J. Paul Johnston and Harvey E. Pasis, eds., *Representation and Electoral Systems: Canadian Perspectives* (Scarborough: Prentice-Hall, 1990). This text contains many of the best articles on electoral reform in Canada, including the seminal article by Alan C. Cairns and the response to the article by J.A.A. Lovink. Any examination of electoral reform must eventually address the work of William Irvine. His *Does Canada Need a New Electoral System?* (Kingston: Institute of Intergovernmental Relations, 1979) is an exhaustive study of electoral reform, and many of his other articles are cited in Barker's paper. Also, Nick Loenen has written a recent study of electoral reform entitled *Citizenship and Democracy: A Case for Proportional Representation* (Toronto: Dundurn, 1997). Finally, the November 1997 issue of *Policy Options* (18: 9) is devoted to the issue of electoral reform.

For a look at the attitudes of Canadians toward the electoral system, one might consult Andre Blais and Elisabeth Gidengil's *Making Representative Democracy Work: The Views of Canadians*, vol. 17 of the Research Studies, Royal Commission on Electoral Reform and Party Financing (Ottawa: Minister of Supply and Services, 1991). Finally, in relation to Canada, students will benefit from an examination of Stephen Harper and Tom Flanagan's "Our Benign Dictatorship," *Next City* (Winter 1996–97). The article reveals the importance of electoral reform to the practice of democracy in Canada.

The experience of other countries with the plurality system and proportional representation is relevant to the discussion of electoral reform in Canada. On this topic, the following might be consulted: Arend Lijphart and Bernard Grofman, eds., *Choosing an Electoral System: Issues and Alternatives* (New York: Praeger, 1984); Vernon Bogdanor and David Butler, eds., *Democracy and Elections: Electoral Systems and Their Political Consequences* (Cambridge: Cambridge University Press, 1983); and Michael Dummett, *Principles of Electoral Reform* (Oxford: Oxford University Press, 1997). Also, special attention may be given to an article mentioned above and in the Hiemstra and Jansen article: Arend Lijphart, "Democracies: Forms, Performance, and Constitutional Engineering," *European Journal of Political Research* 25 (1994). What makes this article so central to the debate is that it denies that one must concede a decline in the effectiveness of government in order to introduce PR.

PART FIVE

PUBLIC POLICY

Does Canada need the CBC?

Should universities be privatized?

Is workfare sound public policy?

Is employment equity fair and necessary?

ISSUE**TWENTY**

Does Canada Need the CBC?

✔ **YES**
DAVID TARAS, "We Need the CBC," in *Policy Options* (September 1995)

✘ **NO**
BARRY COOPER, "Rethink the CBC," in *Policy Options* (September 1995)

The Canadian Broadcasting Company (CBC) was created by the Conservative government in 1932. The CBC was essentially an effort to find a middle road between two different models of broadcasting policy–the European model of state monopoly over television broadcasting and the American model of a regulated communications industry based on private ownership. Thus, while the CBC was to be publicly owned and funded, it was to compete in the market place with privately owned stations and networks.

The mandate given to the CBC is a multifaceted one. According to section 3 of the 1968 Broadcasting Act, it is to "serve to safeguard, enrich and strengthen the cultural, political, social and economic fabric of Canada." At the same time, the CBC is to "be a balanced service of information, enlightenment and entertainment for people of different ages, interests and tastes covering the whole range of programming in fair proportion."

Despite its broad mandate, the CBC has struggled with the issue of financing nearly from the beginning. Unlike its public sector counterparts in most European countries, CBC television relies for a significant part of its revenues on the sale of airtime for commercial advertisers. Although this additional source of revenue is not available to public broadcasters in other countries, this has not always worked to the CBC's advantage. In some ways the CBC's mixed revenues have diluted its distinctiveness from commercial networks. At the same time, the availability of alternative sources of revenues has made the CBC the target of frequent government cuts, based in part on the assumption that the CBC should boost its revenues from commercial sources. As a result, the CBC has been underfunded since 1953. Although the Liberal government of Jean Chrétien promised in its Red Book in 1993 to support the CBC, it undertook a series of drastic cuts in 1996 that triggered extensive staff and programming cuts and led to the closure of some regional stations.

For the CBC, the dilemma is this: The CBC is mandated to reinforce national values and promote national unity and to counter the growing americanization of television programming. However, to appeal to a broad audience and generate advertising revenues, the CBC, like private broadcasters, feels compelled to rely on the use of popular imported American shows. Furthermore, the CBC is expected to provide programming that caters to regional, ethnic, and other minority interests. This goal is difficult to reconcile with the need to provide programming with broad popular national appeal that will generate adequate advertising revenues.

In the article below, David Taras, who is a specialist on the role of the media in Canadian politics, sets out the reasons why it is important that the CBC's funding problems be dealt with in a way that preserves the agency's role in the political and social development of Canada. This is followed by an article by Barry Cooper, who thinks that the funding crisis at CBC is an occasion to rethink the role of the CBC, and perhaps even to ask if it has outlived its usefulness.

✔ **YES**
We Need the CBC
DAVID TARAS

The CBC is again at a crossroads. The government and the new president, former Tory cabinet minister Perrin Beatty, will have to choose from among quite a number of very different visions. There are those who would like nothing better than to see the CBC put under the surgeon's knife. I think the CBC is one of Canada's greatest resources, worth fighting for.

Those who advocate abolition or radical reorganization usually muster the following arguments.

1. The principal argument for dismantling the CBC is that, in a time of shrinking budgets, monies spent on the CBC are a "frill" that can no longer be justified. There is no shortage of budget-cutting suggestions. CBC should be melted down to its core —CBC Newsworld, national and local radio, and perhaps national news programming. Its headquarters in Ottawa should be closed. CBC should dismantle its costly distribution system in favour of broadcasting over cable. Its main TV channel could be shut down and the CBC splintered into a number of pay-TV services.

Others would transform CBC into a granting agency that would dispense funds for Canadian programming or into a production house that would sell its programs to other outlets. The private networks would like the CBC to vacate coverage of professional sports and to forgo advertising revenue so that its "purity" is maintained. Still others prefer the PBS model—a network that would solicit corporate advertising for entire programs and emphasize only news, current affairs, and perhaps children's television.

2. Private networks and stations have argued for years that the CBC is unfair competition because it is heavily subsidized by parliament. As the CBC takes advertising dollars from the private sector, it drains away profits that might otherwise be reinvested in brave new programming. This same lament has been heard endlessly now for decades. But even when there are sizable profits, the brave new world of commitment and excellence in Canadian programming never materializes. The programs that brought CTV its largest audience in the period from September 1994 to April 1995 were *E.R., America's Funniest Home Videos, Larroquette,* and *Roseanne.*

3. Some think the CBC is too dominated by a Toronto perspective. This argument simply does not hold water. The CBC's great value is that it is one of the great reflectors of the country. *Morningside, Cross Country Checkup, Newsworld* and national and regional news programs are bursting with sounds and images from around the country. The CBC has played a particularly important role in connecting northern communities to each other. One has to ask whether private television and radio have the will and resources to make nearly the same efforts. The cynic would argue that left to their own devices, the private networks would con-

nect Canadians with Los Angeles sooner than they would Toronto or Montreal, let alone St. John's.

4. The CBC's opponents also argue that the coming 500-channel universe will doom the CBC in any case. They contend that busting up the CBC and allowing others to scoop up its advertising revenues will allow for redeployment in a way that releases new energies and opens new opportunities. Government regulation would ensure that new channels and services would be just as Canadian. The CBC has the structure and is the model of a 1950s approach to broadcasting. What is needed is a new decentralized "niche" entrepreneurship best left to the private sector.

In reality, however, the much vaunted 500-channel universe may be a mirage. Most viewers can only cope with a limited number of channels and some of the new services are attracting audiences that are so small as to be almost negligible. If the 500-channel universe does unfold, all the more reason to harness resources, energies, and talent in one or two channels that will produce high-quality programming. It should not be forgotten that the CBC has been capable of extraordinary innovation. At the beginning of the 1980s, for instance, the CBC was able to ride the wave of change with respect to TV newsmagazines when it established *The Journal*. Its format and style set an example that was to be copied throughout North America. Undoubtedly, another leap of imagination is now needed.

There are important arguments in favour of a strong CBC that are often overlooked.

1. Public broadcaster plays an increasingly important role at a time when a small number of large corporate empires dominate the presses and the airwaves. One of the important media developments of the 1990s is not only the convergence that is taking place with regard to media technologies but the convergence of media companies into still larger ownership groups. Not everyone sees powerful media owners such as Ted Rogers, Conrad Black, Edgar Bronfman Jr., or Rupert Murdoch as trusted protectors of the public interest. A strong CBC is needed to ensure there will be competition and that voices other than just those of the powerful can be heard.

The existence of the CBC is also of enormous benefit to journalists working for other organizations who might be under much stricter control if the CBC was not there setting a different journalistic standard and providing competition. Journalists who are cheerleaders for various schemes to dismantle the CBC are extremely shortsighted. Not only would the Canadian journalistic world be smaller, but the quality of journalism would likely spiral down.

2. Many news outlets produce news that is cheaply put together, homogenized and inoffensive. In the fight for the bottom line, voyeurism or "feel good news" beats investigative reporting almost every time. The CBC is often the only news source willing to probe deeply into public issues, and take the risk of making political leaders and large numbers of listeners and viewers somewhat uncomfortable. Programs such as *Witness, Prime Time News, The Nature of Things,* and

The Fifth Estate, among others, probably upset audiences at least as much as they comfort them. The politicians would have preferred not having had to contend with the Somalia Affair and the breakdown of authority in the Airborne regiment —a story that CBC did its share in pushing. They would probably have preferred that *Prime Time News* not air its recent five-part series on the future of the Canadian health care system or the discussion that it hosted on why high-wage jobs are disappearing. In the end, however, people receive more of what they need to know as citizens from CBC, a benefit that is difficult to quantify in dollars and cents but is critical to the functioning of a healthy democratic society.

3. At a time when almost all Canada's institutions have come under concerted attack, we should not forget the CBC's many accomplishments. The corporation succeeds best perhaps when it is funny, warm, charming, irreverent, on the edge, or off the wall. *Rita and Friends, Kids in the Hall, Coach's Corner,* or *This Hour Has 22 Minutes* are good examples of when CBC hits the mark. CBC is at its worst when it imitates American trends.

The CBC also provides a vital electronic record of the country's important moments. This past February, for instance, it described and analyzed the federal budget with a depth and a clarity that was simply unmatched by its radio and television rivals. The same could be said for its commemoration of the 50th anniversary of the end of the Second World War, which took place this past May. At its very best moments, the CBC is a kind of national town hall—an ongoing conversation—that binds the country together.

Dismantling the CBC in a substantial way will create deep holes in Canada's cultural fabric and in the way that Canadians communicate with one another which might never be repaired. Endless cutting without new strategic investments in talent, ideas, and ultimately good programs will be very damaging. A more sharply focussed mandate is long overdue, but if the country is now too poor to protect its cultural identity and has lost the courage and imagination needed to preserve it, then we have already lost more than we can imagine.

✗ **NO**
Rethink the CBC
BARRY COOPER

In May of 1995, a preliminary report and recommendations put together by a House of Commons Committee on Canadian Heritage under the chairmanship of Liberal M.P. John Godfrey was leaked to the media. It was the first fruit of a year-long study of the role and financing of CBC and was filled with sound advice. CBC should, it said, get out of local and regional TV news and get out of all sports televising. CBC should also shut down its transmitter and provide feeds to the cable networks and satellites, for a fee. At the same time as the Godfrey committee was still doing its work, another "task force" was announced by the prime minister. Under the guidance of Pierre Juneau, this group will review the mandate and "synthesize" a number of studies, including the Commons committee's.

Don't expect much. Juneau is a former president of CBC, a former chairman of the CRTC, and began his association with the National Film Board as long ago as 1949. A second member, Peter Herrndorf, is a former CBC producer and senior manager who brought us *The Journal,* who believes strongly in a central (and centralized) role for CBC in the diffusion of "Canadian culture," and who, as head of TVOntario, ought to have seen that he was in a conflict-of-interest situation inasmuch as his company and the CBC compete for a finite pool of taxpayers' dollars. The third member, Catherine Murray, has been involved with Decima Research, the Women's TV Network, and, though educated in Ontario, she lives in B.C. All three have spent most of their earning years in the public sector. Juneau said flatly that he won't be bound by the government's budgetary targets in making his recommendations. As one observer put it, if Brian Mulroney, assisted by Mike Wilson, were asked to report on the FTA, we would have a pretty good idea what they would say.

A third report is also due to be released before the end of the year. This is a forensic audit of CBC by the Auditor General. A forensic audit is more than a bookkeeping exercise because it examines the question of value for money. The last time anything like this was done was in 1981, when Stanley J. Leibowitz, an economist at the University of Rochester, completed a report for the Department of Communications. The news that CBC-owned stations were about 233 percent more expensive to operate than affiliated or private stations so shocked CBC senior management and department officials that the results were not published until 1985, when the Fraser Institute brought the report into the public domain. Incidentally, Mr. Juneau was Deputy Minister of Communications at the time the Leibowitz report was squashed.

We should make no mistake: the chief component of the current crisis is financial. The flurry of committees, reviews, task-forces, and audits, as well as rapid turnover in senior executives are but symptoms. The numbers are so large as to be almost meaningless to mere mortals. How much is $1.1 billion? A lot. More to the point, when we speak of CBC being in a financial crisis we are really talking about TV, especially English-language TV. And it is in a crisis because not enough people are watching it. French-language TV, with a budget about 40 percent of that allocated to English-language TV, doesn't help much to balance the books. But it is French. Perhaps it should be looked at as another kind of interregional transfer and charged to the Official Bilingualism account.

The financial plight of the CBC is exacerbated by technological changes, usually symbolized as a "500-channel environment" or more dramatically as a "death star," but that should simply concentrate our minds. What is the rationale for taxpayer-supported TV in this multi-channel context anyhow?

To answer this question I would like to make two points, neither of which can be justified adequately in the space available. The first is that, in my opinion, Neil Postman was right, without doubt or qualification: all TV can do is entertain, whether one considers news reports or hockey or the coverage of the Commons Committee on Canadian Heritage, the medium and what it can do always overwhelms the message. *Masterpiece Theatre, The Simpsons,* and *Newsworld* are all produced to be consumed by persons who have distinct tastes. Some tastes are elevated and refined and are entertained by elevated and refined productions; some aren't. But it's all just entertainment.

The second point, which also takes more space to justify than is available now, is that the terms of the Broadcast Act are unrealistic in the precise sense that they have virtually nothing to do with the reality of TV and what it is capable of doing. Section 3(d)(i), for example, says that the Canadian broadcasting system should "serve to safeguard, enrich and strengthen the cultural, political, social and economic fabric of Canada." Likewise s. (3)(m)(vi) says with respect to CBC in particular that it should "contribute to shared national consciousness and identity." Now, this is the public law of Canada, not some ministerial directive or political wish list, and no TV can possibly fulfill that ominous "should."

All one need do to reflect on the impossibility of compliance with the Act is to consider the meaning of the term, culture. Culture is something that grows from below by means of the active participation of individuals. Whatever its contents, it does not get absorbed by couch potatoes watching transmissions from Toronto or other elsewheres. Or again, "national consciousness and identity" are terms meant to evoke a meaning that Canadians can experience as real. But as Northrop Frye pointed out several years ago, our identities (like our cultures) are local, not national. Accordingly, CBC-TV can do nothing about a non-existent "national identity." Bearing that in mind, when we read a statement such as that of Gérard Veilleux, one of the recent presidents through the revolving door, that "if we don't use the instruments of public broadcasting to define ourselves, to give ourselves our own identity, then somebody else will define us," we should pay more attention to his expressions of fear than his conceptual clarity.

CBC, in my opinion, has good reason to be afraid. As Jan Brown remarked in the House of Commons when she introduced her private members bill to privatize CBC, "public television is facing a reality jolt. Canadians are being asked to make priority choices." Specifically, she said, "CBC has hit the wall. It is continuing to lose its audience support at least in its English television market." Who disagrees?

If Postman is correct about the nature, the very essence, of television and if Frye is correct about the nature of identity and of culture, the Broadcast Act is simply asking the impossible. Does this mean that billions of dollars have been wasted in pursuit of a statutorily defined chimera? It does. Does it mean that Canadian tax-payers must throw good money after bad? Fortunately we have no money to throw, which means we have an opportunity to rethink the role and place of CBC in Canadian life, particularly of the big-ticket items, namely English and French TV.

Let me conclude by saying that help in such rethinking is available. To give just one example, Colin Hoskins and Stuart McFadden, of the University of Alberta business school in Edmonton, proposed a scheme for restructuring CBC that also will be published by the Fraser Institute. It proposed rewriting the mandate so as to provide a commercial-free and reduced schedule of high-quality information, drama, variety, and children's programs. It would cut local, regional, foreign, and sports programs, sell at auction CBC infrastructure of stations and transmitters, and eliminate in-house production. The cost savings would be in the order of $350 million a year, roughly what the cuts in appropriations would be by 1998–99.

With funding in flux, the mandate under review, low morale, a new president, and a feckless minister, this may be just the time for some strong and clear voices from the West to be heard.

Postscript

Barry Cooper suggests that the Broadcasting Act is asking the impossible of the CBC. In examining this debate, a good starting point is to look again at the mandate of the CBC and ask to what extent the network has been successful in meeting its objectives. Has it been successful in promoting Canadian values and national identity? Has it been successful in counteracting the Americanization of Canadian culture? Has it been successful in promoting national unity while reflecting regional diversity in the country? Has it been successful in providing "a balanced service of information, enlightenment and entertainment for people of different ages, interests and tastes covering the whole range of programming in fair proportion"? These questions beg a more fundamental question—given the growing complexity of the communications industry today, how do you measure the success of the CBC in such broad areas?

An important question to address in examining this issue is whether the problems of the CBC are primarily related to its chronic underfunding or to something more fundamental. For example, it can be argued that budget reductions by the government, which led the CBC to close some regional stations, have directly undermined its ability to reflect regional diversity within the country. Thus, an increase in CBC funding should address the problem. Or, as Barry Cooper suggests, is there a more fundamental problem with the CBC that is rooted in the very nature of television and culture themselves? If this is the case, then no amount of spending on the CBC will address its problems.

This issue highlights for us the impact that rapidly changing technological and economic forces can have on public policy. Given such developments, has the proliferation of cable channels and specialty programming largely made the CBC irrelevant? It might be argued that by granting licences to specialty channels like the Women's Network, Vision TV, the Discovery Channel, and, more recently, an all-news network by CTV, the Canadian Radio-television and Telecommunications Commission (CRTC) has been able to achieve many of the same objectives through other means than the CBC. How would the face of communications change in Canada if the CBC were to disappear tomorrow?

A number of resources dealing with the role of media in Canada provide useful background for this issue. Especially helpful are Richard Collins, *Culture, Communications and National Identity* (Toronto: University of Toronto Press, 1992); Ross Earman, *Channels of Influence* (Toronto: University of Toronto Press, 1994); and Marc Raboy, *Missed Opportunities: The Story of Canada's Broadcasting Policy* (Montreal: McGill-Queen's University Press, 1992). For an insider's view of the history and role of the CBC, see Knowlton Nash, *The*

Microphone Wars: A History of Triumph and Betrayal at the CBC (Toronto: McClelland and Stewart, 1994). Finally, an insightful discussion of the defence of Canadian culture from Americanization can be found in John Meisel, "Extinction Revisited: Culture and Class in Canada," in Helen Holmes and David Taras, eds., *Seeing Ourselves: Media Power and Policy in Canada* (Toronto: Harcourt, Brace, 1996).

ISSUE**TWENTY-ONE**

Should Canada's Universities Be Privatized?

✔ **YES**
DOUGLAS AULD, "The Overregulation of Higher Education"

✘ **NO**
WILLIAM BRUNEAU, "Privatization in School and University: Renewal or Apostasy?"

In a recently released book entitled *Petrified Campus*, three respected scholars declare that Canada's universities "are in deep trouble." High operating costs, declining government funding, higher tuition fees, and a perception of declining standards add up to a troubling climate for higher education in Canada. Perhaps the most serious problem is the seeming inability—or unwillingness—of universities to change, to challenge the old ways and to consider new practices. Yet, say the three authors, change is exactly what universities must contemplate. Moreover, they must try to accomplish what is being demanded of many public institutions: to do more with less.

Some might believe that this exaggerates the actual situation, but most concede that universities need to rethink how they go about fulfilling their responsibilities. The present situation essentially involves government providing the bulk of funding for universities and attaching certain conditions to this funding, and it is this arrangement that has now come under scrutiny. One proposal for changing the way universities operate revolves around the notion of *privatization*. In the context of universities, privatization relates to a number of actions that lessen the dependence of universities on the public purse and relax government regulation of higher education. Privatization means allowing universities to set tuition levels without government interference. It also means universities entering into arrangements with corporations that involve the latter providing funds in return for some say in how the funds are used. In its more ambitious form, privatization means private interests establishing institutions of higher learning bereft of government funding and participation—in other words, founding purely private universities. More generally, privatization means *decreasing* the role of government in university life and *increasing* the role of private or nongovernmental forces.

For its supporters, privatization offers many benefits. With the emergence of new private universities, students would be given greater choice, and, presumably, existing institutions would be spurred on to better performance because of the new entrants into the university market. The deregulation of tuition fees would allow universities to vary fees depending on the cost and demand of the programs involved; no longer would the same fees be charged regardless of the program of study and the expected rate of return of the educational experience. Relations between private funding sources and universities would offer additional financial resources to the universities, and lead to a more directed program of research, one that clearly meets an identified need. More broadly, privatization increases the flexibility of universities, allowing them to adapt quickly to the changing demands of society.

Seen this way, privatization seems irresistible, too good to pass up. Yet, some caution might be in order. At present, universities are *public* institutions, funded largely by government and administered by university bodies accountable to the larger community. Under this arrangement, the public interest is looked after. But privatization, almost by definition, erodes the public quality of universities, changing them into entities that are focused on one private interest or another. With privatization, there is a fear that the university becomes more a reflection of the whims of the market and less a product of the wishes of society. In the world of privatized universities, the research activities of faculty follow the corporate donations, the curriculum registers only the demands of the job-conscious student, and the student body as a whole increasingly reflects an individual's ability to pay.

In the readings, Douglas Auld, president of Loyalist College in Belleville, presents the case for privatization. William Bruneau, a member of the education faculty at the University of British Columbia and president of the Canadian Association of University Teachers, outlines the problems with privatizing Canada's universities.

✔ YES
The Overregulation of Higher Education
DOUGLAS AULD

INTRODUCTION

All forms of educational monopoly and stereotyping are fatal to that spirit of freedom, alertness and expectations which must characterize a progressive civilization, in which the achievements of the present and the aspirations of the future, though in close touch with the past, are ever going beyond it.

—G.M. Grant, Principal of Queen's University, 1900

The close of the twentieth century marks one of the exceptional learning revolutions in the history of civilization: the introduction of publicly funded and managed postsecondary education on a massive scale. Whereas at the end of the nineteenth century only a few people, mostly male, graduated from almost exclusively private colleges and universities, today countries throughout the world graduate hundreds of thousands of women and men, most of whom completed their studies at public institutions. The knowledge empowerment of several generations of young and sometimes not-so-young people is cause for celebration.

The celebration should be tempered somewhat because, in the process of achieving this intellectual emancipation, many countries have created a public monopoly that has the potential to become the antithesis of higher education.

Colleges and universities, more than ever, need to be highly flexible, market-driven institutions, places where creativity and innovation in learning and teaching and in the assignment of work are encouraged. They need to be places where risks can be taken without the threat of public-sector retaliation. It is in the universities and colleges that we find highly professional, dedicated teachers and scholars who devote their lives to thinking about learning and education. It is these people who should be the leaders in higher education.

In many jurisdictions today, governments decide how the flow of public monies will be distributed to colleges and universities. Governments often approve or appoint governing councils, boards of governors, or trustees. In some instances, governments approve programs to be offered and decide on what educational or academic standards the institution must meet. Governments set the price of the service, then allow institutions to compete for customers.

Such control and management has led to the politicization of higher education, has shackled creativity, and has forced colleges and universities to operate with rules that result in unwise economic and financial decisions and erode the pursuit of the fundamental goals of higher education. Only by rethinking the elemental purpose of higher education *and* what the role of government ought to be in the affairs of the academy will society be able to develop true centres of learning and research.

A PRIMER ON THE ECONOMICS OF REGULATION

There is a rich and well-established literature pertaining to government regulation that is rooted in economics, political theory, property rights, and public administration. The economic component focuses primarily on whether government control improves efficiency, and on how control may influence the distribution of wealth in society. Political theory provides important philosophical underpinnings for the role of government in democratic states. Public policy analysis highlights the importance of the social and cultural objectives of regulation. None of these approaches operates in isolation from the others, and the confluence of various approaches is what makes the theory of regulation so rich and at times so confusing.

From an economic perspective, there is a defensible rationale for regulation in three areas, all of which bear directly on efficiency. The first of these involves the possible existence of a *natural monopoly*. Simply put, the theory states that if a monopoly, a single firm, is clearly more efficient than a system of individual firms competing one with the other, because the lowest possible operating cost can only be achieved by one firm, a regulated monopoly may be preferred to the competitive model. Even this guideline must be moderated by examining how accountability and the preferences of consumers are affected by a single firm. What is known about the economics of colleges and universities suggests that within a state, province, or country there are no significant economies of scale that suggest the creation of a single, government-regulated monopoly.

If a natural monopoly is not a viable means to ensure maximum efficiency, does that fact therefore imply that a multitude of colleges and universities of all sizes and kinds will ensure maximum efficiency? One school of thought argues that many firms attempting to attract the attention of a limited number of customers results in *destructive competition*. This occurs when the intense competition for students results in "wasteful" advertising and, possibly, a reduction in standards in colleges and universities. Intense competition occurs in many markets, and what is wasteful versus useful advertising is partly a matter of interpretation. If product information is easily and inexpensively attainable, then customers will quickly move away from shoddy products and services, forcing the suppliers of those services to go out of business or improve the level of service.

Finally, intervention in the market is justified if there are *externalities*. Positive externalities exist when the benefits of a consumption or production activity by one person or firm result in benefits accruing not only to those who purchase the product or service but also to others in society who do not pay directly for the benefit. Consequently the *social benefits* of an activity exceed the *private bene-*

fits. If government supports the activity in question, consumption or production is stimulated and, in theory, at just the right level of support the social and private benefits will be equal.

There is a widespread consensus that higher education bestows positive externalities on society and is a legitimate candidate for public support. In most countries this support is manifested by the public management and direct funding of institutions of higher education. This is not the only way to ensure that society reaps the full benefits of higher education.

The contribution of political theory and public policy to the debate regarding the public sector's management of higher education is also important. For example, political parties bring to the legislature a particular view on how wealth and income should be distributed in society. Higher education can be one of the instruments used to carry out a political agenda, but should it be? If so, is the direct management of higher education the most effective method? What are the costs of this type of management? Policy goals can also be achieved by assigning special "envelopes" of funding for higher education in areas of research, new programs, and access. Does this limit academic freedom and the right of the institution to set its own goals and objectives?

In summary, government control over the price of education, programs, access, and research funding, coupled with, in some jurisdictions, insurmountable barriers to the establishment of new degree-granting institutions, spawns a system of higher education that resembles a cross between an oligopoly and a regulated monopoly. Higher education is a knowledge enterprise where there is no rationale for a regulated natural monopoly. Financial support for higher education can be defended, but there are far better ways of achieving this than by controlling the institutions themselves.

Examples of how the regulatory framework inhibits creativity and creates additional costs are several. One university, in trying to respond to a strong demand for a professional program, advocated charging a higher tuition fee: students were willing to pay for the program. The government prevented this from occurring. A college that has the ability and the vision to offer an applied degree program cannot launch such a program, even though it is identified by the business sector in Canada as important to economic growth. More generally, by trying to create methods to respond to the requirement for accountability, several provinces have created regulations that in terms of time and money are imposing huge costs on colleges and universities.

The first goal is to deregulate higher education.

METHODS OF DEREGULATING HIGHER EDUCATION

The deregulation of higher education can be achieved by increasing competition, changing the nature of the relationship between government and higher education and privatizing existing universities and colleges.

Creating New Institutions

To increase competition, governments should eliminate legislative restrictions that prevent the establishment of new degree-granting institutions. In place of such restrictive legislation, it would be far more appropriate either to transfer the approval of new institutions to a branch of government dealing with the approval of new companies or to set out clearly the conditions to be met for the establishment of new degree-granting institutions.

In Canada the opposition to private universities (and degree-granting institutions in general) is widespread. New institutions, it has been argued, would quickly find themselves in need of a "handout" from government, and this would spread the scarce resources of the public sector among a greater number of colleges and universities. There is also the concern that, through other linkages with government, considerable public funding would find its way into private colleges and universities, as it has in the United States. It is important, however, to distinguish between public subsidies and the involvement of the public sector in higher education. A contract between a government agency and a college to provide a specific education or training program or to undertake research is very different from providing general operating grants to the institution based on a broad indicator such as enrolment. In today's climate of restrictive public funding, it is unlikely politicians at either the federal or provincial government level would be anxious to "bail out" a private college.

Another concern relates to quality. There would be, it has been argued, no check or control on the academic quality of a private school, no regulation of standards and competencies. The major benefit of the Canadian university system is the consistency of its quality, which is due to quality regulations. At the graduate level, quality regulation is to a large extent administered by the academic institutions themselves through their provincial associations or internal quality management standards. It is not as widespread or formalized at the undergraduate level. Some provinces do have specific criteria for the establishment of new undergraduate programs. Defenders of the all-public Canadian system point to the plethora of second- or third-rate private U.S. universities and relate this phenomenon to the "unregulated" system of higher education in the United States.

This is a somewhat spurious argument since, if privatization of higher education were to occur in Canada, a variety of checks and balances would quickly come into play, as they do with private primary and secondary schools. Self regulation would be an option. In Canada, the Canadian Education Standards Institute (CESI), composed of those private primary and secondary schools that join, has established a rigorous set of criteria that institutions must meet to gain entry to CESI and sustain their membership. The loss of CESI status is a clear signal of failing quality. Schools may operate outside CESI (within provincial corporate guidelines) but they do so without the quality assurance of CESI. In the United States, statewide accrediting associations also provide some level of quality assurance. And, as educational institutions move into the world of ISO 9002 certification, international standards of quality are being established. In the end, the market would decide which institutions would survive.

Does the availability of private capital limit the ability to establish private colleges or universities? It might be difficult to locate sufficient private funding to replicate the University of Toronto or the University of British Columbia, but the capital start-up costs of a small liberal arts university are not excessive. Given the excess supply of reasonably good physical capital suitable for a small school and the availability of information technology to enable the delivery of courses in the early years, a new degree-granting institution would not be an enormous fiscal challenge.

Such an institution would, initially, require only those laboratory facilities needed for undergraduate courses. Faculty could align themselves with research teams and facilities in major research-intensive universities, and schedules could be arranged to provide scholars with the opportunities to establish research programs in concert with their undergraduate responsibilities. Furthermore, a significant component of the research "equipment" for the humanities and social sciences is found on the Internet. Applied research facilities could be established by arranging partnerships with private corporations.

Bricks and mortar are no longer the key building blocks as far as the physical structure of higher education is concerned. The virtual undergraduate—and even graduate—university program can be developed using very little space and a solid complement of information technology. Athabasca University in Alberta is one example of such an institution.

Privatizing Existing Institutions

Total privatization of an existing university, for example, would involve severing all ties with government with the exception of the normal reporting associated with a not-for-profit corporation. Such an institution would decide which programs to offer; would develop its own policies on governance, research, and curricula; and would set its own prices for various education and research services. It might also be expected to pay back the value of the depreciated capital financed by the public sector in the past. On the other hand, if it will not receive any future public funding for capital, a government may wish to "forgive" such debt in view of the future savings realized by the privatization of the institution.

How would such an institution survive? Tuition fees would be the main source of income, and, with no public funding, they would have to rise significantly. If, however, the government chose to abandon all formula-based funding for one or even all institutions and channel that money to the students in the form of vouchers, the increase in tuition would be cushioned substantially. It is important to keep in mind that the privatization and deregulation of higher education does not de facto mean no government involvement. We saw earlier that because of the divergence of private and social benefits from higher education, it is to society's advantage to support attendance at colleges and universities. Vouchers for qualified students is the simplest way to achieve this goal.

This arrangement gives the college or university the flexibility to modify tuition fees depending on cost and demand factors. The implicit research funding that accompanies most formula funding would be gone if students received a voucher that reflected only the cost of their education.

Since basic research is important to the long-term benefit of society, it is efficient that the public sector fund some level of research. This could be done in the form of block transfers to universities and internal competition for the available funds.

In short, any existing university or degree-granting college or institution could be privatized, and the students could receive the subsidy by way of a voucher. The bureaucratic links between government and higher education would be severed, autonomy would be enhanced, and the encouragement of higher education maintained. The basic role of the public sector is to encourage participation in higher education and provide some level of support for basic research. Anything else could be negotiated as a partnership agreement with any institution. If a government wished to encourage a particular group in society to participate to a greater extent in higher education, that could be accomplished through the use of a special voucher.

SUMMARY AND CONCLUSION

Universities and colleges contribute significantly to the economic, social, and cultural life not only of the nation but also of the communities where they are located. Universities and colleges are the wellsprings of knowledge, contributing immeasurably to our comprehension of biological and physical phenomena, as well as to our understanding of the arts and humanities. In addition to transferring knowledge from one generation to another, higher education provides an environment where, in many programs, students learn to blend specific skills with the more generic skills of critical thinking, understanding the integration of the social and physical world, and learning about themselves and others. Because it is so important, institutions of higher education must be flexible and responsive.

The "capture" of large parts of higher education by governments does not serve the long-term interests of society. There is no logical foundation for the management and control of colleges and universities by government departments and ministries. The case for public support, however, is strong; such support provides students with financial assistance, thereby encouraging attendance at college or university, and ensures there is a solid foundation for basic research, unfettered by either government or private-sector control. Through the privatization of existing institutions or the establishment of new universities and colleges, government can ensure that higher education will contribute to the economic, social, and cultural well-being of society.

✗ **NO**
Privatization in School and University: Renewal or Apostasy?
WILLIAM BRUNEAU

In Greek mythology, Proteus was a sea god, the "herder of seals" who could change shape whenever necessary. His ability to find nourishment, to escape punishment, and to attract the kindly attention of the gods all depended on his ever-shifting appearance.[1] Privatization—the replacing of public ownership and/or regulation with private ownership and/or deregulation—has all those Protean qualities. Just when we think we have it nailed down, described, and defined, "privatization" changes shape and escapes to live another day.

I begin with an "exemplary" case of privatization, this one from the field of elementary and secondary public schooling in the United States. I turn then to Canadian examples, and finally to the university.

I

In Boston's Chelsea suburb in the spring of 1989, the public school board agreed to hand the operation of its entire school system over to a private corporation. The decision produced a shocked chorus of opposition: teachers' unions, politicians (especially older ones), and many parents made it clear they were not ready for so radical a change. Reaction would have been even more severe but for the fact that privatization had become an acceptable topic, and sometimes an acceptable option, in political and academic circles during the previous decade.

The ideas of privatization and client control gained strength with the election of the Thatcher government in the United Kingdom (1979), the ascendancy of the new "market economics" of the Chicago School (Milton Friedman in the lead), and the rise of "reform" movements in New Zealand, Australia, parts of Canada, and many North and South American countries. An entire branch of the American civil service (the air controllers) had come near to being privatized in 1982, and, after 1985, there had even been calls for privatization of the corrections system, an idea that shocked defenders of the public interest.

In all of these movements and cases, the driving idea was that efficiencies and lower taxes would follow from the destruction of government. The popularity of that idea had by 1989 softened opposition to the "marketing" of education.

Under privatization, teachers in the Chelsea District would be paid by Education Alternatives, Inc. Corporation, as would school maintenance and technical staff. In some (but not all) cases, unions would have successor rights in the new system. The privatized schools' effectiveness would be tested by a battery of nationally administered tests in all subjects and grades. Education Alternatives, Inc. would be expected to improve educational performance in comparison to that of the public administration it was replacing. The privatized schools would be required, of course, to teach the officially mandated curriculum. Teachers would spend more time "on task," and they, too, would be tested using "performance indicators." Unnecessary bureaucracy would be eliminated, dropout rates would fall, the rapid turnover of teachers and principals in the region's demoralized districts would end, and taxpayers would be content.[2]

As it turned out, the corporation has not, on average, turned a profit,[3] and, despite its best efforts, has not improved educational results. The cost to taxpayers has not varied even fractionally during the change from public to private control.[4] And performance indicators didn't work either, since teachers already were working at 100 percent capacity in this tough, suburban district.

Meanwhile, businessmen and businesswomen on the board of directors at Education Alternatives, Inc. found it impossible to satisfy the schools' clients. By far the most active critics and opponents of privatization came from Boston's Latin-American community and from Boston University.[5] The crucial point was that parents and taxpayers who sought to influence decisions about spending on computers, libraries, school nurses, and teacher salaries found they were blocked. The idea that privatization would give power to clients turned out to be false. Only two things counted in a privatized school system: profits and test results.

In the end, the Chelsea experiment failed to achieve the objectives set for it, as did similar experiments in Baltimore, Maryland[6]; Dade County, Florida; Hartford, Connecticut; and Minneapolis, Minnesota. In Massachusetts, school board trustees and state legislators began to see after about 1994 that public control and public regulation were not as wasteful and backward as privatizers had claimed. Above all, the Boston story shows how the original objectives of public education were quickly obscured by the necessities of business, and how different "client control" was from "public control."[7] It was not terribly surprising when research began to show the school privatization movement was "fizzling."[8]

Chelsea was, of course, privatization of the brutal kind. But think of Proteus. What of the school system that gives cafeteria and food distribution to the private sector, laying off its own employees and contracting with an outside company to do the work? This is modest privatization, presented under the guise of "restructuring." Is there anything wrong with it, considering this "reform" might save money and might even improve the quality of the cafeteria food school children eat?

What about the Toronto School Board's argument in 1994 about whether to give Pepsi Cola exclusive right to soft-drink distribution in that city's schools in return for a significant annual fee? Still more subtle, what about the 1991 decision in the Vancouver School Board to assign school food preparation to a private firm after a public competition to find the company able to supply the best food for the lowest cost in Vancouver's inner-city schools? Is there anything terribly wrong here, especially considering that public school funding has been in decline for years in Toronto and in Ontario? Why not take the companies' money and run?

The argument against Pepsi Cola in Toronto was that it was the thin edge of the wedge. What looked like a simple monopoly of soft-drink distribution would surely end by giving pupils and their teachers a series of utterly noneducational messages: that healthy diet was less important than consuming commercially popular foods; that profit taking is in the public interest (or is synonymous with public works); and that critical thinking is fine in history class or English literature studies, but not when it comes to advertising.

Now, this will sound extreme and unlikely, as do many thin-edge-of-the-wedge arguments. But within months of the Pepsi deal (and there *was* a deal), Toronto was asked to join hundreds of American cities in welcoming commercial news on cable television aimed explicitly at school-age children, and the same arguments were made again. In the end, Toronto refused the TV sets and the computers, and did not accept the children's commercial cable news service. The difficulty was that in accepting the news service, Toronto would have been accepting more than just news. It would have been accepting a whole *way* of presenting the news, predigested and preselected for the "television generation," and presumably friendly to the values of the stockholders of the company that produced it.

As to contracting out food services in Vancouver and other cities, the argument has been that it is an attack on unions and on working people, since so many school districts employ unionized work forces. Some will argue that contracting out is also the thin edge of yet another wedge, this time referring to the creeping tendency to misunderstand or to undermine the very idea of the "public interest" and the "public service."

Suppose the thin-edge-of-the-wedge argument is correct. If so, then the last stages of privatization would have several key features. Curricula would be driven by considerations of employability and profit alone. Control of education would reside with stockholders. Democratic civic education would be a luxury reserved for schools where parents insisted on it. Schools for the rich would look different from those for the poor, and it would become less and less likely that minority groups and disadvantaged persons were as well educated as the rest.

This doom-laden forecast is, like all forecasts in human affairs, uncertain. It does, however, gain force if one considers the popularity, among privatizers anyway, of a device called the "education voucher." Under a voucher system, every school-age child in a provincial or national jurisdiction would receive a "basic public grant" of money that could be spent at any educational institution whatsoever, whether it be "public" schools, private schools, new schools, home schools, and so on.[9] The enactment of a voucher scheme means the triumph of "consumer orientation in education" (to quote a recent announcement by an American proponent of privatization in public schools). This in turn implies, as Peter Schrag writes, "[a] shrinking regard for education as an integrating community enterprise."[10]

But are all the dangers of privatization in public education present at the postsecondary level? Would privatization make sense in universities? And what would it look like?[11]

II

The university occupies a political "space" quite different from that of public schools. But if universities differ from the public schools in important ways, they can still learn from the recent history of privatization at elementary and secondary levels.

Universities differ most obviously from schools in that university clients are adults, not minors. This means the Ministry of Education need not control or supervise the university's curriculum, nor has it the right to insist on any particular pedagogical approach in teaching that curriculum.

Universities, however, claim much more than a negative freedom, that is, mere freedom *from* government control. They also insist that their job *demands* positive freedom. The work of university teachers, they say, is a combination of teaching, research, and community service. They say that a university teacher *must* usually be a researcher—although the term "researcher" may be broadly understood. The advancement of knowledge is the work of the whole academic community, teachers and students and public together. Teaching and publication are the usual ways of subjecting ideas and arguments to criticism and discussion. Thus, without teaching and publication, research cannot be of the highest quality. And without doing research, teacher-publishers will have nothing new to say.

In any true university, teaching, research, and publication must *all* be done under a condition we call "academic freedom." Unless researcher-teachers have the assurance they will not be punished (fired, demoted, disciplined, or reprimanded) for freely speaking their minds, they will hesitate or even refuse to carry out work that may put their careers (or even their lives, in some countries) at risk. There are limits on academic freedom, but perhaps the easiest way to understand them is to spend a moment with the definition given by the Canadian Association of University Teachers in 1977:

> The common good of society depends upon the search for knowledge and its free exposition. Academic freedom in universities is essential to both these purposes in the teaching function of the university as well as in its scholarship and research. Academic staff shall not be hindered or impeded in any way by the university or the faculty association from exercising their legal rights as citizens, nor shall they suffer any penalties because of the exercise of such legal rights. The parties agree that they will not infringe or abridge the academic freedom of any member of the academic community. Academic members of the community are entitled, regardless of prescribed doctrine, to freedom in carrying out research and in publishing the results thereof, freedom of teaching and of discussion, freedom to criticize the university and the faculty association, and freedom from institutional censorship. Academic freedom does not require neutrality on the part of the individual. Rather, academic freedom makes commitment possible.

> Academic freedom carries with it the duty to use that freedom in a manner consistent with the scholarly obligation to base research and teaching on an honest search for knowledge.[12]

Academic freedom by this definition also requires that universities and colleges will enjoy curricular autonomy, independence in the hiring and firing of academic and other staff, and full financial authority over their own affairs.

It would be too much to expect that governments would hand over large chunks of taxpayers' cash to universities without some assurance that those funds were well spent. That assurance is provided in at least the following ways: the research records and teaching practices of staff members are (or should be) entirely open to the public; the financial records and practices are (or should be) entirely open to public scrutiny; and the curricular and administrative decision making of universities should take place in public bodies (academic senates and boards of governors) and in public view.

I think privatization in higher education, in any of its several possible forms, threatens academic freedom. It discourages the transparency or openness I have just outlined, and it undermines academic freedom.

This may sound a bit odd, since so many universities, some of them very well known and "excellent," are already private. Examples would include Harvard and Stanford universities in the United States, Oxford and Cambridge universities before 1944, and most Canadian universities before 1914. (After 1944 in the United Kingdom, and after 1914 in Canada, public funding accounted for an increasingly significant proportion of these universities' budgets.)

But the big problem is not the existence of private universities; rather, the big problem is privatizers' attacks on free scholarship and public accessibility in post-secondary education. In what follows, I consider three types of privatization and show how and why privatization produces these attacks. I also show how and why privatization is likely to beget intellectual mediocrity, to encourage a decline—not an increase—in accountability to the public, and, in the last analysis, to be wasteful of human and financial resources.[13]

I begin with the voucher system, in which Proteus pretends to be client centred and market sensitive. I then deal with cases where universities sell their property or their research capacity to private interests and persons. I conclude with the subtlest case of all, where private persons and corporations make "donations" in return for having their names attached to buildings or programs of teaching and research.

III

At the moment (1997), no province has yet brought in a system of vouchers, although Ontario is talking about it. By contrast, there are numerous examples to show that the other two forms of privatization (sale of university property and university research capacity, and sale of the names of university buildings or programs) are spreading quickly across the land. Vouchers nonetheless deserve our attention, if only because they are always mentioned when privatizers get together to plot the future governance and finance of universities. Besides, there is much talk at the moment of a near-voucher system, the so-called Income Contingent Repayment Plan (ICRP). Under this plan, students would be permitted to incur a certain amount of debt (probably in the order of twenty-five thousand dollars or more) and to repay this debt through an income surtax over an unspecified future period. Those who earn high salaries would repay student debt more quickly than those who find themselves in minimum-income jobs.[14]

Proponents of the voucher system for university and college students say that universities would thereby become more "accountable" for their activities, and far more efficient. Under a voucher scheme, universities would no longer receive public grants to subsidize their teaching activities. All money now given to universities in Canada in support of teaching would simply be divided into (roughly) a half-million parts and distributed to "client students." Universities would have to compete for students and the money students bring with them. Efficiencies would follow, as universities sought to attract the best students. The *best* universities could attract not only the most students and vouchers, but also students who could pay tuition and living costs in excess of the basic voucher amount. Wealthy students would find it worthwhile to pay the extra amount since a degree from the "best" place would be most likely to produce the best jobs.

Poor students and minority students would have opportunities, voucher enthusiasts argue, equal to those of majoritarian, middle-class students under present arrangements. The reason (they say) is that a voucher system would ensure universities contract with "clients" to provide specific and measurable results ... or else. Students might insist the University of X provide them knowledge and know-how that *guarantees* future employment or else those students would have the right to sue the university for nonperformance of duty. Everyone is equal before the law; therefore, a voucher system ensures equality.

Vouchers mean privatization since government requirements for *transparency* in university governance would be replaced by client *control* of universities. Anyone who knows the recent history of privatization schemes in public education will remember the consequences of corporatization in Chelsea and elsewhere. But in the case of universities, there is an argument that the consequences would be even more sweeping and even more severe.

If students came to universities with the calculated demand that they receive only training that would ready them for instant employment, what sort of training would that be? For one thing, it would be training, not education. A university education implies the study of advanced forms of reason and inquiry in various academic disciplines. Given the pressures of the marketplace, would a voucher-bearing student tolerate a leisurely and excellent curriculum? Or would she prefer to study only those fields that could be applied in the occupation in which she intends to work? Would she check with her future employers to make sure that she studied only the applicable bits? If she was planning to spend the next decade of her life in Sudbury extracting nickel from the deep reaches of the Canadian Shield, would she feel she had the luxury to learn a foreign language? And if she succeeded in forcing the university to offer only narrowly "relevant" training, what would happen to the research that usually informs teaching? Her teachers would feel no particular need to present research-based teaching to our imaginary student.

A last point about vouchers, no less serious than all the rest: the economy is changing at blinding speed. Training for occupation X may be suitable for the job of 1999, but will it work for the job of 2005?

IV

What about the sale of a university's property or research capacity to private interests?[15] At the University of British Columbia (UBC) under the administration of David Strangway (president from 1985 to 1997), the board of governors was persuaded to lease a significant chunk of university land to a private corporation, which it helped to found. That corporation in turn built a series of high- and low-rise condominium apartment buildings on that land. The proceeds of the lease will fund a perpetual endowment for research at UBC.

Here is Proteus, but under a subtler guise than was seen in the voucher system. The background is that government funding has declined radically, in real dollars, since 1971. The decline has been so lengthy and so severe that UBC has found itself compelled to find new sources of funds.

In the 1980s, UBC raised fees for foreign students, and then raised fees for everybody. Throughout the 1980s and 1990s, UBC pushed hard to find new sources of research and development grants, many of them from private, non-governmental sources. Each of these decisions had consequences for the curriculum. Some departments in arts, science, and education have been mauled, others not; the reasons have little to do with the real educational interests of students and the public and a lot to do with funding sources. The lease or sale of public lands is just one more in a long series of privatizing moves whose effects will be little different from those I described earlier, except that the effects are on a relatively small scale and are not immediately noticeable.

A related, but even less noticeable, form of privatization is the sale of research capacity to the private sector. Universities have been in the business of selling their research and development *results* to the private sector for hundreds of years. Just as universities have moved at increasing speeds to adjust to changes in the medical, legal, teaching, and other professions, they have also moved more and more quickly to answer the call of government and industry to supply knowledge and skill when and where it is most needed. There's nothing much to worry about here, since the universities have aimed in all these cases to keep their independence.

It's a different story when a private entity "buys" a university laboratory's research staff and their future intellectual work. That entity is buying the ability, the capacity, of the university to make new knowledge. At the University of Toronto, for example, the Nortel Corporation recently proposed a master plan for collaborative R&D (research and development).[16] The idea was that Nortel would offer several million dollars to subsidize the creation of new scientific laboratories whose work would be limited to be useful to Nortel but also to fit with some of the university's curricular aims. In a separate agreement, Nortel proposed to underwrite three permanent professorial appointments in areas of science it had chosen; in return, Nortel wished to have some influence over who would be appointed and over the decision whether those appointees would receive tenure. There was also uncertainty whether the research results of these laboratories and professors would be published in the usual fashion (that is, quickly).

Many Canadian academics learned about the Nortel proposals from news stories in the University of Toronto's student paper, the *Varsity*. There was an immediate storm of protest, since the Nortel proposals would have given this private company influence over academic decisions previously in the hands of the university's academic board (elsewhere called the Senate). In the end, the proposals were modified to retain the traditional separation of public and private powers. The Nortel story is important, however, for two main reasons. First, it shows how the usual standards of scientific and academic work *always* come under pressure when a university "sells" its research capacity to the private sector. Second, the growing pressure to privatize has led to the devising of contracts in private, which has serious implications for the public good of teachers and students alike. But how many contracts are being arranged without public scrutiny, and with the effect of making the university a less transparent place?

V

Lastly, what about the naming of buildings and programs after major donors? At the University of Toronto, the centre for management was named after Joseph L. Rotman after he donated about fifteen million dollars in cash, and much more than that in equivalent real estate values.[17] By any standards, these were generous acts. Over the past thousand years, universities have gratefully accepted this sort of generous help, and have become better for it.

Once again, in the course of several months of journalistic investigation in 1996 and after several speeches by the president of the University of Toronto Faculty Association, it became clear that Rotman's donation had strings attached. The Rotman School of Business was to be compelled within ten years to achieve world-class status, according to the judgment of Rotman and a committee, or else face financial consequences. Further, its staff were expected to demonstrate a strong commitment to the "mission" of the school. Under considerable public pressure, these conditions were modified, and it now seems the requirements of academic freedom have been satisfied.

As with the Nortel affair, the public learned details of the Rotman agreement well after the university administration had begun negotiations for the donation, and for the school. The risks of accepting the money and the requirement to name a building after a donor would have been hugely reduced if the whole matter had been public from the start.

Such events lead to straightforward recommendations about naming buildings and programs: all discussions about such matters should be on the public record, subject to public discussion in academic decision-making bodies, and arranged so that the eventual donation does not require teachers and researchers to give up even a fragment of academic freedom and autonomy. The naming of programs of instruction (as opposed to buildings) probably crosses the boundary of the acceptable, since it ties the interests and values of the donor so publicly to the research plans and the curriculum of the department concerned. Because so many "chairs" have been named after the people who produce the millions of dollars required to support them, it's probably too late to change that particular practice.

Where, then, is the borderline? One last example from the University of Toronto will help here. Consider Peter Munk's 1997 donation (once again, to the University of Toronto) in support of a centre for international studies and the naming of a building (the Munk Centre?) to memorialize the event. This donation also was proposed in private, and the contract pried from administration hands only after an application under Ontario's Freedom of Information Act.[18] Here again, the question was whether a nonacademic committee would have strong influence over the studies Munk wished to support. Whether to put emphasis on this aspect of the university's curriculum had not been discussed by the academic board. After public debate, the contract was modified to ensure the university's academic autonomy and to place emphasis on collegial decision making. The donor must have found the whole debate distasteful, and more than a little surprising. As a *Varsity* journalist put it,

> [t]he ability to strike a delicate balance between ... university autonomy and ... the desires of private sector friends is becoming the key test of administrative integrity in an age of fundraising mania.[19]

The final, revised Munk contract solved most of the problems raised in public debate.

Turning to matters where the public/private borderline is still more blurry, what of the University of British Columbia, where Coca-Cola was given a monopoly over soft-drink supply in return for a hundred thousand dollars? At that same university, privatization has also made available external funding for forest products research, cancer research, and cement products research—and its visible effects are large buildings in which that research can go on. In each case, these apparently modest steps toward privatization have been joyously welcomed by a university administration desperate for funding as federal and provincial grants decline or disappear. Privatization is increasingly Protean, increasingly risk-laden.

In British Columbia, the creation of two new universities without any provision for academic senates and no provisions for academic freedom, Royal Roads University and the Technical University of British Columbia, show yet another of Proteus's faces. TechBC, by late 1997 under a boycott organized by Canada's university teachers, was explicitly committed to "the requirements of industrial and economic development in British Columbia." Here a government has *itself* chosen to eliminate essential ways of protecting the public interest, simply ignoring basic requirements of modern university governance. This is a case of the state dismantling itself, and, by definition, it's therefore a matter of privatization.[20]

VI

I have tried to show that privatization, behind its changing exterior, has a darker purpose—the dismantling of the instruments of the public interest. That dismantling would go beyond the selling off of public institutions, in whole or in part. Its final effect would be to weaken the very *idea* of the public interest.

In recent Canadian history, members of the public have shown that they continue to like their public services, even if they are skeptical about the very institutions and instruments that provide those services. Public universities are seen, as is the entire enterprise of public instruction, to be central to the survival of democratic practice and democratic community in Canada. Privatization in the university, as it has developed in the past quarter-century, is a direct and dangerous threat to both that practice and that community.

NOTES

1. Cf. "Proteus," in Sir P. Harvey, *The Oxford Companion to Classical Literature* (Oxford: Clarendon Press, 1937), p. 350.

2. General Accounting Office, Government of the United States, *Private Management of Public Schools: Early Experiences in Four School Districts: Report to Congressional Committees* (Washington, DC: GAO/Health, Education, and Human Services Division, 1996), pp. 1–76. The Education Alternatives, Inc. contract in Chelsea runs for ten years, 1989–1999.

3. Educational Alternatives stock was listed at one point near $US 45 3/8, falling in the summer of 1997 to $US 4 5/8.

4. Economic Policy Institute, "EPI Report Finds School Privatization Experiments Costly and Have Failed to Improve Public Education; Authors Propose Options for Improving the Educational Reform Process, July 23, 1996" (Washington, DC: Economic Policy Institute, 1996 *[http://epn.org/epi/epriskyb.html]*).

5. G. Jacobs, "History, Crisis, and Social Panic: Minority Resistance to Privatization of an Urban School System," *Urban Review* 25, no. 3 (1993): 175–198.

6. L.E. Leak and L.C. Williams, "Private Management of Public Schools: The Baltimore Experience," unpublished paper at the Annual Meeting of the American Educational Research Association, Chicago, Illinois, March 25, 1997 (Education Research Information Centre [ERIC] no. ED407731). Leak and Williams describe how Education Alternatives, Inc. (EAI) provided management of nine of Baltimore, Maryland's 180 public schools between 1992 and 1996. EAI's contract was terminated in 1996 when it became clear that its schools were not producing better test results for pupils.

The decision to privatize on the basis of test scores, or to make the system public on the basis of test scores, is itself a revealing one. Surely public education is about many things, not just numerical scores on standardized national and international tests. The Baltimore case shows how privatization narrows and transforms the very idea of any public enterprise it touches.

7. J.A. Gliedman, "The Choice between Educational Privatization and Parental Governance," *Journal of Law and Education* 20, no. 4 (1991): 395–419. Gliedman argues that Chelsea's privately run system is at least as open to parental "input" as was the preceding public system. His views should be contrasted to those of Jacobs in "History, Crisis, and Social Panic."

8. P. Schrag, "'F' is for Fizzle: The Faltering School Privatization Movement," *The American Prospect* 26 (1996 May–June): 67–71. Schrag describes the circumstances under which EAI contracts in Hartford and Baltimore were cancelled.

9. For an energetic defence of vouchers, see S. Easton, *Education in Canada: An Analysis of Elementary, Secondary, and Vocational Schooling* (Vancouver, BC: Fraser Institute, 1988), pp. 1–122. For a critical discussion, see W. Bruneau, "British Columbia's Right Wing and Public Education," *Our Schools/Our Selves: A Magazine for Canadian Education Activists* 1, no. 4 (1989 August): 94–106.

10. P. Schrag, "'F' is for Fizzle," 70. See also P.D. Houston, "Making Watches or Making Music: Arguments Against Private Management of Public Schools," *Phi Delta Kappan* 76, no. 2 (1994 October).

11. *Cf.* G. Williams, "The Many Faces of Privatisation," *Higher Education Management* 8, no, 3 (November 1996): 39–57.

12. Policy Statement on Academic Freedom. Approved by the Council of the Canadian Association of University Teachers. May 1977.

13. I have not dealt with the foundation of private universities, although see note 20, below. Canada's only private university, Trinity Western University of British Columbia, is likely to remain the only private foundation for some time. Besides, my concern is with *public* institutions and the pressure to move them *out* of the public sector.

14. For an extensive and nuanced debate on ICRPs, see E.G. West, C. Duncan, and J.R. Kesselman, *Ending the Squeeze on Universities* (Montreal: Institute for Research on Public Policy, 1993).

15. J. Doctrow et al., "Privatizing University Properties," *Planning for Higher Education* 24, no. 4 (Summer 1996): 18–22; G.B. Biddison, "When Your Dorms Become Their Business," *Trusteeship* 4, no. 3 (May–June 1996): 19–23.

16. For background to the Nortel donation, see the National Research Council press release for June 10, 1996, "Business, Universities, and Government Team Up to Meet Tomorrow's Software Challenges."

17. "U of T's Business Showcase: University Puts Management School at Head of the Class," *Toronto Star,* September 21, 1995; "Business Schools Seek Corporate Aid," *Toronto Star,* September 28, 1995.

18. V. Monty, "Due North: Issues in Access to Government Information: A View from Canada," *Journal of Government Information* 23, no. 4 (July–August 1996): 491–97.

19. Meg Murphy, "U of T Backtracks on Munk Contract: University Falters in Fundraising Balancing Act," *Varsity News,* December 1, 1997, p. 1.

20. W. Bruneau, "Technical University of British Columbia," unpublished paper, Annual Meeting, Western Regional Conference of University Faculty Associations, Vancouver, October 18, 1997 [http://www.caut.ca].

Postscript

Auld presents an attractive picture of privatization efforts in the area of university education. With privatization, institutions of higher education would be given greater freedom to carry out their responsibilities, and students would be provided with greater choice and arguably a type of education more suited to their particular needs. Nevertheless, a certain uneasiness may develop in some who read Auld's effort. The move toward privatization may lead to what might be called "education by e-mail," a development that may not be in the long-term best interest of students and society. More unsettling, there is a sense that access to the world of privatized universities may depend largely on a student's financial resources. The Canadian university system has been fairly successful in making itself accessible to all would-be students, but such accessibility may disappear if privatization becomes prevalent.

Finally, Auld's call for "market-driven institutions" may not be greeted warmly in some quarters, for a market-based approach may be inconsistent with the traditional goals of higher education in Canada. Such an approach induces a certain mindset about universities, one that suggests that universities are essentially corporate forms in the business of selling a particular good. Recently, a dean at one of Canada's most prestigious business schools announced that all the spots in the school had been "sold." This is not how admission to universities has typically been conceptualized, but this is how privatization may force universities to think.

In his article, Bruneau offers a vigorous—and compelling—critique of the various attempts to introduce elements of privatization into higher education. Yet, as with Auld, the presentation may not be wholly convincing. Bruneau is suspicious of what he calls "client control," which is essentially allowing the client—the student—greater say over the offerings of universities. With more client control, Bruneau fears the end of the well-rounded liberal arts curriculum, to be replaced by a more job-oriented course of study. But this concern sounds almost paternalistic, a claim that students do not really know their own interests. Also, some might accuse Bruneau of being unrealistic, that in times of decreasing public funding universities may be forced to bend on certain traditional principles in order to secure necessary funding from private sources.

To begin an investigation of the issue of privatization and universities, students might consult David Cameron's history of universities in Canada. The text, which is entitled *More Than an Academic Question: Universities, Government, and Public Policy in Canada* (Halifax: Institute for Research on Public Policy, 1991), provides the necessary background for assessing the debate topic. Another helpful text for introducing universities is Harry Kitchen and Douglas Auld, *Financing Education and Training in Canada* (Toronto: Canadian Tax Foundation, 1995). The next step is to gain some understanding of the present state of universities in

Canada. For this, one might read the Commission of Inquiry on Canadian University Education, *Report* (Ottawa: Association of Universities and Colleges of Canada, 1991). Though somewhat dated, the analysis contained in the report is still relevant. For an example of a more up-to-date analysis, a 1996 publication of the Ontario Ministry of Education and Training entitled *Future Goals for Ontario Colleges and Universities: Discussion Paper* (Toronto: Ministry of Education and Training, 1996) might be useful. A more provocative analysis of universities is contained in David Bercuson, Robert Bothwell, and J.L. Granatstein, *Petrified Campus: The Crisis in Canada's Universities* (Toronto: Random House of Canada, 1997). Unlike the aforementioned studies, which tend to be rather circumspect in their analyses, this one pulls no punches (as the title itself suggests).

Finally, the student should confront directly the issue of privatization and universities. To do this, one needs to grapple with the meaning of privatization, for this is a rather slippery term. A serviceable discussion of privatization can be found in Joseph Murray, *The Privatization of Schooling: Problems and Possibilities* (Thousand Oaks: Corwin Press, 1996), ch. 2. A more sophisticated treatment of the concept is offered in E.S. Savas, *Privatization: The Key to Government* (Chatham, N.J.: Chatham House Publishers, 1987). On the topic of privatization and universities, some of the texts mentioned in the preceding paragraph are relevant. In addition, Peter C. Emberley's *Zero Tolerance: Hot Button Politics in Canada's Universities* (Toronto: Penguin Books, 1996) contains chapters that deal with various aspects of privatization (and other chapters include insightful analyses of higher education in Canada). Douglas Auld has written a monograph on the issue entitled *Expanding Horizons: Privatizing Universities* (Toronto: University of Toronto, 1996). John Ralston Saul, in his book *The Unconscious Civilization* (Toronto: Anansi, 1995), also has some interesting things to say about the effect of corporations on universities.

ISSUE**TWENTY-TWO**

Is Workfare Sound Public Policy?

✔ **YES**
MICHAEL KRASHINSKY, "The Role of Workfare in the Social Safety Net"

✘ **NO**
ERNIE S. LIGHTMAN, "Workfare: It's Jobs, Not Pathology"

Over the past few decades, spending on welfare and social assistance has increased quite dramatically in Canada. In the early 1980s, about 1.4 million Canadians were recipients of welfare payments; ten years later, that figure had jumped to 3 million. With the increase in welfare caseloads, expenditures on social assistance rose to $67 billion, representing about one-fifth of all government spending. A number of reasons have been offered to explain this troubling development, one of which revolves around the operation and structure of welfare programs. A key to dealing with the welfare problem, it seems, lies in reforming the welfare system.

Welfare reform can involve a number of components. For example, eligibility requirements may be changed, or benefit levels can be adjusted. One particular reform that has received a great deal of attention recently in Canada and the United States is *workfare*. Under a workfare arrangement, welfare recipients are required to carry out a designated activity. Sometimes the activity relates to job search or training, but in many workfare proposals it means doing some kind of actual work, be it collecting garbage, sweeping streets, or shovelling snow. For governments who advocate workfare, the hope is that it will help build a work ethic among welfare recipients, and better prepare them for future opportunities in the job market. A more immediate aim is a lessening of costs. Workfare may lead to fewer welfare recipients as it aids some in making the jump to real jobs; also, it may deter others from even applying for welfare because of the work requirement.

In Canada, some provincial governments have eagerly embraced workfare. Perhaps the most ardent supporter of the policy is the government of Ontario. In 1995, the Progressive Conservative Party of Ontario won office partly on its promise to introduce workfare. Its pledge to put welfare recipients to work struck a chord with many voters, and the result was electoral victory. Other provinces, too, have introduced elements of workfare, and in the United States a major overhaul of welfare included an important workfare component.

Notwithstanding this popularity, workfare is not without its critics. The compulsory quality of workfare suggests that recipients of social assistance are unwilling to work, yet it is argued that this is false. The problem lies not with the recipient, or even with the welfare program, but rather with the absence of jobs. Workfare, in other words, misspecifies the problem. The claims of cost savings are also viewed critically, for most experiences with workfare reveal *additional* costs, not lower costs. More generally, some view workfare as essentially mean spirited: it punishes those who have been unable to find a job or are not capable of working.

This last criticism leads perhaps to the most important reason for the emergence of workfare. In Canada, and other countries as well, an important value is that "you don't get something for nothing." To be paid, one must work. That applies to *most* people, and the popularity of workfare suggests a desire in the electorate for this to apply to *all* people, including those on welfare. The question, though, is whether this is a fair sentiment, when there might not be work for all.

In the readings, Michael Krashinsky, an economist at the University of Toronto, presents some arguments for workfare. As will be seen, Krashinsky accepts that workfare has its failings, but nevertheless argues that it is in the public interest. Ernie Lightman, a professor of social work at the University of Toronto, contends that workfare is a badly flawed policy.

✔ YES
The Role of Workfare in the Social Safety Net*
MICHAEL KRASHINSKY

I. INTRODUCTION

Canada's welfare system is currently under scrutiny, both because of the financial pressures on all levels of government and because of the resulting high levels of taxation on Canadians. Governments face large deficits and must therefore cut expenditures, and the high cost of current welfare programs makes them an attractive target. Canadian taxpayers face rising taxes and shrinking paycheques, and often resent people collecting welfare instead of working.

Both reactions are based on real concerns and neither is inappropriate. Increasingly, concern about the high cost of the welfare system is cutting across party (and ideological) lines. Across all levels of government, public sector expenditures were about 48 percent of GDP in 1995, and taxes and other government revenue accounted for about 44 percent of GDP, generating a deficit equal to 4.1 percent of GDP. Taxpayers with long memories might recall times when government revenues took a significantly smaller chunk out of their gross paycheques: in 1980, government revenues accounted for 37.5 percent of GDP, while in 1960 the equivalent number was 27.1 percent.[1] Since not all of GDP is taxable,[2] and maintaining work incentives requires that those with low incomes pay little, if any, tax,[3] the marginal tax rate is quite high for average Canadians: for most provinces in 1993, the combined federal and provincial marginal tax rates on income over $30 000 were well in excess of 40 percent. And, since the personal income tax accounts for only about 40 percent of total taxes paid by Canadians (who also pay payroll taxes, sales taxes, property taxes, and other charges, as well as bearing a large portion of the taxes on businesses), the true marginal rate is significantly higher.[4]

Of course, the problem certainly cannot be blamed entirely on the welfare system. Yet, expenditures on social assistance have been a significant burden on the government, especially during recessions. In 1991 (the first year of a recession), spending on social services[5] in Canada totalled just over $67 billion, about 22 percent of government spending in that year (not including the Canada and Quebec Pension Plans; if interest on the debt is omitted, the figure is over 27 percent), and about 10 percent of GDP! And the problem appears to be getting worse. In 1982, the first year of the previous recession (and hence comparable to 1991),[6] spending on social services was about 8 percent of GDP.[7]

Out of all this has come a natural interest in some form of work requirement for those on welfare. Politicians and taxpayers see this as a way to reduce expenditures, since if welfare recipients were working and earning incomes, then welfare payments could presumably be reduced. The savings could be applied to deficit reduction and might also finance tax cuts. And hardworking taxpayers see work requirements as a simple matter of equity: most adult Canadians work for a living, so why shouldn't those on public assistance also be asked to help support themselves?

These arguments have been quite powerful politically. In the 1995 Ontario election, Mike Harris and his Conservative Party found the issue of workfare was of concern to many voters, and it quickly became a centrepiece in a successful campaign. But although the new government acted quite quickly in a number of areas (including slashing the level of welfare benefits), it did not move quickly to implement workfare. This suggests—correctly, I will argue—that work requirements may not be the "quick fix" that was suggested in the easy rhetoric of an election, and that the prospective savings for the public purse are, in the short run, illusory.

Despite this, I believe that a convincing case can be made for some form of workfare as part of the welfare system. This case depends more on long-term arguments about labour force attachment and work incentives than on short-term arguments about cutting costs. A work requirement will not reduce expenditures on those at the bottom of the income distribution. But it will keep marginal tax rates at a reasonable level, maintain political support for our social programs, and sustain the work ethic among recipients and their families.

In this paper I will present an economist's perspective on work requirements. The next section will show the inevitable tradeoff between high tax rates and decent support for the disadvantaged. As discussed in the third section, a work requirement can address this problem by allowing marginal tax rates to be quite high on welfare recipients. The fourth section, however, will suggest that work requirements are unlikely to save much money because most welfare recipients do attempt to find work, and because providing daycare to welfare mothers forced to work, generating jobs for those unable to find work, and administering the system will be quite expensive. The final section will then try to draw these two views together and consider how workfare might fit into a reformed welfare system.

II. THE BASIC ECONOMIC CASE FOR WORK REQUIREMENTS

The case in favour of some kind of work requirement for those receiving welfare rests on some relatively simple arithmetic. To understand this, it is important first to become familiar with the way economists think about the welfare system. Every family that cannot support itself will potentially require welfare assistance. As the family is able to work and earn income, welfare is naturally reduced. Of course, we cannot take away welfare too quickly, or the family on welfare will have no incentive to go out and find work. Thus the government must set a "taxback rate," reducing welfare by some fraction of any earned income. At some point, the family earns enough, receives no welfare payments, and pays net taxes to the government.

This simplified version of the welfare system is sometimes called a "negative income tax." In designing such a system for helping the poor, the government must set the support level provided to those without any income and must also establish taxback and tax rates. In setting these, the government has three goals: to provide enough money for the very needy; to set tax rates and taxback rates low enough to preserve work incentives and discourage tax evasion; and to raise enough tax revenue to pay for public services. It has become clear that the government simply cannot meet all three goals. Facing significant taxpayer resistance and a large welfare caseload, the system can no longer be sustained. Requiring work may represent a way out of this trap.

To understand this, it is necessary to build a simple model of the negative income tax system. Economists generally model welfare and the tax system together. This is because a family's disposable income (what the family has available to spend at the end of the day) is equal to what the family earns plus what the family receives in transfer payments from the government (including welfare payments and UIC benefits), minus what the family pays in taxes. Thus the net of taxes and welfare payments is what comes between earned income and disposable income.

A simple example is shown in Table 22.1. Here the family receives welfare payments of $22 000 when there are no earnings, and pays taxes (sales and property taxes, for example) of $2000. As earnings increase, welfare payments fall and taxes rise, but the example is constructed so that the family is never worse off when it earns more income. In this case, the overall gain when income rises is quite small—the family keeps just $2000 out of every extra $10 000 earned because the government effectively takes back 80 percent of what the family earns (in reality, of course, the system may be perverse, so that families in certain circumstances may be worse off when their earnings rise). When income is less than $25 000, welfare payments exceed taxes and the family is a net recipient; when income exceeds $25 000, taxes exceed welfare payments, so that the family's disposable income is less than its earnings (even though it may still be receiving welfare payments). When income is equal to $25 000, welfare payments and taxes exactly balance.

Of course, this example is fictional, but it shows that the system of welfare and taxes can be seen as a single schedule that relates a family's disposable income to what it earns. The two key elements of the schedule are the net payment when earned income is zero and the rate at which "taxes minus welfare" is increased as earnings rise (in Table 22.1, these are $20 000 and 80 percent). This latter rate is the sum of the benefit reduction rate (which we have called the "taxback rate") and the tax rate (the rate at which taxes rise as earnings rise), and is thus a "combined" tax rate. In effect, in the table, it is as if all families were given an initial

TABLE 22.1

EARNINGS, TAXES AND TRANSFERS, AND DISPOSABLE INCOME

EARNINGS	WELFARE	TAXES	TAXES MINUS WELFARE	DISPOSABLE INCOME
0	$22 000	$2 000	–$20 000	$20 000
$10 000	$14 500	$2 500	–$12 000	$22 000
$20 000	$7 000	$3 000	–$4 000	$24 000
$25 000	$3 250	$3 250	0	$25 000
$30 000	0	$4 000	+$4 000	$26 000
$40 000	0	$12 000	+$12 000	$28 000

payment of $20 000 and then were "taxed" on all their earnings at the "combined" tax rate.[8]

Although Table 22.1 is made up as an example, it is not that far off from reality. In Appendix 22.1 are some "back of the envelope" calculations of the kinds of welfare payments and combined tax rates necessary for Canadian governments to operate with approximately balanced budgets. The appendix contains some simple algebra, and is worth the attention of readers who are not put off by numbers. These calculations show the undeniable dilemma facing policymakers. When we provide support of $20 000 to families of four without any other income (and $20 000 is not far off from the poverty line for these families), then we must use a combined tax rate of close to 80 percent to raise the money necessary to pay for other government programs.

There are only three ways to lower this tax rate. The first way is to reduce the basic welfare payment to families with no income below $20 000. But this means essentially accepting the continuation of poverty for families who, for various reasons, cannot earn any money. The second way is to accept large and continuing government deficits. But voters and politicians, as well as international bond rating services, seem to see this as unacceptable. The third way is to disqualify various families from the welfare system. In a sense, this is what workfare tries to do. For families with adult members who are judged capable of working, welfare will not be available unless those adults are prepared to enter the labour force.

Of course, the 80 percent tax rates are what cause this dilemma. It is thus useful to discuss why such rates are problematic. The difficulty is that in the system we have designed, the *marginal* tax rate of 80 percent applies *over the entire range* of earnings. This means that these high marginal rates apply not only to dentists, bank presidents, and university professors, but also to those with middle and low incomes. The incentive problems associated with those kinds of rates are considerable. When rates get up as high as 80 percent, middle income Canadians see little benefit from working, welfare recipients see little point in entering the workforce, and all Canadians have little incentive to engage in activities that will raise their incomes, especially if those activities ("working harder," for example) are not pleasant. And of course, tax evasion becomes more and more serious as tax rates rise, making even higher marginal tax rates necessary to raise the required revenue. The net effect of all this is that productivity falls and our economy grinds to a halt.

Many Canadians are honest and hard working, and will continue to do their best even in the face of near-confiscatory marginal tax rates. But experience suggests that when tax rates get too high, work effort and tax compliance erode over time. What this discussion should make clear is that this problem is a fundamental part of any comprehensive welfare scheme. To raise enough revenue for the public programs other than welfare now in place in Canada, and to provide a reasonable support level for those with no other source of income, we require tax rates that are clearly too high. But to cut those tax rates requires either a dramatic reduction in the support available to the poorest members of society or involves dramatic revenue shortfalls for the rest of the government. Clearly, a generous negative income tax is simply not possible.

Given this fundamental problem with high tax rates, we seem to be caught in a dilemma. Our economy cannot tolerate the kinds of tax rates discussed above. But our sense of social obligation toward the less fortunate members of our society requires a reasonable safety net for those unable to earn a decent living (this safety net was summarized by the figure of $20 000 paid to our poorest welfare recipients in Table 22.1). In the past, the problem was avoided by severely limiting access to the welfare system and providing assistance only to those thought to be "deserving" in one sense or another. The deserving poor were those who, it was felt, could not (or should not) work. This group might include the elderly, people with severe disabilities, and, possibly, mothers with young children. Since everyone else was ineligible for assistance, Table 22.1 would not apply to most families. But our current welfare system expresses our belief that some assistance must be made available to people who are "employable" but either without work or unable to earn enough to escape poverty. And that belief lands us squarely in the dilemma we have been addressing. And of course, the rising costs of other government programs increase the other revenue requirements of the government and increase the tax rates necessary to meet our deficit targets.

The case for some sort of work requirement can now be seen in the context of this dilemma. The only way to reduce high marginal tax rates, as seen in Table 22.1, on most taxpayers is to increase taxback rates on welfare recipients. This can be seen in Table 22.2. The second and third columns simply continue Table 22.1 into the higher income ranges. The fourth and fifth columns show an altered situation with a very high tax rate of 90 percent on welfare recipients combined with a somewhat lower tax rate of 60 percent on those above the welfare cutoff. This latter marginal tax rate is somewhat closer to what Canadians face today and is prob-

TABLE 22.2

EARNINGS, TAXES AND TRANSFERS, AND DISPOSABLE INCOME

EARNINGS	WELFARE SYSTEM: M = 20 000 TAX RATE: 80%		WELFARE SYSTEM: M*= 20 000 TAX RATE: 90% ON FIRST $30 000 AND 60% ON ADDITIONAL INCOME	
	TAXES MINUS WELFARE	DISPOSABLE INCOME	TAXES MINUS WELFARE	DISPOSABLE INCOME
0	-$20 000	$20 000	-$20 000	$20 000
$10 000	-$12 000	$22 000	-$11 000	$21 000
$20 000	-$4 000	$24 000	-$2 000	$22 000
$30 000	+$4 000	$26 000	+$7 000	$23 000
$40 000	+$12 000	$28 000	+$13 000	$27 000
$60 000	+$28 000	$32 000	+$25 000	$35 000
$80 000	+$44 000	$36 000	+$37 000	$43 000
$100 000	+$60 000	$40 000	+$49 000	$51 000
$200 000	+$140 000	$60 000	+$109 000	$91 000

*"M" is the minimum net payment when family income is zero.

ably tolerable both politically and economically. But the extraordinary tax rate on welfare recipients ensures that there will be significant work disincentives for those who cannot earn high wages. And the resulting decision not to work causes tremendous resentment among those whose wages are low and whose work ethic is high. In both cases, the result occurs because working does not lift family income much above the support available to those on welfare. A work requirement eliminates the problem by legislating it away. Those receiving assistance are forced to work; those working do not see able-bodied people not working and receiving welfare payments that make them almost as well off.

The welfare crisis has been delayed only because many people facing low wages and a high taxback rate have still preferred to work because of their work ethic and the stigma associated with being on welfare. But although values change slowly, they do change. Over time, that stigma has disappeared, and some might suggest that the work ethic among those who would otherwise qualify for welfare has been eroded. If that is true, then some kind of a work requirement may be necessary.

III. SOME BASIC LIMITATIONS ON THE CASE FOR WORK REQUIREMENTS

The argument above seems irrefutable: we need work requirements because there is no other way to maintain work incentives while raising the funds necessary to run the Canadian government. Surprisingly, governments—including those ideologically committed to workfare—have been slow to introduce work requirements, and reluctant to expand them to all those receiving welfare. There are two separate explanations for this, depending on whether the economy is doing well or badly.

First, if the economy is doing well—if there are low rates of unemployment—work requirements may be both unnecessary and expensive. Most of those who would be affected are already working, and it will be relatively expensive to get the rest into the labour force.

Low rates of unemployment are about 7.5 percent or less. In this situation, most productive people who want jobs can find them within a reasonable amount of time. Thus, work requirements would be effective only if they forced people to work who were able to do so but who were choosing to receive welfare. But a detailed examination of the welfare rolls over the last few decades reveals very few people who could easily be put in this category.

For example, in 1988, the Social Assistance Review Committee (SARC) in Ontario published a report dealing with welfare reform. SARC found that of the 281 074 recipients in 1987, about 20 percent were unemployed, 32 percent were disabled, and 30 percent were single parents. Among the unemployed (largely on short-term assistance[9]), the average stay on welfare was only six and a half months, while those who stayed longer tended to be older (and thus had more trouble getting a job). SARC also looked at all recipients receiving long-term support.[10] Between 1975 and 1984, an average of 40 percent either entered or left the program in each year.[11]

These statistics suggest that welfare dependency has not been an overwhelming problem in the past in Ontario during good times. SARC concluded that "for the majority of recipients, social assistance fills a temporary need in response to a particular life crisis."[12] When unemployment rates are relatively low, a significant number of those on welfare have gone out and looked for jobs, and have gone off the dole.

This suggests that so long as the work ethic stays where it has been in the past, a work requirement will not be particularly useful when the economy is in relatively good shape, since most of those who can work are already doing so. The largest group of welfare recipients who might be affected by workfare are welfare mothers. But even this group has in the past moved off the welfare roles in significant numbers when jobs are available. Those who remain on welfare are likely to be particularly hard to place, and it is probable that little money will be saved.

The reason for this is straightforward. Mothers who can find relatively high-paying jobs and who can make satisfactory care arrangements for their children are probably working already. Thus, those who remain on welfare are most likely to do so because they cannot find good jobs and cannot make good arrangements for their children. That means that those affected by a work requirement will earn low wages, and that providing childcare will be expensive. Since the state would have to ensure that children are well cared for, it is not clear that significant savings will result. For example, daycare for a preschool child (ages 3 to 5 years) costs about $500 per month, or $6000 per year. A minimum wage job earns about $12 000 per year. Clearly, for a parent with two young children, childcare costs would eat up all of the earnings from low-level employment. If the state pays for daycare, but only "taxes back" part of the earnings, public costs rise when the parent goes to work!

Furthermore, most workfare schemes involve time periods in which participants receive training to increase skills and job readiness. During these periods, there would be childcare expenses but no income. As well, a work requirement would necessitate administration and monitoring costs. Under these circumstances, there is no way that employment can result in higher income for the family and reduced costs for the government.[13]

Second, consider what will happen to workfare if the economy is doing badly—if there are high rates of unemployment that are unacceptable to most voters. Now there are few private-sector jobs for those on welfare. In that case, some kind of government jobs would be necessary, and these may end up increasing rather than reducing government costs.

When unemployment rates are high, it will be difficult for those forced to work to find jobs. In a macroeconomic sense, work requirements do not have any effect on aggregate demand. Any jobs found for those on welfare will simply displace other people with jobs (who will then, presumably, in turn need some sort of public assistance). Thus the policy will neither generate new wealth nor save public money.

Furthermore, even though there are not jobs available, those falling under a work requirement will have to find a job. This means that some kind of public-sector jobs of last resort will have to be made available to welfare recipients. Finding appropriate public work will not be trivial, especially given the number of jobs that will be required when unemployment rates are high. And the cost of providing those jobs will be greater than the wages paid, since productive work requires materials, equipment, and supervision. The logistics of providing a variety of jobs to people with very different skills and degrees of job readiness are staggering. The result—the creation of a new and larger public bureaucracy to administer these jobs—will hardly warm the hearts of taxpayers and policymakers.

The cost of the program is further increased by the fact that daycare will have to be provided to mothers who are required to work. As discussed above, this is costly. But at least during good times, these costs are offset by the productivity of those mothers in private-sector jobs. The offset is, of course, significantly reduced if the mothers are now forced to take low-productivity, public-sector jobs.

IV. THE CASE FOR WORK REQUIREMENT REVISITED

Of course, the previous two sections are contradictory. Section II suggested that the welfare system was in crisis, and that our desire to assist the working poor and extend our welfare programs to all those in need would generate marginal tax rates so high as to endanger our economy and our ability to collect taxes. Section III, however, suggested that work requirements are unlikely either to save much money or to help people find many private-sector jobs. Notwithstanding this fact, work requirements can have real value and are likely, in any case, to be part of most welfare systems in the future. There are three explanations for why work requirements, despite their limitations, can be a useful part of an antipoverty strategy.

The first explanation is that labour force attachment should properly be seen as a type of social capital that can be eroded over time, and that a requirement that able-bodied welfare recipients make an effort to work should be seen as an attempt to prevent that erosion. Although I presented SARC's evidence on the relatively short time spent on welfare by most recipients, it should be remembered that these numbers, while illuminating, are also static. That is, they reflect the state of recipients' motivations at the time (the 1970s and early 1980s), but say little about how that motivation may have changed (and may continue to change) over time.

In the United States, some critics suggest that an erosion of the work ethic has meant that poverty is increasingly caused not by inadequate wages but by the fact that many poor households had no one employed. This suggests the emergence of a permanent underclass, on welfare virtually full-time. These kinds of concerns are already being expressed in Canada. There is public concern that an overly generous unemployment insurance program may itself cause significant unemployment. The SARC document itself suggested that the number of employable welfare recipients has been growing, even during periods of relatively low unemployment.[14] Although SARC blames this on the restructuring of the economy that has eliminated low-skill jobs, no evidence is provided to show that there was an absence of minimum wage jobs over the period. A more alarming possible explanation would be an erosion of the willingness of those on welfare to accept those low-skill, dead-end jobs.

The work-ethic-as-social-capital argument suggests that the current situation is not stable. The design of our welfare programs—which makes the receipt of welfare an entitlement—erodes recipients' work ethic as they begin to realize that they are no better off financially when they accept these low-paying jobs. This is especially problematic as real financial levels of support in most Canadian welfare systems have risen over the decades. That welfare recipients have persisted in trying to work even though they gain little financially reflects a significant work ethic. Over time, this ethic can be eroded if these workers begin to look around and notice that other people are doing as well without working. The worker then begins to feel less satisfaction from his efforts and more of a sense that he is being exploited by the system.[15]

A work requirement addresses this directly. Since it establishes the norm that everyone who is able is expected to work, it reinforces the work ethic among those who have it and avoids inevitable resentment toward those who do not. It also communicates in the clearest possible way to children growing up in welfare homes that labour force participation is normal and expected. Incidentally, high-quality daycare directed toward these children may have significant future benefits if it improves the educational readiness of those children when they reach school age.

The second explanation for why work requirements may be necessary is an extension of the first, and reflects the earlier discussion in section II. The work ethic declines when those who work hard for low wages see little reward for doing so. This problem occurs because the taxback rates facing those on welfare are very high (and thus the rewards for working for low wages are correspondingly low). For example, an 80 percent taxback rate means that a welfare recipient contemplating a minimum wage job (which pays only about $12 000 a year) would gain only $2400 a year, barely enough to cover normal employment-related expenses. In reality, of course, taxback rates are often even higher. In many jurisdictions, welfare recipients lose all benefits when they work full-time, which can push marginal tax rates over 100 percent.[16]

But the point in section II was that these taxback rates are to a large extent determined by the relationship of average tax rates to the combination of welfare support levels and government revenue requirements. This relationship cannot be "repealed" by any amount of wishful thinking. Thus, if taxback rates are reduced for those who receive welfare, then tax rates must correspondingly be raised further up the income distribution. And current concerns about tax evasion and the black market suggest that we have reached the practical limits in Canada on increases in tax rates.

A work requirement offers a partial escape from this dilemma. In effect, a work requirement allows us to set the taxback rate for those on welfare at (or close to) 100 percent. Because labour force participation (or participation in some kind of training program) is required, work incentive effects in this range can be ignored, and marginal tax rates further up the income distribution can be lowered accordingly. In essence, the welfare system for these recipients functions as a wage supplement, ensuring that those who are willing to work will end up with enough income to escape poverty.

The third explanation for the necessity of work incentives is political. Workfare may be necessary to maintain political support for our social safety net, making the low level of any cost savings irrelevant. Support among voters for our social safety net may be eroding because of the increasing number of people on welfare and the perception that these people are capable of work. Again, this is the flip side of the other two issues discussed in this section. If the work ethic is being eroded, then taxpayers will be less inclined to view those who are not working as victims of circumstance. And if taxback rates are too high, taxpayers will resent the fact that those who choose not to work are hardly worse off than those who do. A politically sensitive concern for the poor would suggest that programs must be designed to overcome these objections.

Several comments are worth making about this. The first is that our attitude as a society toward work has changed over time. If 30 years ago we regarded it as appropriate for mothers to stay at home with their children, we now regard it increasingly as the norm that all parents will work to support their families. The second is that some kind of work requirement need not be looked on as a punitive act. In a society where most adults are expected to work, a job—combined with a welfare system that ensures that family income exceeds some minimum level—may well be superior to a handout. That kind of policy reinforces the self-esteem of the recipient, as well as the work ethic.[17] Finally, it may well develop the political support necessary to sustain such a policy through difficult times.

V. CONCLUSION

This paper has suggested that workfare can be useful both in sustaining our social safety net politically, and in overcoming some of the incentive problems associated with high rates of taxation. Such a workfare scheme would include an income subsidy scheme for those who are able to work, coupled with a reduction in benefits to that group if they chose not to work.

It should be emphasized that this kind of approach is unlikely to save us much money, especially in the short run. During good times, most of those who might otherwise be eligible for welfare are already working. During bad times, high-wage jobs are hard to find, so that subsidized public-sector jobs will be necessary. Furthermore, the group on welfare most affected by the program will be single parents. For this group, a high-quality and relatively expensive daycare program will be necessary to allow labour force participation. This may well eat up many of the prospective savings of a work requirement. Finally, a variety of training programs will be needed to ensure job readiness and to develop the skills needed to gain high-paying employment. These kinds of programs will also cost money.

On the other hand, a work requirement may be essential to sustain the fiscal integrity of our tax-transfer system. As has been shown, a comprehensive and reasonably generous system involves extraordinarily high marginal tax rates affecting all Canadians. And these tax rates erode the work ethic and compromise the growth and productivity of the entire economy.

It has become common to view work requirements as a right-wing attack on welfare recipients. But the persistence of poverty and its effects on the family cuts across political lines. Work requirements, combined with remedial training, income subsidies, and quality daycare, may be a way to assist the poor in a way that is less destructive of values held by most Canadians than is long-term welfare dependency.

In the end, despite all the rhetoric, a work-oriented welfare strategy has little to do with cost, especially in the short run. In contrast, it has everything to do with self-respect and the work ethic, and with the political legitimacy of our social programs.

APPENDIX 22.1

To look at some real estimates of these costs, some simplifying assumptions must be made. First, I will assume that all taxes are collected from income.[18] Second, I will assume that all production generates income for households, and all this income is taxed.[19] Third, I will assume that all income is taxed at the same rate.[20] Finally, I will assume that all families consist of exactly four persons.[21]

We can now calculate the cost of a comprehensive welfare program. Begin by using the letter M to represent the amount given to families that have no other income (M is $20 000 in the fictional Table 22.1). As discussed earlier, the simplified welfare-tax system we are discussing gives each family the amount M and then taxes all income. However, we have also assumed that all families pay tax at the same marginal rate, which we can call t.[22] Since we assume that this is the only tax, and that all income accrues to families, we know that the revenue generated by the tax t represents all the revenue received by the government. The *net* tax revenue generated by the welfare-tax system is the revenue generated by the tax t minus the amount necessary to cover the cost of all the M, and this net tax revenue is what the government uses to cover all other expenditures.

This result can also be written in a simple algebraic expression. If REV is the net revenue generated by the welfare tax system, Y_T is the total taxable income in Canada, and n is the number of Canadian families, then

$$REV = tY_T - nM$$

The problem facing the government can be seen by using some "back of the envelope" calculations. I will use data for Canada in 1990, since that was the last full year prior to the most recent recession, and was a year with relatively low unemployment.[23] In this discussion, you should keep in mind that we are constructing a fictitious example using the basic economic data for that year, but pretending that various different policies were being evaluated. We begin by constructing reasonable estimates of Y_T, n, and REV.

In 1990, Net National Product (NNP) in Canada was $570.5 billion. However the government cannot tax all of the NNP. Our income taxes routinely exempt most savings (in pension plans, for example), and our consumption taxes generally do not apply to purchases of investment goods (and clearly cannot touch savings, since savers are not making purchases). Taxing imputed income to owner occupied homes is problematic.[24] In fact, in 1990, assessed taxable income was only $433.6 billion. I will use three possible values for Y_T: NNP ($570.5 billion), assessed taxable income ($433.6 billion), and a midway value of $500 billion.

Determining n is simpler. If we assume that all Canadians lived in families of four persons, there were about 6.75 million such families in Canada.

Finally, we need REV. For the 1990–91 fiscal year (ending March 31, 1991), total spending by all levels of government other than income support (that is, all spending not included in M) totalled $242.4 billion.[25] If we assume that the governments together in 1991 ran a deficit, denoted by DEF, then the revenue requirement (REV in the equation above) will be equal to $242.4 billion *minus* DEF. Plugging these numbers into the equation, we now have

$$(\$242.4 \text{ billion}) - \text{DEF} = tY_T - (6.75 \text{ million})M$$
$$Y_T = \$570.5 \text{ billion, } \$500 \text{ billion, or } \$433.6 \text{ billion}$$

Clearly, once we have set the level of the deficit and the value of M (which is the floor level of welfare for families with no other income), we can derive the value of t necessary to raise the revenue for government programs.

Consider first the deficit. One possible value for DEF is zero. This has been proposed by the Reform Party.[26] On the other extreme, we might imagine that Canadians begin demanding more from governments again in the future and that the deficit is allowed to rise to 5 percent of GDP.[27] In 1990, this would have meant a deficit of $33.5 billion. The actual consolidated deficit in 1990 was $27.2 billion.

Now consider the value of M, the minimum support level for a family of four (that is, the welfare payment received by a family of four with no other source of income). It is useful to remember that $64 237 was the average taxable income per family of four in 1990. In 1990, the National Council of Welfare poverty line for a family of four was $17 380 in rural areas and $25 525 in large cities. If we were to take a rough average and set the poverty line at, say, $22 000, and then were to determine that the minimum income provided to a family with no other sources of support would be equal to that poverty line, this would set M at $22 000. Of course, there is some disagreement with the way the poverty line is measured. Christopher Sarlo, writing for the Fraser Institute, has argued that the standard measurements provide for an ever increasing poverty line in absolute terms. Using the 1961 standard, he suggests that the appropriate measure for 1990 would be $15 525. This would generate an alternative value for M.

Using these alternative possibilities for M and DEF (the maximum welfare payment and the deficit) and plugging them into the previous equation, we can derive various values for the tax rate t. These are reported in Table 22.3.

Most of these numbers suggest an alarming result. For example, if we assume that Canada's current level of debt pretty much requires a zero deficit in the near future,[28] and if we stick with the National Council figure for the poverty line and use current assessed taxable income, this means that we are looking at 90 percent marginal tax rates over the entire income range. Even if we assume that we can increase the income that is taxable halfway to NNP, that would mean a marginal tax rate of 78 percent.[29]

It is important to understand exactly what this means. A marginal tax rate of 80 percent would mean that the average Canadian family with assessed income of $64 237 (the 1991 figure) would pay taxes of $51 390 against an initial transfer

TABLE 22.3

TAX RATES, GIVEN ASSUMPTIONS ABOUT WELFARE, THE DEFICIT, AND THE TAX BASE (1991 DATA)

TAX BASE	MAXIMUM WELFARE NATIONAL COUNCIL ($22 000) ($15 525)		SUPPORT LEVEL FRASER INSTITUTE	
	DEFICIT = ZERO	DEFICIT = 5%GDP	DEFICIT = ZERO	DEFICIT = 5%GDP
Assessed Taxable Income ($433.6 billion)	90.2%	82.4%	80.1%	72.3%
Midway Value ($500 billion)	78.2%	71.5%	69.4%	62.7%
Net National Product ($570.5 billion)	68.5%	62.6%	60.9%	55.0%

payment of $22 000. This translates into a net tax of just under $30 000, or an average tax rate of about 45 percent. Since this includes all taxes, the average tax rate is not all that draconian. This result is not surprising, since this model takes the current level of nonwelfare spending as fixed, and constructs a welfare system that is not that much more generous than our current system at the bottom end; the major difference is that the working poor are allowed to receive some assistance, and that the welfare system is applied to all Canadians, independent of any other criteria.

NOTES

*This paper is a shortened and somewhat modified version of a paper prepared for the C.D. Howe Institute and published in 1995 in *Helping the Poor: A Qualified Case for "Workfare,"* the fifth volume in their series on "The Social Policy Challenge."

1. Canadian Tax Foundation, *The National Finances, 1996* (Toronto, 1996), pp. B:3–B:11.

2. For example, GDP includes depreciation, which should not be taxed, and imputed income to owner occupied housing, which is not (and probably cannot be) taxed.

3. This point is discussed later in the paper.

4. Canadian Tax Foundation, *The National Finances, 1993* (Toronto, 1993), pp. 3:13, 7:22–23.

5. The term "social services" is often used loosely (and incorrectly) as a synonym for virtually all government spending. Here the term refers to various types of transfer payments to individual Canadians, including welfare, public pensions, old age security, and unemployment insurance, as well as a few specific programs like childcare and vocational rehabilitation. Expenditures on education and health are not included in the category of social services.

6. The unemployment rate in 1982 was 11.0 percent, compared with 10.3 percent in 1991 (Department of Finance, 1992, p. 57).

7. Canadian Tax Foundation, *The National Finances, 1993*, pp. 3:17–3:19, 4:5.

8. Of course, this is not what really happens. The family that earns $30 000 in this world, for example, receives no cheque from the government and pays $4000 in taxes. But it is as if the family received the initial $20 000 from the government and then paid $24 000 to the government when they earned $30 000. This somewhat unnatural view of the welfare process allows us to make some relatively easy calculations later in Appendix 22.1.

9. In Ontario, there have been two separate welfare programs: Family Benefits (FBA) delivers assistance to those judged to need long-term support (that is, who cannot be expected to work); General Welfare Assistance (GWA) provides help (at a somewhat lower level) to those needing short-term or emergency support. Thus FBA largely supports the elderly, people with disabilities, and single parents, while GWA supports those without jobs, those who are ill, and those who need emergency help (who, if the situation continues, will end up on FBA). Welfare also assists families who are unemployed and have exhausted their employment insurance benefits (although there would be relatively few of these in "good times").

10. These are the welfare recipients on FBA (see the previous footnote).

11. Social Assistance Review Committee, *Transitions: Report of the Social Assistance Review Committee* (Toronto: Queen's Printer for Ontario, 1988), pp. 43–50, 264–65.

12. Ibid., p. 35.

13. Significant government funding for childcare would also cause the costs per child to rise even further if it pushed up wages among daycare workers and led to calls for improvements in the quality of care. Although both these outcomes might be desirable, they would clearly be more expensive.

14. Social Assistance Review Committee, pp. 42–43.

15. A similar phenomenon occurs in the tax system. When cheating passes some "tipping point" and becomes more of a norm and less of an aberration, then those who do not cheat feel less praiseworthy and more foolish. Preventing cheating is important, not only because of the impact on cheaters but also because of the effect on more honest taxpayers.

16. This occurs when welfare recipients also qualify for a variety of noncash transfers (free prescription drugs, dental care, etc.).

17. It is for these reasons, among others, that the Jewish sage Maimonides argued that the highest form of charity was to help people provide for themselves.

18. In fact, governments derive revenue from taxes on all kinds of activities. They tax individual income, corporate income, sales, property, motor vehicles, cigarettes, and so on. Governments also earn income by marking up and selling alcohol, issuing licences, collecting royalties on Crown land, etc. However, income taxes and social insurance levies account for more than half of government tax revenue. Consumption taxes, which account for another quarter of government revenue, are roughly equivalent to an income tax (ignoring for the moment the fact that goods are taxed at different rates, and that savings are not taxed until they are spent). Taxes on businesses are probably shifted onto consumers, and thus function as another tax on income. And property taxes are related to the value of housing, which is again related to income. Since economists generally assume that all taxes end up being borne by Canadians, and because the revenues generated are highly correlated with income, modelling the entire tax system as a simple tax on income is a useful simplification.

19. In fact, some income flows to corporations, not households, but I will assume that households own the corporations and realize that income (this is consistent with the view of most economists that Canadian taxes ultimately fall on individual Canadians). Of course, not all income is in fact taxed. For example, in 1990, Canadian Net National Product (NNP) was $570 billion (NNP is GNP minus depreciation, which is not properly available for taxation) but assessed income for personal taxation purposes was only $434 billion. The "gap" ($136 billion) includes imputed income to owner occupied housing (taxed through the property tax) and income to corporations (taxed both directly and through capital gains taxes).

20. Of course, the income tax is progressive (at least in principle) and capital gains are incompletely taxed. Furthermore, welfare recipients often face near-confiscatory rates of taxation (since the "combined tax rate" in this system includes the taxback of welfare payments). The assumption of a constant rate simplifies the calculations.

21. Family sizes vary, but smaller families also receive smaller welfare payments. Keeping families the same size allows us to add up all the payments easily across all the families.

22. The marginal rate of taxation is the rate by which taxes (and in this case, taxes are net of any transfer payments to the family) rise when income rises—that is, the marginal rate is the increase in taxes when income rises by one dollar. Although all families pay the same marginal rate of taxation, the average taxes differ among families because of the existence of M. For example, if M is $10 000 and t is 0.40 (a marginal tax rate of 40%), then a family with earnings of $25 000 would pay no net taxes (the tax of 40% on $25 000 would exactly cancel the payment to the family of M). A family with earnings of $35 000 would pay net taxes of $4000, a family with earnings of $45 000 would pay net taxes of $8000, and so on. All these families face a marginal tax rate of 40%, but the average net taxes paid differs significantly among the families.

23. The problems of welfare and work requirements are somewhat different when there are high unemployment rates, as is discussed in the third section of this paper. Although Canada has emerged from the recession in recent years, unemployment rates have remained stubbornly high during the 1990s.

24. The national accounts include in NNP an amount corresponding to the value of the housing services received by people who live in their own homes. That is, the national accounts "pretend" that people who own their homes pay themselves rent, and this rent is included in NNP. Of course, taxing this rent is problematic, since there is no money income generated.

25. Consolidated government expenditure for the fiscal year was $309.5 billion (the Canada or Quebec Pension Plans are left out of the consolidated expenditure data). Of this, $67.1 billion was for social services (again, not including CPP or QPP). This includes transfer payments to people and a number of old age security, unemployment insurance, and welfare payments under the Canada Assistance Plan, and the guaranteed income supplement. It also includes a number of shared-cost programs (childcare, vocational rehabilitation, and so on). If we subtract this from the $309.5 billion, we are left with $242.4 billion in other expenditures. In this paper, all data on government expenditures, taxes, and deficits comes from the Canadian Tax Foundation (1993).

26. In fact, the Reform Party also believes that we must begin paying back the debt, which would require a budgetary surplus. To keep things simple, we will assume that a surplus is not in the political cards right now, and will treat a zero deficit as the extreme result.

27. This is unlikely, given recent rhetoric, but it gives us the other extreme value for DEF.

28. The Liberal, Conservative, and Reform parties all campaigned on a zero deficit in the last election; only the NDP suggested that a zero deficit might not be the only priority.

29. Although the high marginal tax rates emerge from a series of simplifying assumptions, it must be emphasized that changes in the assumptions do not change the overall result. For example, Canada is not made up of neat families of four persons (many family units would be smaller). Introducing other types of families does not change the computations, because the support levels *per person* at the poverty line are not smaller as family size falls (the poverty line for a single person, for example, is only about half of the poverty line for a family of four). Similarly, the model assumed constant marginal tax rates (that is, that the government would take a fraction t of each dollar earned, no matter what the level of income). In reality, rates vary over income. However, the revenue requirements of the government mean that any reduction in t over one range of income must be compensated for by a corresponding rise in t in some other range of income. In practical terms, the way we have sought to keep marginal rates comparatively low for those who pay taxes is to raise the taxback rate on those who are on welfare. Thus, in many jurisdictions, welfare recipients lose most of their benefits when they find full-time work (in effect, they face very high rates of implicit tax), so that people are often better off staying on welfare than getting a job.

REFERENCES

Canadian Tax Foundation, 1993. *The National Finances, 1993*. Toronto.

Canadian Tax Foundation, 1996. *The National Finances, 1996*. Toronto.

Department of Finance, Canada, 1992. *Economic Reference Tables, August, 1992*. Ottawa.

Social Assistance Review Committee, 1988. *Transitions: Report of the Social Assistance Review Committee*. Toronto: Queen's Printer for Ontario.

✗ **NO**
Workfare: It's Jobs, Not Pathology
ERNIE S. LIGHTMAN

INTRODUCTION

Workfare is a concept whose boundaries and meaning are vague, whose political appeal can be substantial, and whose other practical value is negligible. Workfare promises to get people off welfare and direct them to lives of autonomy and economic independence, but in practice simply translates into another assault on the poor and vulnerable. As Mike Harris found in Ontario, the lure of workfare can propel a seemingly irrelevant party of the opposition from obscurity to power, but the grandiose preelection promises subsequently become an embarrassment, as they are fundamentally incapable of being delivered.[1]

This paper begins with a look at the meaning of workfare, as a vast array of programs can be packaged under its label. Considered are the basic premises and assumptions underlying workfare. The paper argues the case against workfare, primarily on practical grounds, examines the reality of workfare, based on experience in both the United States and Canada, and concludes with an assessment of what workfare can and cannot do. Empirical evidence from both countries supports my basic premise that the real, bottom-line goal of workfare is to punish, and nothing more.

THE MEANING OF WORKFARE

There exists a vast array of training, job placement, and educational upgrading initiatives that can be described as "work incentives": all are intended to prepare and facilitate entry (or reentry) into the paid workforce. Workfare represents only a subset of this broader set of work incentives, though the terms are often used interchangeably.

To qualify as workfare, to be distinguished from the many other labour-market initiatives, a work incentive program must satisfy two central conditions[2]:

- Participation must be *mandatory* in practice, rather than voluntary.

- The work or other activities must be done *in exchange for,* rather than as a supplement to, a welfare payment.

The punitive tone of these conditions is clear: if participants see a program as being useful, as providing them with some net perceived present or future benefit, then the compulsion is redundant; life on welfare is not pleasurable or rewarding for the vast majority of beneficiaries, and any avenues that are seen as leading to a life of economic independence and dignity will be rapidly seized.[3] A mandatory condition is required only if the activity is seen as being without reward, meaningless, a dead end.

THE BASIC PREMISE

The basic premise of the economic market is that individuals act in their own self-interest to maximize their net well-being: this is the assumption of rational behaviour, an assumption so beloved by classical economists. We know, of course, that people do not always (or perhaps even often) act in their own best interests, and as a result, we intervene to constrain their actions or choices: this is often known as paternalism.

The ethics or morality of requiring people to do what they don't want to do are complex, and are beyond the scope of this article. Certainly, as a society we have a vigilant court system to limit our intrusion into the lives and property of the middle class and rich. At the same time, we have little difficulty in telling people who are poor how to run their lives in a wide variety of ways—where to live, how to raise their children, and how to spend their money.

Until the recent repeal of the Canada Assistance Act, one of the few things we did *not* do was require people on social assistance to work for their benefits: the act, representing perhaps the high point of morality in the history of the Canadian welfare state, stated that the sole condition for the receipt of benefits was that an individual demonstrate need; once this need was established, no further qualifying conditions could be attached to the receipt of benefits. So, from 1966 (when the Canada Assistance Act was passed) until 1996 (when it was replaced by the Canada Health and Social Transfer, or CHST), workfare was prohibited across Canada. Today, however, there are no legal barriers to its introduction.

The basic premise of this article is profoundly market based: we assume that individuals on welfare will voluntarily (and, indeed, enthusiastically) participate in work, training, or upgrading programs if they perceive that they will be better off by doing so than by noninvolvement. And, indeed, the overwhelming empirical evidence shows clearly that every legitimate and useful training program everywhere is vastly oversubscribed. A recent computer-focused training program in Toronto, for example, had places for one thousand participants, but drew in the range of twelve thousand to thirteen thousand applicants.[4] On the other hand, if claimants perceive that programs are essentially meaningless or unlikely to lead them to attaining their goals, voluntary participation will not ensue.

To argue the case for coercing people to participate in activities they would not undertake on a voluntary basis, one of two assumptions must be met:

- *Poor information.* The programs are not, in fact, meaningless, but rather they will yield benefits that participants do not perceive. This perspective assumes that program planners, politicians, or others know better than the participants about the actual content of the programs and their impacts (the paternalism argument).

Yet, in reality, the goals of the planners, politicians, and others may be fundamentally different from those of participants: "success" of a workfare program can have very different meanings to the various players. Politicians and planners may simply want short-term welfare caseloads reduced, while those involved may desire meaningful and continuing employment. More importantly, the fact that "good" programs are rapidly filled, while "bad" programs remain open over time, suggests that information does filter back through communities, and that potential participants do make informed choices and have better insight into actual program content and the state of the job market than do those more removed from the front lines.

- *Nonrational behaviour.* The alternate assumption for a workfare program is that large numbers of people consciously act contrary to their own self-interest. Rather than pursuing a path that leads to a life of dignity through paid work, many welfare recipients prefer lower incomes, the stigma of being on welfare, and indolence. Compelling people to work is justified as forcing people to act rationally.

The paternalism here is even more difficult to understand, particularly when its strongest proponents are often the most mainstream of economists.[5] While individual cases of irrational behaviour are certainly not hard to find, the general assumption is that in the aggregate, people—almost by definition—act in their own best interests. We shall subsequently examine the empirical evidence about the actual outcomes of workfare.

THE BASIC ARGUMENT AGAINST WORKFARE

The most compelling argument against workfare is simply that it does not work. It does not lead to enhanced job readiness, improved self-esteem, or actual paid employment for the vast majority of participants. In fact, the usual outcomes are directly opposite: participation in activities that are seen as meaningless leads to boredom, lack of interest, and alienation from the labour market; training for jobs that do not exist leads to disillusionment and discouragement; working at pointless tasks leads not to permanent employment, but rather to the emergence of a permanent underclass drifting from one temporary situation to another.

There are numerous reasons why workfare does not "work", some of which have already been alluded to:

- *"Success" is hard to operationalize.* There is little agreement about what a workfare program is intended to achieve. From the perspective of participants, the general goal is to attain continuing paid employment with compensation adequate for a life of independence and dignity. The other players—who include the politicians, bureaucrats, and taxpayers—may have fundamentally different agendas, including the short-term reduction of welfare caseloads or the lowering of the tax bill, all the way through to the punishment of those dependent on the state. Goals to enhance the well-being of participants are not necessarily precluded from the priorities of the other stakeholders, but neither is there any assurance of congruence.

If there is no agreement about what a program is attempting to achieve, there can be little consensus about whether or when success has been attained. This is important because the various goals are not usually mutually compatible, and the attainment of some renders more difficult the achievement of others.

- *The cost is high.* One crucial point upon which all serious participants in the workfare debate agree is that the program does not save money in the short term; its cost-saving potential over time depends, in effect, on its ability to get people off welfare and into the labour force—and in times of chronically high unemployment, the potential for success in this respect is severely limited.

Initiatives in the United States that had even limited success uniformly recognized the importance of spending on childcare, transportation, and intensive training (both of the substantive skills-acquisition and of the job-readiness varieties).[6] The Harris government in Ontario, by contrast, was primarily concerned to limit public expenditure, with the result that its programs contained nothing of value to recipients: most of the spending was directed toward process only—the policing and monitoring of recipients' lives.

Because of what I describe as the "reluctant soldier" problem, the policing costs in any compulsory program will be substantial: unwilling draftees, as the Americans found in Vietnam, do not make good soldiers or win wars; people who do not want to be somewhere do not make good students, or workers, and the risk is high that the entire learning or working environment will be disturbed.[7]

It is, of course, not possible to ensure that participants actually derive benefit from participating in workfare, and so the stress must be on the monitoring process: to ensure that participants attend when and where they are supposed to, that they go through the motions required of them, and that they are not disruptive to others in the neighbourhood. All of this monitoring cost is wasted money, because it produces no tangible outcome except the avoidance of idleness on the part of recipients.

Training, if it is to be successful, must be individualized, as participants are not "widgets" to be slotted into the first available position. The indirect support costs— quality childcare in particular—may be even greater. Some individuals learn slowly, and the time for skills acquisition may be substantial. While we noted that the more "successful" American programs recognized the importance of public investment, there is no evidence of readiness to spend (invest) on the part of any government in Canada.

Without investment, workfare loses any education or training component except that which may be acquired as a random byproduct of working; workfare becomes simply work-for-welfare (as it was called in Ontario for a period of time).

Gone is any pretence of benefit for recipients: the sole rationale for workfare is that of avoiding idleness on the part of those dependent on the state. (Among the rich, by contrast, the pursuit of idleness is to be much admired.) The recipient of welfare must participate in something, however meaningless or demeaning, in exchange for the cheque. Training programs leading to paid work, of course, permit the individual to pay back even more and for a longer period of time, but these are not possible without the initial public expenditure, and this is not to be found in Canada today.

- *It's jobs, not pathology.* Perhaps the most compelling argument against workfare is that it focuses public attention in the wrong direction. Workfare assumes that individuals are unemployed for reasons of individual defect and failing, and that proper preparation and motivation can overcome these deficiencies. The reality, of course, is that most employable individuals are unemployed because there are no jobs.

Workfare reached the peak of its political appeal in the 1995 Ontario election because unemployment was at historically high levels—12 percent of the provincial population in 1993.[8] It was argued by the opposition parties and many business interests that the causes lay in individual pathology, epitomized so well by Prime Minister Chrétien's ill-advised comment about welfare recipients sitting home, watching television, and drinking beer.[9]

Yet, in fact, unemployment was high in the mid-1990s for two reasons, neither of which had anything to do with the unfortunate individuals involved. Firstly, global restructuring, the Free Trade Agreement, and NAFTA led to the elimination of tariff barriers and the substantial drainage of jobs to the United States and farther abroad: the Canadian economy was ill prepared for these changes and the transitional aid to workers promised by Brian Mulroney in the 1988 election never materialized. Canadian—and, in particular, Ontarian—workers were laid off as a result of corporate decisions that they were powerless to influence. Secondly, changes in the rules affecting eligibility for unemployment insurance had a major impact on welfare usage in Ontario: prior to the UI tightening, individuals who became unemployed would have up to a year on the federal program before they were forced to resort to welfare; after the UI tightening, many of these same individuals did not qualify for UI at all, or only qualified for shorter periods of time, with the result that they were thrown onto welfare faster and in great numbers. The increased welfare caseloads among the employable population were a direct consequence of federal offloading through changes to unemployment insurance.[10]

The American experience with workfare in different states persuasively shows the importance of structural labour-market conditions: the likelihood of program "success" was considerably greater in states with substantial economic growth and low unemployment, such as southern California or Massachusetts; in low-growth, high-unemployment areas such as West Virginia, the programs were inevitably failures.[11] And of course, one may ask whether, in a context of rapid economic growth, there is any need for a compulsory program at all: surely, most unemployed people will prefer jobs to indolence if the choice before them is a real one.

THE REALITY OF WELFARE

Theoretical discussions about the benefits that workfare can potentially offer may generate interesting after-dinner conversation, but the relevant policy issue is what happens at ground level. Let us consider some experience:

- The Quebec workfare program excludes workfare participants from the protection of the province's employment laws. Recently, the provincial Superior Court struck down the program as a violation of the Quebec Charter of Rights, which prohibits discrimination on the basis of "social condition." A comparable provision is not found in other provincial human rights codes. The Quebec court was also "extremely critical" of the so-called training programs offered under workfare.[12]

- Ontario municipalities are moving toward the use of workfare participants to replace public-sector employees.[13] In Algoma, for example, Workfare Watch notes that 147 social assistance recipients are painting municipal offices, performing clerical work, and installing wheelchair entrances, all jobs that would otherwise be done by unionized municipal employees. A secret document in the Ministry of Housing explored the possibility of using workfare personnel to replace permanent staff in public housing in Toronto.[14] As the province offloads ever more responsibilities onto the municipalities, the temptation to use free labour will clearly increase. Halton region has identified daycare centres and seniors' residences as possible sites for workfare placements.

Such actions raise major concerns for both the providers and the recipients of workfare-based services. If vulnerable adults and children are to be cared for by untrained and unscreened individuals, there is a clear risk for the well-being, and even the safety, of those receiving the services. Questions of legal liability become important for the municipalities. At the same time, these procedures have the effect of privatizing access to welfare: job supervisors, whether from the public or private sectors, will, in practice, decide if a workfare participant is doing the job correctly, and, hence, whether the individual will remain on welfare or have welfare benefits terminated. The potential for impropriety—sexual harassment, for example, or racial bigotry—is substantial. Particular individuals with limited or no day-to-day accountability will decide who stays on welfare, based on criteria that may be capricious, punitive, or worse.

- In the United States, both Los Angeles and New York make extensive use of nonpaid workfare participants to provide public services formerly delivered by paid staff. The L.A. Bureau of Street Maintenance was only able to maintain its level of services because of "support staffing" from court referrals and workfare placements; in New York City, it is estimated that in 1997 over one hundred thousand welfare recipients would be engaged in workfare, "almost the same number of workers the city employs."[15]

CONCLUSION

There are many things that workfare does *not* do:

- Workfare cannot create jobs. It does, in practice, replace permanent public-service jobs with temporary, unpaid, involuntary labour provided by workfare recipients. The net effect is to eliminate good jobs and substitute instead badly delivered services and badly remunerated labour. Recipients of these services who are vulnerable may be at immediate risk of physical and/or emotional harm.

- Workfare cannot provide links to the labour market as long as unemployment remains high. If there are no (or few) jobs, no program of mass placement or training can possibly treat the backlog of willing, but unplaced, workers. The training, in practice, is minimal or nonexistent.

- Workfare does not strengthen work incentives on a wide basis. For every individual whose motivation increases due to a workfare experience, there are surely many individuals who are demoralized, discouraged, and alienated from the labour force by the requirement to perform tasks that are demeaning and usually meaningless. For an individual who replaces or works with well-paid permanent employees while receiving welfare—compensation that is, in effect, below minimum wage—the incentive to work cannot be enhanced.

- Workfare is more likely to discredit the entire welfare system than to legitimate it. Consider the process used by the Ontario government in its workfare program:[16] after strong language and much rhetoric, the government proved incapable of delivering on its promises. Workfare as it ultimately emerged in Ontario was simply a new name for old programs.[17] The Harris government's experience showed nothing more than the impossibility of quick and simplistic solutions to the welfare "mess." Had it been easy to clean up welfare, the provincial NDP and Liberal governments that preceded the Conservatives would surely have done so, for both tried to do so. Workfare was not a necessary price to retain a welfare system of any sort, but rather it served to discredit the entire program.

- Workfare does not save money in the short term, except by driving people off welfare for their failure to do what is required of them. Whether these people are properly removed from the caseload, whether they are in fact abusing the system and deserve to be terminated, or whether they have legitimate gounds for noninvolvement in workfare or are merely victimized by punitive supervisors is not an issue of much concern to cost-slashing governments. Access to welfare is effectively privatzed and due process for welfare recipients is usually minimal and inevitably after the fact. Long-term savings result only from permanent placement in jobs, which depends primarily on macroeconomic, even global, considerations.

IN SHORT

Workfare is based on a faulty premise, that absence from the labour market is more a matter of pathology than of structural conditions, that the unemployment problem is primarily caused by individual deficiencies that can be remedied by a form of "tough love," coercion, and compulsion.

The reality, however, is that most unemployment is caused by structural conditions that are beyond the capacity of any individual to influence them. If there are jobs and economic growth, the compulsion inherent in workfare is redundant and superfluous; if there are no jobs, no amount of preparedness or compulsion can create them. The result will simply be the replacement of well-paid jobs by cheap, involuntary labour.

The issue, at its simplest, is jobs, jobs, jobs. And forced labour in exchange for menial welfare benefits is not, and cannot be, a substitute for them.

NOTES

1. Phinjo Gombu, "Workfare Far Short of Tory Targets," *Toronto Star,* September 29, 1996; Phinjo Gombu, "Mandatory Workfare Rule Now Uncertain," *Toronto Star,* November 20, 1996; Phinjo Gombu, "Major Flaws May Derail Workfare," *Toronto Star,* November 24, 1996; Laurie Monsebraaten, "Metro Getting Workfare but It Has a Softer Face," *Toronto Star,* March 31, 1997; and Ernie Lightman, "It's Not a Walk in the Park: Workfare in Ontario," in Eric Shragge, ed., *Workfare: A Critique* (Toronto: Garamond Press, 1997).

2. Ernie Lightman, "You Can Lead a UI Recipient to Training but ...," *Financial Post,* November 9, 1994.

3. Jack Lakey, "Forty-three Percent of Ex-Welfare Recipients Have Found Jobs, Metro Finds," *Toronto Star,* February 26, 1997.

4. OneStep (Ontario Network of Employment Skills Training Projects), *Singing for Our Supper: A Review of Workfare Programs* (Toronto: Ontario Network of Employment Skills Training Projects, July 1995).

5. David Brown, "Welfare Caseload Trends in Canada," in John Richards, ed., *Helping the Poor: A Qualified Case for "Workfare"* (Toronto: C.D. Howe Institute, 1995).

6. A. Mitchell, "Workfare: What We Know," *Social Infopac* 14, no. 4 (Toronto: Social Planning Council of Metropolitan Toronto, 1996).

7. Lightman, "You Can Lead a UI Recipient to Training but ..."

8. Brown, "Welfare Caseload Trends in Canada."

9. Lightman, "You Can Lead a UI Recipient to Training but ..."

10. Ontario Social Safety Network and Social Planning Council of Metropolitan Toronto, *Workfare Watch* (1996).

11. Mitchell, "Workfare: What We Know"; OneStep, *Singing for Our Supper;* Thomas Brock, David Butler, and David Long, "Unpaid Work Experience for Welfare Recipients: Findings and Lessons from MDRC Research" (New York: Manpower Demonstration Research Corporation, 1993).

12. Ontario Social Safety Network and Social Planning Council of Metropolitan Toronto, *Workfare Watch* (March 1997).

13. Ontario Social Safety Network and Social Planning Council of Metropolitan Toronto, *Workfare Watch* (December 1996); Ontario Social Safety Network and Social Planning Council of Metropolitan Toronto, *Workfare Watch* (March 1997); and Ontario Social Safety Network (OSSN), *Social Safety News* (various issues, 1996) (Toronto: Social Planning Council).

14. Ontario Ministry of Housing, *Information Paper: OHC "Workfare" Program Options* (Toronto: Ontario Ministry of Housing, Housing Operations Division, December 21, 1995).

15. Ontario Social Safety Network and Social Planning Council of Metropolitan Toronto, *Workfare Watch* (March 1997).

16. Lightman, "It's Not a Walk in the Park: Workfare in Ontario."

17. Gombu, "Workfare Far Short of Tory Targets"; Gombu, "Mandatory Workfare Rule Now Uncertain"; Gombu, "Major Flaws May Derail Workfare"; Monsebraaten, "Metro Getting Workfare but It Has a Softer Face."

REFERENCES

Brock, Thomas, David Butler, and David Long. 1993. "Unpaid Work Experience for Welfare Recipients: Findings and Lessons from MDRC Research." New

York: Manpower Demonstration Research Corporation.

Brown, David. 1995. "Welfare Caseload Trends in Canada," in *Helping the Poor: A Qualified Case for "Workfare,"* in John Richards (ed.). Toronto: C.D. Howe Institute.

Gombu, Phinjo. 1996. "Workfare Far Short of Tory Targets," *Toronto Star,* September 29.

Gombu, Phinjo. 1996. "Mandatory Workfare Rule Now Uncertain," *Toronto Star,* November 20.

Gombu, Phinjo. 1996. "Major Flaws May Derail Workfare," *Toronto Star,* November 24.

Lakey, Jack. 1997. "Forty-three percent of Ex-Welfare Recipients Have Found Jobs, Metro Finds," *Toronto Star,* February 26.

Lightman, Ernie. 1994. "You Can Lead a UI Recipient to Training but ...," *Financial Post,* November 9.

Lightman, Ernie. 1995. "You Can Lead a Horse to Water, but ...: The Case Against Workfare in Canada," in *Helping the Poor: A Qualified Case for "Workfare,"* John Richards (ed.). Toronto: C.D. Howe Institute.

Lightman, Ernie. 1997. "It's Not a Walk in the Park: Workfare in Ontario," in *Workfare: A Critique,* Eric Schragge (ed.). Toronto, Garamond Press.

Mitchell, A. 1996. "Workfare: What We Know," *Social Infopac* 14, no. 4. Toronto: Social Planning Council of Metropolitan Toronto.

Monsebraaten, Laurie. 1997. "Metro Getting Workfare but It Has a Softer Face," *Toronto Star,* March 31.

OneStep (Ontario Network of Employment Skills Training Projects). 1995. *Singing for Our Supper: A Review of Workfare Programs.* Toronto: Ontario Network of Employment Skills Training Projects, July.

Ontario Ministry of Housing. 1995. *Information Paper: OHC "Workfare" Program Options.* Toronto: Housing Operations Division, December 21.

Ontario Social Safety Network (OSSN). 1996. *Social Safety News.* Toronto: Social Planning Council, various issues.

Ontario Social Safety Network and Social Planning Council of Metropolitan Toronto. 1997. *Workfare Watch.* Toronto.

Richards, John (ed.). (1995). *Helping the Poor: A Qualified Case for "Workfare."* Toronto, C.D. Howe Institute.

Postscript

In his contribution, Krashinsky offers a persuasive case for workfare, perhaps in part because he recognizes its failings. For those who expect a quick cost saving, Krashinsky shows that they will most likely be disappointed; he also provides little support for those who think workfare is needed to prevent widespread abuse and fraud in the welfare system. To build his case for workfare, Krashinsky instead relies on some rather long-term considerations, such as maintaining the work ethic and shoring up the political support for welfare expenditures. Here, too, Krashinsky is mostly convincing, though a few questions do arise. For instance, he admits that people will work when employment opportunities are available, yet he argues that workfare is needed to strengthen the work ethic. If welfare recipients do take jobs when they appear, then why is there a need to worry about the attachment to the labour force? Also, he sees workfare as a way of soothing the anger in the electorate felt toward welfare recipients. But this anger may stem from a more general cause, namely the increasing inability of families with stagnant incomes to finance government programs. What people want are *immediate* cuts in government spending, not make-work programs for welfare recipients. Workfare may do little to deal with public resentment toward welfare and social assistance.

Like Krashinsky, Lightman presents a convincing set of arguments. His claim that the goals of workfare are often fuzzy seems on the mark, for governments often appear unsure of what they are trying to accomplish with workfare; indeed, they sometimes have difficulty even defining workfare, first associating it with work, then with work *and* community involvement, and then perhaps with both of the above and a commitment to job search. Yet, one might say that Lightman in his presentation is being too rational, that he assumes too easily that people leave welfare when jobs are plentiful. Though the evidence does suggest that people will work when jobs are available, workfare might be seen as a way of ensuring that the linkage between the individual and the labour force remains intact.

Obviously, it is difficult to resolve the debate about workfare. But the recent introduction of workfare in Ontario may provide a test of competing contentions relating to workfare. In 1997, the Ontario government proposed a new workfare program, called *Ontario Works*, that requires recipients of social assistance to participate in one of three programs (community service, job training, or job search); if they refuse to participate, they risk losing their benefits for specified periods of time. For those eager to come to some conclusions about workfare, the new Ontario program should be given careful consideration.

The recent interest in workfare shown by governments and others has led to a number of publications on the subject. The C.D. Howe Institute, a think tank in Canada, has published a volume of articles that for the most part support workfare: John Richards et al., eds., *Helping the Poor: A Qualified Case for "Workfare"*

(Toronto: C.D. Howe Institute, 1995). A book that takes the opposite view is Eric Shragge, ed., *Workfare: Ideology for a New Under-Class* (Toronto: Garamond Press, 1997). This text includes an excellent overview of the workfare experience in Ontario, written by Ernie Lightman. It also brings readers up to date on relevant developments in the United States.

Other useful sources on workfare are Adil Sayeed, ed., *Workfare: Does It Work? Is It Fair?* (Montreal: Institute for Research on Public Policy, 1995); Sherri Torjman, *Workfare: A Poor Law* (Ottawa: Caledon Institute of Social Policy, February 1996); and James Struthers, *Can Workfare Work? Reflections from History* (Ottawa: Caledon Institute of Social Policy, February 1996). As well, a series of articles on workfare appears in the May 1995 issue of *Policy Options*, including one by Mike Harris just before he became premier of Ontario and author of a newly proposed workfare program in Ontario. For those who might want to put workfare into the larger context of social welfare policy in Canada, Andrew Armitage's text would be helpful: Andrew Armitage, *Social Welfare in Canada Revisited: Facing Up to the Future*, 3rd ed. (Toronto: Oxford University Press, 1996).

Is Employment Equity Fair and Necessary?

✔ **YES**
CAROL AGÓCS, "Employment Equity: Is It Needed? Is It Fair?"

✗ **NO**
JACK ROBERTS, "Employment Equity—Unfair"

Consider the following qualities of employment in Canada. Aboriginal people with university degrees earn on average about one-third less than non-Aboriginal people with comparable levels of education. Women are largely absent in the professions and managerial jobs, yet can be found with little trouble in the clerical and secretarial positions. Visible minorities experience relatively high unemployment rates, and disabled persons are much more likely to remain outside the labour force than others.

For many, these rather uncomfortable truths provide clear evidence of discrimination. Certain social groups in Canada are the victims of practices that deny them equal employment opportunities. If justice is to be served, it is argued, then this situation must be remedied through the introduction of employment equity.

Employment equity is a policy that seeks to eliminate barriers to employment *and* to improve the representation of designated groups in the workplace. Employment equity can include the abolition of unreasonable employment requirements and the provision of services (such as childcare) that facilitate the carrying out of job responsibilities. It can also involve explicit preferential treatment for those traditionally underrepresented in the various occupations. For example, quotas or numerical targets might be set to ensure that women, Aboriginal people, and other disadvantaged groups are both hired and promoted. Employment equity may be voluntarily adopted by private companies, but effective action in this area typically requires the intervention of government.

In the opinion of its supporters, employment equity is a positive step. It not only provides for greater equality, but also has the potential to increase the productivity of organizations and to ensure the supply of skilled employees. A country that fails to capitalize on the abilities and talents of women, minorities, and the disabled cheats only itself.

Others, though, are less enamoured of employment equity. They contend that differences in employment situations may reflect forces other than discrimination.

Age, education, and culture are just a few of the factors that might explain income differences, employment rates, and representation in upper-level jobs. If this is true, then any preferential treatment for certain designated groups constitutes a form of discrimination against those not included in employment equity programs—employment equity fosters discrimination instead of eliminating it.

Critics of employment equity also contest other alleged benefits of employment equity. It has, they say, a detrimental effect on productivity, for it prevents the selection of the most qualified person. As well, it stigmatizes groups designated under employment equity programs; they will be seen as beneficiaries of an unfair policy and unworthy of their position. Perhaps most seriously, the perceived inequities of employment equity programs may create serious societal divisions in Canada.

In our readings, Carol Agócs, an associate professor in the political science department at the University of Western Ontario, argues in favour of employment equity. Jack Roberts, a professor emeritus of law at the University of Western Ontario and adjunct professor of law at Osgoode Hall Law School, argues against it.

✔ YES
Employment Equity: Is It Needed? Is It Fair?
CAROL AGÓCS

Employment equity is the Canadian policy framework that endeavours to bring about equality in the workplace for aboriginal peoples, persons with disabilities, racial minorities, and women—four populations that still experience the effects of historical and continuing discrimination and disadvantage in employment in Canada. By identifying and eliminating discrimination and the disadvantages these groups experience, employment equity seeks to improve their access to employment, their participation in a broader range of jobs throughout the occupational hierarchy, and their opportunity to contribute and be rewarded equally in the workplace.

As it is implemented in the workplace, employment equity is a long-term process of organizational change that involves critical assessment and updating of traditional policies and practices across the whole range of human resource management decisions that affect access to jobs, job assignment, training, compensation, promotion, and terms and conditions of employment. In addition, employment equity entails creating a workplace culture or climate in which women, persons with disabilities, members of racial minorities, and aboriginal peoples (the "designated groups") are accepted and respected as equal participants.

CANADA'S EMPLOYMENT EQUITY LEGISLATION AND REGULATIONS

In Canada in 1998, the instruments of employment equity policy include the Employment Equity Act (1986, revised 1995), which applies to the public service of Canada and to approximately 320 employers and 569,081 employees in the federally regulated sector (Human Resources Development Canada, 1997). In addition, the Federal Contractors Program, in effect since 1987 and revised in 1995, covers employers that employ 100 people or more and sell goods or services worth $200,000 or more to the federal government. About 769 employers, including most universities, and 947,426 employees are covered under the Federal Contractors Program (Human Resources Development Canada, personal communication, Feb. 6, 1998).

In Ontario, employment equity legislation was passed in 1993 and repealed in 1995. The city of Toronto has for many years had employment equity requirements for contractors that sell it goods or services, and for its own workforce. Some provincial governments also have employment equity requirements for the public service and, in some cases, contractors and/or the broader public sector. Some employers in the private and broader public sectors have undertaken voluntary employment equity initiatives.

The Canada Employment Equity Act (1995) and the Federal Contractors Program generally require employers to review their employment policies and practices in order to identify and eliminate barriers to the equal participation of the designated groups in the workplace. (Seniority rights are deemed not to be employment barriers under the Act.) Employment equity also includes measures to ensure that designated group memebers are represented in the workforce in proportions that reflect their representation in relevant labour markets. As a basis for planning equity initiatives, employers are required to use voluntary employee self-identification to collect data on the representation and salary ranges of women, people with disabilities, aboriginal persons and racial minorities in their workforce. The workforce census data are reported annually to the government and are available to the public. Employers must also establish numerical goals and a timetable for the hiring and promotion of designated group members if the data demonstrate that these groups are under-represented. Compliance with the law is reviewed by the Canadian Human Rights Commission.

The Empoyment Equity Act states that employers are not required to implement measures that would cause "undue hardship" to them, or to "hire or promote unqualified persons", or to "create new positions" in their workplace (Employment Equity Act, 1995, Chapter 44, part I, sec. 5-9). Even if the employer has been found to have violated the Act, the employer cannot be ordered to undertake such measures, or to introduce a program to improve the representation of the disadvantaged groups (Canadian Human Rights Act, 1995, sec. 54 (2)). Furthermore, the Commission may not "impose a quota" on an employer. A quota is defined in the Act as "a requirement to hire or promote a fixed and arbitary number of persons during a given period" (Employment Equity Act, 1995, Part II, sec. 33 (1-2)). An employer who violates the Act may be fined, and a tribunal may order them to cease and correct discriminatory practices. In the past, some Canadian employers found by a court or tribunal to have engaged in discrimination have been ordered to hire a fixed percentage (not number) of members of the group that had been discriminated against (e.g., Supreme Court of Canada in *Action travail des femmes v. Canadian National Rail,* 1986).

Prior to 1986 when federal employment equity policy was established, employers very rarely initiated voluntary employment equity programs, although they were permitted to do so under federal and provincial legislation. Furthermore, dealing with discrimination in employment through the individual human rights complaint process has not addressed the issue of systemic discrimination, which creates and perpetuates inequality for entire groups through traditional and unexamined approaches to decision-making in the workplace. (How this occurs will be discussed later in this article.)

Employment equity policy, established by legislation, regulation, or court order, and appropriately implemented and enforced, is needed if the principle of equality in the workplace is to become a reality in Canada. Three national political parties have acknowledged this, since the Employment Equity Act and the Federal Contractors Program were enacted in 1986 by a Conservative government with support for still stronger measures from the Liberal and New Democratic parties, while in Ontario, various employment equity initiatives have occurred under Conservative, Liberal, and NDP governments. Yet there is still a large gap between the spirit of employment equity legislation and policy on the one hand, and the level of employer activity toward equity and the results attained, on the other (Agócs, Burr, and Somerset, 1992: ch. 1; Leck and Saunders, 1992; Leck and Saunders, 1996).

WHY IS EMPLOYMENT EQUITY NEEDED?

Why should there be effective legislation, policy, and enforcement directed toward the goal of equality in the workplace for women, racial minorities, persons with disabilities, and aboriginal peoples? There are four reasons that have been widely acknowledged.

First, at present and over the decade to come, the majority of new entrants to the work force in Canada are and will be women, racial minorities, persons with disabilities, and aboriginal peoples (Johnston, 1991; Harvey and Blakely, 1993). Demographic trends, including rates of labour force participation, the aging of the population, birthrates, and immigration make this a reality. As members of these groups make up an ever growing proportion of the work force it becomes more costly to maintain barriers that impede their access to employment, and that detract from the productivity they would contribute if they were permitted full use of the education and abilities they have to offer. Furthermore, in an economy that is increasingly based on services to a diverse population of consumers and clients, within a global and highly competitive environment, the experience and knowledge that women, minorities, and people with disabilities bring to the workplace will be more and more in demand. Employment equity helps to create a workplace in which all can participate and contribute, and be equitably rewarded.

Second, democratic principles and expectations regarding social justice are important forces for change. Political parties, business firms, governments, the media, and community service agencies and organizations have all found it necessary to become more responsive to public demands that the behaviour of institutions reflect principles of democracy, social justice, and equality. Advocates for the equality of women, racial minorities, aboriginal peoples, and people with disabilities are influencing the policies and practices of public and private sector organizations, just as advocates for the environment and for health have raised awareness and brought about changes in people's behaviour and attitudes, and in government policy.

Third, the legal framework for employment equity is becoming more clearly defined and more explicit as to what employers are required to do in order to ensure equity in the workplace. The Charter of Rights and Freedoms as well as legislation and policy at the federal and provincial levels, and the developing body of case law, are moving Canada ahead of the United States and other countries in requiring employers to take action to ensure that discrimination and harassment on the basis of gender, race, and disability do not create disadvantage in the workplace.

Finally, and most important, there is strong evidence that organizational structures and cultures continue to demonstrate the impacts of discrimination on the basis of gender, race, and disability, and as a result they put women, persons with disabilities, racial minorities, and aboriginal peoples in a position of relative disadvantage in comparison with the traditional working population of able-bodied white males. The evidence shows that the four employment equity groups are disadvantaged in some or all of the following ways: higher unemployment, less access to full-time jobs that offer opportunities for advancement, less job security, representation in a narrower range of jobs, shorter career ladders, poorer pay and benefits, absence from or poor representation in senior management, and harassment on the basis of gender, race, or disability. Research evidence and experience in the workplace also show that racist and sexist organizational practices can be changed and replaced with practices that are fair to all groups, if decision-makers choose to commit themselves to change and to accepting diversity in their organizations.

THREE MYTHS ABOUT EMPLOYMENT EQUITY

Critics of the idea and practice of employment equity often claim that the changes it seeks to bring about are not needed because, they argue, there is no problem of discrimination or inequality in the workplace. Denial of the reality of discrimination and disadvantage is reinforced by myths about inequality in employment that have gained currency in the media and in popular discourse. These misconceptions need to be challenged by facts about how inequality stemming from discrimination and disadvantage continues to affect the employment equity groups. Since it is not possible in this brief overview to review and reference the extensive literature on discrimination and disadvantage in employment, the reader is encouraged to seek out and consider other sources that examine these issues in depth. In the following paragraphs we briefly consider three commonly heard myths about inequality in the workplace.

Myth #1: There's really no problem of inequality. Systemic discrimination based on gender and race is a thing of the past.

An editorial in *The Globe and Mail* (March 21, 1992) illustrates how myth-making about complex issues such as discrimination and inequality can occur. The editorial claims that a 1992 Economic Council of Canada report (deSilva, 1992) tells "the" story of the relationship between race and income in Canada: there is allegedly no evidence of racial discrimination in employment. The editorial concludes with the question, "If there are no significant economic disparities attributable to race or racism, should we be pursuing policies, such as employment equity legislation, which exist to rectify race-based economic disparities?"

The editor's assumption that racism is not an issue does not accurately represent the findings of the ECC study, which itself draws conclusions that are not supported by its own data. The ECC's findings actually show that there is discrimination against some racial minorities, as well as against women.

The ECC study found that immigrants from the Caribbean and East Asia whose education and work experience occurred in Canada are paid significantly less than all other immigrants, and less than the Canadian-born population (deSilva, 1992: Table 4-2). Canadian-educated immigrants from the Caribbean were found to earn 27 percent less than other immigrants, and Canadian-educated immigrants from East Asia showed earnings of 21 percent less, when educational levels and other characteristics were statistically controlled (deSilva, 1992: 33). Although he affirmed the existence of gender discrimination on the basis of his data, deSilva concluded that there was no racial discrimination, and *The Globe and Mail* editor endorsed this unwarranted conclusion as definitive.

A number of other recent studies (e.g., Boyd, 1992; Grayson, 1997; Reitz, 1990) have also found evidence of racial discrimination in employment. Furthermore, the methodological limitations of the ECC study do not support the generalization that there is no racial discrimination in employment in Canada. For example, the ECC study did not examine data for the black population, but only for persons born in the Caribbean or "other Africa" (outside of southern or northern Africa), and the sample used for the study contained very small numbers of specific birthplace groups other than the Caribbean and East Asian categories—too small to support conclusions about the significance of discrimination in Canada (Reitz, 1993). Also, the ECC study did not report a separate analysis of gender effects.

In an analysis of the same 1986 census data, Reitz (1993) found that when education, work experience, language knowledge, government employment, province of residence, urban residence, and weeks and hours worked are taken into account, black males born in Canada have a disadvantage of about 10 percent in earnings. In her multivariate analysis of 1986 census data, in which age, metropolitan residence, and education were statistically controlled, Boyd (1992) found that immigrant women who are members of racial minorities suffer significant income disadvantage compared to men, or to women—both Canadian and foreign born—who are not racial minorities.

Employment equity in Canada has so far not corrected inequality in pay. Data reported by employers covered by the Employment Equity Act show that between 1986 and 1996, the salary gap between Aboriginal men and women and all men and women employees covered by the Act actually *widened*. The same is true for visible minority men, while the salary gap between visible minority women and all women in the workforce has remained about the same from 1986 to 1996 (Human Resources Development Canada, 1997; 25, 33).

There are various ways of studying a complex issue such as discrimination in employment, and it is essential to critically evaluate the claims made as well as the assumptions and methodology on which they are based. Careful research is imperative as a foundation for making weighty policy decisions that affect the working lives of millions of Canadians. When the available research evidence is examined, it is clear that income is influenced by gender and race, and that racial and gender discrimination are realities in Canada. Denying that discrimination in employment exists will not make it go away.

Myth #2: There is still some inequality, but it is rapidly disappearing as a natural consequence of changes in our society and economy. Time will fix the problem.

The lead editorial in *The Globe and Mail* on January 1, 1993, dismissed Statistics Canada's finding of a systematic pay disadvantage of women relative to men, saying, "it's hard to imagine a future in which the wage difference will not continue to narrow." As evidence, it cites the fact that for full-time, full-year workers aged 15 to 24, women's average earnings were 86 percent of men's. In 1995, the ratio was 83% (Statistics Canada, 1997:15). Now, in an age group of women whose labour force participation rate equals men's, whose educational attainment on average exceeds their male peers, and who are too young to have left the labour force for long periods to care for children, a 14 to 17 percent disadvantage doesn't look like equality for women. Despite *The Globe and Mail's* reassurance, it would seem to require considerable imagination to envision a future in which gender equality in pay is a reality even for the youngest generation of workers. Certainly there is little evidence that time alone is correcting the problem of gender inequality in employment.

In a 1987 survey about senior management in ninety-nine Ontario companies covered by the Federal Contractors Program, I found little reason to be optimistic about a major influx of women into positions of corporate power any time soon. Of the 635 senior managers identified in the study, 8 percent were women. But even these women were not equal participants with their male peers in senior management, since they were concentrated in the functional areas that were rated as having the least power and influence on corporate decisions—staff functions such as human resource management. Most of the companies had policies of promoting from within, and women made up a very small proportion of the middle managers in the traditional specialties from which top managers were recruited. A 1997 report on a study of Canadian senior executives found that 62 percent of the women in the group were condidering leaving their jobs because of dissatisfaction with the compensation, advancement opportunities, intellectual challenge, and organizational values presented by their current position (*The Globe and Mail,* Dec. 11, 1997: B15). In 1995, women were paid 69.6 percent of men's average earnings for full-year, full-time work in managerial and administrative jobs (Statistics Canada, 1997: 44). These data again offer no evidence that time alone will correct the problem of women's absence from decision-making roles in organizations.

Myth # 3: There is still some inequality in our society based on gender, race, and disability, but we now have laws that are fixing the problem.

The visibility of so-called "handicapped parking," automatic doors, curb cuts and ramps for wheelchairs, along with a few highly publicized voluntary attempts at "affirmative action" hiring of women and minorities by employers, have met with loud complaints about unfairness to white able-bodied males. Although such visible initiatives are modest in scope and still involve far more talk than action, they have been met with resistance, and with the complacent assumption that current laws and policies are making discrimination and disadvantage a thing of the past.

Many Canadians appear to assume that most employers are subject to affirmative action or employment equity legislation, and that employers must implement what are referred to as "quotas" that require them to ignore qualifications and hire on the basis of gender or race. These assumptions are false and reflect a misunderstanding of how employment equity is actually implemented, or possibly an inaccurate generalization from an example of inappropriate implementation of the concept. Many critics of employment equity also make the mistake of confusing it with past U.S. affirmative action policies. Canada's legal and policy framework is very different from that in the United States, and there are many practical differences between employment equity and affirmative action; hence American examples don't have much relevance to the Canadian context.

It is true that under Canada's Constitution, and under the human rights codes of many provinces, employers are permitted in some circumstances to voluntarily give preferential treatment of various kinds to members of historically disadvantaged groups. But most Canadian employers are not required to implement specific affirmative action or employment equity measures, nor are they held accountable for results. Before it was revised in 1995, employers covered by the Employment Equity Act faced sanctions only for failure to report work-force statistics to the federal government; there were no penalties for lack of action toward employment equity. Perhaps it is not surprising, then, that the work-force statistics submitted by employers covered by the act between 1987 and 1996 have not shown significant improvements in the representation and distribution of the employment equity groups.

As discussed earlier, employers covered by the Employment Equity Act and the Federal Contractors Program are explicitly *not* expected to implement preferential hiring or "quotas." Employers set their own numerical goals, based on their own business needs. Yet there seems to be a widespread misconception that there is wholesale implementation of preferential or quota-based hiring in Canada.

The three myths we have discussed are contradicted by a large body of research evidence, and by the experience of many members of the employment equity groups. To paraphrase Mark Twain, the deaths of gender and racial inequality, and of discrimination on the basis of sex, disability, and race, have been greatly exaggerated. Furthermore, allegations that employment equity is unfair to white able-bodied males, who have traditionally enjoyed privileged access to employment, advancement, and rewards in the workplace, are highly exaggerated and often false. In general, such claims lack credible research support.

Systemic inequality in the workplace on the basis of race, gender, disability, and aboriginal ancestry is still very much with us, as is shown by evidence from a variety of sources including academic research; survey findings and statistical data collected by federal and provincial government departments including Statistics Canada, Employment and Immigration Canada, and various royal commissions and special committees and task forces; records of testimony before the courts and human rights tribunals; and studies conducted by employers and by groups working for the equality of women, people with disabilities, aboriginal peoples, and racial minorities. The literature dealing with patterns of inequality and discrimination is much more extensive for the United States than for Canada, and for women than for groups disadvantaged on the basis of race, disability, or aboriginal ancestry. There is scanty but powerful evidence pertaining to the double disadvantage experienced by women who are also disabled, or members of racial minorities, or aboriginal; this issue has been too often neglected by researchers.

IS EMPLOYMENT EQUITY FAIR?

In order to assess the fairness of employment equity legislation, regulation, policy, and implementation, one must understand their goal or purpose, and have accurate information about what employment equity actually is—in contrast to myths and misconceptions about what it is. Employment equity is not one specific kind of measure, such as preferential hiring of members of employment equity groups, although in some cases, and for defined periods of time, some forms of preferential treatment may be part of an employment equity strategy. Employment equity certainly does not mean that employers are expected to hire individuals just because they are women, minorities, or persons with disabilities, or to hire people who are not able to perform the duties of a particular job. But it does mean hiring without making unfounded and unexamined assumptions about which types of people are able to perform in particular jobs, and it means making an effort to recruit people who may not fit the profile of the traditional employee in a job. It also means providing conditions that will help the new employees to be successful, and that will help the organization to adapt successfully to its changing work force.

Employment equity is a complex change process involving many kinds of actions directed toward identifying and removing the various kinds of barriers encountered by women, persons with disabilities, aboriginal peoples, and racial minorities in the labour market and workplace. Employment equity is therefore a problem-solving process that is based upon data and information about the experience of employment equity group members. Based on this knowledge, a diagnosis of a workplace is developed in order to identify and remove barriers and respond appropriately to diversity.

A careful diagnosis that identifies patterns of inequality and disadvantage on the basis of gender, race, disability, and/or aboriginal ancestry suggests the presence of job barriers—formal and informal employment policies and practices that have discriminatory impacts on the designated groups, whether or not such impacts are intended. The complex of barriers and constraints that continue to limit the access and full participation in the workplace of historically disadvantaged groups has been called systemic discrimination. The purpose of employment equity is to identify and remove these barriers.

Although employment equity is not just a "numbers game," numerical representation is often the first issue that comes up in discussions of inequality and employment equity remedies. Numerical representation is not simply a question of whether women, racial minorities, aboriginal peoples, and people with disabilities are present in an organization. It also includes their concentration in job ghettos, their absence from decision-making positions due to glass ceilings that impede their career advancement, and their lack of access to jobs on career ladders. These groups may be underrepresented relative to the availability of qualified members of these groups in the labour market because of high turnover resulting from sexual or racial harassment, part-time employment or job insecurity, lack of equal opportunity for training or promotion, inequitable pay, failure of the employer to accommodate special needs related to disabilities, or other forms of discrimination.

The culture of the organization clearly influences the numerical representation, distribution, and retention of members of the employment equity groups. The culture of a workplace encompasses its fundamental values, its dominant beliefs and assumptions about people and work, prevailing stereotypes about gender, race, and disability, norms of social behaviour, informal networks through which interaction and communication take place, attitudes toward change, and behaviours surrounding organizational power and politics, cooperation, and conflict. Decisions about people in organizations—their access to employment, job assignment, career development, and daily treatment on the job—tend to reinforce and reflect the values and norms of historically dominant social groups that continue to occupy positions of power and privilege in the organization: typically white able-bodied males (eg. see Cockburn, 1991). For example, have you noticed how often the board members and top managers whose photos appear in corporate annual reports all look alike? Workplaces that are equitable for everyone can exist if organizations make a serious and sustained effort to change traditional cultures in which white able-bodied males are privileged and women, minorities, aboriginal peoples, and persons with disabilities are treated as if they don't really belong.

Employment systems encompass the entire spectrum of organizational rules— policies, practices, and procedures—that affect access to jobs and advancement opportunities for individuals and groups. Employment systems include procedures for recruitment and selection, job assignment, compensation, terms and conditions of employment, scheduling of work, performance appraisal, access to training and development, promotion, transfer, layoff, and termination. There is extensive research evidence from U.S., British, and Canadian settings of discriminatory impacts that employment systems may have in relation to women, racial minorities, and people with disabilities. For example, there have been many studies of how discrimination may be present in recruitment practices, selection criteria that are not job-related, selection interviews, compensation decisions, performance appraisal, promotion, and job assignment (for examples, see Arvey and Faley, 1988; Henry and Ginzberg, 1992; Collinson, Knights, and Collinson, 1990).

Removing discriminatory barriers in employment systems requires a critical examination of how human resource decisions are usually made. For example, are new employees recruited only from traditional sources, so that they are clones of the existing work force? Are criteria for selection and job assignment clearly linked to performance on the job, rather than just criteria that are customary or convenient? Do co-workers and supervisors receive training on how to identify, prevent, and deal with harassment on the basis of gender, race and ethnicity, and disability? Are managers accountable to ensure that performance appraisal, training and development, and promotion practices are free of bias, and that vigorous efforts are made to recruit and retain members of underrepresented groups? Do the leaders and the formal policies and practices of the organization support the principles of equity in the daily life of the workplace as well as in decision-making? Improvements in the representation of disadvantaged groups can occur over time, without unfairness to any group, if barriers in workplace culture and systems are identified and removed, and if decision-makers are sincerely committed to employment equity goals.

FAIRNESS TO ALL: DEALING WITH INEQUALITY IN THE OCCUPATIONAL STRUCTURE

Analyses of data on occupational distribution and income, including multivariate analyses that stastically control for the influence of education, urban residence, and other explanatory variables, show that aboriginal and racial minority populations are consistently disadvantaged in comparison to British, French, and European ethnic groups in Canada (Agócs and Boyd, 1993; Reitz, 1990; McDonald, 1991). The expectation that occupational inequality on the basis of racial minority status would diminish or disappear as disadvantaged groups acquired educational credentials and became culturally assimilated into Canadian society has proved illusory.

Stratification research in Canada, as well as in Britain and the United States, shows that inequality arises primarily from persisting structural constraints that act as barriers to the access and advancement of individuals in the occupational structure. These structural constraints include racial and gender discrimination, which is not only expressed in biased acts toward individuals, but is built into customary patterns of behaviour in a world of work that was designed by, and in the interests of, a white able-bodied male population. Individuals who are not male, white, and able-bodied—and who are now the majority of the Canadian work force—are often disadvantaged by their gender, race or ethnicity, or disability in gaining access to employment, and to the rewards, quality of life, and opportunities for advancement that are attached to occupational status.

A structural perspective redirects the attention of researchers and policy-makers away from the individual worker as the unit of analysis and the object of policy intervention, toward fundamental change in the workplace, beginning with the removal of the structural barriers in organizational systems and culture that serve to maintain occupational inequality on the basis of gender, race, aboriginal ancestry, and disability. Employment equity is an organizational change strategy that can lead to equality by providing remedies for workplace disadvantage that is due to structural barriers. It is a fair policy that reflects and responds to the current reality of the changing Canadian workplace.

REFERENCES

Agócs, Carol and Monica Boyd, "The Canadian Ethnic Mosaic Recast for the 1990s," in James Curtis, Edward Grabb, and Neil Guppy, eds., *Social Inequality in Canada*, 2nd ed. Scarborough: Prentice-Hall, 1993, pp. 330–352.

Agócs, Carol, Catherine Burr, and Felicity Somerset, *Employment Equity: Cooperative Strategies for Organizational Change*. Scarborough: Prentice-Hall Canada, 1992.

Arvey, Richard and Robert Faley, *Fairness in Selecting Employees*. Don Mills: Addison-Wesley, 1988.

Boyd, Monica, "Gender, Visible Minority and Immigrant Earnings Inequality: Reassessing an Employment Equity Premise," in Vic Satzewich, ed., *Deconstructing a Nation: Immigration, Multiculturalism and Racism in the 1990s Canada*. Toronto: Garamond Press, 1992.

Cockburn, Cynthia, *In the Way of Women: Men's Resistance to Sex Equality in Organizations*. Ithaca, New York: ILR Press, 1991.

Collinson, David, David Knights, and Margaret Collinson, *Managing to Discriminate*. London: Routledge, 1990.

deSilva, Arnold, "Earnings of Immigrants: A Comparative Analysis." Ottaw Services Canada, 1992.

Grayson, J. Paul, "Who Gets Jobs? Initial Labour Market Experiences of York ...cs," Working Paper, Institute for Social Research, York University, Jan. 1997.

Government of Canada, Employment Equity Act, 1995.

Government of Canada, Canadian Human Rights Act, 1995.

Harvey, Edward and John Blakely, "Employment Equity in Canada," *Policy Options* (March 1993): 3–8.

Henry, Frances and Effie Ginzberg, "Racial Discrimination in Employment," in James Curtis, Edward Grabb, and Neil Guppy, eds., *Social Inequality in Canada,* 2nd ed. Scarborough: Prentice-Hall, 1993, pp. 353–360.

Human Resources Development Canada, *Annual Report, Employment Equity Act, 1997.* Minister of Supply and Services Canada, 1997.

Johnston, William, "Global Work Force 2000: The New World Labor Market," *Harvard Business Review* 69, no. 2 (1991): 115–127.

Leck, Joanne and David Saunders, "Hiring Women: The Effects of Canada's Employment Equity Act," Canadian Public Policy 18(2), 1992, pp. 203–220.

Leck, Joanne and David Saunders, "Achieving Diversity in the Workplace: Canada's Employment Equity Act and Members of Visible Minorities," *International Journal of Public Administration* 19(3), 1996, pp. 299–322.

Leonard, Jonathan, "Anti-Discrimination or Reverse Discrimination: The Impact of Changing Demographics, Title VII, and Affirmative Action on Productivity," *Journal of Human Resources* 19, no. 2 (1984): 145–174.

Leonard, Jonathan, "Employment and Occupational Advance Under Affirmative Action," *Review of Economics and Statistics* 66, no. 3 (1984): 377–385.

McDonald, Ryan, "Canada's Off-Reserve Aboriginal Population," *Canadian Social Trends* (Winter 1991): 2–7.

Reitz, Jeffrey, "Ethnic Concentrations in Labour Markets and Their Implications for Ethnic Inequality," in Raymond Breton, Wsevolod Isajiw, Warren Kalbach, and Jeffrey Reitz, eds., *Ethnic Identity and Equality: Varieties of Experience in a Canadian City.* Toronto: University of Toronto Press, 1990, pp. 135–195.

Reitz, Jeffrey, "Statistics on Racial Discrimination in Canada," *Policy Options* (March 1993): 32–36.

Statistics Canada, *Earnings of Men and Women, 1995,* Ottawa: Minister of Industry, Jan. 1997 (cat. No. 13-217-XPB).

X **NO**
Employment Equity—Unfair
JACK ROBERTS

INTRODUCTION

Why not employment equity? Why shouldn't the state legislate an employment equity program designed to force every workplace, university, and other institution to "look like Canada," proportionally representing our populace in all its diversity? Because employment equity would be unfair to our society and every person in it. That's why.

From a societal point of view:

(1) The idea that employment equity will promote a nondiscriminatory result by requiring proportional representation of our populace is a myth;

(2) Employment equity will corrode our competitiveness by replacing the ideal of advancement on merit with a "victim culture" that encourages trying to get ahead by marketing our miseries and maladies;

(3) Employment equity will promote a wasteful proliferation of organized "victim groups" lobbying in the legislatures and the media for official government preferences in, for example, admission to higher education, employment, and promotion;

(4) The success of many of these "victim groups" in obtaining official preferences for their members will polarize and fragment our society;

(5) This fragmentation will promote the segregation of our society and its institutions.

From an individual point of view:

(1) Employment equity will officially disadvantage every member of the amorphous majority, i.e., everyone who cannot succeed in convincing the government to grant them official preferences based upon some "victim" characteristic they share with others, regardless of whether they are children of privilege or poverty;

(2) Conversely, employment equity will officially advantage every member of successful "victim groups," regardless of whether they are children of privilege or poverty;

(3) Employment equity is subject to gross manipulation, in that people are classified into one group or another on the basis of information that they personally volunteer;

(4) Employment equity is condescending, in the sense that it suggests that members of official victim groups are incapable of succeeding without being given official preferences;

(5) For the same reason, employment equity casts into doubt the merits of the accomplishments of members of official victim groups—did they get there only because of their ethnic origin, race, gender, etc.;

(6) Employment equity is not a temporary expedient to be suffered by members of the amorphous majority for a short period of time; it will disadvantage them throughout their lifetimes.

THE SOCIETAL REASONS FOR REJECTING EMPLOYMENT EQUITY

(1) The Myth of Proportional Representation

Not too long ago, U.S. President Bill Clinton was trumpeting how he intended to make his cabinet "look like America." There is an undeniable resonance to such rhetoric. It just sounds right: If discrimination never existed, wouldn't our entire population be proportionally represented at all levels of government, industry, and the professions? So why not deliberately create that nondiscriminatory result?

We should not "buy into" this myth. In a country such as Canada, where waves of immigration have created rapidly shifting distributions of population, it is entirely misleading to suggest that a regime of nondiscrimination would ever have created this kind of proportional representation. Immigrants to Canada are selected, *inter alia,* on the basis of having skills and/or investment capital that Canada needs. As a result, many skilled trades, businesses, and professions are heavily laden with relatively recent immigrants. Other occupational categories, where sufficient numbers of Canadian residents have always been available, are not. Unless you take the position that immigration to Canada should not be based upon the needs of the country, a dubious proposition if there ever was one, you can hardly label the result a form of discrimination that needs to be corrected through employment equity.

Add to this the different cultural attributes that immigrants to Canada may bring with them. Some cultural groups may value education more than others, and as a result large numbers of their children may move more rapidly than others into higher education and professional careers. Other cultural groups may not share the modern North American attitude toward careers for women. Most of the first generation of women among these groups may never seek to enter the work force. In neither case would the disproportionate overrepresentation or underrepresentation of the cultural group in the work force represent the outcome of domestic discrimination.

But perhaps most fundamentally, the plain truth is that employment equity never was designed to promote proportional representation of everybody in the populace. You will never see employment equity investigators surveying student populations and work forces to find out, for example, if Roman Catholics, Anglicans, Presbyterians, and/or Jews are proportionally represented at every level. Employment equity is limited to promoting proportional representation of victim groups that, by dint of lobbying efforts or otherwise, manage to make it onto the government's employment equity list. Employment equity is indifferent to the degree of inclusion or exclusion of any other group. They are all rolled into one—an amorphous majority whose members must be held back while the members of the victim groups on the government's list are preferred.

(2) and (3) The 'Victim Culture' and Organized Victim Groups

As can be seen, employment equity places a high premium upon getting on the government's list of victim groups. Get on the list and you have struck gold: you will be preferred, *inter alia*, in admission to higher education, employment, and promotion. Don't get on the list and you will fall into the amorphous majority who must "ride in the back of the bus" and accept being officially disadvantaged at every stage of their careers.

Welcome to the "victim culture," where everyone, it seems, wants to organize a victim group and try to get ahead by marketing their miseries and maladies. When you think about it for a minute, there are lots of reasons why many of us may not have been given a fair shake in employment or promotion—reasons that have nothing to do with the traditional categories of race, ethnic origin, or gender. Perhaps we were regarded as too young or too old (ageism); too bald (follicly challenged); too hairy (hirsutism); too overweight (weightism); too short or too tall (heightism); not good-looking enough (lookism); too quiet or shy (vocalism); not athletic enough (athleticism); or having only experience instead of formal credentials (credentialism).

I mention the above categories because if you have been watching any of the U.S. talk shows on television lately, you would have seen representatives of victim groups organized around one or more of these characteristics lobbying to be added to the U.S. government's victim group list under its affirmative action program.[1] Certainly, you would have seen representatives of another organized victim group, gays and lesbians, parading and lobbying, *inter alia*, to reach this objective.

They are simply following the pattern established by other successful victim groups. Thirty-five years ago, when affirmative action preferences were first mandated by Congress, only blacks and women were on the list. As other groups learned the ropes of victim politics and launched successful lobbies, they too were added. These groups included Native Americans, Hispanics, and most recently, people with disabilities. Fewer and fewer Americans remain in the disadvantaged category of amorphous majority.

Some might say that Americans should encourage this trend. Sooner or later no one would be left in the category of amorphous majority. Everyone—and hence no one—would get preference. Maybe the whole affirmative action program would self-destruct.

Wishful thinking, perhaps, and it begs the real question. That question is, why would we in Canada want to create a "victim culture" like that? Why would we want to destroy the ideal of meritocracy, the ideal of advancement on merit, and replace it with a system where he or she who cries the loudest is the one who succeeds? In a world where international competitiveness will make or break the future of a small trading country like Canada, why would we want to deliver such a crippling blow to Canada's overall potential for economic efficiency?

(4) and (5) Polarization, Fragmentation, and Segregation

The practice of victim politics depends upon creating divisions between people. To succeed, the "victim group" must hive itself off from the amorphous majority and argue that its members are disproportionately underrepresented at the more senior levels of education, government, industry, and the professions because they were oppressed and discriminated against, either overtly or systemically, by the amorphous majority. In the United States, this lobbying effort is usually made by (1) marshalling as many anecdotes as possible of how certain members of the amorphous majority abused, undervalued, overlooked, or held back members of the victim group because of their common "victim" characteristic; and (2) pointing to statistical evidence demonstrating that persons sharing this common "victim" characteristic are underrepresented in the desired areas.

While such evidence does not add up to proof, in any legal sense, that a cultural norm embraced by the amorphous majority promoted oppression of the victim group and actually caused the alleged underrepresentation, the pressure created upon the government through the use of this evidence in an effective lobbying campaign may induce the government to add the victim group to its official affirmative action list. From that point onward, the government will require universities, employers, and other institutions to prefer all members of the victim group at the expense of all members of the amorphous majority, regardless of whether those individuals who are so penalized ever actually committed or benefited from the acts of oppression alleged by the victim group.

It is not difficult to imagine the resentment soon felt by individuals in the amorphous majority who are turned upon in this way. This resentment may be expressed in an emotional "backlash" directed against all members of the victim group. In other words, the victim group and the amorphous majority soon became polarized into opposing camps.

Further fragmentation soon follows. Once again, the United States provides the best example. Because more than one victim group has been officially recognized in the U.S. government's affirmative action program, deep divisions have developed among them. In the world of official victimhood, the question soon becomes, who will be first among equals? If a single job or promotion opens up at a workplace where all official victim groups are underrepresented, from which group will the incumbent be selected? If a university has limited funds available to finance a single additional course in minority studies, which minority victim group will get it? Official victim groups are excellent at reasoning why they should be first among equals in the contest for such scarce spoils. The result? Fragmentation: group against group, all against the amorphous majority.

Next comes segregation, with everybody choosing to "stick to their own kind." If you think I'm exaggerating, take a tour of the campus of any major American university. You won't see black, white, Hispanic, Native American, or Asian students happily intermingling. The students "stick to their own kind." Each minority group exerts considerable social pressure upon its members to ensure that they do not stray into social relationships with others. To the dismay of university administrators, their students have divided themselves into competing collectives and adopted an "us against them" mentality.

And why not? Each group or collective has learned only too well the lessons of victim politics. It has been said that at one university, the Asian students even capitalized upon the fact that the affirmative action classification system of the university depended upon information personally volunteered by the students. They threatened to register as "white" in the next academic year if their demands for an Asian studies program were not met. This would have thrown the affirmative action statistics of the university way out of line, possibly prompting a government inquiry. The university capitulated. The Asian students got what they wanted. Other minorities were not amused.

Collective destinies promote collective identities. Some victim groups have gone so far in this direction as to advocate a deconstruction of democracy as we know it. Rather than proportional representation by geographic area and a legislature based upon one representative, one vote, they advocate proportional representation by victim group, with each victim group either having a veto or more than one vote per representative upon issues they identify as their own.

You may recall the insistence of certain victim groups that they be represented at the table in the last round of negotiations for constitutional reform. You may also recall that traces of their unique philosophy of democracy actually made it into the proposals for an elected Senate. Quebec senators were to be given either veto power or more than one vote per senator upon issues affecting Quebec. It was thought that this would accommodate the Quebec government's concerns about centralization of power in Ottawa, a prospect that had long been anathema to the francophone majority in Quebec. (It is observed in passing that the francophone majority in Quebec is regarded by many as having pioneered the use of victim politics in Canada.)

These are scary proposals. Grouping people by geographic area is relatively benign. Geographic borders within Canada are not exclusive. An Ontarian can become an Albertan simply by moving there, and vice versa. This fluidity prevents the development of strong bloc identities. Not so when you group people according to their official "victim" status. Victim groups are exclusive. If you don't possess the "victim" characteristic that defines the group, you are "out." Strong collective identities are the inevitable result.

Do we really want to condition Canadians to segregate and think collectively in this way? Strong bloc identities promote strong bloc prejudices. The sins of one invariably are laid at the feet of his or her entire bloc. Consider the recent campaign of one victim group that claimed that it wanted to "stop male violence against women." The entire collective of the male sex was sought to be held responsible for the crimes of very few men. Do we really want to unleash the human curses of mistrust, resentment, fear, and hatred between well-defined collectives? Do we really want group mistrusting group, group fearing group, group hating group? This is not my vision for the future of our society in Canada. I hope it is not yours.

EMPLOYMENT EQUITY'S UNFAIRNESS TOWARD INDIVIDUALS

(1) and (2) The 'Head-Count' Orientation of Employment Equity

No race, gender, or ethnic group has a monopoly upon the poor. The same may be said for the rich. While the relative proportions of rich and poor may vary from group to group, it cannot be denied that rich and poor populate every victim group on the government's employment equity list as well as the amorphous majority.

The targets, goals, and quotas of employment equity completely ignore this fact. The only thing that matters is the head-count. What employment equity demands is that an institution or employer prefer persons sharing a particular "victim" characteristic until proportional representation is reached. Whether those who are so preferred are children of privilege or poverty is a matter of complete indifference.

This presents a "double whammy" to the children of poverty in the amorphous majority. Having already begun life at a serious deficit relative to those more fortunate, they now have heaped upon them the further disadvantage of being on the receiving end of official discrimination at every stage of their careers. You can imagine how galling it must be for those who have fought their way up from poverty to be told that they must be held back while a child of privilege from an official victim group is preferred.

If you can't imagine this, let me give you an example from my own experience. In the early 1970s I was a young lawyer in Washington, D.C. Two of my friends, Myles and Art, decided that they would like to go to law school (at the time, Myles was a defence analyst at the Pentagon; Art was a White House aide). Myles had had to fight his way up through the inner-city schools in New York city. Art was a child of privilege. When he was growing up, he lived in mansions. He attended private schools. His father was a successful politician from the southwest. Nevertheless, Myles had the superior academic record and law school admission test score. Myles was rejected by every law school to which he applied. They all accepted Art. He also received warm letters of welcome and multiple offers of scholarships. Today, Myles is still at the Pentagon; Art is a successful lawyer in the southwest. They are no longer friends.

You see, Myles was Jewish. Art was Hispanic. Despite their long history of suffering prejudice and discrimination, Jews never made it out of the amorphous majority and onto the government's affirmative action list. Hispanics did. Under pressure from the government to meet targets for numbers of Hispanics in their student bodies, the law schools were only too anxious to recruit Art. It didn't matter that his prior academic record and law school admission test score fell far below the floors established for applicants from the amorphous majority. It didn't matter that Art was a child of privilege who had never suffered an ounce of discrimination in his life. All that mattered was the head-count of Hispanics.

It seems ironic, doesn't it, that such an inequity between Myles and Art should be worked by a process that Canadians call employment equity? We shouldn't be surprised, though. Employment equity was never designed to be fair as applied between individuals. Its only objective has always been to work for equity on behalf of its official victim groups, in the sense of requiring their proportional representation. It has narrowed the broad concept of equity down to a "numbers game" that is devoid of any sensitivity to other criteria of fairness.

(3) Gross Manipulation of Volunteered Information

In a free and open society, where until recently human rights laws forbade employers and other institutions to ask about an applicant's race or ethnic origin, gathering employment equity statistics can be a touchy subject. Forcing Canadians to carry racial or ethnic identity cards is out of the question. Even requiring Canadians to fill out employment equity questionnaires is unthinkable. Many Ontarians who received such questionnaires from the provincial government reacted with considerable hostility and refused to provide the requested information. As a result, just as in the United States, the government must rely upon information that is voluntarily provided in administering its employment equity program.

Relying upon volunteered information involves considerable potential for gross manipulation of the employment equity program. You will recall the threat of the Asian students at one U.S. university to register as white if they did not get their way. But gross manipulations also occur in other ways.

Not too long ago the press ran a story about two brothers in Philadelphia. They were white. When they applied to join the fire department, they received the highest test scores; however, they were rejected in favour of minority applicants who had not done as well. The next time they applied, the brothers had learned an important lesson. They identified themselves as African American. They were immediately hired. It wasn't until the brothers applied for promotion some time later that grumbling among their colleagues prompted the fire department to require some proof that they were, indeed, African American. When they couldn't come up with any, they were fired.

It is difficult to say how often applicants for admission to university, jobs, or promotions commit such flagrant manipulations, but the temptation at least to embellish the minority aspects of your pedigree must be great. Friends of mine in New York had this happen with their daughter. The daughter, whose academic record was not strong, had been rejected by every university to which she had applied. Then, recalling that her grandmother came from Portugal, she reapplied, stating that she was of Hispanic origin. There were acceptances all around.

These instances raise considerable doubt about the reliability of the statistics that must be used in administering an employment equity program. How many members of the amorphous majority might be "passing" as members of official victim groups? How many members of official victim groups might have chosen to be counted as members of the amorphous majority because of a desire to be seen as advancing solely upon their own merits? How are those people counted who choose not to submit completed employment equity questionnaires? When the voluntary nature of the information-gathering process makes employment equity subject to this much manipulation and, hence, potential for unfairness, why implement it at all?

(4) and (5) Condescension and Doubt

These objections to employment equity probably require little in the way of expansion. Employment equity programs are condescending to members of official victim groups because they imply that without the special preferences of employment equity, they cannot succeed. For the same reason, employment equity programs cast into doubt the achievements of members of official victim groups. The unasked question always lurking in the background is, did they make it on their own or was it because of their official victim status?

(6) No Temporary Expedient

If there is one thing that the past experience of the United States can tell you, it is that employment equity is not a temporary expedient to be eliminated in, say, ten years, when proportional representation of all victim groups is achieved. It is not a "quick fix." Twenty-five years after the implementation of affirmative action, the United States still has not even come close to achieving the goal of proportional representation.

More than a full generation after the fact, it seems clear that the billions of dollars spent in implementing, policing, and enforcing affirmative action programs would have been better invested in improving the living conditions and educational opportunities of, for example, African American children in the urban ghettos of the United States. In other words, the investment should have started at the beginning of youth. The goals, targets, and quotas of affirmative action only begin to apply at the end, when the child reaches university age.

By then, the damage is already done. Very few buck the odds presented by a harsh environment and make it through to high-school graduation. What good are affirmative action goals, targets, and quotas to the rest? They are already ineligible. They are beyond the downward reach of the affirmative action program.

Many U.S. commentators, both African American and white, have noted that because of this, affirmative action mainly helped those who really didn't need it—those African Americans from middle- and upper-class families who would have gone on to university and successful careers anyway. For the most part, the rest remained stuck where they were a quarter-century ago—in the lower rungs of society.

Even the enforcement objective of affirmative action was changed to reflect this phenomenon. No longer was the enforcement objective to reach proportional representation of victim groups in student bodies and work forces, measured on the basis of their proportion of the population, but rather proportional representation was measured on the basis of their proportion of the pool of minimally qualified applicants. It is highly unlikely that, in the present scheme of things, proportional representation on the basis of population ever will occur. Until then, affirmative action will continue as a permanent part of the American landscape.

CONCLUSION

No one disputes that in Canada many people in positions of power may still treat others differently solely on the basis of their race, gender, ethnic origin, or some of the other possible victim characteristics that I set forth earlier in this paper. Because of this, the best qualified people may have been passed over for, *inter alia*, employment or promotion. That is unfair. Something must be done about it.

The only dispute is about that "something." In my submission, employment equity programs are not the way to go. I have set out in this paper extensive reasons for opposing their implementation. Perhaps it is beyond the scope of this paper to explore possible alternatives. It is important, however, to stress that such alternatives exist. One such alternative is to review personnel procedures to ensure that reliance upon tools such as interviews, where subtle prejudices may influence the evaluation, are minimized. Another is streamlined enforcement of anti-discrimination laws. Still another is to do what the United States didn't do—

invest the dollars that would have gone into employment equity into specialized programs designed to minimize the social and educational deficits now suffered by children of poverty. Another is to educate and foster changing attitudes in the workplace to accommodate the needs of different people, for example, the provision of flexible working hours and day care. There obviously are many more alternatives, none of them that involves dividing the people of Canada up into collectives and officially advancing one collective at the expense of another.

NOTES

1. "Affirmation action" is the U.S. term for "employment equity." Actually, employment equity is a broader—and hence more accurate—term, since even in Ontario the government's so-called "equity" initiatives are designed to reach beyond employment to embrace, *inter alia,* university admission.

Postscript

Agócs and Roberts both present credible arguments for their respective positions. Nevertheless, some nagging doubts remain. Let us take the case for employment equity first. Employment equity programs focus on groups, but surely there are members in these designated groups who are not victims of discrimination. (Recall Roberts's story about Art and Myles.) If this is the case, then why not centre on individual instances of discrimination? A related concern with employment equity is its argument about the impact of discrimination. Canadians of Japanese and Jewish descent have in the past been the target of many discriminatory practices, but these people have managed to thrive economically in Canadian society. Such evidence leads one to doubt whether the difficulties women, Aboriginal people, visible minorities, and the disabled experience in the workplace are the fault of unfair employment practices. Lastly, even if discrimination prevails, it is questionable whether reverse discrimination in the form of preferential treatment is a prudent course of action. Two wrongs do not necessarily make a right.

To say that the position for employment equity is less than fully convincing is not to say that the contrary position is sound. At times, critics of employment equity come perilously close to denying the existence of discrimination in the workplace, yet study after study documents its existence. In their book *Employment Equity: Cooperative Strategies for Organizational Change* (Scarborough: Prentice-Hall, 1992), Carol Agócs, Catherine Burr, and Felicity Somerset present the results of a survey of Canadian corporate recruiters and hiring managers in which nearly all the respondents admit to discriminating against potential employees on the grounds of disability, age, sex, and colour. Critics may also be blamed for presenting a narrow conception of employment equity, one that concentrates on quotas and the establishment of proportional representation in the labour force. In reality, employment equity represents a wide range of actions, many of which endeavour only to eliminate barriers and ensure that all have an equal opportunity to secure employment.

For students wishing to acquire an initial understanding of employment equity, the aforementioned text by Agócs, Burr, and Somerset is a good starting point. Though the authors are unabashed supporters of employment equity, they provide a disinterested overview of the meaning of employment equity and existing governmental programs in this area of public policy. Another important reference is Rosalie Abella, *Report of the Commission on Equality and Employment* (Ottawa: Minister of Supply and Services, 1984). This report offers strong arguments for employment equity, and was instrumental in drawing the attention of government decision makers to the issue of discrimination in the workplace. Not surprisingly, the report elicited some critical commentaries, two of which are Walter Block and Michael A. Walker, *On Employment Equity: A Critique of the Abella Royal*

Commission Report (Vancouver: The Fraser Institute, 1985) and Conrad Winn, "Affirmative Action and Visible Minorities: Eight Premises in Quest of Evidence," *Canadian Public Policy* 11, no. 4 (December 1985). Block and Walker also provide a more extended critique of employment equity in their book *Discrimination, Affirmative Action, and Equal Opportunity: An Economic and Social Perspective* (Vancouver: The Fraser Institute, 1982). As well, students may wish to refer to debates on employment equity in Ronald Hinch, ed., *Crosscurrents: Debates in Canadian Society* (Scarborough: Nelson, 1992).

Employment equity programs in Canada have been influenced greatly by developments in the United States. In the 1960s, the American government introduced programs aimed at reducing discrimination in the workplace against Black Americans. These programs, which have expanded to include other groups, come under the name of *affirmative action*. A set of articles entitled *The Annals of the American Academy of Political and Social Science: Affirmative Action Revisited* (Newbury Park: Sage Publications, 1992), edited by Harold Orlans and June O'Neill, offers a good discussion of affirmative action in the United States.

Employment equity and affirmative action have engendered a good deal of philosophical debate about whether these initiatives are consistent with various notions of justice. Two books that address this matter are Michael Rosenfeld, *Affirmative Action and Justice* (New Haven: Yale University Press, 1991) and Kathanne W. Greene, *Affirmative Action and Principles of Justice* (New York: Greenwood Press, 1989).

APPENDIX

How to Write an Argumentative Essay

LUCILLE CHARLTON

Argumentative essays are written to convince or persuade readers of a particular point or opinion. Whether the point is to change the public's mind on a political issue or to convince a person to stop smoking, all argumentative essays have common elements: a well-defined, convincing argument; credible evidence; and a rebuttal of criticism. While most points of general essay writing apply to argumentative essays, there are several special guidelines the writer of a good persuasive essay must consider. The following sections introduce students to six basic steps in writing an argumentative or persuasive essay.

STEP 1: DEFINE THE ARGUMENT

It is very easy to point out that there are two sides to every discussion; however, it is difficult to define precisely one's own opinion on a subject and write about it. First, the writer must be certain that there is, in fact, something to disagree about. For example, Paul Martin is a Liberal cabinet minister; no one can dispute that fact. However, if I claim in my essay that Martin's financial policies have been innovative and have benefited Canadian society, many people would disagree with me. There must be room for disagreement with whatever position is taken, so an argumentative essay has to be more than an affirmation of acknowledged facts. In this way, argumentative writing differs from descriptive or journalistic writing. Also, the writer must state the entire argument in a precise thesis statement that will act as a controlling idea for the entire essay. All ideas expressed in the essay must relate to the thesis statement.

Second, an argumentative essay is more than a restatement of the two sides of the question. A simple recounting of opposing arguments does not give the reader any clear indication of how the writer feels about the subject, and is not really a persuasive statement. For example, a court reporter records every word spoken by the witnesses at a trial. These statements are entered as evidence in the court, but it is up to the lawyers for both sides to interpret the evidence and present it in a persuasive manner to the jury, leaving no doubt about which side they are on. In the same way, the writer first carefully defines the subject, examines the evidence, and then interprets that evidence by writing a precise opinion. An argumentative essay takes one side of a controversial issue; there should be no doubt in the reader's mind where the writer stands on that issue.

STEP 2: GATHER THE EVIDENCE

Arguments need credible supporting evidence, and good persuasive writers assemble a variety of information from different sources. This evidence can be found in statements from authorities, statistics, personal experience, or can be interpreted from research data. The authors found in this book have chosen one or more of these types of evidence to support their positions. These four types of evidence can also be used by student writers in their argumentative essays.

When researching evidence to support a particular position, the writer needs to keep the four *Rs* in mind: *reliable, relevant, recent,* and *referenced.*

First, all authorities used for supporting evidence need to be reliable—that means an acknowledged authority published in a recognized source. Evidence can be suspect if it is published only in unreliable sources, or if a researcher is unable to independently verify the statements. A good writer recognizes acceptable sources and is knowledgeable of the biases normally found in newspapers, magazines, journals, and Internet sources.

Because of the vast amount of material now available through electronic sources, writers must become skilled in evaluating the information presented. Newspaper and journal articles go through a process of editing and evaluation before publication. This acts as a check on information from unreliable sources. Electronic sources are not subjected to such scrutiny, so it is advisable to independently verify information from Internet sources. Consult the Web address at the end of the appendix for information on evaluating the reliability electronic sources.

Reference librarians can assist students in finding a variety of trustworthy sources for essays. Using suspect information will damage the credibility of the writer. A variety of reliable sources adds credibility to the writer's arguments.

Second, sources need to be relevant; that is, they must have something to contribute on the immediate topic. The Economic Council of Canada has expertise in the area of the Canadian economy, but scholars know that the council would be an unlikely source for information on the collapse of the Soviet Union. Writers can easily lose unity in their essays by adding irrelevant quotes or paraphrases just to sound authoritative.

Third, a good writer looks for updated information on the topic. Using outdated information could affect the outcome of the argument. For example, if I were arguing for increased funding for AIDS research, I would not base my essay on statistics from 1990, when fewer cases of HIV were reported. The writer should be familiar with the effects of recent changes on the topic: politicians can reverse their positions, new statistics can change the writer's perspective, and new research can add to the evidence. Internet access greatly enhances a writer's ability to access updated statistics, and instructors expect student initiative in this area.

In addition, a writer must know how much background research needs to be done to introduce the topic to the reader. Background information may be necessary to show how events have progressed over the last few years. The background information should not overwhelm or become the main point of the essay.

Finally, all sources need to be carefully quoted and referenced in an acceptable citation form. There are a few basic rules to follow when using someone else's material:

1. Quotations are the exact words of the original author. They must always be referenced. Consult one of the reference books listed at the end of this appendix for correct formats. If you are unsure how to reference a particular source, consult with your instructor or a reference librarian.

2. Paraphrases are your restatement of the original author's ideas. Paraphrases keep the same idea, but are restated in your own words. All paraphrases must be referenced.

3. Do not take either quotations or paraphrases out of context, thereby misquoting a source. Make sure you have carefully read the entire research document and have understood its thesis statement.

4. Give credit whenever using information that did not originate with you, except for general information or well-known facts. For example, you do not need to acknowledge that Canadian Confederation happened in 1867. However, you must acknowledge statistical data taken from census or research reports used to support your arguments. All of the contributors to this volume have acknowledged their sources at the end of their articles in notes or references.

In gathering the evidence, keep careful notes and records of all your sources. Make sure to acknowledge all of your sources. The reference manuals listed at the end of this article have helpful information on deciding how to cite your sources. Avoid plagiarism. If you are not certain what constitutes plagiarism, ask your instructor for assistance and consult your institution's policy on plagiarism. All colleges and universities have serious penalties for plagiarism.

STEP 3: REFUTE THE OPPOSITION

To be convincing, writers have to support their argument while defusing criticism of it. When researching the argument, the writer also anticipates opposing viewpoints, researches them thoroughly, and is ready to refute them in the essay. Casting doubt on other writers' positions or reasoning can clinch your support. This can be done in several ways. First, the writer can cite authorities who hold opposing views, then refute their arguments by quoting other sources or different statistics. Second, rebuttals of arguments can be constructed through differing personal experiences. A third method is to attack the opposition's interpretation of documents and facts.

Writers often concede some of the arguments an opponent makes, then challenge the opponent with a strong conclusion. Concessions should be included early in the argument. The strongest points should be left for the last, leaving no doubt in the reader's mind of the writer's intentions. Avoiding all mention of the opposing position is not a good strategy.

Whether building support for their own arguments or refuting criticism of their positions, writers must be careful to avoid argumentative fallacies, or mistakes in reasoning or argument. The most common fallacies that appear in essays are overgeneralization, faulty cause and effect, and misrepresentation of the opposition. Various writing manuals contain complete discussions of argumentative fallacies.

STEP 4: OUTLINE YOUR ESSAY

Good essay writers start with an outline that mentions the key ideas expressed in the body of the essay. All argumentative essays begin with an attention getter; the writer quotes an interesting fact, makes a dramatic statement, or even illustrates with the opposite opinion. Robert Martin's use of the words "antidemocratic and un-Canadian" for his essay title in this volume is an example of an attention-getting title. Once the reader is hooked into reading the essay, the writer continues with a thesis statement and proceeds with the arguments.

The body of an argumentative essay can be organized in two ways:

Pattern I

Introduction
Thesis statement
Background (if needed)
Listing of all your arguments with supporting evidence
Refutation of your opponent's points
Reminder of your strongest arguments
Conclusion, including a strong opinion statement

Pattern II

Introduction
Thesis statement
Background (if needed)
Statement of your opponent's first argument, with concession or refutation
Statement of your opponent's second argument, with concession or refutation
Continuation of refutation of your opponent's arguments, in order
Conclusion, with a strong statement of your own opinion

Most of the contributors to this volume follow Pattern II, which is more effective for longer essays. Pattern I is acceptable for shorter essays with fewer points of supporting evidence, because the reader will not get lost following the train of thought from argument to refutation. In both patterns, concessions are made early in the argument, and a strong opinion statement concludes the essay.

STEP 5: DECIDE ON TONE AND STYLE

The tone and style of your essay will depend on your audience. Most writers assume that they are writing for an intelligent audience with an open mind on the topic. Therefore, the tone of the essay cannot be insulting or pejorative. Treat your opposition and your readers with respect.

Examples:

Wrong: As every intelligent person knows ...
Better: Many people believe ...

Wrong: Only children would assume that ...
Better: I do not agree with this position ...

The essay must also be readable. Using language that is either hard to understand or too casual for the audience will not win converts to your point of view. The language used in an essay must be clear, direct, understandable, and free of gender, racial, or other biases.

Examples:

Wrong: Legitimized concerns on this matter were postponed by the committee.
Better: The committee delayed discussion.

Wrong: Those guys really messed up on this one.
Better: The politicians made mistakes in their analysis.

Wrong: A cabinet minister is accountable for his decisions.
Better: Cabinet ministers are accountable for their decisions.

Most academic essays are written in a formal tone, making minimal use of the pronoun "I." However, be sure to know what your audience expects. Sometimes persuasive essays or speeches are directed at a particular group, and the writer can then use a less formal style of presentation.

STEP 6: CHECK AND DOUBLE CHECK

After writing a draft of an essay, follow this basic checklist of items. By working through the list, you can catch errors in your essay.
Argumentative essay checklist:

1. Have I defined the argument?

2. Do I have a well-stated opinion on the topic?

3. Is my thesis statement clear? Does it have sufficient support?

4. Is my essay unified? Do all parts of the essay relate to the thesis statement?

5. Have I avoided argumentative fallacies?

6. Are my tone and style consistent and appropriate?

7. Have I varied my sentence structure and vocabulary?

8. Have I concluded with a strong statement?

9. Does the opening paragraph grab the reader's attention?

10. Have I checked for spelling errors and misused words and expressions?

11. Have I cited all sources in an acceptable style?

12. Have I correctly punctuated my sentences?

SOURCES TO CONSULT ON ESSAY WRITING

Buckley, Joanne. *Fit to Print: The Canadian Student's Guide to Essay Writing.* 3rd ed. Toronto: Harcourt Brace Canada, 1995.

Finnbogason, Jack and Al Valleau. *A Canadian Writer's Guide.* Toronto: Nelson Canada, 1997.

Gibaldi, Joseph. *MLA Handbook for Writers of Research Papers.* 4th ed., 1995. New York: Modern Language Association. 1995.

For ESL Students:

Hall, Ernest and Carrie S.Y. Jung. *Reflecting on Writing: Composing in English for ESL Students in Canada.* Toronto: Harcourt Brace Canada, 1996.

Web sites:

For evaluation of electronic sources:

http://www.science.widener.edu/~withers/advoc.htm

For citation of electronic sources:

http://www.sfu.ca/politics/cite.html

http://www.cas.usf.edu/english/walker/mla.html

For links to various Canadian media resources:

http://www.canpress.ca/canpress

CONTRIBUTORS ACKNOWLEDGMENTS

Permission to reprint copyrighted material is gratefully acknowledged. Information that will enable the publisher to rectify any error or omission will be welcomed.

Issue 1

John Olthuis and Roger Townshend, "The Case for Native Sovereignty," © ITP Nelson 1994.

Thomas Flanagan, "Native Sovereignty: Does Anyone Really Want an Aboriginal Archipelago?" © ITP Nelson 1994.

Issue 2

Paul Nesbitt-Larking, "Canadian Political Culture: The Problem of Americanization," © ITP Nelson 1998.

Anthony A. Peacock, "Socialism as Nationalism: Why the Alleged Americanization of Canadian Political Culture Is a Fraud," © ITP Nelson 1998.

Issue 3

Pierre Trudeau, "Values in a Just Society," in Thomas S. Axworthy and Pierre Elliott Trudeau, eds. From *Towards a Just Society: The Trudeau Years.* Copyright © for the selection, introductions and biographical notes 90562 Canada Ltée and Axiom Strategy Group Inc. 1990. Copyright © this edition, Penguin Books Canada Limited, 1990. Reprinted by permission of Penguin Books Canada Limited.

Paul Marshall, "The Importance of Group Rights," © ITP Nelson 1994.

Issue 4

Nelson Wiseman, "Tory-Touched Liberalism: Political Culture in Canada," © ITP Nelson 1998.

Janet Ajzenstat and Peter J. Smith, "The 'Tory Touch' Thesis: Bad History, Poor Political Science," © ITP Nelson 1998.

Issue 5

Robert Martin, "The Canadian Charter of Rights and Freedoms Is Antidemocratic and Un-Canadian," © ITP Nelson 1994.

Philip L. Bryden, "The Canadian Charter of Rights and Freedoms Is Antidemocratic and Un-Canadian: An Opposing Point of View," © ITP Nelson 1994.

Issue 6

Kathy L. Brock, "The Need for Constitutional Reform," © ITP Nelson 1998.

Michael Lusztig, "Megaconstitutional Reform Is Not Desirable," © ITP Nelson 1998.

Issue 7

Roger Gibbins, "Decentralization and the Dilemma of National Standards," © ITP Nelson 1998.

Ronald Manzer, "'And Dog Will Have His Day': National Standards in Canadian Social Policy," © ITP Nelson 1998.

Issue 8

Paul De Villers, "Why We Must Entrench Quebec's Francophone Heritage," in *Canadian Speeches* 11, no. 1 (April 1997). Reprinted by permission of the author.

Line Maheux, "Why the Distinct Society Idea Is Tearing Canada Apart," in *Canadian Speeches* 11, no. 1 (April 1997). Reprinted by permission of the author.

Issue 9

Justice Charles Gonthier, "Opinion in *Thibaudeau v. Canada*," from the Supreme Court of Canada, *The Supreme Court Report,* 1995-2 SCR 627. Reproduced with the permission of the Minister of Public Works and Government Services Canada, 1997.

Justice Beverly McLachlin, "Opinion in *Thibaudeau v. Canada*," from the Supreme Court of Canada, *The Supreme Court Report,* 1995-2 SCR 627. Reproduced with the permission of the Minister of Public Works and Government Services Canada, 1997.

Issue 10

David J. Bercuson, "Why Quebec and Canada Must Part," reprinted with permission from *Current History* magazine (March 1995). © 1995, Current History, Inc.

David T. Koyzis, "Why Political Divorce Must Be Averted," © ITP Nelson 1998.

Issue 11

Kenneth Kernaghan, "Is the Doctrine of Ministerial Responsibility Workable?" © ITP Nelson 1998.

Hugh Segal, "Ministerial Accountability: Confronting the Myth," © ITP Nelson 1998.

Issue 12

Christopher Dunn, "The Utility of the Institutionalized Cabinet," © ITP Nelson 1998.

Paul Barker, "Problems with the Institutionalized Cabinet," © ITP Nelson 1998.

Issue 13

David Kilgour, John Kirsner, and Kenneth McConnell, "Discipline versus Democracy: Party Discipline in Canadian Politics," © ITP Nelson 1994.

Robert J. Jackson and Paul Conlin, "The Imperative of Party Discipline in the Canadian Political System," © ITP Nelson 1994.

Issue 14

Peter H. Russell, "Canadian Constraints on Judicialization from Without." Reprinted by permission from the *International Political Science Review* 15, no. 2, pp. 165175.

F.L. Morton, "Judicial Policymaking Under the Charter," © ITP Nelson 1998.

Issue 15

F.L. Morton, "Why the Judicial Appointment Process Must Be Reformed," © ITP Nelson 1994.

H. Patrick Glenn, "Parliamentary Hearings for Supreme Court of Canada Appointments?" © ITP Nelson 1994.

Issue 16

G. Grant Amyot, "Democracy Without Parties: A New Politics?" in A. Brian Tanguay and Alain-G. Gagnon, eds., *Canadian Parties in Transition,* 2nd edition (Scarborough: ITP Nelson, 1996). © ITP Nelson 1996.

Vaughan Lyon, "Parties and Democracy: A Critical View," in A. Brian Tanguay and Alain-G. Gagnon, eds., *Canadian Parties in Transition,* 2nd edition (Scarborough: ITP Nelson, 1996). © ITP Nelson 1996.

Issue 17

Tim Schouls, "Why "Group Representation in Parliament Is Important," © ITP Nelson 1998.

John H. Redekop, "Group Representation in Parliament Would Be Dysfunctional for Canada," © ITP Nelson 1998.

Issue 18

Brian Needham, "A Better Way to Vote: Why Letting the People Themselves Take the Decisions Is the Logical Next Step for the West," from *The Future Surveyed,* September 11, 1993, pp. 58. Copyright © 1993 The Economist Newspaper Group, Inc. Reprinted with permission. Further reproduction prohibited.

Mark Charlton, "The Limits of Direct Democracy," © ITP Nelson 1998.

Issue 19

John L. Hiemstra and Harold Jansen, "Getting What You Vote For," © ITP Nelson 1994.

Paul Barker, "Voting for Trouble," © ITP Nelson 1994.

Issue 20

David Taras, "We Need the CBC," in *Policy Options,* September 1995. Reprinted with permission.

Barry Cooper, "Rethink the CBC," in *Policy Options,* September 1995. Reprinted with permission.

Issue 21

Douglas Auld, "The Overregulation of Higher Education," © ITP Nelson 1998.

William Bruneau, "Privatization in School and University: Renewal or Apostasy?" © ITP Nelson 1998.

Issue 22

Michael Krashinsky, "The Role of Workfare in the Social Safety Net," © ITP Nelson 1998.

Ernie S. Lightman, "Workfare: It's Jobs, Not Pathology," © ITP Nelson 1998.

Issue 23

Carol Agócs, "Employment Equity: Is It Needed? Is It Fair?" reprinted by permission of the author.

Jack Roberts, "Employment Equity—Unfair," © ITP Nelson 1994.

To the owner of this book

We hope that you have enjoyed *Crosscurrents: Contemporary Political Issues*, Third Edition, and we would like to know as much about your experiences with this text as you would care to offer. Only through your comments and those of others can we learn how to make this a better text for future readers.

School _____   Your instructor's name _____

Course _____   Was the text required? _____   Recommended? _____

1. What did you like the most about *Crosscurrents: Contemporary Political Issues?*

_____

_____

_____

2. How useful was this text for your course?

_____

_____

3. Do you have any recommendations for ways to improve the next edition of this text?

_____

_____

_____

4. In the space below or in a separate letter, please write any other comments you have about the book. (For example, please feel free to comment on reading level, writing style, terminology, design features, and learning aids.)

_____

_____

_____

_____

Optional

Your name _____   Date _____

May ITP Nelson quote you, either in promotion for *Crosscurrents: Contemporary Political Issues* or in future publishing ventures?

Yes _____   No _____

Thanks!

You can also send your comments to us via e-mail at
college_arts_hum@nelson.com

PLEASE TAPE SHUT. DO NOT STAPLE.

TAPE SHUT

TAPE SHUT

FOLD HERE

Nelson

0066102399-M1K5G4-BR01

ITP NELSON
MARKET AND PRODUCT DEVELOPMENT
PO BOX 60225 STN BRM B
TORONTO ON M7Y 2H1